AT THE ELEVENTH HOUR:
Reflections, Hopes and Anxieties at the Closing of the Great War, 1918

AT THE ELEVENTH HOUR

Reflections, Hopes and Anxieties at the Closing of the Great War, 1918

LEO COOPER

First published in Great Britain in 1998
by
LEO COOPER
an imprint of
Pen & Sword Books Ltd,
47 Church Street,
Barnsley, South Yorkshire S70 2AS

A CIP record for this book is available from the British Library

ISBN
0 85052 6094 Hardback edition
0 85052 6442 Paperback edition

Set in 10 on 11.5pt Sabon by Phoenix Typesetting, Ilkley, West Yorkshire.

Printed in Great Britain by Redwood Books Ltd, Trowbridge, Wilts.

Dedication

To the welfare of all archives, libraries and museums specializing in the acquisition, conservation and public access to materials relating to twentieth century history – against whatever adversity.

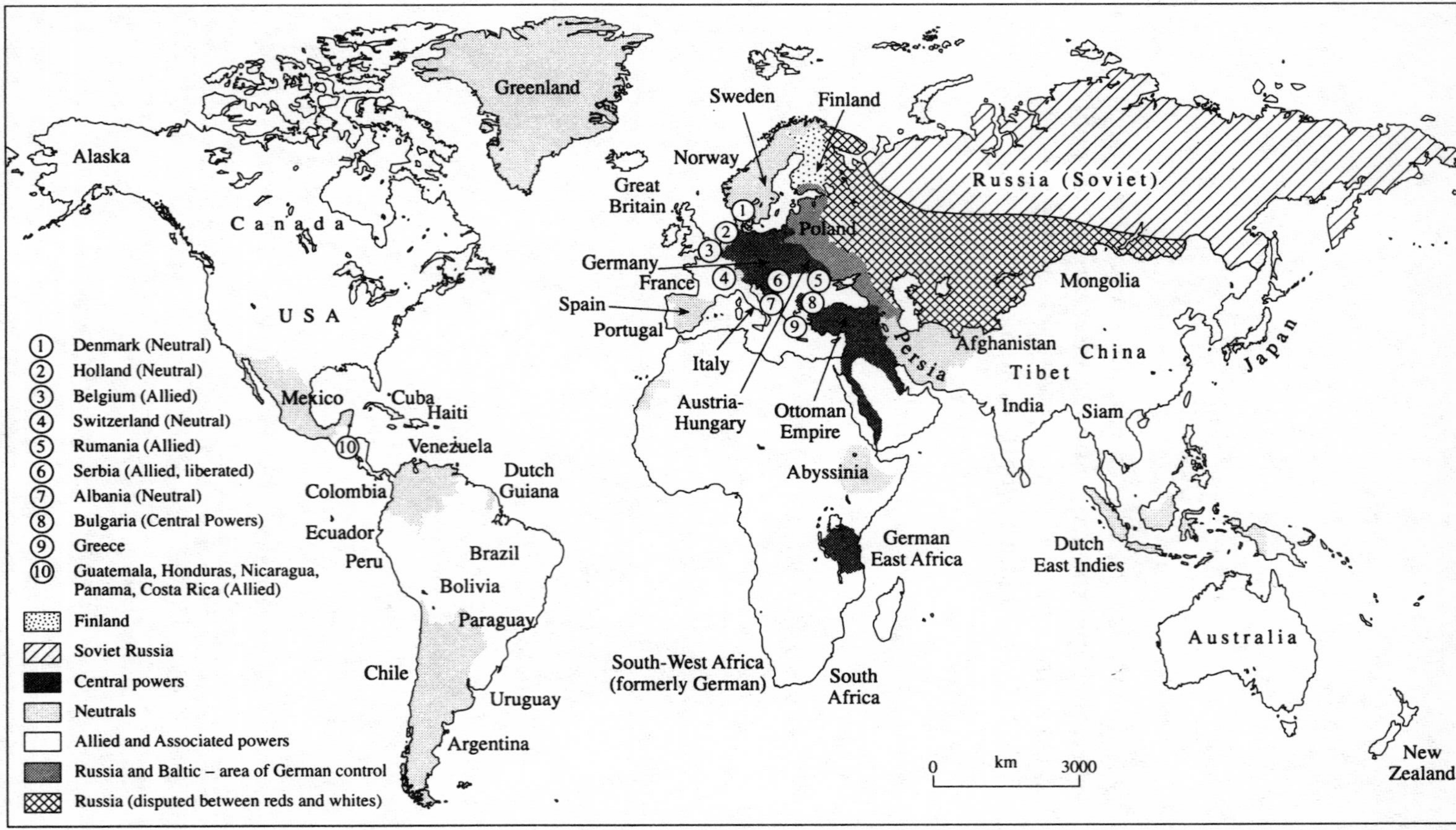

The World at War, November 1918

Contents

List of Illustrations

Illustrations within the text

Plate Illustrations

Between pages 92 and 93

11 November 1918 – left to right Captain Ernst Vanselow, Count Alfred Oberndorf, Major-General Detlov von Winterfeldt, Captain J.P.R. Marriott, Herr Matthias Erzberger, Rear Admiral Sir George Hope, Admiral Sir Rosslyn Wemyss, Marshal Ferdinand Foch, and General Maxime Weygand. (Liddle Collection) (Chapter 2 – Negotiating the Armistices)

3 General John J. Pershing, leaving his headquarters at Chaumont, 1918. (Patrick Gariépy collection) (Chapter 2 – Negotiating the Armistices)

4 Under the eye of French civilians, German troops retreating through Soignies, 9 November 1918. (Chapter 3 – Germany) (I.L. Read, Liddle Collection)

5 German troops in retreat. Note the motor lorry, loaded with as much booty as its occupants could carry off. (Chapter 3 – Germany) (I.L. Read, Liddle Collection)

6 German troops crossing the Hohenzollern Bridge at Cologne, November 1918, to comply with the terms of the Armistice which stated that German forces must retire to the eastern bank of the Rhine. Note the smiling faces and flowers. (Chapter 3 – Germany) (W.K. Rose, Liddle Collection)

7 Revolution on the streets of Berlin. Deserters from the army mix with sailors and armed civilians on the way to the barricades during the Spartacist rising. (Liddle Collection) (Chapter 3 – Germany)

8 The statues of four German soldiers, sculpted by the Munich artist Ernst Krieger, mourn for their lost comrades at Langemarck Germany cemetery, Belgium. Langemarck, the site of fighting on 11 November 1914, was a place of special significance in the Germany of the 1920s and 30s. (Hugh Cecil) (Chapter 3 – Germany)

9 The village war memorial in Bordesholm, Schleswig-Holstein, northern Germany. Erected in 1920 and designed by local architect Harry Maas, the inscription reads "From the Parish of Bordesholm to the fallen. Seed of Hope". Wreaths are laid at the memorial each November on *Toten Sonntag*, the German day of remembrance. (C.L. Harder) (Chapter 3 – Germany)

10 British officers pose together outside Mons, on the morning of 11 November 1918. (M.F.T. Baines, Liddle Collection) (Chapter 4 – Britons Overseas)

11 Father Roger Morrisey, Padre of the 2nd Battalion Royal Munster Fusiliers, outside the battalion's billet in Wargnies-le-Petit on the morning of 11 November. (Liddle Collection) (Chapter 4 – Britons Overseas)

12 A service of thanksgiving in the Collegiate Church at St Quentin, conducted by a padre and a French priest and attended by British soldiers. (French War Office, official) (Chapter 4 – Britons Overseas)

13 Officers of "A" Flight, No 8 Squadron RAF in front of one of their Bristol Fighters, at Malincourt aerodrome on the morning of 11 November. Flight Lieutenant Peffers DFC at the centre. (S. Horscroft, Liddle Collection) (Chapter 4 – Britons Overseas)

14 Time lapse photography has captured this display of Armistice night fireworks by No 10 Squadron RAF, at its base near Reckem, Belgium. (C.E. Townley, Liddle Collection) (Chapter 4 – Britons Overseas)

15 British troops gather in the main square in Baghdad to hear the news of the Armistice in Europe from the GOC Mesopotamia, Lieutenant-General Sir William Marshall. (T.H. Parkinson, Liddle Collection) (Chapter 4 – Britons Overseas)

16 Crowds of Arab civilians are held in check by British and Indian soldiers in Baghdad, 11 November 1918. (F. Everitt, Liddle Collection) (Chapter 4 – Britons Overseas & Chapter 18 – The Arab World)

17 Shortly after hearing the news of the Armistice, British officer prisoners posed for this photograph outside Clausthal POW camp, Germany. The most senior figure here is Brigadier General H.S.L. Ravenshaw, (front row third from left in double breasted overcoat) who was captured in the aftermath of the Battle of Cambrai, November 1917. (R.V. Maudslay, Liddle Collection) (Chapter 4 – Britons Overseas)

18 German sailors aboard the German super-dreadnought battleship SMS *König*, seen from a British ship. For the men of the Royal Navy, the reality of the Armistice was underscored by the German High Seas Fleet surrendering itself for internment on 21 November. Many were struck by the dirty, rusty and generally unkempt appearance of the enemy vessels after two years at their moorings. (L.A.K. Boswell, Liddle Collection) (Chapter 4 – Britons Overseas)

19 A German submarine of the latest ocean-going type, *U112*, enters Harwich for internment, late November 1918, signifying Germany's naval as well as military defeat. (J.M. Heath) (Chapter 4 – Britons Overseas)

20 *U112* with her new British crew. The Royal Navy's triumph over the High Seas Fleet complete at last. (J.M. Heath, Liddle Collection) (Chapter 4 – Britons Overseas)

43 A post-Armistice legacy for France: human remains collected from various parts of the Verdun battlefield rest in a temporary ossuary. (R.C. Money, Liddle Collection) (Chapter 6 – The French)

44 Belgian troops entering Torhout, 19 October 1918. In the background the former *Feldbuchhandlung*, field book store for German troops. (Archives of the Royal Palace, Brussels) (Chapter 6 – The Belgians)

45 Almost as soon as the Armistice came into effect, refugees began returning to the devastated areas, often, like this family, carrying all of their possessions on a single cart. (M.F.T. Baines, Liddle Collection) (Chapter 7 – The Belgians)

46 The Belgian Royal Family at the head of the army entering Ghent on 13 November 1918. The Queen receives a bouquet, while the King acknowledges the cheers of people in the upper storey windows. (Archives of the Royal Palace, Brussels) (Chapter 7 – The Belgians)

47 The British Army and the Belgian Government quickly put up huts like this one, to accommodate Belgian refugees. At first, for much of the returning civilian population, almost everything that they had was supplied to them by the British Army, from housing to tools to items of clothing such as greatcoats. (R.F. Pritchard, Liddle Collection) (Chapter 7 – The Belgians)

48 The Belgian resistance in action. Manneken-Pis is scattering the German armies with the force of his powerful jet of water. Cartoon in the liberal weekly *Pourquoi pas?* (University Library, Leuven) (Chapter 7 – The Belgians)

49 Pilots and enlisted groundcrew of the American 1st Aero Squadron, wearing a collection of German souvenirs, celebrate the news of the Armistice in France. (James J. Cooke collection) (Chapter 8 – The Americans)

50 A shower of tickertape greets news of the Armistice in New York, November 1918. (via Patrick Gariépy) (Chapter 8 – The Americans)

51 Happy to be going home: US troops en route for the States. The US began a rapid demobilization soon after the Armistice. (Patrick Gariépy collection (Chapter 8 – The Americans)

52 A sadder homecoming: an American serviceman being reinterred in the United States. The US was one of the few nations to begin to repatriate its dead after the Armistice. (Patrick Gariépy collection) (Chapter 8 – The Americans)

53 The end of the war came one month early for some Australians: this group is about to leave Bray in France on 10 October 1918 for two months' special furlough in Australia. In September 1918, 'Anzac

Leave' was granted to the 'originals', those men who had left Australia in 1914 and had served four years in the AIF. Some 6000 'originals' left France on home leave, and with the end of the war in November, they were discharged in Australia. (Australian War Memorial, Negative No. E03534) (Chapter 9 – Australians)

54 Part of the immense crowd in Martin Place, Sydney, on Monday 11 November 1918, celebrating news received early that evening of the signing of the Armistice. Boisterous crowds paraded through the streets of Sydney, singing patriotic songs and cheering. They also hanged and burnt effigies of the Kaiser. (Australian War Memorial, Negative No. H11563) (Chapter 9 – Australians)

Between pages 188 and 189

55 Australian prisoners of war, from various AIF infantry battalions, photographed outside the barracks of their camp in Germany, on 16 November 1918, five days after the Armistice. With the end of the war, many such men joined crowds of civilians on the long march back to the liberated territories of France and Belgium. (Australian War Memorial, Negative No. P01981.058) (One of a series of 400 photographs sent by Australian prisoners in German camps to Miss M.E. Chomley, Secretary of the Prisoners Department, Australian-British Red Cross Society, in London) (Chapter 9 – Australians)

56 Australian Army troops and volunteer groups at Adelaide Oval cricket ground celebrating the Armistice on 'Peace Day', 14 November 1918. On this day, which was declared a public holiday following the news of 11 November, a crowd of 40,000 people crammed the Oval to watch a victory parade of returned and invalided soldiers, nurses, recruits, rejected volunteers, militia forces and cadets. Some 6,000 children also joined the display, which culminated in "cheers for the British Navy, the British Army, the Australian troops, and the Allies" – the Adelaide *Advertiser*. (Australian War Memorial, Negative No. H11601) (Chapter 9 – Australians)

57 Premature celebrations in Toronto, 7 November 1918, as people react to early but unsubstantiated rumours that an armistice has been agreed. (National Archives of Canada PA 71198) (Chapter 10 – The Canadians)

58 A Canadian battalion, headed by pipes and drums, enters the town of Mons on the morning of 11 November 1918. The town fell to Canadian troops a few hours before the Armistice came into effect. (National Archives of Canada PA 3572) (Chapter 10 – The Canadians)

69 Africans in Natal assemble to hear news of the Armistice from a local magistrate, November 1918. (*Natal Witness* 23 November 1918) (Chapter 13 – South Africa)

70 Japanese and westerners in Tokyo gather at Hibiya Park to celebrate the signing of the Armistice. A photograph from the newspaper *Tokyo Asahi Shimbun* (via N. Shimazu) (Chapter 14 – The Japanese Response)

Between pages 220 and 221

71 Marshal Józef Pilsudski; in 1918, as Poland emerged independent from the ruins of the German, Austrian and Russian empires, Pilsudski unified into a national army the Polish units which had been fighting for the Austrians, or in the Russian Army or indeed in the Polish Legion under French command. Outside Warsaw in August 1920 this Polish national force repelled the Bolshevik attempt to retake Poland. From a watercolour. (Mrs A. Kurcz) (Chapter 15 – Central and Eastern Europe)

72 Celebrations following the departure of the Germans from Windau on the Baltic, in August 1919, and the arrival of Lettish troops, an event doubtless of infinitely more importance here than the Armistice in the west, the previous November. (R.B. Pargiter, Liddle Collection) (Chapter 15 – Central and Eastern Europe)

73 Captain R.B. Pargiter (centre), of the British Military Mission to Lithuania, with Lettish authorities in Windau, August 1919, shortly after independence. (R.B. Pargiter, Liddle Collection) (Chapter 15 – Central and Eastern Europe)

74 King Ferdinand of Bulgaria, seen here on the left, an inveterate schemer who had led his country to war for territorial and monetary gain. (Hugh Cecil) (Chapter 16 – Bulgaria)

75 General Lukoff, commanding the Bulgarian 2nd Army, and M. Liaptcheff, Minister of Finance, arrive at Janeš in Macedonia to discuss peace terms, 28 September 1918. (Liddle Collection) (Chapter 16 – Bulgaria)

76 Staff cars wait to take away the Bulgarian emissaries, Janeš 28 September 1918. (Liddle Collection) (Chapter 16 – Bulgaria)

77 A Bulgarian officer announces to his men the news of his country's departure from the war. (via Hugh Cecil) (Chapter 16 – Bulgaria)

78 Victor in the Balkans: General Franchet d'Espérey. (via Hugh Cecil) (Chapter 16 – Bulgaria)

79 A subject city: French and British troops mingle with Turkish citizens in a crowded Constantinople street. (L.V. White, Liddle Collection) (Chapter 17 – The Ottoman Empire)

80 Palestinian Arabs, photographed in 1918. What rewards would the Armistice bring for their part in the revolt which assisted in the overthrow of Ottoman rule? (A.B. Fuller, Liddle Collection) (Chapter 18 – The Arab World)

81 British troops watching a victory parade, Alexandria, Egypt, November 1918. Captain Eric Smith MC rides the horse with the white blaze. (E.J. Smith, Liddle Collection) (Chapter 18 – The Arab World)

Between pages 252 and 253

82 Popular celebrations in the Czech capital, Prague, on Independence Day, 28 October 1918. (from Rosický, *Rakouský Orel Padá*) (Chapter 19 – Austria Hungary)

83 One of the Czech national leaders, Isidor Zahradnìk, joins the crowds under the statue of St. Wenceslas, Prague 28 October 1918. (Rosický, *Rakouský Orel Padá*) (Chapter 19 – Austria Hungary)

84 Crowds in Zagreb sing Croatian patriotic songs, having learned that Croatia has severed links with Austria Hungary. 29 October 1918. (Horvat, *Politicka Povijest Hrvatske*) (Chapter 19 – Austria Hungary)

85 Austrian emissaries arrive at Osteria del Termine in Italy to sign the armistice document, 3 November 1918. (Reproduced from *With the 48th Division in Italy*, Lieutenant-Colonel G.H. Barnett, 1923) (Chapter 20 – Italy)

86 The Austrian party reach the Italian lines, Osteria del Termine, 3 November 1918. (Reproduced from *With the 48th Division in Italy*, by Lt. Col. G.H. Barnett, 1923) (Chapter 20 – Italy)

87 Italian troops enter Trento around 5 November 1918, shortly after the Armistice on the Italian Front. (M. Pluviano & I. Guerrini) (Chapter 20 – Italy)

88 Roger Vercel, author of *Capitaine Conan* published in 1934. Vercel at the time of the Armistice was in Sofia, as a French Army legal officer. He travelled extensively between Budapest, Belgrade, Odessa and Istanbul, and based his literary work on his experiences. (Hugh Cecil) (Chapter 22 – Armistice in Literature)

89 R.H. Mottram (right), serving with the British Claims Commission (assessing the civilian claims for damage caused by the army) in Belgium c. 1917. (Norfolk Record Office, Mottram Collection) (Chapter 22 – Armistice in Literature)

90 Crowds gather on Armistice Day 1920 in Richmond, North Yorkshire. (Green Howards Regimental Museum, Richmond) (Chapter 23 – A Changing Meaning)

91 A girl bends to lay flowers at the foot of the Cenotaph, while next to her a widow wears her husband's medal ribbons. 11 November 1920. (*Illustrated London News*) (Chapter 23 – A Changing Meaning)

92 A service of dedication at the Royal Naval Division memorial, Beaucourt sur Ancre, on Sunday 12 November 1922. Veterans of the division, and Royal Marine bandsmen are present, while behind them the devastation of the battlefield is still apparent. (E. Wettern, Liddle Collection) (Chapter 23 – A Changing Meaning)

93 A veteran pays his respects at Northampton war memorial, November 1962. (Liddle Collection) (Chapter 23 – A Changing Meaning)

List of Maps

Acknowledgements

Catching a moment in time, eighty years ago, just as it was being experienced by men and women all over the world - different races, cultures and language - and then drawing upon the expertise of scholars world-wide to re-picture that moment, was always going to be a challenge. We hope that, thanks to the ready understanding of those scholars that this was the goal, the challenge has been effectively met.

We do sincerely thank all the historians listed at the end of this book. For us as editors, co-operation with our contributors has been a pleasure from the first and we are mindful of their readiness to undertake this additional academic burden and fit it in to their over-filled schedule of commitments. We recognize that we were fortunate in the direction of our invitations.

Of those we must thank beyond the range of our contributors, first must come Claire Harder, Secretary to the Liddle Collection, for her presentation to the publishers of the edited text of this book and her professional skill, interest, enthusiasm, loyalty and unflappability. This is the third large-scale book which she has brought towards fruition and we record with relief on our part as well as congratulation that she was awarded her MA between the second and third of those books.

Second we thank Matthew Richardson, the Assistant Keeper of the Liddle Collection. Matthew is to a large extent responsible for drawing together all the illustrative material in this book and locating much of it too. As well as contributing the concluding chapter of the book and fulfilling efficiently, like Claire, an expanding range of Collection responsibilities, Matthew has always responded positively to general and particular questions as this book has moved from concept to final production. Good scholars are to be cherished especially when they work with such enthusiasm and sustained dedication.

To Dr Ian Whitehead we express our appreciation for his compilation of the index, a task he carried out to superb effect in *Passchendaele in Perspective*. In asking Ian to do the index, we knew that this major task was in good hands.

Again Friends of the Liddle Collection have supported this book from the start. In particular Albert Smith, Bob Carrington and Bob Pykett examined references from the Collection's catalogues and checked their appropriateness in the letters, diary entries, photographs and official papers concerned. Carolyn Mumford's transcriptions of tape-recorded recollections once again proved valuable in our research.

Adam Smith, now Director of the Scottish Museum of Flight, scoured Scottish newspapers for contemporary evidence linked to our theme, schoolmaster Martyn Luckwell of Penyrheol Comprehensive School, Swansea, scrutinized South Wales newspapers, and local historian Bill Turner, combed through files similarly in the libraries of East Lancashire's mill-towns. The evidence gleaned from all these sources was invaluable to Peter Liddle.

From his own collection and from wider photograph research, Patrick Gariépy in Eugene, Oregon has been unstinting with his assistance. From Kilmainham Jail Museum in Dublin came by request an exceptionally interesting Irish document and we thank Patrick Cooke and Niamh O'Sullivan for their assistance here and also the help given by Jean Siddall in the Local Studies Section of Burnley Reference Library, staff of the British Newspaper Library at Colindale, London, Matthew Johnson of Newark Museums and Nicola Mills at Beamish Open Air Museum. Staff within the Media Services Department, the University of Leeds copied many of the photographs and documents in the book. Colin Butterfield and David Bailey have done fine work before for our books and have matched it again. We thank them and the Graphics Unit, School of Geography, University of Leeds, for the production of the maps which so helpfully support the text. We are indebted, too, to Professor Ian Nish for his advice.

It is also a pleasure to report our recognition of the excellent service given us by Barbara Bramall of Pen & Sword in overall supervision of the production of the book at every stage towards publication. Our confidence in Barbara, and in Roni and Paul Wilkinson with the cover design and the setting of the illustrations, has been well-placed but we thank too, other staff at Pen & Sword and our volunteer proof-readers.

We would like to thank all copyright holders for their generous readiness to allow material under their control, illustrations, maps or textual, to appear in the book. Every effort has been made by contributors to locate current holders of copyright in text and illustrations but the editors apologize for any omissions which may have occurred in this respect and would welcome information so that amendments can be made in future editions.

It is certainly not as a matter of form that we thank our wives, Mirabel Cecil and Louise Liddle. We are fully aware that our work is made possible not least through the support we enjoy at home. How fortunate we are in this and, as far as this particular book is concerned, in the remarkable team listed here and at the end of the book.

Hugh Cecil and Peter Liddle, University of Leeds, March 1998.

President Wilson's Fourteen Points

President Wilson's Fourteen Points programme for world peace, first made public on 8 January 1918, and amplified by his 'subsequent addresses', formed, under the pre-Armistice agreement between Germany, the Allies and the U.S.A., the accepted basis for future peace terms, subject also to German agreement, which was given, to allow the Allies to reserve the question of Freedom of the Seas, and to pay "compensation .5.5. for damage done to the civilian population of the Allies and to their property by the aggression of Germany by land by sea and from the air".

The Fourteen Points represented President Wilson's Utopian blueprint for a new, open, democratic and liberal international order, through which legitimate national aspirations could be settled through the 'principle of nationality', and through which the pernicious effects of secret treaties and alliances could be removed by a commitment to 'open' diplomacy; certain freedoms, of the seas for example, were laid down as essential to international harmony. The 'subsequent addresses' most importantly included: no annexations, no contributions, and no punitive damages (11 February 1918); impartial justice in international relations; no form of economic boycott or exclusion; publication in full of all international agreements and treaties (27 September 1918).

The pre-Armistice agreement for a peace based on Wilson's Fourteen Points, with certain reservations, was a binding undertaking. It cannot be said that these promises were fulfilled in the final peace settlement, with its glaring inconsistencies over the 'principle of nationality'. Given the conflicting claims among the Allies however, and the state of public opinion among them, the idea that the Allied statesmen could ever have agreed to a peace based fully on Wilson's points – even if the points were all to have been practicable – seems wholly unrealistic; and the draconian terms of the Treaty of Brest Litovsk imposed by Germany on Bolshevik Russia in March 1918, does not suggest that the Germans, had they won the war, would have handled the Allies any more mercifully than they themselves were handled by the Allied negotiators of the Treaty of Versailles.

THE FOURTEEN POINTS:

I. Open covenants of peace, openly arrived at, after which there shall be no private international understandings of any kind but diplomacy shall proceed always frankly and in the public view.

II. Absolute freedom of navigation upon the seas, outside territorial waters, alike in peace and in war, except as the seas may be closed in whole or in part by international action for the enforcement of international covenants.

III. The removal, so far as possible, of all economic barriers and the establishment of an equality of trade conditions among all the nations consenting to peace and associating themselves for its maintenance.

IV. Adequate guarantees given and taken that national armaments will be reduced to the lowest point consistent with domestic safety.

V. A free, open minded and absolutely impartial adjustment of all colonial claims, based upon a strict observance of the principle that in determining all such questions of sovereignty the interests of the populations concerned must have equal weight with the equitable claims of the government whose title is to be determined.

VI. The evacuation of all Russian territory and such a settlement of all questions affecting Russia as will secure the best and freest co-operation of the other nations of the world in obtaining for her an unhampered and unembarrassed opportunity for the independent determination of her own political development and national policy and assure her of a sincere welcome into the society of free nations under institutions of her own choosing; and, more than a welcome, assistance also of every kind that she may need and may herself desire. The treatment accorded Russia by her sister nations in the months to come will be the acid test of their good will, of their comprehension of her needs as distinguished from their own interests, and of their intelligent and unselfish sympathy.

VII. Belgium, the whole world will agree, must be evacuated and restored, without any attempt to limit the sovereignty which she now enjoys in common with all other free nations. No other single act will serve as this will to restore confidence among the nations in the laws which they have themselves set and determined for the government of their relations with one another. Without this healing act the whole structure and validity of international law is forever impaired.

VIII. All French territory should be freed and the invaded portions restored, and the wrong done to France by Prussia in 1871 in the matter of Alsace-Lorraine, which has unsettled the peace of the world for nearly fifty years, should be righted, in order that peace may once more be made secure in the interests of all.

IX. A readjustment of the frontiers of Italy should be effected along clearly recognisable lines of nationality.

X. The peoples of Austria-Hungary, whose place among the nations we wish to see safeguarded and assured, should be accorded the freest opportunity of autonomous development.

XI. Roumania, Serbia, and Montenegro should be evacuated; occupied territories restored; Serbia accorded free and secure access to the sea; and the relations of several Balkan states to one another determined by friendly counsel along historically established lines of allegiance and nationality; and international guarantees of the political and economic independence and territorial integrity of the several Balkan states should be entered into.

XII. The Turkish portions of the present Ottoman Empire should be assured a secure sovereignty, but the other nationalities which are now under Turkish rule should be assured an undoubted security of life and an absolutely unmolested opportunity of autonomous development, and the Dardanelles should be permanently opened as a free passage to the ships and commerce of all nations under international guarantees.

XIII. An independent Polish state should be erected which should include the territories inhabited by indisputably Polish populations, which should be assured a free and secure access to the sea, and whose political and economic independence and territorial integrity should be guaranteed by international covenant.

XIV. A general association of nations must be formed under specific covenants for the purpose of affording mutual guarantees of political independence and territorial integrity to great and small states alike.

THE ARMISTICE TERMS:

Here follows the text of the British translation of the terms of the Armistice signed by the Allied and Associated Powers and by the Germans, effective from 11 November 1918 at 11 a.m. There was also a German translation, the original text being in French. The document required Germany to evacuate the occupied zones of France and Belgium immediately and, by the obligation to surrender war material on land and sea and by the evacuation of the left bank of the Rhine, made it effectively impossible for the Germans under the Armistice terms to resume the fighting against the Allies. To reinforce this, the Entente powers kept up their blockade of Germany until the summer of 1919, and this caused intensified hardship.

The 11 November Armistice was valid for thirty-six days. It was renewed on 12-13 December 1918; the Armistice was extended until 17 January 1919, and the Allied High Command reserved the right to occupy the neutral zone on the right bank of the Rhine, north of Cologne and up to the Dutch frontier. Owing to delays in reaching an agreement on the peace terms to present to Germany, there were two further extensions of the Armistice. After the last of these extensions expired, as long as the final peace terms were still under debate, the Allied powers simply reserved the right to terminate the Armistice at any time, at three days notice. New Armistice conditions imposed during 1919 included the placing of the German merchant fleet under the control and flag of the Allies during the Armistice period, and the requirement that the Germans should abandon offensive operations against the Poles, in the Posen region and everywhere else.

TERMS OF ARMISTICE WITH GERMANY.

(The French text is the official one; the English and German texts are translations).

TERMS OF ARMISTICE WITH GERMANY.

Between MARSHAL FOCH, Commander-in-Chief of the Allied Armies, acting in the name of the Allied and Associated Powers, with ADMIRAL WEMYSS, First Sea Lord, on the one hand, and

HERR ERZBERGER, Secretary of State, President of the German Delegation,
COUNT VON OBERNDORFF, Envoy Extraordinary and Minister Plenipotentiary,
MAJOR-GENERAL VON WINTERFELDT,
CAPTAIN VANSELOW (German Navy),

duly empowered and acting with the concurrence of the German Chancellor on the other hand.

An Armistice has been concluded on the following conditions:—

CONDITIONS OF THE ARMISTICE CONCLUDED WITH GERMANY.

A.—CLAUSES RELATING TO THE WESTERN FRONT.

I.—Cessation of hostilities by land and in the air six hours after the signing of the Armistice.

II.—Immediate evacuation of the invaded countries—Belgium, France, Luxemburg, as well as Alsace-Lorraine—so ordered as to be completed within 15 days from the signature of the Armistice.

German troops which have not left the above-mentioned territories within the period fixed shall be made prisoners of war.

Occupation by the Allied and United States Forces jointly shall keep pace with the evacuation in these areas.

All movements of evacuation and occupation shall be regulated in accordance with a Note (Annexe 1) determined at the time of the signing of the Armistice.

III.—Repatriation, beginning at once, to be completed within 15 days, of all inhabitants of the countries above enumerated (including hostages, persons under trial, or condemned).

IV.—Surrender in good condition by the German Armies of the following equipment:—

- 5,000 guns (2,500 heavy, 2,500 field).
- 25,000 machine guns.
- 3,000 trench mortars.
- 1,700 aeroplanes (fighters, bombers—firstly all D. 7's and night-bombing machines).

The above to be delivered *in situ* to the Allied and United States troops in accordance with the detailed conditions laid down in the Note (Annexe 1) determined at the time of the signing of the Armistice.

V.—Evacuation by the German Armies of the districts on the left bank of the Rhine. These districts on the left bank of the Rhine shall be administered by the local authorities under the control of the Allied and United States Armies of Occupation.

The occupation of these territories by Allied and United States troops shall be assured by garrisons holding the principal crossings of the Rhine (Mainz, Coblenz, Cologne), together with bridgeheads at these points of a 30-kilometre (about 19 miles) radius on the right bank, and by garrisons similarly holding the strategic points of the area.

A neutral zone shall be reserved on the right bank of the Rhine, between the river and a line drawn parallel to the bridgeheads and to the river and 10 kilometres (6¼ miles) distant from them, between the Dutch frontier and the Swiss frontier.

The evacuation by the enemy of the Rhine districts (right and left banks) shall be so ordered as to be completed within a further period of 16 days, in all 31 days after the signing of the Armistice.

All movements of evacuation and occupation shall be regulated according to the Note (Annexe 1) determined at the time of the signing of the Armistice.

VI.—In all territories evacuated by the enemy, evacuation of the inhabitants shall be forbidden; no damage or harm shall be done to the persons or property of the inhabitants.

No person shall be prosecuted for having taken part in any military measures previous to the signing of the Armistice.

No destruction of any kind to be committed.

Military establishments of all kinds shall be delivered intact, as well as military stores, food, munitions and equipment, which shall not have been removed during the periods fixed for evacuation.

Stores of food of all kinds for the civil population, cattle, &c., shall be left *in situ*.

No measure of a general character shall be taken, and no official order shall be given which would have as a consequence the depreciation of industrial establishments or a reduction of their personnel.

VII.—Roads and means of communication of every kind, railroads, waterways, roads, bridges, telegraphs, telephones, shall be in no manner impaired.

All civil and military personnel at present employed on them shall remain.

5,000 locomotives and 150,000 wagons, in good working order, with all necessary spare parts and fittings, shall be delivered to the Associated Powers within the period fixed in Annexe No. 2 (not exceeding 31 days in all).

5 000 motor lorries are also to be delivered in good condition within 36 days.

The railways of Alsace-Lorraine shall be handed over within 31 days, together with all personnel and material belonging to the organization of this system

Further, the necessary working material in the territories on the left bank of the Rhine shall be left *in situ*.

All stores of coal and material for the upkeep of permanent way, signals and repair shops shall be left *in situ* and kept in an efficient state by Germany, so far as the working of the means of communication on the left bank of the Rhine is concerned.

All lighters taken from the Allies shall be restored to them.

The Note attached as Annexe 2 defines the details of these measures.

VIII.—The German Command shall be responsible for revealing within 48 hours after the signing of the Armistice, all mines or delay-action fuzes disposed on territories evacuated by the German troops, and shall assist in their discovery and destruction.

The German Command shall also reveal all destructive measures that may have been taken (such as poisoning or pollution of wells, springs, &c.).

Breaches of these clauses will involve reprisals.

IX.—The right of requisition shall be exercised by the Allied and United States armies in all occupied territories, save for settlement of accounts with authorized persons.

The upkeep of the troops of occupation in the Rhine districts (excluding Alsace-Lorraine) shall be charged to the German Government.

X.—The immediate repatriation, without reciprocity, according to detailed conditions which shall be fixed, of all Allied and United States prisoners of war, including those under trial and condemned. The Allied Powers and the United States of America shall be able to dispose of these prisoners as they think fit. This condition annuls all other conventions regarding prisoners of war, including that of July, 1918, now being ratified. However, the return of German prisoners of war interned in Holland and Switzerland shall continue as heretofore The return of German prisoners of war shall be settled at the conclusion of the Peace preliminaries.

XI.—Sick and wounded who cannot be removed from territory evacuated by the German forces shall be cared for by German personnel, who shall be left on the spot with the material required.

B.—CLAUSES RELATING TO THE EASTERN FRONTIERS OF GERMANY.

XII.—All German troops at present in any territory which before the war formed part of Austria-Hungary, Roumania or Turkey, shall withdraw within the frontiers of Germany as they existed on 1st August, 1914, and all German troops at present in territories, which before the war formed part of Russia, must likewise return to within the frontiers of Germany as above defined, as soon as the Allies shall think the moment suitable, having regard to the internal situation of these territories.

XIII.—Evacuation of German troops, to begin at once, and all German instructors, prisoners and agents, civilian as well as military, now on the territory of Russia (frontiers as defined on 1st August, 1914), to be recalled.

XIV.—German troops to cease at once all requisitions and seizures and any other coercive measures with a view to obtaining supplies intended for Germany in Roumania and Russia (frontiers as defined on 1st August, 1914).

XV.—Annulment of the treaties of Bucharest and Brest-Litovsk and of the supplementary treaties.

XVI.—The Allies shall have free access to the territories evacuated by the Germans on their Eastern frontier, either through Danzig or by the Vistula, in order to convey supplies to the populations of these territories or for the purpose of maintaining order.

C.—Clause Relating to East Africa.

XVII.—Evacuation of all German forces operating in East Africa within a period specified by the Allies.

D.—General Clauses.

XVIII.—Repatriation without reciprocity, within a maximum period of one month, in accordance with detailed conditions hereafter to be fixed, of all interned civilians, including hostages and persons under trial and condemned, who may be subjects of Allied or Associated States other than those mentioned in Clause III.

Financial Clauses.

XIX.—With the reservation that any subsequent concessions and claims by the Allies and United States remain unaffected, the following financial conditions are imposed:—

Reparation for damage done.

While the Armistice lasts, no public securities shall be removed by the enemy which can serve as a pledge to the Allies to cover reparation for war losses.

Immediate restitution of the cash deposit in the National Bank of Belgium and, in general, immediate return of all documents, specie, stock, shares, paper money, together with plant for the issue thereof, affecting public or private interests in the invaded countries.

Restitution of the Russian and Roumanian gold yielded to Germany or taken by that Power.

This gold to be delivered in trust to the Allies until peace is concluded.

E.—Naval Conditions.

XX.—Immediate cessation of all hostilities at sea, and definite information to be given as to the position and movements of all German ships.

Notification to be given to neutrals that freedom of navigation in all territorial waters is given to the Navies and Mercantile Marines of the Allied and Associated Powers, all questions of neutrality being waived.

XXI.—All Naval and Mercantile Marine prisoners of war of the Allied and Associated Powers in German hands to be returned, without reciprocity.

XXII.—To surrender at the ports specified by the Allies and the United States all submarines at present in existence (including all submarine cruisers and minelayers), with armament and equipment complete. Those that cannot put to sea shall be deprived of armament and equipment, and shall remain under the supervision of the Allies and the United States. Submarines ready to put to sea shall be prepared to leave German ports immediately on receipt of a wireless order to sail to the port of surrender, the remainder to follow as early as possible. The conditions of this Article shall be completed within 14 days of the signing of the Armistice.

XXIII.—The following German surface warships, which shall be designated by the Allies and the United States of America, shall forthwith be disarmed and thereafter interned in neutral ports, or, failing them, Allied ports, to be designated by the Allies and the United States of America, and placed under the surveillance of the Allies and the United States of America, only care and maintenance parties being left on board, namely:—

- 6 battle cruisers.
- 10 battleships.
- 8 light cruisers (including two minelayers).
- 50 destroyers of the most modern types.

All other surface warships (including river craft) are to be concentrated in German Naval bases, to be designated by the Allies and the United States of America, completely disarmed and placed under the supervision of the Allies and the United States of America. All vessels of the Auxiliary Fleet are to be disarmed. All vessels specified for internment shall be ready to leave German ports seven days after the signing of the Armistice. Directions for the voyage shall be given by wireless.

XXIV. The Allies and the United States of America shall have the right to sweep up all minefields and destroy all obstructions laid by Germany outside German territorial waters, and the positions of these are to be indicated.

XXV. Freedom of access to and from the Baltic to be given to the Navies and Mercantile Marines of the Allied and Associated Powers. This to be secured by the occupation of all German forts, fortifications, batteries and defence works of all kinds in all the routes from the Cattegat into the Baltic, and by the sweeping up and destruction of all mines and obstructions within and without German territorial waters without any questions of neutrality being raised by Germany, and the positions of all such mines and obstructions to be indicated, and the plans relating thereto are to be supplied.

XXVI. The existing blockade conditions set up by the Allied and Associated Powers are to remain unchanged, and all German merchant ships found at sea are to remain liable to capture. The Allies and United States contemplate the provisioning of Germany during the Armistice as shall be found necessary.

XXVII.—All Aerial Forces are to be concentrated and immobilized in German bases to be specified by the Allies and the United States of America.

XXVIII.—In evacuating the Belgian coasts and ports, Germany shall abandon, *in situ* and intact, the port material and material for inland waterways, also all merchant ships, tugs and lighters, all Naval aircraft and air materials and stores, all arms and armaments and all stores and apparatus of all kinds.

XXIX.—All Black Sea ports are to be evacuated by Germany; all Russian warships of all descriptions seized by Germany in the Black Sea are to be handed over to the Allies and the United States of America; all neutral merchant ships seized in the Black Sea are to be released; all warlike and other materials of all kinds seized in those ports are to be returned, and German materials as specified in Clause XXVIII. are to be abandoned.

XXX.—All merchant ships at present in German hands belonging to the Allied and Associated Powers are to be restored to ports specified by the Allies and the United States of America without reciprocity.

XXXI.—No destruction of ships or of materials to be permitted before evacuation, surrender or restoration.

XXXII.—The German Government shall formally notify all the neutral Governments, and particularly the Governments of Norway, Sweden, Denmark and Holland, that all restrictions placed on the trading of their vessels with the Allied and Associated countries, whether by the German Government or by private German interests, and whether in return for specific concessions, such as the export of shipbuilding materials or not, are immediately cancelled.

XXXIII.—No transfers of German merchant shipping of any description to any neutral flag are to take place after signature of the Armistice.

F.—Duration of Armistice.

XXXIV.—The duration of the Armistice is to be 36 days, with option to extend. During this period, on failure of execution of any of the above clauses, the Armistice may be repudiated by one of the contracting parties on 48 hours previous notice. It is understood that failure to execute Articles III and XVIII completely in the periods specified is not to give reason for a repudiation of the Armistice, save where such failure is due to malice aforethought.

To ensure the execution of the present convention under the most favourable conditions, the principle of a permanent International Armistice Commission is recognized. This Commission shall act under the supreme authority of the High Command, military and naval, of the Allied Armies.

The present Armistice was signed on the 11th day of November, 1918, at 5 o'clock a.m. (French time).

(Signed)—

F. FOCH. ERZBERGER.
R.E.WEMYSS. OBERNDORFF.
WINTERFELDT.
VANSELOW.

11th November, 1918.

The representatives of the Allies declare that, in view of fresh events, it appears necessary to them that the following condition shall be added to the clauses of the Armistice :—

"In case the German ships are not handed over within the periods specified, the Governments of the Allies and of the United States shall have the right to occupy Heligoland to ensure their delivery."

(Signed)—

R. E. WEMYSS, *Admiral.* F. FOCH.

"The German delegates declare that they will forward this declaration to the German Chancellor, with the recommendation that it be accepted, accompanying it with the reasons by which the Allies have been actuated in making this demand."

(Signed)—
ERZBERGER.
OBERNDORFF.
WINTERFELDT.
VANSELOW.

Annexe No. 1.

I.—The evacuation of the invaded territories, Belgium, France and Luxemburg, and also of Alsace-Lorraine, shall be carried out in three successive stages according to the following conditions :—

1st stage.—Evacuation of the territories situated between the existing front and line No. 1 on the enclosed map, to be completed within 5 days after the signature of the Armistice.

2nd stage.—Evacuation of territories situated between line No. 1 and line No. 2, to be carried out within 4 further days (9 days in all after the signing of the Armistice).

3rd stage.—Evacuation of the territories situated between line No. 2 and line No. 3, to be completed within 6 further days (15 days in all after the signing of the Armistice).

Allied and United States troops shall enter these various territories on the expiration of the period allowed to the German troops for the evacuation of each.

In consequence, the Allied troops will cross the present German front as from the 6th day following the signing of the Armistice, line No. 1 as from the 10th day, and line No. 2 as from the 16th day.

II.—*Evacuation of the Rhine district.*—This evacuation shall also be carried out in several successive stages :—

(1.) Evacuation of territories situated between lines 2 and 3 and line 4, to be completed within 4 further days (19 days in all after the signing of the Armistice).

(2.) Evacuation of territories situated between lines 4 and 5 to be completed within 4 further days (23 days in all after the signing of the Armistice).

(3.) Evacuation of territories situated between lines 5 and 6 (line of the Rhine) to be completed within 4 further days (27 days in all after the signing of the Armistice).

(4). Evacuation of the bridgeheads and of the neutral zone on the right bank of the Rhine to be completed within 4 further days (31 days in all after the signing of the Armistice).

The Allied and United States Army of Occupation shall enter these various territories after the expiration of the period allowed to the German troops for the evacuation of each : consequently the Army will cross line No. 3, 20 days after the signing of the Armistice. It will cross line No. 4 as from the 24th day after the signing of the Armistice : Line No. 5 as from the 28th day : Line No. 6 (Rhine) the 32nd day, in order to occupy the bridgeheads.

III.—*Surrender by the German Armies of war material specified by the Armistice.*

This war material shall be surrendered according to the following conditions :—The first half before the 10th day, the second half before the 20th day. This material shall be handed over to each of the Allied and United States Armies by each larger tactical group of the German Armies in the proportions which may be fixed by the permanent international Armistice Commission.

Annexe No. 2.

Conditions regarding communications, railways, waterways, roads, river and sea ports, and telegraphic and telephonic communications :—

I.—All communications as far as the Rhine, inclusive, or comprised, on the right bank of this river, within the bridge-heads occupied by the Allied Armies shall be placed under the supreme and absolute authority of the Commander-in-Chief of the Allied Armies, who shall have the right to take any measure he may think necessary to assure their occupation and use. All documents relative to communications shall be held ready for transmission to him.

II.—All the material and all the civil and military personnel at present employed in the maintenance and working of all lines of communication are to be maintained in their entirety upon these lines in all territories evacuated by the German troops.

All supplementary material necessary for the upkeep of these lines of communication in the districts on the left bank of the Rhine shall be supplied by the German Government throughout the duration of the Armistice.

III.—*Personnel.*—The French and Belgian personnel belonging to the services of the lines of communication, whether interned or not, are to be returned to the French and Belgian Armies during the 15 days following the signing of the Armistice. The personnel belonging to the organization of the Alsace-Lorraine railway system is to be maintained or reinstated in such a way as to ensure the working of the system.

The Commander-in-Chief of the Allied Armies shall have the right to make all changes and substitutions that he may desire in the personnel of the lines of communication.

IV. *Material.*—(*a.*) *Rolling stock.*—The rolling stock handed over to the Allied Armies in the zone comprised between the present front and Line No. 3, not including Alsace-Lorraine, shall amount at least to 5,000 locomotives and 150,000 waggons. This surrender shall be carried out within the period fixed by Clause 7 of the Armistice and under conditions, the details of which shall be fixed by the permanent International Armistice Commission.

All this material is to be in good condition and in working order, with all the ordinary spare parts and fittings. It may be employed together with the regular personnel, or with any other, upon any part of the railway system of the Allied Armies.

The material necessary for the working of the Alsace-Lorraine railway system is to be maintained or replaced for the use of the French Army.

The material to be left *in situ* in the territories on the left bank of the Rhine, as well as that on the inner side of the bridge-heads, must permit of the normal working of the railways in these districts.

(*b.*) *Permanent way, signals and workshops*.—The material for signals, machine tools and tool outfits, taken from the workshops and depôts of the French and Belgian lines, are to be replaced under conditions, the details of which are to be arranged by the permanent International Armistice Commission.

The Allied Armies are to be supplied with railroad material, rails, incidental fittings, plant, bridge-building material and timber necessary for the repair of the lines destroyed beyond the present front.

(*c.*) *Fuel and maintenance material.*—The German Government shall be responsible throughout the duration of the Armistice for the release of fuel and maintenance material to the depôts normally allotted to the railways in the territories on the left bank of the Rhine.

V. *Telegraphic and Telephonic Communications.*— All telegraphs, telephones, and fixed W/T stations are to be handed over to the Allied Armies, with all the civil and military personnel and all their material, including all stores on the left bank of the Rhine.

Supplementary stores necessary for the upkeep of the system are to be supplied throughout the duration of the Armistice by the German Government according to requirements.

The Commander-in-Chief of the Allied Armies shall place this system under military supervision and shall ensure its control, and shall make all changes and substitutions in personnel which he may think necessary.

He will send back to the German Army all the military personnel who are not in his judgment necessary for the working and upkeep of the railway.

All plans of the German telegraphic and telephonic systems shall be handed over to the Commander-in-Chief of the Allied Armies.

General Staff,
War Office,
November, 1918.

The Western Front, November 1918

Part I

Introductory

Chapter One

Armistice: National Reactions and Reflections, September/November 1918

Hugh Cecil and Peter Liddle

At the Eleventh Hour is a book about the armistices of 1918 which ended the Great War. It is not a book specifically of military or diplomatic history, but rather, a study of popular attitudes, worldwide, towards the coming of peace – the exultation, fears, hopes, expectations, disappointments and sorrows of service personnel and civilians after a terrible and prolonged struggle. Nor is the canvas confined simply to responses in Europe and the Western world; it covers the Near and Middle East, India, Japan, Southern Africa and the Antipodes as well. The object of the book is to capture a moment in history: that is the eve of the armistices, the armistice days themselves, and the weeks which followed, during which people were accustoming themselves to a world without war.

It will be noted that we speak here of 'armistices' and not simply of the best-known armistice – that of 11 November – which did not come until after there had been a succession of cease-fires between Germany's lesser partners and their antagonists. The first to sue for peace – at the end of September – was Bulgaria; then in late October and the beginning of November, Turkey and Austria. These cease-fires showed that the previous united front of Germany with her allies was dissolving, as their interests separated from those of the mighty but crumbling Hohenzollern Empire, under Kaiser Wilhelm II, whose reign, like that of other crowned heads of state, was shortly to end. The 11 November Armistice followed.

This present volume, *At the Eleventh Hour*, provides also a study of how societies, accustomed, some of them over more than four years, to their countries' total involvement with the war effort, began the process of disengagement from this all-entangling web; and how they looked on the world when released, for the first time in years, from its obfuscations or dubious protection. Clearly there was a great variety of responses.

The reactions of such eminent figures as Lloyd George and Georges Clemenceau to the Armistice are well-recorded – their triumph and their apprehensions about the world that lay ahead. Apart, however, from general comments in memoirs about frantic rejoicing or depression in defeat, the immediate responses of the general public in every country have attracted little serious study. In recent years there has been one vivid portrait of opinion at this particular moment in history, Stanley Weintraub's *A Stillness Heard Round the World* (1985).[1] This draws largely on the voluminous published sources – letters, diaries, memoirs and fiction by eyewitnesses – as well as valuable interview material assembled by the author.

At the Eleventh Hour, relies more on contemporary unpublished material – personal papers both of obscure individuals and of prominent public statesmen and those soon destined to make history. It also uses official papers, and national and local newspaper reports – European, Far Eastern, Antipodean, South African and North American. There is a greater emphasis, too, on the economic and social factors overshadowing the daily lives of the populations involved; and *At the Eleventh Hour* benefits from the specialist knowledge of the contributors, most of them nationals of the countries about which they are writing.

In the popular imagination, the Armistice is summed up in photographs of riotous celebration or in flickering newsreels, taken in subsequent years,

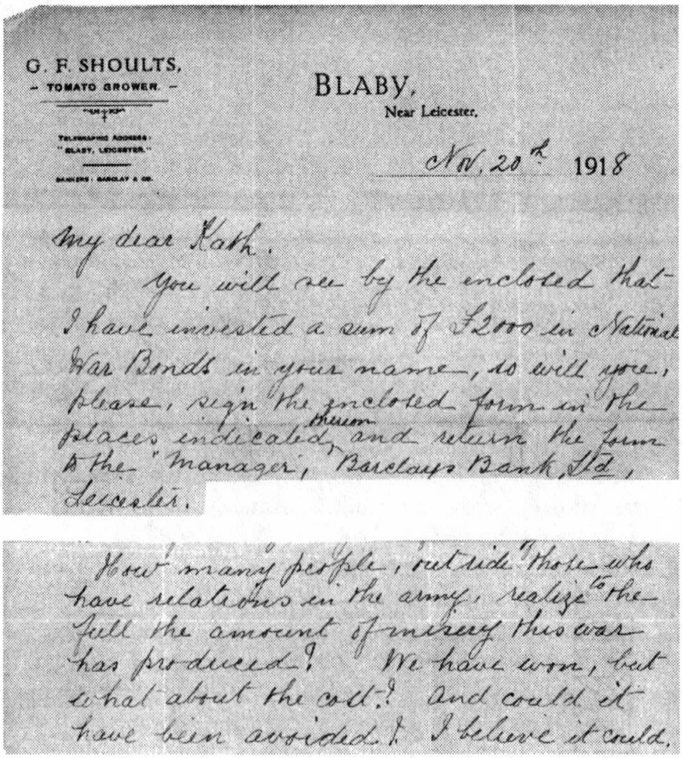
G. F. SHOULTS,
– TOMATO GROWER. –

BLABY,
Near Leicester.

Nov. 20th 1918

My dear Kath.

You will see by the enclosed that I have invested a sum of £2000 in National War Bonds in your name, so will you, please, sign the enclosed form in the places indicated thereon and return the form to the "Manager," Barclays Bank, Ltd, Leicester.

How many people, outside those who have relations in the army, realize to the full the amount of misery this war has produced? We have won, but what about the cost? And could it have been avoided? I believe it could.

i "But what about the cost?" A Leicestershire man asks his daughter. (K. Shoults, Liddle Collection) showing solemn Remembrance Day services round the Cenotaph. The general picture which emerges from the studies in the present volume is far more complex. Even for the victors, the nature of the war prevented 11 November being, for any nation, the day of unalloyed triumph to which all sides had looked forward in August 1914. There had been no Trafalgars, no Agincourts. To this day, historians dispute whether the Somme, Jutland or Third Ypres were victories for the Allies. The overwhelming German defeat of the Russians at Tannenberg in 1914, was indecisive in its consequences. The German High Seas Fleet had stayed for most of the war in harbour. A huge Anglo-French force was locked up for years in an inconclusive campaign in Salonika. Furthermore, what had decided the outcome seemed to be less the almost unimaginable courage shown, month by month, by so many men in arms, than the impersonal forces, such as industrial power, economic blockade and the *threat* of an enormous army of American soldiers, many of whom never had to fight.

Although the ordeal of war failed to obliterate sense of duty, national loyalties, or indeed, idealism – as can be seen from the surge of hope for a better world when the war ended – the old innocence and romance were gone. The trenches were an indelible symbol of the desolation of modern war. To be liberated from 'all that', to have survived, was, of course, as good a reason for rejoicing as any, but many found it hard to extricate themselves psychologically from the morass.

On the other hand it is an over-simplification to the point of untruth to say, as George Panichas has done: "Not a transfiguring nobility but a sense of disgust beyond despair marked the temper of Europe by November 11, 1918".[2] The actuality was that from top to bottom of every society doubt mingled with triumph, and hope with depression. Among the defeated Germans, Ernst Jünger, warrior extraordinary, is named here as being one of those who as a junior officer at the end of the war "had a feeling of despair about the lost war, the lost values and ideals";[3] yet, like the then more obscure Corporal Hitler, he was quick to recover his belief in his country's destiny, personified in the army to which Jünger continued to belong. High-ranking German nationalists, too, took a crumb of consolation from the fact that the principle of nationality, embodied in Wilson's Fourteen Points, gave full justification for their humiliated land to pursue a great purpose for the future – to unite all the German-speaking territories of Europe. Even on the left, hardly sympathetic to dreams of military glory, there was sorrow at the defeat – but also hopes for a new socialist Germany: the expressionist artist Käthe Kollwitz, who for years lived, of choice, in a working-class district of Berlin, wrote in her diary for 11 November: "Agreement between the Majority Socialists and the Independents, thank God! Further publication of the terrible Armistice conditions. All we can hope is that peace will bring better conditions".[4]

For the victors, likewise, the emotions felt were mixed. Could they have broken Germany more completely by not letting them have an armistice and by taking the war into their own country? Had the chance of a lasting peace been missed? Georges Clemenceau, the French Premier, indomitable enemy of Germany, recalled that at the first news of the German requests for an armistice "I almost went mad... with joy!"[5] Yet on the night of the Armistice, when his daughter Madeleine found him silently brooding, and begged him: "Tell me you're happy, Papa!" he replied: "I can't tell you that, because I'm not... It will not have done any good".[6]

At the Eleventh Hour is divided into four parts. The First, which is introductory, consists of this chapter, and a second one, '*Negotiating and Signing the Armistices*' by the American historian Bullitt Lowry; Lowry puts the armistices in their overall context, outlining the sequence of the events and negotiations as the war efforts of the Central Powers and their supporters successively collapsed. He makes it clear that the variation in priorities among the Allied and Associate Powers, particularly as between the U.S.A. and the others, was a considerable obstacle in bringing the war to an end on terms acceptable to the victors and enforceable – in every Ally's opinion – on the vanquished.

Part Two deals with those countries most involved in the 11 November Armistice. For Germany, the reality of defeat, the inexorability of its penalties, the pain to Germans everywhere and the clamour to avoid or apportion blame are themes running through Heinz Hagenlücke's Chapter Three, which ends with a chilling conclusion: "The war was not over yet". Hagenlücke conveys vividly the despair at defeat expressed at the level of High Command and even down to the German long-term P.O.W.s, but at the same time he corrects a widely-held view that German soldiers marching home were not received with honour in the homeland. He also points out many soldiers' lack of ready identification with the new, republican Germany. It was a world far-removed from the fraternity of active service and herein lay a prime attraction of the *Freikorps* which were being formed. At the same time there were those who saw the ending of the war as an end also to the capitalist enslavement of the workers and for many ex-soldiers the Communist movement, too, offered brotherhood and a cause. Had the day dawned for a revolution to overthrow bourgeois democracy now that the military autocracy lay in ruins? Many socialists, expressing solidarity with their Russian Bolshevik brothers, reckoned so. Other socialists, the majority, like most of their fellow-citizens, thought better, in the end, of yet another armed struggle.

It might be anticipated that the servicemen of Britain, who, with their French comrades, had borne for so long the brunt of the struggle to halt Germany's bid for European dominance, would have given way to unconfined triumphalism in the days of victory. In fact, as Peter Liddle shows in Chapter Four, those soldiers in forward positions in France were fighting to the end and were in no frame of mind or body to indulge in abandoned revelry. As so many commentators recorded, too much had been endured and lost – and how certain was the peace? Amid the cheering there was great weariness and much foreboding.

RESOLUTION PROPOSED AT THE VICTORY CELEBRATION OF THE 15TH NOVEMBER, 1918, BY THE MAYOR OF GEORGETOWN (HONOURABLE NELSON CANNON, M.C.P.), AND SECONDED BY THE HONOURABLE J. B. LAING.

We, the Government Officers, Mayor and Town Council of Georgetown, elected representatives and people of British Guiana, assembled in public meeting in the Capital of the Colony, respectfully tender to His Gracious Majesty King George the Fifth the renewed expression of our loyalty and devotion to the Throne. We ask God's blessing upon him and upon Her Gracious Majesty Queen Mary and the Royal Family in this momentous hour.

We desire to convey to Their Majesties and to the Government of the United Kingdom our congratulations upon the issue of the war for human liberty and British honour. After more than fifty-two months of slaughter, civilisation has been saved by the downfall, through crushing military defeat, of a despotism which, working under many forms, threatened to enslave the world. Our honoured dead will not have died in vain. The swiftness and fulness of the retribution have stricken us with awe and we are humbled by this manifestation of the Providence of God.

We desire to express our gratitude to Admiral Beatty, Field Marshal Sir Douglas Haig, Lieut.-General Allenby and their colleagues and to the professional and non-professional soldiers and sailors of the Army and Navy of the Empire, as well as to the dauntless men of the Red Ensign. We of this Colony owe to them our property, our liberty and our lives.

We offer our congratulations to the Allied Nations. We hail the resurrection of Belgium, Serbia, Bohemia and Poland. Above all we greet heroic France, who has suffered most and longest from the terrible German menace but whose dark night of vigil has ushered in a glorious dawn. We are glad that the end of the rivalry of a thousand years has been recorded for all time by the advance of the British Armies to final victory under the supreme command of the greatest of the Marshals of France.

We trust that the league of Nations and Classes which has brought success in war may guide the march of civilization towards the solution of the vast problems of peace. We hope that it may lead to such measures of International Brotherhood as will prevent the liberty and honour of any country from being again threatened by an ambitious Prince or by a greedy or unbalanced People.

We rejoice that the dangers through which His Majesty's Empire has passed have only made more strong the links of patriotism and friendship which bind its various races and nations to the Mother Country and to one another.

We acknowledge in humility and thankfulness the hand of God in all these tremendous events.

Resolved:

That copies of this Resolution be sent to the Secretary of State for the Colonies for transmission through the proper channels.

ii The "crushing military defeat ... of a despotism which ... threatened to enslave the world". A proclamation from Georgetown, Guiana. (J.B. Laing, Liddle Collection)

On those fronts where the fighting had ceased some weeks before, informal and official celebrations to mark the end of the war had taken on a more planned, relaxed and reflective tone. However even this was widely affected by sickness and uncertainties about getting home and about the future. Indeed, on some fronts hostilities continued, and so a general picture of the British overseas response to the Armistice is multi-hued.

Similarly, the scene on the British Home Front in Chapter Five has many more variations than is conveyed by the familiar images of cheering crowds. The influenza scourge, the sheer concentration of bereavement in the United Kingdom, and economic, social and political anxieties, are the sobering context in which Liddle enables us to see, regionally, in Scotland, Wales, Ireland and throughout England, how both crowds and individuals greeted the end of the war. He shows the conflicts within Ireland emerging through attitudes to the Armistice at the time – Sinn Fein hostile to the celebrations, Ulster loyalists passionately enthusiastic, but, more surprisingly, many Nationalist communities proud of the victory and of the feats of local boys, though resolute for a more independent Ireland.

It is appropriate here to touch briefly on the domestic political scene in Britain and France in the weeks following the Armistice, which is not covered in the chapters on these two countries. The anxieties felt about national and imperial security by Lloyd George and Clemenceau, as the Premiers of Britain and France, and by the other leaders of their two countries, were destined to dominate the 1919 Peace Conference which opened in January and was concluded on 28 June. Personal ambition apart, these anxieties were in large measure the reason for Lloyd George's drive to have his country firmly behind him at the Peace Conference, so as to counterbalance effectively the moral advantage enjoyed by the American President Wilson's lofty international liberalism and by martyred France. So important was this to the British Prime Minister that he conducted a notoriously jingoistic campaign in the General Election of December 1918, in which there was much talk of hanging the Kaiser – a course greatly favoured by the voters at the time – and above all making Germany bear the full costs of the war. Lloyd George himself never used the phrase about squeezing the German lemon "till the pips squeak" but he encouraged such sentiments and they were popular in a country in revanchist mood and anxious about the economic future, especially employment. The result was an overwhelming parliamentary victory for Lloyd George's coalition administration, with a majority of 340. Politicians thought to be 'pro-Hun' such as Labour's Ramsay Macdonald or insufficiently belligerent, such as the Liberal ex-Prime Minister Herbert Asquith, lost their seats. Even so, although the Labour candidates included many whose loyalty had been doubted and who were not re-elected, their party emerged as second in the parliamentary race with 60 seats, twice as much as Asquith's depleted Liberal following.

International idealism was not completely at a discount. The idea of a League of Nations to prevent future wars met with widespread approval. Moreover the country, though fervently patriotic, was far from militaristic.

Demobilization was the most burning issue of all and the British intervention in Russia against the Bolsheviks was destined to be unpopular.

The election result however was to shackle Lloyd George during the Peace Conference to promises to the British public that Germany would pay for the war, promises which, he must have been well-aware, could not be carried out. Clemenceau, with a much stronger case, was confident of his support. According to the normal schedule, there were due to be French Parliamentary elections in 1918. These elections were suspended, however, until after the signing of the peace, for he wished to deal with *députés* whom he knew and who would be more biddable during the Conference if they faced an election in a few months.

Allain Bernède, in Chapter Six on the French, concentrates initially on the very moments when front-line French soldiers first learned of the German emissaries suing for a cease-fire; then he turns to the response of generals and leading politicians. Among soldiers in particular, the competing feelings of disbelief, joy, incomprehension, triumph and reflection, in varying measures, are brought home to the reader, together with quintessentially French scenes of comedy worthy of films by Jean Renoir or Jacques Tati.

On the civilian front, Bernède's canvas stretches far outside Paris to include many of the provinces. He conveys, picturesquely, the spreading news of the war's end: church bells in remote rural communities distracting peasants from their agricultural labour; or a postman hurrying across a field, waving a flag and shouting "It's over, it's over". The divided loyalties of the newly liberated Lorrainers contrast disturbingly with the battle-scarred but triumphant French cockerel.

Belgium paid an immense price for victory in her occupied territory and in the 'free' area collectively defended from the first to last day of the war. Early in Mark Derez's Chapter Seven, on Belgium, he makes the point that few Belgian soldiers were ever able to go on home leave. Their homes were all too often in a war zone or occupied by the Germans – or both. Towards the end of his chapter he pictures the soldiers' eventual return – in all likelihood to a landscape of desolation. Some of the English proposed that it should remain so, round Ypres, as a memorial to British and Empire dead, as Verdun was to the French fallen. Continuing the destruction to the end, the Germans sometimes gas-shelled Belgian villages after retreating from them, or left booby-traps – '*cadeaux d'adieu*' – behind, some of which, despite the stipulations of the Armistice, went unrevealed, exploding with fatal effect even weeks after the war was over. The harrowing accounts of the days leading up to the Armistice, the story of the liberation of Belgian villages, towns and cities, have not overestimated the ordeal of their peoples as they survived to reach that November day, and indeed played a part in its achievement.

Derez also illustrates vividly a wide range of personalities and reactions in the last weeks of war and the days of transition into peace: the hero-king Albert, enjoying an unique and possibly undeserved adulation, and his ministers, Belgian literary celebrities and ordinary people all figuring on the same ravaged stage, somewhat sardonically observed.

Derez is unequivocal over the suffering endured by all the Belgian people under the yoke of their oppressors who were expelled at last, four years, three-and-a-half months after their destructive invasion. He highlights also the tensions innate in Belgian society and exacerbated by the war – such as those between Flemings and Walloons; but revolution, despite the presence of insurgent German soldiers preaching universal brotherhood as they retreated, did not take fire in Belgium, and socialist fervour was neutralized in a postwar democratic compromise.

In their reaction to the Armistice the Americans were conditioned by distinctly different factors from those influencing the British or the French response. Civilians in the West and Midwest States were remote both physically from the struggle in France, and spiritually from those idealistic enthusiasts on the Eastern Seaboard who had joined up believing in the France of Lafayette and England of the Mayflower. Ethnically, too, many Midwesterners were of German extraction. This extreme variation of origin was one factor in conditioning the responses of American soldiers drawn far and wide from urban and rural locations; another was the stage which their soldierly experience had reached by 11 November: whether it were simply training in the States, or encompassed transit to, and training in, Europe and active service experience in France. All this is considered by James Cooke, writing in Chapter Eight. He also emphasizes the rapidity with which the U.S. Government began to disengage itself militarily from the European Alliance after the Armistice. The President's administration had always signalled his nation's wish to keep its distance by terming it an 'Associated' rather than an 'Allied' power. Moreover the Americans made it clear that they had no wish to continue with the joint economic arrangements over shipping and blockade matters. Members of a free enterprise society *par excellence*, their leaders were keen to whittle down the state-directed war machine which had sprung up over the last two years. This was to have serious implications for the Europeans who were relying on American support in the anxious period of transition to a postwar international system. For the American people, too, it created difficulties. Most of the troops who were called up never saw active service – a considerable disappointment for some, but even those disillusioned by army life and anxious to get out of army uniform felt aggrieved that, after the dislocation of leaving their civilian occupations, they were being dumped unceremoniously back on the labour market without guarantee of gaining the employment which they believed their country owed them.

The Great War, nonetheless, was an important rite of passage for Americans individually and for their youthful nation as it emerged as a world power. The War too, provided a formative experience for the newly emergent nation states belonging to the British Empire – Australia, Canada, New Zealand and South Africa – and for British India. In the case of Australia the picture provided by contemporary personal documentation of the reaction of their soldiers to the cease-fire mirrors that offered by the evidence of soldiers of other dominions and from the United Kingdom – some variations, but in France, in general: "we were a quiet crowd". Ashley Ekins in Chapter Nine charts celebration where it occurred but, as an historian closely concerned with examining the disciplinary record of the Australian soldier, he does not hesitate to emphasize the escalation of misbehaviour among troops already with an extraordinarily disproportionate number of men in military prisons in France and Belgium.

In the immediate aftermath of the war, the storming of a Field Punishment Compound near Le Havre and a Military Prison at Rouen was chiefly the responsibility of Australians and efforts also had to be maintained to bring in the marauding gangs of Australian deserters plaguing what had been the 'rear areas'. Even on the ships taking Australians home for demobilization, there were serious incidents of disorder and, when all account had been taken of dead and missing Australian servicemen, there were still 900 "illegal absentees" who remained unaccounted for, following upon the Armistice. It is in this context that overseas Australian reaction to the ending of the war has to be examined.

Ekins informs us that very few Australian units were sent to Germany for occupation duties. However, he does provide evidence on one area of grim labour upon which Australian soldiers were engaged post-Armistice, that of Graves Detachment work. In his concluding summary, the author of this chapter describes homeland city celebrations but, sociologically, they were the herald, in Australia as for so many other victor nations, of hard times and a sense of loss rather than benefit from the huge endeavours called for by the Great War.

In Chapter Ten, Dean Oliver demonstrates how the Canadian troops, commonly acknowledged to have played a leading role in the victories of the 'Hundred Days', in 1918, were from a nation increasingly troubled by fractures in its identity – not just French-British but socialist-capitalist too. Additionally, prolonged combat and a general weariness help to explain why the triumph recognized by the Armistice was not greeted by Canadian soldiers with any notable display of enthusiasm. As Oliver puts it "Peace stole quietly over the men of the Canadian Corps".

Across the Atlantic, in Toronto, Ottawa and elsewhere in Canada, there were scenes of jubilation but for Canadian soldiers in France [and in Britain] there was to be a sobering postscript to this record of fine, hard-earned victories; delayed repatriation and an accumulation of grievances would lead to tragic disturbances. Ironically, and despite the lasting symbolism of Vimy, this would be in keeping with Canadian reflections on the war and its outcome, "more on the edge of tears than joy".

In the eleventh chapter, on India, Sanjoy Bhattacharya writes of "the anxious peace" which came to the Indian sub-continent and which is evident from the commentaries of the Nationalist press. Although Indian Army regiments had acquitted themselves well in the war and had sustained serious casualties, and although there was much genuine pride as well as orchestrated rejoicing among the Indian population, there were strong economic and political pressures which worked in an opposite direction, away from loyalty to the British. Trade – particularly agricultural – was depressed and the livelihood both of the peasants returning from the front, and of the Indian middle classes, was uncertain. The pressures for Indian independence were mounting, and within a year both rioting and a campaign of unarmed resistance had begun. The government authorities faced a new struggle, though one entirely different from that through which the Indians had passed as part of the Imperial armed forces in Europe and the Middle East.

Knowing that, proportionately, the service of New Zealand's young manhood in the First World War outmatched even the impressive record of the other Dominions, we should not be surprised to learn from Chris Pugsley, in Chapter Twelve, that the New Zealand soldiers reacted to the end of the war more with relief that they were safely through it than with any other emotion. In England, on 11 November, New Zealand soldiers cast discipline to the winds, assisted by alcohol, but there were others like Major A.E. Alexander who pondered on the significance of the experience through which they had passed, and a quieter reaction prevailed in France too.

In Macedonia, for many New Zealand soldiers, malaria interfered with the prospect of enjoying victory fireworks in any sense. In Palestine particular tensions and the frustration of delay in returning to their longed-for homeland played their part in a tragic and scandalous affair at Surafend. For some New Zealanders, like the Canadian demobilization disturbance and ensuing tragedy at Kinmel Park, North Wales, after superb achievement under the most demanding Western Front circumstances, it proved impossible to maintain self-control under the irksome tedium, for citizen soldiers, of peacetime in khaki.

Whereas the Australians, Canadians and New Zealanders experienced no fighting on their own soil, and had a close involvement and identification with Britain and with the war in Europe, the South African presence in Europe was relatively small, though distinguished, and Bill Nasson, in Chapter Thirteen, reminds us of South Africa's distinctively different military experience. South African troops served on several of the subsidiary fronts too in the war – there was a sizable South African deployment in East Africa against the German forces under Major-General von Lettow-Vorbeck and in South-West Africa, which, like the Tanganyika territory, was a German possession. In fact, in South- West Africa (now Namibia) the fighting was soon over. An early armistice in the war – in 1915 – took place between the German Imperial defence force there and the South African Government, after the Germans had decided that their cause in this location was beyond hope. In Africa in fact, the South African soldiers' feelings for their German enemies were more sympathetic, as fellow white colonialists, than they were on the Western Front, after years of heavy fighting and high casualties.

The black Africans had high hopes that their service and support (in contrast with that of a partly pro-German Boer population) would bring them a better deal after the war, but for the South African Native National Congress, the coloured elite and for victor or vanquished askaris on either side, there was no direct political gain.

Nasson also draws attention to a particular point of interest, the paradox that the famous two minutes' silence, which was for years – and is now again – a central focus of Armistice Day remembrance, was derived from an Empire ritual of 1916 in South Africa, despite that country's remoteness from the war in Europe.

Further east, Japan, an emerging great power allied to Great Britain, played only a minor, though significant, part in the world conflict. Nearly all the action that her forces had seen was in the Far East. Geographically remote, her people viewed the European war with detachment, and were bemused by western manifestations of joy at the Armistice, as Naoko Shimazu stresses in Chapter Fourteen. Their mood at the time of Armistice was one of hope: that at the forthcoming peace conference Japan's status as a great power would be confirmed and the entitlement of the Japanese race to equal treatment in international affairs would be embodied in the new League of Nations Covenant.

The third part of *At the Eleventh Hour* deals with the other armistices – the Bulgarian, Turkish and Austrian, and with the reactions in the Balkans, Italy, Eastern Europe and the Near East. Imanuel Geiss, in Chapter Fifteen, draws a picture of the general state of Eastern Europe and Asia Minor at this time. The 11 November Armistice with Germany was the climax of the defeat of the Central Powers, following the downfall of Bulgaria, Turkey and Austria-Hungary; but though the *great power* military struggle was over, other wars immediately began to follow, chiefly between the 'successor' states of the empires broken up by the war. Professor Geiss's chapter offers a survey of these conflicts on the redrawn map of the Balkans, and of the former Russian, Ottoman and Austrian imperial lands, not leaving out the involvement of Germany, which was to lose territory to the east, and remained pivotally important even in defeat. The general lesson, that the end of Great Power conflict – as with the Cold War thirty years later – merely opens the floodgates to release endless minor conflicts, and that small wars lead to Great Wars, brings home to the reader just how dangerous our world remains.

Writing of Bulgaria in Chapter Sixteen, Richard Crampton demonstrates how the economic misery of that country and her lack of success in the field drove her to seek an armistice in late September, in the hope that, in exchange for her withdrawal, the Allies, led by President Wilson, would secure her the territories for which she had gone to war. Bulgaria's ignominious fate and subsequent political difficulties are described in this chapter.

Germany's contrasting capacity to endure for so long the weight of the military burden in this war was undeniably impressive. So too was the resilience of the Turks. The Ottoman war effort was rendered particularly arduous by the widely separated fighting fronts, by the over-extended, sometimes incomplete and always vulnerable communications, by the ethnically mixed populations, some of which were potentially or actually 'disloyal', by the Empire's backward agriculture and by its inadequate industrial base. The Great War had taxed soldiers and civilians to the limit. Erik Zürcher in Chapter Seventeen, describes how the flawed edifice of empire cracked beyond repair in wartime but how as a nation Turkey still possessed the residual potential for regeneration shortly thereafter. Zürcher charts the Turks' last hours at war: the ironical turn of fate whereby the British found themselves assisting the Turkish emissaries to make contact with their government; and the moment of cloak and dagger melodrama as Ottoman leaders slipped quietly from the scene. Initial lack of resentment shown by the Turks towards the British and French troops in occupation soon gave way to hostility.

As the Ottoman Empire lay defeated, its Arab peoples had high expectations of achieving independent status, purchased by their military effort in assisting the Allied cause against the Turks. In Chapter Eighteen, Avihai Shivtiel catalogues the Arab hopes and frustrations, in the face of conflicting British and French promises and ambitions, during the weeks and months after the war's end. The story can be seen as both a cynical betrayal of tribal peoples used for Allied ends and as the inevitable tendency of competing Great Powers to seek both compensation for their wartime endeavours and security for vital economic and strategic assets.

In Chapter Nineteen, the complexity of the consequences of military defeat for the Austro-Hungarian Empire is revealed by Mark Cornwall in the bewilderingly rapid sequence of events in different locations throughout the Habsburg Empire. His concern is with the reaction to those events by men seeking to take advantage of the situation, in the interests of their ethnic or political grouping, and by those desperately anxious to stem or divert the flood of change. As far as 'nationalisms' are concerned, it seems that 'flood' or 'torrent' is the right word, pushing aside any alternative solution. The tribes of Europe would have their nationhood, come what may, except, at the time, the Germans. Their turn came later but the pursuit of a new order by an Austrian former soldier in the German Army is not part of Cornwall's brief.

Of all the victor powers, Italy emerged from the war seemingly the most forlorn and yet, in Chapter Twenty, Irene Guerrini and Marco Pluviano show that with victory coming almost unexpectedly after the near-conclusive defeat at Caporetto a year before, the reaction from Italian soldiers was "joyous and triumphant". However the dampeners on celebration were powerful too: among others, the 'Spanish influenza' plague; the difficulties facing undernourished Italian P.O.W.s attempting to return from remote parts of the disintegrating Austro-Hungarian Empire or from Russia; and the widespread dissatisfaction with the government's incapacity to deal with inflation and unemployment which fuelled the arguments of revolutionary agitators. Using personal experience evidence, Pluviano and Guerrini demonstrate that the Italians were chiefly relieved that the war in which they had been involved so unnecessarily had come to an end. There were some who looked to Germany and Russia for the example of social and political revolution, but there was also a genuine pride in the fact that after a long period of military defeat they had finally overcome their traditional enemy, the Austrians; and there were also those who expected to see their nation rewarded with islands and cities on the other side of the Adriatic.

The Fourth, and final part of *At the Eleventh Hour* deals with the *legacy* of the Armistice. John Bourne in the twenty-first chapter looks at its long-term historical significance. The problems of arriving at a satisfactory peace might be said to be chiefly the problems inherent in the attitudes of the principal belligerents who were prisoners of their outlook in wartime and earlier.

France, for example, was obsessed with her vulnerability to Germany, economically, in demographic terms, and in geographical position, a situation unalterable unless she could succeed in wresting the Rhineland away from Germany and under French tutelage. There were problems too about incorporating the liberal idealistic vision of the American President Wilson into a peace settlement alongside the national passions, sense of history and ruthless pragmatism of the Europeans. The consequences of the Armistice were to prove ambiguous and difficult to the victors and immediately catastrophic for the defeated. All too soon it became clear that in the short term what was important about the Armistice was not that it brought peace, which was transitory, but that it was attended by economic dislocation, outbreaks of revolution and civil disorder, all of which led eventually to international conflict again.

In the twenty-second chapter, Hugh Cecil examines the way in which feelings about the Armistice have been expressed in British, French, German and American novels and poetry – at the time and long after the event. These writings demonstrate much the same range of response – from jubilation and hope for a new society to anxiety, sorrow, disgust, disappointment and just plain relief at survival – as is to be found commonly in diaries, letters and memoirs from the period. One such work of literature is Siegried Sassoon's magnificent poem 'Everyone Sang' which was not about the end of the fighting as is commonly believed, but about the possible dawn of a new socialist Britain on the lines laid down in the *Daily Herald* – an example of a piece of writing being hijacked in the popular imagination to fit a stereotype about reactions to the end of the war.

It is the story of Armistice Day commemoration in Britain which, in the final chapter, Matthew Richardson sketches from its beginnings, through the days of mourning between the wars, and through the later 1960's when it began to be played down, leading to the abandonment of the two minutes' silence; then recently, to a new spirit, far more respectful than in the immediately preceding decades, albeit distant from the emotionally charged early days. There is nothing particularly traditionalist about this spirit, nor militarist nor even nationalistic, but it embodies a close interest in Britain's past, and gratitude to the servicemen and women of both wars for their defence of this country. The very fact that those who served and died in Korea, Indonesia and the Falklands are also now commemorated, and enjoy the same respect from the public, demonstrates the continuity of the Armistice ceremony as an important feature of our national life, though not, it should be emphasized, a triumphalist one; nor is there any longer the interwar mood of public mourning.

The old feelings have faded away; but it must be remembered that the 11th November Armistice with Germany was one of the greatest emotional moments in modern history. It brought to an end the bloodiest war then known to man, and, although we know better now, it really did seem to most people as though all the fighting were over, and that there could never be a war like this again. A vast number reacted to the news with an act of reverence – a prayer of thanksgiving, a religious service, a ritual drink or meal, or the clasping of hands with a comrade or an ally from another country. One such was Sir Esmé Howard, the British Ambassador in Sweden who has described his visit to Paris on the way back to Britain, early on the eleventh of November. In a moving passage in his memoirs he highlights concisely the different responses of the three principal victor powers, Britain, France and the USA – the old world tragic but inwardly exultant, the new world hopeful and enterprising:

> I reached Paris very early in the morning. The Gare de Lyon seemed almost deserted. An old porter took one of my handbags, I took the other. We made our way slowly to the exit of the station. As we reached it he suddenly dropped my bag and held up his hand: '*Écoutez*', he cried, '*Les canons du Mont Valérien. Ils vont signer*'. The guns of Mont Valérien were telling the people of Paris that the Armistice would be signed that day, November 11th.
>
> Many have recounted their experiences of Armistice Day but few, I think, can have been so touched as I was by that old porter with tears of emotion in his eyes. If I had not been an unhappy Anglo-Saxon suffering like all my people from inhibitions regarding the expression of emotion of any kind, I should have flung my arms round the old man's neck. As it was I dropped my bag and clasped hands for some moments in a silence that meant much more than words. Then he told me that he had lost two sons in the War but had two more whom he hoped now to see again.
>
> Driving to my hotel near the British Embassy I saw little stir as yet in the streets until I passed the statue of St. Joan of Arc with the uplifted sword [near St. Augustin's Church], where some American soldiers, always the first in the business that was afoot, were already decorating it.
>
> On that day and with the sound of the guns of St.Valérien still in our ears, that act had a peculiar significance. The Americans were right to be the first to do it.[7]

Endnotes

1 Stanley Weintraub, *A Stillness Heard Round the World: The End of the Great War*, November 1918, London, Allen & Unwin, 1985.

2 George Panichas (ed.), *Promise of Greatness,: The War of 1914–18. A Memorial Volume for the Fiftieth Anniversary of the Armistice*, London, Cassell, 1968, p. xxxv.

3 See this volume, Chapter 4.

4 Jutta Bohnke-Kollwitz (ed.), *Käthe Kollwitz, Die Tagebücher*, Siedler Verlag, 1989, p. 381.

5 Jean Martet, *Le Tigre*, Paris, Albin Michel, 1930, p. 152.

6 Georges Wormser, *La république de Clemenceau*, Paris, Presses Universitaires de France, 1961, p. 341.

7 Lord Howard of Penwith, *The Theatre of Life,* vol. 2: *Life seen from the Stalls*, London, Hodder & Stoughton, 1936, pp. 271–272.

Chapter Two

Negotiating and Signing the Armistices

Bullitt Lowry

The great German spring offensive of 1918, after coming within a hair's breadth of winning the First World War, ground to a halt in June. After 8 August 1918, the day that German general Erich Ludendorff called "the black day of the German Army in the history of the war", the Allied and Associated Powers steadily forced the Germans back.[1] With their armies retreating, the other Central Powers suing for peace, and the United States shipping hundreds of thousands of fresh soldiers each month to France, the German leaders decided they must seek an armistice.

What strikes a retrospective eye is how quickly the Germans collapsed between the beginning of October, when they asked President Woodrow Wilson to arrange an armistice for the purpose of making a peace based on his Fourteen Points, and 11 November, when they signed it. During October, while negotiations over that armistice were taking place, the Allied and Associated Powers continued their military operations, and by the end of the month, they had clearly defeated the Germans both strategically and tactically.

As important as any military event was the pressure German public opinion was putting on the German leaders. Once the leaders publicly sought an armistice, there was no turning back; the German soldiers and the German public became increasingly reluctant to remain in a war their leaders had declared was lost. Outbreaks of revolution in Germany's cities at the beginning of November and the end of the monarchy on 9 November flowed from the original decision to ask for an armistice, and radicalism erupted because German morale, both military and civilian, had dwindled away to nothing.[2]

That wild German plunge downhill caught the Allied leaders by surprise. They had made a start at setting forth what they wanted in a peace, but no draft of armistice terms existed in any capital. The leaders simply had not conceived of an armistice to allow the negotiation of a preliminary peace, which is what the Germans requested.

Now, with the German request for an armistice, the Allies saw the opportunity to implement their most cherished war aims, which they inserted into the armistice document, effectively creating a preliminary peace. When what they wanted did not accord with President Wilson's famous Fourteen Points, it was the Fourteen Points that were supplanted, either directly or covertly. When Allied and American negotiators completed a draft document on 4 November, it demanded a German surrender so abject that most Allied leaders believed the Germans would refuse it initially and the war would continue into 1919.

Yet the Germans did sign it. Public pressure and revolution left them no choice. The document that the Germans signed on 11 November 1918, gave the Allied and Associated Powers absolute dominance over land and sea, and hinted that in addition the Allies would demand great tracts of German territory and enormous reparations.

The cascade of armistices with the Central Powers began with Germany's allies. The Austro-Hungarians lacked supplies, munitions, and any sort of will for combat. In mid-September, the Austro-Hungarian foreign minister sent a circular letter to the other Central Powers stating that his nation must leave the war before it collapsed internally, and then he unilaterally proposed non-binding peace talks to the Allied and Associated Powers, a proposal that the United States and the Allies promptly rejected.[3] At the same time in the Near East, the British were rolling back the Ottoman Empire from both south and east, and the Turkish army was now fighting not far from its ethnic Anatolian borders. But it was Bulgaria, least of the Central Powers, which left the war first.

A massive attack that the Allies launched against Bulgaria's southern front on 15 September cut through the Bulgarian armies, the Bulgarian war effort being hampered by the Germans having practically stopped sending military aid. Even more compelling, rebellion had broken out among the Bulgarian soldiers on the southern front and was spreading. With the Bulgarians having no reason to stay in the war and good reasons to leave it, they signed the Salonika Armistice on 29 September.[4] Its terms were moderate. The Bulgarians must pull back to their prewar boundaries, demobilize all but three divisions of soldiers, and allow the Allies the right of transit across their territory to attack Austria-Hungary.

The news that the Bulgarians had signed an armistice contributed to the growing despair at German headquarters.[5] The army needed men, and there were none immediately available. They needed food and other supplies which the Allied blockade was preventing them from getting. In sum, they needed peace, and to that end, General Ludendorff urgently demanded that the German leaders immediately seek an armistice.[6]

The Germans had been seriously discussing some sort of peace initiative since August. Now, with the need imperative, the German political leaders had three choices: they could work through President Wilson, address the Allies through a neutral nation, or send military envoys directly to the Allied military commanders. The Germans decided to ask Wilson to intercede with the Allies to arrange an armistice so that the warring nations could make a peace based on Wilson's Fourteen Points, a shrewd move.[7] In the best possible outcome, his Fourteen Points might set limits to Allied exactions.[8]

Wilson's Fourteen Points constitute one of the most extraordinary documents in modern history.[9] Contrary to customary diplomatic and political practice, Wilson drew up his Fourteen Points and promoted them, while giving little or no consideration to whether they advanced the narrow interests of the United States or his own political fortunes. Wilson's was a disinterested idealism, for he intended to eradicate the causes of war.

With his Fourteen Points, he aimed at problems that had caused war in the past. His first five points dealt with general matters. He would end secret diplomacy, support neutral rights on the high seas, end trade wars, stop arms races, and settle colonial rivalries. The next eight points were more specific and were aimed at removing territorial conflicts that might be particular threats to peace. The great powers would settle the territorial problems of Europe and the Ottoman Empire through a consideration of nationality, modified by historical claims. Finally, since new problems inevitably would arise, Wilson proposed the creation of a League of Nations to deal with unanticipated situations.

His program caught the public's fancy. Certainly, a number of persons saw his Fourteen Points as irredeemably idealistic and impractical, but others, looking at the chaos and tragedy of the war, felt Wilson's program was the hope of the world. Wilson, therefore, had a strong international following which the politicians of the Allied nations felt they must appease.

When Wilson received the German request, he responded non-committally, beginning a series of exchanges which continued for more than two weeks before he decided that the German request was genuine, and not some subterfuge.[10] In the process, General Ludendorff changed his position entirely, demanding that the Germans reject any armistice and fight on, but by now the situation was irretrievable. Ludendorff resigned on 26 October. Meanwhile, on 23 October, Wilson forwarded the German request to the Allies.

At the time when Wilson received the First German Note, on 6 October, the Allied prime ministers were meeting in Paris to discuss the new situation created by the surrender of Bulgaria.[11] When the news broke that the Germans were seeking an armistice, the Allied leaders set themselves to drafting armistice terms. Yet they were conscious that to grant an armistice for the purpose of writing peace terms would remove the greatest diplomatic advantage winning nations had: the threat to pursue the war until the losers agreed to whatever terms the victors demanded. In theory, a victorious nation could reopen a war that an armistice had stilled, but it would require motivating the armies and home fronts once again to make great sacrifices, perhaps for some point the public might not consider worth the pain.

Not entirely convinced that the German overture was serious — this German note was not the first peace overture of the war — the Allied leaders worked on what they wanted armistice terms to contain.[12] Underlying their actions was fear that President Wilson, who had what they thought was a perverse streak in his thinking, might somehow give the Germans some advantage. They also had no great faith in his peace programme, which had never been a subject for direct Allied consultation. The French Prime Minister,

Georges Clemenceau, thought the Fourteen Points were unrealistic and even evil to the extent that they might limit Germany's atoning for the war through reparations and territorial cessions.[13] The British Prime Minister, David Lloyd George, was less certain that the Fourteen Points should be dismissed out of hand. Indeed, he thought that Wilson's programme generally was a good one, at least in so far as it followed his own, which he had presented a few days before Wilson issued the Fourteen Points.[14]

Clemenceau went to the Commander-in-Chief of the Allied Armies on the Western Front, French Marshal Ferdinand Foch, and asked him to draw up terms.[15] Foch did so, showing little mercy to the Germans. They must evacuate Belgium, Luxembourg, and France (including Alsace and Lorraine, ceded to Germany in 1871 following defeat in the Franco-Prussian War) and carry out that evacuation so rapidly that their armies would in fact be disrupted. The Allies would occupy that evacuated territory and the left bank of the Rhine and bridgeheads across the river. The Germans must surrender all the military equipment and supplies which could not be evacuated, and surrender very large quantities of railway equipment, engines and rolling stock, limiting any subsequent mobility.

Foch's draft would make its way almost unchanged, although with many additions, into the final armistice document. At this point, on 9 October, the prime ministers adjourned, having neither approved nor disapproved any draft of armistice terms. They were not convinced that the military situation would allow them to impose Foch's terms on Germany, but they were equally certain that they were unwilling to settle for anything less.

After 9 October, there was little debate in Allied circles over whether to grant Germany an armistice; the general feeling was that they had no reason to fight on if such an armistice included the significant items they wanted. What was a significant item, however, was defined elastically, and not everything that would be demanded had surfaced on 9 October. For example, one group, the British admirals, had been poorly represented at Paris, and their demands soon became insistent.

The First Sea Lord, Admiral Sir Rosslyn Wemyss and the Commander-in-Chief of the Grand Fleet, Admiral Sir David Beatty, entered the deliberations with passion. Beatty believed that the naval terms should have the same effect on Germany's naval strength as the loss of an out-and-out battle, thus giving Britain naval security and demonstrating British naval supremacy.[16] An armistice, many British leaders were beginning to say, should approximate the terms of peace, and Beatty appropriated that slogan. Whether the public supported continuing the war, if needs be, to attain those ends was never clear, but the leaders assumed that the public demanded a victorious conclusion to the war for which they had sacrificed so much.

Beatty hurried down from the great Scapa Flow naval base in the Orkneys to promote his views to the War Cabinet.[17] Germany, he argued, must be reduced to the status of a second-rate naval power by requiring the surrender of her most modern warships and all of her submarines. The Cabinet members temporized because they were frightened of rejecting, indirectly, an armistice with Germany by asking for impossible conditions and equally frightened that they might not achieve the British war aim of ending the German naval challenge. In the end, the cabinet agreed upon a formula that was useless. "The naval conditions of the armistice should represent the admission of German defeat in the same degree as the military conditions recognize the corresponding admission of German defeat by land".[18] All that formula guaranteed was that the admirals would keep up the pressure for harsh naval terms.

The cabinet also heard from Britain's two most important military leaders, the Chief of the Imperial General, Staff Sir Henry Wilson and the Commander-in-Chief of the British Expeditionary Force, Sir Douglas Haig. Sir Henry would grant Germany an armistice only on very stringent terms, while Haig counselled moderation, because he was convinced that the Germans still possessed significant military power and he feared that the brunt of any further fighting must fall on the British.[19] "The British alone", he commented, "might bring the enemy to his knees. But why expend more British lives—and for what?"

In France, Clemenceau approved in its entirety Marshal Foch's draft. On 25 October, on Clemenceau's instructions, Foch called together the commanders of the Allied armies and of the American Expeditionary Force less to get their approval than to see whether any of them would oppose him publicly.[20] Philippe Pétain, commanding the French armies, supported him, and so did John J. Pershing of the United States. Only Haig dissented, continuing his advocacy of moderate terms; he suspected (incorrectly) that Foch was trying to reject an armistice by proposing impossible terms.[21] In any event, Haig's opposition, unsupported by the other generals, was not enough to sway Foch. He stood by his terms which would shortly be presented to the Allied and American political leaders for approval.[22]

When President Wilson forwarded the German request to the Allies on 23 October, he pointed out that any response had to include two parts: whatever military and naval terms the Allies and the United States thought desirable, and Allied agreement to the Fourteen Points.[23] "[I]f those [Allied] Governments are disposed to effect peace upon the terms and principles indicated", he wrote, then they should draw up terms for Germany which would leave the Allies and the United States "in a position to enforce any arrangements that may be entered into and ... make a renewal of hostilities on the part of Germany impossible".

During the last year, Woodrow Wilson had deliberately postponed discussion of his Fourteen Points for fear of causing a rift in unity at the height of the war. Now, that deficiency had to be remedied, and to that end, he sent his intimate friend and adviser, Colonel (honorary) Edward M. House, to Europe to represent him in talks with the Allies. Wilson gave House no directions. "I have not given you any instructions", he told him just before House sailed for Europe, "because I feel you will know what to do."[24] Of course, Wilson could not leave it at that. On 28 October, he telegraphed House, who by then was in Paris getting ready to meet with the Allied prime ministers who were gathering to consider armistice terms. Wilson ordered House to support any terms which would prevent Germany from renewing hostilities, "but which will be as moderate and reasonable as possible within those limits . . .".[25] House and the Allied prime ministers began their meetings on 29 October. Lloyd George adamantly opposed the Freedom of the Seas, and both he and Clemenceau wanted reparations from Germany, which the Fourteen Points, strictly interpreted, precluded. The Italians, who were also represented at these Paris meetings, objected to applying the Fourteen Points to any settlement with Austria-Hungary, because Wilson's programme would block Italian territorial gains for which they had gained British and French approval in 1915.[26]

House's position was not easy, for he had Wilson from across the seas insisting that the Allies adhere to his Fourteen Points, and daily, beginning on the twenty-ninth, he had to face the Allied prime ministers who stridently refused to accept Wilson's programme. With the Allies standing firm, House even went so far as to threaten that the United States would make a separate peace, but to no effect.[27] Eventually, he accepted the British refusal to agree to the Freedom of the Seas, acceded to the claim for reparations, and left it uncertain whether the Fourteen Points bound the Italians. By default, the Allies accepted the rest of the Fourteen Points, although that programme was less precise, and hence less binding, than many contemporaries assumed. For example, armaments, Point Four read, should be "reduced to the lowest point consistent with domestic safety", whatever that level was and whoever should decide it. That latitude was clear to the Allied prime ministers. As Lloyd George said of the Fourteen Points, "They were wide enough to allow us to place our own interpretation on them".[28]

Several days of further negotiations would elapse before the final deal on the Fourteen Points was struck, but the British and French prime ministers set the outlines in the first day of discussion. With reparations added and with the Freedom of the Seas deleted, they would agree to accept the Fourteen Points, if they were interpreted loosely, and as long as they got what they wanted in the final armistice terms. For the French, that meant the return of Alsace-Lorraine and control over the German Rhineland, which the military occupation described in Foch's draft terms, would give them. For a number of the British, any armistice must dictate the destruction of German sea power.

The British admirals used their dominance over the Allied Naval Council to push their claims for Draconian naval terms.[29] The Allied Naval Council agreed to recommend to the Allied leaders and House that the terms should require the surrender of all Germany's submarines, six battle cruisers, ten *Dreadnought*-type battleships, and a number of lesser vessels. "The naval terms", Admiral Wemyss noted, "are stiff — but not more than they should be nor more than we deserve. It is good for Europe".[30]

This insistence on harsh naval terms caught the prime ministers and House in a dilemma: although the British, especially the admirals (who had strong political support), wanted the destruction of the German navy, they did not want Germany to reject the armistice terms, and they thought that the military terms were more important in securing Allied safety than the naval. Lloyd George went back and forth, first insisting that British public opinion demanded harsh naval terms and then saying that the admirals were asking for too much. The admirals stuck to their demands. As Lloyd George put it, "[O]ur admirals have their tails up and will not move".[31] After much agonizing, the prime ministers and House agreed to require the surrender of 160 submarines, which was about the total German number, and to intern the battleships, battlecruisers, and lesser vessels in a neutral port.[32]

On that proposed internment hangs a tale. Worried that requiring internment in a neutral port — the way the terms originally read — might come to grief if no neutral country would accept the responsibility, the leaders added the phrase "or failing them [neutral ports] Allied ones".[33] The British diplomats thereupon set out to make certain that no neutral nation would accept the German ships.[34] Thus, the British would come to supervise the internment of the German vessels at Scapa Flow, and would be able to do little but watch the Germans scuttle those warships seven months later.

The other critical piece on which the Allies and House had to reach agreement was Foch's demand for the left bank of the Rhine and bridgeheads across that river. It seems likely that House traded Clemenceau his support in return for Clemenceau's agreeing to the Fourteen Points.[35] House's support overrode Lloyd George's reluctance concerning the occupation, and the final terms provided for Allied and American military occupation of the left bank, a neutral zone on the right bank, and occupation of bridgeheads at Köln, Koblenz, and Mainz.

While the Allied leaders and House were dealing with the Fourteen Points and terms for Germany, they also spent time discussing the Ottoman Empire. When the Allied leaders had met earlier in October, they had drafted terms for Turkey. Throughout the month, there had been serious dispute between the British and the French over the terms and how to deliver them to the Turks. Both Allied nations had designs on territory in the Near East, and both sides wanted more than their wartime arrangements had given them. Nevertheless, Turkish delegates came to the island of Mudros, and on 30 October, they signed the Mudros Armistice, which went into effect the following day.[36] Anglo-French controversies did not end with the Mudros Armistice, but for the moment they were muted in the glow of victory.

The second of the Central Powers had now fallen, but although the victory required the Turks to demobilize their army, give up their warships, allow occupation of strategic points, and allow free passage through the Straits, the submission of the Ottoman Empire had no immediate, direct effect on Germany.[37] In the long run, the fall of Turkey could affect events, because the Allies could now move into the Black Sea and push up the Danube, bringing Rumania back into the war on the Allied side, but that was not a project that could be completed quickly.

More immediate in its effect on Germany was the surrender of Austria-Hungary. For all intents and purposes, that country and its multi-national army had already collapsed. In the autumn of 1918, the demolition of the Dual Monarchy had moved forward relentlessly. The Austro-Hungarian Government renewed its plea for peace, and the Allied leaders and House drafted terms that were formally delivered to the Austro-Hungarians on the afternoon of 31 October.[38] Drafting that armistice was difficult for the Allied leaders and House, because they had to deal with the newly emergent successor nations and the additional welter of Italian territorial ambitions, Italian-French animosity, and Italian-Serb/Yugoslavian hatred.

Those terms that were finally drafted required the demobilization of the greater part of the Austro-Hungarian army, which had already disintegrated into its national components; the surrender of large quantities of material and a number of warships; Allied right of transit; and what was the most controversial element, the military occupation of a zone that exactly corresponded with the Austro-Hungarian territory allotted Italy in the Treaty of London.[39] The Serbs, who were allowed to attend some of the sessions at this Paris meeting, protested bitterly against that provision because it gave over to Italian control territory the Serbs and Yugoslavs wanted and to which they had a strong ethnic claim. House should have objected to that occupation zone on the grounds that it foreshadowed Italian annexation and violated self-determination, but he did not. The Italians got the occupation of their Treaty of London line, but as events in the next few months would show, they wanted even more.

On 3 November, the Austro-Hungarian delegates signed the Armistice of Villa Giusti, named after the place where the envoys met outside Padua. The third of the Central Powers had now fallen, although several serious questions remained, chief among them, the leaders of the newly-proclaimed Hungarian nation refusing to admit that the Villa Giusti terms applied to their republic.[40] The Allies refused to let Hungary escape the Austrian death-grip, although they did negotiate a separate convention with Hungary ten days later, the Military Convention of Belgrade.[41]

The surrender of Austria-Hungary, unlike that of Turkey, could have a military impact on Germany because it opened the southeastern German frontier to Allied attack through Austria- Hungary. The prime ministers and House oversaw planning for a Bavarian Offensive, but it was an exercise in optimism. Launching it would have been far more complicated than they assumed, and it would have taken far longer to be effective than they hoped. To begin with, the imminent onset of winter would delay any effective action till the following spring. However, whatever obstacles lay in the path of the Bavarian Offensive, the surrender of Austria-Hungary made the German position ultimately untenable in a military sense.

With the surrender of Austria-Hungary buoying them up, the Allied leaders and House debated further on the wording concerning the Fourteen Points and other matters, and they added clauses covering financial factors and the Eastern Front. The financial clauses began with a reservation preserving all future reparations claims, so reparations were embedded in the armistice terms themselves. On the Eastern Front the Allies decided, after some debate, to require that Germany withdraw its forces within its 1914 boundaries, but this would be changed later.

So all the pieces had come together, but the accord on the Fourteen Points was uncertain. Although House and the Allies had reached agreement, they had done so only by stressing how malleable the terms were, how they could be interpreted to mean whatever the Allies wanted them to mean. What happened in the future would depend on who had the power to enforce definitions. Nevertheless, both Lloyd George and House claimed victory on the Freedom of the Seas, so perhaps from that perspective, the arrangement was a good one.[42] Wilson reluctantly acceded to the Allied position on the Fourteen Points; "I accept the situation", he cabled to House.[43]

The terms to which the Allied leaders and House had agreed — the military, naval and all the rest — were Carthaginian. Did the Allies and House really expect Germany to accept them? The answer seems to be, no.[44] They did not know the extent of Germany's internal weaknesses, nor did they have reliable intelligence on the spread of the German revolution, which had caught fire on 30 October. They expected Germany initially to refuse these terms, but accept them in 1919 after further military action.

Did the terms meet the need of providing security for the Allied and American forces? They did and more than that. When House queried Foch on whether it was better to have an armistice or to continue the war, Foch had replied, "I do not make war for the purpose of making war, but for the purpose of getting results...". If the armistice conditions contained what he thought was necessary, "I am satisfied. No one has the right to prolong the bloodshed longer".[45] The armistice conditions now contained what Foch thought was necessary, what the British admirals thought was necessary, and what the financial advisers thought was necessary. Nothing more was needed to safeguard Allied and American interests.

The Allied leaders and House appointed Foch and an unnamed British admiral (it would be Wemyss) to meet with the Germans and to communicate the terms to them. Then they sent a message to Wilson agreeing to the Fourteen Points, except for Freedom of the Seas and reparations and asked him to tell the Germans to make arrangements to meet Foch.[46]

On 8 November, a military escort brought the German delegation headed by Matthias Erzberger (whom German nationalists would murder in 1921 for his part in the Armistice) to a railroad crossing in the Forest of Rethondes, just outside the village of Compiègne. There, in railroad carriages brought in for the occasion, Foch and Wemyss waited for the Germans.

When the Germans came into the carriage, Foch forced them to ask him formally for an armistice.[47] When they had done so, Foch's chief of staff read the proposed terms to the Germans, who visibly paled. The first thing the Germans did was to request a ceasefire while negotiations continued. Foch refused the German request and then they accepted the Armistice in principle, sending the text off to Berlin by courier. What would happen to the terms there, was anybody's guess, since Berlin was convulsed by revolution, and the most recent chancellor was about to declare the abdication of the Kaiser in absentia just before he himself resigned. The Kaiser was in seclusion at army headquarters in Belgium, but at dawn on the morning of the tenth, he would take his train to the Netherlands and seek asylum. So whether there were a German government to stand behind the execution of armistice terms was uncertain.

The German delegates failed to get Foch to raise the blockade, [although he did agree to consider supplying food to Germany], but they were able to

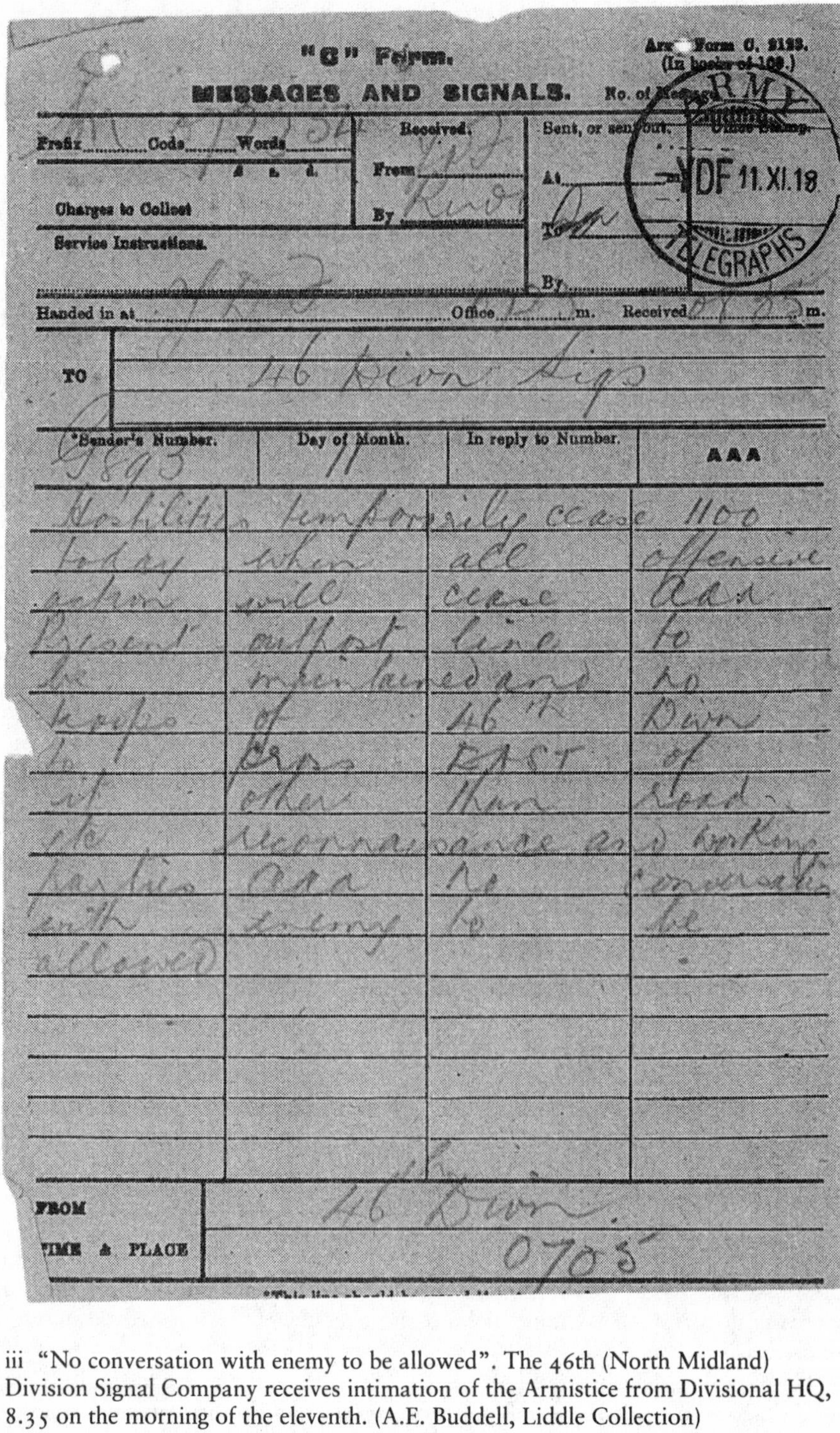
"C" Form.
MESSAGES AND SIGNALS.
Army Form C. 2123.
(In books of 100.)
No. of Message
Prefix Code Words
Received. From By
Sent, or sent out. At To By
Office Stamp.
ARMY TELEGRAPHS YDF 11.XI.18
Charges to Collect
Service Instructions.
Handed in at Office m. Received m.

TO 46 Divnl Sigs

*Sender's Number.	Day of Month.	In reply to Number.	AAA
9893	11		

Hostilities temporarily cease 1100 today when all offensive action will cease AAA Present outpost line to be maintained and no troops of 46th Divn to go EAST of it other than road etc reconnaissance and working parties AAA No conversation with enemy to be allowed

FROM 46 Divn
TIME & PLACE 0705

iii "No conversation with enemy to be allowed". The 46th (North Midland) Division Signal Company receives intimation of the Armistice from Divisional HQ, 8.35 on the morning of the eleventh. (A.E. Buddell, Liddle Collection) negotiate some modifications in the armistice terms. Foch and Weygand agreed to reduce, modestly, the material that the terms required Germany to surrender, and to reduce, again modestly, the speed with which the German army was required to evacuate the Western Front. Foch did grant one important change to the clauses for the Eastern Front. Ostensibly to protect the civilian population of the old Russian Empire from Bolshevism, Foch told the Germans not to withdraw their forces from that area until the Allied nations ordered it sometime in the future. Therefore, instead of withdrawing to their 1914 frontiers in the east, the Germans would remain, temporarily, in Russia, controlling all the gains they had made in the Treaty of Brest-Litovsk.[48] That delay in requiring the Germans to return to their borders led to severe problems the following spring.

At 5.10 a.m., the Germans, Foch, and Wemyss signed the Armistice. The news went out from the great radio station in the Eiffel Tower, and after 1,567 days of war, at 11 a.m. on 11 November, the guns on the Western Front fired their last rounds and fell still.

Lloyd George in London read the armistice terms to a cheering House of Commons, and before leading the members to Westminster Abbey, expressed the spirit of the hour with a personal summary, "Thus at eleven o'clock this morning came to an end the cruellest and most terrible War that has ever scourged mankind. I hope we may say that thus, this fateful morning, came to an end all wars".[49]

House believed he had won a great victory. The diplomatic battle with the Allies, he wrote, "has resulted in complete victory".[50] The Armistice gave military victory to the Allies, true enough, but House was thinking of American diplomacy, and victory for the Allies in that sphere was far less clear. Nevertheless, on the other side of the Atlantic on the evening of 11 November, Wilson stood at the White House gates looking at the jubilant crowd surging down Pennsylvania Avenue. "In his countenance", wrote an associate, "there was an expression not so much of triumph as of vindication".[51]

Clemenceau, alone among the great leaders, kept a sense of proportion, perhaps even a prescient vision. "We have won the war...", he told his chief military aide. "[N]ow we must win the peace and that will be perhaps more difficult".[52]

Endnotes

1 Erich Ludendorff, *My War Memories, 1914–1918*, London, Hutchinson, 1919, vol. 2, p. 679. President Wilson insisted that the United States was a power Associated with the Allies (France, Great Britain, Imperial Russia, and so on), not another Ally.

2 For fascinating suggestions on deeper causes of the collapse of German morale, see Jay Winter and Jean-Louis Robert, eds., *Capital Cities at War: Paris, London, Berlin 1914–1919*, Cambridge, Cambridge University Press, 1997, pp. 333–341, 353–356, 531.

3 Ludendorff, *My War Memories*, vol. 2, pp. 702–703. Ekengren, 16 September 1918, transmitting Note from K/k Government, United States, Department of

State, *Papers Relating to the Foreign Relations of the United States, 1918*, Supplement I, *The World War*, Washington, Government Printing Office, 1933, vol. 1, pp. 306–309; and response, Lansing to Ekengren, 17 September 1918, ibid., pp. 309–310; this source cited hereafter as *Foreign Relations, 1918, World War.*

4 Petko M. Petkov, *The United States and Bulgaria in World War I*, Boulder, East European Monographs, 1991, pp. 78–79. Admiralty, Berlin, 27 September 1918, RM 40/144, Bundesarchiv/ Militärarchiv, Freiburg, Germany. Franchet d'Esperey to Clemenceau, 27 September 1918, and Clemenceau to Franchet d'Esperey, *idem*, 6 N 71, Service historique de l'armée de terre, Vincennes, France. France, État-major des armées, Service historique, *Les armées françaises dans la Grande Guerre*, Tome 8, Paris, Imprimerie Nationale, 1934, vol. 2, pp. 913–914, 980.

5 Following the German decision-making process at army headquarters is very difficult, owing to the destruction of the relevant records in an Allied air raid on Potsdam in 1945; see preface to PH1, Bundesarchiv/ Militärarchiv, Freiburg. See also Sir John Wheeler-Bennett, *Hindenburg: The Wooden Titan*, London, Macmillan, 1936, pp. 157–178, although Sir John may put too much stress on Ludendorff's "mental deterioration". On the civilian side, see Carnegie Endowment for International Peace, *Preliminary History of the Armistice*, New York, Oxford University Press, 1924, pp. 40–48; this source cited hereafter as PHA.

6 Ludendorff, *My War Memories*, vol. 2, pp. 712–718.

7 Not all the German leaders agreed with the procedure; the new Chancellor, Max of Baden, claimed he wanted to approach the enemy in general, Conference, 6 October 1918, PHA, p. 49.

8 The Supreme Command was willing to use the Fourteen Points as a general guide, but demanded resistance to anything in them that would lessen Germany. That is, they resisted integral acceptance of the Fourteen Points. See Major von dem Busche, Notes, Conference, 3 October 1918, Erich Ludendorff, *The General Staff and Its Problems*, London, Hutchinson, 1920, vol. 2, p. 637.

9 Address, 8 January 1918, *Foreign Relations, 1918, World War*, vol. 1, pp. 15–16. He made additional speeches in 1918 which technically form part of his peace program, but public attention focused on the Fourteen Points speech and collectively his programme was usually referred to as the Fourteen Points.

10 The First German Note reached Wilson through the Swiss on 6 October 1918, Oederlin to Wilson, 6 October 1918, *Foreign Relations, 1918, World War*, vol. 1, pp. 337–338, and the First Wilson Note (his response) went as Wilson to Oederlin, 8 October 1918, ibid., p. 343. The Austro-Hungarians also requested that Wilson arrange an armistice, 7 October 1918, ibid., p. 341.

11 I.C.–77, 6 October 1918, CAB 28/5, Public Record Office, London (Kew). Because the subject of discussion was Bulgaria with which the United States was not at war, no American representative was present.

12 Maurice Hankey, *The Supreme Command, 1914–1918*, London, George Allen and Unwin, 1963, vol. 2, p. 853.

13 Jean-Baptiste Duroselle, *Clemenceau*, Paris, Fayard, 1988, p. 641; David S. Newhall, *Clemenceau: A Life at War*, Lewiston, Edwin Mellen, 1991, pp. 376–377, 401.

14 Speech, Caxton Hall, 5 January 1918, *The Times* (London), 6 January 1918. See Minutes of Danny Meeting, 13 October 1918, Cabinet Paper G.T.–5967, CAB 24/66, Public Record Office. Lloyd George's later apparent conversion to

Wilsonianism is seen in *Memoirs of the Peace Conference*, New Haven, Yale University Press, 1939, vol. 1, pp. 38–50.

15 Appendix 1 to I.C.–80, Conference of Prime Ministers, 8 October 1918, CAB 28/5, Public Record Office; Ferdinand Foch, *Mémoires pour servir à l'histoire de la guerre de 1914–1918*, Paris, Plon, 1931, vol. 2, pp. 270–272. See also, Maxime Weygand, *Idéal vécu*, vol. 1 of *Mémoires*, Paris, Flammarion, 1953, p. 623; and *idem*, *Foch*, Paris, Flammarion, 1947, p. 260.

16 Beatty to Wemyss, 17 October 1918, BTY/13/40/7, National Maritime Museum, Greenwich, London.

17 War Cabinet 489A, 21 October 1918, CAB 23/14, Public Record Office; Beatty to Hankey, 23 October 1918, Cabinet Paper G.T.- 6107, CAB 24/68, Public Record Office.

18 War Cabinet 491B, 26 October 1918, CAB 23/14, Public Record Office.

19 War Cabinet X–29, 19 October 1918, CAB 23/17, Public Record Office.

20 Conference, Senlis, 25 October 1918, United States, Department of the Army, *The United States Army in the World War*, Washington, Government Printing Office, 1947, vol. 10, pp. 19–22.

21 Unsent letter, Haig to Foch, 23 October 1918, Douglas Haig Papers, H132, National Library of Scotland, Edinburgh.

22 Foch to Clemenceau, [26 October 1918], René L'Hôpital, *Foch, l'armistice et la paix*, Paris, Plon, 1938, pp. 60–65; Weygand, *Idéal vécu*, p. 636.

23 Lansing to Oederlin, 23 October 1918, *Foreign Relations, 1918, World War*, vol. 1, pp. 381–382.

24 Charles Seymour, ed., *The Intimate Papers of Colonel House*, Boston, Houghton Mifflin, 1926–28, vol. 4, p. 88.

25 Wilson to House, private code series 1, 28 October 1918, Woodrow Wilson Papers, Library of Congress, Washington, D.C.

26 In the Treaty of London, 1915, the agreement under which Italy had entered the war. For the text, see Réné, Albrecht-Carrié, *Italy at the Paris Peace Conference*, New York, 1938; reprint, Hamden, Archon, 1977, pp. 334–339.

27 I.C.–83, Notes, 29 October 1918, CAB 28/5, Public Record Office; Maurice Hankey diary, 29 October 1918, HNKY 1/6, Churchill College Archives, Cambridge University.

28 I.C.–83, 29 October 1918, CAB 28/5, Public Record Office.

29 Allied Naval Council, Report of the Sixth Meetings Held ... October 28th to November 4th, 1918, BTY/7/11/9, National Maritime Museum.

30 Wemyss, Notes, 27 October–3 November 1918, WMYS 7/11/4, Churchill College Archives, Cambridge University.

31 Notes of a Conversation, 3 November 1918, House Collection, Yale University.

32 I.C.–93, 4 November 1918, CAB 28/5, Public Record Office. The final terms were amended to require the surrender of all Germany's submarines.

33 5 November 1918, 6 N 42, Service historique de l'armée de terre. Efforts to discover who proposed that addition have been unsuccessful. The initiative did not come from the navy; the best guess is that it came from Lloyd George or one of his aides.

34 Foreign Office to Sir A. Hardinge, 14 November 1918, FO 371/3446, Public Record Office.

35 Such an agreement must be inferred, Henri Mordacq, *Le ministère Clemençeau: Récit d'un témoin*, Paris, Plon, 1930–31, vol. 2, p. 297; House to Lansing for Wilson, 12, 30 October 1918, Wilson Papers, series 2, Library of Congress.

36 Calthorpe to Admiralty, 31 October 1918, ADM 1/8541/276, Public Record

Office; for drafts of the Mudros Armistice and the document as signed, see Henry Newbolt, *Naval Operations*, vol. 5, *From April 1917 to the End of the War*, Committee of Imperial Defence, Historical Section, London, Longman's, Green, 1931, pp. 418–423.

37 Sir Frederick Maurice, writing later, commented that this victory was one of the most complete the British ever won, *The Armistices of 1918*, Oxford, Oxford University Press, 1943, p. 26.

38 I.C.–85 (SWC), 31 October 1918, CAB 28/5, Public Record Office.

39 The Germans were required to evacuate Austro-Hungarian territory within fifteen days. For the text of the Armistice of Villa Giusti, including the important attached protocol, see Sir James E. Edmonds and H.R. Davies, *Military Operations, Italy, 1915–1919*, Committee of Imperial Defence, Historical Section, London, 1949; reprint, Nashville: Battery Press for the Imperial War Museum, n.d., pp. 426–434.

40 Bogdan Krizman, "The Belgrade Armistice of 13 November 1918", *Slavonic and East European Review* 48 (1970), pp. 67–87.

41 Gen. Jean Bernachot, *Les armées françaises en orient après l'armistice de 1918*, Ministère des armées, État-major de l'armée de terre, Service historique, Paris, Imprimerie nationale, 1970, vol. 1, p. 20; Paul Azan, *Franchet d'Esperey*, Paris, Flammarion, 1929, pp. 225–232. For the text, see United States, Department of State, *Foreign Relations of the United States, 1919, The Paris Peace Conference*, Washington, Government Printing Office, 1942- 47, vol. 2, pp. 183–184.

42 House diary, [3 November 1918], House Collection, Yale; Lloyd George, *Memoirs of the Peace Conference*, vol. 1, pp. 44–46.

43 Wilson to House, private code series 9, 4 November 1918, Wilson Papers, series 2, Library of Congress.

44 I.C.–87, 1 November 1918, CAB 28/5, Public Record Office; War Cabinet 497 (Imperial War Cabinet, 36), CAB 23/8, Public Record Office; Derby diary, 5 November 1918, 920 DER(17) 28/1/1, Liverpool Record Office, Liverpool.

45 Probably said at a meeting on 31 October 1918 where no secretary was present, but confirmed in Weygand, *Idéal vécu*, p. 635, and Foch, *Mémoires*, vol. 2, p. 285.

46 *Foreign Relations, 1918, World War*, vol. 1, pp. 468–469.

47 Foch quotes his official report in his memoirs, *Mémoires*, vol. 2, pp. 288–320; Waffenstillstandkommission, 1918–1919, *Der Waffenstillstand, 1918–1919*, Berlin, Deutsche Verlagsgesellschaft für Politik und Geschichte, 1928, vol. 1, pp. 1–57. See also Weygand, *Idéal vécu*, p. 639; Matthias Erzberger, *Erlebnisse im Weltkreig*, Stuttgart, Deutsche Verlagsanstalt, 1920, pp. 330- 335; and Mordacq, *Le ministère Clemenceau*, vol. 2, pp. 343–352.

48 Most of the British and French civilian leaders had wanted that evacuation, I.C.–91 (SWC), 2 November 1918, CAB 28/5, Public Record Office.

49 *Parliamentary Debates* (Commons), 5th ser., vol. 110, cols. 2452–63.

50 House diary, 4 November 1918, House Collection, Yale University.

51 Joseph Tumulty, *Woodrow Wilson as I Know Him*, Garden City, New York, Doubleday, Page for the *Literary Digest*, 1921, p. 321.

52 Mordacq, *Clemenceau*, vol. 3, p. 5; the original is italicized.

Part II

The Eleventh of November Armistice

Chapter Three

Germany and the Armistice

Heinz Hagenlücke

The very same day the Armistice between the Allies and the German Empire was signed in the early hours of 11 November 1918 at Compiègne, a group of illustrious scholars, government officials and bankers had gathered in Berlin to celebrate the 70th birthday of one of the most famous German historians, Hans Delbrück. In the aftermath, one of the guests, the theologian Ernst Troeltsch, recalled the event as being awkward, more like a funeral than a birthday party. Everyone was in a grim mood, particularly Delbrück himself. The speaker who was chosen to congratulate Delbrück could not find or utter any words; he was openly weeping. Delbrück, responding, said that at that very moment they were witnessing the end of the glorious monarchy Frederick the Great had created, to which all Delbrück's own political thinking and his belief in Germany's future had been connected. Although Prussia had undergone some very difficult moments in its history, it was never so bad as now. The historian's faith in all his previous criteria and preconditions had been shaken. However, he found some relief in Goethe's words, that neither force nor time dismembers the carved shape which being alive has developed.[1] Troeltsch, who by the way carried a gun because he was afraid of the revolutionary situation that day in the German capital, left the birthday party in a shattered frame of mind, since all his faith was rooted in the form of government which had just been crushed.[2]

Indeed, for most Germans 11 November 1918 was a sad day. There were no jubilant bells ringing, no bonfires burning, no cheering crowds on the Berlin boulevard, *Unter den Linden*, as there had been in August 1914 and no thanksgiving services in the churches. The war was lost, the Kaiser had abdicated, the seemingly rock-solid old Wilhelmine order was destroyed, the future uncertain. The loss of the war appeared the greatest catastrophe in German history since 1807. Yet, there was also some hope for a new future in a democratic and possibly socialist Germany; finally, expressions of relief that the war was over – for better or worse – could be overheard. This chapter therefore will try to examine the manifold reactions to the Armistice in a country which was believed by the Allies and some German far-left politicians to be chiefly responsible for the outbreak of the Great War.

To understand the events that took place in the German Army leading to military defeat in November 1918, one must note that the Imperial Army of 1918 was no longer the same as that of 1914. As a result of attritional warfare, the *Materialschlachten* of the second half of the Great War, the Army had ceased to be the exclusive organization it had been up to 1914. Former class barriers and social differences were levelled out, the community of the *Frontsoldaten* had replaced the old *Klassenheer*; the Imperial Army was transformed into a militia.[3] At the same time, the physical and moral exhaustion of the troops had become more and more serious. The desire to end the war and secure peace grew ever stronger; desertions and signs of weakening discipline occurred to an extent nobody had ever dreamed possible. In late 1917 for instance, up to 10% of the soldiers who were being transferred from the Eastern to the Western Theatre seized this opportunity to go absent without leave; the High Command (*Oberste Heeresleitung*) found itself unable to deal with the problem.[4] Nevertheless, it is also worth noting that during the preparatory phase of the last great German offensive, the *Michaels-Offensive*, the general mood of the troops seemed in good order. The tempting vision of finally ending this long and gruesome war with one last and huge effort, apparently mobilized the last strength of the troops. For a brief moment, the soldiers at the Front as well as the Germans at home overcame their generally resigned mood. On 5 May 1918, *Unteroffizier* (Sergeant) Fiessmann wrote from the Western Front:

> The daily advance has an encouraging and stimulating effect on the soldier's mind (*Gemüt*) which has been desiccated by the over-long duration of trench warfare. Once again this gives rise to the hope that the newly-begun war of movement could bring the final decision, the long-awaited return home, to the beloved family, to the once familiar civilian work. This fair bargain strengthens body and soul and makes the unsettled and disordered life [at the Front] much easier to bear.[5]

Similarly, the representative of a *Landsturmbataillon* noticed on 23 March 1918: "Every hope we have is based on the forthcoming offensive in the West, which it is believed will end this war, and it is clear that these expectations leave no room for serious grumbling".[6] Even the traditionally sceptical mood in the nation's capital had changed during the early days of the offensive. Reports which reached the Chief of the Berlin Police, Heinrich von Oppen, of the general mood of the crowd, emphasized that confidence in winning this war had increased and peace seemed to be imminent. On 22 April 1918, it was even reported that due to the rapid advance of the German troops in France and Belgium, "we can claim that now the English are finally being made to pay their debt in blood".[7]

Despite the initially amazing success of the German offensive in March and April 1918, it became clear relatively soon that Quartermaster-General Ludendorff's strategic aim of breaking through the Allied lines had not been accomplished. On the contrary, in July and August the strategic initiative for the rest of the war had been lost to the Entente. In July at Villers-Cotterets and even worse near Amiens on 8 August 1918 – the *dies ater* of the German Army – the Army was demonstrably beaten. But still, Ludendorff refused to accept the bitter truth. Although he later wrote in his memoirs that the war now had turned into a gamble *(Hasardspiel)* and therefore had to be ended as quickly as possible,[8] he did not finally make up his mind to tell his emperor or the Chancellor that the war was lost. Instead, at a conference in GHQ at the Belgian resort, Spa, on 14 August 1918, where the soldiers were joined by the Kaiser, Crown Prince Wilhelm, the Chancellor, Count Hertling and the Secretary of State, Admiral Hintze, he summed up the situation as not so unfavourable. Count Hertling interpreted General Field Marshal Hindenburg's assessment of the military situation as being "that we could not hope to break the enemy's will by military operations and therefore our conduct of war must be successively to paralyse the enemy's *Kriegswillen* by strategic defence".[9] Towards the end of the conference, Hindenburg finally declared that the Army would manage to hold on to French soil and thus force Germany's will upon her foe.[10] It was agreed to come forward with another German peace offer when the military situation had improved – which was to be expected in early October. However, the contrary happened. On 2 September, the troops had to be withdrawn to the Siegfried-Line; 10 days later, St. Mihiel was lost, and on 26 September, a major combined Anglo-French attack against the whole front from Rheims to the Maas began. As if this were not enough, the bad news of the Bulgarian demand for an armistice reached the German H.Q. and clearly Ludendorff had to take action. On 28 September at 6 p.m. he visited Hindenburg in his study and told him that Germany must ask for a ceasefire. The Field Marshal told him that he had come to the same conclusion.[11] Ludendorff later described the scene: "The General Field Marshal and I separated with a firm handshake like men who had buried their dearest but who were determined to stand together in the worst as well as in the best hours of human life".[12]

Although it was generally recognized among the high-ranking officers of the General Staff that the military situation had progressively deteriorated ever since August 1918 and hope of winning the war had vanished, Ludendorff's bid for peace caused a shock among his entourage. There is a vivid description by Colonel Albrecht von Thaer of the reaction to Ludendorff's admission that the Reich had lost the war. He recapitulated the scene:

> Terrible and appalling! It is so! Indeed! As we [the officers in Spa] gathered together, Ludendorff stood up in our presence, his face was pale and filled with deep worry, but his head was still held high. A truly handsome Germanic hero figure. I had to think of Siegfried with the mortal wound in his back from Hagen's spear. He said roughly the following: It was his duty to tell us that our military condition was terribly serious. Any day now, our Western Front could be breached ... the war could no longer be won, but rather an unavoidable and conclusive defeat awaited ... Our own Army had

> unfortunately also been heavily contaminated with the poison of Spartacus-socialist ideas, and the troops were no longer reliable ... It was thus foreseeable ... that the enemy in the near future, with the help of American troops anxious to fight, would succeed in a great victory, a breakthrough in grand fashion. As a result, the West Army would lose its last hold and retreat in disorder across the Rhine and carry the revolution back to Germany. This catastrophe, he said, must be avoided by all means ... Therefore, the Supreme Army Command demanded of His Majesty the Kaiser and of the Chancellor that the proposal for bringing peace should be made to President Wilson of America without delay, for an armistice on the basis of his 14 points ... At present, then, we have no chancellor. Who will fill this position is yet to be determined. I have, however, asked His Majesty the Kaiser to bring those political cliques into the government whom we can mainly thank that we have come to this. We will now see these gentlemen brought into the Ministries. They should make the peace that must now be made. They made their bed, now they must lie in it!

Thaer then continues to describe the emotions he felt at this moment:

> The effect of these words on the listeners was indescribable! As L. spoke, quiet sobbing and moaning was audible. Many, probably most, had involuntary tears running down their cheeks. I stood to the left of General Director Gen. von Eisenhart. We instinctively grasped one another by the hand. I almost pressed his hand flat. After his last words, L. lowered his head slowly, turned and went to his adjoining room. Since I had an appointment to report to him afterwards, I followed him and – since I'd known him so long – grasped his right arm with both hands, something I never would have done under other circumstances, and said: 'Your Excellency, is that the truth? Is that the last word? Am I awake or dreaming? That really is too terrible! What will happen now?' I was completely beside myself. He remained calm and gentle and said to me with a deeply sorrowful smile: 'Unfortunately, that is how it is, and I see no other way out'.[13]

Apparently, most of the officers had been unaware of the seriousness of Germany's military situation and found themselves in a state of shock when they were confronted with the terrible news. But one has to ask how the lower ranks, particularly the *Mannschaften* (enlisted) of the Army, reacted.

As already mentioned, the desire for peace had grown still stronger since the proven failure of the last offensive. On the other hand, there was still a certain readiness to hold out (*Durchhalten*) until the war was over, one way or the other.[14] However, when the news from Spa reached the front, the overwhelming majority of the soldiers had only one wish – to go home. Older soldiers in particular, those who had wives and family to return to, could not wait for the war to be over; 'peace at any price' being the motto. Captain Loose, for example, delivered a detailed account of the collapse of soldier morale at the *Heeresgruppen* Gallwitz and Duke Albrecht on 5 November 1918. The spirit was very bad, he reported to OHL, the Army was not willing to fight anymore:

In the cinemas, no pictures of the Kaiser, Hindenburg and Ludendorff can be shown. Everyone whistles. When a picture of Hindenburg was shown in an area of the Corps, shouts of 'Lights out, Knives out, two mess kits to catch the blood'[15] allegedly could be heard ... All in all, the morale at the Army Groups is of the kind that the enlisted (*Mannschaften*) will not fight any more if we do not reach a peace agreement at once ... [16]

These realistic descriptions of the Army's condition obviously did not reach the fantasy world of the German Headquarters in Spa where the leading officers of the Army and the Kaiser and his entourage had gathered. On the contrary, in early November, the most absurd proposals emerged. Count Friedrich von der Schulenburg, Chief of Staff of the Crown Prince's Army Group, expressed the opinion that if the Armistice could deliver a breathing space for the weary troops, they could be motivated to strike against the 'Bolshevistic' mutineers at home. A few reliable divisions for instance could take the City of Cologne and through that restore order in the whole Reich. It was left to General Groener, who had succeeded Ludendorff as General Quarter Master on 30 October, to tell the Kaiser the truth: "Sire, you no longer have an army" he stated. To strengthen Groener's assessment, Colonel Wilhelm Heye, later to be chief of the *Reichswehr* from 1926–1930, bluntly stated that the troops "remain loyal to His Majesty, but they are tired and indifferent and want nothing but rest and peace. At the present moment they would not march for Germany, even with Your Majesty at their head, they do not even march against Bolshevism, they want one thing only – an armistice at the earliest possible moment. For the conclusion of an armistice every hour gained is of importance".[17]

Indeed, the military breakdown in late 1918 was not caused by revolutionary agitators who stabbed a glorious army in the back, as right-wing parties in particular, claimed after 1918, but it was a "general strike of a hopelessly defeated army" as Wheeler-Bennett noted in 1953.[18]

However, notwithstanding the bad shape of the fighting troops, the German units at the front continued fighting until virtually the last hours, against Allied attacks maintained until the end. When the Armistice became effective at 12.00 hrs German time, no signs of jubilation or festivities could be detected. There are some reports of German and Allied troops meeting between the positions reached at that time and exchanging cigarettes or food, but this was a rare occurrence.[19] Most men simply left what was not easily carried and, as units, commenced the long trail home. The withdrawal from Belgium and Northern France it seems, was conducted in an orderly manner. Reports from Holland confirmed that the men marched calmly and silently, discipline being maintained everywhere.[20] This was partly due to the fact that the Soldiers' Councils of the Army organized the retreat very effectively.[21]

However, not all of the soldiers shared that strong longing for peace and the return home. Friedrich Sieburg, then a young officer on the Western Front, related his feelings as a soldier who suddenly was to be demobilized after four years of trench fighting: "I am happy I am not going on leave, I never again want to go home", he wrote on 11 November:

> I would like to live my life walking along these country roads, searching the sky, measuring the world by co-ordinate squares and division combat sectors, evaluating the daylight hours by the strength of the artillery fire. The tremor when they attack near Zonnebeke! Those calls in the night 'Feldflieger 218?' or 'Divisionsstab 28?' or 'Attention! Wire' ... My Germany begins where the flares go up and ends where the train for Cologne departs ... I can't go home again and live the old life.[22]

Indeed, some soldiers may have shared these feelings of despair when they learned about the Armistice. In particular, younger and well-educated officers who had volunteered in August 1914 and served in the elite-regiments of the Army like Sieburg or Ernst Jünger had a feeling of utter desolation – about the lost war, the lost values and ideals, about bourgeois existence which had become deeply unattractive to them. Many feared losing the familiar stability of soldier front-line comradeship (*Frontgemeinschaft*). In general, these people were later to find their way into the so-called Free Corps (*Freikorps*). For them, the war was not over at all. It is interesting to note that the very first of these units was established on Armistice Day.[23] Although the figures are not certain, it has been estimated that in the summer of 1919, there existed over 100 of these *Freikorps*, a total of some 250,000 men.[24] Some were engaged in the *Grenzschutz* against Polish troops in the Posen Area, but most of them operated in the Baltic States. Here, quickly, a special situation had developed and the war continued. As a result of the provisions of the Brest-Litovsk Peace Treaty of March 1918, Russia had granted the Baltic states their independence. From March to October 1918, the German Government however, made several appeals to secure German influence in that area, especially in Latvia. Once the Soviets realized that Germany would certainly lose the war, Soviet Russian troops occupied the Baltic states in late 1918, the Soviet Government having repudiated the Brest-Litovsk Treaty on 13 November. The Baltic governments and their leaders fled and asked the Allies for help. It was in these circumstances that Article XII of the Armistice was brought into play. According to this, "all German troops at present in territories which before the war formed part of Russia, must likewise return to within the frontiers of Germany ... as soon as the Allies shall think the moment suitable, having regard to the internal situation of these territories". In the light of the above, there were some German troops left in the Baltic States, especially in Latvia,[25] who would stop the attack of the Red Army at the order of the Allied Powers.[26] They managed to do this in the Spring of 1919. It soon turned out that the regular 8th Army stationed there was unsuitable for the fulfilment of this task. The men had only one thought in mind: to get home.[27] The only units available and fit for action were *Freikorps*, whose task was originally to cover the retreat of the 8th Army. Soon, more and more men arrived from the Reich joining the *Freikorps*, mostly attracted by the Latvians' promise that every single combatant would receive his own property in the country after he had served there for only four weeks. Great numbers of them were simply criminals who hoped to escape from the German police. Anyway, the *Freikorps* caused much trouble for the German and the Allied governments, until they finally agreed to withdraw in December 1919. Some of these units, only three months later, played an active part in the Putsch of Kapp and Lüttwitz.

In a different but related way, the war was not over on 11 November for the 772,000 German soldiers taken prisoner during the four-and-a-half years of fighting. To return from Allied P.O.W. camps, from Morocco to Siberia, sometimes took them more than a year; for instance a last ship of prisoners arriving from Japan, carrying the former Governor of Kiaochow on board, reached Hamburg as late as 25 May 1920.[28] More than half of the number originally captured failed to return, a reflection of the conditions they had endured. Most of those who were returning were as shocked as the people in Germany when they learned that the Fatherland had laid down its arms. Hermann Reese, who had been imprisoned in Western France since 1915, reported his feelings when he heard: "Wilson, the Armistice offer, the emperor in Holland, revolution in Germany, these are words which fly around, words whose meaning is difficult to grasp. How could all that happen? The iron Germany, the people in arms beaten, at the mercy of her enemies! (*ein Spielball der Feinde*). And here we sit in sheer helplessness".[29] The young Edwin Erich Dwinger, who served as an ensign at the Russian Front and was captured early in 1915 at the age of 17, noticed a widespread depression among his comrades in his camp in Siberia as the news of the Armistice finally had reached the Far East: "Collapse in Germany! Am I crazy? Am I imagining things? In the yard an active *Oberleutnant* stands without coat and cap. He has put on all his medals, beats himself jingling on his chest and keeps on shouting: it was all for nothing ... it was all for nothing ... it was all for nothing".[30]

The fact that more than two million German soldiers were killed during the Great War, their sacrifice in vain, caused in many men a powerful feeling of hate and a demand for revenge. The most famous report of these feelings was undoubtedly written by the "unknown soldier of the Great War", Corporal Adolf Hitler, at the time in question recovering from a temporary blindness in the military hospital in Pasewalk: "Everything went black before my eyes", was how he recalled his state of mind when learning about the war being lost:

> I tottered and groped my way back to the dormitory, threw myself on my bunk and dug my burning head into my blankets and pillow ... so it had all been in vain ... There followed terrible days and even worse nights ... In these nights hatred grew in me, hatred for those responsible for this deed. In the days that followed, my own fate became known to me ... That night I resolved that, if I recovered my sight, I would enter politics.[31]

After the war, the revolutionary soldiers, the SPD and, most of all, the Jews – the 'November criminals' – became the target of fanatical hatred and anger particularly of the nationalists on the right, since the former had allegedly stabbed the German Army in the back, thus being responsible for the defeat. It is very interesting to notice that once military defeat had become a fact, there was a remarkable upsurge of anti-Semitism in the Reich, the Jews becoming the scapegoat for all that went wrong during the war. The extreme nationalist *Alldeutscher Verband*, which up to 1918 still refused formally to incorporate anti-Semitism into political matters, decided in late 1918 to make use of the *Judenfrage* (the Jewish Question) as a propaganda factor. General von Gebsattel, Vice-Chairman of the *Alldeutschen*, demanded in October 1918 that "the situation be used as a fanfare against Judaism and that Jews be used as scapegoats for every injustice" *(die Lage zu Fanfaren gegen das Judentum und die Juden als Blitzableiter für alles Unrecht zu benutzen)*.[32]

It has been often argued that the homecoming of the soldiers was a humiliating event. Allegedly, the German population did not welcome their soldiers or at least did not honour them in the way they deserved. Quite a few officers' memoirs contain descriptions of how their decorations, epaulettes and badges were torn off by revolutionary *Spartacist* or other *Pöbel* (mob). However, recent research into contemporary accounts from November and December 1918, reveal a very different picture.[33] When the troops finally crossed the border, they were often greeted by an enthusiastic reception with bands playing the traditional German marches and patriotic hymns, flags swaying and the crowds cheering the *feldgraue*. When the battery of Lieutenant Bräutigam for instance, which was on its way home back from the Maas to Germany, crossed the border at the small town of Echternach near Luxembourg, he stated that they could hardly have been granted a warmer welcome if Germany had won the war![34]

The Prussian Secretary of War informed the deputy *Generalkommandos* in late November 1918 about the widespread wish of the population to demonstrate the Fatherland's gratitude by giving the veterans a warm welcome in their old garrison towns. Consequently, the Ministry instructed the deputy *Generalkommandos* to organize appropriate ceremonies in close co-operation with the local Workers' and Soldiers' Councils (!).[35] These ceremonies seemed to have been quite successful. On 30 November 1918, the Supreme Command of the *Armee-Abteilung* C informed the *Oberpräsident* of the Rhine Province: "The warm welcome which the population everywhere granted the troops returning from the fronts has been acknowledged gratefully by all members of the Army".[36] Finally, in January 1919, the Prussian Secretary of War wrote to the West-German *Regierungspräsident* (District governor): "The first-rate welcome which the German troops have found on their march back home from the west [by all parts of the population in the areas concerned] has been warmly appreciated by the troops".[37] It was no less a figure than the future President, Friedrich Ebert, who welcomed the troops in Berlin on 11 December 1918, declaring: "I salute you who return unvanquished from the field of battle".[38]

To move from the soldiers returning to the Fatherland to Home Front reaction to defeat, we need to look first at the official intimations of impending disaster. On 2 October, three days after the military was informed about Germany's request for an armistice, a certain Major von dem Bussche of OHL notified the leaders of the *Reichstag* parties of the calamitous situation.[39] They reacted exactly as the soldiers had done. Prince Max von Baden, soon to become the last Imperial Chancellor, described their reactions: "The deputies were absolutely broken; Ebert turned as white as a sheet and did not utter a single word; the MP Stresemann looked as if he had an accident ... Secretary v. Waldow[40] is believed to have left the room uttering: 'the only thing left to do is to shoot oneself in the head'".[41]

As a consequence of the new conditions, the old Chancellor, Count Hertling, formerly Bavarian Prime Minister, decided to resign; a new man had to be found to replace him. The only appropriate candidate was the liberal, Prince Max. The Prince, however, was at first adamant in his refusal to take up the heavy burden, since he did not want his Chancellorship to be stained by making an appeal for peace. In consequence, he informed the *Kabinettschef*, von Berg, that he could not become Chancellor because the request for an Armistice was a "fatal mistake".[42] Berg replied: "You have never been my candidate, but I do not know of anyone else". For a while, the Prince refused to take the office. When the situation was discussed in Berlin on 2 October, the Emperor and the former government being present, Prince Max again stated that he was strongly opposed to the peace offer. Kaiser Wilhelm II answered him: "The High Command deems it [the request for the Armistice] to be necessary, and you have not come here to get the High Command into trouble".[43] Since nearly everyone, civilians and military alike, urged Prince Max to take the responsibility, he finally agreed and on 3 October was appointed Imperial Chancellor. He was to be the last one. In his memoirs, he depicted his state of mind after the appointment: "When I woke up on the morning of the 4th, I felt like a man who had been sentenced to death and forgotten about it while he had been asleep".[44] But, there was no alternative to sending the government's request for peace to President Wilson. The cable which asked Wilson to mediate an Armistice based upon his 14 Points left the German capital on the night of the 3/4 October 1918.[45] The German public did not know that it had been the military High Command which had urged an immediate ceasefire. On the contrary, it appeared to them that it was a step taken by the civilian government, with or without questioning the High Command. Ludendorff's plan to exempt the military from responsibility worked as he had intended, a fact which later played an important part in the so-called 'Stab-in-the-back' legend.

In German historiography, it has long been the received view that German military defeat took the home front completely by surprise and hence unprepared. However, there are indications which suggest that at least the working class was not all that surprised. Again, the Berlin Police President, von Oppen, had to admit on 24 September, that the great majority of Berliners no longer believed in a decisive German military victory and therefore were entirely ready to support a peace of reconciliation. Furthermore, he added that the Austrian peace note from 14 September was welcomed.[46] In mid-August 1918, the writer Josef Hofmiller observed: "Nobody believes any more that we can win the war. Everybody knows that we have lost it, but no one spells it out".[47]

Research into the atmosphere within the Grand Duchy of Württemberg seems to confirm this.[48] It is quite obvious that the educated classes, the Wilhelmine *Gebildeten*, were particularly surprised and hit by the bad news, as they had believed in the Imperial propaganda until the bitter end. Of course there was a difference between the voices which did not believe in military victory any more and those which thought the war was definitively lost. Further research has to be done on this subject, but it appears that far more Germans were aware of the true state of affairs concerning the military situation than has hitherto been realized.

Meanwhile, after the public had learned about the step the German government had taken, a new thought concerning Germany's fate was brought up. On 7 October 1918, Walter Rathenau, at that time Chief of the huge electricity concern AEG and later to become the Foreign Minister who signed the Treaty of Rapallo, launched an article entitled *Ein dunkler Tag* (A dark day) in the liberal *Vossische Zeitung*, demanding that a comprehensive national defence as in the 1813 campaign against Napoleon should be organized if the Allies' answer to the German peace proposal proved to be unacceptable.[49] The matter was instantly discussed inside the cabinet and it was agreed that it should be postponed for the time being. This great patriot's *Herzensschrei* (a cry from the heart), as Prince Max later put it, though being totally unrealistic considering Germany's military situation, found many supporters particularly among the right-wing parties, who could not believe that four years of warfare had been for nothing. But it was not just radical nationalists who endorsed such a hazardous final step. In the western provinces of the Reich, where an occupation by Allied forces was expected – perhaps with black French colonial troops causing a particular reaction among the populace – committees were hastily formed in October, proposing such a national defence. In the Rhenish city of Düsseldorf, for instance, a so-called *Volksausschuß für nationale Verteidigung in Deutschland* (People's committee for the national defence in Germany) was formed in mid-October, which managed to traverse the old party cleavages which had determined the political situation in that city ever since late in the final decade of the 19th century. The *Volksausschuß* united all existing parties except the Social Democrats and appealed in various leaflets to the population to show themselves as worthy as their fathers and grandfathers had been in 1870 and 1813.[50] As the French plans for a possible cession of the Rhineland from the Reich were rumoured, the last lines one of these leaflets read: "We are German and we want to stay German!"[51]

After the first German note requesting an Armistice on the basis of the Fourteen Points, an intense exchange of diplomatic notes took place between Berlin and Washington in order to specify the terms of the Armistice. Soon it became clear that the American Government was encouraging a change in the nature of the German Government, culminating in the 3rd note of 23 October, which seemed to urge the Germans to alter their political system into a republic. The Government of the U.S.A., it read, could not "trust the words of those who have hitherto been the masters of German policy" but only "true representatives of the German people ... If it must deal with the military masters and the monarchical autocrats of Germany now, or if it is likely to have to deal with them later in regard to the international obligations of the German Empire, it must demand, not peace negotiations, but surrender".[52] Although President Wilson did not directly demand the abdication of Wilhelm II, the German public as a whole believed that this was in fact the case. Ethel Cooper, an Australian woman who for unknown reasons was allowed to spend the whole war in the Saxon city of Leipzig, wrote in a letter of 20 October 1918: "One only hears two questions this week – 'Have you escaped the Grippe [the flu] so far?' And 'Is the Kaiser going?'" This question could only fully be appreciated by anyone who knew Germany and the Germans. She continued: "I can really suggest no parallel to it – or perhaps if you can imagine 75 million members of the Salvation Army massed on the south coast, seeing the heavens above them torn, and waiting for the Lord above to fall with a splash into the English channel, you may have an idea of the atmosphere here".[53] After the German Government in its reply assured the USA that the peace negotiations would be conducted by a true *Volksregierung* (Government of the People), people were 'obsessed' with only one thought in their minds: if the Kaiser abdicates, Germany will get a better armistice.[54] The first party to react was the SPD. Philipp Scheidemann, later to become the first elected Prime Minister of the Weimar Republic, encouraged Chancellor Prince Max, in a letter of 29 October, to call for His Majesty's abdication as the only means by which Germany would receive tolerable armistice conditions, but the Prince – for the time being – refused to do so. It was not only voices from the left which demanded the Kaiser's abdication, but also 'realistic' politicians from the right and the centre urging Wilhelm II to resign, since that was the only way to preserve the Monarchy.

The Kaiser, however, reacted to the emerging clamour for his abdication by his flight from reality and arrival at German military headquarters in the Belgian town of Spa, on 29 October, where he gathered with his military entourage, although Prince Max and other politicians had strongly advised him to stay in Berlin. He was never to return.

A few days earlier, another event occurred which, only a few weeks before, would have been unimaginable: Quartermaster-General Erich Ludendorff was dismissed. As a reaction to President Wilson's note of 23 October, the High Command had issued an order to the Army, denouncing the note as unacceptable and demanding the continuation of the struggle by every means.[55] The next day, 25 October, Hindenburg and Ludendorff both came to Berlin – although Prince Max had advised them to stay in Spa, urging Vice Chancellor von Payer (Prince Max was ill with the flu) to break off the negotiations.[56] On 26 October, the Generals were called to the Kaiser and confronted with their unauthorized action.[57] After a very sharp interview with their Supreme Warlord, Ludendorff, on the verge of forgetting himself in the presence of Wilhelm II, was finally dismissed, while Hindenburg was persuaded to remain in his post. For more than two years, Ludendorff had been something like a 'Silent dictator' of the German Empire, although he was never able or sometimes willing to conduct the course of German policy all by himself. Now, his resignation caused no stir, showing that to a great extent the powerful position of the OHL was due to its promise to win the war. Once this promise was proved ill-founded, a strong position had become shaky.

In the last days of October 1918, the German Admiralty decided to engage the High Seas Fleet in a grand-scale final battle against the British Fleet, a battle which would include major deployment of U-Boats.[58] This 'Death or Glory' sortie idea was accompanied by wild rumours among the enlisted, that a raid was being planned from which nobody would return; that Armistice negotiations must be thwarted, that the Admiralty planned a rebellion against the Government and so on. All these rumours were to a certain degree true, but most of all, discipline had broken down among the 'war-service only' men in the German battleships. With the Armistice seemingly only a few days away, nobody wanted to die in a senseless heroic doomsday gesture. Very soon, the first signs of mutinies could be detected; on 29 October 1918, the Red Flag was hoisted in the Dreadnoughts *Thüringen* and *Helgoland*. The movement soon seized the whole German High Seas Fleet, the majority of the civilian workers in the ports displaying sympathy with the sailors. On 3 November, after a bloody confrontation with regular troops, the sailors took Kiel and were joined by garrison troops. From Kiel, the movement spread over all Northern Germany. In the beginning, apart from their refusal to take part in a last forlorn effort, the sailors had no political, let alone revolutionary, demands; all they wanted was to improve basic service conditions in the Fleet – for example better and more food. However, as the uprising moved beyond Kiel in the early days of November, more and more socialist workers of the leftist USPD joined the sailors, now demanding the abdication of the Kaiser, a revolution in Germany's political system with the establishment of soldiers' and workers' councils. At the same time, independently of the events in

iv German celebrations; fireworks rain down, fired from ships of the High Seas Fleet in Wilhelmshaven, at the announcement of the German Republic. (*Die Woche*, 16 November 1918, Liddle Collection)

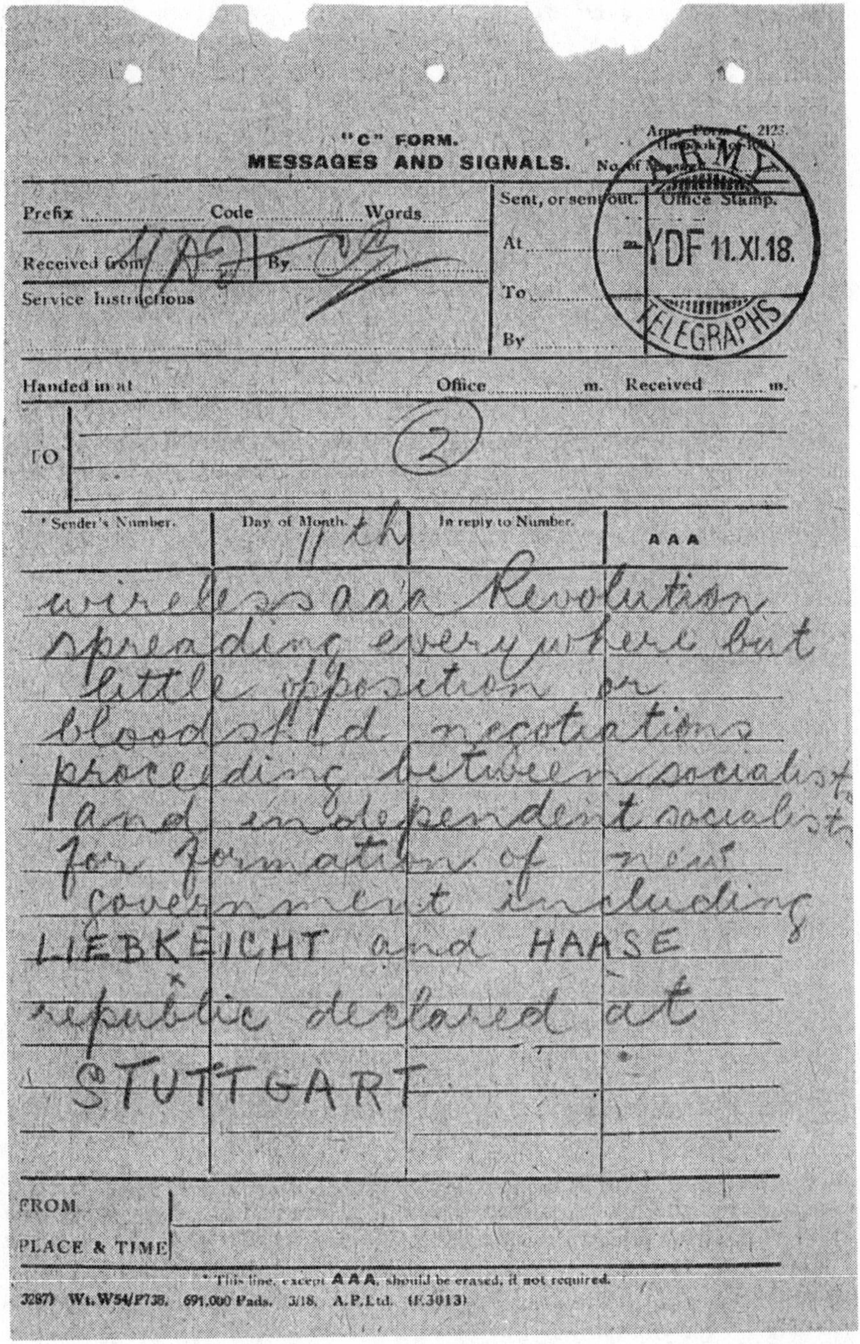

"C" FORM.
MESSAGES AND SIGNALS.

Army Form C. 2123.

No. of Message

Prefix .... Code .... Words ....

Received from .... By ....

Service Instructions

Sent, or sent out. | Office Stamp.

At .... m.

To ....

By ....

ARMY YDF 11.XI.18. TELEGRAPHS

Handed in at .... Office .... m. Received .... m.

TO (2)

* Sender's Number.	Day of Month.	In reply to Number.	AAA
	11th		

wireless aaa Revolution spreading everywhere but little opposition or bloodshed negotiations proceeding between socialists and independent socialists for formation of new government including LIEBKEICHT and HAASE republic declared at STUTTGART

FROM

PLACE & TIME

* This line, except AAA, should be erased, if not required.

3287) Wt. W54/P738. 691,000 Pads. 3/18. A.P.Ltd. (E.3013)

v "Republic declared at Stuttgart". An intercepted German wireless message tells of Germany in revolution, 11 November 1918. (A.E. Buddell, Liddle Collection)

Northern Germany, the revolution broke out in Bavaria, and finally, on 9 November 1918, Prince Max announced to the public that the Emperor had abdicated. Social Democrat Philipp Scheidemann proclaimed the German Republic from the *Reichstag* balcony. The Monarchy had ceased to exist.

Just one day after their victory, the Berlin Workers' and Soldiers' Council, which was the most important centre of power at that time in the German capital, gathered on 10 November 1918 at the Circus Busch to discuss nothing less than the future of the German Reich. Should Germany be governed by the councils – following the Soviet example – or should it become a parliamentary republic, led by the SPD? In a dramatic atmosphere, the crowd of between two and three thousand, finally decided to support the Ebert administration, which shared power with the Independent socialists in the so-called *Rat der Volksbeauftragten*. In their proclamation to the German people, the workers expressed their admiration for their Russian comrades. It was particularly emphasized that by following the example of their Russian brothers, they had managed to preserve the old claim of being pioneers of the *Internationale*. Indeed, many socialists expected that from now on, a new era of international solidarity would arise and that the comrades in the Allied countries would do everything they could to help their German brothers. In consequence, the Berlin workers had every confidence that "the proletariat of the other countries will use all its power to prevent the German people from being violated *(Vergewaltigung)* at the end of the war".[59]

Still, the preconditions of the coming Armistice were not known, and this prompted the circulation of the wildest rumours concerning Germany's future. On 6 November, the German delegation left for France; on 8 November, the conditions were handed over to them. On the evening of 10 November, special issues of the newspapers printed the conditions.

The result was an universal cry of despair. The rightist *Rheinisch-Westfälische Zeitung* denounced the Armistice terms as the "most brutal conditions of an Armistice that history knows"; compared to that, even the Tilsit Peace of 1807, after which Prussia had ceased to be an European Great Power, was "a piece of cake".[60] Germany was going to be the pariah of the whole world. The left-liberal *Berlin Tageblatt* complained about the "outrageously cruel conditions", the continuation of the blockade being an "unequalled act of inhumanity".[61] In a telegram of 12 November, the *Bayerische Volksstaat* (Bavarian Republic) under its Prime Minister, the Independent Socialist, Kurt Eisner, sent perhaps the harshest statement of all. "All hopes that we had of the success of the Revolution, are destroyed. The new republic will, if these dreadful conditions prove to be unalterable, end in ruination and chaos in a very short time".[62] The German Government, now led by Friedrich Ebert, shared the general opinion of the people. In a Cabinet meeting of 10 November, the only topic discussed was whether the Armistice conditions should be accepted or not, Ebert pointed out that there was nothing left for Germany but to sign the Armistice. But he stressed that the sacrifices which were imposed upon the country were so harsh that "they must end in the destruction of our people".[63]

To a certain degree, the surrender of the fleet, submarines, machine-guns

Mittags-Ausgabe.

Die Freiheit

Redaktion und Expedition: Berlin NW 6, Schiffbauerdamm 19.
Die „Freiheit" erscheint zweimal täglich, morgens und nachmittags, an Sonn- und Festtagen nur morgens. Der Bezugspreis beträgt bei freier Zustellung ins Haus für Groß-Berlin monatlich 2 Mark, nach außerhalb (Zusendung unter Streifband) 4 Mark. Bestellungen sind bis auf weiteres ausschließlich an die Expedition zu richten. Für die Erledigung auswärtiger Bestellungen ist vorherige Einsendung der Bezugsgebühr erforderlich.

Berliner Organ

Fernsprecher: Amt Norden Nr. 110 07, 110 08 und 110 48
Inserate kosten die siebengespaltene Petitzeile oder deren Raum 70 Pf. „Kleine Anzeigen" das fettgedruckte Wort 30 Pf., jedes weitere Wort 15 Pf. Teuerungszuschlag 30 Prozent. Bei Familienanzeigen und Versammlungsankündigungen von Gewerkschaften und politischen Organisationen fällt der Teuerungszuschlag fort. Inserate für die Morgenausgabe müssen bis 5 Uhr abends am Tage zuvor, Inserate für die Nachmittagsausgabe bis vorm. 11 Uhr bei der Expedition aufgegeben sein.

der Unabhängigen Sozialdemokratischen Partei Deutschlands

Jahrgang 1 | Berlin, den 15. November 1918 | Nummer 2

Für ein Bündnis des Weltproletariats.

Ein Aufruf der russischen Regierung.

Revolution und Volkswirtschaft.

Von Ed. Bernstein.

Zu den vielen erfreulichen Erscheinungen unserer Revolution gehört auch die, daß sich fast auf allen Seiten ihrer Vorkämpfer ein volles Verständnis für die volkswirtschaftlichen Notwendigkeiten zeigt, die der Sieg der Revolution bedingt. Die Erlasse des Rates der Volksbeauftragten der preußischen Volksregierung, des Arbeiter- und Soldatenrates von Berlin und der Provinz, die Kundgebungen der süddeutschen Revolutionsregierun-

Wie wir von informierter Seite erfahren, erläßt das Volkskommissariat des Auswärtigen in Rußland einen Aufruf an die arbeitenden Klassen Deutschlands und Oesterreich-Ungarns sowie der okkupierten Gebiete zu einem Bündnis, dem sich später auch die arbeitenden Klassen der übrigen Länder anschließen sollen.

Arbeiterklasse begrüßt der Allgemeine Arbeiterbund die deutsche Republik. Dieses historische Ereignis muß das Ende der Gewalt-

Sammlung des Bürgertums?

Der Sieg der Revolution war für das Bürgertum eine Ueberraschung. Einen derartigen Zusammenbruch des alten Systems hatte man nicht erwartet und beeilt sich nun, sich auf den Boden der neuen Regierung zu stellen. Die Bereitwilligkeit weiter Kreise der Beamtenschaft und der Intellektuellen zur Mitarbeit darf aber nicht darüber täuschen, daß es auch Strömungen gibt, die sich keinesfalls mit der jetzigen Lage abgefunden haben. In rechtsstehenden Blättern, z. B. der „Deutschen Tageszeitung" und der „Deutschen

vi *Die Freiheit*, newspaper of the German Independent Socialist Party, calls for solidarity among the working peoples of the world (Liddle Collection) and other war material as provided by the Armistice conditions had been expected by the German people. It was not so much the handing over of these military means, but the deliverance of the 5,000 locomotives, 150,000 wagons, 5,000 motor lorries and a huge merchant shipping tonnage in combination with the continuation of the Allied blockade, which upset the people. Considering the ever-worsening food situation since the notorious turnip-winter of 1916/17, people in Germany hoped that the end of the war would mean the end of hunger. In the main, as a result of the blockade, the supplies of food had to be reduced by some 50 per cent in 1918. A decline in the population and an increase in disease had been evident since 1914, and in late 1918 Germany was threatened by famine. In November 1918 for instance, more than 3,500 people were dying each day of hunger and malnutrition in the Reich.[64] If all these wagons and trucks were to be surrendered, how would the big cities be supplied with food? It was in particular these conditions of the Armistice which resulted in the feeling among many Germans that the war was far from being over.

Jo Mihaly, a famous German ballet dancer in the 1920's, depicted a scene where she, then just sixteen years old, met an old friend in the East-Elbian town of Schneidemühl on 14 November 1918, the friend being about to be demobilized. When she asked him where he would go from there, he replied:

> 'Home. Have you read the Armistice conditions?' – 'No!' I said, rather surprised. 'Is it bad?' – 'Even worse!' He drew a crumpled piece of newspaper out of his pocket. 'You can keep the document of shame. You will be amazed. We will bleed to death over this'. – 'We already did', I murmured. – 'Now, it is our children's turn. You know, we are just simple soldiers, but we are intelligent enough to know that this is a very stupid deal ... Damn it! It's not over yet, *Fräulein*!'[65]

Under these circumstances it is not surprising at all that Armistice Day never had even a chance of becoming a national holiday. Generally speaking, it is the date of 9 November to which so many different, and sometimes tragic events of modern German history are connected. But neither the ninth nor eleventh of November was officially commemorated during the Weimar Republic. This does not mean, however, that on these dates it was business as usual, for 11 November 1914 was also the day of one of the most influential German myths of the Great War, the day of *Langemarck*.[66] Near that small village in Flanders, regiments consisting of very young soldiers, recently students – the 'Schoolboy Corps' according to some British sources – had allegedly attacked the enemy lines with the hymn *Deutschland, Deutschland über alles* on their lips. It is not the place to discuss what really had happened there[67] but Langemarck, above all, was to become the symbol of Germans in the full bloom of youth who collectively sacrificed themselves in a heroic gesture for the good of the Fatherland. During the Weimar Republic, whilst the former Allies celebrated 11 November as Armistice Day, the 'true, real' Germany, represented by its youth, commemorated 11 November as the day of Langemarck; to some degree it was the Anti-Armistice Day in Germany.

In fact, the myth of Langemarck was so strong that as late as 28 January 1943, *Reichsmarschall* Hermann Göring sent a radio message telegram to the encircled 6th Army at Stalingrad, praising their *Todesmut* as equal to that of the young regiments 29 years before.[68] The fact that most Germans commemorated 11 November as the day when several thousand young men were slaughtered for a strategically questionable or at best inconsiderable goal, rather than celebrating the end of the First World War, reveals a lot about the revisionist mentality in the 1920's and 1930's in Germany. The war was not over yet.

Endnotes

1 '*Und keine Macht und keine Zeit zerstückelt geprägte Form, die lebend sich entwickelt.*'
2 Ernst Troeltsch, *Spektatorbriefe*,Tübingen, 1924, pp. 24–25.
3 Erich Ludendorff, *Meine Kriegserinnerungen*, Berlin, 1919, p. 516.
4 *Ibid.*, p. 434.
5 Quoted in Bernd Ulrich / Benjamin Ziemann (eds.), *Frontalltag im Ersten Weltkrieg: Wahn und Wirklichkeit; Quellen und Dokumente*, Frankfurt am Main, 1994, p. 197.
6 *Ibid.*
7 Report to the Berlin Chief of Police, 15 and 22 April 1918, in: *Dokumente aus geheimen Archiven*, Band 4 1914 – 1918. Berichte des Berliner Polizeipräsidenten zur Stimmung und Lage der Bevölkerung in Berlin 1914–1918. Bearbeitet von Ingo Materna und Hans-Joachim Schreckenbach, Weimar, 1987, pp. 272–273.
8 Ludendorff, *Kriegserinnerungen*, pp. 551–552.
9 Ludendorff, *Urkunden der Obersten Heeresleitung über ihre Tätigkeit 1916–18*, Hutchinson, London, p. 501.
10 Ludendorff, *ibid.*, p. 503.
11 Eberhard Kessel: Ludendorffs Waffenstillstandsforderung vom 29 September 1918, in *Militärgeschichtliche Mitteilungen* 4 (1968), pp. 65–86.
12 Ludendorff, *Kriegserinnerungen*, p. 583.
13 Albrecht von Thaer, *Generalstabschef an der Front und in der OHL. Aus Briefen und Tagebuchaufzeichnungen 1915–1919*, Herausgegeben von Siegfried A. Kaehler, Göttingen, 1958, pp. 234–235. Diary-Note from 1 October 1918.
14 Anne Lipp, "Friedenssehnsucht und Durchhaltebereitschaft", in *Archiv für Sozialgeschichte* 36 (1996), pp. 279–292.
15 '*Licht aus, Messer raus, zwei Kochgeschirre zum Blutfangen*!'
16 Quoted in Ulrich / Ziemann, *op. cit.*, pp. 204–205.
17 Wilhelm Groener, *Lebenserinnerungen. Jugend, Generalstab, Weltkrieg*, Göttingen, 1957, p. 462.
18 J.W. Wheeler-Bennett, *The Nemesis of Power. The German Army in Politics*, London, 1953, p. 15.
19 Stanley Weintraub, *A Stillness heard round the World. The end of the Great War: November 1918*, London, 1985, p. 325.
20 *Ibid.*, p. 386.
21 Ludwig Lewinsohn, *Die Revolution an der Westfront*, Berlin, 1920, pp. 5–16.
22 Friedrich Sieburg, *Es werde Deutschland*, Frankfurt am Main, 1933, pp. 20–21.
23 The Freikorps Volck in Lüneburg. Cf. Hagen Schulze, *Freikorps und Republik 1918–1920*, Boppard, 1969, p. 26.
24 *Ibid.*, p. 36.

25 After the Red Army had conquered this country, it was declared a Soviet republic on 13 December 1918.
26 Warren E. Williams, "Die Politik der Alliierten gegenüber den Freikorps im Baltikum 1918–1919", in *Vierteljahreshefte für Zeitgeschichte* 12 (1964), pp. 147–169.
27 *Die Aufzeichnungen des Generalmajors Max Hoffmann.* Herausgegeben von Karl Friedrich Nowak. Vol. 1, Berlin, 1929, pp. 217–224. The last lines in his diary read: "The troops do not want to fight anymore".
28 Ulrike Klein, *Deutsche Kriegsgefangene in japanischem Gewahrsam 1914–1920.* Phil. Diss. Freiburg, 1993, p. 288.
29 Hermann Reese, *Kriegsgefangen!* Berlin, 1930, p. 98.
30 Edwin Erich Dwinger, *Die Armee hinter Stacheldraht. Das Sibirische Tagebuch*, Jena, 1929, p. 280.
31 Quoted in Weintraub, *op. cit.*, p. 141.
32 Heinz Hagenlücke, *Deutsche Vaterlandspartei. Die nationale Rechte am Ende des Kaiserreiches*, Düsseldorf, 1997, p. 410.
33 Cf. Richard Bessel, "The Great War in German memory: The soldiers of the First World War, demobilization and Weimar political culture", in *German History* 6 (1988), pp. 20–34.
34 Otto Bräutigam, *So hat es sich zugetragen. Ein Leben als Soldat und Diplomat*, Würzburg, 1968, p. 94.
35 Preußisches Kriegsministerium to deputy *Generalkommandos*, 26.11.1918, in Hauptstaatsarchiv Düsseldorf (HStAD) Nr. 15109.
36 Generalleutnant Fuchs to *Oberpräsident* of the *Rheinprovinz*, 30.11.1918, in *ibid.*
37 Prussian Secretary of War to all *Regierungspräsidenten* in West-Germany and the Governments of Württemberg, Bavaria, Hesse and Oldenburg, 18.1.1919, in *ibid.*
38 Heinrich August Winkler, *Von der Revolution zur Stabilisierung. Arbeiter und Arbeiterbewegung in der Weimarer Republik 1918 bis 1924*, Bonn, 1984, p. 100.
39 His speech is printed in Ludendorff, *Urkunden*, pp. 535–538.
40 The Secretary of the *Kriegsernährungsamt* (War Food Office).
41 Prinz Max von Baden, *Erinnerungen und Dokumente*, Stuttgart, 1968, pp. 328–329.
42 *Ibid.*, p. 323.
43 *Ibid.*, p. 332.
44 *Ibid.*, p. 338.
45 It is printed in *ibid.*, p. 337.
46 Stimmungsberichte, p. 289.
47 Quoted in Ernst Johann (Hg.), *Innenansicht eines Krieges. Bilder, Briefe, Dokumente*, Frankfurt am Main, 1968, p. 324.
48 Cf. Felix Höffler, "Kriegserfahrungen in der Heimat: Kriegsverlauf, Kriegsschuld und Kriegsende in Württembergischen Stimmungsbildern des Ersten Weltkrieges", in Gerhard Hirschfeld a.o. (eds.), *Kriegserfahrungen. Studien zur Sozial- und Mentalitätsgeschichte des Ersten Weltkrieges*, Tübingen, 1997, pp. 76–79.
49 Printed in Prince Max von Baden, *op. cit.*, pp. 362–363; Peter Graf Kielmansegg, *Deutschland und der Erste Weltkrieg*, Frankfurt am Main, 1980, p. 671.
50 HStAD Regierung Düsseldorf Nr. 15081.
51 *Ibid.*
52 FRUS 1918 Supplement Part 1 Vol. 91, pp. 382–383.

53 *Behind the Lines. One Woman's War 1914–1918. The Letters of Caroline Ethel Cooper*, edited and with an introduction by Decie Denholm, London, 1982, Letter from 20.10.1918.
54 Prince Max von Baden, *op. cit.*, p. 484; Diary of Richard Stumpf, *Erinnerungen aus dem deutsch-englischen Seekriege auf SMS Helgoland*, Berlin, 1928, (16 October 1918), p. 300.
55 Printed in Prince Max von Baden, p. 470.
56 Friedrich von Payer, *Von Bethmann Hollweg bis Ebert. Erinnerungen und Bilder*, Frankfurt am Main, 1923, pp. 141–144.
57 Ludendorff, *Kriegserinnerungen*, pp. 613–614.
58 Kielmansegg, *op. cit.*, pp. 686–688.
59 Printed in *Die Regierung der Volksbeauftragten 1918/19*, Erster Teil, eingeleitet von Erich Matthias, bearbeitet von Susanne Miller unter Mitwirkung von Heinrich Potthoff, Düsseldorf, 1969, pp. 31–33.
60 *Rheinisch-Westfälische Zeitung* 15.11.1918, Nr. 934.
61 *Berliner Tageblatt* , 11.11.1918, Nr. 578.
62 Telegram of the Bavarian Government to the Entente, 12 November 1918, printed in *Rheinisch-Westfälische Zeitung*, 12 November 1918, Nr. 936.
63 Notes of Cabinet meeting from 10 November 1918, printed in *Regierung der Volksbeauftragten*, p. 25.
64 N.P. Howard, "The Social and Political Consequences of the Allied Food Blockade of Germany, 1918–1919", in *German History* 11 (1993), pp. 161–188.
65 Jo Mihaly, ... *da gibt's ein Wiedersehen! Kriegstagebuch eines Mädchens 1914–1918*, München, 1986, p. 375.
66 Colin Fox, "The myths of Langemarck", in *Imperial War Museum Review* 10 (1995), pp. 13–25.
67 For the facts cf. *Karl Unruh, Langemarck: Legende und Wirklichkeit*, Koblenz, 1986.
68 Walter Kempowski, *Das Echolot. Ein kollektives Tagebuch Januar und Februar 1943*, Band II, München, 1993, p. 508.

Chapter Four

Britons Overseas

Peter Liddle

In a letter written on Armistice Day to his father, Major S. C. Marriott recorded:

> We shall not forget the number 11, because by a curious coincidence hostilities closed officially on the 11th. month at 11 o'clock in the morning of the 11th. day, and the 11th. Battn. of the Manchesters, belonging to the 11th. Division, were by that time back in billets after going through a very hectic experience. We got orders late last night to push on at day-break, and it was expected that we might be in action before long. So the Battn. had fallen in and marched off. As 2nd. in command I was busy at the end of the Column getting the Companies off at proper intervals, and marshalling the Transport into place. I was the last man to ride out of the village, next to Malplaquet, amidst cheers, handshakes and good wishes of the villagers, who had assembled to see us off. The column stretches about half a mile these days, because we march in file with long intervals between companies, to make it less deadly if bombed by aeroplanes and after marching about half a mile, I suddenly saw the C. O. and Adjutant retreating back down the column, and then I heard terrific cheering, and saw hundreds of caps thrown into the air. I guessed at once what it was and my first thought was to tell those villagers, so I turned my old horse round, and galloped like blazes down the road towards our last village. I shouted the news to a gang of R.E. repairing a blown up bridge, who threw their tools, picks, shovels, hats etc. into the air and cheered. The people in the village heard it, and as I came up I shouted "C'est fini", somebody put a French flag into my hand, and on I went as far as my billet and Hd. Qrs. shouting the news all round, and the people went absolutely mad. By this time the Battn. was forming up to march back, as hostilities had ceased, and with the C. O. who arrived about two minutes behind me, we went to rejoin it and bring it back. And back came the men amid indescribable scenes, they were cheering, firing off signal rockets, and one chap produced a Union Jack, and the band played a lively march. We were accompanied by a whole squadron of planes, who swooped down, round and over us, sometimes only a couple of yards above

us, looping the loop, firing signals and going completely mad, and in this fashion we marched through the village. Then came a march past and the Marseillaise, and the people wept and cheered alternately. We were decked with flowers and kissed ... In spite of all this it will take us a long time to realize that the war, which has been present to us for so long a time, is now a thing of the past.[1]

The scenes depicted are those which, today, one would readily associate with the Armistice through a kaleidoscope of remembered images from flickering films screened in television documentaries, descriptions in books and recollections handed down within families. However, Marriott's letter precisely contradicts what is sometimes assumed of the final hours of an indisputable watershed in history and contains striking differences from the way many soldiers in France or Flanders described the reaction in their zone.

It is sometimes assumed that the troops in France were waiting for an imminent cease-fire. Marriott makes it abundantly clear that his battalion was expecting to be involved in further action soon and that they had just been through 'a very hectic experience'. This, as will be seen, is confirmed again and again by contemporary letters and diaries. Among the great number of retrospective accounts which support Marriott's report is the striking statement of Tom Traill, an R.A.F. fighter pilot crossing the Channel on Home Leave on 10 November. 'While I realized that we seemed at last to be winning there was deep in my mind a feeling that war was a permanent state. I had not really considered that we might soon be at peace'.[2] Of course there were rumours of peace but, meanwhile, the war went on, hopes and fears were personally to be suppressed as today's realities continued to command bodies and to a large extent minds.

For some weeks, even months, it had been a different war, one of movement, perhaps even more fatiguing physically even if bestowing a sort of vulnerable freedom from the trenches. Casualties were still being suffered, in fact in far heavier numbers than in holding the line, but there was a new spiritual reward. Things were visibly going better; steady, sometimes even swift strides forward were being taken and then, suddenly, more in fulfilment of hope than anticipation, the fighting was over. Any idea we may have today of the B.E.F. drawing breath in the rumours of German home front troubles and, [towards the very end], the sailor mutinies, is well adrift. The debate continues over the degree to which the German Army in France had been militarily beaten but there can be no argument that the British soldier was convinced in the late Autumn of the year that he was winning the battles he was called upon to fight, until, from on high, he was ordered to stop – precipitately according to the diary or letter record of some in khaki.

We shall return to this idea of troops 'waiting' for an Armistice because it must be emphasized that the outcome of the war looks so much clearer to us now than it was to those at its forefront at the time. It will also be shown that the prevailing reaction of the British soldier to the cease-fire was sometimes a good deal less exuberant than the terrific cheering and throwing of caps in the air described by Marriott. The very message by which the news was imparted has the implication of tension maintained rather than of casting all care aside. 'Troops will stand fast on the line reached at that hour which will be reported to Corps HQ. Defensive precautions will be maintained and there will be no intercourse of any kind with the enemy'.[3] This does not sound like an invitation to organize a celebration party.

The limitations of the scene described in Marriott's letter should also be appreciated: there are of course no sailors; airmen are but fleetingly mentioned; British women, in uniform or not and all those on the Home Front, are conspicuously absent. Absent too is the still-wider active service context. There had already been an armistice in Macedonia producing its own reaction in the conduct and emotions of British troops there. For these troops, [their part in beating the Bulgars insufficiently recognized they considered], there was an air of unreality in celebrating the distant victory over the Germans – still the war was over and that was something. For British troops victorious over the Turks in Palestine and Mesopotamia, they too were celebrating a second armistice and some of them were actively engaged in complex consequences of the war. The same of course could be said for those forces in or en route for North Russia but certainly there was one more European front where November the eleventh had been preceded by a cease-fire on sectors where British troops were involved, the surrender of the Austro-Hungarian forces engaged in Italy. This chapter will show how much variation there was in individual response according to place and circumstance.

Writing on 12 November in France, an officer of the 9th Battalion Royal Welsh Fusiliers, B. H. Puckle, noted that "I've seen no signs of rejoicing or revelry by night whatever you would almost imagine ... people took it so quietly. I think perhaps it is because we have not collected our ideas as yet and haven't quite realized what has happened to us".[4] Bombardier Mortimer sought a contrast on national lines with French celebrations: "the English took it all very soberly and made no demonstration beyond expressions of pleasure at the cessation of hostilities".[5]

Whether or not it were expressed by many men, E.G. Bates surely wrote what was in the minds of the majority in any uniform and on any front: the Armistice had found him: "still alive and kicking for which I suppose I must be thankful".[6] Unpublished memoirs frequently reflect what J.L. Hampson described as a 'calm' reaction to the news. He was in Tournai, newly liberated after a German rearguard action to hold that sector. The city had suffered and so did the celebration it had suddenly to stage to mark the end of the war, a very subdued response as Hampson remembered.[7] A.M. Boyd also used the word 'subdued' in his account but he went further; he and his comrades: "were sceptical" of the permanent nature of the Armistice.[8] Bates, referred to above, had added quizzically to his letter in reference to disturbances in Germany: "How damned easily it might have been England! I wonder how many people think of that!!"[9]

Lest the impression be given that all was sober appraisal, it should be made clear that at Heule, about two miles from Courtrai, British troops certainly celebrated. "The whole of the pipe bands of the battalions were out playing one against another, men lighting flares, firing Verey lights and rockets, all searchlights flashing, singing shouting rattles" and with civilians making their own contributions to this uproar, according to Sergeant A.J. Butler.[10] On the march from Celles, the celebrations were similar with the addition of church bells and "the people taking us into their houses and giving us bread and coffee etc., flags flying everywhere, horses and waggons decorated, everybody in good spirits".[11]

It may be that troops not so recently engaged in action were more receptive to the jubilation of citizens who themselves in these last days had not been under the additional strain of a German fighting withdrawal through their streets. We should however return to A.M. Boyd's scepticism. The letter written by Captain Oliver Sichel on 16 October foreshadowed such sentiment. "The Peace terms are all rot and we are all against it out here. Why should not Foch finish it".[12] Though writing far from France, F.S.G. Barnett was on an active front and in mid-October he had been "terrified of this Peace Offensive". He considered Wilson's fourteen points all very fine and lofty but "until Germany's armies are really beaten in the field, her line broken and if possible her country invaded ... until she unconditionally surrenders it will be an awful mistake to stop".[13] A mild-spirited private in the 14th Battalion Royal Fusiliers, H.S. Innes, revealed in his letters as an unwilling conscript,

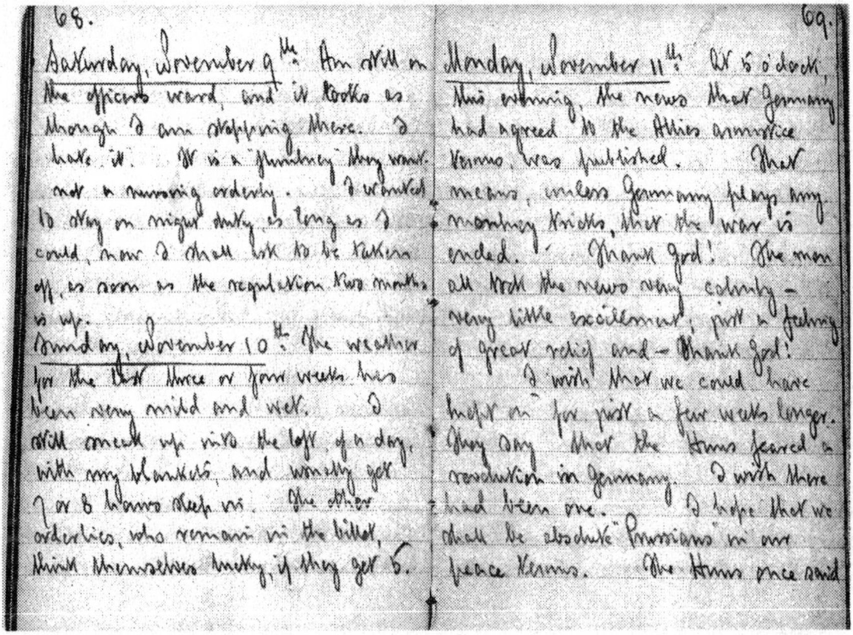
68.

Saturday, November 9th: Am still on the officers' ward, and it looks as though I am stopping there. I hate it. It is a "flunkey" they want, not a nursing orderly. I wanted to stay on night duty as long as I could, now I shall ask to be taken off, as soon as the regulation two months is up.

Sunday, November 10th: The weather for the last three or four weeks has been very mild and wet. I still sneak up into the loft of a day, with my blankets, and usually get 7 or 8 hours sleep in. The other orderlies, who remain in the billet, think themselves lucky if they get 5.

69.

Monday, November 11th: At 5 o'clock this evening, the news that Germany had agreed to the Allies armistice terms, was published. That means, unless Germany plays any monkey tricks, that the war is ended. Thank God! The men all took the news very calmly – very little excitement, just a feeling of great relief and – thank God!

I wish that we could have kept on for just a few weeks longer. They say that the Huns feared a revolution in Germany. I wish there had been one. I hope that we shall be absolute "Prussians" in our peace terms. The Huns once said

vii The diary of Pte C.J. Woosnam, RAMC, for 11 November 1918. "I wish that we could have kept on for just a few weeks longer". (C.J. Woosnam, Liddle Collection) was on Armistice Day scarcely less judgmental. He was "thrilled with the justice, the logic, of meting out the very punishment which the enemy thought could never be his".[14]

No one could express more clearly his readiness to continue enduring the misery of the war in order properly to punish Germany than R.A.M.C. Corporal Woosnam. He had served on the Western Front from early in 1915 till late in 1917 but was now, in November 1918, in Italy. In his diary for 7 November he reminisced over the scenes of destruction he had witnessed in France and the civilians killed: "but there was always the thought, at the back of one's mind, that one day – it might be a long way off – but one day, Germany would receive the same treatment. And I hate to think of peace being made, and those smug German towns escaping Scot free".[15]

As with the soldiers, for R.A.F. personnel there was no gentle wind-down of action before the Armistice. The diary of an Intelligence Officer for 9 November reports that with improved weather at last, and with pursuit of the enemy across the Scheldt, there was a "Great rush as many patrols sent out and they take the best photographs we have had for a long time. We lose two observers, one killed and the other slightly wounded in a scrap with twelve Huns. Report that we are just outside Mons and in Maubeuge. Orders come in at 8 o'clock that no more bombing is to be done at which no one weeps".

This officer, Captain C.E. Townley, then recorded on the following day: "that we may hear of the Armistice in the evening". When the sound of cheering is heard, he rang up and was informed that the Armistice had been signed and a great party ensued. "Mess full of semi-intoxicated officers, soldiers and Belgians". Unfortunately they were later: "given to understand that all was as yet unofficial and that we were to carry on with the work in the morning". One can imagine the scratching of sore heads when no early confirmation was received in the morning but, in due course, the news arrived, no further reaction to it being described in this diary.[16]

The Chaplain to Number 149 Squadron also had problems, but they were coincident with, rather than in consequence of, the Armistice; at least we are given no reason by the Reverend P. Gardner Smith to link the cessation of hostilities to his personal discomfiture. "The whole German Navy has mutinied and it is said that the Kaiser has abdicated. No one knows what may happen next, these are stirring times. Much worried at the complete disappearance of my washing".[17] Like Captain Townley, Gardner-Smith recorded on 10 November that the Armistice was signed but his misfortunes continued: "Going out I fell into a ditch full of dirty water which damped my body if not my spirit". Interestingly, at a time of such thankfulness, he noted: "very small attendance at the Services today".[18]

One high-spirited action by an R.A.F. pilot in celebration should not go unrecorded. Captain Ronald Ivelaw Chapman acquired a football from mechanics at his squadron and piloted his Armstrong Whitworth for the observer to throw it out for British troops in forward positions. His logbook formally states: "Saw the last few minutes of the War. Our troops halted at

11.00" but he recalled his pleasure in watching the troops kicking the ball around "having dropped their rifles on the ground".[19]

For some soldiers and airmen the cease-fire threw into still sharper relief their loss of a brother or dear friend on active service and there were no longer urgent military tasks to discipline their grief into the background. Such a case was Lance Corporal H.G. Morris of the Wiltshire Regiment. The news of the Armistice encouraged his friends to have a real 'flare-up' but he "was not taking any part in it as I feel too broken-hearted over poor Alb's death. I had great hopes of us all getting through alright but it's God's will so we must bend our heads. God grant that Mother will bear up under this terrible blow".[20]

Away from France, reaction to the German Armistice demonstrably lacked the sense of abrupt change, even surprise with which it was greeted on the Western Front. Certainly there were scenes which the ordnance department would not have envisaged with equilibrium. Although vast quantities of flares and verey lights illuminated the skies on all fronts and shells were even fired from coastal positions into the Eastern Mediterranean, the 11 November Armistice celebrants in Mesopotamia, Palestine or elsewhere seemed to have been able to take a more measured look at the years past and at the future, albeit with a new factor of uncertainty: would transportation problems or occupation force duties and the very scale of the demobilization problem mean frustrating delays to their return home when this was finally authorized? Could they in fact be home for Christmas, this time, Christmas 1918?

In Italy, Major Rory Macleod, even before the Armistice was signed, was expressing to his wife his anxieties and hopes for the future. The prospect of a reduced Regular Army was certainly a worry as was his concern for his wife if he were sent to India. At the same time he was "almost off my head with joy at the thought of having you now for the rest of my life, and no more war worries". Macleod expanded on this in a way which we might not expect from a professional soldier keen to remain in the Army and concerned about its likely contraction. "Time and again men have been killed within a yard or two of me, sometimes almost touching me and all the time I have come through without a scratch, except at Le Cateau. I have indeed a lot to be thankful for".[21]

It has to be said that D.B. Watson, a Middlesex Regiment Officer in Cairo, was considerably less reflective in his diary for 11 November. "Very busy all day. Played tennis in the afternoon with Pryce. Germany signed the Armistice. Everyone took it very quietly. A good dinner, rained very heavily during the night".[22]

Just as 'matter of fact' were the observations in the diary of Corporal Mather of the 8th Oxford and Buckinghamshire Light Infantry on the Macedonian Front where armistice conditions seem in his view to suggest that "we are the beaten party as anything the Bulgars want doing has to be done, whilst we have more or less to go on bended knee for whatever we want, a state of affairs which arouses much righteous indignation on our part". On 6 November, accumulating rumours reached such a pitch that "we all feel justified in dreaming of peace universal very soon. Life here continues more or less monotonous. Was lucky enough to get hold of some more eggs" and on 7 November, encouraged by still more rumour though it lacked confirmation, "in celebration I have a rattling good breakfast". His diary marks 10 November as *Der Tag* but again neither on this day nor the next is there any more momentous observation than "I suppose we shall have to hang on until Germans are out of Rumania for which they have 36 days".[23]

In East Africa there were special circumstances which influenced reaction to the ceasefire. First, the German force, led by Major-General von Lettow-Vorbeck, did not present itself for surrender until 25 November. Second, tropical diseases and the impact of influenza seriously coloured the diaries of hospitalized men like Second Lieutenant E.W. Hancock, a 'debility case' in hospital at Dar es Salaam, who wrote on 11 November: "Armistice declared with Germany. I don't propose to effervesce over this. Everybody knows what everybody else feels and thinks about it. My pulse is very variable just now; between 64 and 104!"[24]

Another factor which may have curbed the expression of unbounded pleasure at the ending of hostilities in East Africa was potentially the remoteness of the location from which letters or diaries were being written and the writer's awareness that even if demobilization authorization were to come with relative swiftness, logistical arrangements to give effect to it were not likely to be of a similar order. A Medical Officer, Quintus Madge at Lindi,

THE BALKAN NEWS

Price One Penny | *Salonica, Tuesday, November 12th, 1918* | *No. 10 Fourth Year*

Armistice With Germany Signed

2nd. day of the general armistice.

To-Morrow's Sun and Moon
Sun rises 0715 Sets 1710
Moon rises 1352 Sets 0116
Full Moon, Nov. 17.

THE GREAT VICTORY

There is Peace. Not yet a certain, settled Peace, but a cessation of arms. But let no one think to-day only that there is Peace. There is more than that. Peace might be a black thing bringing regret, despair, anger as it must be for the Germans. No, it is not on the silence of our guns that we should lay stress but on their victory. It is not only for the end of the fighting that we should have glad hearts but for the glory of having won in that fighting. We had a terrible enemy and we have laid him low. He has come in to our terms, and our terms have certainly in them just severity and punishment. By them he is certainly made impotent for all harm for the immediate future. His sting is drawn. And for the remoter future, when again the world is settled in an been much nearer to military defeat than he ever was until, nation by nation, he was actually defeated. Time after time he has had startling partial successes which gave him hope and which seemed for a moment to retrieve his first failure. We have had an uphill fight all the four and a half years until the enemy's sudden catastrophic rush downhill and collapse. It has not been a happy time as we all know for our peoples. Yet our peoples have stuck it. They have not broken as the enemy peoples have done. They have shown more character, more firmness, more grit because, to start with, they were more civilised. And because also they were sure all along that they had right and justice on their side

This victory, then, the Allies have won by fighting better than the enemy on land and sea and in the air, and by the greater endurance and finer character of their peoples But it has been won also by two personal things that must never be forgotten. It has been won by the military genius of Marshal Foch And it has been won also by those hundreds of thousands of our gallant brothers-in-arms who, in winning it, have died and to whose souls God will without doubt give Peace.

The Victory of the Allies

Cessation of Hostilities with Germany

Paris, Sunday.— *(Official)*. **THE GERMAN COURIER ARRIVED THIS MORNING AT 10 A.M. AT GERMAN GRAND HEADQUARTERS.**

Paris, Monday.— *(Official)*. **AN ARMISTICE WITH GERMANY WAS SIGNED AT 5 A.M. THIS MORNING, AND HOSTILITIES ARE TO CEASE AT 11 A.M. (FRENCH TIME) TO-DAY NOV. 11.**

Signed MARSHAL FOCH
Commander-in-Chief.

At 1 p.m. yesterday by Salonica time hostilities with Germany ceased. The units of the Allied Fleets in the harbour dressed ship. At 7 p.m., 12 hours after the signing of the armistice, the Allied naval units fired a salute of 21 rockets.

London, Monday—A Copenhagen telegram despatched at 9.45a.m.Nov. 10 (Sunday) stated that it was officially reported from Berlin that the German courier bearing the armistice terms from Marshal Foch to German Grand Headquarters had not yet arrived. It was assumed that some acci-

viii British soldiers and nurses at Salonika learn news of the Armistice on 12 November. In fact, the previous day's edition of the Balkan News had carried information only of the Kaiser's abdication (Liddle Collection) recorded that his Mess was "now full of discussion as to how long the next stage of the proceedings will last" as they had been anticipating a five-day train journey to a port from which a troopship would take them to take part in the same campaign from a different location. Nevertheless, a celebration did take place at Lindi with rockets, lights and African dances.[25]

From another relatively remote location, Entebbe, Lieutenant Stansfield of the King's African Rifles recorded a reaction which serves as a reminder to us today that the pride felt in Empire surfaced quite naturally at such a moment in history. He found it "a little thrilling to think how one great wave of British joy swept round the world and found its way to every nook and cranny". He added, "No one was more delighted than our Askaris who cheered themselves hoarse and then held ngomas [tribal dances] galore".[26]

Still further away, in India, Private H.H. Hill in the Machine Gun Corps, was serving at Deolali. He was later to record that he "wept with joy" on the great day. He also wrote that celebrations continued for a fortnight, culminating in "thousands of spectators, English and Indian, gathered round a great arena to watch humorous races and other events. At dusk there was a colourful pageant called Britannia and her Allies and our band provided the appropriate patriotic music for it. When the pageant's final tableau was in position a rocket gave the signal to 5,000 Indian soldiers waiting on a nearby hill. They lit their torches and marched towards the arena cheering tumultuously all the way. Simultaneously the hilltops burst into fire with scores of bonfires and shower after shower of coloured stars fell from the sky as rocket after rocket soared through the air. It was an impressive occasion".[27]

It was a moment of unanimity too [though here viewed through English eyes], unanimity which would rapidly be forgotten in the following year as the fierce political storm over Amritsar exercised its dramatic and lasting influence.

In Mesopotamia, Captain E.C. Rycroft of the Army Dental Corps, precisely records in his diary the sense of expectation of the German Armistice which conditioned the general reaction. There had been so much uproarious behaviour on 2 November, "the air electric with hope and expectancy" released with the G.O.C.'s proclamation of the conclusion of hostilities with Turkey, that, by 9 November, "there is a certain amount of reactive depression today, quite apart from the fact that no official news of Germany's fall has arrived! In any case it was good practice for when it does arrive". On 11 November, although there had been a severe thunderstorm and flooding, a river boat party was arranged but "despite singsong, hooting the syren, [sic] lighting signals of distress etc. things seemed to be too ordinary".[28]

In Salonika the jubilation was predictably more international. C.E. Shipton, a Seaforths officer, was having lunch at the *Cercle Militaire* when naval guns and ships' syrens in the bay announced the end of the war. "Several times during the meal officers of various nationalities got up and proposed the health of the Allies whereupon the whole room rose and cheered wildly". Poor Shipton had to retire to bed with another attack of malaria but the doctors at one military hospital gave their nurses a dance and champagne supper and General Service V.A.D. nurses in the officer hospitals "broke loose and held an informal concert on the roads of the camp and the tin whistles and drums were going like mad for a time and in addition every ship in the harbour was letting off rockets".[29] One feels admiration for Shipton that he made no reference to the effect all this noise must have had on his malarial headache.

Self-induced headaches from "a variety of disorders perpetrated" in an officers' mess in Zeitoun on 11 November, may have dulled thinking for the morrow, but, Captain Wingham wrote of his awareness of immediate and long-term problems.

> Work is to go on as usual, but you can realize that the situation in a School of Instruction becomes a little difficult now. How can one expect the civilian soldier to maintain any interest in military studies now that the whole purpose of his life is changing? However, it is obviously of the utmost importance that some sort of work is pursued and I hope all soldiers will realize this. We can't afford to go to rot at this stage when cool thinking is so much in demand to solve the mighty problems that are arising.[30]

He might have mentioned demobilization, as one of those problems, though, by date, this particular problem falls outside the remit of this book. Brief mention should perhaps be made of related troubles ahead in Calais, and in the British Channel ports, in North Wales, in North Russia and something less than enchantment, even if falling short of serious unrest, in many overseas areas where British troops fretted for release. One man may here be allowed to speak representatively of the evidence from North Russia on 17 January 1919; "Much trouble with the men's letters. They are becoming horribly fed up with life, hearing that so many soldiers with little service are being discharged in England and having no idea that we are to get back. R.C. Padre has spread the news that we are to be here another year. Heaven forbid".[31]

In contrast with the soldiers, the officers and ratings of the Royal Navy had no captured guns, cowed prisoners or a Trafalgar to their credit, proof of their part in the achievement of victory. A different sort of triumph would be theirs but they would have to wait ten days for it and then it would be so unimaginable, so tense an experience, that for many it was filled with awe rather than one which excited exuberance – this was the approach to British waters of the High Seas Fleet for internment, initially in the Firth of Forth, on 21 November.

Able Seaman J.L. Jenkins of the Dreadnought battleship, *H.M.S. Sovereign*, then at Rosyth, nicely summarized the Naval reaction in his diary account on 11 November. "No news of signing armistice. Comes however at 09.45. Received with reserve and suspicion. Is the signature sufficiently weighty and authoritative?"[32] Paymaster Lieutenant C.H. Longden Griffiths, [*H.M.S. Forward* in the Eastern Mediterranean], on learning in advance of the great news, expressed his disgust: the British fleet was "deprived of the opportunity for which it has been waiting for over 4 years – to thrash the German High Seas Fleet".[33]

At Ardrossan, a west coast of Scotland naval base, J.E. Nicol told his mother that he had felt "overwhelming sadness mingled with a great sense of thankfulness on hearing the news". His sadness was over the loss of two brothers. He consoled his mother with the thought that "their sacrifice has not been in vain".[34]

The Commander in Chief's signal to 'splice the main brace' was recorded in diaries or letters wherever ships were serving but a congratulatory message from the Admiralty included a warning about "German submarines, possibly still at sea, and ignorant of the Armistice". The Lords of the Admiralty concluded that with the work of escorting surrendering ships in for internment and the continuing task of sweeping for mines it was plain that no officers or men could be spared from their duties until the safety of their country at sea was assured.[35] Predictably there would be disquiet over this douche of cold water over any expectation of swift demobilization for the 'hostilities only' enlisted men.

For anyone with a sense of tradition it is pleasing to read in Surgeon Probationer Christopher Andrews' diary [*H.M.S. Marigold* at Rosyth] that amidst the noise of the sirens and rockets and the flashing searchlights playing on a figure of the Kaiser strung from yard-arm "Many matlows dancing hornpipes on focsle-heads".[36]

There were more warlike circumstances at Baku with the revolutionary imbroglio there. The British Caspian Naval Force, with its confiscated merchant vessels flying the Russian ensign to identify with the White Russian cause and now armed for war, was in action on 11 November. An officer, A.B. Lee, recalled:

> we were bombarding a troop train hemmed in a tunnel to the South of Baku and it was terribly cold. In fact in the heavy weather the ice was forming as soon as the water came over, [on deck] thick ice forming on even a single rail and on our guns. We even had to keep putting hot water on the guns. We [were firing] there all day long and then there was a disturbance because the wireless operator broke out the news about the Armistice.[37]

Lee remembered that the news had led to a disagreement on board but unfortunately did not expand upon this.

The diary of a wireless operator, B.C. Bishop, aboard the merchant ship *Laomedon*, reminds us of another danger, distinct from mines or U Boats: the sea itself could dictate its own emergencies even on Armistice Day. On 10 November in convoy Eastbound across the Atlantic, such were the "huge rollers ahead all day" that *Laomedon* "had to heave to". On 11 November, *Laomedon* was "chasing convoy all day and catch it up in evening. 4 ships still missing". Then Bishop records: "Get NEWS OF PEACE in evening". There was great excitement the next day, the weather improved and only one vessel, the Scotian was still missing".[38]

In the Grand Fleet, officers and ratings recorded their puzzlement at the absence of a *final throw* by the High Seas Fleet. Lieutenant Frank Bowman [*H.M.S. Colossus*] considered it "astounding that a great fleet like theirs which could choose the time and circumstances of an action to some extent should never have come out. One surmises that their method of discipline has not been able to 'wait', that their morale has been wasted in barracks by too strict discipline on the lower deck and self-indulgence on the part of the officers."[39]

When 21 November arrived and with it the High Seas Fleet for closer inspection, Frank Bowman's assessment based on the widespread knowledge of the disaffection in the German Navy was confirmed by Wallace King Brown, Surgeon Probationer *H.M.S. Grenville*. In this instance the observations are representative of the evidence of almost all witnesses though King Brown states that from Grenville they had the "best view of anyone in the Fleet as we steamed right along their line". He counted five battlecruisers and nine battleships, seven light-cruisers and forty-nine destroyers,

> the most impressive sight I have ever seen and somehow it made one's opinion of the fighting efficiency of the German fall to practically nothing to see the way their fleet steamed in without any blow being struck at all. I think there is no doubt that the Hun is absolutely demoralised, and from what I saw as I was on board several destroyers [as it was said they had some wounded on board] there seemed to be no discipline left and in some cases it would appear that the officers had very little say in the matter, the men seeming to be in charge in everything but name.[40]

British prisoners of war in Germany were also close observers of the breakdown of military authority in the country. Though differentiation between the captivity conditions of one man and another cannot be attempted here, we should be aware of it because it might well have an influence upon a man's feelings at his release. There were men who had been used virtually as forced labourers in no regular camp as the Germans retreated. In particular, this could relate to those captured in the German attacks from late Spring 1918. Many of these men were under-nourished, weary and in poor condition. There were also long-established camps for men in the ranks, some well-run and some the reverse, and then there were the officer camps usually adequate and some seemingly quite comfortable. There were British prisoners in Bulgaria, in Austria and of course in Turkey. We need also to be mindful of the Britons interned in Holland for a variety of reasons, the exchanged long-term or wounded P.O.W.'s here and in Switzerland and the British civilians interned since November 1914 at Ruhleben camp on the outskirts of Berlin at Spandau. It was in this camp, Ruhleben, where unpromising conditions initially had been transformed into a British community which throve in recreation, educational and cultural activity and to some extent as a self-governing entity. No general picture is intended of this camp with about five-thousand inmates if one were still to say that amidst all the rejoicing at the prospect of freedom there will still have been groups of men and individuals faced with an emotional dilemma on 11 November; musical and drama groups rehearsing for some performance, sporting teams leading in some competition or league, students working for externally moderated examinations, craftsmen producing some artefact or work of art.

Of soldier P.O.W.'s, the listlessness of the really weary is caught in the diary of a private in the 6th Battalion Manchesters, O.G. Billingham. He is at work behind the German lines, often on the move and largely reliant on French civilians for food. He records being "wet through and whacked", "not feeling well, headache and rotten cold". He learns on 10 November of the Armistice and his diary on that day could scarcely be less dramatic. "Not feeling well. Carried on as yesterday. Signed for pay. Rumours of moving tomorrow".[41]

In an established camp, unlike Billingham, was Lance Corporal Pat Salisbury, 1/1 Cambridgeshire Regiment, and he was in far better shape, writing on 10 November to his mother that he was "in the best health. By the way events are shaping I should not be surprised if I am home before you receive this".[42]

P.H.B. Lyon, a 6th Battalion D.L.I. officer in Graudenz, described events as he experienced them there, news changing every hour as he recorded it.

> Rumour is of course rife, not only in the camp, but in the town outside as well – so that we cannot even rely on news brought in by our guards. This crisis outside is not unaccompanied by inside disturbances, though of course we hear less of this than we might. But we hear enough to increase our restlessness and uncertainty tenfold. Our considerations are perhaps naturally rather selfish, and riots and such-like do not favour a speedy home-coming.

Between 8 and 10 November for which the above was written, he sang solos at a concert and attended the funerals of two officers who had died from influenza. The children who besought the British officer for biscuits day and night were increasingly clamorous and Lyon heard that a socialist meeting was being held in the town on the evening of 9 November. Then, later on 10 November:

> one of the interpreters has brought in strange news. The soldiers in the town are wearing red cockades and a republic seems well on the way. The Kaiser appears to have abdicated and Ebert the Social Democrat is the new Chancellor – hardly any trains are running and a soldiers and workmens committee has been formed. Aeroplanes have been flying over with red flags flying – Prisoners have been released in the town. What will happen to us? We seem backwatered in a curious way while all these things are happening. But we may yet have to take active part.

On the following day his forebodings multiply until, assured of immediate repatriation, they are dispelled like mist by the morning sun. "The feeling here is absolutely indescribable. It is like a dream come true". It is clear that the arrival of their parcels earlier feared looted, played a part in this release of anxiety and the confirmation of new privileges. Lyon's final entry for this Armistice Day in Graudenz is "This morning the Commandant walked into the camp in 'civvies' and raised a trilby hat to the sentry – Oh Gilbert, oh Sullivan".[43]

As the war was ending and revolution in Germany flourishing, British civilian internees at Ruhleben were asked by the guards there for a Red Flag to demonstrate their new identity. In exchange for the Imperial Standard, they were given a tablecloth dyed red by those who had learned that skill in the camp school. It seems the guards still needed the help of the interned because two Merchant Marine officers duly raised the proletarian emblem.[44]

In many camps, P.O.W.'s and internees were addressed by a representative of the new Germany asking them not to have bad feelings over the time they had languished away from their loved ones because "if the peoples at last realize that it is not each other who are their enemies but the ruthless forces of Imperialism and Capitalism, of Militarism of all sorts, of Jingo Journalism that sows falsehoods, hatred and suspicion, then this war will not have been fought in vain".[45] There is an ironic Armistice Day recollection from Ruhleben internee, J.S. Messent, that celebrating the revolution in Germany had created an atmosphere in Berlin which appeared as full of rejoicing and holiday atmosphere as was no doubt the case in Britain but for rather different reasons.[46]

Among British uniformed non-combatants abroad there were many women serving as nurses, doctors, clerks, cooks or drivers who also witnessed the coming of the Armistice. From France, Dr Elizabeth Courtauld [Principal Anaesthetist at the Scottish Women's Hospital at Royaumont near Paris] wrote of being driven by ambulance from her hospital into Paris to see the capital city's delirious crowds, but at the hospital itself she makes clear that the celebration was no less joyful. The bell on the roof was rung continuously by patients and a great assembly in 'Canada Ward' of hundreds of patients and staff gathered for speeches, anthems and toasts before they paraded into the park and burned an effigy of the Kaiser. "It was a lurid scene. At last the Kaiser fell backwards and a perfect howl of hate rose from the patients. Some jumped as soon as the fire was low on to the burning remains of [the] Kaiser and trampled him with curses and execrations". The hospital was for French wounded and this mature English doctor from a Huguenot family added in her letter, "I fancy the French are a more revengeful race than the English. In fact we have often been laughed at for feeling so little personal spite, but then the English have not had the cause the French have".[47]

The Kaiser's image came in for more restrained punishment in Sofia, Bulgaria, where V.A.D. cook, Miss C.M. Fisher, could scarcely credit that they were in "an enemy country celebrating peace, even dining in a room with large portraits of the Kaiser and King Ferdinand on the wall – but we turned them upside down! A bottle of champagne was produced and we drank to a lasting peace and then a silent toast to those 'who had made it possible'".[48]

An ambulance convoy of twenty-two walking wounded was received on 11 November at No. 3 Stationary Hospital, Rouen, where Elizabeth Oswald was a V.A.D. nurse. Her diary records the orderlies going 'mad' but the nurses taking it "rather more quietly but equally happy". She got permission to take the afternoon off and, before going off to have a "hilarious time" opened a letter informing her of the death from wounds of a close friend. "I went out in sheer desperation – the same feeling that makes the men go out and get drunk sometimes…".[49]

In the Women's Auxiliary Army Corps, clerk Nora Steer had no such sad discordance to influence her reaction. For her, 11 November was a day of "Great excitement. No work at the office. Had dickens of a time. Band played round the depot. Capt Mackie carried shoulder high. Left office at 4.30 pm had bon tea. After tea got poshed up for the dance. Joe and Jack came up and all had gay time finishing at 10 pm. Some day!"[50]

Similarly uncomplicated rejoicing is recorded by a lady, Mrs J.B. Brown, working for the Scottish Churches Huts. "When the great news came through the whole camp paraded and received it from the C.O …. we gave out free teas all afternoon and had a concert also arranged by the authorities". On the following day there were sports and a dance but, not surprisingly, thoughts turned to home. "Just longing to hear what people are thinking of the great news in Glasgow".[51]

Just as these two women in their carefree rejoicing do not necessarily express the totality of reaction in France, we may gauge that Mrs Brown's anticipation of Home Front reaction was limited in its perspective. However, there remains a significant point to be made about those serving overseas and the way in which later they came to look upon their active service now being concluded.

A phrase in Sir Douglas Haig's Special Order of the Day, issued on 12 November, may be chosen to point out the irony of Armistice Day 1918 being both the threshold of ex-soldier disillusionment as well as a portal through which to proceed to a world at peace. The Field Marshal assured his Expeditionary Force of almost two million men, that "Generations of free peoples, both of your own race and of all countries, will thank you for what you have done".[52] Did the words register at the time with those to whom they were addressed? Probably not, except for those few with a conscious sense of the continuity of history. However, as the men came home, mentally wearing their war ribbons of endeavour for King, Country, community, family and self-respect, they expected the appreciation of society and of their Government. They looked for what they felt was their due, some practical improvement in their lives contrasting favourably with their pre-war circumstance and, wider, some change beyond the punishment of the foe, a moving away from the bellicose stance of great powers in arms like pit bulls snarling to be unleashed.

The writer of this chapter recently received from the daughter of a First World War veteran her father's personal papers. She concluded her letter with a vignette: "The only time I saw my father in tears was during the radio announcement at the start of the 1939–45 war". Among those who had held apprehensions on Armistice Day 1918 were some who feared that while the Armistice terms might seem deserving of a herald's trumpet blast, a roll of drums and then the proclamation of a lasting peace, it could be but a pause of unknown duration before the resumption of unfinished business.

Endnotes

All references marked L.C. are from the Liddle Collection, Brotherton Library, University of Leeds, U.K.

1 Major S.C. Marriott, 11th Battalion Manchester Regiment, letter 11.11.18, L.C.
2 Air Vice Marshal T.C. Traill, [1918 Acting Captain No. 20 Squadron R.A.F.], recollections, L.C.
3 Message received by 102nd Battalion M.G.C., L.C.
4 Lieutenant B.H. Puckle, 9th Battalion Royal Welsh Fusiliers, letter 12.11.18, L.C.
5 Bombardier G.M.M. Mortimer, R.G.A., letter 17.11.18, L.C.
6 Captain E.G. Bates, 9th Battalion Northumberland Fusiliers, letter 12.11.18, L.C.
7 J.L. Hampson [Sergeant Intelligence Police, Second Army], recollections, L.C.
8 A.M. Boyd [Pte 2nd / 1st London Field Ambulance, R.A.M.C.], recollections, L.C.
9 See endnote 4.
10 Sergeant A.J. Butler, Lowland Division, Signal Company, R.E., letter 8.30 pm 11.11.18, L.C.
11 Private Frank Ridsdale, 89th Field Ambulance, R.A.M.C., diary 11.11.18, L.C.
12 Captain Oliver W. Sichel, 2nd / 5th Battalion Royal Warwickshire Regiment, letter 16.10.18, L.C.
13 Temporary Captain F.S.G. Barnett, R.F.A., letter 13.10.18, L.C.
14 Private H.S. Innes, 14th Battalion Royal Fusiliers, letter 11.11.18, L.C.
15 Corporal C.J. Woosnam, R.A.M.C., diary 7.11.18, L.C.
16 Captain C.E. Townley, 11th Battalion Suffolk Regiment, attached R.A.F., diary 9–10.11.18. L.C.
17 The Reverend P. Gardner Smith, Chaplain, No. 149 Squadron R.A.F., diary 9.11.18, L.C.
18 *ibid*, 10.11.18.
19 Captain Ronald Ivelaw Chapman, No. 10 Squadron R.A.F., log 11.11.18 and [Air Chief Marshal Sir Ronald Ivelaw Chapman] recollections, L.C.
20 Lance Corporal H.G. Morris, 5th Battalion Wiltshire Regiment, diary 11.11.18, L.C.
21 Major R. Macleod, R.F.A., letter 8.11.18, L.C.
22 Captain D.B. Watson 2nd / 10th Battalion Middlesex Regiment, diary 11'12.11.18, L.C.
23 Corporal W.D. Mather, 8th Battalion Oxford and Buckinghamshire Light Infantry, diary, L.C.
24 Second Lieutenant E.W. Hancock, Gordon Highlanders, diary 11.11.18, L.C.
25 Captain Q. Madge R.A.M.C., letter 11.11.18, L.C.
26 Lieutenant F.O. Stansfield, King's African Rifles, letter 16.11.18, L.C.
27 H.H. Hill [Private M.G.C.], memoir, L.C.
28 Captain E.C. Rycroft, Army Dental Corps, diary 2–11.11.18, L.C.
29 Lieutenant C.E.C. Shipton, 1st Garrison Battalion Seaforth Highlanders, diary 11.11.18, L.C.
30 Captain E.G.R. Wingham, M.G.C., letter 12.11.18, L.C.
31 Lieutenant T. Lethem, M.G.C., diary 17.1.19, L.C.
32 Able Seaman J.L. Jenkins, R.N., *H.M.S. Royal Sovereign*, diary 11.11.18, L.C.
33 Paymaster Lieutenant C.H. Longden Griffiths, R.N.R., *H.M.S. Forward*, diary 10.11.18, L.C.
34 Lieutenant J.E. Nicol, R.N.R., letter 17.11.18, L.C.
35 From the papers of J.G.D. Ouvry, Lieutenant R.N., *H.M.S. Constant*, L.C.
36 Surgeon Probationer C.H. Andrews, *H.M.S. Marigold*, diary 11.11.18, L.C.

37 Captain A.B. Lee [Lieutenant A.B. Lee R.N.R.], tape-recorded recollections, L.C.
38 B.C. Bishop, Merchant Marine, Wireless Operator, *H.M.S. Laomedon*, diary 11.11.18, L.C.
39 Lieutenant Frank Bowman, R.N., *H.M.S. Colossus*, diary 13.11.18, L.C.
40 Surgeon Probationer Wallace King Brown, *H.M.S. Grenville*, letter 25.11.18, L.C.
41 Private O.G. Billingham, 6th Battalion Manchester Regiment, diary 10.11.18, L.C.
42 Lance Corporal Pat Salisbury, 1st/1st Battalion Cambridgeshire Regiment, letter 10.11.18, L.C.
43 Captain P.H.B. Lyon, 6th Battalion Durham Light Infantry, diary 10/11.11.18, L.C.
44 Harold Redmayne, [Ruhleben internee], manuscript recollections, L.C.
45 'A Parting Word' leaflet issued at Giessen P.O.W. camp. From the papers of Quarter Master Sergeant J. Carney, 2nd/2nd Battalion Northumbrian Field Ambulance, R.A.M.C., L.C.
46 J.S. Messent [Ruhleben internee], typescript recollections, L.C.
47 Elizabeth Courtauld, Principal Anaesthetist, Scottish Women's Hospital, Royaumont, letter 14.11.18, L.C.
48 Miss C.M. Fisher [V.A.D. cook in hospitals on the Macedonian Front, but on 11 November 1918 visiting a hospital established by the Germans in a school in Sofia], typescript recollections, L.C.
49 Miss E.A. Oswald, V.A.D. Nurse, No. 3 Stationary Hospital, Rouen, diary 11.11.18, L.C.
50 Nora Steer, Worker WAAC, 1st A.M.T.D., diary 11.11.18, L.C.
51 Mrs J.B. Brown, Scottish Churches Huts, Cayeux, letter 13.11.18, L.C.
52 Special Order of the Day by Field Marshal Sir Douglas Haig, 12.11.18, L.C.

Chapter Five

Britons on the Home Front

Peter Liddle

The news of the Armistice was greeted in almost every city, town, village or hamlet of the United Kingdom with people leaving their homes to come together to express their joy. For London, the scenes were memorably captured by ciné film, but in all the large centres of population, huge crowds gathered uninhibitedly celebrating the end of the protracted tribulations of war. Such scenes must dominate any picture recreated today of how, in general, people on the Home Front reacted but we should not lose sight of what lay beneath the acclaim of a victorious end to the war, the sense of relief and of quiet thankfulness. We should remember too that reduced energies were but momentarily regenerated within weary folk now cheering, singing, lighting bonfires, hurrying to city vantage points for announcements, speeches or impromptu parades. We should be aware too of those left grieving and others preoccupied, even at such a time, by political and social problems unresolved from the past, but temporarily submerged by the demands of war or other newly emergent problems which some saw like distant storm clouds approaching with threatening speed.

Dissolution of parliament and a General Election were common currency for speculation well before 11 November and now their imminence and concern about whether the terms of the Armistice could be transmuted into conditions for a lasting peace settlement, were the most obvious foci for such anxieties. There were others, discussed in war hospitals, public houses, on the streets and in living rooms as well as in formal places for debate; employment in an economy now to be geared for peacetime needs, the current influenza scourge, pensions, housing, political power for representatives of the working classes and, soon to remind anyone who might have thought that it could be dealt with in an ordered, considered way, the problem of Ireland.

It may be thought that a concentration upon reactions discordant with the national rejoicing is inappropriate as a starting point but retrospectively there is a spice to observations which exposed the base metal of the national self-applause at winning a conclusive victory which seemed to sweep aside all problems of the shaping of a brighter British future in the new world without war. What irony is held in Miss E.M. Selby's little volume which periodically she used as a diary. She actually stops writing at the end of the war with sentences including the thought that the joy was almost too much to bear, "one could hardly keep from crying – and when one thought of all the boys who will never come home . . .". Then, on the very same page, is written "June 7 1940 Another war. Same enemy".[1]

A Quaker, Kate Courtney, who put up her own small banner of a dove, offered a large one to Chelsea Town Hall. "Doubt if they will take it. I hope the temper, which has been odious, will now change and become more generous and just" but she was "amazed at the light-hearted way our junker class have driven Germany into revolution by harsh terms – they may rue it". It was not long before her second point was strongly advocated by some but more immediately she was soon proved right with her first. Her banner, with its olive branch in too, was brusquely rejected.[2]

As for the lack of restraint on the day, an Army Officer on Salisbury Plain, Second Lieutenant E. Ansell, thought that the men in uniform there misjudged what was called for on such a day.

> There is a lot of stupid horseplay going on tonight: Verey lights are being fired and crackers and bombs going off; also there is much looting going on. I have little sympathy with this kind of thing . . . Some of the mobs are quite mad and have utterly lost their heads. Collectively they do things which, individually, they would not dream of doing. No, no, this is not the time for thoughtless revelry. Too many of the best have given their lives for this hour and it should be one of thanksgiving rather than tomfoolery.[3]

Gladys Hutchinson kept up her diary intermittently and for Armistice Day and the days following she was late by a month but she catches something of the awe felt by some and then the swift strike of sickness. "It is hard to describe the weight removed, the sense of God's greatness . . . influenza broke out in the village [Catterick] about a week after, almost every house. Thousands have died in the country from it. Sometimes four or five in one house".[4] The influenza pandemic was indeed to have something of the immediate, local impact which we might associate with that of a medieval plague.

An extreme case of rejection of the idea of anything having been won by the war, was poor Phyllis Iliff. Bereft on Armistice Day, as she had been since the death of her fiancé in action at the end of June that year, Phyllis Iliff left a record of searing bitterness.

> So it has come – the day when this war which has wrecked my life and altered my whole character [has ended] and what does it mean to us, us, who have lost our all in this fight, a fight which is not won. It is wickedly unfair to our dead, you dear boy are the only one I think of, of course, but very soon will England have to answer for this base piece of treachery in which millions of brave lads like yourself went "West" only to have been sold as the English Government would sell anybody or any thing. But

England's day is over, the Throne shakes, Ireland openly hates England and will soon be out of their power, Scotland silently hates the English and is working swiftly but steadily for the time when they will be free also. France, Italy and all other "allied" countries turn away from England to – America, the country which will in a few years head the world. How America despises England which pretends to be so clever, while with her bad ruling, petty strikes and pigheadedness is losing trade and every other thing which makes a country famous.

And here – on the night when all are laughing and enjoying themselves, left alone I sit and think of what it would have been had you not been taken away and my heart were not slowly breaking. This night when "everyone is happy" as people say. Dear Lord! have mercy it is not in human nature to stand so much.[5]

Phyllis Iliff's inconsolable sense of loss places her in a great host of women, and of men too, coping in varying degrees with their bereavement. In the sense that this marked them as distinctly separated from the throngs of carefree Armistice celebrants, there is a parallel with a much smaller group.

In civil prisons throughout the United Kingdom, apart from Ireland to which the provisions of the Military Service Acts had not been extended, young men were incarcerated for their refusal, on the grounds of conscientious objection, to fulfil their statutory military service obligations. They were known as 'absolutists' who had also refused the opportunity of alternative service under the Home Office Scheme. These 'C.O's', numbering perhaps a thousand, awaited with uncertainty a different sort of demobilization. When would they be freed and, despite the strength of their convictions, how would they be received outside of the protection of loving families and like-minded people? They could of course celebrate the ending of war but from a standpoint which disqualified them from kinship with the crowds gathering at the focal points of the cities in which their forbidding prisons were situate.

In Wandsworth Prison, four days after the Armistice, Quaker Malcolm Sparkes assured his wife that circumstances had not made him restless or unhappy. "I feel pretty sure that none of my letters complain of hardship – or of injustice – they only express an intense desire to render the service I feel called to render. It is a great pity that so much of the agitation for release of C.O.'s is based upon tales of hardship and so forth. Not a man of us desires pity and this sort of agitation does not come from C.O.'s ourselves but from people who are trying (quite genuinely no doubt) to befriend us". Sparkes asked his wife: "Has thou joined the Labour Party?" as he thought they ought to, and, "if we get a really just and democratic Peace, with something of Pres. Wilson's idealism in it, then we shall be able to rejoice in the overthrow of capitalism, but it will not be force that has done it but constructive goodwill".[6]

Sparkes's letter is appropriate as a corrective to the impression which one might reasonably have of all C.O.'s being frustrated, unhappy and desperate for release. In his case inner contentment was the fruit of his faith and it was paralleled in many C.O.'s. Eric Southall for example, in Walton Gaol,

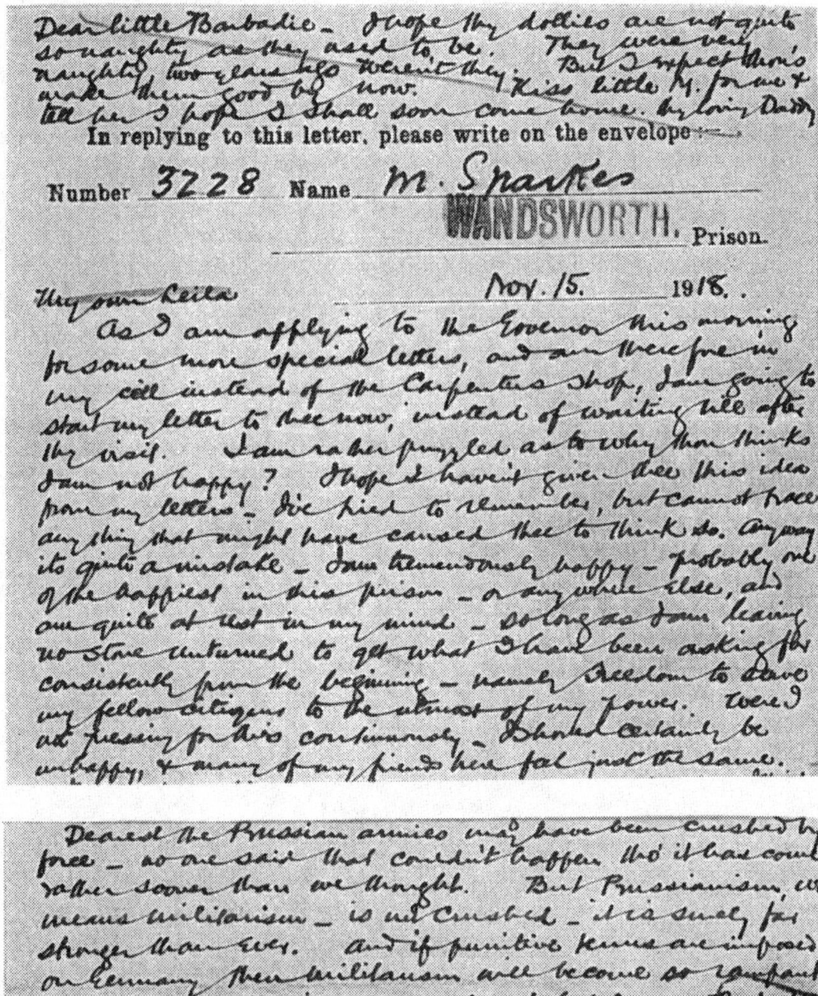

Dear little Barbadie – I hope thy dollies are not quite so naughty as they used to be. They were very naughty two years ago weren't they. But I expect thou's made them good by now. Kiss little M. for me & tell her I hope I shall soon come home. My loving Daddy

In replying to this letter, please write on the envelope :—

Number 3228 Name M. Sparkes

WANDSWORTH. Prison.

~~My own Leila~~ Nov. 15. 1918.

As I am applying to the Governor this morning for some more special letters, and am therefore in my cell instead of the Carpenters shop, I am going to start my letter to thee now, instead of waiting till after thy visit. I am rather puzzled as to why thou thinks I am not happy? I hope I haven't given thee this idea from my letters – I've tried to remember, but cannot trace anything that might have caused thee to think so. Anyway its quite a mistake – I am tremendously happy – probably one of the happiest in this prison – or anywhere else, and am quite at rest in my mind – so long as I am leaving no stone unturned to get what I have been asking for consistently from the beginning – namely freedom to serve my fellow citizens to the utmost of my power. Were I not pressing for this continuously – I should certainly be unhappy, & many of my friends here feel just the same.

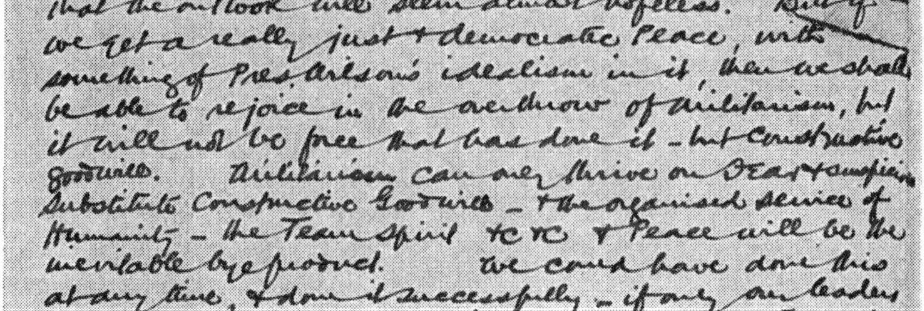

Dearest the Prussian armies may have been crushed by force – no one said that couldn't happen tho' it has come rather sooner than we thought. But Prussianism, which means militarism – is not crushed – it is surely far stronger than ever. And if punitive terms are imposed on Germany then militarism will become so rampant that the outlook will seem almost hopeless. But if we get a really just & democratic Peace, with something of Pres. Wilson's idealism in it, then we shall be able to rejoice in the overthrow of militarism, but it will not be force that has done it – but constructive goodwill. Militarism can only thrive on fear & suspicion. Substitute constructive Goodwill – & the organised service of Humanity – the Team spirit &c &c & Peace will be the inevitable bye product. We could have done this at any time, & done it successfully – if only our leaders had had the courage & the vision. Yes – the question

ix "... militarism ... is not crushed ... it is surely far stronger than ever". Conscientious Objector, Malcolm Sparkes, writes to his wife on prison notepaper, 15 November 1918. (M. Sparkes, Liddle Collection)

Liverpool, wrote that he was quite calm on the subject of his release. "I fix no dates – neither earliest nor latest – for my discharge; in no event do I mean to worry overmuch – not at all if I can help it – and as yet I am certainly serene and very well in health".[7] Whether from religious, moral or political objection, or a combination of all three, serenity or obduracy, stimulated by excitement at the dawn of new possibilities for mankind, characterise the response to the Armistice of most Conscientious Objectors. This is not to remove from them the personal ache of family separation on such a day, a poignancy illustrated from a child's point of view by Freda Peet.

> I was nearly four years old, living with my mother on a farm near Llangaddock, Carmarthen. We had left London to be near my father, a conscientious objector, working in a labour-camp, higher up the valley. [It had been raining heavily and we were soaked]. Midmorning the church-bells began to ring – and ring – and ring echoing all round the hills and valleys. We all ran out into the roadway and I can still remember the feel of the icy black mud squelching up between my bare toes. I had no idea what the bells meant but I knew from the shouting of the farm people, one to another, that something important was happening. When at last the bells stopped we trooped back into the farmhouse kitchen to find that our forgotten boots were not only bone-dry but had become so small we couldn't get them on. Armistice Day for me ended in tears as I vainly tried to force my feet into the shrunken leather, and I got my second scolding of the day. Bells ringing, icy mud and the pain of trying to put on my dried-up boots make up my memory of November 11th 1918.[8]

Quite apart from C.O.'s and the bereaved, there were others conscious of the turbulence of events and who seemed bewildered like Louisa Harris who recorded for the day: "a glorious peace it will be, alas though mixed with sorrow for so many". She thought "a new page in the history of the world" had been turned over but was clearly thunderstruck that now, the third of three great royal dynasties had been overthrown in "an incredibly short space of time".[9] Hilda Craven too, a V.A.D. nurse at the Crescent Hospital in Croydon among the massed crowds outside Buckingham Palace who cheered the King, the Queen, Princess Mary and the Duke of Connaught, the next day found it "hard to realize that after four years of terrible anxiety and slaughter the war is over at last and the fighting finished with. The heavy clouds which always hung over us on waking up are all rolled away ... "[10]

Another V.A.D., Winifred Kenyon, witness to the overflowing joy of the crowds in Oxford Street, the buses, taxis, lorries, private cars filled inside and festooned outside with cheering, waving figures, could not avoid having to swallow a lump in her throat at "the suffering which has brought this day".[11] Untroubled by her enjoyment of the unprecedented scenes in London was post-office van driver, Florence Schuster, who soon had people sitting on the top of her van. "We saw a procession of High Pots of the Army going away from the Palace in cars and one car full cheered my party and van. I was much elated".[12] Florence's diary of events in central London also describes the dancing in the streets.

Hoardings which had protected statues from bombing were torn down and burned and Guy's hospital staff seem to have indulged in an orgy of incineration. A young woman wrote to her mother of wheelbarrows and laundry trolleys and everything which was at hand being gathered and set alight. "It was the first real bonfire they have had since the war so we all made the most of it and one of them rang up the Fire Stations so we had about 7 fire engines round in about two minutes and then they rushed and closed the gates in their faces after stealing one of the firemen's helmets to put on old 'Guy's' [statue]".[13]

One girl wrote later in the month that on Armistice day afternoon, "it was positively unsafe to go up Whitehall and the Strand. The soldiers were embracing every girl they met and vice versa ... Luckily it rained in the evening which damped the crowds a bit". It may be added that this girl declared she "would not have missed being in town for anything...".[14]

Girls from Gipsy Hill Training College travelled up from Wimbledon by train to join the crowds in the city. One of the students, Molly Macleod, first mentioned in her letter how hard it was on families like "the Inneses who have no one left to welcome home. You can't help remembering them", but then described so well all that she had seen and done. "We actually managed to get into a shop and had an unrestricted pre-war tea at pre-war prices". On 12 November, they joined the throng trying to get into the Thanksgiving Service in St Paul's and "got a bird's eye view of the King and Queen ... a band of Royal Welsh Fusiliers in khaki played the music, I never heard anything so thrilling as the roll of drums just before the National Anthem". Molly's family home was in Cambridge where the "Cambridge Magazine" had published support for pacifism. How glad her two soldier brothers would have been, she recorded, to learn that this newspaper's shop windows had been broken.[15]

The excitement in Cambridge had included the burning of an effigy of the Kaiser and of a telephone booth in Market Place "while a large crowd of soldiers and civilians, undergraduates dressed as V.A.D.'s and WAACs dressed as undergraduates frolicked around".[16]

The Yorkshire Telegraph and Star newspaper, in a late edition on 11 November, reported from its Rotherham branch office that the great news had interrupted a court hearing of an application by a wife against her husband for a separation order. "Mr Fenoughty, who represented the man, made the observation that 'since peace seems to be in the air the complainant may be glad to sign an armistice'". The advice was not accepted but the paper went on to report that "at noon the alarm buzzers were blown and the other steam sirens joined to swell the noise". The reporter sought to explain the absence of church bells offering their carillon with the fact that the ringers were at various works. "Steps were taken to get them together for the early afternoon".[17]

In Batley, West Yorkshire, people had streamed out of the mills and a general holiday was declared. There was a huge bonfire but the father of

November 11th, 1918.

x Female students gather round a bonfire, Cambridge 11 November 1918. An illustration from Newnham College magazine. (*Thersites* No. 57, 6 December 1918. A. Cotterill-Davies, Liddle Collection)

Bombardier Mortimer was more concerned to write to his son about the chance of his being demobilized and the way Lloyd George was manipulating the coming election. "I should like Asquith to get a majority and form a Government. The election will soon be on. We do not know how it will turn out there being so many women voters", wrote Mr Mortimer who was keen to get his three sons home from the Army and "for ever have done with militarism".[18]

A reporter for the *Liverpool Evening Express* wrote effusively that "it was a magnificent day for the Dove of Peace to unfold its wings – balmy and sunny with scarcely a breeze to mar the splendour of the Autumn morn", but some paragraphs later he descended from such flights of fancy: "It seems that at the shipyards and repair works, the men had given the signal 'knock off' with certain other joyous phrases which need not be repeated".[19]

In Waterfoot, Rawtenstall, a nice touch of commercial enterprise combined with Lancashire humour matching the hour was recorded of the proprietor of a "tripe and pea refreshment house". He was well-known for his original window advertisements but surely excelled himself with a banner strung across Burnley Road, "Peas perfect peas". Not everything here however had so light a touch: the Red flag which a socialist conscientious objector had challengingly draped from his upstairs window so irritated an Army pensioner that he "affixed a light to a clothes prop and reaching up to the flag, set it on fire".[20] Relatively near, in Blackburn, another discordant incident was reported, a firework so startling a soldier recovering from shell-shock that he "collapsed and was carried back to hospital by ambulance".[21]

Such untoward incidents may appropriately remind us that while the newspapers graphically illustrate the great news giving rise to almost instant civic and informal celebration, their columns also report on the very same pages a more sober context for the mayoral addresses and cheering crowds. Every local paper carried tidings of the devastating influenza epidemic concurrent with the Armistice. *The Accrington Observer and Times*,[22] for example, advertised that 150 bottles of Beswick Flu Mixture "sent to Southport, Liverpool and Birkenhead today, where scores are dying, is saving 150 lives". Sadly, it does not seem to have saved Accrington's own Lancashire County cricketer, a Mr Worsley, who was reported by the paper four days later as having died and been buried with his wife who too had fallen victim to the scourge.

The editor of the same paper gave note on the twelfth that he was preparing a roll of honour for the town and district, even at the very time that his paper was still learning of the deaths in action of local men. A comprehensive list for the war was now necessary. Relatives were asked to send in details and there would be "no charge" for this service. This melancholy note was reinforced in an editorial column oberving that the war had "seared our hearts too deeply and left upon too many of our hearths and homes its ineffaceable shadow" to permit any display of abandoned rejoicing in the streets.

On the material rather than spiritual front, in Lancashire and elsewhere, coal was in short supply and the Government's Coal Controller wrote to the Blackburn Trades and Labour Council that the serious shortages could not justify any increase in the allowance for small houses. It was not only coal which was restricted and in short supply; an advertisement again in the *Accrington Observer and Times* stated that: "1 oz of butter a week will not satisfy you but Dorsella Lactic Cheese will give all the necessary nourishment" and no ration coupons were needed for this "uncontrolled Dorset produce". Another advertisement was addressed specifically to the munitions workers of Accrington and district among whom "skin troubles such as eczema, blotches, pimples are now alarmingly prevalent". Mr Hadfield, a Preston chemist, put these problems down to the lowering of bodily resistance in overworked people but, happily, he had an ointment cure.

These munition workers had other worries consequent upon the news preempting the need for their continued employment. The Ministry of Munitions immediately announced restrictions upon further production and also a temporary non-contributory unemployment pay scheme which offered men over eighteen 24 shillings a week and women of the same age 20 shillings. Much would be expected from the Ministry's announcement of "The great task before the country [being] the transformation of industry from war to peace".[23]

The Accrington Observer and Times in several ways showed sensitivity to the local consequences of both the war and its ending. It expressed concern that, in Clayton le Moors, the closing of the factories for celebration would mean that "in many a home the wages lost will be sorely missed" and then counselled at length on the subject of how to regain energy among "workers who feel weak". The article made the point that debility is not only distressing to the individual but it is a loss and a waste of national energy, sternly issuing the warning that "stimulants do not give real help. They only spur you on for a while to use up your reserve strength, but this effort in turn leaves you weaker than before".

It has to be said that this Accrington newspaper's concern for its readers did not extend to Mr John Marshall of 51 Warner Street whose seven shillings and sixpence fine was reported as being imposed on 11 November for having a light showing from his premises on 7 November and yet we are also left to muse upon the paper choosing not to print in its correspondence column a letter from a war-bereaved Accrington parent because "at the present juncture [it would] we fear, serve no useful purpose".

A fifty per cent increase on current wages was the weavers' claim reported in the *Burnley News*[24] during Armistice week. It had been "rejected by the masters" and so Union officials had submitted their case to the Committee on Production. Time would tell whether the end of the war would mark the ebbing of their opportunity to press their case but wages and secure employment were well within the concern of those cheering the end of hostilities as dramatic productions at Burnley's Palace, Arcadia and Empire theatres were delayed by special announcements, speeches, cheers, tributes and singing of the National Anthem.[25]

In the North East there was an aerial dimension to the festivities. An R.A.F. officer, F.C. Penny, in honour of the Armistice, had had all the klaxon horns available to him fitted to his aircraft. The machines of his flight then took off and from low altitude shrilled out their alarm call over Sunderland, Durham and then North to the Tyne and Newcastle. Penny arranged a special *do* for the other ranks and N.C.O.'s, while the Officers dined at the well-known Tilly's restaurant in Newcastle, a policeman holding back the crowds for the uniformed men to enter with a commanding 'Make way for the Flying Corps'. "The crowd cheered and we felt somewhat like heroes".[26]

At Sunderland, the Mayor, Alderman Vint, declared a holiday, asked tradesmen to close their shops and "the schoolchildren to be set at liberty". *The Sunderland Daily Echo* also reported that the children from the east end of the town and the women from the roperies, "as is their wont on such occasions let themselves go" and impromptu fancy-dress costume parades were soon in full swing. The paper however also reported visitors to their offices reflecting tension and tragedy – a father bursting into tears of relief as he had four sons in France, and a soldier on leave reporting his brother's death in action, sorrowfully remarking that news of the Armistice was "too late for me".

In Nottingham, it was considered that:

> the licensing restrictions prevented a repetition of the orgies associated with the relief of Mafeking, even had the people been in a mood to indulge in them. Moreover, bereavements caused by the war have been so terrible that great as is the relief experienced at its termination, the public are not likely to give way to unrestrained merriment. Many public houses did not open at all today, the shortage of beer, coupled with the fear of riotous behaviour, leading many prudent licensees to decide to keep their doors closed.

However, in one respect, Nottingham indulged itself: "The passing [i.e. ending] of the lighting restrictions was formally sanctioned by the Mayor's suggestion that every blind should be left up this evening and the city thereby flooded with light".[28]

In no way was South Wales left behind. From Swansea, the *South Wales Daily Post*, Stop Press, announced that the "military and naval authorities discharged a gun from the beach at 11 o'clock and there were numerous fireworks, detonators left [sic] off all over the town". The Mayor declined the request of some temperance advocates to close the public houses but he appealed for restraint. Both a "First Peace Concert" and a "Great Thanksgiving Service" were advertised prominently for the actual day when this paper claimed to be the first "by many minutes" to announce the great news to the people of Swansea and West Wales. On the following day, the twelfth, in his notes and comments, the Editor considered that the British people had proved the fibre of their race was as tough as ever and "with ever-growing responsibilities the capacities of a ruling race have developed". However, he reminded his readers that the nation had had a close call: "The 'blond beasts' are down but they are numerous and breed fast. They may come again...". For more than one reason such admonition reads uncomfortably today but then so does the reported concern of Roger Beck, Chairman of the Swansea Harbour Trust, that "we must never let the men who have saved us come to want". Arguably, the hollowness of these words would resonate soonest in South Wales. [29]

From Cardiff, the *Western Mail* reported on 12 November that the presiding magistrate had discharged almost all the defendants on the previous day and from Abergavenny, Abertillery, Barry, Blackwood, Blaina and many more localities, the celebrations were described. In Blaina: "Practically every house exhibited a flag. Cannon went off throughout the day ... and business establishments closed". It seems that no irony was noticed in the news snippet two columns away from this detail that the Blaina strike was spreading: "Ten Thousand Workmen Now Idle".

From newspaper evidence it seems as if chapel and church thanksgivings in South Wales, and the expression of religious sentiment at public declarations of the Armistice there, played an especially prominent role but nevertheless "South Wales came perilously near the Mafficking type of jubilation...". It was recorded that most people went to sleep late having satisfied themselves "that they had done the celebration of peace in a right worthy fashion".[30]

Something of the Mafeking type of jubilation was experienced in Leith Street, Edinburgh, where:

> the boisterous spirit of the sailors and soldiers found vent in a great variety of frolics, but especially daring were the men who ... halted a lorry laden with beer barrels, and abstracted one of the barrels. The lorryman was helpless in the midst of the jostling crowd, who vastly enjoyed the incident and there was a scene of great merriment as the men in uniform proceeded to 'broach the admiral' on the pavement.

The Edinburgh Evening News reporter of this incident thought that it was "the good humour that attended the audacity of the act that saved the situation". Elsewhere however, the celebration had been the occasion of tragedy. In Moffat, a lady with three soldier sons "was so overjoyed by the news that she had a sudden seizure and died before medical aid could be obtained".[31] Like the *Edinburgh Evening News*, the *Scotsman* drew attention to poignant figures contrasting with the general mood. "Amongst those, for instance, who stood at one of the street corners and waved a white handkerchief to a joyous company of soldiers who had commandeered the top of a [tram] car was a young widow attired in black".

In Dundee, the *Scotsman* reported crowds had sung the "National Anthem with fervent goodwill, and, amidst a forest of flags, cheers were given for 'Haig and the boys at the front'". The evident tone of thankfulness was indeed recorded but with it, as in South Wales, there was a self-confidence, "a deeper stronger note that the British cause was triumphant", something made manifest by the flags displayed from the "windows of hundreds of little houses in mean streets".

In Aberdeen, the great bell, Victoria, was rung for the first time since Hogmanay 1914 and in Glasgow, a city which the *Scotsman* considered had exercised "commendable restraint" for more than four years, celebrations on the streets and public addresses at the city's institutions expressed judgements on the past; ["The Kaiser ought to be tried and when found guilty made to pay the penalty for his misdeeds" declaimed John Hodges (Minister of Pensions) at the City Chambers], and serious concern about the future, [John Murray, Chairman of the Chamber of Commerce earnestly hoping that "they would stand solid in the great work of reconstruction that was before them otherwise they would not reap the full fruits of the glorious victory which had been achieved]. [32]

Returning to Edinburgh and the *Edinburgh Evening News*, a reporter commented upon the city's admirable fund-raising endeavour and, in the last week of the war, on the swift campaign change of title from "Feed the Guns" to "Thanksgiving Loan Week". He congratulated the citizens on their achievement, noting that "perhaps the truest indicator of the confidence and support of the general public, to say nothing of the thrift of the most stable section of the general community" was the investment in £5 bonds and War Savings Certificates.[33] For all these people there was at least one certain reward in store because *The Haddingtonshire Courier* reported on 15 November that from the first of December "bakers can manufacture and sell Genuine Scotch Currant Bun", indeed "Only Genuine Scotch Currant Bun can be made".[34]

South of the Border, practical concerns animated Londoner Mrs Pendley too, but in her case these concerns were with regular employment rather than a fruit and flour-baked staple. In her letter to her soldier son, Charles, she wrote anxiously of wanting him safely home and in work too! She had some assurance for him in this matter. "Well dear when do you think you may be coming home? I hear that the boys with jobs to come back to will stand a better chance. I still hear from the Bank so your job is still alright".[35]

For another young soldier, Gunner Frederick Wall and his fiancée, Daisy, employment was not a major concern on Armistice Day. It was their Wedding Day and they were to experience problems consequent upon such an unplanned circumstance as the national day for celebration coinciding with their own special day. At his fiancée's home, while he champed on the bit at St Luke's Church, Old Street, London, no carriage turned up for the bride. Her father anxiously telephoned the horse-drawn carriage firm in question, only to be told that all the drivers had stopped work. Replacements could not be found. In the emergency, the bride's brothers were allowed to fetch and drive the carriage but the late arrival at the church had displeased the Minister in charge. The sorry story worsened as the wedding photographer failed to turn up and the photograph, shown in this book, had to be taken in a subsequent visit to a studio. The national cause of joy on this very special day seems to have got in the way of at least one personal celebration.[36]

From the particular of the newly-wedded Walls to the general and the reaction of people from the Emerald Isle to the Armistice, here we are in a more politically coloured circumstance – Green and Orange – than anywhere else in Britain. Home Rule, and, some might say, Civil War, had been forestalled by the eruption of war on the continent in August 1914. Now, in November 1918, committed Irish nationalists and those of equally strong Unionist persuasion were aware that a divergent destiny beckoned or threatened them.

The Orange cause had certainly distinguished itself in loyal, costly service to the Crown, but the Green too had seen many thousands enlist in the British armed forces. Now with the last shots fired in France, Irish newspapers trumpeted discordant tunes.

The Unionist *Ulster Gazette and Armagh Standard* [37] scorned the fact that there had been "very little exultation in the Nationalist parts of the city" [of Armagh] and while *The Daily Express and Irish Daily Mail*[38] in Dublin, used the headline "Dublin Delirious with Joy" to describe scenes in the city which might well pass for those in London, it also made reference to a Sinn Fein gathering at the Mansion House leading to a minor clash, the demonstrator's flag being trampled by girls bearing the Union flag and then "a slightly more respectable crowd of youths paraded with the rebel colours in Dawson Street and Grafton Street, and seeming to gain in courage when the police did not interfere with them, burst into song".

The Unionist *Irish Times*, on 12 November, reported on Trinity Students commandeering a hearse and putting in it an effigy of the Kaiser wrapped in a Sinn Fein flag and then, on 14 November, Sinn Fein crowds provoking soldiers into attacks on Sinn Fein Headquarters, Liberty Hall, and on the Mansion House, bewilderingly to the Lord Mayor, unless, he said, it was because he "flew the American flag there". In fact the Lord Mayor knew well why the Mansion House might have been attacked. He was under pressure from Sinn Fein to recognize that a new opportunity was presented for Ireland – different from Easter 1916. In a letter on Sinn Fein notepaper headed 6 Harcourt Street Dublin on 22 October under the signature 'Maloney', it was stated that this new opportunity was offered by President Wilson's answer to Austria wherein he deals with:

> the case of the Czechs and Slavs and shows that they are belligerents etc. We urged the L[ord] M[ayor] to call his M[ansion] H[ouse] Conference together to hear our views. We intend to out Cromwell Cromwell and persuade these Gentlemen to declare for 1. Absolute Independence 2. The Evacuation of Ireland by the Armed Forces of England and 3. The release of all Irish Political Prisoners.

Maloney added that the men who made these claims could then be considered "Miniature George Washingtons" and reaffirmed this American link with information that: "we have just sent a cable to President Wilson asking [for] our place in the sun". Maloney doubted whether the cable would be sent for them so that another means of communicating its detail to Wilson would have to be found. However, "the news has just come to hand that Wilson has agreed to Germany's last note so that we may expect the Armistice at any moment". The implications of Maloney's next sentence: "We will soon know if that Armistice is to be observed here", seem clear enough without call for further comment.[39]

In Belfast, the Unionist paper with the oldest pedigree and biggest circulation, the *Belfast Newsletter*,[40] concentrated upon the city's loyal support of the British War Effort and the reports of unbounded rejoicing everywhere in

Ulster. By contrast, the strongly nationalist *Connaught Telegraph*[41] offered low profile reports of Armistice celebrations, stressed that America, not 'England' had won the war and called for unity in Nationalist ranks to secure Home Rule. "The game in England is to keep Ireland in subjection and make her pay for the war. Will the people of Ireland play the game?".

The Connaught Telegraph counselled its readers towards constitutional resolution of the great issue at stake. *The Dungannon Democrat*[42] was not to be so readily satisfied. "Constitutional, weak, apologetic methods have brought no results from the strong predominant partner. No prospect of justice or even fair or honest treatment will ever come from begging from England. Consequently, an appeal to the Democratic people of the world is called for".

However, *The Cork County Eagle and Munster Advertiser* – the famous 'Skibbereen Eagle',[43] demonstrated that Irish political nationalism could be comfortable with news of the victorious end to the European war: "It can truly be said that nowhere was the unconditional surrender of Germany heard of with more genuine pleasure than in Skibbereen ... the Macaura Volunteer Silver Band turned out and a torchlight procession was formed which included several tar barrels, and paraded the principal streets". A local solicitor, Mr Sheehy, made a speech celebrating the glory of Ireland in combatting the Kaiser, and lamented that Redmond had died before seeing the victory, disappointed by conflicts of his fellow countrymen.

It should not be assumed that there were strong reactions throughout Ireland. Malcolm Bickle, a Pensions Officer for the Customs and Excise at Castletownbere, County Cork, related in his diary that he had motored around his district telling "several people the war was over. The answers were 'It's a good job' or 'it's time for it as it was going on a long time' – not the slightest enthusiasm or excitement".[44]

Of the political ferment bubbling elsewhere in Ireland in the weeks following the Armistice, there is one contemporary statement which stills further comment here. Irish Quaker artist, Josephine Webb in Dublin, was:

> longing for the day when the two nations will be quite separate, living in friendly relations to each other side by side like Sweden and Norway. They found it better to separate and did so quietly and sensibly. We are palpitating with excitement politically over here and the people are getting a most excellent training in self-control – I fervently pray that the more hot-blooded and feather-headed may not do anything rash, against the councils [sic] of their leaders – that would lead to a massacre of the people by the soldiers I fear.[45]

When proper account has been taken of the fact that, in November 1918, Britons in Ireland present a distinctive case, is it possible to make general observations of the way in which citizens in the United Kingdom recorded their response to the historic cessation of hostilities on 11 November? It is easy to state without question of contradiction that there was joy, relief, thankfulness, but it must be said there were other elements too. There was too much emotional turbulence in these particular waters categorically to state that all was flowing in a flood of euphoria. If, at certain locations, there were to seem simply a surge of celebration, there was also likely to be an undertow of quieter relief tinged even with suspended belief, certainly unpreparedness for such news. There were swirls and eddies of apprehension relating to immediate and also more distant issues, some personal, some collective. There were back-currents of reflection, awareness of loss, slack water of tired indifference, even pools of despair at the mockery of one's own grief in bereavement by the rejoicing of others.

What of course united everyone, the exultant, the thankfully relieved, and the forlorn, was that this war, now over, had been the war to end all wars, so terrible that another was unthinkable. Such was the mood of the hour. The cruel dismantling of that shared confidence lay ahead, not far ahead, because the infants joining in the excitement of that November day in 1918 would, in two decades, be called compulsorily to train to face a demonstrably approaching second conflict, their surviving fathers and mothers involved too – truly the shattering of that unifying 1918 Armistice illusion.

Endnotes

All references marked L.C. are from the Liddle Collection, Brotherton Library, University of Leeds, U.K.

1 Miss E.M. Selby, V.A.D., diary, week ending 15.11.18, L.C.
2 Kate Courtney, privately published diary 1914–19 [11.11.18], L.C.
3 Second Lieutenant E. Ansell, Kings Liverpool Regiment, attached 5th Royal Irish, diary 11.11.18, L.C.
4 Miss Gladys Hutchinson of Catterick, North Yorkshire, diary, 18.12.18, L.C.
5 Phyllis Constance Iliff, writing on 11.11.18, L.C.
6 Malcolm Sparkes, Absolutist Conscientious Objector, Wandsworth Prison, letter 15.11.18, L.C.
7 Eric P. Southall, Absolutist Conscientious Objector, Walton Gaol, Liverpool, letter 21.11.18, L.C.
8 Freda Peat, daughter of a Conscientious Objector, recollections, L.C.
9 Louisa Charlotte Harris, diary 11.11.18, L.C.
10 Hilda Craven, V.A.D. Nurse, Crescent Hospital Croydon, diary 11/12.11.18, L.C.
11 Winifred Kenyon, V.A.D. Nurse, typescript diary, 11.11.18, L.C.
12 Florence Schuster, Postal van driver, diary 11.11.18, L.C.
13 'Pops' Sparkes, letter to her mother, 21.11.18, L.C.
14 'Linda' in letter 30.11.18 to Miss I.K. Rankine, a V.A.D. at Fovant, L.C.
15 Miss M.L. Macleod, student at Gypsy Hill Training College, letter 12.11.18, L.C.
16 Robin Wilson, officer on leave, letter 13.11.18, L.C.
17 *Yorkshire Evening Star and Telegraph*, 11.11.18, L.C.
18 The father of Bombardier G.M. Mortimer, letter from Hanging Heaton, 13 and 26.11.18, L.C.
19 *Liverpool Evening Express*, 11.11.18, L.C.
20 *The Rossendale Free Press*, 16.11.18, The Rossendale Collection, Rawtenstall Library.
21 *The Blackburn Times*, 16.11.18, Blackburn Library.
22 *The Accrington Observer and Times*, 12.11.18, Accrington Central Library.

23 *ibid*, 16.11.18.
24 *The Burnley News*, 13.11.18, Burnley Central Library.
25 *The Burnley Express and Advertiser*, 13.11.18, Burnley Central Library.
26 F.C. Penny [Lieutenant F.C. Penny, R.A.F.], typescript recollections, L.C.
27 *Sunderland Daily Echo*, 11.11.18, L.C.
28 *The Nottingham Evening Post*, 11.11.18, L.C.
29 *The South Wales Daily Post*, 11–12.11.18, L.C.
30 *Western Mail*, 12.11.18, L.C.
31 *The Edinburgh Evening News*, 12.11.18 [Edinburgh Central Library].
32 *The Scotsman*, 12.11.18 [Edinburgh Central Library].
33 *The Edinburgh Evening News*, 13.11.18 [Edinburgh Central Library].
34 *The Haddingtonshire Courier*, 15.11.18 [Haddington Library].
35 Mrs C. Pendley, letter 18.11.18, L.C.
36 Manuscript recollections of Daisy Wright who married Gunner Frederick Wall at St Luke's Church, Old Street, London on 11.11.18, L.C.
37 *Ulster Gazette and Armagh Standard*, 16.11.18 [British Museum Newspaper Library, Colindale, London].
38 *Daily Express and Irish Daily Mail*, 12.11.18 [British Museum Newspaper Library, Colindale, London].
39 Maloney letter 22.10.18 [Archives Department, Kilmainham Jail Museum, Dublin – ref. 18LR IB13 09].
40 *Belfast Newsletter*, 12.11.18 [British Museum Newspaper Library, Colindale, London].
41 *The Connaught Telegraph*, 16.11.18 [British Museum Newspaper Library, Colindale, London].
42 *The Dungannon Democrat*, 13.11.18 [British Museum Newspaper Library, Colindale, London].
43 *The Cork County Eagle and Munster Advertiser*, 16.11.18 [British Museum Newspaper Library, Colindale, London].
44 M.E. Bickle, journal for November 1918, L.C.
45 Josephine Webb, letter 4.1.19, L.C.

Chapter Six

The French

Allain Bernède

During the autumn of 1918, as the Allied general offensive was developing, Paris sensed that the *Marseillaise's* precious 'jour de gloire' was getting closer and hope of victory increased. On 18 October, an immense crowd gathered at the Place de la Concorde to celebrate the liberation of Lille in front of the statue representing the city. Two days later, at the review of the 1920 class recruits, the Parisians were full of enthusiasm.

At Military Headquarters however, though the atmosphere was more cautious, information began to come in and Jean de Pierrefeu[1] learned that, according to a dispatch from Berne, "the Germans have decided to ask for an armistice...".[2]

Of course, the information was difficult to credit and still, highly secret. However, it quickly became a topic of all discreet conversation. On 27 October, Berlin was said to have asked the President of the United States of America to "handle the peace process...".[3] Despite all the evidence, the High Command prudently warned the armed forces against rumours leaked by enemy propaganda agents. Nevertheless, at 00.30 hrs on 6 November, a radiotelegram picked up by the Eiffel tower monitoring station indicated, at last, the names of the plenipotentiaries who would meet Marshal Foch. As well as being an initial contact, the text offered the information that the Germans "would be most satisfied, in the interest of humanity, if the arrival of the German delegation on the Allied front could bring a temporary cease-fire".[4]

Informed on the morning of 7 November that the German emissaries were to appear at the 1st French Army lines in La Capelle-Guise sector between 16.00 and 17.00 hrs, General Debeney took the necessary step for a local and temporary suspension of fire. Meanwhile, Marshal Foch, General Weygand and three staff officers, together with the British naval delegation led by Admiral Wemyss, went by special train to the forest of Compiègne. So, it was in Rethondes, his train diverted to an artillery railway siding, that the Allied Commander-in-Chief was to wait for the German delegation to present them with the text of the Armistice as decided by the Allied governments on 4 November.

At the front, the first news had come in the following fashion: on 7 November, from a forward observation post, Sergeant Maître reported:

> Suddenly, at exactly half past eight in the evening, while a card game was going on among these gentlemen, a call was heard in the distance and then soon much nearer till it was loud and clear near our command post... 'They wouldn't run over us would they?' Captain Lhuillier cried out. Standing on the running boards of the car, there were two Boches each sounding in turn cease-fire with a silver bugle, at least 5 feet long, much like a Jericho trumpet. While one was blowing, the other one was waving a large white cloth by way of a pennant.[5]

On the captain's order, the German trumpeter was replaced by Corporal Sellier: "And now, throughout the night, bugle calls of the *171ème* R.I. [Régiment d'Infanterie], the 19th and 26th *chasseurs à pied*, and of all the units of the 166th infantry division resound in turns, cheerfully and triumphantly ... and soldiers run across the fields...".[6]

At 22.00 hrs, after a frugal dinner at the Homblières presbytery, the German delegation was led to General Debeney's Command Post. The mission was accomplished for the 166th infantry division, and the cease-fire remained effective for the next 8 hours! On the morrow, at 06.00 hrs, whilst the German delegation was to be received by Marshal Foch three hours later in dining car 2419D arranged as a meeting room in the Forest of Compiègne, the advance was to be resumed. Even so, just before the last shells were fired, Lieutenant Moulin, commanding the 5th company *171ème* R.I., together with one NCO and three soldiers, was to be killed near La Capelle.

In the forest of Compiègne, Raymond Recouly reported that: "By 7 o'clock in the morning, on the 8th, at the very dawn of an autumn day, the people with Marshal Foch can see the red light of the German train looming up. The train drives up the siding backwards; the rear brake van, being the first coach, draws level with the Marshal's engine".[7] Shortly after the meeting had begun, and on the German express request for an armistice, Marshal Foch presented the conditions but refused all kinds of suspension of hostilities, even a provisional one, until the convention itself was signed. Then, at half past two, the Marshal gave the Allied Commanders-in-Chief[8] confirmation of his intention to pursue the "feldgrauen with a sword at their backs. The enemy, being disrupted by our repeated attacks, is losing ground on all fronts. It is important to maintain and hasten our advance".[9]

However, although the Communiqué dated 9 November informed the French that "the enemy has got seventy-two hours to reply", people were quite conscious that nothing was certain yet, and the war could still continue and in fact, on the morrow, while Major Vuillemin of 12 Squadron successfully bombed Philippeville and Marienbourg, another machine of 14 Squadron was never to return from its mission over Givet! On the banks of the river Meuse, Second Lieutenant Laurent of the *415ème* R.I. was killed on his return from convalescence; Sergeant d'Holler, who postponed the leave he had planned on the occasion of the birth of his third child because "it wasn't a suitable time to leave his companions",[10] was killed too.

However, at 05.00 hrs, on 11 November, the convention was signed, at last. Jérôme Carcopino, wounded in July 1917 while in the Armée d'Orient, was on duty at the War Ministry that night. He recorded and transmitted the last war communiqué[11] to the Elysée as well as to the rue Franklin where Clemenceau was residing. Army commanders are immediately informed by telephone.

At 07.00 hrs, Foch left Rethondes taking the Armistice convention back to Paris. He arrived at the War Ministry dressed in field uniform, and with Admiral Wemyss and General Weygand. Here, it did not take him long to hand over to Clemenceau, who was most moved, the green books containing the Armistice conventions.[12] Then, Foch's party crossed the river Seine, heading for the Elysées to meet the President of the French Republic. When Clemenceau finally joined them, Raymond Poincaré, who did not have much affection for the latter, nevertheless held him in a warm hug. The 'Tiger' being now obviously moved and elated, called out to him: "I've been embraced by more than five hundred young girls!"[13] At noon, on the Avenue de Saxe, when Foch arrived to have lunch with his wife and honour the memory of his son and son-in-law killed during the war, an enthusiastic crowd would shower him with flowers!

Meanwhile, at the front and in forward positions, the engine of war was still in action. At 07.00 hrs on the eleventh, the Colonel commanding the *80ème* R.I. received the telegram announcing that the Armistice was to come into effect at 11.00 hrs. After the news was notified to the troops, the advance was to resume at 09.00.[14] At the same time, in Lorraine, whilst a few men of the *162ème* R.I. were bustling about a field kitchen, a messenger from division cried out : "'That's it, the war ends at 11!' 'Shut up', the cook retorted! 'And why don't they come over here and have a drink?'"[15] Later on, at about 08.00 hrs, the telephone rang at the *163ème* R.I. on the banks of the river Meuse. Corporal Guillermi, the telephone operator, took the message: "Get your unit into order. Be ready to resume advance. Further instructions to follow". Needless to say liaison officers could not help being sarcastic at this: "And you thought peace was to be signed on Sunday morning".[16] However, at 10.10 hrs, a messenger ran into the Command Post of the 3rd battalion of the *415ème* R.I. and cried out: "That's it . . . signed . . . ended, 11 o'clock". Captain Lebreton took the document and impassively read it out in a loud voice:

> Quarter to ten, Marshal Foch's wire:
> 1. Hostilities shall cease on all fronts as from November 11th at 11 o'clock, French time.
> 2. Allied troops shall not pass the line reached at this date and time unless ordered to the contrary. Report this line in every detail.
> 3. Any communication with the enemy is forbidden until further instructions to army commanders.[17]

Since the last victorious attacks, everyone was well aware that the decisive moment could be near. On 9 November, German aircraft had dropped over the lines of the 1st French Army leaflets which read: "The German people offer peace" but, peace propaganda was so much feared at this time that nobody dared to believe that at last "we've got 'em!"

Soon, at the outposts of the *163ème* R.I., as in a great number of units, the search was on for a bugle. It had been long since that the liaison officers had had access to such an instrument. However, one soldier remembered a man called Delahuque who might have one. Someone went and fetched him. Luckily he had still got his bugle with him. He crept back carefully to Captain Lebreton for the German machine-guns were shooting at whatever moved. It was almost the appointed time. Watches had been set by telephone but Delahuque was silent, he couldn't remember the call. The last time he had played it was on the firing range in 1911! The Captain whistled the first notes but Delahuque had now lost his bugle mouthpiece. Finally, he found it , in a pocket, but clogged with tobacco. By now it was 10.59 hrs. A burst of heavy shells passed over their heads. A few seconds later, on the Captain's signal, Delahuque started sounding the regiment's chorus: "*Ils z'en ont plein le c...*".[18] Then, as he was standing up: the *Garde-à-vous*: "*A droite la musette, à gauche le bidon, nous sommes la classe et demain nous partons*". A pause elapsed, the Cease-fire: "*T'as tiré comme un cochon...*". Another pause: "*T'auras pas de permission*" (No leave for you).[19] Still standing up and now standing straight: "*AU DRAPEAU!*" (to the flag). Delahuque went on repeating these calls, facing the east, and then facing the north, and again facing the east. German bugles replied with their classic *Ta ta ta ta ... Ta ta ta ta ...* The *Marseillaise* burst out almost everywhere from occupied shell holes. Warrant officer Chambaz commented: "Our youth has come to an end".

At noon, Father Guitton, the divisional chaplain, celebrated a *Te Deum* in Dom-le-Mesnil church which had been occupied by the Germans on the previous day. Only General Boichut, his staff and a few villagers attended. Although everyone felt a great relief, there was no explosion of joy for, at the same time, the funeral of Lieutenant Dupin and telephone operator Charreton were taking place. They had been killed a few hours before.[20]

Elsewhere things were different. In Guise, soldiers of the *39ème* R.I. burst out joyfully singing the *Chant du Départ*.[21]. However, instead of the words: "*La victoire en marchant, nous ouvre la barrière*", they improvised the following chorus: "*C'est fini, c'est fini, c'est bien, c'est bien fin-i, (bien fin-i); c'est bien fini, mais oui, c'est bien fini...*".[22]

The Armistice had been signed and, faced with this incredible event, everyone rejoiced or mourned, or did both at the same time. However, some circumstances at least inspired humour. Having received the order to leave Epinal fortified camp in order to stage an attack to keep the offensive going, the *47ème* R.I. stopped off at the village of Frizon on 10 November in the evening. There, at dawn on the eleventh, the Colonel was roused from slumber and, while still in pyjamas, had the operator on duty read the official

TROISIÈ

43ᵉ ANNÉE. - Nº 15.253

DIRECTION & ADMINISTRATION :
16, 18, 20, 22, rue d'Enghien, Paris

Téléphone : Gut. 02.73 - 02.75 - 15.00
Adresse télégraphique : Petitsien-Paris

La publicité est reçue
à l'OFFICE D'ANNONCES
29, Bd des Italiens, Paris. Tél. Gut. 17-99

ABONNEMENTS	3 mois	6 mois	1 an
Seine et S.-et-O.	8.»	15.50	30.»
France & Colon.	9.»	16.50	32.»
Etranger.....	10.»	18. »	35.»

Le Petit

10 Cent

LE PLUS FORT TIRAGE DES

C'EST

(Officiel). — *L'armistic*
Les hostilités ont été

LES CONDITIONS DE L'ARMISTICE

Voici un extrait des conditio. de l'armistice :

1. Entrée en vigueur six heures après la signature.

2. Evacuation immédiate de la Belgique, de la France et de l'Alsace-Lorraine, et cela dans un délai de quatorze jours. Les troupes qui se trouveront dans ces territoires après ce délai seront internées ou faites prisonnières de guerre.

3. Doivent être remis 5.000 canons, tout d'abord de gros calibre, 30.000 mitrailleuses, 3.000 lance-mines et 2.000 avions.

4. Evacuation de la rive gauche du Rhin. Mayence, Coblence et Cologne seront occupées dans un rayon de trente kilomètres de profondeur.

5. Constitution d'une zone neutre sur la rive droite du Rhin d'une profondeur de 30 à 40 kilomètres. Evacuation dans les onze jours.

6. Rien ne doit être enlevé de la rive gauche du Rhin. Les fabriques, chemins de fer, etc. doivent rester intacts.

7. Cinq mille locomotives, 150.000 wagons, 10.000 camions automobiles doivent être remis.

8. Entretien par l'Allemagne des troupes ennemies d'occupation.

9. En Orient, toutes les troupes doivent être retirées derrière la frontière du 1ᵉʳ août 1914. Il n'y a pas de délai fixé pour cette opération.

10. Renonciation aux traités de Brest-Litowsk et de Bucarest.

11. Capitulation sans conditions en Afrique orientale.

xi The newspaper *Le Petit Parisien* carries news at last of the Armistice signing, 12 November 1918. (Liddle Collection)

:DITION

Parisien

:NAUX DU MONDE ENTIER ★★★ 10 Cent.

MARDI
12
NOVEMBRE 1918
Saint René
SOLEIL : lev. 6 h. 55 ; couch. 4 h. 14
LUNE : pl. le 18 ; der. quart. le 25
Temps probable : brumeux
1562e JOUR DE LA GUERRE

SIGNÉ !

été signé lundi matin à 5 h. 40.

ndues à 11 heures.

PARIS ACCUEILLE l'heureux événement dans un débordement d'enthousiasme

Sur les boulevards, la joie est délirante et la foule acclame particulièrement nos Alliés

C'est au son du canon, dans l'allègre sonnerie des cloches, que Paris a appris, hier matin, vers 11 heures, la nouvelle de la signature de l'armistice. L'heureux événement qui met fin aux jours d'angoisse était depuis la veille escompté, mais les cœurs, étreints par tant d'heures douloureuses vécues, hésitaient à laisser déborder leur joie. Tout le monde était calme et patient, guettant l'annonce joyeuse qui allait dissiper définitivement le cauchemar et sonner l'heure triomphante des réparations, acquise au prix de tant de sacrifices et de tant de deuils.

De même qu'aux soirs tragiques de 1914, c'est sur les boulevards que la foule s'est portée, certaine de surprendre là les premiers frémissements de joie de la ville, comme elle y avait vécu, voilà quatre ans, ses premières angoisses. Dès dix heures, les trottoirs étaient noirs de monde. Les camelots vendeurs de cocardes ou d'insignes étaient assaillis. On s'arrachait les petits drapeaux vendus par les marchands ambulants et que déjà des groupes agitaient joyeusement. Aux fenêtres, c'était une éclocommuniqué from the window of the presbytery where he had stayed for the night.[23]

"Even before the German plenipotentiaries had reached the French lines, the rumour in Paris was that the Armistice was signed".[24] By 10.00 hrs, at the time when the official communiqués were traditionally posted, newspaper directors (*Le Matin* at the boulevard Poissonnière and *L'Echo de Paris* at the Place de l'Opéra) having been informed of the news by telephone, had the following sign posted: "The Armistice is signed". Cars decorated with small tricolor and Allied flags immediately begin scurrying to and fro across the city. Suddenly, at 11 sharp, a great detonation could be heard throughout the city. It's the gun! The gun, soon followed by Notre-Dame's great bell and then by all the capital's church bells, announcing the longed-for news!

> I was walking down the Champs-Elysées, Adrien Chevalier reported in the *Journal de Die et de la Drôme* issued on the following day.[25]* A man I didn't know came up to me and said: 'That's it. The armistice is signed'. We shook hands, as many Parisians did all day long. What a day! Paris has never appeared to me so fantastic. From the people around the guns assembled at the Place de la Concorde,[26] you could feel emotion rising all the time. We were longing for the news but it would not come. Tension was at its utmost! Finally, yesterday, bells and guns broke the news that Germany had surrendered. And then the explosion, an explosion of joy which still could not fully comprehend the news. Shouts, songs, hurrahs! ... And a crowd of people thronging, feverishly, with their eyes and hearts full of joy ... It is much like a carnival, with a little of the grotesque and a lot of the sublime. Actually, Paris as it is, with her patriotic exhilaration, being full of friendly and Allied soldiers, sounds fantastic and incredible.

Paris was soon decorated everywhere with flags! From the Saturday, already, people had queued for flags in the department stores[27]. In working-class neighbourhoods, factory hooters took over from the bells so that the news spread even quicker. Workers had left their workshops. The *grands boulevards* were now thronged with those women who had replaced men at their work place. Even the pandemonium of drums and trumpets could not shut out the *Marseillaise's* "*Le jour de gloire est arrivé*" (The day of glory hath come) and the crowd went on in a sort of liberating uproar of: "*On les a eus!*" (We've got 'em!).

At the Place de la Concorde, the Belgian soldiers' "*Brabançonne*", the Americans' "*Over there*" and the British "*Tipperary*" melodies mixed with the French "*Madelon*".[28] The Strasbourg statue, draped with a black cloth since 1871, was unveiled. Now, at last, the 'captured trophies', the German guns, could be laughed at. These spoils of war were dragged around the streets.

Some kicked the guns in revenge, others bestrode them to demonstrate that they were no longer objects of fear. As hours passed, Parisians had a better sense of it *all being really true*. They walked in the streets. All public spaces, streets, cafés, churches, were thronged with people. At Notre-Dame, a young lady amidst the crowds was about to buy a candle. She related, half a century later:[29] "a man was standing near me. Suddenly, as if to free himself from a secret, he started talking: 'I have been waiting for this day for over forty years, he said, ... I promised Notre-Dame de Paris to come to Her and thank Her when France got back Alsace ... I was a cavalryman and I charged at Reichshoffen."

At the front, soldiers burst out in a great uproar of relief. Though natural, this exhilaration was soon tempered by the recall of friends gone forever. Very often, men were in utter disarray. Nobody seemed to know exactly what to do next. In many places, officers called up their 'poilus' just to shake hands and thank them for what they did for France. That's all!

Those men, from the muddy trenches, hard-mouthed, cheerful, cocky, familiar, slovenly-looking as they were, but still France's soldiers, did not know what would now be expected of them because no one had ever experienced an armistice before! Furthermore, very little guidance could be found in daily operation orders.[30]

Typical entries were, for example; for the *6ème* regiment de Cuirassier à cheval: "Received order to cease fire and remain on the spot";[31] for the *217ème R.I.*: "In the morning, the regiment was informed an armistice had been concluded on November 10th at 2300 (sic) between maréchal Foch and German plenipotentiaries. Rest and cleaning tasks".[32]

As for the enemy, they were in the immediate vicinity too! There was no fraternizing, or scarcely any, on the eleventh of November. A poilu jotted down in his notebook: "about fifty boches came in the village. They were shouting, singing and wanted to join us in a dance ... They said they had not been eating for 48 hours ; we gave them bread. Up to 11 o'clock, several hundreds came over. We kept them prisoners as the war was not over. Then, we did not allow any more to come over".[33] Lieutenant Bonneval confided that, as he was surveying the lines along the banks of the river Meuse just after the cease-fire had been sounded, he had met a German major in full dress who told him in excellent French "it is my duty [as a German soldier] to pay tribute to soldiers who have sacrificed their lives on the last but one day of war and have fought well".[34]

As for Moriba Doumbia,[35] a Guinean NCO of the *68ème* bataillon de tirailleurs senegalais, resting in the rear after the terrible bayonet charges at Epernay in July, he was overcome with joy and like others of his regiment, he was laughing: "*Abana, abana* (it's over, it's over). We win war completely".[36] In some areas, in the evening, in order to work off tension, flares were fired by way of a firework display. Elsewhere, the poilu remained on guard, in silence, out of habit. Those were his orders and one never knew!

At Pétain's Headquarters in Provins, Pierrefeu, responsible for the daily communiqué returns to Provins GQG, was back from Chantilly, the Allied GHQ, to which he had been summoned in the morning by Pétain. Just before 11 was struck, he hastily wrote[37] the very last war communiqué. Then, General Pétain not being back, he looked for the Major-General to get his authorization, but General Buat was at his HQ like other generals. Thus, it was from his sector of the front that Buat was notified of and approved the last war communiqué, a communiqué which he thought would have been written under Pétain's close supervision.[38]

> On the 52nd month of an unprecedented war in history, the French Army together with Allied powers has defeated the enemy. Our troops, in the purest sacrificial spirit, have, for four years of uninterrupted struggle, proved sublimely enduring and have shown daily heroism in fulfilling the task invested in them by the country. Now facing enemy assaults with undiminished energy, and then attacking to bring victory, they have, after a four-month decisive offensive, stopped, defeated and pushed the powerful German army out of France so that it was compelled to sue for peace. All the conditions imposed for hostilities to be suspended having been accepted by the enemy, the armistice has come into force this morning at 11 o'clock.

The document had already been telephoned to Paris and published by newspapers when General Pétain signed it, adding sardonically: "Victory close-down".[39]

In Macedonia, on the banks of the river Vardar, the *Armée d'Orient*, had for some time, been under no stress as the Salonica Armistice had been signed on 29 September. However, it was widely accepted that the outcome of the war would be decided on the French front. It was during a card game that the soldiers of the 227*ème* *R.I.*, in charge of pushing supplies forward in the Vélès region, received information, thanks to the 'Paris-Balkans' newspapers issued on 10 November, of: "Armistice with Germany ... Belgium and Alsace-Lorraine evacuation". Immediately, while Zouave, Clémençon, was uncorking the wine containers, soldiers ran up to the Bulgarian prisoners: "War over! *Franzous*, ... Paris!" Out of their slumber, the unfortunate P.O.W.s asked: "Germans, *kapout*?" "Ja, Ja, like Ferdinand" the French replied.[40] The next day, when the news was confirmed, there was jubilation everywhere. In Salonica, French and British officers took over barouches to go joyfully parading through the town. One of the French officers, the shrewd and pragmatic Second Lieutenant Norbert Cassagne, had a billiard cue in hand so that he could teasingly menace the British barouches and keep guard over the French ones.[41*] At the same time, Sergeant Mangelle, an air observer of the *Armée d'Orient*, was surprised in Rome on his way home on leave. He rejoiced too and remembered being more "plastered" than he had ever been before.[42*]

At sea, the morale of the navy, a major part of which was absorbed in tasks aimed at maintaining the lines of communication of the *Armée d'Orient*, was seriously depleted. The great decisive battle that Admiral Boué de Lapeyrère had dreamt of in 1914 had never materialized. The serious losses[43] inflicted by the U-boats had undermined the self-confidence of the French Navy and its "battleships were stationed in Corfu, Mudros and Salamis harbours behind protective stockades and steel nets".[44] However, the fleet, after all, had fulfilled a transportation and submarine warfare rôle, and had not suffered embarrassing defeats in surface actions so it was particularly shocked not to be mentioned in the victory speeches. Though Georges Leygues, the

1. 'Here on the 11 November 1918, succumbed the criminal pride of the German Empire. Vanquished by the free peoples which it had aspired to rule'. A plaque in the forest glade at Compiègne marks the spot where the emissaries met. For France the fact that Germany should be humiliated was a crucial part of the peace - so much so that on that historic occasion Foch actually made the German delegation ask him for an Armistice. (Liddle Collection) (Chapter 2 - Negotiating the Armistices)

2. An artist's impression of the signing of the Armistice inside the railway carriage at Compiègne, early in the morning of 11 November 1918 - left to right Captain Ernst Vanselow, Count Alfred Oberndorf, Major-General Detlov von Winterfeldt, Captain J.P.R. Marriott, Herr Matthias Erzberger, Rear Admiral Sir George Hope, Admiral Sir Rosslyn Wemyss, Marshal Ferdinand Foch, and General Maxime Weygand. (Liddle Collection) (Chapter 2 - Negotiating the Armistices)

3. General John J. Pershing, leaving his headquarters at Chaumont, 1918. (Patrick Gariépy collection) (Chapter 2 - Negotiating the Armistices and Chapter 8 - The Americans)

4. Under the eye of French civilians, German troops retreating through Soignies, 9 November 1918. (I.L. Read, Liddle Collection) (Chapter 3 - Germany)

5. German troops in retreat. Note the motor lorry, loaded with as much booty as its occupants could carry off. (I.L. Read, Liddle Collection) (Chapter 3 - Germany)

6. German troops crossing the Hohenzollern Bridge at Cologne, November 1918, to comply with the terms of the Armistice which stated that German forces must retire to the eastern bank of the Rhine. Note the smiling faces and flowers.
(W.K. Rose, Liddle Collection)
(Chapter 3 - Germany)

7. Revolution on the streets of Berlin. Deserters from the army mix with sailors and armed civilians on the way to the barricades during the Spartacist rising.
(Liddle Collection) (Chapter 3 - Germany)

8. The statues of four German soldiers, sculpted by the Munich artist Ernst Krieger, mourn for their lost comrades at Langemarck German cemetery, Belgium. Langemarck, the site of fighting on 11 November 1914, was a place of special significance in the Germany of the 1920's and 30's. (Hugh Cecil) (Chapter 3 - Germany)

9. The village war memorial in Bordesholm, Schleswig-Holstein, northern Germany. Erected in 1920 and designed by local architect Harry Maas, the inscription reads "From the Parish of Bordesholm to the fallen. Seed of Hope". Wreaths are laid at the memorial each November on Toten Sonntag, the German day of remembrance. (C.L. Harder) (Chapter 3 - Germany)

10. British officers pose together outside Mons, on the morning of 11 November 1918. (M.F.T. Baines, Liddle Collection) (Chapter 4 - Britons Overseas)

11. Father Roger Morrisey, Padre of the 2nd Battalion Royal Munster Fusiliers, outside the battalion's billet in Wargnies-le-Petit on the morning of 11 November. (Liddle Collection) (Chapter 4 - Britons Overseas)

12. A service of thanksgiving in the Collegiate Church at St Quentin, conducted by a padre and a French priest and attended by British soldiers. (French War Office, official) (Chapter 4 - Britons Overseas)

13. Officers of 'A' Flight, No 8 Squadron RAF in front of one of their Bristol Fighters, at Malincourt aerodrome on the morning of 11 November. Flight Lieutenant Peffers DFC at the centre. (S. Horscroft, Liddle Collection) (Chapter 4 - Britons Overseas)

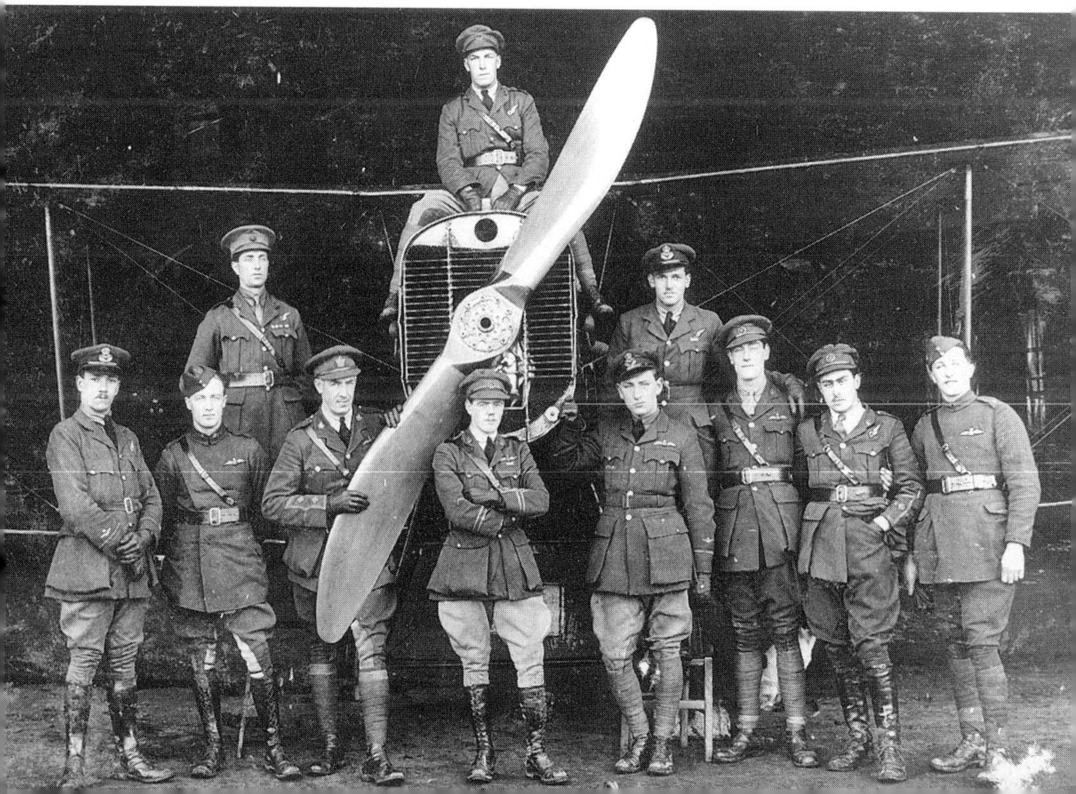

BRATION OF ARMISTICE 10 · 11 · 18 10 p.m.
UADRON R.A.F. BELGIUM.

14. Time lapse photography has captured this display of Armistice night fireworks by No 10 Squadron RAF, at its base near Reckem, Belgium.
(C.E. Townley, Liddle Collection) (Chapter 4 - Britons Overseas)

16. Crowds of Arab civilians are held in check by British and Indian soldiers in Baghdad, 11 November 1918.
(F. Everitt, Liddle Collection) (Chapter 4 - Britons Overseas & Chapter 18 - The Arab World)

15. British troops gather in the main square in Baghdad to hear the news of the Armistice in Europe from the GOC Mesopotamia, Lieutenant-General Sir William Marshall.
(T.H. Parkinson, Liddle Collection) (Chapter 4 - Britons Overseas)

17. Shortly after hearing the news of the Armistice, British officer prisoners posed for this photograph outside Clausthal POW camp, Germany. The most senior figure here is Brigadier General H.S.L. Ravenshaw, (front row third from left in double breasted overcoat) who was captured in the aftermath of the Battle of Cambrai, November 1917.
(R.V. Maudslay, Liddle Collection)
(Chapter 4 - Britons Overseas)

18. German sailors aboard the German super-dreadnought battleship *SMS König*, seen from a British ship. For the men of the Royal Navy, the reality of the Armistice was underscored by the German High Seas Fleet surrendering itself for internment on 21 November. Many were struck by the dirty, rusty and generally unkempt appearance of the enemy vessels after two years at their moorings.
(L.A.K. Boswell, Liddle Collection)
(Chapter 4 - Britons Overseas)

19. A German submarine of the latest ocean-going type, *U112*, enters Harwich for internment, late November 1918, signifying Germany's naval as well as military defeat.
(J.M. Heath, Liddle Collection) (Chapter 4 - Britons Overseas)

20. *U112* with her new British crew. The Royal Navy's triumph over the High Seas Fleet complete at last.
(J.M. Heath, Liddle Collection)
(Chapter 4 - Britons Overseas)

Navy minister, appeared in person before the *Chambre des Députés* on 31 October to announce the clauses of the Armistice with Turkey, opening the Dardanelles and the Bosphorus and giving access to the Black Sea to the French navy, the mere congratulatory motion that was tardily adopted on 4 December by the Navy Committee alone, had a disastrous effect on naval self-perception. With the Armistices signed,[45] the feelings of disappointment and bitterness became seriously acute when seamen realized, on anchoring before Constantinople on 13 November, that they would not be sailing back to France and their demobilization was indefinitely postponed. It is thus easy to understand the discontent that caused the dreadful and humiliating Black Sea mutinies. Those seamen, deprived of mail for so long and now employed "as dockers alongside Bulgarian prisoners",[46] had become aware of the violent criticizms some Parisian politicians were uttering against the involvement of the Second French fleet in the Black Sea against the Bolsheviks.

In Lille, the northern capital, the great surge of emotion caused by the liberation was already three weeks past. The population, badly affected by the occupying forces' drastic requisitions and with many suffering from tuberculosis, had now resumed work. On 17 October, the newspaper, *L'Echo du Nord*, was published again. Public services were now in operation, schools and city administration open again. However, even if the newspaper, *L'Illustration*, claimed that tradesmen were displaying all the "odds and ends that were shrewdly concealed from the most drastic German requisitions ... evidence of the triumph of native wit over brute force",[47] people were not enjoying a comfortable recovery from their experience of occupation. The thousands of men and women who were sent to work-camps in the Ardennes and Laon region from April 1916 returned to "a dead city ... at the end of a desert", as the *Morning Post*[48] correspondent wrote in December 1918.

In the south of France, things were quite different. In its 12 November issue, the newspaper, *Le Journal de Die et de la Drôme*,[49*] reported: "The good news that was telephoned yesterday just before 10 o'clock to one of our fellow men is now spreading like a flash of lightning". Everywhere, in France, once the official communiqué was known, people put out flags. As in Paris, church bells started ringing, French and Allied flags were put out at the windows of public buildings as well as private houses. To cries of "Long live France! Long live England! Long live United States!", the crowds invaded the streets of every town, whether big or small, breaking into patriotic choruses. In Chartres, at half past four in the afternoon, the Mayor, together with local councillors, decided to offer the Prefect of Eure et Loir the city's testimonial to civil and military leaders who led the republican armies to victory. Preceded by the city's brass band, the Mayor was welcomed by the Prefect himself in the main courtyard. After the *Marseillaise* was played, with the bareheaded audience standing in an impressive silence, the Mayor addressed the following words to the Government representative:

> Now that Victory has crowned the immense efforts of Allied armies, the members of the City Council, their hearts overflowing with joy, enthusiasm and pride, are honoured to express their admiration and eternal gratitude

to the armies, the army chiefs, Maréchal Foch, our fellowman Georges Clemenceau, Prime Minister and Minister of War whose vibrant patriotism, unflagging energy and most realistic viewpoint together with commanders' genius and the valour of the troops have safeguarded France. To the men killed in action whom we shall never forget, we pay our most heart-felt tribute. Glory to all of them, Glory to the victors in the Great war![50]

The Prefect replied:

Ladies and gentlemen, we are experiencing events on a mighty scale. After four years of superhuman endeavours and unspeakable sufferings, we have reached the end of this gigantic fight. Germany confesses and signs its defeat and proclaims our victory. Glory to everyone to whom we owe this colossal achievement. Glory to our wonderful soldiers, to our heroic poilus. Glory to all those who were killed to defend the land of France, supreme homeland of human liberties. Glory to our great Allies, to our distinguished civil and military leaders who wrought out this apotheosis for us, the triumph of democracies against despicable regimes based on lies and tyranny. Glory to the victorious and liberating Republic and to eternal France.[51]

The Nîmes bar, seven members of which were killed in action and one of whom was missing, sent to the Prime Minister and Marshal Foch, a telegram expressing "their deeply-felt homage and grateful admiration".[52]

In Die, in the Drôme department, "all afternoon long, *processions* were to parade through the town. At night, bonfires and farandoles. Scenes of *fraternité*. Most of those taking part were women. Poilus and lively young girls from all backgrounds took part in this general rejoicing. The *Marseillaise*, *Girondins*,[53] *Madelon* and other airs were sung. Banquets took place in major hotels", the local newspaper reported.[54]*

In villages, it was usually the postmaster who, as in Arbois, a small village in Jura, ran into the Mayor's office to hand him the official communiqué. But, even if the post office were closed, the message got out! "It's thanks to Saint-Gaudens church great bell that the inhabitants of Valence[55] were informed of the conclusion of the Armistice by noon. The Mayor immediately ordered the ringing of the church bells".[56]

Of the soldiers on leave on 11 November, soldier Martignac of the *Armée d'Orient*, remembered being on leave in Cantal. His first thought when he heard the victory bells was that he was through the war unwounded and he shouted: "I won the war!".[57]* [Martignac still survives, he is a hundred years old!]

Elsewhere, a bugler was operating a threshing machine.[58] He recalled that: "On All Saints' day, we, together with our comrades of the *41ème R.I.*, celebrated a mass to the memory of the dead. Then, we took the soldiers leave-train at Heygem station. The train crossed the sinister Yser battlefield where we could see the scanty walls still standing in Ypres". The former bugler continued:

The connecting train initially departed from Dunkerque. There, we could read big posters announcing that Turkey and Bulgaria had capitulated. We did not dislike the idea at all. An officer even told us we were the lucky ones for the war would be over before we returned ... Near Creil, I secretly changed train in Noisy-le-Sec[59] and finally arrived at home. Rumours of an armistice were circulating widely. One day, on my way to the neighbouring town,[60] I saw workers from a rubber factory walking out of a café, some carrying others on their backs, and cheerfully singing: 'It's over! It's over!' but that was a false alarm. Two days after that, I was operating the steam threshing machine when, at half past eleven, B., my neighbour of the 41st B.C.P. on leave too, came up to me crying with joy: 'That's it! That's it!' This time, it was true. The threshing machine stopped as if by itself. I was puzzled and wondering what would happen next. Deep down inside, I would have preferred people to take part in the general rejoicing on this memorable date. However, on my actually proposing nothing and the food being ready for everyone, work continued normally to the end of the day.

When his leave expired, this soldier briefly took up again his bugle and knapsack, but was demobilized on 20 February, 1919.

During the days following the announcement of the Armistice, resolutions of support for the Government were voted as in the village of Malissard in the Rhône valley, east of Valence:

Malissard city council, on behalf of the population, unanimously sends the government, and particularly Monsieur Georges Clemenceau, its patriotic homage and gratitude. This tribute is also directed to our valiant marshals and generals for their leading our brave poilus to victory, liberating our country and our brethren residing in Alsace and Lorraine. Long live France.[61*]

A woman, thirteen years old at the time and living in the small village of Bernède in the Gers department, has given her account of the period. In the afternoon, whilst she was busy helping her parents on the farm, she heard Lannux bells pealing out and then the Bernède[62] bells in their turn. At this moment, Juchort, the postman, from across the field, was waving a small blue, white and red flag, and shouting: "*Es acabat ! Es acabat!*" (It's over! It's over!).[63]

In Heurs, a village in the Marne department, inhabitants were far from being surprised, remembered René Pignart. [He was eleven years old at the time]. His brother, Robert, a prisoner who had been repatriated just the day before, had announced the war would end any time now. The news had been gossiped widely so that when bells started to ring, no one was surprised. In no time, farmers had their ploughmen back home. Nobody worked on this afternoon, whether in the fields or at school. On the following Sunday, the church was packed for a mass in memory of the twenty-one local men[64] who would never return – the price of victory. At Talus-Saint-Prix, another village in the marshes of Saint-Gond,[65] Mrs Domenichini,[66*] [eleven-and-a-half at the time], has recalled that whilst she was watching over the cattle, she heard the pealing of the bells of the surrounding villages and saw at the foot of the hill a small train decked with French *tricolour* flags passing by. At midday, while she was driving the herd back home, she heard the Mayor had ordered the *garde-champêtre* to proclaim the war had ended. There, as in Rivesaltes,[67] and in many other places, this country policeman read out in public, between two bugle calls, the official message, concluding with declamatory cries of "Long live France! Long live the Republic!"

The relief was inexpressible. However, many Talus-Saint-Prix families were still living in anxiety as they had not received any news from their sons at the front. Others were in mourning, like that of the cartwright whose son's death had been learnt two days earlier. No celebration took place in this village, so, on 11 November 1918, the youngest sister who, like many other peasants' children, was in the fields in the morning, attended school in the afternoon.

Of the Rhône department, Victor Mercier, related of that day when he had been a nine year old schoolboy:[68]

> The weather was calm. There was an autumn mist, but rather foggy in the early morning. By ten or eleven o'clock, the schoolmaster told the pupils: 'the war is over, you may go back home'. Bells started pealing. I heard the bells of surrounding villages. The folk in this small village were apparently very surprised. At Saint-Symphorien d'Ozon, the neighbouring town, the Martinmas fair[69] had attracted people from throughout the vicinity and people here were generally embracing one another. A feeling of happiness founded in a deep relief was manifest everywhere. In one family the father had been mobilized since August 1914 and had not been home on leave for thirty two months.

Sometimes the news was not believed. Boisterous children were sometimes sent out of school as a disciplinary measure. One such, Jacques, lived next to the school with his mother. On 11 November, late in the morning, he was returning home when his mother shouted at him: "'What have you been doing this time?' – 'Nothing', he replied sheepishly, 'but the teacher told us we could go back home because the war is over' – 'You should have found some better excuse!' his mother angrily retorted. 'Lying is a very bad habit! Come here, I'll take you back to school and we'll see *what's what*!"[70*] However, on this occasion, the boy's story proved true.

In Bordeaux, the military hospital's walking-wounded went into the city to take part in the rejoicing but one soldier, Maurice, "was a double amputee of the legs, so his friends carried him up to the *Girondins* monument.[71] After stopping at several cafés, they were in no state to bring him back, so Maurice had to drag himself back on the pavement across a town *en fête*".[72]

As for French losses, the newspaper, *Le Journal de Die et de la Drôme*, emphasized their place in the current jubilation: "May inconsolable people, wherever they may be, be comforted. In spite of this rejoicing, the dead did not fall into oblivion, neither our own dead nor our Allies's dead since we owe them everything, Liberty in particular".[73*] Roland Dorgelès, the novelist, who was to write "*Croix de Bois*", was thought insane when he cried out:

"Long live the dead!" as he was caught up in the unbridled display at Place de l'Opéra. No doubt demonstrations of joy were excessive but it could not be other than difficult to balance the joy of victory with an awareness that it was achieved by losses within the families of those greeting the end of the war.

The newspapers of course could be expected to be reflective upon the war newly ended: "After more than four years of a terrible war, the civilized world can breathe again", *Le Pays de France* stated. "When the Armistice was signed, that is on the 1561st day of war, our valiant troops, with the assistance of our brave allies, had almost totally reconquered France. On the morning of the 11th of November 1918, only a very narrow strip of our land was still remaining in the Boche's hands". While *L'Illustration* gave a dispassionate version of the facts in the 16–23 November issue, the local and regional press reacted more vehemently. *La Dépêche d'Eure et Loir*[74] and *Le Pays de France*, took up the theme of the enemy's barbarity: "The Boche had just shown new evidence of their own barbarism and stupidity. Whereas the Armistice they had insistently requested had already been signed and cease-fire was expected at any time, they kept on bombarding Mézières and Charleville with gas shells though they had only just ordered the evacuation of both cities and 22,000 civilians were still left behind".[75] However, the most dominant theme in the newspaper was the anthem, *La Marseillaise*. *Le Républicain du Gard*, reported on 19 November that at the opera house in Nîmes, the management had organized special entertainment after the usual performance. "Mr Angel fervently sang *La Marseillaise*. In order that the setting was worthy of the singer and the purpose of the performance, the painting representing Rouget de Lisle singing La Marseillaise at Strasbourg city hall, was put on the stage. Then, the apotheosis: the scenery parted to reveal, illuminated by Bengal lights, the figure of the Republic, holding the French flag".[76]

In France, some celebrated victory, others the end of the war, each in his or her own way. In smart districts, Clemenceau and Foch were warmly toasted whereas, in taverns, people indulging in pints of beer and glasses of wine shouted repeatedly: "Another one the Boche won't have!" No doubt *Madelon* was much more cheered with toasts and other songs away from the war zone than it was near the front where there was an amazing absence of the noise of guns but, it has to be said, there was the same old food and drink – rabbit, swedes and *ersatz* coffee without sugar. Moreover, poilus did not even have their quarter of red wine to celebrate the Armistice!

In Paris, "at Rue Royale, fashionable restaurants had their windows protected by the police against the flow of diners ... Wine waiters kept on uncorking bottle after bottle and, as customers encouraged them to share their champagne, they were increasingly unsteady on their feet".[77] Famous people were there, of course, but in Montparnasse bars as well as on the *grands boulevards*, people of all sorts were celebrating.

Eugène Lefebvre, a young inhabitant of Lille who had been evacuated by the Germans at the end of 1917 to the Malmédy-Stavelot region and who had come back to France in September 1918, had now found accommodation near Orléans. He remembered cadets dancing a sarabande in the neighbouring military camp as well as the boisterous exuberance of American soldiers in Orléans, normally a rather quiet city.[78*] However, according to a well-known saying, *dura lex sed lex*, rejoicing had to have limits. The Police Superintendent of Nîmes reminded the public that, according to a local regulation dated 10 July, 1836, selling and lighting fireworks, firecrackers, rockets, etc. was forbidden in public places on national holidays. As a matter of fact, the *Journal du Midi* reported that window panes were broken, a man injured and a hundred-franc coat[79] burnt.

On that night, while the splendidly good-looking Marthe Chenal, "draped in a flag and with an Alsatian headdress on",[80] was singing *La Marseillaise* on the steps of Paris Opéra, others, like the French poet, Paul Léautaud, was mourning in silence the death of a dear friend or relative killed in action or carried off by Spanish influenza, as in the case of Guillaume Appolinaire.[81]

Of Saint-Hippolyte-du-Fort, Marcel Barral remembered: "Bells started ringing in the afternoon: the war was over! Out! Out! Pupils ran out of school into Lamouroux's shop ... they bought all kinds of firecrackers and rockets". While the rejoicing was going on, a boy was left forlorn: "you are all happy. Your father is to come back, but mine is dead".[82]

At about three o'clock in the afternoon, bells were pealing everywhere in France. Didier Baudillon, then six years old, still remembers it but knew that his father, Pierre Baudillon, a soldier of the *35ème* de la Coloniale, would not be back, nor would ninety-six other men of the village of Vix-en-Vendée.[83*]

Of French prisoners in Germany on 11 November 1918, somewhere in Bavaria, Théophile Barès [also known as Etienne], a prisoner since 1914, was obviously surprised when Hans, a young German, respectfully greeted him: "Bonjour Etienne" on the morning of 13 November. 'What was up?' he wondered. Of course, the French prisoner knew the mischievous boy, now a teenager, who used to shout when he saw him: "*Paris kaput! Paris kaput!*". However, Hans had grown up now and would not indulge in the same tricks, after all he now drove a horse and carriage. Something new had happened. It was the farmer's wife who informed Etienne the war was over and he would soon be able to go back to France. The Armistice was signed! The war was over! It was such a joy! Prisoners ran to spread the news. They gathered their belongings ... and so did Etienne who didn't forget the small bird and the lanterns of the first Christmas he had spent in captivity and which he had kept and treasured. He also secretly promised himself that he would give the bird to his first child for he could, at last, marry Alice, his home village cobbler's daughter.[84]

Some prisoners had mixed feelings about their liberation. For example, one man, a native of the Pyrénées,[85] had been sent to a farm in Pomerania. There, the old man whose ancestor had been a soldier in Napoléon's army could speak a few words of French. Ties of friendship had developed to bind them together so that he came home late, after the winter of 1919. For others, private dramas added to national misfortunes. They knew their homes would be empty or full of new-born children. A Radiguet-like scenario![86]

A phrase common to so many soldiers' letters of the time was: "I am alive!" "At least I've come through; my bacon is saved. I can't really credit it. By the skin of my teeth I've made it and that's the important point ... so a kiss to fate and hurrah!"[87*]

Lieutenant de Franclieu of the *88ème* R.I. wrote to his mother two days after the Armistice while his regiment was stationed in Guise after they had crossed the Hindenburg line: "At the 88th, the Armistice has been welcomed with great satisfaction but calmly because there are no civilians or shops for miles so we couldn't toast our victory. Moreover, we're all exhausted and would rather rest than rejoice".[88*]

The soldier Roux wrote a postcard to his eight year old daughter: "At last, it's over. Who could have imagined it would have lasted so long. When are we to come back? Nobody knows, nobody tells us anything. All we know is that we're sick of it. But I'm happy for it's over for good. I'm looking forward to the great day when I don't need this scrap of paper to send you my kisses".[89*]

Yet, some men did not ask questions or write with impatient longing. They just jotted down notes like: "From the 28th of October, I'm on leave. The Armistice is signed on November 11th. I'll be back at the battery in Chaintrix [in the Marne]".[90] Others, whether optimistic or pessimistic, wondered: "When you see the conditions of the Armistice, I tell you the enemy won't be

xii A cartoon from the magazine *La Vague*, of 14 November 1918, shows the soldier returning to his wife and child, ploughing starting once again, and the weapons of war being destroyed, while the light and warmth of peace shine down on town and country. (via Allain Bernède) a danger to us for a long time". Or: "It's incredible what we imposed on them. Those fellows won't be a menace for a while now". Or, conversely, as a Colonel wrote: "What armistice? What peace guarantees have we got? Before rejoicing, we'd better know whether we'll be rewarded for our sacrifices".[91]

For these men who had endured the war for so long, their joy was coloured by a feeling of resignation even if the occasion stimulated high-flown sentiments: "The war to end all wars! Die for your country!" as Nobécourt[92] was to write later. For men in November 1918, "we beat 'em!" was enough.

To return to Paris; immediately before the Senate as well as the *Chambre des Députés*, Clemenceau reaffirmed the theme of "France, one and indivisible", born as a result of the 1789 French Revolution and with, "Alsace and Lorraine at last restored, ... the work of our dead ... Thanks to them! They shall never fall into oblivion, and, if given the power, I shall create a commemorative day in their honour".[93] The myths of the poilu as a national hero and that of Alsace-Lorraine were being created and enshrined for commemoration on this eleventh of November. A Deputy, Chéron, was frantically applauded when he read the text of the protestation made before the National Assembly at Bordeaux in 1871 by representatives of the French provinces lost in the Franco-Prussian war.

In Alsace-Lorraine, on 11 October, Philippe Husser[94] was already writing: "Victory is complete, our enemy is rejoicing ... Alsace-Lorraine is going to get autonomy ... Provided it is not too late. It seems Wilson has made some proposals to the French".[95] As a matter of fact, the word armistice only appeared in the Alsatian teacher's diary on 2 November: "the conditions of the Armistice are not yet known. However, it seems the Allies require territories which have been occupied and Alsace-Lorraine to be handed over ... In the cities, people are happy to be French again though in the countryside in particular, many reservations are expressed".[96]

From Friday 8 November, it was clear a page in history had been turned when the Reichsbank closed down in Mulhouse. On Saturday, rumours of an armistice were spreading and, on the following night, there were many demonstrations. On Sunday morning, it was even said that people who had acquired a bad reputation during the occupation were being harassed and there was a tense situation when soldiers' councils were set up. However, while local authorities were asking the population to keep cool, three-coloured cockades were appearing for the first time.

On Monday, 11 November, Husser recorded:

> The Armistice starts as from 11 o'clock. There is no more black-out. All kinds of goods that previously could not be seen now appear in shop windows. Prices are already going down. Out of forty-nine pupils, thirty-one are here. They behave correctly and have come without a cockade. All reminders of the war have been taken off the walls of the classroom ... The special war benefit (660 and 350 marks for each daughter)[97] has been paid in municipal bonds. Two friends of mine, of German origin[97] ... asked for retirement benefits. The conditions of the Armistice have been published. They are more severe than anyone feared though they were accepted. The

> German defeat is total; Germany is ruined and is completely at the mercy of her conquerors. After such sacrifices, there was nothing else we could expect.[99]

On the next day, Husser wrote: "on the front, we can see blue, white and red flares rising in the sky. Scenes of fraternization are developing".[100]

Meanwhile, the occupation regime was in its death-throes, removal vans were slinking away, German administration closing down and soldiers were packing or selling off cheaply their possessions and equipment. Others were preparing to adapt to a new future.

In Mulhouse, a delegation arrived at the French camp to ask that the city's security be safeguarded as soon as possible. On 15 November, the newspaper, *Landeszeitung*, printed its first article in French: "On the eve of our liberation ... And, when, within a few hours, we shall have the pleasure of greeting our brothers from France, they will know that their brothers in Alsace-Lorraine, separated from them for forty-seven years, have faithfully kept them in their hearts!"[101]

On 17 November, French troops arrived in Mulhouse. The city bells were pealing and people were shouting: "Long live France" and "Long live Alsace". However, Husser recorded:

> many soldiers look tired and remain unconcerned whereas almost all passers-by are wearing a three-coloured cockade, even those who, a few hours before, were still displaying their *Verdienstkreutz*.[102] Amongst troops and cars, girls in traditional Alsatian dress were following the parade. Other sorts of girls were endeavouring to be noticed by soldiers ... [103]

Husser added his belief that they were lamenting that they could not speak French. Anti-German graffiti appeared, native Germans and compromised Alsatians were threatened. In the afternoon of 22 November, General Castelnau arrived in Colmar. "On his chest, many decorations were glittering: grand croix de la Légion d'Honneur, Médaille Militaire, Croix de Guerre, Médaille des Vétérans de 1870".[104] He was welcomed by the Mayor, Doctor Lehmann. On the façade of the city hall the 1871 original inscription *Hôtel de Ville* was displayed anew. France was taking up her responsibilities in a region again French. French newspapers such as *Le Petit Parisien* or *Le Journal* were published again. Supplies were on the increase and so were the witch-hunts. Not surprisingly, opportunists seized their chance. Administrative blunders arising from political mistakes were frequent.[105] *Laissez-passers* were required again and Alsatian soldiers returning home were arrested for their identity to be checked. In early December, the French border was closed because of the Bolshevik threat. "Mulhouse is safeguarded by Negroes. The city is preparing to welcome the President. Two thousands pupils are to sing *La Marseillaise*"[106] was Philippe Husser's description of the changed circumstances.

In all this we should not forget the issue of French national thanksgiving. The *Journal de Nîmes*,[107] issued on 15 November, reported its hope that, "the *Te Deum* will be followed by our national anthem, *La Marseillaise*. For our priests, pastors and rabbis were singing *La Marseillaise* when going into battle and many of them sacrificed their lives as the price of the final triumph of our immortal *Patrie*". On the same day, Clemenceau, who was in Lille on a visit, accepted the invitation for the *Te Deum* to be celebrated there the next day.[108] However, as Monsignor Amette, the Archbishop of Paris, was sending the State's highest authorities invitations to attend a "thanksgiving *Te Deum* for the victory of France and her Allies"[109] in Notre-Dame, Marshal Joffre had to send an apologetic letter of reply stating that unfortunately the Constitution precluded his attendance.[110]

However, on 19 November, General Pétain[111] attended the *Te Deum* celebrated in Metz by Monsignor Pelt,[112] Vicar-General, [also a native of Lorraine], together with the whole cathedral chapter. Pétain also attended the one in Strasbourg on 25 November, still swathed in his blue cape, with no apparent decorations, standing straight and obviously moved.

France was indeed showing herself to be a strange country. On Sunday 17 November, the first Sunday after war had ended, *Te Deums* were celebrated everywhere at the front[113] and in the rear, all in an atmosphere of general fervour, although the Church and the State in France had been separated since 1905.

The end of the war brought classically together the concept of victory and its cost. Though bells were pealing and people were singing *La Madelon de la Victoire*,[114] the French knew that huge numbers [in fact over two million] were physically or mentally wounded, or worse, they would never come back. Madame Edmée de la Grandière wrote: "All the young men of our family had died ... all my mother's friends were widowed, except one ... I have to say that, after 1915–1916, we were no longer so directly concerned by the war".[115*]

After a few exhilarating hours, the country simply got on with work. "Demonstrations gave rise to no incidents. Workers of the chemicals factory, who had been granted a day off, have quietly resumed work" the Salingres [Gard] station master wrote.[116] A reaction set in later on, when trade-unions claimed, in early December, a seat at the peace conference. However, at this stage, the response of workers to disputes was patchy. If, in the mining region of Alès, the C.G.T.[117] were to lead 70% of miners into a strike, only 40% of such workers went on strike in Rochebelle and a demonstration in Alès gathered no more than 700 people.[118]

After the extraordinary experience of the Great War, people's feelings of course varied but, overall, many remained reserved rather than excessively demonstrative. R.G. Nobécourt wrote in *La Onzième Heure*:[119] "One finds it amazing to be still there, with both one's legs and arms. We embrace each other, just like kids. And many of us cry". "It's a miracle. To come back from where I was, what extraordinary luck! Me ... why me?" "You see that, we haven't died". On the 1561st day of war, France was like the little girl in Abel Faivre's cartoon;[120] she was wondering: "Does Papa know we've won the war?"

Endnotes

(*) . Indicates that the information was collected on the occasion of an historical investigation directed by the author of this chapter among a panel of French Mayors and Associations between July and October 1997).

1 Assigned to the G.Q.G. (Grand Quartier Général) from 23 November 1915, after he had been wounded, Jean de Pierrefeu was in charge of writing the official daily Communiqué.

2 Jean de Pierrefeu, *G.Q.G., secteur 1*, *L'édition française illustrée*, vol. II, Paris, 1920, p. 235.

3 Nobecourt R.G., *L'année du 11 novembre*, Robert Laffont, Paris, 1968, p. 22.

4 Maréchal Foch, Mémoires pour servir l'histoire de la guerre 1914–1918, Paris, Plon, vol.II, 1931, p. 289.

5 "L'année 1918, Les derniers mois de la guerre, l'armistice du 11 novembre", in *Les Cahiers de l'Histoire*, no. 80, issued November 1968, p. 114.

6 After Gustave Babin in *L'Illustration*, issued 16–23 November 1918, p. 464.

7 Quoted by Louis Cadras, in *Les Cahiers de l'Histoire*, issued November , p. 106.

8 Pétain, Commander-in-Chief of the French armies, Haig, Commander-in-Chief of the British Expeditionary Force, Pershing, in command of the American Expeditionary Corps, Degoutte, Major-General in the Belgian Army and Commander-in-Chief of the Flanders task force (a group set up from 19 September).

9 Maréchal Foch, *op. cit.*, p. 291.

10 Nobecourt R.G., *op. cit.*, p. 362.

11 Jérôme Carcopino, *Souvenirs de la guerre en Orient*, Avant-propos, Hachette, Paris 1970, p. 9.

12 The only witness, apart from the members of the delegation, was General Mordacq, head of Clemenceau's military cabinet.

13 After Marie-Jeanne Viel in *L'Armistice du 11 novembre 1918, Le Roman Vrai de la IIIème et de la IVème République*, col. Bouquins, Robert Laffont, vol.1, 1991, p. 1214.

14 Marie-Jeanne Viel, *op. cit.*, p. 1223.

15 Paul Constant's account in *L'Almanach du Combattant*, Durassié, 1968, p. 58.

16 Lieutenant André Bonneval's account in *L'Almanach du combattant*, Durassié, 1968, pp. 51–53.

17 Maréchal Foch, *op. cit.*, p. 319.

18 We've screwed 'em up!

19 Soldiers, mischievous as they are, had tacked choruses to their tastes on prescribed calls.

20 Albert Bruner's account in *L'Almanach du Combattant*, Durassié, 1968, pp. 53–54.

21 A very popular song during the French Revolution. NDT: "Marching to victory lifts the barrier…".

22 André Bonneval, *op. cit.*, pp. 51–53. ["it's over … it's really over."]

23 C. Larchevesque's account (class 1899) in *L'Almanach du Combattant*, Durassié, 1968, pp. 55–56.

24 Nobecourt R.G., *op. cit.*, p. 56.

25 An account collected by Bernard Piccoli, city of Malissard, Drôme.

26 Since, on 18 October, a subscription to national defence had been launched and celebrations of the liberation of cities in northern France and in Belgium had been organized, guns, machine-guns and aircraft seized from the enemy were

assembled between the Arc de Triomphe, the Place de la Concorde and the Tuileries pond.

27 "In May, as a sales attendant puts it, they were queueing to buy trunks". After Nobecourt R.G., *op.cit.*, p. 56.

28 A very popular song among soldiers during the war. It was written in Paris in 1914.

29 Quoted by Lieutenant-Colonel Mabille du Chesne, in *Revue historique de l'Armée*, no. 4, 1968, p. 118.

30 *Journaux de marches et opérations*, set up by ministry's directive dated 5 December, 1874. According to 1892 regulations, they were to be anonymously held by a Lieutenant-Colonel and written by NCOs. The aim was to record "with no blanks or blots" the chronology of daily events. Out of a hundred documents analysed (at regimental level and below from 62 divisions over the front and rear lines), more than 50% make no particular reference on 11 November 1918, 25% mention the Armistice and less than 20% give some brief information. Service historique de l'Armée de Terre, Vincennes, shelf-mark 26N 501 to 26N 1252.

31 Service historique de l'Armée de Terre, Vincennes, ref. 26N 888.

32 Service historique de l'Armée de Terre, Vincennes, ref. 26N 717, booklet no. 15.

33 *Revue historique de l'Armée*, no. 4, 1968, p. 177.

34 André Bonneval, *op cit.*, pp. 51–53.

35 He was appointed Lieutenant in 1939 and was killed in action during the Battle of the Somme on 24 May 1940, in the service of his country.

36 Quoted by Colonel Rives in *Un légionnaire guinéen*, Lieutenant Moriba Doumbia, in *La Cohorte*, a publication of the Légion d'Honneur mutual aid association, no. 142, May 1997, p. 14.

37 Pétain had been staying in Chantilly for two days.

38 Pierrefeu, *op.cit.*, p. 239.

39 Pierrefeu, *op.cit.*, in annex.

40 André Ducasse's account, in *L'Almanach du Combattant*, éd. Durassié, 1968, pp. 50–51.

41 (*) An account of Second Lieutenant Norbert Cassagne's nephew, Général Jacques Cassagne.

42 (*) Sergeant Mangelle had once been wounded on the French front near Valmy. He fought for the Resistance during the Second World War and survived the ordeal of deportation. An account by his son, Général André Mangelle and his son-in-law, Colonel Saint-Martin.

43 Five battleships, 5 cruisers, 15 destroyers, 8 torpedo boats, 14 submarines, 5 gunboats or chasers, 70 trawlers almost half of which were sunk on minesweeping missions.

44 Philippe Masson in *Histoire militaire de la France*, PUF, Vol. 3, 1992, p. 243.

45 The major part of the French navy being in the Mediterranean, they were particularly affected by the Mudros Armistice signed on 30 October and Villa-Guisti Armistice signed on 3 November.

46 Philippe Masson in *Histoire militaire de la France*, PUF, Vol. 3, 1992, p. 249.

47 In *L'Illustration*, p. 448, issue no. 3949 dated 9 November 1918.

48 Quoted by Félix-Paul Codaccioni, in *Histoire d'une métropole, Lille, Roubaix, Tourcoing*, Editor: Louis Trénard, Private Publication, 1977, p. 404.

49 (*) Bernard Piccoli, *op.cit.*

50 Chartres local archives, extracted from the minutes of the Local Council, meeting of 11 November 1918, ref. H9 390.

51 *La Dépêche d'Eure et Loir*, issue no. 5465 dated November 1918, Chartres local archives, ref. H9 390.
52 *Le Républicain du Gard*, issue of 13 November 1918.
53 A song of the French Revolution boasting the "indomitable glory of the Republic".
54 (*) Bernard Piccoli, *op.cit.*
55 Foch's birthplace in the department of Haute-Garonne.
56 According to Henri Cossira, in *L'Illustration*, issued 16–23 November, 1918, p. 470.
57 (*) An account collected by Major Pierre Marcel.
58 (*) Extracted from an anonymous manuscript entitled "Mémoires d'un vieux brancardier-musicien des 29ème et 59ème B.C.P.", 175 hand-written pages, held by Association Mondement.
59 A railway station in the eastern suburb of Paris.
60 The author was living in the hamlet of Marsangis, the neighbouring town was Romilly-sur-Seine, in the Aube department.
61 (*) Bernard Piccoli, *op.cit.*
62 An account collected by Jean Dessans, Mayor of Bernède, department of Gers.
63 At that time, French countrymen in the main spoke regional dialects. Here, Gascon, a dialect of French spoken in Gascony. It belongs to the Langue d'Oc family.
64 Out of one hundred and thirty who went off to war.
65 The Saint-Gond swamps are located in the south of the Marne department, beyond Epernay. It is the place where the Xth army commanded by Foch went into action in September 1914.
66 (*) An account collected by her son, Lieutenant-Colonel Domenichini, President of the Association Mondement.
67 Joffre's birthplace in the department of Pyrénées Orientales, in *L'Illustration*, issued 16–23 November, 1918, p. 478.
68 An account collected by A. Sardat, the Mayor of Corbas, Rhône department.
69 A regional fair traditionally held on 11 November, the feast of St. Martin.
70 (*) An anonymous account collected by *La Sabretache*.
71 A monument erected to the glory of the so-called deputies during the French Revolution. They had their heads cut off during the 'Terror' in 1793. This monument is located more than ten kilometres from the hospital.
72 *Revue historique de l'Armée*, issue no. 4, 1968, p. 176.
73 (*) Bernard Piccoli, *op.cit.*
74 *La Dépêche d'Eure et Loir*, issue no. 5465 dated November 1918, Chartres local archives, ref. H9 390.
75 *Le Pays de France*, 5th year, issue no. 214 dated Thursday 21 November 1918, section "La semaine militaire" (Military week), Association Mondement's archives.
76 *Le Républicain du Gard*, issued on 19 November, 1918.
77 Marie-Jeanne Viel, *op.cit.*, p. 1223.
78 (*) An account collected by *La Sabretache*.
79 i.e. worth a four-year subscription period to the newspaper.
80 Marie-Jeanne Viel, *op.cit.*, p. 1222.
81 Second Lieutenant in the *96ème* R.I., Appolinaire, seriously injured in the head in a trench near Berry-au-Bac, died in Paris on 9 November 1918.
82 Interview with Marcel Barral (18 September, 1994) in Abbal (Odon), *Il était une*

fois Saint-Hippolyte-du-Fort et la Grande Guerre,. Lib. Coubron, 1994, pp. 98–99.

83 (*) An account collected by Pierre Drapeau, Deputy-Mayor of the village of Vix-en-Vendée.

84 The author's family remembers Théophile Barès alias Etienne was mobilized in Marmande in the Lot-et-Garonne department; he was caught prisoner near Rouvres in the Oise department in October 1914 during the fighting known as the 'race to the sea'; since that date, he had been working in a farm in Bavaria. It must be added that his wedding had been scheduled for the Summer of 1914, but on the day he was caught prisoner, the soldier Etienne had been in action for the first time and in fact had to take the place of his platoon corporal who had been killed.

85 (*) His son's account.

86 Raymond Radiguet was born in 1903. He supposedly seduced the wife of Gaston Serrier, an officer in the *151ème* R.I. This adventure, published by Grasset Publishers in 1923 under the title *Le Diable au Corps* (The Devil in the Flesh) was a best-seller. The author sent a copy to Roland Dorgelès bearing this provocative inscription: "To Mr Dorgelès who wrote the only book about the war – this war I looked at from the other side. Signed: Raymond Radiguet". One theme of Dorgelès' novel, *Les Croix de Bois*, was a soldier's betrayal by his wife. Dorgelès' mistress deserted him in the war for a Belgian.

87 (*) Bernard Piccoli, *op.cit.*

88 (*) Account and family documentation communicated by Général de Franclieu, Lieutenant de Franclieu's son.

89 (*) Bernard Piccoli, *op.cit.*

90 Service historique de l'Armée de Terre, Vincennes, shelf-mark 26N 664.

91 *Revue Historique de l'Armée*, issue no. 4, 1968, p. 174.

92 His work "Les fantassins du Chemin des Dames" received an award from the Académie Française.

93 *La Dépêche d'Eure-et-Loir*, issue no. 5465 dated 12 November 1918.

94 As from the beginning of the war, Philippe Husser kept a sort of diary. Born in 1862 near Colmar, he was a protestant, of German culture as well as a liberal. His diary was written in German up to 4 December 1918 and published by one of his grandsons in 1992. This document presents the split identity of the Alsatian population.

95 Philippe Husser, *Journal d'un instituteur 1914–1951*, Livre de Poche, 1992, p. 141.

96 Philippe Husser, *op.cit.*, p. 147.

97 Husser was married and had three daughters.

98 After 1871, many German immigrants settled down in Alsatian cities.

99 The author is referring to press articles published on the same day describing reprehensible actions by German troops in occupied territories.

100 Philippe Husser, *op.cit.*, p. 150.

101 Philippe Husser, *op.cit.*, p. 153.

102 The German Cross of merit.

103 Philippe Husser, *op.cit.*, pp. 157–158.

104 *L'Illustration*, issued on 30 November 1918, p. 500.

105 In the judgement of the French victors, a plebiscite was certainly not necessary. The 1918 victory simply overturned the consequences of the Treaty of Frankfurt dated 10 May, 1871.

106 Philippe Husser *op.cit.*, p. 165.

107 *Journal de Nîmes*, Gard Department archives. Ref. 357–150–135.
108 According to the newspaper *Le Gaulois*; the information was echoed in the following day's issue of *Le Journal de Nîmes*.
109 The last *Te Deum* to be celebrated in Notre-Dame in Paris was in 1859 to honour the victories of the army in Italy.
110 Joffre's operation journal, 1916–1919, document presented by Guy Pédroncini, *Service Historique de L'Armée de Terre*, Vincennes, 1990, p. 291.
111 It was in Metz on 8 December, that Raymond Poincaré, Président of the French Republic, gave Pétain his Marshal's baton.
112 Monsignor Brensler, the German bishop, had left.
113 Service historique de l'Armée de Terre, Vincennes. 26N 717.
114 New words were added to the song *La Madelon*, in particular the now famous: "*On les a eus!*".
115 (*) An account collected by Association Mondement.
116 His report to the Prefect of the department of Gard dated 16 November, Gard department archives, ref. 1 M 878.
117 Confédération Générale du Travail, a French Trade Union.
118 According to the Gard Prefect's report to the government, Gard department archives, ref. CA 148.
119 *Revue historique de l'Armée*, issue no. 4, 1968, p. 173.
120 It was published in *L'Echo de Paris* issued on 2 November and in *L'Illustration* no. 3950–3951 issued on 16–23 November 1918, p. 486.

Chapter Seven

Belgium: A Soldier's Tale

Mark Derez

On 28 September 1918, the final offensive began in Flanders.[1] That same day *L'Histoire du soldat* had its premiere in Lausanne. A mimed narration about a soldier marching homeward, it had a libretto by C.F. Ramuz and music by Igor Stravinsky.[2] This poetic fairy tale on the theme of *le retour du soldat* was a great success. The work was written for a small ensemble with a mobile mini-theatre which was intended to travel from village to village. The day after the opening, however, the players went down with influenza; the Spanish flu was raging in Europe, and the play never did go on tour.

Ten years later 'The Soldier's Tale' was on the programme of the *Vlaamsche Volkstooneel* (Flemish Folk-Theatre). Its productions of authentic popular theatre were no less appreciated by the Flemish rank and file than by the elite of Brussels and Paris. This ensemble had its roots in *Fronttooneel* (The Theatre at the Front) which had performed for Flemish soldiers during the war. In September 1918 it had put on Oscar Wilde's *The Importance of Being Earnest*, though some questioned whether such English humour might not be considerably over the heads of Flemish foot-soldiers.

On 4 July 1929, the *Vlaamsche Volkstooneel* gave a command performance of this soldier's tale for King Albert and Queen Elisabeth in the theatre of the royal residence at Laken.[3] This was the high point of a triumphal tour which had taken *L'Histoire du soldat* to the villages and towns of *la Flandre profonde* where the war years were still fresh in people's minds. The play owed its success to the familiarity of its basic theme, embodied in the little recurrent marching-song:

Down a hot and dusty road
Tramps a soldier with his load.
Ten days' leave he has to spend,
Will his journey never end?
He's been marching all the day,
Happy now he's home to stay.[4]

The Belgian soldiers of course had leave. They went to Paris or to London – if they had money – or to Lourdes in the Pyrenees for a pilgrimage, but never home. Home was occupied by the Germans. News from the home front only arrived in dribs and drabs. The English had only to 'pop over the Channel for afternoon tea and back again', so to speak. The Belgians, however, had no chance of passing through the German lines to reach home and hearth, though it was sometimes only a stone's throw away. This was demoralizing. To be home: that could only happen after the offensive to liberate Belgium, but then it would be for good. "To fight with body and soul, with no thought of the cost, that was their wish and their passion. To thrust through iron and steel, to worm their way through flames and poison gas, to get it over with and go home, go home, go home".[5]

That was how the Flemish writer of popular novels, Edward Vermeulen, put it in *Piot*, his war novel published in 1923. His short, repeated 'go home' (Dutch '*naar huis*') was no less staccato than Stravinsky's music. The *piot* of the title means 'foot soldier'. Almost seventy percent of these infantrymen were Flemish, they formed the core of the front line soldiers and they could hardly be restrained now that the home front was within reach.[6] Survival gave them impetus.[7] In another novel, we read: "Never had life been so dear to us as now, standing here facing home. We can smell the stables; all we want now is to eat, to sleep and rest, and then to charge again, until we are there".[8]

That was literature. A more sober account is that given by a veteran from the village of Voormezele, Jules Leroy, born in 1894:

> We started out from Gijverinkhove. At a country tavern, 'The Empty Pocket' (*de Blote Zak*) between St. Julien and Langemark. I knew that area well. It was the night of the 27th to the 28th of September '18. The evening of the 27th they gave us wine and spirits, as much as we wanted. I said to some of the boys: 'Don't drink that. You're going to have to hold out, because it's going to be tough'. It was about eleven when the lieutenant went from man to man. The King himself would give the signal to attack. There was a big cannon in the park of the Thibault de Boesinges' castle in Boezinge. The third cannon shot was the signal for the attack. We charged and we went through the first line in no time, and the second line too. Things didn't get hot until the plateau of Passchendaele-Westrozebeke. There the resistance was fierce and there a lot of our men fell.[9]

From other witnesses, too, we learn how successfully the offensive began.. A cannon rumbling at half past two in the morning, flares that 'set the night on fire'[10] and a king who gave the sign to attack. The weather was familiar: the rain came down in buckets, but spirits were not dampened. All the rebelliousness and the apathy of the past year were gone. "The energy, discipline, courage, patriotism, and the self-sacrifice of all classes are beyond all praise", wrote the British ambassador.[11] It was as though the enthusiasm of 1914 had returned.

King Albert was in fact the only head of state involved in the war who actually took personal command, in conformity with the constitution of Belgium which gave the king authority over the armed forces in time of war.[12] His rather literal interpretation of the constitution was contested by the head of his government, but the King stood firm. Belgium may well have imported its dynasty from England, taking along the British parliamentary system in the same sweep, but Albert's predecessors on the throne of Belgium had kept a much tighter grip on politics than their cousin Victoria in England.[13] In contrast to his crowned colleagues King George V and Kaiser Wilhelm, Albert, the supreme commander of his troops, stood at the peak of his power.[14] His kingdom, however, had been reduced to a sodden polder in a far corner of the country, *un bout de sol dans l'infini du monde*, as the national bard, Emile Verhaeren, put it. The government had been transferred to far-off Le Havre. Parliament was dispersed across the Front and in the diaspora. The King, standing alone with his army at the River Yser, represented the beating heart of the nation. Out of this constitutional background grew the *image d'Epinal* of the King-Knight which would later be devised by Hergé, the Belgian national cartoon-strip artist *par excellence*, best known as the creator of Tintin.[15]

This king without a country was his own master during the war.[16] Up to now he had refused to be harnessed to the Allied High Command. As long as he had his own army, hope of the recovery of his country remained alive. In November 1914, Albert had resolutely rejected Foch's proposal to incorporate the Belgian army into the French forces at a ratio of one Belgian brigade per French division.[17] He refused to take part in dubious offensives, and cautiously kept his soldiers in the trenches behind the Yser, where they were more likely to perish from mud, cold and homesickness than from the enemy's shells. For the final offensive, he did allow the reins to pass out of his hands because the outcome seemed certain, and thus the survival of his army and his country would be guaranteed.

In the event, King Albert nevertheless found himself under the wing of Marshal Foch, the general co-ordinator of the offensive that was to spread out from Ypres (Ieper) to the River Meuse. He himself came to stand at the head of the *Groupe d'Armées de Flandre* which was intended to liberate the area between the coast and the River Lys (Leie) and thrust through toward Brussels.[18] These Allied military forces consisted of the Belgian troops, General Plumer's Second British Army and two French corps under the command of General Degoutte, who was immediately installed as Albert's Chief of Staff. In that way the King would be accorded all honour, and could enter city after city at the head of his men. Above all, the King wished to prevent ruthless foreign troops from retaking his country by fire and sword. Finally, he aimed to oust the Allied troops as soon as possible after the war was over. Just before the offensive commenced, one more message from the King was read to the troops: "Side by side, and supported by the heroic English and French forces, the task is now yours to drive out the conquerors who have oppressed your brothers for more than four years".[19] As an extra incentive, the soldiers were promised that those who came from the liberated villages would be given leave to visit their families and friends.

Now that they were at last heading homeward, the Belgian troops appeared to be at the top of their form. The army, having numbered 117,000 mobilized men at the beginning of the war, had been reduced to a mere 52,000 after the

Battle of the Yser in October 1914. In the subsequent years of trench warfare, the army had been thoroughly reformed and replenished by, among others, some 30,000 volunteers from the occupied territory who had escaped from Belgium via the Dutch frontier and then managed to return to re-enlist. By 1918 the army numbered 167,000 men. It had eleven hundred guns and as many as a hundred aeroplanes. Everyone and everything was mobilized for the offensive, even a company comprised of artists.

On that 28 September the attack began with eight Belgian infantry divisions in the front line. By evening, Houthulst Wood, which the Germans had transformed into a huge machine-gun nest, had been cleaned out, and the main enemy position, the *Flandern II Stellung*, had been breached in parts. Four British divisions had struck between Ypres and the River Lys. The Salient was retaken by sundown.

The next day the Belgians made almost no progress. Their artillery was bogged down in mud. On the thirtieth their advance brought them just in front of the second German line, the *Flandern I Stellung* at Roulers (Roeselare). Here their progress stopped. From now on the offensive would encounter frequent interruptions caused by the condition of the terrain and the Belgian command's lack of organization, for they were not prepared for the dynamics of an offensive movement. The fireworks of 28 September threatened to end in a splutter. The troops had lost their drive and their initial fighting spirit seemed to have evaporated. At the end of this first phase there were already 15,000 men who had been put out of action. The King decided that his army had made a sufficiently great sacrifice.[20] For the second and third phases the Belgian forces were only to provide protection for the flanks of the French troops which would have to take over the main task.

From now on the Belgian troops would be deployed as support for offensives directed more to the east. On 14 October the offensive was restarted with the decisive battle of Tielt, the town where the Kaiser had made vain preparations for his entry into Ypres. The Belgians deviated toward Ostend and Bruges, whereas the English went into action around Courtrai (Kortrijk). On 31 October, following vigorous German resistance at the River Lys, the third phase of the offensive was begun, moving in the direction of the River Escaut (Schelde).

The fighting was still heavy on the strongly defended hills between the Escaut and the Lys ('between the mountains' wrote Pastor Slosse from Rumbeke in the flat land of Flanders).[21] The British occupied the banks of the Escaut as far as Oudenaarde which was captured by an American division of the French army on 2 November. With an eye toward making a breakthrough south of Valenciennes, Marshal Foch asked King Albert to allow the Second British Army to be put back under the command of Field Marshal Sir Douglas Haig as from 5 November. From now, the attack became a floodtide that the Germans were unable to stop. Ever since 2 November, persistent rumours were circulating about negotiations and an approaching armistice. Early on the morning of 11 November, Ghent was taken without a blow being struck. The front now stretched from Ghent to Mons and then on to Sedan and Verdun.

Front Belge, le 18 octobre 1918.

CHANSON DU FRONT BELGE

DERNIÈRE OFFENSIVE

Air : « Légende des Flots Bleus »

I

Elle se déclanche et la brute prussienne
A notre bord
S'est élancée et jette à perdre haleine
Ses cris de mort.
Partout, partout, l'incendie ravage
Chaque maison
Et le canon qui tonne en bruit d'orage
Dans l'horizon
Parfois le bruit s'éteind, — pour reprendre plus loin
Ici dans les fossés les patrouilles se glissent
En bravant le danger ; Ah ! Dieu, les balles sifflent.
Allez ! Voyez !
Aux appels des blessés de sa note plaintive,
Un clairon répondait au lointain sur la rive

REFRAIN

Ils sont tombés sur les bords de l'Yser,
Héros obscurs dont le pays est fier,
Pour le Drapeau, méprisant les revers
Ils sont tombés sur les bords de l'Yser.

II

La nuit survint éclairant la bataille,
On lutte encore
Et les canons semant feu et mitraille
Sèment la mort.
Ces pauvres Belges tiennent et montent de garde
Dans cet enfer !
Les maudits boches sous la lune blafarde
Passent l'Yser !
Et d'un terrible assaut leur tombent sur le dos.
Plus d'un dans la tranchée jette.it le cri d'alarme
Mais la Prusse enragée se moque de leurs larmes,
Allons ! Français !
Et notre armée enfin dans un ciel qui se rose
Voit les soldats de France en une Apothéose

REFRAIN

Si votre sang a coulé dans l'Yser,
Héros obscurs dont le pays est fier !
Le monde entier veut venger vos revers
Ils sont tombés sur les bords de l'Yser.

III

Reveille toi, noble peuple énergique
Auprès de toi
Avec la France la vaillante Amérique
Est au combat.
Depuis quatre ans, ton Roi et ton Armée
Avec honneur
Ont su braver cette brute enragée
L'envahisseur
Bientôt dans tes faubourgs, sonnera le retour
Ecoute ces canons, dans tes plaines qui s'avancent
Au lointain tes clairons sonnent ta délivrance
Ta liberté !
Et l'aigle germanique, devant Coq Gaulois
Doit fuir la Belgique, pauvre martyr du droit.

REFRAIN

Petits enfants de la Démocratie
Souvenez-vous ! souvenez-vous ! longtemps
Que l'Allemagne et puis l'Autriche-Hongrie
Furent bourreaux de vos bons vieux parents.

Aux Armées de la Victoire

PAR

LÉOPOLD LAGASSE

Ex. 3e Chasseurs à Pied Z. 206 G. A. T. A. Armée Belge. *En campagne.*

xiii A Belgian Army war song, dated 18 October 1918, for use on the occasion of the final offensive: *Et l'aigle germanique, devant Coq Gaulois / Doit fuir la Belgique, pauvre martyr du droit*. Note that the French are welcomed, but the British are ignored! This document is hand printed on the reverse of a disused staff map. (University Library, Leuven)

It seemed that during the last days of the occupation the Germans did their utmost to leave behind the most disagreeable impression. In the summer, school-children had to pick stinging nettles to serve as raw material for the German textile industry. In late September they had to gather acorns, beech-nuts and chestnuts. The requisitions and confiscations which had been sucking the country dry, especially since September 1916, were intensified: wagons, carts, hay, straw, potatoes and eventually cattle. All horses had to be handed over. The Belgian dray-horse was an object of national pride. Its breeding was now endangered. Things went so far that the municipal hearse of Assebroek near Bruges had to be drawn by a dairy cow.[22] But cows too were impounded. Finally, it was the able-bodied men who were summoned, often for digging new trenches.

In Izegem the local *Kommandant* locked several hundred men in the church. They were pushed in through the main entrance. The Germans had seized the keys of the church, but forgot to lock the sacristy door. In one door, and out the other, for when the *Kommandant* went into the church to cast an eye on his catch, there was none.[23] The tale was one to glory in. It mirrored the image the Flemish liked to project during the war: at the front a sort of *Soldier Schwejk*, but above all an *Eulenspiegel* in occupied territory, roguish and clever, poking fun at tyranny. This was passive resistance with humour as its weapon. The image was one of folk who were almost childishly innocent, with "roguishness as a sign of their spirit of independence".[24]

The *Eulenspiegel* spirit, however, was a poor match for blatant terror. German reprisals were often fierce, with manhunts, house searches, hostage-taking, deportations. In the last days of the war they forbade the populace to flee, and then bombarded the villages with gas-shells. English lorries brought hundreds of victims with burnt lungs to Courtrai, where they slowly died of suffocation.[25] Most despicable were the hidden mines, true time-bombs, which were often set to explode many days after the Germans had withdrawn. '*Leur cadeau d'adieux*', the newspaper *Le Soir* called them.[26] In Courtrai, German officers revealed the location of the bombs as Article 8 of the Armistice Treaty required. They had been hidden everywhere, even in the cinema, where one was due to explode on 6 December, St. Nicholas Day![27] Thus a catastrophe was avoided here, whereas, in the railway stations of Brussels, entire trains were blown up on 19 November.

Did all this lead to a craving for revenge? In the national press, yes, to some extent, but it remained within bounds. *La Libre Belgique*, which had appeared clandestinely during the war, claimed that one German had been lynched in Bruges, though no other source confirmed this. It also printed what purported to be the sentiment of the people, "*Nos soldats doivent aller en Allemagne, ces maudits nous ont trop fait souffrir*".[28] Was that the *vox populi* speaking? In any event it was not the view of King Albert, who was more than reluctant to see his troops marching off to the Rhine. Nor was it shared by the Catholics, the Socialists or the radical Flemish, the '*Flamingants*'. All of them had their own brand of anti-militarism built into their ideology, and this was a potent antidote to the revanchism of certain French-speaking groups which had developed an unusually chauvinistic type of Belgian nationalism during the war. This did not prevent booing and hissing at German prisoners of war. Moreover the Mayor of Bruges found it prudent to caution against the maltreating of defenceless Germans, calling it "cowardliness unworthy of Flemings".[29]

Reprisals then, were hardly a problem. The Flemish writer, Stijn Streuvels, had already foreseen this in September when, on the eve of the liberation, he took the pulse of his people. Streuvels, the baker-author who was nominated for the Nobel Prize several times, brought the West-Flemish countryside to life in his stories. He knew its inhabitants inside-out:

> Some find it good that the Entente will win, but they want to see the fighting done over there [at the old Front area – translator's note], so they can sit here quietly and see what happens. The others – the fanatics, that is – can't wait to leave everything, let their farms go to ruin and go with the victorious French to Germany and there ... take their revenge – those are just words however – *meanwhile they sit quietly by the hearth and smoke their pipes*. (Italics added)[30]

Streuvels had not foreseen that the forward movement of the front and the change of command would entail such heavy going. Many of his contemporaries, too, had expected not a military campaign, but a triumphal entry. The human mind cannot adequately picture evils to come. Streuvels, it seems, imagined the liberation as a kind of changing of the guard. The reality was not nearly as orderly. In the villages it began with the town crier announcing that all were to stay indoors and not to leave town, or just the opposite: forced evacuation, which was often an excuse for plundering by both the occupier and just as frequently the fellow-countrymen who stayed behind – old standards went unheeded everywhere. In and round the villages, then, there was plundering and arson ("We won't leave a thing for the Tommies!"[31]), and burnt-out windmills reminiscent of the hells of Hieronymus Bosch. Church towers and other land-marks were blown up at the last minute ("The work of beasts". "No it isn't! Dogs only make water against the tower; Germans knock it down".[32]) Orphans roamed about ("We make our hearts into stones"[33]). On top of all this, Allied bombardments (bombs, mortar-shells and to boot, leaflets saying "Whatever you do, don't flee"). There was shelling from both sides and, finally, fighting in the streets. All this lasted many days which the inhabitants spent in their cellars, praying earnestly. The English stormed into Streuvels' house on 26 October with bayonets at the ready. Half an hour earlier there had been a German standing in the stairs to the cellar.

In the long run, everyone fled. Upon entering a place, the British would call out, "*Allemands parti?*". What the liberators intended as a question, "Have the Germans left?", the villagers understood as a command: "*Alleman parti!*", i.e. "Everybody out!", and most of them hurried away.[34] Fleeing had become second nature. It was part of the war psychosis. Even sedentary Streuvels ultimately left his village, Ingooigem, which lay in the area between the Escaut and the Lys – the military theatre of the last phase of the liberation offensive:

> We went together with relatives from Avelgem, on a farm wagon with all our household things and the mothers and the children, pulled by a steer which had never been in a yoke, with two men to keep the animal in line and a third with the whip and a prod to push him along. It was a comic spectacle, to see this animal zigzagging right and left down the road, that long road from Courtrai to Mouscron. *But nobody felt like laughing*. (Italics added)[35]

Nor had those Flemish soldiers, who found themselves in their native region in the first days of the offensive, cause for rejoicing, for this area had been in the line of fire all through the war. Stravinsky's soldier, approaching his native village with its familiar bell-tower, found that he had been gone not three days, but three years. The Flemish soldier, who had thought he would be away for four months and back by Christmas of '14, was away for four years. There was nothing to be seen of the church or its tower; where his family's cottage had stood, not a stone was left standing. Soldier Achiel Mylle, who was given a few hours to visit his parents' farm in Zonnebeke, found their iron plough, rusty but undamaged, leaning against the remains of a thorn-bush.[36] There was nothing else. Nothing remained of the cosy countryside of his childhood – a landscape that English travellers had already begun praising in the eighteenth century as the Garden of Europe.

The English now proposed that the Ypres Salient be left as it was, and that it be made into an extensive place of pilgrimage for British and Empire veterans, as at Verdun for the French. Memorialists, in their writings, say that the destruction was indescribable. They did their utmost, nevertheless, with metaphors and exhaustive descriptions, borrowing from the Apocalypse and Dante's infernal circles. Limiting ourselves to the realm of the organic, we find rats as big as cats gnawing at the corpses, and swarms of birds feasting on the worms at the same source.

Nor did the returning soldiers have words for what they found. Kamiel Masschelein, upon entering Beselare on the traditional *kermesse* Sunday, 6 October 1918, called upon a non-existent French-German bastard term which he then twisted into a Flemish neologism: the unutterable *verdimmolierung*, a word with the punch of a curse and the compressed aggression of an expressionist war-painting.[37] With difficulty he located the spot where his house must have stood. When asked by a British officer if he were looking for something he had lost there, he explained that his regiment having advanced to Moorslede, he was given permission to visit his village and his parents' house. He then left his birthplace and, while retracing his steps, his thoughts went to his family in France. Let them stay where they were!

The refugees themselves, of course, were filled with an irresistible desire to return home. No one believed the rumours about the poisoned earth and the unexploded shells – not until, that is, a few of them went reconnoitring and came straight back totally demoralized.

Everyone, in those last weeks, wanted to escape from that sinister battlefield zone and return to the inhabited world. The soldiers of the Allied armies, however, were stuck there for more than a fortnight until the *Flandern I-Stellung* was taken on 14 October. On that day, Roulers (Roeselare) became the first Belgian city to be liberated, but most of the inhabitants had been evacuated on 30 September. The French – real live Frenchmen, the chronicler exulted – were delighted to come upon a few citizens, at last, to whom they could announce that liberation was at hand.[38] An anti-climax came a few weeks later, in spite of the presence of the King and the French President. These lofty dignitaries avoided the town hall and ignored the local notables. This made a poor impression on the few bystanders, and the reception ceremony was devoid of warmth and cheering. The war, it seemed, had become a matter of paying homage, and it was the military leaders who swept up all the honours for themselves. This was a dissonant note in the otherwise fairly unison singing of the Flemish 'choir'.

On 15 October, the German army collapsed behind Roulers. The men of the *Groupe d'Armées de Flandres* had advanced seventeen kilometres. The zone of destruction was behind them at last. Standing on the heights of Staden and Hooglede, the so-called Ridge of Flanders, they saw a different landscape, an untouched world, so inviting with its trees and houses and homely shutters. Yet this too was no-man's-land with not a soul to be seen in the villages. The Belgians proceeded through a landscape where everything seemed to be abandoned. Moving east, they arrived in Torhout. The first inhabitants they met thought they were English. The Germans had told them there were no Belgian soldiers left.[39] Torhout was the first town along their way which had not been evacuated. They made their entry on 19 October under the command of General Grendell.[40] This was no triumphal entry. The soldiers were as moved as the people. Here at last they felt that they were well and truly the liberators of their own people. This emotion was also present when, somewhat later, the King came to the town. A grave silence reigned. The West-Flemish are reputed to be serious and dour. The King too wore a serious expression and the men respectfully removed their caps. It was clear to see that everyone felt the solemnity of the moment. Only then did the jubilation begin.

A poem in graceful script was placed in many a window. The rhyme was in doggerel (French *lion* rhyming with 'Wilson', *guerre* with *bière*) and the phrasing bordered on the hilarious, but it was in deadly earnest. The self-appointed poet of victory had done his best to distribute praise to all the Allied armies. He admonished his readers never again to drink Rhenish wine, and to imbibe only champagne and Bordeaux after the war. This was revanchism in its mildest form, the rhyming worker transforming his famished homeland into a land of plenty, the 'Land of Cockaigne' rhyming with 'champagne'. And this was written at the moment when people began to venture out of their cellars to carve up the carcasses of horses which had died of their wounds. Soon thereafter Allied rations began to find their way to some of the inhabitants. They had their first tinned fruit, their first corned-beef. This was the taste of victory.

It appeared that the liberation would bring back normalcy. Expectations were high, yet they were not totally gainsaid, by post-war statistics. The government's food policy saw to it that the food-supply problem was solved by the end of 1919. By 1921 the daily intake of calories was 6% higher than it had been in 1910.[41] It was not the working classes' consumption of champagne that had increased, but their intake of beef, eggs, milk and butter. As we shall see, this too was related to the Armistice. The versifying worker from Torhout was a visionary.

On the same day, 19 October, troops entered Tielt. Though people were hoping there that they would be liberated by 'our boys', it was the French who occupied a virtually empty city. They were equally welcome. At ten-thirty the bells began to ring – the bells of triumph. Soon thereafter, the tone changed, a bell tolling for the dead; it continued the whole afternoon. There were at least thirty casualties – mourning in juxtaposition with euphoria. The French were received with bouquets of flowers and bottles of wine, with apples, pears and boxes of matches. To his great surprise a General from Bordeaux was treated to a *Château d'Yquem*! *"Rien n'est trop bon pour nos libérateurs!"*[42] In the provinces the good burghers had cautiously hidden their better bottles when the war started. In Brussels such bottles had been seeing active duty throughout the war, out of pure patriotism, if we are to believe another Frenchman, the novelist Henri Bordeaux, given to praising the pleasures of bourgeois sociability. The point was to keep these precious bottles from falling into the hands of the forces of occupation.[43]

In the meantime the Belgians tramped on towards the coast, the *Flandern Küste* which the German navy had now abandoned. The villages along the way were festooned with flags, in all haste, and the local brass bands reassembled, proud of having hidden their horns from the Germans. Friends and relatives were pulled out of the ranks of the soldiers, or even dragged off their horses, the better to be kissed. Many took brief leave, with or without permission, to see their father or mother. It is noteworthy that some soldiers first stopped by at friends' houses, or even spent the night there before going home, as though they dreaded the emotion that was to come.[44] The cherished son who had left his childhood behind and survived the war, mature at an early age, his illusions gone, now hesitated to meet his parents, prematurely aged by hunger and the sufferings of war. For most, however, it was quite natural to be back home. Octaaf de Vreese told how his brother came back to the Tielt area:

> On the Sunday after October 14th I saw a young soldier with backpack, rifle and grenades at his belt coming up the road. I was at the front door. Mother, I cried, Achiel is back! Father and mother were silent. Achiel told us about the muddy trenches when his hands and feet were so soaked they were like mother's hands after spending the whole day at the wash-tub.[45]

The author of this chapter is reminded of another Achiel: my own great-uncle, Achiel Vereecke, born in 1890, whose return home was immortalized in a long poem dedicated to my great-grandparents. It tells of the sorrows of the war that are soon forgotten:

als die motto stille viel	when the motorcycle stopped
en gij samen hebt gekreten,	and together you cried out,
'Ach, waarachtig 't is Achiel!'	"Ah, it truly is Achilles!"

As children we found that extremely moving. In translation, rhythm and rhyme are gone, but that is no great loss. Even in the original, literary merit had to retreat before sentimental impact. Sentimental? Did not Graham Greene maintain that what we label as sentimental actually has to do with a feeling we ourselves do not share? This scene of the unexpected return must have been repeated hundreds of times over, and was later endlessly recounted at family gatherings, in a kaleidoscope of variations, but always with the same action and an echo of the same emotions. Here was yet another *image d'Epinal*, that would imprint itself on the collective memory.

In Bruges 'our boys' were welcomed by the Victory Bell.[46] The belfry tower flew pennants plundered from the German ships. The Victory Bell had not rung since 4 March 1918, when the Germans had renamed it the *Friedensglocke* on the occasion of the Peace of Brest-Litovsk. For Belgians, that had been a rather misleading announcement of peace, since it rang in the German spring offensive on the Western Front. Now, on 19 October, as its peals once again resounded over the city, the Victory Bell was truly announcing peace.

The ringing of bells was a new sound in the air. During the occupation the tolling of bells had been forbidden. Now people could not get enough of the welcome sound. They were, after all, the people "from the Land of Chimes" as Hardy fondly imagined in his "Sonnet on the Belgian Expatriation".[47] On Sunday 27 October, the only entry in the diary of Octaaf de Zutter from Tielt was: "the carillon started ringing yesterday".[48] In Courtrai on 25 October, the market square was packed with people who had come out to hear a concert played by British military bands – the Belgian national anthem on bagpipes, so to speak.[49] The city responded with '*God Save the King*' played on the carillon, a fitting tribute to the country that had taken all those tinkling Belgian carillons and made of them a national trademark. As early as 1914, Edward Elgar composed *Carillon*, a piece for full orchestra to accompany a song by the celebrated Belgian poet, Emile Cammaerts.[50] The work was hugely successful in its own right, notwithstanding its being performed by Lala Vandervelde, the wife of the Belgian Minister, who graced the music-hall stage from time to time.[51] It was a piece composed especially for Belgium, with an appeal to continue the resistance. And continue they did. Here, for once, reality and propaganda coincided. After four years of war the stereotype image of a brave people choosing freedom instead of comfort and security had remained more or less intact. One thing, however, remained unfulfilled. The *entrée triomphale à Berlin* of Cammaerts' text never did take place.

Courtrai was presented with the banner of the 12th Irish Rifles, the regiment that had liberated the city, and in return it bestowed honorary citizenship upon Lieutenant-General H.E. Watts, commander of the British XIX Corps. All in all, there was much ceremonial bowing back and forth. The governing of the city was in the hands of an English Town Major of Belgian descent, bearing the markedly Flemish name, Van Cutsem.[52] An ancestor had married an English girl after Waterloo, and a fluke of fortune had now brought him back. Such are the workings of history, weaving generations and nations together, from the Battle of Waterloo to the Battle of Courtrai.

Yet Albion remained just a fraction foreign even here, close to the Ypres Salient which was practically an overseas territory, and even in Courtrai, which had harboured a colony of English flax merchants from times immemorial. There was the language barrier, and there were differences of mentality. The Belgians had never paid much attention to rules and regulations; now they soon found that British administration was no more tolerant in this respect than the German. Streuvels, who had been so impressed by the German officers at the beginning of the war, now reacted crustily to the billeting of English soldiers. He scribbled in his diary, "Anglo-Saxons no connections through 700 (years) – estranged".[53] This was not over-friendly on the part of a writer whose *Deutschfreundlichkeit* is still a matter of discussion today.

Love of Albion was not universal and it was also recent. Only a decade earlier, the British diplomat, Sir Roger Casement, had been King Leopold II's *bête noire* during the 'Congo question'. Moreover, Casement was an advocate of Irish nationalism, with which the Flemish intellectuals were in sympathy, as previously they had been with the Boers of South Africa. That it was just the British who were now the great liberators, required on the part of some, a certain mental adjustment.

The French did better, especially in the towns where, at least since Napoleon's time, a French-speaking upper-class held the reins. The French revelled in this positive discrimination, perhaps too visibly. At the ceremonial entry into Bruges even the Belgian flag had been forgotten, and the King reviewed the troops against a backdrop consisting only of the French banner of the *Groupe d'Armées de Flandres*.[54] Chief of Staff Degoutte did claim to feel a bit ill at ease with regard to the British officers.[55] This notwithstanding, the General undoubtedly had his own political agenda. It was he who urged that Foch follow a policy of continued presence. In effect, this was anchored by a French-Belgian military agreement which was chummily arranged in January 1920 in – of all places – Ypres. It would soon become the cause of much bad feeling in Flanders.[56]

The final offensive was costly for Belgium, all things considered: 253 officers and 3,085 soldiers were killed or died of wounds, and 750 officers and 25,973 soldiers were wounded.[57] Jules Leroy, the veteran whose words we have already heard, reported that he had a photo of his company, taken by Lieutenant Dewinde a few days before the great offensive. The Lieutenant had said, "We are marked men. I know that some of us will die. This will be a souvenir for those who survive".[58] Twenty-seven made it. Certainly more than forty did not come through. Lieutenant Jules Dewinde himself (born in

Merchtem in 1893) was one of those who died, the very first day, on 28 September 1918. Along the Poelkapelle-Westrozebeke road there is a monument to him.[59]

To die at the moment of victory has become a literary commonplace, a tried recipe that has retained all its savour. In Remarque's *Im Westen nichts neues*, the young Paul Bäumer dies on 11 November 1918. It also happened that the Armistice came too early, as in the best-known of the Flemish 11 November stories, *Zijn derde ster* (His Third Star) by Jozef Simons, for this prevents the hero, a lieutenant, from being made a captain and thus receiving his third star.[60] In most cases, however, peace came too late, as in the anti-war novel *De miskenden* (The Unsung) in which a stretcher-bearer who has risked his life daily, dies on the last day of the war.[61] Nor were poets such as Wilfred Owen of the bitter *Dulce et decorum est (pro patria mori)* the only ones who died during the last week of hostilities.[62] Marie Beck (1893–1973), from Westouter in the hinterland of the Salient, told what happened during the celebrations on 11 November: "We had our own party, just us, Belgian refugees, family. For once we ate well. In the evening a *dépêche* came. The party was over. Hector Fever was shot five minutes before eleven, out of his trench too soon. You can just imagine, he was the brother of Daniel who was married to our Germaine..."[63]

This is the *Lefebvre Hector † 11.11.18* of the inscription on the war memorial in Westouter. Of course he was not the only one. Jules Leroy tells a similar story of joy and sorrow on the day of the Armistice: "Our joy was incredible. But we couldn't drink. We didn't have anything. And after the first wave of joy was past, the sadness came because boys had died even on the last day. Up to the last minute. My cousin died on the eleventh of November at eleven o'clock. On the Baasrode bridge".[64]

Yet life demanded to be lived. In infantryman Jules Leroy's tale there is also what we might expect, a sense of relief:

> We had got as far as the canal of Landegem. I was sitting in the cellar of a doctor's house. I had never had a better rifle position. I could see the whole canal. Suddenly there were bugles blowing on all sides. What was that? It came so unexpectedly. First we were mystified. Finally, off to the side of us, we saw Germans coming out. Unbelievable! It was over! *We had survived!* We had been saying, 'That'll stay with us for the rest of our lives. The misery, the hunger, the cold and people dying before our eyes every day. More than four years long.' And then it was suddenly over. (Italics added)

Edmond van Lede (1896–1965), one of the many seminarians from Bruges, served as a stretcher-bearer and thus was close to the enlisted men. He sketched the atmosphere at the front thus:

> *Enfin, nous pouvons respirer à l'aise, nous pouvons enfin dormir en toute sécurité; nous reposer sur les deux oreilles comme on dit. L'armistice est signée: Hip, Hip, Hip, Hourra. Ah, vous décrire l'enthousiasme qui animait*

les hommes, hier au soir, lorsqu'ils apprirent la nouvelle, m'est impossible; la joie ressenti par tous est indescriptible.[65]

At the front near Ghent, the soldiers reacted indifferently, not seeing what the difference could be between armistice and peace. They wouldn't have to start again, would they? Was this a reason for stopping their card-game? Most of them dropped exhausted on their straw-filled sleeping-bags. Some of them were so war-worn that they could not even imagine what peace could be! "*Où sont nos rêves des boues de l'Yser, quand nous parlions de cette paix qui, fatalement, devait 'éclater' un jour? Les plus sobres songeaient à quelque entrée triomphale, tandis que d'autres goûtaient d'avance les plaisirs d'une noce carabinée à faire pâlir l'éclat des baccanales!*"[66]

The Belgians abroad were more enthusiastic. Achille van Acker was a working-class youth from Bruges, a basket-maker by trade, pro-Flemish but not exactly Christian, a healthy lad who freely visited bars and bawdy-houses though never, by his own statement, going upstairs; he would also be one day a Socialist Prime Minister. In November 1918 he was working in a munitions factory in Le Havre:

> And suddenly, like a bomb, the news reached us that the years of slaughter were at an end. In our barracks the garde-chambre pulled out his accordion. The brigadier put aside his dignity just this once and started marching brandishing a broom that took the place of a victory banner.
>
> Singing, the whole group followed him, first inside and then outside the barracks, where we joined the other groups. Some of the non-commissioned officers wanted to stop this, bring back order. It was as though they did not exist.
>
> In the days that followed, everything was turned upside-down. Everybody was trying to get in touch with the occupied territory and get news of their families. Everybody had only one thought: to be back in the fatherland as soon as possible.[67]

Marie Beck, whom we have already encountered, was also in France, one of the 325,000 Belgian refugees there:[68]

> The people came together in the market square. What a lot of people. A real carnival. You can imagine. Four years of misery. Over! The French and many Belgian refugees. The cafes were more than full. They earned a pretty penny that day. And the singing!
>
> There was somebody who got up and stood on a chest. He had an accordion. 'La Guerre est finie' he sang. You know, 'La Guerre est finie – ie – ie'. I was thinking, that fellow doesn't know what he's singing about. Marie has seen the war. It's miserable. Nothing fine about it. 'Nos héros ... ' Our heroes. Yes, there were heroes, people who did what they had to do, and were brave and cold and hungry. But no heroes like in that song. Nobody takes risks like that for glory. 'Nos héros ...' Heroes. People who, like everybody, felt oppressed by such horrible things. In no time at all, everybody was singing along. A lot of people got drunk that day.[69]

Maria Govaere, born in Ardooie in 1896, was one of the 162,000 Belgians who fled to England:[70]

> There is a lot you forget, but the eleventh of November '18, that I'll never forget. I was in Birmingham, where I worked in a munitions factory. At eleven in the morning the sirens began to hoot, ... and all the church-bells started ringing. Everybody was mad with joy. My legs were trembling beneath me. In the evening the buses that were all lit up drove round the city. They carried no passengers, only a huge photo of the King and Queen. That evening I drank whisky for the first time. The English really had a party.[71]

In the liberated part of Belgium, the Armistice wrought no such effects. In the hard-hit Lys region, where many victims of gas attacks lay in agony, the British already began shouting "War is over!" in the late evening of 10 November, the blaring of their bugles announcing the Armistice.[72] Streuvels no longer cared. He found the bugles annoying.[73] In Aartrijke, a village near Bruges, 11 November came and went unnoticed. School was once again open. Jules Depuydt, a brewer's son, noted in his war journal, that the municipality was registering the men born between 1894 and 1899 "to make little soldiers of them, for sure", he wryly remarked. On 12 November the news came trickling through, and our village chronicler observed the reaction: "The people here should have been wild with joy, but they weren't. All these great happenings, one right after the other, have made people lose their balance. Nobody can believe that it's true. It's more like a dream!"[74]

By the next day the villagers had recovered, and they were unanimous in their intent to make full use of the freedom they had regained. With movement restrictions rendered obsolete, they ran back and forth and went on trips to their hearts' content. Many crossed the Yser to the region that had not been occupied to purchase all manner of things: cows, horses, petrol, bicycle tyres, coffee, soap. Jules Depuydt had someone bring back a young pig, having paid 165 francs for it – "that's the price of a fat hog!".

November the eleventh is also the feast-day of Saint Martin, the Roman centurion whose popularity in West Flanders rivals that of Saint Nicholas. He is the patron saint of countless churches there, the best-known being the cathedral of Ypres. The English architect, G. A. T. Middleton, considered that the cathedral, together with the Cloth Hall, formed the most beautiful complex of buildings in Europe, Westminster and the Houses of Parliament excepted, of course.[75] The English Town-Mayor now had a notice put up with the warning, "This is Holy Ground, no stone may be taken away". All that the Austrian writer Stefan Zweig saw there, were lumps of stone "like decayed teeth, black and rooted there, outlined against the sky".[76] Many came to look. Louise Parmentier from Dranouter (born in 1895), a working-class woman who may not have had an eye for monuments but who was not insensitive, naturally, to the sight of total destruction, refused to go and gawk. The thrills of disaster tourism were not for her; she preferred resignation. "'Been to Ypres to look?' people would often ask. I never went to look. We didn't need to go anywhere. We had enough of that right here. We weren't curious about going to look. It was all misery anyway. The people there were like us, and we like them".[77]

The Catholic priest, Cyriel Verschaeve, was curate in a village behind the Yser. He was the most renowned of the *petits vicaires*, those priests who spoke with more passion about Flanders than about Christ, or so his bishop maintained.[78] Verschaeve was not only the drama critic who commented on the *Fronttooneel*, the Flemish travelling theatre group at the Front; his rectory, situated a stone's throw from the King's headquarters, was the meeting-place throughout the war of young Flemish intellectuals in the army. Some of them had even refused to become officers so that they might stand closer by "their people". They started the Front Movement, which agitated for equal rights for Dutch-speakers in the army. Their motto was "Here is our blood; when – our rights?" The Front Movement was forced underground in 1917, resulting in its becoming more radical. In an open letter to the King it demanded a Flemish army along with a Walloon army.[79]

The King paid little attention to the Flemish lamentations, for they could endanger the discipline and the striking capacity of his army. The refusal to recognize Flemish rights quickly set the Front Movement on the path of Activism, the collaborating minority of Flemish radicals in the occupied territory.[80] An admixture of idealism and opportunism, Flemish Activists set up a Flemish university (1916) and Flemish self-government (1917) with the help of the Germans but without popular support. Verschaeve was no less radical. German help must be permitted if it helped the Flemish cause. It was in this spirit that, as late as March 1918, he had produced "The Flemish Nationalist's Catechism" in question-and-answer form, which was anonymously distributed among the troops.[81] The curate, who saw wartime as action time, was now left with nothing to do. A few days after the Armistice he complained that it had become so quiet behind the Yser. Peace meant that he would get to see his sister and his friends, but would peace bring a solution for Flanders?[82] Verschaeve may have seemed like an isolated shepherd in a God-forgotten parish, but in the long run the ideas of his catechism would not be without influence on some of his flock.

Emile Vandervelde, a Minister of the King and President of the Second International, though he was at the opposite end of the country, and at the opposite pole of the political spectrum, was nevertheless in the grip of the same melancholy.[83] When the war broke out, he was attached to the war cabinet in his capacity as a Crown Councillor with the title of Minister of State, and soon he would become one of the first socialist ministers in the history of Europe. In 1910, at the time of his first speech from the throne, the King had been welcomed by the socialists not with *Vive le Roi!*, but with the cry, *Vive le suffrage universel!* It was the same monarch who brought Vandervelde into the Crown Council. The promise of universal suffrage was made to Vandervelde when he actually became a full cabinet member in 1916, the same year that his British friend, Arthur Henderson, was taken into Lloyd George's cabinet.

This suited the King well. He had had enough of the Catholics who had been in power for thirty uninterrupted years. Moreover, he wished to integrate the workers in the country's social system under the sign of *l'union sacrée*. Two flies at one blow: this would demonstrate the impartiality of the Monarchy and would strengthen the unity of the populace in the face of the enemy.[84] Vandervelde personified the incorporation of socialism in the national state. During the entire war he shuttled between Le Havre and the Front. In 1917 he exerted himself on the Eastern Front to convince the Russians that above all they must fight to the very end, till the German empire fell. Now that the war was actually over, he found himself, like the curate, Verschaeve, in a black hole, so to speak. It was all over. An era in his life was past, and a feeling of emptiness came over him.[85] Yet there was another role awaiting him, and it would be the very type of socialism which he embodied that would garner the fruits of its loyalty to the nation.

A new period seemed to be at hand. Monarchies collapsed in Central Europe one after the other. Mutiny in the fleet at Kiel spread to other German cities. On 9 November 1918, the Republic was proclaimed in Berlin and the Kaiser fled to the Netherlands. That was front-page news. The papers noted that twenty-two German kings, princes, grand-dukes and dukes had lost their thrones, and that soldiers' and workers' councils were set up everywhere under the red banner. Behind all these tottering thrones lay the revolution in Russia, where the Tsar and his family had been executed in July. *L'exemple de Russie est plein de dangers*, King Albert had noted in his *carnets* in October 1917.[86] The fate of the Romanovs had not, in fact, particularly touched him. Many of his subjects, however, had placed their savings in tramways in Saint Petersburg or Odessa, and the Société Générale and Solvay saw their investments disappear like smoke.

The simple threat of social unrest was sufficient to invoke the spectre of Bolshevism from Warsaw to Lisbon. Even before the revolution had begun in Germany, the British military leadership had determined that the real danger would not be German but Bolshevik.[87] Now that the war between Wilson and Wilhelm II was over, the war between Wilson and Lenin could begin, so the papers predicted in Switzerland, where a general strike was in progress. The Belgian artist, Frans Masereel, was staying in Switzerland as a semi-deserter. He had just published in Geneva his first albums of woodcuts on the topic of the war (*Debout les morts* and *Les morts parlent*). As he and Stefan Zweig strolled through Zurich on Sunday, 10 November, they were in what seemed to be an occupied city. There were soldiers and machine-guns, and everywhere the good citizens were hoping that they would start shooting "at that pack of Bolshevists".[88] Nearer home, in that other neutral country, the Netherlands, the bourgeoisie was no less nervous, and here too the government made military preparations. On 10 November, workers held meetings in Rotterdam demanding votes for women and an eight-hour workday. In Parliament on the twelfth, Troelstra, leader of the Socialist Party, would allude to a possible take-over by the proletariat. There was reason to believe that the revolution would not stop at the German border, but would overflow into the un-

21. Sailors and Marines of the pre-dreadnought battleship *HMS Agamemnon* (the vessel aboard which the Turkish Armistice had been signed at Mudros on 31 October), in the Black Sea off Sebastopol, November 1918.
(W.T. Henson, Liddle Collection) (Chapters 4 -Britons Overseas & Chapter 17 - The Ottoman Empire)

22. A crowd gathers to hear the announcement of the Armistice in Europe outside the House of Assembly at Hamilton, Bermuda.
(Adm. Sir Morgan Singer, Liddle Collection) (Chapter 4 - Britons Overseas)

23. Lieutenant General Watts' XIX Corps, headed by a Belgian Army band, parade through the town of Courtrai in celebration of the Armistice, 13 November 1918.
(C.E. Townley, Liddle Collection) (Chapter 4 - Britons Overseas and Chapter 7 - Belgium)

24. A Victory Tea celebrating the end of the war. Cyril Street, Consett, November 1918
(Beamish - North of England Open Air Museum, 71898)
(Chapter 5 - Britons at Home)

25. A group of children dressed for victory celebrations outside the miners' cottages in Low Prudhoe Rows, Low Prudhoe [South Tyneside].
(Beamish - North of England Open Air Museum, 70341)
(Chapter 5 - Britons at Home)

26. The news is proclaimed from the Town Hall steps, Burnley, on the morning of 11 November 1918.
(By permission of Lancashire County Library. Burnley Division. Via W. Turner) (Chapter 5 - Britons at Home)

27. The bonfire constructed by Royal Engineers at Beacon Hill, Newark, to celebrate Armistice night.
(Newark Museums Service) (Chapter 5 - Britons at Home)

28. Wounded soldiers and female workers celebrate news of the Armistice at the Fairoak Dairy Produce Company, Eastleigh, Hants, on the morning of the eleventh.
(D.E. Williams, Liddle Collection)
(Chapter 5 - Britons at Home)

29. The Mayne family and their neighbours in Meanwood, Leeds, celebrate in their own way, posing outside their terraced house in a motley selection of mens' clothes borrowed for the occasion.
(Yorkshire Post Newspapers)
(Chapter 5 - Britons at Home)

30. Bunting decorates trawlers in the harbour at Dundee, 11 November 1918.
(S.J. Wallis, Liddle Collection) (Chapter 5 - Britons at Home)

31. Crowds by the dockside at Dundee - 11 November 1918.
(S.J. Wallis, Liddle Collection)
(Chapter 5 - Britons at Home)

32. Armistice Celebrations in Harrogate - high-spirited officers it seems.
(Liddle Collection)
(Chapter 5 - Britons at Home)

33. Wounded men feature prominently in this photograph taken in Knaresborough on 11 November. (Liddle Collection) (Chapter 5 - Britons at Home)

34. Soldiers in Norwich raise a cheer for HM the King on Armistice Day. (Liddle Collection) (Chapter 5 - Britons at Home)

35. Wounded soldiers at Netley hospital seem in imminent danger of causing themselves further injury as a result of these Armistice high-jinks.

(T.E. Hulbert, Liddle Collection)

(Chapter 5 - Britons at Home)

36. Signal flags are flown in celebration from the mast at RN Airship Station Howden, East Yorkshire. 11am 11 November 1918.

(S.J. Rosser, Liddle Collection) (Chapter 5 - Britons at Home)

37. Gunner Frederick Wall and his wife Daisy, photographed around 13 November 1918. They were married on Armistice Day, but this was to be their only 'wedding' photograph, as the official photographer had not arrived at the ceremony.

(D.E. Goodlet, Liddle collection)

(Chapter 5 - Britons at Home)

38. The Spoils of War: schoolboys look on as German field guns are put on show in the town square, Chipping Norton, in December 1918.

(R.L. Fudger, Liddle Collection) (Chapter 5 - Britons at Home)

39. Peace: crowds line the route of a procession as it passes along Lambeth Road, South-East London, marking the formal end of hostilities with the signing of the Treaty of Versailles in June 1919.

(A. Green, Liddle Collection) (Chapter 5 - Britons at Home)

conquered countries that were known precisely for the quiet respectability of their burghers.[89]

Revolution, it appeared, was at the door. Not only were the neighbours' chimneys ablaze, smouldering had already begun indoors. In Brussels, retreating German soldiers began to mutiny on that same Sunday, 10 November. The Belgian nationalist press was fearful of contamination from the German Spartacists who, it was said, got their inspiration from the Bolsheviks. A workers' and soldiers' council did, indeed, occupy the *Kommandantur*. Soldiers threw their weapons away or sold them to the Belgians. Officers were stunned to be disarmed by their own men and to have their badges of rank torn from their uniforms. They fled on foot or by motorcar. Soldiers stopped the cars, forced the officers out, took their sabres and got into the stolen vehicles. The Dutch envoy, Van Vollenhoven, saw some of the humiliated officers crying like children.[90] The most characteristic emotion during these days was one of bewilderment: the authorities were bewildered that they could so swiftly lose command, the insurgents that they could so easily acquire such unexpected power.[91] Even the revolutionaries were surprised by the revolution, and the bystanders were perplexed. Minister plenipotentiary Van Vollenhoven, *seigneur* of Cleverskerke, had to stand by and watch as the new men in power sat in deep armchairs in the majestic *Palais de la Nation*, seat of the Belgian Parliament, singing the 'Internationale' and drinking whisky and *chartreuse*.[92] In the afternoon a throng of soldiers, red flags flapping up ahead, marched along the boulevards, followed by people from Brussels who may have been curious, hangers-on or supporters – it was hard to say. Supporters filled with the spirit of fraternity – that is how they appeared in the account written by Karel van de Woestijne who was the Flemish correspondent in Brussels for the Dutch liberal newspaper, *Nieuwe Rotterdamsche Courant*:

> The orderly mass of people starts moving in the direction of the Exchange, growing all the time as soldiers join them on the way. The blood of the Brussels citizen runs cold. He thinks of that dreadful word: Bolshevism. But this word, does it not now mean liberation, our liberation, a liberation in spite of everything, and even without an armistice?[93]

Some observers nevertheless found it a bit strange to see inhabitants of Brussels cheering at the troops "who had shot at our boys only yesterday". Such was, indeed, the tone of things: not a shred of rebellion against the establishment, only a somewhat gratuitous, perhaps, sense of brotherhood in general. Van de Woestijne, who was not only a journalist but above all Flanders' greatest poet, gave his feelings free rein:

> The joy is uncontrollable; it goes gusting through the streets, spiralling up like a hurricane, then fading to the murmur of a summery sea in the quieter streets. The general feeling finds expression in the words of an old man of the people, walking arm-in-arm with a German. 'Why are you doing that?

It's dishonourable!' an incensed priest screams at him. 'Ah, milord, we're all of us poor bastards!' is his good-natured reply.[94]

On Monday, 11 November, *le lendemain de la fête*, Brussels felt the repercussions of the previous day's delirious Bolshevism. Herman Teirlinck, another Flemish man of letters, witnessed nervous German soldiers, machine-guns at the ready, clearing people out of the square in front of the North Station.[95] The actual facts of the matter are not known. Nor were things any clearer in Louvain (Leuven), where, on the night of 8/9 November, a train trimmed with red flags and on its way from Berlin to Brussels with insurgent soldiers, stopped.[96] Here too the mutineers exuberantly sought *rapprochement*. The populace, used as they were to the strict occupation rules, could hardly believe their eyes, and kept their distance. Only in a few working-class sections did the marchers find any encouragement. One could not be sure that revolutionary violence might inexplicably turn against the people. The Rector of the University feared a repetition of the horrors of August 1914 when the town was set on fire and citizens were executed as a reprisal for the actions of what the Germans presumed to be sharp-shooters.[97] Officers of the retreating German Sixth Army were convinced that the clergy had incited the people of Louvain to come up with a new plot against the Germans, and that this would be carried out as soon as the Armistice was signed. The ghost of 1914 was hovering in the background.[98] It was rumoured among the Germans that 500 rifles had been discovered in the house of the Mayor. The Jesuit Community was under surveillance by machine-gunners. On the evening of 11 November the soldiers' council was in favour of taking hostages as in 1914. Not until General Lübbert, who had been appointed the local commandant, offered to be a hostage himself, did the dangerous mood come to an end.

In Louvain as well as in Brussels, the Belgian socialists lay low. They had no truck with communists. The Walloon socialist, Jules Destrée, who had been a diplomat in Russia, deemed Lenin to be part Hun and part Mongol.[99] These social-democrats had no use whatever for either the Spartacists nor an operetta revolution like the Troelstra effort in Holland. They were hoping to cash in on their loyal war efforts and achieve a legal take-over of power using parliamentary methods. They had been agitating for a reform of the electoral system for more than thirty years, and it was in Louvain that five had died for this cause in 1902.

The first minister to arrive in the capital was Vandervelde, on 14 November. As recently as July 1914, in their *Maison du Peuple*, the socialists had proclaimed a war against war. Now their red roses had given way to red-yellow-and-black cockades. Vandervelde was home again. He was in radiant health. One of those present remarked that the *patron* clearly had not suffered from a shortage of potatoes. "So much the better for us" was his comrade's reply. "Their" minister had good news for them. The 1914 army of paupers had been reshaped into a true army of the people consisting of all sectors of society. This army had now come back, conscious of what it had acquired, of the right for which it had fought: the right to vote.[100]

Universal suffrage was on its way – one man, one vote without respect of wealth or education. That had already been decided, *en petit comité*, at a much higher level. This had occurred not in Victor Horta's renowned *Maison du Peuple*, that bastion of democracy and workers' palace in *Art nouveau* style, but in the Neo-Gothic castle of Loppem near Bruges, the fanciful product of the English architect, Edward Pugin, but above all the futile reflection of a class-society already threatened with extinction. There, on 11 November, King Albert received delegates from within the country, messengers of the new era.[101] One was a progressive liberal, Paul Emile Janson. He represented first of all the National Committee for Assistance and Food which had organized provisioning during the war and had formed a kind of shadow-government in the occupied territory. This was a powerful club of bankers and industrialists who wanted to start reconstructing the country's economy as soon as possible. Edward Anseele was an authentic socialist captain of industry who had brought into being a veritable opposition force consisting of co-operatives and socialist firms. Despite the co-operative fishing-fleet that he commanded in the 1920's, the 'Red Fleet', he was in fact the personification of 'beef-steak socialism', a distinctly reformist brand of socialism. The bankers and industrialists looked for dividends; the socialists wanted work; the King sought quiet, the re-establishment of order and social peace, and only the socialists could guarantee that. All were raring to go. Now more than ever, the final phrase of Zola's *L'Oeuvre* resounded: *Allons travailler!*[102] No finer consensus could be imagined. So it was, too, during the consultation. Anseele inquired familiarly of the King what time it was, for in Ghent they were still on German time that the occupier had imposed, and he added jovially: *Sire, je mets ma montre d'accord sur la vôtre. J'espère qu'elle le restera longtemps.*[103] Janson was unable to detect the least bit of insubordination.

The conservative forces claimed that the King had allowed himself to be duped by Anseele and Janson and, what was worse, that he had ceded to their threats. It was inconceivable that the Soldier-King should be found wanting in civic courage. Faced with the menace of a popular revolt, however, he had had to give in. Serious historians have tried to show how the Conference at Versailles was dominated by the fear of an escalation of the communist revolution, and that for this reason the eight-hour work-day was inserted into the Treaty.[104] In the present instance, however, we must incline to one of historiography's basic categories: chronology. The spectre of the October Revolution certainly did make its presence felt in Versailles' Hall of Mirrors, but that was in 1919. Whether it drifted about in the castle of Loppem in November 1918 is another matter. Painstaking research has revealed that this was a gothic novel, so to speak, originating in the brains of recalcitrant conservatives who, unable to read the signs of the times, persisted in viewing the war as a parenthesis, and who rationalized their loss of power by grasping at a ghost story.[105] In any event, at the end of 1918, everyone in the Allied countries was so inebriated by victory and by peace that wild tales of the revolution went without an audience.[106] Just how decisive was this intoxication with victory, will become evident in what follows.

The aura surrounding the King-Knight was almost blinding. His image was flawless.[107] The secret negotiations Albert had conducted with his German brother-in-law, unbeknownst to the government, had produced no results.[108] The people would not have believed this in any case. Likewise, the inhabitants of Bruges would not believe that the bombs that fell on them in 1918 were dropped, as the king had noticed, by British aircraft[109] The entire royal family was fantastically popular. At no time since then have they been able to bask in such undivided popular favour. Young Crown Prince Leopold, who had been somewhat of a troop mascot at the Yser, was now given the status of a national treasure. The Prince could not appear in public without being grasped to numerous bosoms so that he always came late for parades, *'avec des joues humides et dévorées'*.[110] The King-Knight, the Nurse-Queen and the Mascot-Prince were living legend. How could the socialists compete with that? The republic and class struggle were phrases fit for a preamble or a closing resolution, but they were in fact out of harmony with the reformist practices of a modern social-democracy.

The King could see for himself how popular he was when he entered Ostend, Bruges and Tournai.[111] Well and good, but that was in the provinces and the countryside. Yet even the reports issuing from Brussels were not that ominous. With regard to the German Spartacists, he received a note from his Chief of Cabinet reporting that he had been most politely received by the Soldiers' Council (*Soldatenrat*).[112] Its spokesman, Carl Einstein, author of expressionistic anti-novels, regretted the German invasion of Belgium, promising to see that the murderers of the English nurse and resistance fighter, Miss Cavell, would be punished and to set all the wrongs that had been done right, in the shortest possible time. A German in penitential garb: if that were the new Germany ... We know now that the illusion was not long-lasting. Einstein himself, fleeing from the Nazis in 1940, committed suicide.[113] This leftist German had not concealed his admiration for King Albert. One is reminded of that other German who, at about the same time, made a proposal that Albert be crowned Emperor of Germany.[114] Jaspar, the Catholic minister, sent the King a missive in which he correctly assessed the circumstances: *La situation politique actuelle est sérieuse sans être grave.*[115] As communications go, it was hardly alarming. The danger could be avoided if the government followed a clearly democratic course in consultation with the socialists.

That was precisely the intention of the King and the new cabinet. As early as 13 November, the day after Troelstra's abortive attempt at revolution in Holland, the King was already looking to get a new government off the ground. The actual formation took place on about the twenty-first, the day before the triumphal entry into Brussels. Henceforth the head of government would be called Prime Minister, following the British model.[116] Nor was that the main one among the changes. The Catholics were countered by a strong group of socialists and liberals. The Flemish were under-represented, and it was not the former ministers who had been in Le Havre who had a say, but those who had been members of the National Committee for Assistance. This allotment reflected the distribution of power and the policy options. The government felt that waiting any longer to make reforms would be *une impossibilité morale*.[117] Paul Emile Janson spoke soothingly of *un coup d'état parlementaire*.[118] The conservative right dropped *parlementaire* and spoke boldly of a leftist take-over.

At top speed and side-stepping the formalities, universal suffrage was whisked through Parliament along with the eight-hour work-day and an expanded right to strike. Measures were also taken to promote a sizable increase in purchasing power and in the standard of living in accordance with that acknowledged principle, *Erst kommt das Fressen, und dann die Moral.* This was a form of populism that had its counterpart in the *ouvriérisme* of the Belgian Labour Party. Success guaranteed! The socialists, who happily contributed to the mythologizing of Albert I, made him into a Marxist hero, *le protecteur des prolétaires*.[119]

Marxism, however, no longer had the wind in its sails. The socialists having been welcomed with open arms, in no time at all the working-class was integrated into parliamentary democracy and into the capitalist economy of consultation.

For the women, it was back to where they had been before.[120] They had taken upon themselves many tasks – as bread-winner, nurse, spy, war-widow – in a society that, owing to the cruelty of war, had assumed, paradoxically, a masculine character. The men, those on the left as well as the right, were still convinced believers in the *Kinder, Kirche, Küchen* syndrome. The conservatives hoped they would be strengthened if women were allowed to vote. The liberals and socialists considered the women to be under the thumb of Church and tradition and feared they might shift the balance to the right. Consequently, women would have to be content with voting in local elections only, right until after the end of the Second World War. A kind of cold comfort was accorded them in the form of general access to higher education. The bishops no longer blocked their entry to the Catholic University of Louvain. There, after matriculating, they were promptly put into "female residences" under the watchful eye of ... German nuns.

The Flemish, too, were left empty-handed.[121] Twice the King had promised equality before the law, first in his address from the throne at the beginning and then at the end of the war. The politicians only paid this lip-service – perhaps because they could not address all problems at the same time. The Flemish, brought into discredit by the collaboration of a minority, were refused any sort of hearing. In the long run, this eventually led to the disintegration of the unified Belgian state. The war had revealed that people and *patrie* in this relatively young kingdom were by no means equivalent terms. Verschaeve's prayer in his Soldier's Prayer Book is well-known: "My God, as I love Mother's nook in Father's house, so I love Flanders in Belgium". In the course of the war, the pious motto that Flemish soldiers wrote at the top of their letters or journal entries, AVB-BVK (All for Belgium-Belgium for Christ), was gradually replaced by the original AVV-VVK (All for Flanders-Flanders for Christ).[122] The close relatives of war dead were faced with a similar quandary when they had to decide what inscription to place on the tombstone: "died for the fatherland" or "died for Flanders", *Vaderland* or *Vlaanderland*?[123]

The war had sown confusion in people's hearts. The German invasion of this small country whose neutrality was considered to be eternal and sacrosanct, had sparked furious indignation which in turn had produced a surge of patriotism.[124] From this understandable love of country there developed, toward the end of the war, a nationalism with characteristics that were not fatherland-like at all. Take, for example, the ridiculously arrogant 'Annexionists', whose design was to tear large patches of territory out of the neutral Netherlands, though Flemish public opinion, grateful for the hospitality which their northern neighbours had so recently extended to refugees, was against this.[125] Quite different from this staggeringly revengeful Belgian nationalism was a budding Flemish nationalism. It had been fostered by the same war, but had fed on the frustrations of intellectuals at the front and the disdain shown by the French-speaking officers toward the many soldiers who spoke only Flemish (*et pour les Flamands la même chose*). It was further stimulated by the Germans' *Flamenpolitik* in occupied territory.

The radical Flemish Front Movement, which never had more than a few hundred members, grew totally desperate at the time of the final offensive. The leader was taken prisoner by the Germans, and the militants were completely separated in their various units. The collaborating Activists, terrified by the wrath of the citizenry and the repression to come, scampered to the safety of Berlin or the Netherlands. There, in the 1920's, they continued to revile the Belgium they hated. The Front Movement, however, was not quite *une histoire sans lendemain*: the veterans regrouped in a Front Party which was slow in starting and did not have the initial success they had hoped for. These Flemish nationalists gave great emphasis to the humiliation they had endured at the Front; they minimized the collaboration of the activists; claiming the right of self-determination – that of Wilson, not of Lenin – they demanded home rule for Flanders.[126]

The slightest concession to the Flemish, however, was booed down on the grounds that they had received enough concessions from the Germans during the war. The University of Ghent, which had indeed been made Flemish (i.e. Dutch)-speaking by the Germans, would not revert to being a Dutch-speaking institution until the 1930's. There was a brand-new Flemish newspaper, *De Standaard*, which certain intellectuals who had fled to England had launched with the hope of producing a Flemish 'Times'.[127] On 5 December 1918, its second issue, it published a Flemish minimum programme, calling for Dutch to be made the language of instruction, of the courts and of the administration in Flanders. This was, in fact, a moderate programme which remained strictly within the boundaries of the Belgian unified state. The reaction of the French-language press was furious: *Le programme minimum consacre la division pure et simple de la Belgique telle que l'avaient conçue les Allemands et que voulaient la réaliser les activistes.*[128] This was the *ultimate* accusation, but it was not the *last* time it would be brought to bear. Even today, Flemings who wish to remain loyal to the Belgian state believe that the disunion of

Belgium is a consequence of the German occupation and a posthumous triumph of Nazism and the German Empire.[129] Thus the Great War continues to influence political developments and how they are perceived.

To return to the troops in the field: in the eyes of Chief of Staff of the Allied armies of the *Groupe d'Armées de Flandre*, the French General Degoutte, the Armistice was coming too soon. He was about to miss the award of another star. *L'armistice me laissera-t-il le temps?* he asked himself.[130] He had planned a major exploit for 11 November: pressing on to Brussels in hot pursuit of the foe, a pursuit which would result in the capture of hordes of cavalry, thousands of soldiers and hundreds of guns. The Armistice undid all his calculations. The General and his forces were immobilized in East Flanders. In Ghent, however, a city known for its flower-growing, the royal couple were showered with orchids on 13 November. *Les Flamands que l'on disait froids se sont échauffés!*[131] The Armistice, having been declared for a period of six days, the Allied troops could not start moving again until the seventeenth. Not until 22 November did they reach Brussels and there all the celebration organ-stops were pulled out.

Meanwhile, the Belgian soldiers who had leave, converged on the capital. The people of Brussels were also unable to wait. Whole families set out in their Sunday best with the intention of meeting up with their very own hero in his new khaki uniform.[132] They really believed they would find their dear son in, say, Ghent or along the way. They followed their illusion on a journey by foot which turned out to be as long as sixty kilometres. Amazingly enough, in some cases the illusion turned into reality, and many long-absent soldiers did actually fall into the arms of their families who then walked home beside their dear ones as though beside a being from another world or of a higher order. Later, at table on the home front, a certain alienation might become apparent when the home-guard and the returnees discovered they spoke different languages. One talked of attacks, raids and patrols, the other of soup kitchens, coarse bread and the price of butter.[133]

Out in the countryside there never had been many flags in evidence – in Belgium, as in France, patriotism was particularly a sentiment of the urban middle classes. Now, however, the whole road between Brussels and Ghent seemed as if it were one long flag. The provincial town of Alost (Aalst) took an international view, flying flags of England, America, France and Italy, while not neglecting the higher powers by displaying Sacred Heart banners depicting Jesus with a bleeding heart.[134] Belgium and France were consecrated to the Sacred Heart of Jesus. In France, in the nineteenth century, the *Sacré Coeur* had already been enlisted in the struggle against the Godless republic – a question of rehabilitation after the Commune and the Revolution. Even so, in Belgium, this object of veneration was about to be positioned in the front line against nuisances and rowdies, namely the Bolsheviks, who were causing the heart of Christ to bleed. Certainly at the time of the liberation it was a powerful icon, both political and religious. It appealed to the *piété patriotique,* which Cardinal Mercier had in a sense devised, and which was now bearing fruit.

As for the people of Brussels, they went wild: *la réception du Roi avait été*

25 CENTIMES LE NUMÉRO.

LE PATRIOTE ILLUSTRÉ

ABONNEMENTS.

Prix provisoire : 1 fr. 25 par mois.

ADMINISTRATION

Montagne-aux-Herbes-Potagères, 12

BRUXELLES

Annonces : 3 francs la ligne.

LA GRANDE JOURNÉE

Le Roi et la Reine font leur rentrée Triomphale à Bruxelles.

xiv The front page of the illustrated weekly, *Le Patriote Illustré,* (8 December 1918), showing the King and Queen on their triumphal entry into Brussels. (University Library, Leuven) *chaleureuse à Bruges, enthousiaste à Gand. À Bruxelles, ce fut du délire.*[135] The sculptors of Brussels had outdone themselves, managing to have no less than seven huge statues ready in time for the great day. There was even one in the *Grand Place* in front of the *Maison du Roi,* whose ancient, now-vanished inscription *A pestis, fame et bello libera nos Maria pacis* would have now been quite apposite.[136] Shop windows displayed plaster effigies of Albert and Elisabeth as well as cartoons lampooning Wilhelm and his Germania who had now bled to death. Everywhere, one heard a variation on the German triumphal song, "Gloria! Victoria! The Kaiser, he's got cholera!" Copies of the words of Belgium's un-singable national anthem were distributed, a measure that met an obvious need. All the seamstresses of the capital, on the other hand, seemed to have learnt English in order to warble out the original text of "God Save the King".

The Allies, at the request of the Americans, made themselves highly visible. Brussels' most famous citizen, *Manneken-Pis*, was promoted to corporal in the French army and dressed in the appropriate uniform. The lad appeared minus his clothes but all the more virile for that, in a cartoon in the liberal weekly magazine *Pourquoi pas?*. The imperial armies were shown splattered to bits by the force of his powerful jet of water. This hero of the resistance had made his debut in the issue published on 13 August 1914, went on to have a revival in 1918 at the time of the liberation[137] and made his ultimate come-back in September 1944. If this life-loving tot, symbol of *la Belgique joyeuse* could personify the Belgian resistance, then he must have corresponded to the Belgian self-image which saw itself as something of an anti-hero, even in the resistance. Literature produced during the war was rife with the legends of *Eulenspiegel* and Belgium's heroic 'King Without a Country', and they too were cut from the same cloth.[138] The country that had sweated water and blood under the Teutons' yoke now chose as its idols Manneken-Pis and the Sacred Heart. This was a baroque combination that would not have been out of place in the works of Ensor or Ghelderode, artists who excelled in portraying the national character, known as *belgitude*.

Jules Leroy from Voormezele, whom we met at the very beginning of this account, was still on the march. He was there when the offensive began on 28 September, and he was still there on 22 November when the army entered Brussels.

> We went into Brussels with the King out in front. Nobody will ever experience such a thing again! In the trees, on the fences, everywhere, people! We had to march in file. The King up ahead on his horse. At the gates of the palace he stopped. There an old man came up to me. 'Are you one of the carabineers?' 'Yes.' 'From which regiment?' 'The third'. 'Do you know a Frans Hernalsteen?' 'I know him well, he's a corporal in my platoon, but in another section'. 'And do you know where he is?' 'He has gone to the commander to ask for permission to go home'. 'That's my son'. The old man practically ran.[139]

With this *tableau vivant* we conclude our great parade on a rather intimate note: a cry from the heart of an old man in the Great War.

In Stravinsky's *Histoire du soldat*, the soldier is taken in tow by the devil. On the way, he trades his violin for a magic book. The Flemish soldier did not sell his soul, either to the Front Movement or to Bolshevism. He was not very literate. What good, then, to him were the 'magic books', 'The Flemish Nationalist's Catechism' or 'The Communist Manifesto'? The Flemish soldier did not lose his bearings but marched bravely on, homeward, toward his mother, his wife, his sweetheart and, if the King so wished, even to Germany for the 'Watch on the Rhine'. Soon he was home. The curtain fell, winter came and a shroud of snow fell upon Flanders Fields.[140] Streuvels, who went biking through the battle-fields, had no use for such sentimental imagery. Streuvels was more inclined to the rugged realism and crude power that would make his works such steady sellers in post-war Germany. Churlish as ever, he wanted no part in the euphoria. His journal entry is grim: "The world is lying there like a huge beast that rests in deep sleep after a strenuous effort, and no one knows if it is dead or wounded".[141]

EPILOGUE

For some unfathomable reason – be it a burst of self-denial or self-pity – the Belgian state chose, at first, the fourth of August as its day of national rejoicing – the anniversary of the German invasion. As of 1922, however, it was the eleventh of November, a day more appropriate for commemoration, which became the day officially for memorializing the war and its victims.[142] On 11 November 1922, following the French and British example, the mortal remains of the Unknown Soldier were laid to rest. This was preceded by a selection process involving much sombre ceremony and a theatricality the pathos of which may well give rise to mixed feelings today. Five coffins, chosen at random, were taken from various military cemeteries and transported to Bruges, where the First Class railway waiting-room was transformed into a funerary chapel.[143] The coffins contained the unidentified remains of soldiers who had fallen in battle near Liège, Namur, Antwerp and the Yser, or during the liberation offensive in Flanders. Their rank was not known, and no one would ever be able to find out if the anonymous hero were Walloon or Flemish. A blind veteran of war chose one of the five coffins. This coffin, containing the remains of the Unknown Soldier, was carried by eight war invalids – four having lost their left arm, and four their right – and was placed on the train to Brussels. One is reminded of those veteran composers who wrote pieces for veteran pianists, pieces for the left hand – so many right hands having been victims of the Great War.[144]

In Brussels, the Unknown Soldier was put in his resting-place at the foot of the Congress Column on 11 November at eleven o'clock. King Albert was naturally present at the ceremony, though he was not at all keen on all those monuments and commemorations, *les horreurs de la guerre*, as he called them in an unguarded moment, the horror instead of the honour of war. The King-Knight who, in fact, did not like that title, was once again the citizen-king, the image by which he had been portrayed before the war. Mixed feelings could also be observed at the Flemish satirical weekly, *Pallieter*, which solemnly announced the founding of a pension fund for the widow of the Unknown Soldier.[145] This went like a dagger to the heart of all well-meaning Belgian patriots – yet another indication of how painful were the wounds of war inflicted on the nation.

Endnotes

The author of this chapter is grateful to several individuals and institutions providing documents and literature for his work: Jan Dewilde and Roger Verbeke of the Documentation Centre "In Flanders Fields" in Ypres (Ieper), Dr Gustaaf Janssens, keeper of the Archives of the Royal Palace in Brussels, his colleagues Els Scheers and Monique Baetens in the University Archives of the Catholic University Leuven, Franky Bostyn who guided him through the Ypres Salient on 11 November 1997 and the author and, not least, the editors are most grateful to Mrs. Ardis Dreisbach for her translation.

1 *België en de Eerste Wereldoorlog. Bibliografie*, (eds. P. Lefèvre and J. Lorette), Brussels 1987; H. Pirenne, *La Belgique et la guerre mondiale*, Paris-New Haven 1928; E.H. Kossmann, *The Low Countries 1780–1940*, Oxford 1978; L. Schepens, "België in de eerste wereldoorlog", in *Algemene Geschiedenis der Nederlanden*, Haarlem 1979, vol. XIV, pp. 19–39; L. Schepens, *14/18 Een oorlog in Vlaanderen*, Tielt 1984; G. Durnez, *Zeg mij waar de bloemen zijn. Beelden uit de Eerste Wereldoorlog in Vlaanderen*, Leuven 1988; L. de Vos, *De Eerste Wereldoorlog*, Leuven 1996; S. de Schaepdrijver, *De Groote Oorlog. Het koninkrijk België tijdens de Eerste Wereldoorlog*, Amsterdam – Antwerpen 1997 (brilliantly written!).

2 E.W. White, *Stravinsky. The Composer and his Works*, London 1966, pp. 47–48, pp. 226–237.

3 H. Vanderheyden, *Een bijdrage tot de geschiedenis van het Vlaamse Volkstoneel*, thesis University Leuven 1972; documents on the performance in the archives of the Vlaamsche Volksbond in KADOC (Catholic Documentation Center) Leuven.

4 *Histoire du soldat The Soldier's Tale. Texte de C.F. Ramuz. English version by M. Flanders & K. Black Musique de Igor Stravinsky* (ed. J. Carewe), London 1992, pp. 1–6.

5 E. Vermeulen, *Piot*, Leuven 1923, pp. 292, quoted in F. Deflo, *De literaire oorlog. De Vlaamse prozaliteratuur over de Eerste Wereldoorlog*, Aartrijke 1991, pp. 126.

6 *The Flemish Movement. A Documentary History 1780–1990* (eds. T. Hermans, L. Vos & L. Wils), London 1992, p. 19; L. de Vos & H. Keymeulen, "Een definitieve afrekening met de 80%-mythe? Het Belgisch Leger (1914–1918) en de sociale en numerieke taalverhouding onder de gesneuvelden van lagere rang", *Revue belge d'histoire militaire*, 1988–1989 (several articles); C. van Everbroeck, "Een bewustzijn geboren uit het vuur". Vlaamse slachtoffers van de Eerste Wereldoorlog", in *De grote mythen uit de geschiedenis van België, Vlaanderen en Wallonië* (ed. A. Morelli), Berchem (Antwerp) 1997, p. 221.

7 D.S. White, *Lost Comrades*, p. 21.

8 J.-G. Gheuens, *De miskenden*, Kortrijk 1938, p. 204, quoted in F. Deflo, *De literaire oorlog*, p. 126.

9 *Van den Grooten Oorlog. Volksboek* (ed. Elfnovembergroep), Kemmel 1978, p. 265. A real source-book of oral history!

10 F. de Backer, *Longinus*, Hasselt 1963, p. 60, quoted in F. Deflo, *De literaire oorlog*, p. 125.

11 Private letter of Villiers to A. Nicholson, 12 August 1914, in *British Documents on the Origins of the War*, vol. XI, p. 350, quoted in J. Stengers, "La Belgique", in *Les Sociétés européennes et la guerre de 1914–1918. Actes du colloque organisé à Nanterre et à Amiens du 8 au 11 décembre 1988*, Nanterre 1990, p. 84.

12 See J. Stengers, *L'action du roi en Belgique depuis 1831. Pouvoir et influence*, Brussels 1996; or J. Stengers, *De koningen der Belgen. Van Leopold I tot Albert II*, Leuven 1997 (Dutch translation).

13 *The Flemish Movement. A Documentary History 1780–1990* (ed. T. Herman, L. Wils and L. Vos), London 1992, pp. 20–21.

14 J. Stengers, *De koningen der Belgen*, p. 264.

15 P. Werrie, *La légende d'Albert Ier, roi des Belges* (Préface du Lieutenant-Général Pontus – Dessins de Hergé), Tournai-Paris (1934).

16 J. Stengers, *De koningen der Belgen*, p. 92.

17 T. Luykx, *Politieke geschiedenis van België van 1789 tot 1944*, Antwerpen 1985, p. 268.

18 M. Weemaes, *De l'Yser à Bruxelles. Offensive libératrice de l'Armée belge le 28 septembre 1918*, Marcinelle 1969; M. Weemaes, *Van de IJzer tot Brussel. Het bevrijdingsoffensief van het Belgisch leger 28 september 1918*, Marcinelle (1969) (Dutch version); R. Verbeke, "De laatste oorlogsdagen in 1918", serial of articles (I-X) *Het Volk*, 30 Oct.–12 Nov. 1978; *Beknopte Uiteenzetting over Enkele Verrichtingen in Vlaanderen tijdens den Veldtocht 1914–1918* (ed. Generale Staf van het Leger), Brussel 1939; A. Deseyne, *Oorlog in de Ieperboog*, Zonnebeke 1987.

19 M. Weemaes, *Van de IJzer tot Brussel*, p. 76.

20 M. Weemaes, *Van de IJzer tot Brussel*, p. 196.

21 L. Slosse, *Oorlogsdagboek van Rumbeke in 1914–1918*, Brugge 1962, p. 163.

22 About horses: *De Standaard*, 4 Dec. 1918 (nr. 1!); about the milkcow: J. de Smet, *Brugge onder de Oorlog 1914–1918*, Brugge 1955, p. 107.

23 J.M. Lermyte, *Geschiedenis van Izegem*, Izegem 1985, p. 366.

24 K. van de Woestijne, *Verzameld journalistiek werk*, vol. IX: *Nieuwe Rotterdamsche Courant. Maart 1916-september 1919* (ed. A. Deprez), Gent 1992, p. 114.

25 E. van Hoonacker, *Kortrijk 14–18. Een stad tijdens de Eerste Wereldoorlog*, Kortrijk 1994, p. 430.

26 *Le Soir*, 10 Nov. 1918.

27 E. van Hoonacker, *Kortrijk 14–18*, p. 432.

28 *La Libre Belgique*, nr. 169, Oct. 1918.

29 J. de Smet, *Brugge onder de Oorlog 1914–1918*, p. 110.

30 S Streuvels, *In oorlogstijd. Het volledig dagboek van de Eerste Wereldoorlog*, Brugge-Nijmegen 1979, pp. 656–657.

31 R. Halewyn, *Torhout onder de oorlog 1914–1918*, Torhout, s.a. (no pagination).

32 L. Slosse, *Oorlogsdagboek van Rumbeke in 1914–1918*, p.161.

33 S. Streuvels, *In oorlogstijd*, p. 662.

34 S. Streuvels, *In oorlogstijd*, p. 665.

35 S. Streuvels, *In oorlogstijd*, p. 663.

36 A. and A. Deseyne, *Zonnebeke 1914–1918*, Zonnebeke 1976, p. 466; See also the letters of Franz Hosten about his parents' house in Diksmuide in *Oorlogsdagboeken uit de streek tussen IJzer en Leie* (ed. L. Devliegher) Brugge 1972, pp. 126–127.

37 *Gedenkboek aan Beselare in de Eerste Wereldoorlog 1914–1918*, (ed. J.H. Maes), Beselare 1960, pp. 85–87.
38 A. Denys, *Geschiedkundige oorlogskroniek van Rousselare en 't Ommeland. Vierde Boek*, Roeselare 1994, p. 205 and p. 231.
39 *Van den Grooten Oorlog*, p. 280.
40 R. Halewyn, *Torhout onder de oorlog 1914–1918*, no pagination.
41 P. Scholliers, "België dreunt in zijn voegen. Sociale en politieke troebelen 1914–1921", in *Mensen in oorlogstijd* (ed. F. Vanhemelryck), Brussels 1988, p. 151–173.
42 *Een streek in oorlog. Oorlogsdocumenten uit het Tieltse 1914–1918*, Tielt 1980, p. 398.
43 H. Bordeaux, "L'Armistice du 11 novembre 1918 à l'Armée de Flandre. Fragments de mémoires", *La Revue des deux mondes*, Nov.-Dec. 1950, p. 31.
44 *The Story of a War Bird, New York 1918*. Added letters of a soldier from Leuven (Louvain).
45 *Een streek in oorlog*, p. 388.
46 J. de Smet, *Brugge onder de Oorlog 1914–1918*, p. 47 and p. 110.
47 *King Albert's Book. Een hulde aan den koning der Belgen* (Dutch version) (The Daily Telegraph) London 1914, p. 21.
48 *Een streek in oorlog*, p. 396.
49 E. van Hoonacker, *Kortrijk 14–18*, p. 426.
50 *King Albert's Book.*, pp. 85–92.
51 W. Geldolf, *Stockholm 1917. Camille Huysmans in de schaduw van titanen*, Antwerpen 1996, p. 158.
52 E. van Hoonacker, *Kortrijk 14–18*, p. 425.
53 S. Streuvels, *In oorlogstijd*, p. 662 (25 Oct. 1918).
54 Marcel Weemaes, *De l'Yser à Bruxelles*, p. 367.
55 *Rapport du général Degoutte au maréchal Foch*, in M. Weemaes, *De l'Yser à Bruxelles*, p. 372.
56 G. Provoost, *Het Frans-Belgisch militair akkoord van 7 september 1920 en zijn invloed op de Belgische buitenlandse, militaire en binnenlandse politiek (1920–1937)*, doctoral dissertation University Gent 1975, p. 151.
57 L. de Vos, *De Eerste Wereldoorlog*, p. 156.
58 *Van den Grooten Oorlog*, p. 265.
59 M. Jacobs, *Zij, die vielen als helden Inventaris van de oorlogsgedenktekens van de twee wereldoorlogen in West-Vlaanderen*, Brugge 1996, vol. II, p. 430.
60 J. Simons, *Zijn derde ster*, first edition 1926. See: *De Grote Oorlog. Novellen over 14–18* (ed. A.G. Christiaens), Leuven 1994.
61 J.G. Gheuens, *De miskenden*, Kortrijk 1938. See F. Deflo, *De literaire oorlog*, p. 132.
62 P.& W. Chielens, *De Troost van Schoonheid. De literaire Salient (Ieper 1914–1918)*, Groot-Bijgaarden 1996, p. 28.
63 *Van den Grooten Oorlog*, p. 301.
64 *Van den Grooten Oorlog*, p. 297.
65 G. Cooman, "De 'kaki-seminaristen'. West-Vlaamse seminaristen tijdens en na de Eerste Wereldoorlog", *Trajecta. Tijdschrift voor de geschiedenis van het katholiek leven in de Nederlanden*, 1997, p. 283.
66 L. Gorremans, *Mosaïque de guerre 1914–1918*, Antwerpen (1936), pp. 164–165.
67 A. van Acker, *Herinneringen. Jeugd in oorlogstijd*, Antwerpen 1967, pp. 154–155.
68 L. Schepens, "België in de eerste wereldoorlog", p. 27.

69 *Van den Grooten Oorlog*, p. 301.

70 L. Schepens, "België in de eerste wereldoorlog", p. 27; P. Cahalan, *Belgian Refugee Relief in England during the Great War*, New York 1982.

71 *Van den Grooten Oorlog*, p. 301.

72 E. van Hoonacker, *Kortrijk 14–18*, p. 432.

73 S. Streuvels, *In oorlogstijd*, p. 664.

74 *Het oorlogsdagboek van Jules Depuydt Aartrijke 1914–1918*, Zedelgem 1997, p. 204. See also D. Jonckheere, *Aartrijke 1914–18*, Aartrijke 1964, p. 58.

75 G.A.T. Middleton, *Ypres as it was before the Great War. Being and Appreciative description written in 1913*, Antwerpen 1919, p. 5; A. Bras & J. Cornillie, *Sint-Maartenskerk van Ieper voor, onder en na den wereldoorlog*, Ieper s.a.

76 H. Speliers, *Dag Streuvels. "Ik ken den weg alleen"*, Leuven 1994, p. 437.

77 *Van den Grooten Oorlog*, p. 313.

78 C. Verschaeve, *Oorlogsindrukken* (ed. D. Vanacker & R. Vanlandschoot), Gent 1996, p. 141.

K. van de Woestijne, *Verzameld journalistiek werk*, vol. IX: *Nieuwe Rotterdamsche Courant. Maart 1916 – september 1919* (ed. A. Deprez), Gent 1922, p. 427.

K. van de Woestijne, *Verzameld journalistiek werk*, p. 429.

K. van de Woestijne, *Verzameld journalistiek werk*, p. 430.

79 A. Debeuckelaere, *Open Letter to the Belgian King 1917*. See Document 33, in *The Flemish Movement*, pp. 227–237. For the last episode in the complicated discussion about King Albert's attitude towards the Flemish demands, see L. Wils, "De taalpolitiek van Koning Albert", *Wetenschappelijke Tijdingen op het gebied van de Vlaamse Beweging*, Sept. 1996, pp. 197–203.

80 L. Wils, *Flamenpolitik en activisme. Vlaanderen tegenover België in de Eerste Wereldoorlog*, Leuven 1974; W. Dolderer, *Deutscher Imperialismus und belgischer Nationalitätenkonflikt. Die Rezeption der Flamenfrage in der deutschen Öffentlichkeit und deutsch-flämische Kontakte 1890–1920*, Messungen 1989; D. Vanacker, *Het Aktivistisch avontuur*, Gent 1991.

81 C. Verschaeve, *The Flemish Nationalist's Catechism 1918*. See Document 35, in *The Flemish Movement*, pp. 240–253.

82 C. Verschaeve, *Oorlogsindrukken*, p. 140.

83 J. Polasky, *The Democratic Socialism of Emile Vandervelde. Between Reform and Revolution*, Oxford-Washington 1995, p. 135.

84 H. Haag, "La Belgique en novembre 1918", *Revue d"histoire moderne et contemporaine*, Jan-March 1969, p. 153–160; H. Haag, "De 'staatsgreep van Loppem'", *Spiegel Historiael*, 1981, pp. 140–145.

85 E. Vandervelde, *Souvenirs d'un militant socialiste*, Paris 1939, p. 275.

86 Quoted in L. Michielsen, *Geschiedenis van de Europese arbeidersbeweging*, Gent 1980, vol. III, p. 264.

87 P. Renouvin, "L'Europe au lendemain des armistices de 1918", *Revue d'histoire moderne et contemporaine*, Jan.-March 1969, pp. 10–11.

88 J. van Parijs, *Masereel. Een biografie*, Antwerpen-Baarn 1995, p. 81.

89 H.J. Scheffer, *November 1918: journaal van een revolutie die niet doorging*, Amsterdam 1968, 312 p.; H. Haag, "De 'staatgreep van Loppem'", p. 142.

90 M.W.R. van Vollenhoven, *Memoires. Beschouwingen, belevenissen, reizen en anecdoten*, Amsterdam-Brussel-London-New York 1946, p. 361.

91 G. Haffner, *Die verratene Revolution. Deutschland 1918–1919*, Bern-München-Vienna 1968, pp. 62–63, quoted in P. Staes, *Het socialisme in Leuven tijdens de Eerste Wereldoorlog*, thesis University Leuven 1982, p. 159.

92 M.W.R. van Vollenhoven, *Memoires*, p. 364.
93 K. van de Woestijne, *Verzameld journalistiek werk*, vol. IX: *Nieuwe Rotterdamsche Courant. Maart 1916 – september 1919* (ed. A. Deprez), Gent 1922, p. 427.
94 K. van de Woestijne, *Verzameld journalistiek werk*, p. 429.
95 K. van de Woestijne, *Verzameld journalistiek werk*, p. 430.
96 P. Staes, *Het socialisme in Leuven*, pp. 160–164.
97 *Journal de correspondance de mgr. Ladeuze du 19 juin au 22 décembre 1918* (the Rector's diary) in the University Archives of the Catholic University Leuven (Louvain).
98 F. van Langenhove, *Comment naît un cycle de légendes. Franc-tireurs et atrocités en Belgique*, Lausanne-Paris 1916, according to Marc Bloch and Jean Stengers a model of sociological analysis and "psychologie collective". See also M. Derez, "The Flames of Louvain. The War Experience of an Academic Community", in *Facing Armageddon. The First World War Experienced*, London 1996, pp. 617–629.
99 E. Witte & J. Craeybeckx, *Politieke geschiedenis van België sinds 1830*, Antwerpen 1983, p. 210.
100 K. van de Woestijne, *Verzameld journalistiek werk*, pp. 447–448.
101 H. Haag, "Le choix du roi Albert à Loppem", in *Actes du colloque Roi Albert. Bruxelles Bibliothèque royale Albert Ier 26–29 mai 1975*, Brussels 1976, pp. 170–191; *Histoire de la Belgique contemporaine 1914–1970*, Brussels 1974; C.H. Hoejer, *Le régime parlementaire belge de 1918 à 1940*, Uppsala-Stockholm s.a.; E. Gerard, *De Katholieke Partij in crisis. Partijpolitiek leven in België 1918–1940*, Leuven 1985, pp. 62–70.
102 K. van de Woestijne, *Verzameld journalistiek werk*, p. 449.
103 P.E. Janson, *Lophem* (extrait de la Revue *Flambeau*), Brussels 1926, p. 29.
104 A.J. Mayer, *Politics and Diplomacy of Peacemaking, Containment and Counter-Revolution of Versailles 1918–1919*, London 1968.
105 See the articles of H. Haag.
106 P. Renouvin, "L'Europe au lendemain des armistices", p. 10.
107 J. Stengers, "La Belgique", in *Les Sociétés européennes et la guerre de 1914–1918. Actes du colloque organisé à Nanterre et à Amiens du 8 au 11 décembre 1988*, Nanterre 1990, pp. 75–91.
108 H. Haag, *Le comte Charles de Broqueville, Ministre d'État et les luttes pour le pouvoir (1910–1940)*, Louvain-la-Neuve – Brussels 1990, pp. 492–494.
109 H. Bordeaux, "L'armistice du 11 novembre 1918", p. 19.
110 Princesse Marie-José, *Albert et Elisabeth de Belgique, mes parents*, Paris 1971, pp. 303–305.
111 *Rapport du général Degoutte au maréchal Foch*, in M. Weemaes, *De l'Yser à Bruxelles*, pp. 372–373.
112 Note of the comte d'Arschot-Schoonhoven for the King, 13 Nov. 1918, see Archives of the Private Secretary of King Albert and Queen Elisabeth, 275 in the Archives of the Royal Palace in Brussels.
113 *The ideological crisis of expressionism: the literary and artistic German war colony in Belgium 1914–1918* (eds. R.R. Rumold & O.K. Werckmeister), Columbia 1990 mentioned in S. de Schaepdrijver, *De Groote Oorlog. Het koninkrijk België tijdens de Eerste Wereldoorlog*, Amsterdam-Antwerpen 1997, p. 244.
114 K. Grünebaum, "Le roi Albert et l'opinion allemande. Un relevé de quelques faits de appréciations", in *Actes du colloque Roi Albert*, Brussels 1976, p. 289.

115 Note of minister Henri Jaspar 15 Nov. 1918, see Archives of the Cabinet of King Albert, 883 in the Archives of the Royal Palace in Brussels.
116 T. Luykx, *Politieke geschiedenis van België van 1789 tot 1944*, p. 275.
117 T. Luykx, *Politieke geschiedenis van België van 1789 tot 1944*, p. 296.
118 H. Haagn "La Belgique en novembre 1918", p. 155.
119 About the mythology on King Albert, see G. van den Abeelen, "Le roi Albert: naissance et avatars d'une mythologie", in *Actes du colloque Roi Albert*, Brussels 1976, pp. 19–33; M.R. Thielemans, "De legende van Albert I", in *De grote mythen uit de geschiedenis van België*, Vlaanderen en Wallonië (ed. A. Morelli), pp. 159–173; L. van Ypersele, *Le roi Albert. Histoire d'un mythe*, Ottignies – Louvain-la-Neuve 1995.
120 D. de Weerdt, *De vrouwen van de Eerste Wereldoorlog*, Gent 1993; K. Celis & A. Godfroid, *Vrouwen en oorlog 16ᵉ–20ᵉ* Eeuw (catalogue exhibition General Archives of the Realm), Brussels 1998.
121 H. Haag, "La Belgique en novembre 1918", pp. 159–160.
122 See G. Cooman, "De 'kaki-seminaristen'", p. 282.
123 M. Jacobs, *Zij, die vielen als helden . Cultuurhistorische analyse van de oorlogsgedenktekens van de twee wereldoorlogen in West-Vlaanderen*, Brugge 1995, vol. I, pp. 73–78.
124 J. Stengers, "La Belgique", pp. 78–79; see also J. Willequet, "Belgique et Allemagne, 1914–1945", in *Sentiment national en Allemagne et en Belgique, XIXe-XXe siècles*, Brussels 1964, p. 60.
125 M. Bossenbroek et al., *Vluchten voor de groote oorlog. Belgen in Nederland, 1914–1918*, Amsterdam 1988.
126 Flemish Committee, *Telegram to President Woodrow Wilson* (1919). See Document 36 in *The Flemish Movement*, pp. 254–257.
127 G. Durnez, *De Standaard. Het levensverhaal van een Vlaamse krant*, Tielt 1985, p. 97.
128 *Le Vingtième Siècle*, 5 Dec. 1918 quoted in E. Gerard, *De Katholieke Partij in crisis. Partijpolitiek leven in België (1918–1940)*, Leuven 1985, p. 94.
129 L. Wils, *Vlaanderen België Groot-Nederland. Mythe en geschiedenis*, Leuven 1994, p. 473.
130 H. Bordeaux, "L'Armistice du 11 novembre 1918", p. 18.
131 H. Bordeaux, "L'Armistice du 11 novembre 1918", p. 25.
132 K. van de Woestijne, *Verzameld journalistiek werk*, p. 459.
133 L. Gorremans, *Mosaïque de guerre 1914–1918*, p. 166.
134 K. van de Woestijne, *Verzameld journalistiek werk*, p. 461. See M. Jacobs, *Zij, die vielen als helden* , vol. I, p. 127. About Cardinal Mercier and the Holy Heart see also *Gazet van Antwerpen*, 24 Nov. 1918; documents on the National Manifestation of Gratitude for the Holy Heart of Jesus in Brussels in the Archives of the Secretariat of King Albert (1919–1924) in the Archives of the Royal Palace in Brussels.
135 M. Weemaes, *De l'Yser à Bruxelles*, p. 384.
136 H. Bordeaux, "L'Armistice du 11 novembre 1918", p. 29.
137 *Pourquoi Pas? Pendant l'Occupation par un des trois moustiquaires. La Vie Bruxelloise de 1914 en 1918*, Brussels 1918, 216 pp.
138 C. Bronne, *Albert Ier, Le Roi sans terre*, Paris 1965; F. Deflo, *De literaire oorlog*, passim.
139 *Van den Grooten Oorlog*, p. 302.
140 See A.& A. Deseyne, *Zonnebeke 1914–1918*, p. 397.
141 S. Streuvels, *In oorlogstijd*, p; 664.

142 G. Janssens, "De Belgische nationale feestdagen en de monarchie", *Museum Dynasticum*, 1997, pp. 7–8. See also L. Macdonald, *1914–1918 Voices and Images of the Great War*, London 1991, pp. 324–329.
143 W. Degrande, "Assebroek en de Onbekende Soldaat", *Shrapnel (Western Front Association België)*, Dec. 1995, pp. 3–8.
144 H. Triebels, "De grote oorlog", *Muziek en Woord*, Aug. 1994, p. 7–8.
145 *Pallieter*, 5 Nov. 1922.

Chapter Eight

The Americans

James Cooke

Leslie Langille was a student at the University of Illinois when the United States declared war on Germany on 6 April 1917. A devout young man from Chicago, Illinois, Langille decided, as did many of his fellow students, to enlist in the service of his country. He joined Battery B, 149th Field Artillery Regiment of the Illinois National Guard, and served in the 67th Artillery Brigade of the 42nd Infantry Division. Langille fought in every major battle the Division was committed to from the Champagne in July 1918, to the Ourcq River to St. Mihiel and to the Meuse-Argonne. His regiment was in sight of Sedan on 10 November 1918, when word came that fighting would end on the morrow. He recalled that "The news was received without any violent outbursts or insanely joyous demonstration. It was received quietly and with the sentiment, 'we are glad', upon the lips of every man there assembled".[1] Eighteen months earlier he would have cheered a touchdown by the University of Illinois football team, but on that November Langille and his comrades were beyond cheers.

Langille represented what the United States had to offer to the Allied cause in World War One. He was young, vigorous, healthy, and unjaded by the trenches of the Western Front. When America entered the war in the spring of 1917 she was totally unprepared for the conflict. The army numbered around 250,000 men, nearly half being National Guard (or militia). The Regular Army was scattered over the vast expanse of the United States and on posts in the Philippine Islands and elsewhere. Only two hundred regular officers were trained for staff duty, and none had practical experience above the regimental or brigade levels. The U.S. Air Service had sixty officers; only half knew how to fly. The eighteen aircraft of the 1st Aero Squadron were obsolete and could not be sent to France. There were not enough rifles, artillery pieces, shoes, uniforms, or any of the other sinews of war. The Americans had manpower, and they had General John J. Pershing to mould the raw clay of youth into the stern soldiers needed for France.

Pershing was the archetypical American. Born in rural Missouri in 1860, he eagerly sought an education and graduated from the United States Military

Academy in 1888. He achieved the rank of Major-General, a great success in an army where earning rank was agonizingly slow. His instructions, which would carry him to the Armistice in November 1918, had been simple, almost absurdly so — build an American army to fight under American commanders in an American sector of the Western Front.[2] The Americans did not come into the war as Allies, they came as Associates, and this would complicate the picture during the Armistice. President Woodrow Wilson, an idealist and a reformer, had tried to keep the United States from the war in Europe. Having failed, he went before Congress to ask for the declaration of war, but it was unclear what influence Wilson would have on post-armistice diplomacy and negotiations. Much to the distress of interventionists, Wilson had named Newton B. Baker of Ohio, an outspoken pacifist, as Secretary of War in 1916. To cloud the issue, on 8 January 1918, Wilson made his famous "Fourteen Points" speech which set forth American war aims based on national self-determination, no annexation of territories, democracy, and basic human freedoms. The Allied commanders found Pershing difficult to deal with, and there was every indication that Woodrow Wilson would be as well. Americans were still to some extent an unknown cypher as the war drew to a close.

There was no question that Pershing was committed to seeing the war through to the end. When, on 15 July 1918, the Supreme War Council at Versailles issued a document entitled the "Allied Plan of Campaign for Autumn and Winter of 1918 and Summer of 1919",[3] Pershing embraced it with an almost religious passion because the plan stated that the American Expeditionary Forces (AEF), in view of the overall Allied manpower situation, would be a decisive factor. Pershing informed Washington of his belief that, by the opening of the 1919 fighting, the AEF should have 100 combat divisions, or 2,800,000 men. While the United States War Department targeted from 60 to 80 divisions as the number which would be available, it was clear that the vast reservoir of manpower would be enough to submerge German military resources.[4] As the Allied offensives developed in the fall of 1918 there were very few indicators that the Germans were actually collapsing. The American view was firmly set as far as the year 1919 was concerned. At Chaumont, General Headquarters of the AEF, (GHQ, AEF), minds were focused on the Meuse – Argonne struggle and on the training of those millions of American troops who would be arriving throughout the winter of 1918–1919.

The Meuse – Argonne battle did not go well for Pershing and the AEF. When the battle opened for the 1st US Army it became apparent very quickly that the units committed to the 26 September assault were by and large unprepared, from the staffs of divisions down to the individual infantryman. Within a few days the attack ground to a halt. Pershing firmly believed that the years of trench warfare had sapped the fighting spirit of the British and French, and he preached a doctrine of open, or manoeuvre, warfare. Only when, reasoned General Pershing, the infantryman with his rifle and bayonet left the trenches and fought in the open, could victory be won. The reality in the hills, thickets, and ravines of the Meuse – Argonne was simply that motivated, well-trained Germans, taking advantage of good cover and observation, using machine-guns and artillery to maximum advantage, were able to inflict serious casualties and break up attacking American divisions. Two days after the Meuse – Argonne battle opened, Pershing confided to his diary, "Our advance is *somewhat* [author's italics] checked by rather persistent action of Germans with machine guns. This is due to a certain extent [to] the lack of experience and the lack of push on the part of the division and brigade commanders".[5] By the end of September the American attack halted to "reorganize".

On 4 October the American advance began again, but that night Pershing wrote in his diary, "Met considerable resistance; advance very slow ... There is no course but to fight it out taking the best possible advantage of the ground which now lays to the advantage of the Germans".[6] By mid-October this attack ended with even more casualties. By the end of the month the AEF began another assault phase, this time driving the Germans back—not because they were beaten, but because their internal situation forced them to consolidate. But there was a lesson to be learned from the piles of American dead and from the wreckage of AEF divisions. Pershing and the AEF could throw troops into a battle of attrition which the Germans could not possibly hope to win. By the spring there would be perhaps two-and-a-half million more American troops ready for the fight.

Pershing's desire to show the Allies that American forces were making a great difference was of little consequence for the American soldiers in the Meuse – Argonne. Food was short, poor, muddy roads meant that the wounded faced agonizing hours, if not days, before receiving medical care, and every soldier was wet and chilled. Elmer Sherwood of Indiana, serving in the 149th Artillery Regiment, recalled that, "Not being content to firing H.E.'s into us, the enemy added gas. His airplanes came over often and dropped some bombs".[7] Neither Sherwood nor Leslie Langille, both serving in the 67th Artillery Brigade, had great concern over the higher lessons of coalition warfare. They just wanted the war to end, and to go home.

Word of the impending armistice filtered down to the troops quickly on 10 November, and when the dawn of the next day broke there was a grim wish by the individual soldier that he should not be the last man to fall before the guns went silent. Sergeant Walter Williams of Pennsylvania, serving with the 27th Aero Squadron, Pursuit, recorded in his diary "It seems funny, we hear no artillery shooting. All is quiet, even the ground is at rest ... It is a fact, NO MORE WAR".[8] Closer to the front, Sergeant Calvin Lambert of Kansas, an original member of the 117th Ammunition Train, saw little different in the day until he and his buddies wandered, "to a German bathhouse where we tried to drown our cooties [lice]. The bath house had a tiled floor,steam heat, and in the officers bathroom was a real tub".[9] There seems to have been more celebration during the daylight hours among the troops who had yet to be committed to battle.

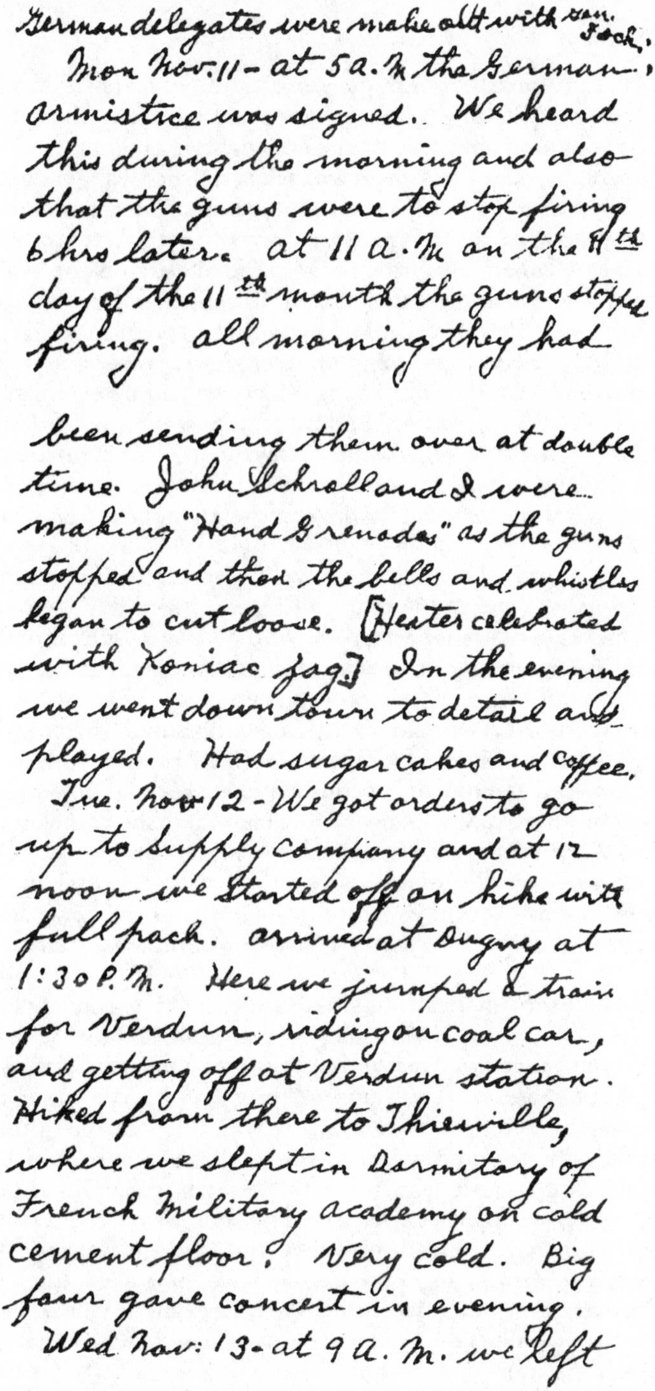
German delegates were make alt with Gen. Foch.
Mon Nov. 11 - at 5 a.m. the German armistice was signed. We heard this during the morning and also that the guns were to stop firing 6 hrs later. at 11 a.m. on the 11th day of the 11th month the guns stopped firing. all morning they had been sending them over at double time. John Schroll and I were making "Hand Grenades" as the guns stopped and then the bells and whistles began to cut loose. [Hester celebrated with Koniac jag] In the evening we went down town to detail and played. Had sugar cakes and coffee.
Tue. Nov 12 - We got orders to go up to Supply company and at 12 noon we started off on hike with full pack. arrived at Dugny at 1:30 P.M. Here we jumped a train for Verdun, riding on coal car, and getting off at Verdun station. Hiked from there to Thierville, where we slept in Dormitory of French Military academy on cold cement floor. Very cold. Big four gave concert in evening.
Wed Nov: 13 - at 9 a.m. we left

xv "... making hand grenades as the guns stopped and then the bells and whistles cut loose ...". An American soldier, Private T. Wolf, records the events of 11 November 1918 in his diary. (T.Wolf, Liddle Collection)

For the infantryman fighting in the wet and cold Meuse-Argonne, the armistice came as a life-saving release. For those who flew above the battlefields in highly flammable reconnaissance, fighter, or bomber aircraft the ceasefire meant an end to stress, and when the armistice was announced there were more sighs of relief than raucous celebration. The reaction of Captain Percival Gray Hart of the combat-experienced 135th Aero Squadron was fairly typical of American airmen. He recalled that on the night of 11 November he and a number of pilots and officer-observers went to the city of Nancy to a favourite café called the *Liegeois*. Hart remembered that there, the officers, " ... celebrated the end of an era in our lives, an era of adventure and romance such as in our younger days we had never dreamed could come to pass—filled with memoirs and friendships which only death itself can take from us".[10] On the night of 11 November First Lieutenant Gustaf Lindstrom of the 90th Aero Squadron noted how many new, untested, officers there were, and he spent the day remembering those who would never return from France.[11]

The United States had been in the war a little over a year-and-a-half and the home front was three thousand miles away from the Western Front. Americans had experienced scarcely any of the negative effects of war—the ever-present spectre of widows in black, the legions of maimed veterans, critical food and fuel shortages, the depression in morale caused by four years of unrelenting bloodshed. They had no real foundation upon which to gauge the course of the war, either. A few days before the Armistice, Lily Lutman of Clymer, Pennsylvania, wrote to her cousin, Private Blair D. Connor, who was at the front with the 306th Engineer Regiment and she complained about gasless days when no petrol was available. Connor wrote back, "You was talking about your gasless Sundays over there now and that people were getting their buggies out and using them. I guess a girl will be glad to go in anything back there now if she is lucky enough to have a beau that is not in the army".[12]

It was difficult for Americans to sense how the AEF was doing in combat because of censorship. Experience such as that possessed by the British and French simply did not exist. They had a vague idea about the St. Mihiel offensive in early September 1918, and citizens knew that the AEF was in the midst of the Meuse-Argonne operation, but that was all. What news did appear came from heavily censored dispatches from the AEF and from European news agencies which dealt with the entire front in general and usually in glowing terms. Lily Lutman received a very typical letter from Private Connor which stated, "I guess you can see how they [the AEF] are doing the Germans. I think if we keep them going back like we have for a while longer we will make the Kaiser want peace worse than he does now".[13] That was all the censoring officer would allow, and it certainly did not tell Lily Lutman much of value about the war.

The authoritative *New York Times* was as helpful as Private Connor. On the front page, on 1 November 1918, the paper announced a "Teuton collapse hourly expected",[14] but one looked in vain for specific news about the AEF. In the same edition the so-called Military Expert of the *New York Times* stated, "Our own losses have also been extremely heavy", but at no time did this expert even speculate on numbers of Americans killed or wounded. It was clear from his comments that there were no figures coming from the AEF General Headquarters at Chaumont.[15]

Edwin L. James of the *New York Times*, with the 1st U.S. Army in the Meuse-Argonne, reported in the 2 November edition the Germans' retreat and the quantity of prisoners and material captured by the AEF, but was unclear as to where exactly the AEF was, and what casualties had been suffered.[16] When casualties were listed in the newspapers the statistics were six to eight weeks old. Six days prior to the signing of the Armistice the *New York Times* carried a list of local soldiers who had been killed or wounded prior to the St. Mihiel Offensive of 12 September.[17]

Press releases from Washington, Paris, and London focused on the evolving armistice terms and President Woodrow Wilson's role in transmitting terms to Germany. The American people, continually kept in the dark as far as the battlefield was concerned, were well-prepared to receive the welcomed news of the ending of the fighting. When the word came that the Armistice had been signed there were wild demonstrations in every American city, as would be expected. The smaller towns also joined in the euphoria of the day. Cadet Herbert R. Hamm of the Student Army Training Corps at the University of Maine related to his mother that during the morning of 11 November cadet drill was stopped, the boys were loaded onto buses and taken to Bangor, Maine, for an impromptu parade. "We paraded all over the city I guess. My goodness there was an awful crowd in Bangor it seems", Hamm wrote to his mother a day later.[18]

While the citizens of Bangor, Maine, were celebrating, the people of Tupelo, Mississippi, in the deep South, were equally caught up in the joys of the moment. The sister of Private Elijah L. Cosby, [the first soldier from Tupelo to arrive in France], described in a childish hand the events of the night of 11 November:

> The night of the peace the red cross had a parade and school children had a torch apease and march around town and then down to ... Tupelo High [School] and had a sham battle with romalin candles and cannons and fire-crackers. Then some girls danced down in town and then they came up town and danced ... I tole mamma when you come home I would git you to teach me to dance.[19]

In a few days the dancing in Tupelo gave way to more sombre reflections, however. Private Cosby's cousin wrote, "So many boys from Miss[issippi] and Tenn[essee] have been killed in battle ... They are going to turn all the boys out of camp in the states in two weeks. Gordon Gilaspy was killed in battle the 18th of Oct. I only knew him when he was a baby ...".[20]

That night in France, however, there were ceremonies of a sort in the American lines. Flares were fired and wine was drunk — everyone did that. There was immense satisfaction in building a fire at night, and vehicles drove with their lights on.[21] By dusk of Armistice Day there were more rumours.

Many of the old divisions, which had seen the most fighting and suffered the heaviest casualties, were not going to be the first to go home. They were going to Germany, to various locations on the west bank of the Rhine, as a combat/occupation force. Pershing had his doubts about ending the fighting with an armistice, but he had not been fighting since 1914! What he did do was create the U.S. 3rd Army for occupation duty on the Rhine. The Armistice of 11 November 1918, was just that, an armistice, and fighting could begin again should peace discussions break down. His decision to send troops was based on solid military judgement. If combat broke out again, the most experienced, battle-hardened troops should be in the vanguard of the AEF. Consequently, the old divisions — 1st, 2nd, 3rd, 4th, 42nd, 32nd, 89th, were brought up to full strength in a very few days, and were set on the road to Belgium, Luxemburg, and then Germany. With an army headquarters in Coblenz, under the able command of Major General Theodore G. Dickman, the Americans settled in for occupation duties.

Despite much Armistice Day speculation on when American troops would return home, there was not much complaining among the Americans detailed for duty in Germany. The United States of the early twentieth century was mainly rural, small-town, isolated from the outside world. The AEF was very young, and duty on the Rhine, the land of the enemy, was seen as a great adventure. They had seen France, the war- ravaged countryside, the villages, less than spic and span, though very few had seen Paris, where they all wanted to go. As the combat divisions marched into Germany they were greeted by a land that had not been ravaged by war – there were no trench systems, buildings were neat and pavements were cleaned by industrious Hausfrauen, and they admired the pink- cheeked girls. For the young men from Alabama, Iowa, New York, South Carolina, and Colorado the change was dramatic indeed. Poor France, which had suffered since August 1914, seemed now a dirty place, a place of death, and deprivation.

Corporal Maurice Moser of Little Rock, Arkansas, a combat veteran of the 355th Infantry Regiment, had his first real encounter with the "hated Hun" on 15 December 1918. He recorded in his diary that "The German people gave us coffee, bread, butter, marmalade jam and blackberry punch. Some job trying to understand them as they speak a different dutch than other towns we have been at".[22] It appears that food, one of the universal obsessions of all soldiers, became a bridge between the American soldier and the Germans. Private Everett Scott, a farm boy from Iowa, told his mother that "We have a nice room in a big house and I can stand on the porch and watch the boats go up and down [the Rhine], the people treat us real nice ... I am sleeping on a little white bed that makes me think of the one we have in the north room at home".[23] Young men from the deep South were taught to ice skate and build snowmen by pretty German girls. Despite the constant efforts of the American High Command, a good relationship began between the Doughboys and the German people.

The United States Congress, which had voted vast sums of money to sustain the eighteen month effort, was in no mood to keep large numbers of troops in Europe any longer than necessary. With Woodrow Wilson's relationship with Congress deteriorating, it became imperative to show a restive and budget-minded congress that the great burdens were coming to an end. A large number of the divisions in Germany were either National Guard or National Army (conscript), and there was a feeling that these units should be back in the United States as soon as possible.

The course of AEF – Allied relations did not need to be complicated any more, but it was, and by forces which Pershing could not control. On the afternoon of 11 November, Pershing received a stunning cable from Washington. There would be no more troops sent to Europe, and those that were in training in the United States would be sent home as quickly as possible. On 12 November, all over-time pay work would cease and all work on Sunday would end. If replacements were needed for those divisions going to Belgium, Luxembourg and Germany, then they would come from the AEF, not from the United States.[24] Congress and the various bureaux of government, including the War Department, acted very quickly on 11 November to scale down the American commitment to the European war effort. The government, with a one-sided perception of the problem, believed that once the Armistice was signed it was a matter of getting troops home in order to save vast sums of money. Not all of the fault rested with Washington, however. Because of the complexities of waging war so far from home, Pershing had assumed many of the prerogatives which would have normally belonged to Congress or the bureaucracy. He had not communicated well with the War Department, and they had little idea of what the actual progress of the war was or what Pershing had committed to the Allies. Newton Baker, the Secretary of War, visited France a number of times during the war, but very seldom did he question Pershing about his dealings with the Allies. That breakdown of communications between Washington and Chaumont came back to haunt Pershing and the Allies on the very day the Armistice went into effect.

While these were internal American political matters, the desire to save money would very quickly affect the British and the French. Pershing had to announce that all contracts with European firms for war materiel were cancelled.[25] On 12 November, the AEF informed all air units training in Britain, France, and Italy they were to cease operations and prepare for immediate return to the United States. Items which could not be returned or sold were destroyed in the haste to depart. Sergeant Walter Williams of the 27th Aero Squadron was aghast at the pace. He recorded in his diary: "On salvage duty today. Oh my dont the aviation intend to do any more flying?? of all the planes being destroyed and disposed of. Why not sell them cheap to persons that still want to fly. As a civilian I would not mind having one, perhaps a SPAD".[26]

The French government, which had provided vast quantities of equipment, weapons, and aircraft for the AEF, was stunned, and the British government was outraged by AEF actions. In regard to the large number of American aero squadrons training in Britain, the London government informed Pershing that they fully expected the United States to abide by a 5 December 1917 agreement which stated that the British government would be in charge of releasing

U.S. air units. The cost to the British would be huge if all operations ceased only a few days after the Armistice.[27] On 15 November, Pershing complied with directives from Washington and ordered that all purchasing and contracts be discontinued.[28] This caused great irritation among French contractors who had agreed to build buildings and roads for the AEF training facilities.

Throughout the war Pershing had been a difficult Ally to deal with. His orders to build an American army which would fight under its own commanders in its own sector meant that he resisted any attempt to use U.S. troops to bolster the depleted armies of the British and French. Pershing believed in the mission and, at times, thoroughly frustrated his counterparts. He was a stern man, a man saddened by the tragic death of his wife and daughters in a fire in 1915. He imposed his personality on the AEF and drove them hard. Convinced that trench warfare had sapped the fighting spirit of the British and French, he unwisely pushed the AEF into a series of battles – St. Mihiel and the Meuse-Argonne – which became battles of attrition.

No British or French officer ever doubted the élan or the courage of the Doughboy. Since Pershing adopted the doctrine of "open warfare", his soldiers did too. In their minds it was their sacrifice that made final victory possible. Certainly the unending source of manpower tipped the scales for the Allies, and Pershing believed that over two million, eight hundred thousand combat soldiers would enlarge the AEF by the spring campaign of 1919 which would simply smother the war-weary Germans. As the Americans returned home they carried with them the sense that they had made the difference.

Most of the soldiers also had a sense that the home front had little idea what they had actually done in France. Pershing had imposed strict security measures on the AEF in the fall of 1917. In each unit there were officers appointed to be mail censors, and precious little information concerning the actual fighting was sent home by mail. Newspaper reporters, by and large, limited their stories to non-combat situations. Families and friends in the United States had little grasp of the actual conditions at the front. Private B.A. Hunt of West Point, Mississippi, who saw combat service with the 114th Field Signal Battalion, wrote to his sister:

> I really feel sorry for the soldiers when they get back to the States for with all these experiences and the stories they will have to tell will win us the name of the "biggest" fibbers in the world, but lots of it is so, even if it does seem hard to believe. If you would see it for yourself you would say that a man wouldn't live through it, if he was [not] in the best of health.[29]

The effects of censorship were two-fold. First, there was a basic ignorance about what the Doughboys went through. Second, this lack of appreciation for the hardships suffered on the Western Front increased the sense of isolation and alienation which the soldiers felt upon returning to the United States. The picture painted for the home front was basically one of the soldiers in

France enjoying themselves. Countless thousands of French–English dictionaries were produced for the soldiers which seemed to indicate that the Doughboys would spend their time ordering meals, wines, and engaging in polite conversation about the weather, politics, and the like. One of the most popular songs of World War One was "How Ya Gonna Keep 'Em Down on the Farm?" which the soldiers in France were not too fond of. One of the lines went, "They'll never want to see a rake or plow, And who the deuce can parley vous a cow. How ya gonna keep'em down on the farm, after they've seen Paree?"[30] Even during the Armistice period very few soldiers visited Paris, but that was not the popular perception of the life of the Doughboy. Nor were women who served in the AEF immune from the popular view of the French experience. One popular song, "Oh Frenchy", telling the story of an ambulance nurse, stated that she, " ... met a chap named Jean, a soldier from Paree, when he said 'Parle [sic] – vous, my pet', She said, 'I will, but not just yet ... ".[31]

During the eighteen months that America was a belligerent, people on the home front were called upon to make sacrifices for the war effort. On 24 April 1917, Congress passed the First Liberty Loan Act, which totalled 5 billion dollars in loans. There were four such liberty bond acts, and rallies were held all over the United States with popular entertainers exhorting the crowds to buy more bonds. A War Industries Board was established in July 1917 to oversee the American industrial effort, and in August 1917 the Lever Food and Fuel Act was passed. This law aimed at the conservation of foods and fuels, establishing such measures as a "wheatless Monday, a meatless Tuesday, and a porkless Thursday". In theory, this conservation of food would assist in feeding the large number of troops either in training in the United States or in Europe with the AEF. Once the Armistice was signed on 11 November 1918, the controls were lifted despite the precarious status of the ceasefire.

The conscription act which went into effect immediately after the April 1917 declaration of war was basically a fair law. It had a "work or fight" provision and exempted only those men who were engaged in necessary war-related industries and businesses. As more and more men were drafted, however, their places were taken by others, men and women, and little was done to insure that a returning AEF veteran could get his old job back. Those men released from training camps directly after the Armistice stood first in line to get jobs, and there were few left for those combat veterans who had served on the Western Front and in Germany. It seemed to be a land of prosperity except for those who had fought! After serving in contact with the enemy since February 1918, Leslie Langille expressed his feelings about his homecoming thus:

> ... a grateful government gives us an honorable discharge from the army — and sixty dollars. What a burst of patriotism must have prompted our solons to pass a bill giving each discharged soldier sixty dollars with which to start a new life ... On the train, headed for Chicago, with just enough money to buy a suit of civilian clothes, the thought of another and different kind of a battle faces us. How about a job?[32]

When the Armistice was announced on 11 November almost all military training stopped in the United States. Many men were in fact sent home immediately. Military schools were terminated as cost-saving measures went into effect. Within a few days those ex-soldiers, who had seen no service in France, were seeking employment. However, many of those who had joined in the joyous celebrations of 11 November found that the next day they had a deep sense of embarrassment at not being in the great battles of the Western Front. A week before the Armistice took effect, American newspapers carried such headlines as "Heavy Blows by Pershing ... a dozen towns are freed".[33] On 8 November there was a false report of the signing of the Armistice and an end to the fighting, and there were scenes of wild, shouting parades. The mayor of New York City ordered all saloons to be closed to stop disorders.[34] Once it was clear that the report was in error, newspapers, which were the only source of information for the public, continued with stories from Pershing's headquarters that the offensive went on at a furious pace. All of the reports were vague as to what ground was taken, and never were there reports of battle casualties.[35] Once the actual Armistice was signed, and the euphoria of the day subsided, there was the realization that, after 11 November, the Great War—the great adventure—had passed them by. They really could not answer the question, "What did you do in the Great War?"

Despite their early employment and release from service, many of those who did not serve in France felt a deep resentment that the returning veterans would find hard to comprehend. Not to be a part of the "Big Parade" was viewed as a slight on their manhood, their patriotism. A terribly embarrassed officer wrote a bitter poem about his feelings. It was published in the official classbook of the Officer Training School at Camp Gordon, near Atlanta, Georgia, in November 1918. His lament was fairly typical of those who saw the Armistice of November 1918 as the end of their hopes for overseas service. This unnamed soldier wrote:

The unlucky ones in this great war
Are not the men who are killed
Nor wounded ones, be they Allies or Huns
No matter what blood they have spilled
The most unfortunate man to-day
Is the man who jumped at the chance
To fight like hell from the tap of the bell
But who'll never see service in France.[36]

For those who returned from the Meuse – Argonne those lines could only show how little was known of the reality of active service in France.

Even worse was the sense of distance and alienation many felt from their own families. Those who remained at home had no concept of the conditions under which the soldiers had lived. The strict policy of censorship in the United States, coupled with the stringent AEF policies of censorship, actually hid the gruesome nature of the World War One battlefield. While civilians saw posters supporting such things as the four Liberty Loans or voluntary rationing, they had no idea what the Western Front was like. The vision of Paris, pretty French girls, and French wine was conjured up by the popular press and popular music. The government had seen fit to suppress the actual casualty figures from the Meuse – Argonne Offensive, and unless a family had lost a loved one the full magnitude of the effort was hidden from view. Books by soldiers were mainly humorous ones like Edward Streeter's *Dere Mable* and *Thats me all Over Mabel*, which were stories of camp life as told by a semi-literate private to his fiancée, Mabel. Streeter served in the 77th Division in combat. *Conscript 2989: Experiences of a Drafted Man* was another popular book which recounted life in a conscript division. These books were written in the United States; the Western Front produced little light-hearted literature.

In 1918, for example, a popular song was "You'll Have to Put Him to Sleep with the Marseillaise and Wake Him Up with a Oh-la-la". Reflecting the inherent silliness in popular music in any age, this one, which sold a lot of sheet music copies, had lines such as, "You better learn to parlez – vous when your soldier boy comes back to you. Girls he has learned a lot of things in France". What he learned was high explosive shells, mustard gas, and short rations. How could one overcome the popular image of the Great War experience? It was easier to draw inward and not try to communicate the reality of the conflict. The veteran had his own music — "Over There", "A Long Way to Tipperary" — and he had probably never heard many of the tunes which his family had heard, bought, and played on the piano.

The combat soldiers of the Armistice never called themselves a "lost generation". That would be the province of writers like Ernest Hemingway or F. Scott Fitzgerald. They saw themselves as common men who were called upon to fight in the Great War, and once it was over they sought wives, jobs, and some way to forget the battlefield. Some of their number, of course, went on to serve again in various capacities in the next world war!

What then did the Armistice of 11 November 1918, mean for the Americans? For John J. Pershing and the ranking officers of the GHQ, AEF, it meant a vindication of the American soldier as a fighting man, equal to any in the world. The bravery and the élan were there, but they fought with little skill. The doctrine of open warfare, which Pershing adamantly believed in, caused battles of attrition. By the end of the Meuse – Argonne fighting, the AEF was nearly played out. But, on the other hand, there were millions of American combat troops ready to pour into France during the winter of 1918 – 1919 prepared for the great offensive of the spring of 1919. That massive number of healthy young soldiers, coupled with Pershing's willingness to commit them to battle as the AEF, made eventual victory inevitable on the Western Front. Of course, the Armistice that November meant that Pershing could never prove what he held as a matter of doctrine.

The impact on the reputation of the United States as a member of the community of nations is much less clear. European leaders felt that they would have trouble with Woodrow Wilson the idealist, the author of the Fourteen Points, but few could have envisaged how rapidly the United States would begin the processes of disengagement from the Great War. The immediate halting of troops for the AEF followed by the ending of contracts and construction was an unpleasant surprise for the British and French. The Armistice did not at that stage mean a permanent end to the war, but Washington gave every indication of believing this. British and French leadership had reason to wonder about the level of American commitment to European security in the immediate aftermath of the war. It seemed that the United States was demonstrating its status as an Associate, not one of the Allies. Certainly Pershing sent the 3rd U.S. Army to Germany and troops to guard the Lines of Communication, but that continued presence was seriously reduced in the spring of 1919 when most of the National Guard and draftee divisions went back to the United States. Was the United States truly now an isolationist state again, and were great matters of mutual concern guided by money issues alone?

Then there was the effect of the Armistice on the men who fought in the Great War. Does the term 'Lost Generation' apply to those men who served in France? Certainly they never applied the term to themselves, but the veterans were disillusioned with the course of world and national politics. Their reaction, especially those in the combat divisions, was muted. The night of 11 November saw rocket firing and much wine drinking, but the men were too tested in the crucible of battle to react flamboyantly. Sergeant Calvin Lambert, who had been in France since the fall of 1917, wrote in his diary:

> Last night the town was lit like a drunken colonel. Fires were burning and there was no attempt to hide from the dutch avions. I heard men yell "lights out", but the only response was a cheerful "Go to Hell" ... I slept soundly last night but I couldn't realize that there were no more planes to fear, no more shells to dodge, no more camoflage, and no more wondering when the war will end.[37]

Lambert, who went on to a career in journalism in his native Kansas, was pretty typical of the American soldiers. He differed in one respect: he knew he had a job when he returned to the United States. The employment situation was a critical one and would remain so, especially for those who served in the forces in Germany until the spring of 1919. Problems adjusting to their families and a sense of isolation plagued the veterans for years to come. For the United States the Armistice meant a return to business as usual, and American withdrawal into an isolationist shell.

In the long run, the Armistice caused more problems for the United States than it solved. The brief foray of America into world affairs was unsatisfying for everyone concerned and raised serious questions about the ability of the U.S. to make a commitment and stick to it. The army of the United States, so massive in manpower, was allowed to shrink very rapidy because of a shortage of funds granted by an economy-minded congress. Those Americans who served on the Western Front were embittered by their reception and lack of employment. It would be twenty-three years before the United States would be propelled into another world war, and with many of the lessons of the

Great War and the Armistice of 1918 lost and having to be painfully relearned.

Endnotes

1 Leslie Langille, *Men of the Rainbow*, Chicago: The O'Sullivan Publishing House, 1933, pp. 167–68.
2 John J. Pershing, *My Experiences in the World War*, I, Blue Ridge Summit, PA: Tab Books, Military Classics Reprint, 1989, pp. 37–40.
3 "Allied Plan of Campaign for Autumn and Winter of 1918, and Summer of 1919," in the Briant Harris Wells Papers, U.S. Army Military History Archives, Carlisle Barracks, Pennsylvania.
4 Donald Smythe, *Pershing: General of the Armies* (Bloomington: University of Indiana Press, 1986), pp. 144–45.
5 Diary Entry, 27 September 1918, in the Pershing Diaries, The Papers of John J. Pershing, the Library of Congress, Washington, DC.
6 Diary Entry, 4 October 1918, *ibid.*
7 Elmer Sherwood, *Rainbow Hoosier*, Indianapolis: Printing Arts Co., 1925, p. 134.
8 Diary Entry, 11 November 1918, in the War Diaries of Sgt. Walter S. Williams, in the Air Force Historical Agency Archives, Maxwell Air Force Base, Alabama.
9 Diary Entry, 11 November 1918, in the Calvin Lambert Diaries, Emporia, Kansas, Public Library.
10 Percival Gray Hart, History of the 135th Aero Squadron, Chicago: Chicago Law Printing Co., 1939, p. 154.
11 Peter Kilduff (ed.). "Observations: The War Diary of Lt. Gustaf L. Lindstrom", *Cross and Cockade Journal* XIII (Summer, 1972), pp. 126–127.
12 Letter from Blair Connor to Lily Lutman, 29 October 1918, in the Blair Connor Letters (James Cooke, personal collection).
13 *Ibid.*
14 *New York Times*, 1 November 1918, p. 1.
15 *Ibid*, p. 2.
16 *Ibid*, 2 November 1918, pp. 1–2.
17 *Ibid*, 5 November 1918, p. 9.
18 Letter from Hamm to his Mother, Orono, Maine, 13 November 1918, in the Cadet Herbert R. Hamm (SATC) Letters (James Cooke, personal collection).
19 Sister to Pte Elijah L. Cosby, Tupelo, Mississippi, 13 November 1918, in the Cosby Family Papers (James Cooke, personal collection).
20 Susan Sandifer to Pte Elijah L. Cosby, Tupelo, Mississippi, 18 November 1918, *ibid.*
21 John B. Hayes, *Heroes Among the Brave*, Loachapoka, Alabama: Lee County Historical Society, 1973, p. 41.
22 Diary entry, 15 December 1918, in the Maurice Moser Diaries (James Cooke, personal collection). Editorial note: this evidence contrasts markedly with British personal documentation recording considerable hardship.
23 Letter from Everett Scott to his Mother, Niederbreisig, 17 December 1918, in the Everett Scott Letters (James Cooke, personal collection).
24 Cable from the U.S. War Department to Pershing, Washington, 11 November 1918, in Records Group 18, U.S. Air Forces, Entry 96, National Archives, Washington, DC.
25 G5, Air Service, AEF, Report on Demobilization of Training, c. 15 December

1918, in Records Group 120, Records of the AEF, Entry 640, National Archives, Washington, DC.

26 Diary Entry, 22 January 1919, Walter S. Williams Diary, see endnote 8.

27 Captain H.G. Leslie, Report of Training of American Aviation in England, c. 15 December 1918, in Records Group 120, Entry 640, National Archives, Washington, DC.

28 Cable from Pershing to the War Department, Chaumont, 15 November 1918, in Records Group 18, Entry 96, National Archives, Washington, DC.

29 Letter from B.A. Hill to his Sister, Souilly, 2 December 1918, in the B.A. Hill Letters (James Cooke, personal collection).

30 "How 'Ya Gonna Keep 'Em Down on the Farm?" by Joe Young, Sam Lewis, and Walter Donaldson. New York: Waterson, Berlin and Snyder Co., 1919.

31 "Oh Frenchy," by Sam Ehrlich and Con Conrad. New York: Broadway Music Corporation, 1918.

32 Langille, *Men of the Rainbow*, *op. cit.*, pp. 190–91.

33 *New York Times*, 2 November 1918, p. 1.

34 *Ibid.*, 8 November 1918, pp. 1, 3.

35 *Ibid.*, 10 November 1918, p. 5.

36 "Interned — C.O.T.S.", in *Lest We Forget, C.O.T.S., Camp Gordon, GA* (Camp Gordon: Camp Printing, January,1919), p. 3.

37 Diary Entry, 12 November 1918, The Calvin Lambert Diary. See endnote 9.

40. French soldiers gather for a ceremony of thanksgiving in Lille, after the liberation of the town (Collection Archives departementales du Nord, CL 15 FI 1427 J 322) (Chapter 6 - The French)

41. Parisians celebrate in *Fête de l'Armistice, place de la Concorde, le 11 Novembre,* painted by Paul Seguin-Berthault [1869-1964]. (Musée Carnavalet, Paris) (Chapter 6 - The French)

42. Marshal Philippe Pétain reviews the march past of triumphal French soldiers as they enter Metz, on 19 November 1918. As the troops file past, General Fayolle, the Army Commander, shakes the hand of the Commander-in-Chief, while on the horse nearest the camera General Buat looks on. (Le Miroir, 1 December 1918) (Chapter 6 - The French)

43. A post-Armistice legacy for France: human remains collected from various parts of the Verdun battlefield rest in a temporary ossuary.
(R.C. Money, Liddle Collection) (Chapter 6 - The French)

44. Belgian troops entering Torhout, 19 October 1918. In the background the former Feldbuchhandlung, field book store for German troops.
(Archives of the Royal Palace, Brussels) (Chapter 6 - The Belgians)

45. Almost as soon as the Armistice came into effect, refugees began returning to the devastated areas, often, like this family, carrying all of their possessions on a single cart.
(M.F.T. Baines, Liddle Collection) (Chapter 7 - The Belgians)

46. The Belgian Royal Family at the head of the army entering Ghent on 13 November 1918. The Queen receives a bouquet, while the King acknowledges the cheers of people in the upper storey windows. (Archives of the Royal Palace, Brussels) (Chapter 7 - The Belgians)

47. The British Army and the Belgian Government quickly put up huts like this one, to accommodate Belgian refugees. At first, for much of the returning civilian population, almost everything that they had was supplied to them by the British Army, from housing to tools to items of clothing such as greatcoats.
(R.F. Pritchard, Liddle Collection) (Chapter 7 - The Belgians)

Pourquoi Pas ?
GAZETTE HEBDOMADAIRE PARAISSANT LE JEUDI SOIR

48. The Belgian resistance in action. Manneken-Pis is scattering the German armies with the force of his powerful jet of water. Cartoon in the liberal weekly *Pouquoi pas?*
(University Library, Leuven)
(Chapter 7 - The Belgians)

49. Pilots and enlisted groundcrew of the American 1st Aero Squadron, wearing a collection of German souvenirs, celebrate the news of the Armistice in France.
(James J. Cooke collection)
(Chapter 8 - The Americans)

50. A shower of tickertape greets news of the Armistice in New York, November 1918. (via Patrick Gariépy) (Chapter 8 - The Americans)

51. Happy to be going home: US troops en route for the States. The US began a rapid demobilisation soon after the Armistice. (Patrick Gariépy collection) (Chapter 8 - The Americans)

52. A sadder homecoming: an American serviceman being reinterred in the United States. The US was one of the few nations to begin to repatriate its dead after the Armistice. (Patrick Gariépy collection) (Chapter 8 - The Americans)

53. The end of the war came one month early for some Australians: this group is about to leave Bray in France on 10 October 1918 for two months' special furlough in Australia. In September 1918, 'Anzac Leave' was granted to the 'originals', those men who had left Australia in 1914 and had served four years in the AIF. Some 6000 'originals' left France on home leave, and with the end of the war in November, they were discharged in Australia. (Australian War Memorial, Negative No. E03534) (Chapter 9 - Australians)

54. Part of the immense crowd in Martin Place, Sydney, on Monday 11 November 1918, celebrating news received early that evening of the signing of the Armistice. Boisterous crowds paraded through the streets of Sydney, singing patriotic songs and cheering. They also hanged and burnt effigies of the Kaiser. (Australian War Memorial, Negative No. H11563) (Chapter 9 - Australians)

Chapter Nine

Australians at the End of the Great War

Ashley Ekins

When the guns of the Western Front fell silent on 11 November 1918, there were almost six and a half million men in the Allied armies on that front, over four million of them combatants.[1] The British Expeditionary Force (BEF) contained 56 divisions and covered a front of some sixty miles in France and Belgium.[2] Within these massive armies, the Australian Corps, then numbering less than 100,000 soldiers, was a minuscule though integral formation. Yet by the end of the war the five divisions of the Australian Imperial Force (AIF) had achieved a fighting reputation which belied these numbers. An Australian commander wrote in 1919 that during the final months of the war the Australian Corps, although comprising less than 10 per cent of the total strength of the BEF, defeated 39 German divisions, advanced 37 miles, liberated 116 villages and towns, and captured almost a quarter of all the German prisoners and guns captured by the British armies.[3] Some in England dismissed these claims as "Australian boasting" but in time they became popularly accepted as part of the image of the Australians. The basis of some of the claims requires re-examination.[4] Excessive focus on the combat performance of Dominion troops has, until recently, tended to obscure the very real achievements of the British Army in securing victory in 1918.[5] However, there is no doubt that the Australians were regarded as a *corps d'élite* and their five divisions were successful as spearhead troops in many of the battles which led to the German surrender.

In their final battles of the war, the Australian Corps, together with the British III and IX Corps, breached the formidable German defences of the Hindenburg Line in late-September and early-October. On 5 October, eleven Australian battalions, although depleted to a fighting strength of about 260 men, drove through the Beaurevoir Line, the reserve system of the Hindenburg Line, and captured Montbrehain village.[6] However, their sustained advance had taken a heavy toll. The Australian Corps suffered almost 35,000 casualties, including over 7,000 dead, in the four months' fighting from 1 June to 5 October.[7] Eleven of the 60 Australian infantry battalions were disbanded in May and September 1918 due to a lack of reinforcements following the failure of the Australian government's campaign to introduce conscription in December 1917.[8] All five Australian divisions were exhausted. They were withdrawn from the front line by 5 October and sent to Abbeville for rest and refitting. Only Australian support units remained fighting with the advancing armies up to 11 November.[9]

The Australian infantry divisions began their return to the front on 5 November one month after their October withdrawal. By 11 November the 1st and 4th Australian Divisions were arriving near their new Corps headquarters in Le Cateau. They were delayed by demolished bridges and junctions and few Australian troops were at the front when the Armistice was announced. Official historian Charles Bean wrote that most men were too stunned or emotionally drained to celebrate the news: "For the troops there [in France] the change went too deep for outward rejoicing; on the surface, life continued as usual except for the cessation of actual fighting. Neither [in the rear at Le Cateau], nor at the front, was there any general demonstration – the sound of guns ceased; the gates of the future silently opened".[10] Another historian concurs: "Hardly a man anywhere reacted to the momentous news".[11] Similar reactions are ascribed to British and American troops on the Western Front. The news of the Armistice, according to one account, precipitated "an orgy of celebration and rejoicing in Britain. The troops in the front line remained calm and sober. It was over. That was enough".[12]

This remains the common perception of the general reaction to the Armistice – civilians indulging in wild celebrations while soldiers received the event with a numb bitterness. But as one scholar has shown, the reality was more complex than this image would suggest.[13] The varieties of individual responses were quite diverse and it seems that the enthusiasm of Australian celebrations tended to increase with distance from the front line.

Many Australian soldiers displayed only slight or unenthusiastic reactions. One recorded proudly in his diary on 11 November the success of his mule team in the previous day's sports competition: "the old grey donks pulled off the prize, bringing home the Blue Ribbon for the third time, also a couple of Gold Medals". Almost as an afterthought, he added that the cessation of hostilities was announced to his unit on parade: "There wasn't a cheer, not even a handshake. The trouble is, it has been expected so long, and is such great news that the crowd can't believe it".[14] Another reported that on receiving the news, "the men just stood quiet and looked at one another, as though they couldn't take it in. One felt like crawling away on his own, the relief was so great. Some of the boys got drunk, but the majority just seemed stunned as though they were afraid it might not be true. We were a quiet and subdued crowd".[15] A soldier of the 17th Australian Battalion laconically wrote, "*The day of days.* We had two victory's today. We won the War and defeated the 5th Field Company at Soccer. The news of the Armistice was taken very coolly ... nobody seemed to be able to realize it".[16]

However, there were also joyful responses. An Australian gunner wrote of his battery, "The result came out about 10 am and we went into Amiens and had a good time. Everyone went mad".[17] An Australian medical officer described celebrations in Rouen in similar terms:

> We went quite mad. We cheered and we sang and we went into Rouen. And what a sight it was. Rouen had come out *en masse* and the streets were nothing but a seething happy mass of all sorts of people – civilians, Tommies, Jocks, Diggers [Australians], Canadians, Indians etc. – all waving flags, singing, cheering, dancing, kissing. All restraint was thrown off and the people went wild with joy and happiness. Wine flowed freely ... and in the middle of all the crowd was an Australian band playing 'Australia will be there'.[18]

An Australian soldier of the 20th Battalion described his part in joyful celebrations in the French town of Vignacourt where his unit was billeted: "an Armastice signed great fun with French people, a mate and I went to the

Drawn by A. Storr.

UNLUCKY.

"Cripes! there's stiffness fer yer! We've just finished building this bonzer possie, stove and all, ready for the Winter, and now they go and make an Armistice!"

xvi A cartoon from a post-Armistice edition of the Australian soldiers' magazine, *Aussie.* (via H.P. Cecil)

Church and climed up to the steple, and hoisted the French and Australian flags, there were over 1,000 Australians around the church at the time all the 5 Brigade, the band played the National Anthem, and god save the king".[19] On the following day all his unit attended a Thanksgiving service and a Brigade sports day.

An Australian gunner with the Australian 105th Howitzer Battery described to his mother how his unit had been marching through Péronne on 11 November as the Armistice was announced and "all the train whistles blew, and kept blowing for about a quarter of an hour, you never heard such an awful row in all your life". He added, "You don't know how pleased we are at being out of the fighting at last, thank God".[20] Another Australian gunner in Péronne that evening recorded in his diary, "Tonight flares and rockets are going up and whistles are shreiking all over the place".[21] Significantly perhaps, his diary has no entries for the following four days. Yet another Australian, ruefully noted that as his unit was in a deserted village, they could not "even buy a bottle of soda water to celebrate the joyful news ... Cheers are floating round the camp just as well we are not near an inhabited city they would run amuk with joy".[22]

Some Australian troops did indeed run amok and their behaviour in the rear areas strained the tolerance of both military and civil authorities. According to one account, Australian soldiers from a convalescent camp in Boulogne celebrated the Armistice by breaking into stores of beer and then raping the women in a brothel in the rue de St Pol and setting fire to their furniture. The military police arrived late and none of the Australians appear to have been arrested.[23] This incident, with its echoes of the notorious 'battle of the Wazza' in Cairo in 1915, seems to have confirmed the worst fears of the British High Command about the potential behaviour of the 'wild colonials' in peace time.[24] One week later the Adjutant-General of the BEF issued a warning to all units that offences such as looting or molesting local inhabitants constituted 'war crimes' under the general laws of war. Such offences would be dealt with by military courts which could, he warned, "award any civilized punishment, including death, but not corporal punishment".[25]

These sanctions did not apply in the United Kingdom where over 60,000 Australian soldiers were based at the time of the Armistice. Over the previous four years the Australians had acquired in Britain a reputation for lawlessness which had tarnished their initial reception by the British public during the Gallipoli campaign. However, according to one historian, the Australians' indisciplined behaviour was largely a perception of the British imagination. He concludes: "Overall, Australians appeared before civilian magistrates on petty charges of no great consequence ... more evidence of high-spirits and thoughtlessness than of criminality".[26] It has to be said that this judgement defies his own evidence of drunkenness and riots, theft and bashings, and even rape and murder of British civilians by Australian soldiers. Moreover, most Australian soldiers who were charged with such offences in the United Kingdom did not appear before the civil courts. They were charged with civil and related offences under military law and dealt with by courts martial. There were over 9,000 courts martial of Australian soldiers for crimes committed in the United Kingdom during the war years. Although the majority was for charges of absence without leave, a substantial number involved crimes against civilians, drunkenness, theft, assaults, robbery with violence, fraud, indecency, resisting arrest and escaping confinement.[27] The number and content of the AIF courts martial records forces the conclusion that, in Britain at least, the Australians' reputation may have been deserved.

Australian soldiers' actions during the Armistice celebrations in London further confirmed that reputation. As the rejoicing continued into the evening of 12 November, Dominion soldiers ransacked bus signs and road dumps for timber and at around midnight built bonfires at the base of Nelson's Column in Trafalgar Square. The huge blaze left scars on the monument which are visible today. Although the incident confirmed the popular image of Dominion troops as the worst behaved soldiers, it appears that many British troops were also among the rioters.[28] An Australian infantry officer on convalescent leave in London observed the bonfire, for which Australians were later blamed, but which he claimed was led by a New Zealand soldier who urged on the crowd.[29] In fact the story was soon appropriated by many Australian soldiers who seemed to glory in their reputation. An Australian gunner, who was not present, wrote from France to a friend, "I suppose you saw the account of the joy fire the night of the Armistice near Nelson's monument in London. We hear, as usual in all horseplay, the Aussies were in command".[30] Members of the British War Cabinet were not so amused when they discussed the incident shortly afterwards. Colonial Secretary Walter Long remarked that the Australians "apparently intended to make their behaviour in Cairo in 1915 a standard for future action"; he urged that Australian soldiers should be removed from London as soon as possible.[31]

The indiscipline of Australian soldiers had been a constant concern to the British High Command throughout the war. At the time of the Armistice the number (per thousand strength) of Australians in military prisons in France and Belgium was eight times that of British troops and four times that of all the other dominion troops combined – and the number of Australians in military prisons was rising steeply.[32] Within days of the news of the Armistice, Australian prisoners were involved in disturbances in military prisons which appear to have been provoked by the belief that prisoners would be released upon the cessation of hostilities. On 14 November a mob of between 500 and 1,000 soldiers from the 39th General Hospital at Le Havre stormed a nearby No. 1 Field Punishment Compound and released 33 prisoners. Seven Australian soldiers and one British soldier were arrested as ringleaders; five were found guilty and received sentences ranging from 2 years imprisonment with hard labour to 5 years penal servitude. On 19 November a more serious riot occurred at No. 2 Military Prison in Rouen during which the Prison Governor and his staff drew their revolvers and threatened to shoot prisoners. The incident resulted in 23 Australian soldiers and 15 British and Canadian soldiers being charged with mutiny. One Australian escaped before his court martial but the remaining 37 soldiers received sentences ranging from 56 days Field Punishment No. 1 to 3 years 9 months penal servitude.[33] The severity of military punishments in the BEF was clearly not relaxed with the coming of the peace.

Australian divisional artillery and trench mortar batteries, continued to support the advancing British Fourth Army's attacks on the retreating German army right up to the Armistice. These batteries served with the II American and the IX British Corps until the battle of Le Cateau on 4 November. For the support units each advance meant the need to bring up vast quantities of ammunition and rations along with horses and fodder. The new war of movement brought new dangers and discomforts and a steady toll in casualties. The retreating German armies had devastated and booby-trapped the towns and villages and the artillery batteries and ammunition supply columns had to seek shelter each night in open country, often utilizing makeshift trenches to protect themselves from the cold and harassing enemy shellfire.[34] "Before, we had dugouts to live in", according to one gunner, "but when we were going forward we had to depend on any shelter we could get. Sometimes we would have to sleep under the guns and trust to luck".[35] An Australian ammunition column driver recorded how his unit was caught in an enemy barrage while transporting ammunition to the front line:

> We sheltered in a sunken road. We tied our teams to waggon wheels and sheltered in dugouts. It was a living Hell for a time. Two of our gunners had to be sent back or else they would have gone mad. It was awful to see men in such condition. Their nerves were completely gone. They could only crouch in the corners of the dugout and keep up a continual moaning.[36]

One Australian gunner's battery had gone into action near Busigny on 17 October and suffered heavy gas casualties from German shelling before being withdrawn on 22 October. He wrote, "We only pulled out yesterday because we couldn't carry on. The men and horses are absolutely knocked up. Believe two or three batteries have been wiped out and we are paying dearly for this advance".[37]

Australian salvage companies, sappers and tunnellers also worked in the forward areas, repairing the damaged bridges and disarming and disposing of hundreds of delayed-action mines and booby traps left behind by the Germans during their retreat. Five men of the 1st Australian Tunnelling Company were killed and five wounded while constructing a tank bridge over the Sambre-Oise Canal near Le Cateau, one week before the Armistice. They were among the last Australian battle casualties of the war.[38] When the news of the Armistice reached them, many soldiers who had been through the heavy fighting of 1918 were simply glad to have survived. On 11 November an Australian bombardier whose unit had been in action 24 hours before, wrote to his parents, "Hostilities ceased this morning at 11 am. It seemed almost too good to be true ... you cannot imagine the feeling of all us boys to think that we have pulled through safe and sound ... now we are all looking forward to getting back home again".[39]

News of the Armistice quickly reached Allied prisoners in German prison camps. According to an Australian sergeant-major who was released in

September 1918, after two years as a prisoner of war in Germany, "The best fed man in Germany is today the British prisoner of war – his Red Cross parcels arrive regularly".[40] Not all prisoners would have agreed with his judgement, especially in 1918. An Australian, captured in May, recorded months of hunger and hard labour as a prisoner in various camps as well as his punishment of 14 days bread and water in solitary confinement when he was recaptured after escaping.[41] With the news of the Armistice, of course everything changed as prisoners refused to take orders from the guards, many of whom soon abandoned their posts. Another Australian prisoner wrote that his group learnt of the Armistice from civilians; they were told two days later by the German officer in charge, "that we were free and could go wherever we pleased but to stay and wait for the British and that he had placed us in charge of the Bergomaster".[42] Given the treatment of some prisoners by the Germans it seems likely that some retributions occurred at the time of the Armistice but most prisoners soon joined the lines of hungry civilian refugees winding their way back to France and Belgium. An Australian soldier in the forward areas described how the roads near Ponchaux were crowded with hundreds of British POWs released by the Germans and thousands of women and children travelling west from the liberated territories: "The Tommies and Aussies shared their blankets and rations with these unfortunate people".[43]

In addition to relocating civilians and prisoners of war after the Armistice, all nations faced the problem of demobilizing their huge armies in the field. This presented difficulties for the Australian government whose troops were serving at great distances from Australia in the main theatres. At the end of the war there were between 167,000 and 185,000 Australians on service overseas.[44] They were deployed in three main areas. The largest group comprised between 87,000 and 95,000 men of the AIF in the British field army in France and Belgium; there were also between 60,000 and 63,000 Australians in hospitals, training camps and depots in the United Kingdom; and there were some 30,000 in Egypt, Mesopotamia, in the lesser theatres and aboard troopships at sea. In addition, there were between 4,000 and 5,000 Australian munition workers and war workers in the United Kingdom; over 4,000 Australians were serving in the Royal Australian Navy; and 3,000 were serving in the four squadrons of the Australian Flying Corps.[45] Over 1,500 Australian military nurses were serving in bases from India and Salonika to Egypt, Italy, France and the United Kingdom.[46]

One fortunate group of Australian soldiers had begun their passage home a month or more before the Armistice. In September 1918, 'Anzac Leave', consisting of two months' special furlough in Australia, was granted to the 'originals', those Australian troops who had left Australia in 1914. The first contingent of 800 men withdrawn from their units was in fact ordered on the eve of a major attack on the Hindenburg Line. This contingent left the Western Front battlefields on 14 September, the departure leaving some units seriously depleted for combat. Over the following weeks some 6,000 'originals' left on home leave to Australia.[47] An Australian officer wrote that some, however, elected to stay in England: "All the 1914 boys have gone to Aussie. Some of them are having their spell in Blighty. In that case they get

75 days leave, 75 days pay in advance, 3s a day exes, and 25 per cent of their deferred pay. I think that an extremely liberal thing too".[48]

For all of them, the war would be over before their leave expired. They were discharged in Australia. Many of the returning soldiers first heard of the Armistice while on board troopships at sea. One young signaller on "Anzac leave" celebrated his twenty-second birthday and the Armistice on the same day, "somewhere in the Indian Ocean". He had enlisted in Sydney in September 1914 at the age of 17. At 18 he took part in the Gallipoli landing on 25 April 1915. By his 19th birthday he was a veteran of the Gallipoli campaign and at 21 he fought in the decisive battles which halted the German advance at Villers-Bretonneux in April 1918. On 11 November 1918 he was sailing for home, having survived four long years of war. At the time of his death on 10 December 1997, aged 101, Signaller Ted Matthews was Australia's last surviving "original Anzac".[49]

Repatriation of the remaining 200,000 Australians still overseas at the time of the Armistice became the concern of the Australian Corps commander, Lieutenant-General John Monash, who was appointed Director-General of Repatriation and Demobilization on 21 November.[50] Many problems had to be resolved: the early return of convalescents; the discharge of some soldiers abroad; the occupation and entertainment of troops waiting in camps; and their education and recreation on the long sea voyage. For the soldiers of course, the crucial issue was that of the order of embarkation. After considering the return of the AIF by regiments, the guiding principle Monash decided upon was the democratic one of "first to come out, first to return". This seemed fairest to most men. Despite the shortage of shipping for the long journey to Australia, a steady stream of embarkations was departing for Australia within a month of the Armistice. Initial planning indicated that it would take eighteeen months to transport all the Australians home but, through masterful staff work, most had embarked within eight months and the task was virtually completed within a year. By the end of 1919 over 177,000 soldiers, munition workers, war workers and their families had embarked for Australia from the main theatres and only 7,000 remained.[51]

About 60,000 Australian dead and missing servicemen did not return home. Their loss would be mourned in Australia for a generation. A further 6,000 Australians remained abroad, many of them electing to be discharged overseas.[52] Over 900 Australian soldiers remained unaccounted for, having been declared 'illegal absentees' during the war.[53] Their number lends credence to the persistent belief that by the end of the war gangs of Australian deserters were marauding in the rear areas of France, raiding camps and dumps and evading the military police.[54] There were numerous attempts to capture these deserters in the final months of the war.[55] One week before the Armistice, the 5th Australian Division mounted a secret operation to round up absentees believed to be in the Australian Corps area and "mixing with the troops".[56] The operation appears to have had limited success.[57] Similar operations continued over the following months. A British officer records that on 9 January 1919, two companies of his battalion were sent fully armed to

Sailly Laurette on the Somme to search for "a nest of Australian deserters, who had been terrorising and living on the neighbourhood".[58] They succeeded in capturing only two men who were handed over to the Australian authorities. An Australian officer described in early-November an "organized search and round-up for all absentees and deserters" in which he led his battalion in beating Carillon Wood. They made no captures but he recorded that the 4th Pioneers exchanged revolver shots with eight deserters in Ailly sur Somme, one of whom, dressed as a corporal of his battalion, was shot and killed.[59] Having defied such attempts to capture them, at least 750 Australian deserters remained at large twenty years after the end of the war.[60]

There were also disciplinary problems aboard the returning troopships, perhaps inevitable in transporting to Australia some 180,000 soldiers. Many troopships contained groups of potentially refractory soldiers: there were the 'incorrigibles' weeded out from units and deported home;[61] there were large numbers of Australian soldiers who had been serving with their units under suspended sentences previously awarded by courts martial;[62] and there were also the inmates of military prisons and detention barracks in France and Britain who were transported under custody.[63] Such men sometimes had to be accommodated in ships without adequate detention cells and containing other Australian soldiers being repatriated with their wives and families.[64] The British wife of an AIF officer later wrote a vivid recollection of her nightmare journey to Australia on board such a troopship:

> H.Q. has unloaded a whole gang of prisoners on us, and I don't suppose there are a worse set of fellows in the whole A.I.F. than this little lot. Some were in for murder and some for theft and some for deserting, and some for other things ... They're just about the scum of the A.I.F., and lots of them have never seen a day's active service. They joined up as late as they could and saw to it that they spent their time in gaol, finding it a pleasanter proposition than France.[65]

The prisoners soon openly flouted the authority of their guards and they broke out and rioted in Port Said and Colombo. Breakouts occurred on a number of other Australian repatriation troopships visiting Colombo. One of the most serious was that aboard the hospital ship *Morvada* in early–1919 when hundreds of men escaped to shore. The ship's commandant later reported that the only way of preventing the incident would have been to fire upon and kill some of the mutineers, but he drily remarked that he did not think that a massacre of returning diggers "would have been in accordance with the wishes of the Australian authorities".[66] The quarantine of troopships in Australian harbours due to the influenza epidemic was, according to the official historian, "the severest test to the discipline of the A.I.F. during demobilization".[67] Soldiers' frustrations at being delayed on board ships in sight of their homeland led to several troopship riots in Australian waters. The most notorious was a mutiny on the *Somali* in January 1919 at Semaphore, Adelaide, led by Gunner George Yates MHR, a member of the Australian federal parliament. Yates was tried by court martial and awarded 60 days detention while others received lighter sentences.[68]

While the quotas of troops were selected and transported home, there remained the problem of occupying Australian fighting troops now idle in the field or languishing in camps, depots and prisons. For now that the war was over, the soldiers had changed expectations; most simply wanted to return home to Australia without delay and resume their civilian lives.[69] Many soldiers, who had enlisted only for the duration, were in no mood to carry on with regular soldiering. One Australian soldier noted in his diary on 20 November, "nothing of very great interest has happened ... and the daily routine, is, if anything, worse since the Armistice was signed, than when we were boxing on. By the look of things, I wouldn't be surprised if there was a bit of a row amongst the various units".[70]

Some officers made attempts to smarten up their units through tightening discipline and imposing 'spit and polish' regulations. Their orders were generally met with sullen resistance and even strike action in Australian units. Less than one week after the Armistice, the men of the 5th Divisional Artillery held a mass meeting and forced their general to cancel his long list of orders that they polish their hat and collar badges, Blanco their waggon drag ropes and Brasso the wheelcaps of their limbers, and so forth.[71]

On the day of the Armistice the BEF Commander-in-Chief, Field Marshal Sir Douglas Haig, impressed upon his Army Commanders, "the importance of looking after the troops during the period following the cessation of hostilities [warning that] very often the best soldiers are the most difficult to deal with in periods of quiet!"[72] Haig suggested ways to keep the men occupied and amused. Some Australian units, such as the Army Service Corps, medical units and those units which had the maintenance of horses, were kept busy through the nature of their work, which did not cease with the end of fighting.[73] Attempts to involve men in an AIF vocational education scheme were only partially successful although several thousand men took advantage by learning new skills and trades for civilian employment.[74] Most fighting troops, however, had to be occupied artificially in various tasks now that military training no longer had any purpose Such occupation could take many forms. Early in January at least one Australian battalion in France provided men to help local farmers harvest their sugar beet crop; they astonished the French by accomplishing six-days' work in a single morning.[75]

Another small group of Australian soldiers was employed from the early months of 1919 on essential but grim labour with the Graves Detachment. A 19-year old Australian soldier, who arrived in England with a reinforcement draft four days after the Armistice, was posted to the Graves Detachment in March 1919. He wrote that they had "the roughest lot of officers they could find in the AIF with this unit and by jove they want them, it is the roughest mob I have ever seen, they would just as soon down tools as not. We are getting on pretty well with our job though, about 400 bodies in so far".[76] The young soldier recorded his unit's dismal work: "Found a grave with 18 men in it, no crosses only 4 had identification on them";[77] and the pitiful visits of relatives to the cemeteries:

> Last Wednesday an English lady came here looking for her son's grave, she found out we were reburying him at the Adelaide cemetry, she went round after we'd knocked off and found him lying in a bag on the ground, there was a load just came in and we didn't have time to bury them, she fainted when she saw him and is in hospital suffering from shock, so English people are forbidden to travel in the battle areas now.[78]

Few soldiers had even this melancholy labour to occupy them. One month after the Armistice an Australian junior officer's tone was despondent as he recorded that his days now began with "Brekker in bed" and consisted of little more than playing cards and the occasional sports afternoon: "Gee this life is monotonous. Wish we could visit some decent places and take some interest in things. As it is we have nothing to do and so get lazy".[79] The longer this inactivity persisted, especially through the winter, the more disaffected Australian soldiers became and their boredom sometimes turned into disobedience. One Australian wrote to a battalion mate from France in March 1919, describing a strike against what they viewed as military excesses:

> we are camped at a village called St Maxent and it is a bitch of a possie, would bog a duck ... We are getting easy times now. The heads were making it a welter some weeks ago and the troops went on strike, we all stood on our dig, also made our own terms, and stood out until we got them, it was as good as a circus. Our platoon officer gave us five minutes to get all of the billet on parade. The mob never moved an eye lid, so he gave it up for a bad job. We won the game at the finish ... We do sweet F.A. now, just a march of a morning.[80]

He added that they had abolished afternoon parades and that in the evenings dancing classes were being held "in a big marki tent with a floor in it. Most of the lads are learning to dance, as to myself I am a dud". Troop morale was sustained in diverse ways in the Great War but this image of Australian soldiers partnering each other in waltzes makes a striking contrast with the popular view of the tough fighting troops of the AIF.[81]

One of the most potentially serious disciplinary incidents after the Armistice took place in January 1919 when the entire complement of the 3rd Australian Divisional Artillery, about 500 men, refused all duties, held mass meetings and made a number of demands of their commanding officer. This action was treated as "defiance of authority" by their commanders who exacerbated matters by arresting soldiers. A senior officer sent to resolve the trouble, attributed it to "a want of appreciation by the officers ... of the unrest and mental change which took place amongst all the men after the cessation of hostilities". He noted with wry appreciation, "The whole thing was organized on the lines of an Australian strike and well done too. They spoke of 'being out' not being insubordinate ... The men now consider ... themselves civilians – I have told the officers they are to work on them as citizen soldiers".[82] Friction was eased when the protagonists, including some commanders, were replaced and occupation, education, sports and amusements were organized for the men.

In assessing this incident later, the commander of the Australian Corps wrote, "there is no question that there is a good deal of unrest throughout many units of the AIF"; he acknowledged that the men "are perhaps difficult to handle", due to "all they have gone through, and their great desire to return to Australia at the earliest possible moment". But he considered that AIF

xvii Front cover of the Christmas 1918 issue of Australian soldiers' magazine *Aussie*, celebrating the imminent return home of the AIF. (via H.P. Cecil) officers could prevent more serious trouble arising "by attending to the small things which affect the comfort and wellbeing of the men": "In nearly every case that has come before my notice so far, the cause has been the want of experience, tact and judgment, or want of attention and sympathy towards the men on the part of the officers".[83]

This approach by senior Australian officers reflected a directive by the Australian Prime Minister that in the primary task of returning the nation's soldiers, one principle should be foremost: "Our men are no longer soldiers in the strict sense of the word; they are citizens of Australia, who, having done their duty, are returning to their own country. They should be treated, therefore, as far as consistent with the maintenance of discipline, as citizens and not as soldiers".[84] This policy may largely explain why the AIF, despite its high rate of indiscipline generally, experienced no large scale demobilization riots;[85] such riots did occur in the British and Canadian forces.[86]

Demobilization unrest, however, did not prevent the use of other Dominion forces as occupation troops in Germany, leading the Australian Prime Minister later to claim that "mistrust of the Australians' discipline accounted for their divisions not being sent to Germany".[87] Very few Australian units went into Germany with the occupation army, although some Australians seem to have gone absent without leave in order to tour Cologne.[88] But the prospect of moving to Germany as an occupation force failed to appeal to most Australian soldiers. One Australian wrote, "The Troops are not too keen on being kept on as Occupation Troops. It may be an Honor, as the Heads try to impress on us, but it is Australia we are looking for".[89] Another Australian wrote home three weeks after the Armistice, "we seem lost without the war. When it was on we always had something to occupy our minds, but now it is different ... we seem to be living another life ... We are still in Amiens and having a good time but we seem to be discontented. I think that we must all be homesick, for nothing seems to satisfy us".[90]

In the homeland for which most Australian soldiers now yearned, the reaction to the news of the Armistice had been joyful and prolonged. The celebrations in Australia began three days early due to a false alarm. News of an armistice reached Sydney on the morning of 8 November and precipitated boisterous celebrations throughout the city. Several thousand people cheered as an effigy of the Kaiser was hanged and burned; despite the correction of the earlier news, festivities continued long into that night.[91] The confirmation of the actual signing of the Armistice was received in the eastern Australian cities on the early evening of Monday, 11 November. A spontaneous outpouring of emotion quickly swept the cities, with crowds parading through the streets, singing patriotic songs and cheering.[92] Huge crowds gathered in Sydney's Martin Place, creating a deafening din with their voices and tin can bands. Returned or invalided soldiers in the crowd were feted and once more effigies of the Kaiser were burnt or hanged to the delighted roars of crowds all over the city. A public holiday was declared for 14 November in New South Wales and celebrations continued in the cities and country towns over several days.[93]

One writer who was a child at the time, recalls that in Melbourne, as the news was received, church bells began to ring out along with factory hooters throughout the city and suburbs.[94] Celebrating crowds ran wildly out of control in the city and attacked tramcars, derailing one and crashing another through the front window of an office building. Hundreds of people then surged into the Chinese quarter breaking into barricaded stores and stealing fireworks. The Melbourne *Age*, on the following day, appealed to people not to explode fireworks, "in the interests of invalided soldiers and particularly those suffering from shell shock".[95] A more dignified celebration took place in Melbourne on the following Sunday afternoon when a commemorative service was conducted in the Commonwealth Parliament. The Governor-General and the Governor of Victoria officiated over a service which merged imperial triumphalism and mourning: opening with the Royal Salute and a Guard of Honour, the service incorporated the improbable medley of Chopin's funeral march, the Dead March from 'Saul' and the Last Post. A Church of England chaplain read from 'The Order for the Burial of the Dead', while chaplains of other denominations led prayers and hymns; significantly, in a nation which had seen passionate sectarian divisions during the war, Roman Catholics were not represented.[96] The service concluded with all singing the national anthem, 'God Save the King'.[97]

In Adelaide on the night of 11 November, crowds gathered outside the Post Office to greet the arrival of the official cablegram confirming the signing of the Armistice.[98] On the Adelaide Oval three days later, Australian Army troops and various volunteer groups celebrated on 'Peace Day', 14 November 1918. A public holiday was declared for the occasion and a crowd of 40,000 people crammed the oval to witness a victory parade of returned and invalided soldiers, nurses, recruits, rejected volunteers, militia forces and cadets. Some 6,000 children also joined the display which "concluded with cheers for the British Navy, the British Army, the Australian troops, and the Allies", reported the Adelaide *Advertiser*.

Throughout these celebrations was the relief that Australia's surviving soldiers would be coming home. Among those returning to Australia were many who carried new hopes and expectations for their nation now that the intensities of war had passed. Many believed that the post-war world would require a return to fundamentals. An Australian officer, who had served through the entire war from the Gallipoli campaign to the Armistice, pondered the changes the Armistice would bring for the future:

> Peace! For the multitude I suppose it simply means the end of all this awful murder and destruction. I do not think that people really see what it means more than this. For four years now the world has lost its equilibrium ... the way in which we have lived during the last four years has all been a false existence and the bump back to reality, the levelling up, will be jolly hard to take.[99]

But in the wake of the war most Australian soldiers' responses to the peace were purely nationalistic. An infantry soldier, travelling into Belgium with his unit after the Armistice, was appalled by the sight of starving refugees and war-damaged towns. He wrote of the town of Bohain, "this place is shelled to pieces, the church is about levelled to the ground, the people almost starving and very thin, the Germans have taken everything away from them".[100] The experience confirmed his belief in the rightness of the Allied victory over Germany: "plenty of French and British prisoners arriving, in an awful state, women and children dragging all sorts of veacles, it is a very pitiful sight, my thoughts are of Australia, and I am very pleased I came away to do my bit to keep the Germans away from wife and children and the people of Australia".[101]

An Australian gunner wrote to his mother several weeks after the Armistice, "Nobody can realize what a cruel war this has been unless he has been in it ... now that it is all over and I've come through safely, I can tell you candidly it was a rotten business. There have been times when I'd have given anything to get out of it. But now that it is finished I'm not sorry I came".[102] One veteran recalled almost 80 years after the Armistice that his experiences as a soldier of the AIF left him with a life-long abhorrence of war; but he never doubted the rightness of the cause for which he had enlisted.[103] Most surviving Australian soldiers viewed the victory in such clear terms: they believed they had defeated Prussian militarism and thwarted German imperialist war aims. For a brief period it seemed that they were right.[104]

Despite the hopes in victory for post-war Australia, in many ways the inter-war years would be what one writer has aptly called "the grey years".[105] On virtually every level, cultural, economic, political and social, the sombre after-effects of the Great War were apparent for almost a generation. Culturally, in the inter-war years Australia was characterized by a sense of arrested development: the promises of the social advances and welfare in the early years of the century were never realized. Most Australians continued to harbour divided loyalties towards Britain and their own nation, despite federation in 1901 and the emergent foundation myth of the birth of the Australian nation on Gallipoli.[106] The war also had lasting economic effects. Although Australian farmers had prospered during the war from British advance purchases of primary produce, Australia was left with the burden of a substantial war debt to Britain. After a brief post-war boom, living standards fell, unemployment rose and Australia sank into an economic recession which lasted until the late 1930's.[107] The war had also brought bitter political division to Australia over the question of conscription for war service. It had intensified imperial loyalist sentiment amongst the supporters of the war and ex-servicemen while also heightening sectarian opposition to British rule in Ireland. The war left Australia a divided society despite the illusion of the unity at the announcement of the Armistice.[108]

The social effects of the war were profound and enduring. Almost half the eligible male population of Australia enlisted during the war and over 330,000 of them embarked for service overseas. Almost two-thirds of those who served abroad became casualties, the AIF having the highest proportion of battle casualties of all the forces of the British Empire.[109] About 60,000, or one man in five of those who served abroad, died on active service. Of those who returned, more than half had suffered some sort of wound.[110] Together with the loss of those who died and the devastation to the living, the war left a legacy of sorrow. Thousands of families were left with only the memories of men – husbands, fathers and sons – who did not return. Many grieving women never remarried. War-damaged veterans were a visible reminder of the war in Australian society throughout the inter-war years.[111]

In time the Great War receded in Australian popular memory. The only conspicuous evidence of its impact remained in the hundreds of war memorials which were erected in every city and in country towns all over the nation. By the 1930's there were over 1500 of them.[112] Personal grief and civic pride had mingled in this impulse to commemorate Australia's soldiers in stone and bronze. The memorials provided a symbolic reminder of the official justification and meaning for the war; and many small town memorials also offered families and communities a focus for their grief as 'substitute graves', a means of keeping alive the memories of their loved ones who remained buried on the other side of the world.[113] The memory of the Armistice of November 1918 was slow to fade in Australia. The significance of that event in Australia's past was symbolically recognized on 11 November 1993. On that day, 75 years after the Armistice of 1918, an unknown Australian soldier disinterred from the soil of the Western Front was ceremonially entombed in the Australian War Memorial in Canberra.[114]

Endnotes

1 John Terraine, *To Win A War: 1918 The Year of Victory*, London, Sidgwick & Jackson, 1978, p. 260, n. 26.

2 Paddy Griffith, *Battle Tactics of the Western Front: The British Army's Art of Attack, 1916–18*, New Haven & London, Yale University Press, 1994, pp. 218–19; C.N. Barclay, *Armistice 1918*, London, J.M. Dent & Sons, 1968, pp. 118–19.

3 Lieutenant General John Monash (Commander Australian Corps), *The Australian Victories in France in 1918* (published 1920), quoted in Terraine, *To Win A War*, pp. 185–7. Monash's claims are repeated in Bill Gammage, *The Broken Years: Australian Soldiers in the Great War*, Ringwood Vic, Penguin, 1975, p. 204, and P.A. Pedersen, *Monash as Military Commander*, Melbourne, Melbourne University Press, 1985, p. 292.

4 The Australians captured 29,144 prisoners and 338 guns in over six months (27 March–5 October 1918); these totals represent 15 per cent (prisoners) and 12 per cent (guns) of the totals of 188,700 prisoners and 2,840 guns captured by the British armies in less than four months (July-November 1918), from figures in C.E.W. Bean, *The Australian Imperial Force in France During the Allied Offensive, 1918*, vol. VI, *The Official History of Australia in the War of 1914–1918*, 12 vols, Sydney, Angus & Robertson, 1942, pp. 1044, n. 19, 1051, n. 16. For the reception of Monash's book in London, see Geoffrey Serle, *John Monash: A Biography*, Melbourne, Melbourne University Press, 1982, pp. 418–19.

5 See for example: Shelford Bidwell & Dominick Graham, *Fire-Power: British Army Weapons and Theories of War 1904–1945*, London, George Allen & Unwin, 1985, pp. 131–3; Robin Prior and Trevor Wilson, *Command on the Western Front: The Military Career of Sir Henry Rawlinson 1914–18*, Oxford,

Blackwell, 1992, Part VI; and Griffith, *Battle Tactics of the Western Front*, pp. 83, 192–200.

6 H. Essame, *The Battle For Europe 1918*, London, B.T. Batsford, 1972, p. 191.

7 Bean, *The Australian Imperial Force in France During the Allied Offensive, 1918*, p. 1044, n. 19.

8 An enquiry into recruiting in Australia reported in March 1918 that the Australian Imperial Force (AIF) needed to enlist 5,400 volunteers per month to maintain its strength and 8,233 per month to make up deficiencies; but from January to October 1918, enlistments averaged only 2,776 per month. F.W. Perry, *The Commonwealth armies: Manpower and organization in two world wars*, Manchester, Manchester University Press, 1988, p. 157; Ernest Scott, *Australia During the War*, vol. XI, *The Official History of Australia in the War of 1914–1918*, 12 vols, Sydney, Angus and Robertson, 1939, pp. 443–5, 872.

9 Bean, *The Australian Imperial Force in France During the Allied Offensive*, 1918, pp. 1044, n. 18, 1047–9, n. 5, 8–11.

10 C.E.W. Bean, *Anzac to Amiens*, Canberra, Australian War Memorial, 1946, p. 515; and Bean, *The Australian Imperial Force in France During the Allied Offensive, 1918*, p. 1053.

11 Gammage, *The Broken Years*, pp. 264–5. Gammage states that of the 1,000 collections of letters and diaries he studied, 46 Australian soldiers wrote from France at this time; about half gave the Armistice merely token acknowledgement and only three expressed joy at the news.

12 J.M. Bourne, *Britain and the Great War 1914–1918*, London, Edward Arnold, 1989, p. 101. See also personal accounts in Terraine, *To Win A War*, pp. 256–8; Barrie Pitt, *1918: The Last Act*, London, Corgi, 1962, pp. 245–7; John Toland, *No Man's Land: The Story of 1918*, London, Eyre Methuen, 1980, pp. 576–80; and Stanley Weintraub, *A Stillness Heard Round The World. The End of the Great War: November 1918*, New York, Truman Talley Books, E.P. Dutton, 1985.

13 Adrian Gregory, *The Silence of Memory: Armistice Day 1919–1946*, Oxford, Berg, 1994, pp. 63–6.

14 Sergeant John Linton, 3rd Divisional Ammunition Column AIF, diary entry dated 11 November 1918, from John Stewart Linton (ed.), *A Soldier's Tale: One Man's War 16 February 1916 – 12 June 1919*, Kalamunda, WA, J.S. Linton, 1997, p. 129.

15 Sapper Harry Dadswell (no unit given, enlisted in AIF in September 1915), quoted in Patsy Adam-Smith, *The Anzacs*, Melbourne, Sphere, 1981, p. 431.

16 Private T.J. Cleary, 17th Battalion AIF, quoted in Gammage, *The Broken Years*, p. 265.

17 Gunner Charles Rea, 17th Battery Australian Field Artillery AIF, diary entry dated 11 November 1918, PR00184, Australian War Memorial (hereafter AWM).

18 Captain Keith McKeddie Doig, MC (RMO 60th Battalion and 8th Field Ambulance AIF), letter to his fianceé, dated 16 November 1918, from No. 1 Australian General Hospital France, PR00317, AWM.

19 Private Alfred W. Binskin, 20th Battalion AIF, diary entries dated 22 October, 11 November 1918, PR83/47, AWM.

20 Gunner Kenneth R.G. Downes, 105th Howitzer Battery AIF, letter to his mother dated 22 November 1918, Item 6987, 3DRL, AWM.

21 Corporal Robert Addison, MM, 46th Battery Australian Field Artillery AIF, diary entry dated 11 November 1918, PR00442, AWM.

22 Gunner Alexander S. MacKay, 8th Brigade Australian Field Artillery AIF, diary entry dated 11 October (should be November) 1918, Item 441, 1DRL, AWM.

23 Weintraub, *A Stillness Heard Round The World*, p. 243.

24 Anzac soldiers rioted and set fire to the Wazza brothel district of Cairo in April 1915, see Kevin Fewster, "The Wazza riots, 1915", *Journal of the Australian War Memorial*, No. 4 (April 1984), pp. 47–53.

25 Lieutenant G.H. Fowke, Adjutant-General, "War Crimes", circular memorandum issued by GHQ, 20 November 1918, Item 783/1, AWM 25.

26 This assessment is based upon civilian magistrates' court reports from a small sample of British provincial newspapers, Michael McKernan, *The Australian People and the Great War*, Melbourne, Nelson, 1980, pp. 145–8, 231.

27 There were 9167 courts martial of Australian soldiers for offences committed in the UK from 1915–1920; in 58 per cent of these cases the first charge was absence without leave; of the individuals charged, 82 per cent were privates or equivalent rank, 16 per cent were NCOs, and 2 per cent were officers. Figures collated from author's database of AIF courts martial proceedings files examined under conditions of Special Access granted under the Australian Archives Act. Further details are contained in the author's study of AIF discipline and punishment currently in progress.

28 Gregory, *The Silence of Memory*, p. 65. Gregory writes that the bonfire occurred on Armistice night. The incident took place two days after the Armistice according to Gammage, *The Broken Years*, p. 264. Another historian attributes the bonfire solely to Canadian soldiers, A.J.P. Taylor, *The First World War: an illustrated history*, Harmondsworth, Penguin, 1966, p. 251.

29 W.D. Joynt, VC (Lieutenant, 8th Battalion AIF), *Saving the Channel Ports 1918*, Melbourne, Wren Publishing, 1975, pp. 213–4.

30 Gunner Alexander S. MacKay, 8th Brigade Australian Field Artillery AIF, letter dated 20 November 1918, Item 441, 1DRL, AWM.

31 Cabinet minutes quoted in Eric Andrews, *The Anzac Illusion: Anglo-Australian relations during World War I*, Cambridge, Cambridge University Press, 1993, p. 195.

32 See chart, "Military Prisons in the Field. B.E.F. France", in War Office 'Most Secret' publication, *Statistical Abstract of Information regarding the Armies at Home and Abroad*, War Office, London, 1st October 1919, facing page 596, IWM 83558, Imperial War Museum.

33 Details from author's database of AIF courts martial proceedings files examined under conditions of Special Access granted under the Australian Archives Act. These incidents are treated more fully in the author's study of AIF discipline and punishment currently in progress.

34 Terraine, *To Win A War*, pp. 190, 226–7. For a firsthand account of conditions within advancing artillery batteries, see Gunner Keith S. Dowling, 107th Howitzer Battery AIF, letter to his mother dated 30 September, Item 259, 2DRL, AWM.

35 Gunner Charles Rea, 17th Battery Australian Field Artillery AIF, letter to his mother dated 2 December 1918, PR00184, AWM.

36 Driver John Henry Turnbull, Divisional Ammunition Column AIF, transcribed diary entry, dated 4 October 1918, PR91/015, AWM.

37 Gunner Charles Rea, 17th Battery Australian Field Artillery AIF, diary entry dated 22 October 1918, PR00184, AWM. Twenty men of Rea's battery were evacuated, all but two of them suffering the effects of gassing.

38 Ronald McNicoll, *The Royal Australian Engineers 1902 to 1919: Making and*

Breaking, Canberra, Corps Committee of The Royal Australian Engineers, 1979, pp. 154–5.

39 Bombardier W.R. Leach, 31st Battery Australian Field Artillery AIF, letter to his parents dated 11 November 1918, PR00441, AWM.

40 From a letter published in the Melbourne Argus, 12 October 1918, quoted in Brian Lewis, *Our War: Australia during World War I*, Melbourne, Melbourne University Press, 1980, p. 320.

41 Private J.F. Court, 34th Battalion AIF, captured 8 May 1918, diary, PR00403, AWM.

42 Private J.F. Court, 34th Battalion AIF, diary entry dated 11 November 1918, PR00403, AWM.

43 Driver John Henry Turnbull, Divisional Ammunition Column AIF, transcribed diary entry, dated 25 November 1918, PR91/015, AWM.

44 Definitive figures are unavailable because as one scholar has observed, "No strength figures for the AIF appear to have survived and British sources are suspect", Perry, *The Commonwealth armies*, p. 158.

45 Estimates collated from figures in: Bean, *Anzac to Amiens*, pp. 516–7; Bean, *The Australian Imperial Force in France During the Allied Offensive, 1918*, p. 1057, n. 29; Scott, *Australia During the War*, p. 825; A.G. Butler, *Special Problems and Services*, vol. III, *The Australian Army Medical Services in the War of 1914–1918*, 3 vols, Melbourne, Australian War Memorial, 1943, pp. 710, 882, 891; and Clem Lloyd and Jacqui Rees, *The Last Shilling: A History of Repatriation in Australia*, Melbourne, Melbourne University Press, 1994, p. 116.

46 Estimate based upon figures in Butler, *Special Problems and Services*, Ch. XI, esp. pp. 544, 579–80. A total of 2139 nurses served overseas in the Australian Army Nursing Service (AANS) from 1914–1918, see Butler, *Special Problems and Services*, p. 882; and Jan Bassett, *Guns and Brooches: Australian Army Nursing from the Boer War to the Gulf War*, Melbourne, Oxford University Press, 1992, pp. 94–5.

47 Bean, *The Australian Imperial Force in France During the Allied Offensive*, 1918, pp. 878, 895–6, 937. Two months' leave in Australia was granted to men with four years' service in the AIF, preference being given initially to married men with wives in Australia.

48 Second Lieutenant Cyril Lawrence, MC, 1st Field Company Engineers AIF, letter to his mother, dated 13 October 1918, in Peter Yule (ed.), *Sergeant Lawrence Goes To France*, Melbourne, Melbourne University Press, 1987, p. 181.

49 Signaller Ted Matthews, 1st Brigade and 4th Division Signals AIF, telephone interview with author, 29 October 1996; Ashley Ekins, "Date with destiny", [Sydney] *Daily Telegraph*, 13 November 1997; Tony Stephens and Steven Siewart, *The Last Anzacs: Gallipoli 1915*, Sydney, Allen & Kemsley, 1996, pp. 60–3; *Australian*, 11 December 1997.

50 The issues surrounding repatriation, demobilization and civil rehabilitation of Australian soldiers are covered in: Scott, *Australia During the War*, pp. 824–8; Bean, *The Australian Imperial Force in France During the Allied Offensive, 1918*, pp. 1053–62; Lloyd and Rees, *The Last Shilling*, pp. 109–32; Butler, *Special Problems and Services*, pp. 706–22; and A.G. Butler, *The Western Front*, vol. II, *The Australian Army Medical Services in the War of 1914–1918*, 3 vols, Melbourne, Australian War Memorial, 1940, pp. 790–5.

51 Butler, *Special Problems and Services*, p. 721. The repatriation process required 176 voyages in 137 different ships, Scott, *Australia During the War*, p. 827 (203 voyages according to Lloyd and Rees, *The Last Shilling*, p. 121).

52 Butler, *Special Problems and Services*, p. 891; Lloyd and Rees, *The Last Shilling*, p. 119.

53 Butler, *Special Problems and Services*, p. 891.

54 According to one historian, the wastes of the Somme battlefield were "colonized by a freebooting gang of Australians, who lived by raiding military dumps and eluded the search of the military police for many months, some say until the end of the war", John Keegan, *The Face of Battle*, Harmondsworth, Penguin, 1978, p. 317; see also Gammage, *The Broken Years*, p. 218. Similar claims are made about Australian and other soldiers in the Second World War, see John Ellis, *The Sharp End of War: The Fighting Man in World War II*, Newton Abbot, David & Charles, 1980, p. 367, n. 65.

55 Australian military police arrested a total of 49 Australian absentees in two round-ups in the Corbie area in October 1918 and reported that the round-ups would be continued. In the three months, August, September and October 1918, the Australian Corps in France had an average of 689 absentees (although weekly totals of Australian absentees fell over this period from from 760 on 18 August to 578 on 26 October; no further figures are recorded after that date). Data collated by author from Assistant Provost Marshal War Diary, Australian Corps, 1917–18, Item 13, WO 154, PRO.

56 'Secret' communication, Assistant Adjutant and Quartermaster-General 5th Australian Division to 5th Division HQ, 31 Oct 1918, Item [1/1], AWM 25.

57 5th Australian Division records show 70–71 absentees weekly for the period, 26 October to 23 November 1918 with a temporary drop to 63 in the week following the round up, Weekly Reports from Deputy Assistant Provost Marshal 5th Australian Division, Item [233/6], AWM 25.

58 Captain J.C. Dunn, *The War the Infantry Knew 1914–1919: A Chronicle of Service in France and Belgium with The Second Battalion His Majesty's Twenty-Third Foot, The Royal Welch Fusiliers: founded on personal records, recollections and reflections, assembled, edited and partly written by one of their Medical Officers* [first published 1938], London, Cardinal, 1989, pp. 573–4.

59 Captain Daniel S. Aarons, MC and Bar, 16th Battalion AIF, diary entry dated 2 November 1918, Item 7047, 3DRL, AWM.

60 By 1940, 152 of the 902 AIF "illegal absentees" had been discovered, Butler, *Special Problems and Services*, p. 891.

61 See for example, AIF Fifth Army signal to Australian Section GHQ, 3rd Echelon BEF, 17 December 1918, instructing: "Party of about 40 undesirables being sent you shortly by Aust. Corps for deportation...", file 79/900/86, bundle 212, box 35, AWM 23.

62 In November 1918, 192 men in the 2nd Australian Division and 253 men in the 4th Australian Division were reported as serving under suspended sentences. Figures collated by author from Nominal Rolls requested under General Routine Order 5210, files 29/2100/6, bundle 64, box A40 and file 29/4100/13, bundle 66, box A41, both in AWM 23. Equivalent records for the other three Australian divisions do not appear to have survived, but these figures indicate on average that there were over 1,000 men in the Australian Corps serving under suspended sentences at the time of the Armistice.

63 Bean, *The Australian Imperial Force in France During the Allied Offensive, 1918*, pp. 1054, n. 24; and evidence from AIF courts martial proceedings files examined under conditions of Special Access granted under the Australian Archives Act. Further details of the numbers and circumstances of Australian soldiers in

military prisons are contained in the author's study of AIF discipline and punishment currently in progress.

64 Australian soldiers were marrying in the UK at the rate of 150 per week by mid–1919; about 20,000 wives, fianceés and children of soldiers and munition workers were transported to Australia by the end of 1919, Bean, *The Australian Imperial Force in France During the Allied Offensive, 1918*, p. 1061.

65 From the autobiographical novel by Angela Thirkell, *Trooper to the Southern Cross* [first published under the male pseudonym of Leslie Parker in 1934], London, Virago, 1985, p. 57, and Introduction by Tony Gould, p. vii. Thirkell travelled with her husband, an AIF captain, aboard the *SS Friedrichsruh* which left England in January 1920. See also the perceptive critique in Robin Gerster, *Big-noting: The Heroic Theme in Australian War Writing*, Melbourne, Melbourne University Press, 1987, pp. 166–71.

66 Lloyd and Rees, *The Last Shilling*, pp. 131.

67 Bean, *Anzac to Amiens*, p. 519; and Bean, *The Australian Imperial Force in France During the Allied Offensive, 1918*, p. 1073. The Spanish Influenza pandemic killed between 20 and 30 million people worldwide in the post-war years.

68 Bean, *The Australian Imperial Force in France During the Allied Offensive, 1918*, p. 1073, n. 93. [Melbourne] Argus, 20, 25, 26, 27 February, 4, 5, 6, 10 March 1919; Gunner G. Yates MP Court Martial, Item 172.13 [7], AWM 27.

69 Gammage, *The Broken Years*, pp. 265–6.

70 Sergeant John Linton, 3rd Divisional Ammunition Column AIF, diary entry dated 20 November 1918, from Linton (ed.), *A Soldier's Tale*, p. 132.

71 Driver John Henry Turnbull, Divisional Ammunition Column AIF, transcribed diary entries, dated 14–16 November 1918, PR91/015, AWM.

72 John Terraine, *Douglas Haig: The Educated Soldier*, London, Leo Cooper, 1990, p. 480.

73 Bean, *The Australian Imperial Force in France During the Allied Offensive, 1918*, p. 1069, n. 77.

74 Bean, *The Australian Imperial Force in France During the Allied Offensive, 1918*, pp. 1062–72; Lloyd and Rees, *The Last Shilling*, pp. 122–8; and Butler, *The Western Front*, pp. 797–8, n. 41.

75 Robin S. Corfield, *Hold hard cobbers: The story of the 57th and 60th and 57/60th Australian Infantry Battalions 1912–1990*, vol. one 1912–1930, Glenhuntly, Vic, 57/60th Battalion (AIF) Association, 1992, p. 194.

76 Private William Frampton McBeath, 12th Reinforcements of 58th Battalion AIF, typescript copy of letter to his mother dated 23 April 1919, PR00675, AWM. McBeath noted that in its first few weeks the Graves Detachment soldiers had already held two strikes to obtain better means for handling the bodies, better food, and to cut out ceremonial parades. [typescript copy of letter to his mother dated 19 April 1919, PR00675, AWM].

77 Private William Frampton McBeath, 58th Battalion AIF, typescript diary entry dated 16 April 1919, PR00675, AWM.

78 Private William Frampton McBeath, 58th Battalion AIF, typescript copy of letter to his mother dated 19 April 1919, PR00675, AWM.

79 Lieutenant Keith Probert, 5th Pioneer Battalion, AIF, diary entries dated 12–17 December 1918, quotation 13 December, PR00779, AWM.

80 Letter dated 28 March 1919 (signed 'your true cobber Bob'), to Private George Isbister, 41st Battalion AIF, PR 90/001, AWM.

81 A study of concert parties, unit journals and other troop diversions is found in

J.F. Fuller, *Troop Morale and Popular Culture in the British and Dominion Armies 1914–1918*, Oxford, Oxford University Press, 1990.

82 Brigadier-General Harold W. Grimwade, letters to Major-General Sir John Gellibrand, Commander 3rd Australian Division AIF, dated 17, 18 January 1919, in "3rd Aust Division Artillery Incident – Unrest and trouble occurring in this Divisional Artillery, Dec. 1918/1919", Gellibrand papers, Item 58, 1473, 3DRL, AWM. I thank Dr Gary Sheffield for drawing this file to my attention.

83 Lieutenant-General J.J. Talbot Hobbs, letter to Gellibrand, dated 11 January 1919, in "3rd Aust Division Artillery Incident – Unrest and trouble occurring in this Divisional Artillery, Dec. 1918/191"', Gellibrand papers, Item 58, 1473, 3DRL, AWM.

84 From instruction by W.M. Hughes, PM of Australia, December 1918, quoted in Butler, *Special Problems and Services*, p. 711; also, Lloyd and Rees, *The Last Shilling*, pp. 118–19.

85 One writer claims that there was a mutiny by Australian soldiers at Larkhill Camp on Salisbury Plain in January 1919, news of which was suppressed in the press under military censorship, Andrew Rothstein, *The Soldiers' Strikes of 1919, London, 1980*, p. 56. The author has found no evidence of this incident in the courts martial records of the AIF.

86 This unrest stemmed mainly from rank and file boredom, frustration with delays and muddle over demobilization, grievances over poor pay and camp conditions, and fear of post-war unemployment, see Julian Putkowski, *The Kinmel Park Camp Riots 1919*, Clwyd, Flintshire Historical Society, 1989; Douglas Gill and Gloden Dallas, *The Unknown Army: Mutinies in the British Army in World War I*, London, Verso, 1985; and Christopher Pugsley, *On the Fringe of Hell: New Zealanders and Military Discipline in the First World War*, Auckland, Hodder & Stoughton, 1991, pp. 285–95.

87 Bean, *The Australian Imperial Force in France During the Allied Offensive, 1918*, p. 1072, n. 91.

88 The official historian notes that Australian absentees were "ignored" by the local military police, Bean, *The Australian Imperial Force in France During the Allied Offensive, 1918*, p. 1072, n. 91.

89 Driver John Henry Turnbull, Divisional Ammunition Column AIF, transcribed diary entry, dated 16 November 1918, PR91/015, AWM.

90 Gunner Charles Rea, 17th Battery Australian Field Artillery AIF, letter to his mother dated 2 December 1918, PR00184, AWM.

91 McKernan, *The Australian People and the Great War*, pp. 201–202. For the origin of the false rumour of an armistice, see Toland, *No Man's Land*, pp. 547–50.

92 Scott, *Australia During the War*, p. 473.

93 McKernan, *The Australian People and the Great War*, pp. 203–205.

94 Lewis, *Our War*, pp. 324–5.

95 Cyril Pearl, *Australia's Yesterdays: A look at our recent past*, Sydney, Reader's Digest Services, 1974, p. 308.

96 Catholic pride in war-service was displayed at the St Patrick's Day march in Melbourne in 1920 which was led by thirteen Victoria Cross winners in full AIF uniform and mounted on greys, see A.W. Martin assisted by Patsy Hardy, *Robert Menzies: A Life, Volume 1, 1894–1943*, Melbourne, Melbourne University Press, 1993, pp. 55–56.

97 Order of ceremony, "In Memoriam service for All who made the Supreme

Sacrifice in the Great War 1914–1918", Thanksgiving Sunday, 17 November 1918, Commonwealth Parliament Houses, Melbourne, PR84/068, AWM.

98 This account is from David Hood, "Adelaide's First 'Taste of Bolshevism': Returned Soldiers and the 1918 Peace Day Riots", *Journal of the Historical Society of South Australia*, No. 15, 1987, pp. 42–53.

99 Second Lieutenant Cyril Lawrence, MC, 1st Field Company Engineers, AIF, letter to his sister, dated 17 November 1918, in Peter Yule (ed.), *Sergeant Lawrence Goes To France*, Melbourne, Melbourne University Press, 1987, p. 184.

100 Private Alfred W. Binskin, 20th Battalion AIF, diary entry dated 25 November 1918, PR83/47, AWM.

101 Private Alfred W. Binskin, 20th Battalion AIF, diary entry dated 22 November 1918, PR83/47, AWM.

102 Gunner Charles Rea, 17th Battery Australian Field Artillery AIF, letter to his mother dated 2 December 1918, PR00184, AWM.

103 Signaller Ted Matthews, 1st Brigade and 4th Division Signals AIF, telephone interview with author, 29 October 1996.

104 See the assessment of John Robertson, *Anzac and Empire: The Tragedy & Glory of Gallipoli*, Port Melbourne, Hamlyn, 1990, pp. 266–7.

105 McKernan, *The Australian People and the Great War*, ch. 9, pp. 207–24.

106 These assessments are based on Geoffrey Serle, *From Deserts The Prophets Come: The Creative Spirit in Australia 1788–1972*, Melbourne, Heinemann, 1973, pp. 89–91, 100, 114–16, 119–31, 152.

107 Scott, *Australia During the War*, pp. 495–6; Marnie Haig-Muir, "The economy at war", in Joan Beaumont (ed.), *Australia's War, 1914–18*, St Leonards, NSW, Allen & Unwin, 1995, pp. 93–124, esp. 98–9, 114; and Barry Smith, "What if Australia had not participated in the Great War? An essay on the costs of war", in Craig Wilcox (ed.), assisted by Janice Aldridge, *The Great War: Gains and Losses – ANZAC and Empire*, Canberra, The Australian War Memorial and The Australian National University, 1995, pp. 179–95, 195.

108 Joan Beaumont, "The politics of a divided society", in Joan Beaumont (ed.), *Australia's War, 1914–18*, St Leonards, NSW, Allen & Unwin, 1995, pp. 35–63.

109 Jeffrey Grey, *A Military History of Australia*, Cambridge, Cambridge University Press, 1990, pp. 118–19.

110 From a total population of about four and a half million people almost 417,000 men enlisted. Over 330,000 members of the AIF embarked from Australia, about 60,000 died on service and 93,000 were repatriated for various reasons by the end of 1918. Over 264,000 soldiers were returned to Australia, about 156,000 of whom had been wounded or injured, Butler, *Special Problems and Services*, pp. 707, 891, 895–7, 903–4, 957.

111 By 1920, two years after the Armistice, over 90,000 veterans, about one third of Australia's over 270,000 "returned men", were receiving disability pensions; by 1926, almost 23,000 were in hospital and by 1939 this number had grown to almost 50,000, Gammage, *The Broken Years*, Appendix 2, p. 283. Barry Smith, "What if Australia had not participated in the Great War? . .", in Wilcox, *The Great War: Gains and Losses – ANZAC and Empire*, pp. 179–95; see also Butler, *Special Problems and Services*, ch. XVI; and Lloyd and Rees, *The Last Shilling*, ch. 7.

112 K.S. Inglis, "World War One Memorials in Australia", *Guerres mondiales et conflits contemporains*, No. 167, July 1992, p. 55; see also, K.S. Inglis, *Sacred Places: War Memorials in the Australian Landscape*, Melbourne, Miegunyah Press/Melbourne University Press, forthcoming November 1998.

113 K.S. Inglis, "The Great War and the Australian Landscape", unpublished lecture, Australian National University, 23 May 1979, copy of text in AWM library, pp. 1–3; K.S. Inglis and Jock Phillips, "War Memorials in Australia and New Zealand: A Comparative Survey", *Australian Historical Studies*, vol. 24, no. 96 (April 1991), pp. 179–91.

114 See Ashley Ekins, "The Unknown Australian Soldier: Memory and Meaning", *La Grande Guerre: Pays, Histoire, Mémoire. Bulletin du Centre de recherche, Historial de la Grande Guerre*, Pèronne, No. 7, June 1994, pp. 3–5.

Chapter Ten

A Canadian Armistice

Dean Oliver

The Armistice was desperately needed, and not just for the obvious reason that Canada was running out of men. The conscription election in December 1917 had left a bitterly divided country in its wake.[1] In the months which followed, the Unionist government of Sir Robert Borden had struggled to keep the victorious Canadian Corps at full strength. It was winning the war, pro-conscriptionists argued, and with it a place for Canada in post-war international affairs. However, its sacrifice was also ripping the nation asunder. In the most overtly racist election campaign in Canadian political history, the Liberal Party of Sir Wilfrid Laurier foundered on the rocks of English-Canadian patriotism, drowning amidst a chorus of anti-French epithets and insults. French-Canadians were certainly not enlisting in numbers proportionate to their share of the national population, but those responsible for recruitment had never really attempted to accommodate their concerns. In an English army with English officers and English flags, there were few inducements for heroism by *les habitants*. Sam Hughes, Minister of Militia and Defence, had likened Canada's call to arms to the fiery cross travelling through the Scottish highlands in days of yore; that such imagery would have meant nothing to the residents of Trois-Rivières or Rimouski was sadly indicative of a youthful, intolerant nationalism.

Militant Protestants thought otherwise but by 1917 Quebec's sons were by no means the only ones loath to enlist. The casualty toll and the government's broken promises of volunteer service had seen to that. Tens of thousands of farmers, labourers, and immigrants now also refused to show up after being called to the colours. The English-born had constituted a majority of Canada's first divisions overseas, but the second wave proved decidedly less enthusiastic. The first conscription campaigns were thus monumental failures: a paltry few thousand troops in exchange for a near-mortal wound on the Canadian body politic. The alternative — reducing the size or combat effectiveness of Canada's army overseas — was indeed the greater evil, as Borden correctly argued, but, in implementing with vigour English Canada's vengeance on French-Canadian 'slackers', Ottawa stoked the fires of sectional discontent for decades to come.[2]

Conscription was one component of Canada's wider malaise in 1917–18. In a country woefully unprepared for armed conflict in 1914, the stresses and strains of four years of fighting had become all too evident. Labour unrest, inflation, political partisanship, vicious public battles within both government and opposition ranks, regionalism, and religious strife all marked the latter war years. An influenza outbreak in September 1918 added to the country's travails and left thousands dead and dying. National pride in the accomplishments of the troops overseas was thus tempered by the glaring imperfections of life on the home front. The 1920s, some historians would later argue, pushed the senior Dominion to the verge of collapse, but the foundations of such a dangerous situation had been laid in the moment of the young country's greatest triumph.

Brooke Claxton, a future defence minister, was an artilleryman in 1918 and knew then that the war had made him an unrepentant Canadian nationalist.[3] However, in the days after men of the Third Canadian Division at Mons heard the news of the Armistice, he lapsed into a prolonged and intense depression that well reflected the turmoil brewing in his country an ocean away. Waiting for repatriation intensified his loneliness and disaffection. The demobilization riots by Canadian troops in the winter of 1918–19 proved that Claxton was not the only Canuck so affected.

Canada was scarcely a defeated nation in the late summer of 1918, as the triumphant headlines from Amiens and Canal-du-Nord revealed, but it was a disillusioned one. The nation's faith in impending victory grew but slowly, such slowness influenced by the sheer cost of those victories of 'the hundred days'. Britain's bookish tank specialist, J.F.C. Fuller, was busy prophesying armoured legions that would fight the war into 1919 or 1920. Had Canadians known of such official pessimism they would not have been surprised; the Ludendorff offensives in early 1918 had taught everyone the futility of grand predictions. Corner-store patriarchs talked of patience and of 'seeing things through'. My own grandfather would smile thinly in remembrance of that time, humming 'Onward Christian Soldiers' to echo a common spiritual injunction to worldly endurance; it would be the first hymn played at his funeral sixty years later. Budding writers and disgruntled Bolsheviks were already pronouncing on the futility of it all, much to the soldiers' disgust. Fearful politicians, sensitive to the boasts of Marxist labour organizers, wondered if the war were making radicals of a generation of young men.

They may not have been far wrong. In one of the most controversial assessments of this period, Canada's leading labour historian concluded that the seeds of a Marxist-inspired labour revolt did exist in Canada in 1918–19, a revolt that "was national in character" and whose seeds "were not rooted in any unique regional fermentation".[4] Only an aroused and repressive capitalism forestalled the 'revolution'. It was into this maelstrom that peace intruded in late 1918 and against its backdrop that the reactions of Canadians to the ceasefire must be judged.

Even before the suddenly swift arrival of peace, rumours that the end was near had appeared and dissolved like ghostly apparitions, drawing crowds to the streets for a brief but boisterous rendezvous only to send them shuffling along again when the next bulletin spoiled the revelry. November 7 was the greatest of these, sending thousands into the town squares and dry taverns — all provinces except Quebec were under prohibition in 1918 — in anticipation of the end. By nightfall, truth intervened. Half a world away, German artillery, machine-guns, and snipers continued their toll of Canadian manhood as Toronto bankers and Montreal railwaymen trundled back to hearths and homes. The Canadian Corps was now moving on to Mons and imminent victory but the beaten, battered German army had the poor grace not to recognize its predicament.

The realization of what was about to transpire spread slowly through the

xviii Canadian cavalry attempt to protect German prisoners of war from an angry crowd of civilians in the outskirts of Mons, November 1918. An incident described and illustrated in the memoirs of Russell Rabjohn, a Canadian veteran. (Canadian War Museum) ranks on 10–11 November. At 6:30 am on the eleventh, Canadian Corps Headquarters received official word of the impending Armistice and proceeded to relay the news to its various sub-units. It moved with remarkable speed, although some battalions did not receive notice until late morning, and then it was greeted with a distinct lack of ebullience. Contemporary accounts are difficult to interpret on this point, though many speak of the silence that accompanied the news. They are vaguely unsatisfying. One wants to sense, indeed to feel, the unbridled joy and relief of those who, receiving the military's terse memorandum, must have leapt or wept for joy, whose every physical and mental faculty must have been overcome by the long-awaited news. Surely, one might reason, the arrival of peace would have been cathartic for the troops in some measurable or observable way.

Such accounts do exist. Ralph Green of the 4th Battalion relates the delighted anguish of no less a participant than General Arthur Currie, the Corps commander, during the latter's address to First Canadian Infantry Brigade an hour before the Armistice took effect. "He cried like a baby, his emotions were so great", Green recorded in his unpublished World War One 'Autobiography'.[5] Some units, like the 10th Battalion, fired their weapons wildly into the air;[6] others yelled or threw impromptu parties. All perhaps celebrated in some small degree, but the relative paucity of such examples tells another story: in fact, peace stole quietly over the men of the Canadian Corps.

It was a reflective moment, although few would mimic the introspection of Claxton, whose post-Armistice depression soon led him to discover in the works of Thomas Carlyle a secular, intellectual antidote to the war's fearful legacy. For many the Armistice was simply insufficient to drive them too far from their established routines for it seemed to imply impermanence. Military discipline would not have countenanced dereliction of duty in any case. "Carrying on same even tho [sic] Armistice is signed", noted signaller Gorden S. Bennett near Arras.[7] "I to stables in the am", noted C.S.L. Hertzberg, a future general, "and in barracks all afternoon". "Celebrated peace but got home sober".[8] No Germans were yet surrendering, after all, though many could be seen heading home, and the fighting might still resume. Advancing through Mons on the night of 10 November, the 42nd (Highland) Battalion received notification that a ceasefire would go into effect the next day. "With a brief cheer the platoons carried on up a ridge to establish an outpost line on the high ground".[9] There was no time for celebration. "Among some of the men an underlying mistrust of the Armistice impinged upon the noisy merry-making", Vincent Goodwin recorded in his diary. What would happen if the Germans counterattacked? With only a couple of men from his battery of 2nd Canadian Motor Machine-Gun Brigade still sober after an extended liquid lunch, Goodwin refrained after a dram or two and spent the night on guard.[10]

More than duty or fear, however, the real constraint on jubilation was stunned disbelief: after so long could it really all be over? Pandemonium seemed grossly inappropriate as a memorial to the fallen; prayer came closer and most survivors, padres in tow, were, for once, not shy in their devotions. "Word of the armistice brought no wild scenes of joy in the Regiment", wrote the historian of the Princess Patricia's Canadian Light Infantry. "Rather it was received in silence, almost in disbelief. It seemed that men who had seen so much could not, on 11 November, bring themselves to rejoice in victory".[11] Major Warren of the 38th (Ottawa) Battalion agreed:

> There was little enthusiasm. The war had long since ceased to be an adventure, and had become merely a terribly necessary routine. Now the necessity had been dealt with – there was need no longer. Besides, a state of peace and safety was a new thing, and had to be remembered and learnt all over again. It could not be grasped in a moment ... [12]

Their families back home displayed no such reluctance and in the records of cities, towns, and villages across the country one finds the popular

– WHAT A CELEBRATION!
THOUSANDS OF CIVILIANS
TRYING THERE BEST TO DO
SOMETHING FOR YOU. FOOD, WINE,
BEER, ARM IN ARM MARCHING
FURTHER INTO MONS. STILL
WONDERING CAN IT REALLY
BE TRUE.

xix Canadian soldiers and Belgian civilians celebrate in Mons as news of the Armistice reaches them. An illustration from the memoirs of Russell Rabjohn. (Canadian War Museum) outbursts and spontaneous demonstrations that might have been expected, intuitively at least, amongst the long-suffering soldiery. Commonalities in these accounts abound: church bells chiming, parades, speechifying by local politicians, the consumption of illegal spirits, dancing in the streets. It was all there, evidence of a tired country's relief that its trial by fire had ended. Rejoicing in the war's apparent conclusion Canadians dismissed momentarily the social, economic, and political cleavages occasioned by the conflict. It was a brief but glorious respite filled with frenzied merrymaking and in its shadow, as Jonathan Vance has argued, lay the seeds of powerful, nation-forming wartime myths.[13] They wanted desperately to believe in a Canada the war had largely destroyed, Vance argues, and in doing so, saddled Borden's government with expectations no post-war regime could meet.

"Toronto Hails Peace in Delirium of Joy", reported the *Toronto Star* on 12 November.[14] In its exuberance, however, the crowd overturned a delivery wagon, pushing it through the front window of a downtown shoe store. The city's patriotic but selectively law-abiding citizens paused momentarily in their enthusiasm to loot the unfortunate establishment of its winter boots. In Montreal, a Canadian Pacific railroad engine moved from Windsor Station along city streets blowing its whistle to announce the peace. Benign chaos ensued as a planned Victory Loan parade metamorphosed into a Victory Parade instead.[15] In Ottawa, military and civilian bands assembled on Parliament Hill to play the 'Maple Leaf Forever'. "The scene was one of extreme beauty", noted the *Ottawa Evening Citizen*. "Overhead, the star-strewn heavens were faintly tinged with the approaching light of dawn".[16] Amidst a cacophony of musical instruments, bells, bands, car horns, and human screaming, from Sydney, Nova Scotia to Victoria, British Columbia, Canadians rang in peace with a bang. Here, if not in Mons, relief was palpable and loud.

Canada's noisy Armistice day in fact differed little from England's or America's, though in Canada's case it is tempting to posit an inverse relationship between vigorous celebration and the perilous state of the country's social and economic fabric. There is little evidence that ordinary citizens saw it that way, of course, so although civic holidays and thanksgiving services may have merely glossed over wartime differences, it is also clear that the cultural touchstones provided by the war and the Armistice were for many profoundly integrative in their effects. Canada really *was* born on Vimy Ridge, to paraphrase Pierre Berton and others,[17] despite the deceptive simplicity of this view. One might append, perhaps, in a typically Canadian concession to what the war had wrought on the home front, that it was born 'warts and all' but the extent to which Canadian leaders at the time appreciated the effects of battlefield deeds on nation-building is striking, even if one dares to dismiss as jingoistic or foolhardy the sentiments underlying their acts. "I appreciated the national pride our country would have if we finished the war with the old battlefield in our possession", Currie wrote to Borden in reference to Mons, "and though we were anxious to take it, we did not care to suffer many casualties in doing so".[18]

In the aftermath of the ceasefire and the thanksgiving services that soon swept the land, civilians at home tried to bring their lives back to normal, despite the enormous changes peace would bring. For military personnel overseas, peace meant anything but normality. Months of waiting on the continent for the machinery of repatriation would be followed for many by additional months in England. Canada's troops had no reputation for patience. Politics, so impassioned in the Canada of 1918, had never been absent from the army's ranks, as the 1917 election campaign demonstrated,[19] but, like concern for the future, worries about unemployment, and anger at the lack of shipping for the voyage to Canada, it entered the ranks with a vengeance in the wake of victory, adding a vaguely militant — and wholly ominous — edge to the usual grumpiness of trained soldiers forced to languish in rain-sodden idleness. To talk of socialist dissent in the embarrassing riots is "nonsense", argued Desmond Morton: "There was no bud to nip. There was no conspiracy". But it was tempting to see in the disturbances a profound danger to the state. "Dramatic events also deserve dramatic causes", Morton noted.[20] Ottawa would view the following year's Winnipeg General Strike in precisely this fashion. Official fear of a 'Red' menace would persist in the corridors of power for decades.

It was this curious mixture of intense national pride tinged with national angst that perhaps distinguished Canada's Armistice from others. Canada was hardly unique in facing with trepidation the uncertainties of the post-war period, but its domestic bloodletting over conscription had left it peculiarly susceptible to paranoia. It was not that individual Canadians delighted any less in the return of peace, but merely that its outlines were so worryingly unknown. This could not fail to affect military personnel overseas, whose fears were accentuated by waiting for repatriation. The spontaneous celebrations which swept the country from Halifax to Victoria from 7 November onward were nevertheless genuine indications of relief. Military formations overseas shared in the experience, though for soldiers who, just hours or minutes before, had been engaged in active combat, the actual moments of transition from war to peace were qualitatively different. At once more cerebral and more mundane, the experience of exhausted but grateful troopers as they sang, danced, embraced, reflected, and guarded against renewed hostilities conveyed much about the comradeship in arms amidst squalid surroundings that had attended Canada's first 'good' war. It also spoke to the vast gulf that had emerged between the country's professional soldiers and the citizenry from which they had come. There was no ticker tape in the shallow, fetid trenches east of Mons on the evening of November 11, 1918.

"You must have had thrilling experiences too", George Parkin wrote to his son in the Canadian Corps after describing the raucous victory celebrations in London, England on 12 November. There is no extant reply. As Parkin noted elsewhere in the same correspondence, "where thoughtful men met together there was something much deeper – more on the edge of tears than joy".[21]

Endnotes

The author wishes to thank Barbara Dundas for valuable research assistance and Professor David Beatty for material from his personal collection.

1 See J.L. Granatstein and J.M. Hitsman, Broken Promises: *A History of Conscription in Canada* (Toronto, 1977).

2 Robert Craig Brown and Ramsay Cook, Canada 1896–1921: *A Nation Transformed* (Toronto, 1974), pp. 250–74.

3 David Jay Bercuson, *True Patriot: The Life of Brooke Claxton, 1898–1960* (Toronto, 1993), pp. 22–43.

4 Gregory S. Kealey, "1919: The Canadian Labour Revolt," *Labour/Le travail* 13 (spring 1984), p. 15.

5 National Archives of Canada [NAC], William Green Papers, "An Autobiography of World War I", p. 11.

6 Daniel G. Dancocks, *Gallant Canadians: The Story of the Tenth Canadian Infantry Battalion, 1914–1919* (Calgary, 1990), p. 196.

7 NAC, Gordon S. Bennett Papers, vol. 2, Diary, entry for 11 November 1918.

8 NAC, C.S.L. Hertzberg Papers, vol. 1, file 18, Diary, 10 May – 15 November 1918, entry for 12 November 1918.

9 Paul T. Hutchison, *Canada's Black Watch: The First Hundred Years, 1862–1962* (Montreal, 1962), p. 136.

10 David Pierce Beatty, *Memories of the Forgotten War: The World War I Diary of Pte. V.E. Goodwin* (Port Elgin, New Brunswick, 1986), p. 201, 203.

11 Jeffery Williams, *Princess Patricia's Canadian Light Infantry* (London, 1972), p. 30.

12 NAC, 38th Ottawa Infantry Battalion war records, 1917–1919, File "Story of the 38th Battalion" by Major Warren, p. 57.

13 Jonathan F. Vance, *Death So Noble: Memory, Meaning, and the First World War* (Vancouver, 1997), passim.

14 *Toronto Star*, 12 November 1918 (last edition), p. 5.

15 *The Gazette* (Montreal), 12 November 1918, "Cohesion of Many Nations Feature of Grand Parade", p. 4.

16 *The Ottawa Evening Citizen*, 11 November 1918, "Ottawans Joined Celebrations as Never Before", p. 5.

17 Pierre Berton, *Vimy* (Toronto, 1986).

18 NAC, Sir Thomas White Papers, vol. 21, file 89, Currie to Borden, 26 November 1918, p. 5.

19 Desmond Morton, "Polling the Soldier Vote: The Overseas Campaign in the Canadian General Election of 1917", *Journal of Canadian Studies/Revue d'études canadiennes* 10 (November 1975).

20 Desmond Morton, "'Kicking and Complaining': Demobilization Riots in the Canadian Expeditionary Force, 1918–19", *Canadian Historical Review* 61 (September 1980), p. 351.

21 NAC George Robert Parkin Papers, vol. 57, George Parkin to son Raleigh, 12 November 1918.

55. Australian prisoners of war, from various AIF infantry battalions, photographed outside the barracks of their camp in Germany, on 16 November 1918, five days after the Armistice. With the end of the war, many such men joined crowds of civilians on the long march back to the liberated territories of France and Belgium.
(Australian War Memorial, Negative No. P01981.058) (One of a series of 400 photographs sent by Australian prisoners in German camps to Miss M.E. Chomley, Secretary of the Prisoners Department, Australian-British Red Cross Society, in London) (Chapter 9 - Australians)

56. Australian Army troops and volunteer groups at Adelaide Oval cricket ground celebrating the Armistice on 'Peace Day', 14 November 1918. On this day, which was declared a public holiday following the news of 11 November, a crowd of 40,000 people crammed the Oval to watch a victory parade of returned and invalided soldiers, nurses, recruits, rejected volunteers, militia forces and cadets. Some 6,000 children also joined the display, which culminated in "cheers for the for the British Navy, the British Army, the Australian troops, and the Allies" - *The Adelaide Advertiser*.
(Australian War Memorial, Negative No. H11601) (Chapter 9 - Australians)

57. Premature celebrations in Toronto, 7 November 1918, as people react to early but unsubstantiated rumours that an armistice has been agreed.
(National Archives of Canada PA 71198) (Chapter 10 - The Canadians)

58. A Canadian battalion, headed by pipes and drums, enters the town of Mons on the morning of 11 November 1918. The town fell to Canadian troops a few hours before the Armistice came into effect. *(National Archives of Canada PA 3572)* (Chapter 10 - The Canadians)

59. Soldiers of the 42nd Battalion Canadian Expeditionary Force take a rest in the main square of the town of Mons, shortly after the news of the Armistice. It was on this very pavé in the square, where the men of the original BEF rested on their way to the Battle of Mons, on a hot August morning over four years earlier.
(National Archives of Canada PA3570) (Chapter 10 - Canadians)

60. A crowd scene on Yonge Street, Toronto, photographed on the morning of 11 November 1918. Amid the celebrations, small excited groups pause to discuss the news.
(National Archives of Canada C16934) (Chapter 10 - Canadians)

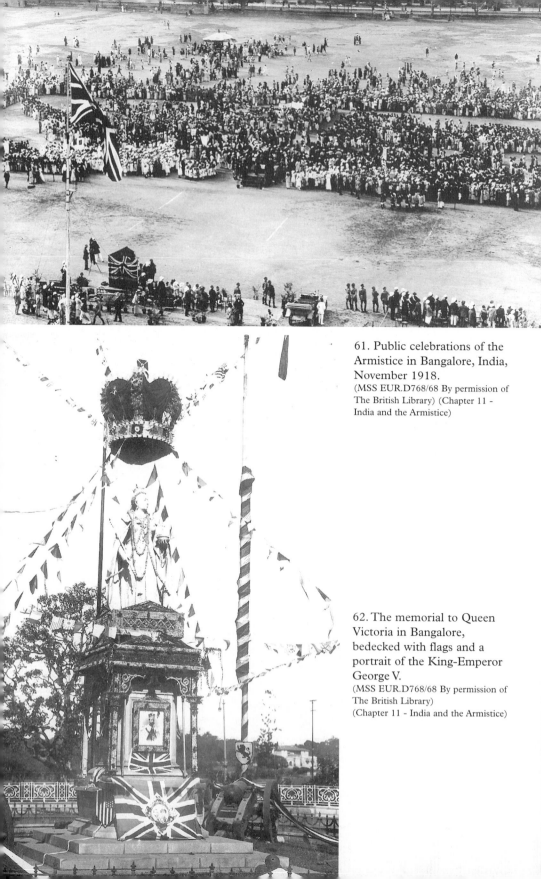

61. Public celebrations of the Armistice in Bangalore, India, November 1918.
(MSS EUR.D768/68 By permission of The British Library) (Chapter 11 - India and the Armistice)

62. The memorial to Queen Victoria in Bangalore, bedecked with flags and a portrait of the King-Emperor George V.
(MSS EUR.D768/68 By permission of The British Library)
(Chapter 11 - India and the Armistice)

63. New Zealand artillery moving forward over a temporary bridge, during the final advance in 1918. (QE II Army Memorial Museum, Waiouru) (Chapter 12 - New Zealand)

64. New Zealand soldiers' graves, Roman Road, Jericho, at the end of the First World War. (Alexander Turnbull Library, Wellington, New Zealand. F-106342-1/2) (Chapter 12 - New Zealand)

65. New Zealand troops marching across the Hohenzollern Bridge in Cologne, subsequent to the Armistice. The New Zealand Division was one of those selected to take part in occupation duties in Germany.
(QE II Army Memorial Museum, Waiouru)
(Chapter 12 - New Zealand)

66. The village of Surafend the morning after it was attacked by men of the New Zealand Mounted Rifles, resulting in some thirty to forty Arab dead. December 1918.
(QE II Army Memorial Museum, Waiouru)
(Chapter 12 - New Zealand)

67. The impact of the war would cast a long shadow: The Governor General of New Zealand, Admiral Lord Jellicoe, visits wounded men still convalescing in the early 1920's. Queen Mary's Hospital, Hamner Springs.
(QE II Army Memorial Museum, Waiouru) (Chapter 12 - New Zealand)

68. The armistice in German South West Africa, 1915. Governor Seitz and his party alight from their train, to be met by Louis Botha (far right) in front of the tent in which the surrender document would be signed. (Cape Archives Depot) (Chapter 13 – South Africa)

69. Africans in Natal assemble to hear news of the Armistice from a local magistrate, November 1918. (*Natal Witness*, 23 November 1918) (Chapter 13 – South Africa)

70. Japanese and westerners in Tokyo gather at Hibiya Park to celebrate the signing of the Armistice. A photograph from the newspaper *Tokyo Asahi Shimbun.*
(via N. Shimazu) (Chapter Fourteen - The Japanese Response)

Chapter Eleven

Anxious Celebrations: British India and the Armistice

Sanjoy Bhattacharya

It has often been pointed out that the experience of the First World War created, and sharpened, numerous contradictions between British and Indian interests in colonial South Asia. As the war affected different sections of the Indian people in separate – sometimes opposite – ways, it kindled tensions within Indian society as well.[1] The pressures of war on the Indian economy were undeniable: there was a 300 per cent increase in the defence expenditure, which not only heralded the imposition of war loans, but also caused a sharp rise in taxes and a modification of the entire financial structure. Military recruitment increased dramatically and the size of the wartime army rose to 1.2 million men, of whom the Punjab contributed 355,000 soldiers. While this recruitment drive injected money into selected localities, the outfitting of the wartime army caused severe difficulties in other parts of the country. For instance, the export of grains and other raw materials for the military's use often caused local shortages. One report, dated as late as January 1919, from Sir George Lloyd, the governor of Bombay, to Edwin Montagu, the Secretary of State for India, stated that "Large quantities of valuable fodder are being exported from here to Mesopotamia by the Army ... Luckily the Horniman Press [a reference to B.G. Horniman, the editor of the nationalist *Bombay Chronicle*] have not tumbled to the fact that fodder is being exported while the Deccan starves".[2]

Moreover, the wartime transport bottlenecks and disruption, primarily in the form of a sharp fall in shipping-space available for non-military needs, caused a sharp fall in imports, and contributed to the general inflationary trends.[3] At the same time, the export prices of Indian agricultural goods did not go up in the same proportion due to the dislocation in world economic relations. The consequent shift in conditions of trade against agriculture, adversely affected the well-to-do peasants who produced for the market. Poorer peasants and landless labourers were affected in a different way: the prices of coarse foodgrains, which constituted their staple food, went up dramatically. The high prices of foodstuffs affected other occupational groups as well. Artisanal labour, in particular, was badly hit, and ironically, even the industrial workers attached to businesses benefiting from wartime demands, suffered. Although employment in organized industries and plantations went up from 2,105,824 in 1911 to 2,681,125, wages remained low in a period of high prices and super-profits for employers. For instance, in the C.N. Wadia Century Mills – an Indian concern – an 80 to 100 per cent increase in foodgrain prices was counterbalanced by only a 15 per cent increase in wages between 1914 and 1918, even though the enterprise had made a 100 per cent profit on its capital investment of 1918.[4] Indeed, some select businesses benefited greatly from wartime demands, the decline in foreign competition, the price-differential between agricultural raw materials and industrial goods, and the stagnation or decline in real wages. In eastern India, for instance, British jute mill magnates gained from the boost in the price of jute manufactures (like sandbags and canvas), and the cotton textile industry of Bombay, Ahmedabad and Sholapur went through a period of decisive growth at the expense of the Lancashire mills.[5] In addition, a rising group of Indian, primarily Calcutta-based Marwari businessmen, also accumulated considerable wealth during the war through speculation in jute and other commodities. In fact, two of them – G.D. Birla and S. Hukumchand – would utilize these windfall profits to start the first Indian-owned jute mills soon after the war. It is against this background that we must view the responses in India towards the news of the Armistice.

As the First World War affected different groups in substantially different ways, it was perhaps inevitable that the attitudes of different sections of British Indian society to the Armistice were going to be very mixed. Driven by specific, and, in the main, widely divergent expectations from a post-war scenario, they often disagreed with each other's standpoint about 'peace', 'democracy', 'freedom' and 'constitutional advance'. This is well illustrated by a piece in the *Tribune*, a 'Hindu' paper published from the capital of the militarily important province of Punjab, which celebrated the ceasefire by declaring that:

> ... we must be thankful for the successful end to the war ... It is no small gratification to us Indians that we have taken a substantial share in bringing about the present victory ... it is the Indian valour and Indian blood that produced momentous results in France and in Turkey. India's rejoicings on the present occasion will, therefore, be no less than those of England or America.[6]

The congratulatory tone of the article tended to hide the many social tensions that had been brewing throughout the war, and would explode into the open soon after 11 November 1918. The significance of India's contribution to the war, which was continually reiterated in many other 'native' papers,[7] would soon degenerate into caustic disagreements about what Britain now 'owed' India.

A relieved Government of India sponsored widespread celebrations to mark the Armistice. In Simla, on 12 November 1918, this involved an

xx A newspaper (top) produced in Urdu for Muslim Indian soldiers fighting in Palestine, and (below) also one in Hindi, for Sikhs and others. Racial tensions between ethnic groups which had fought so successfully together would emerge on their return to India after the Armistice. (Liddle Collection)

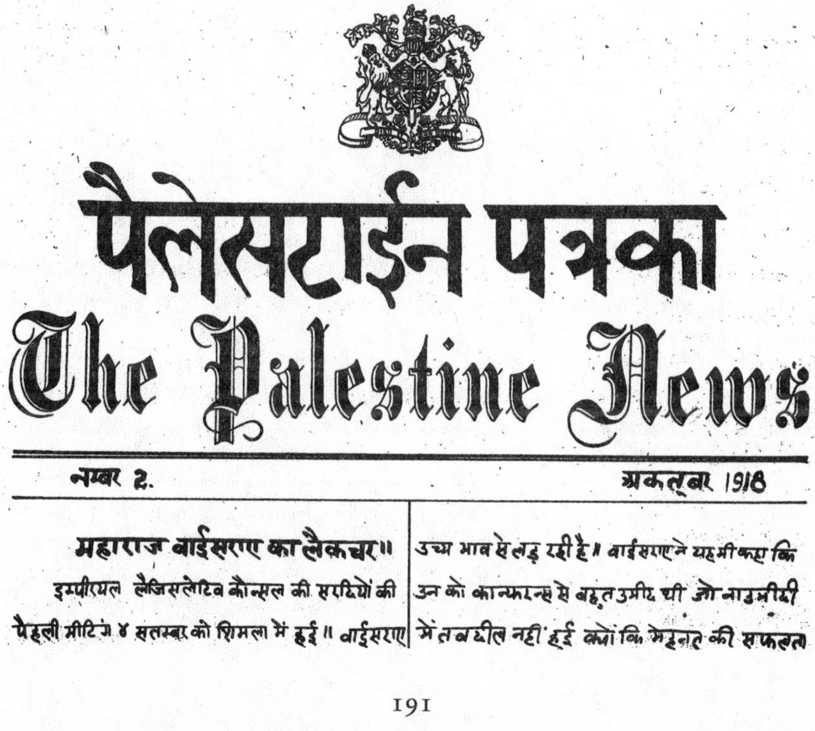

"extraordinarily large assembly", where the Viceroy of India described the Armistice as the "supreme event" that had "assured peace". In Calcutta, the news of the cessation of hostilities caused the "wildest enthusiasm" and:

> there was the greatest rejoicing in all parts of the town. All public buildings and mercantile firms hoisted Union Jacks and motors and carriages were decked with Allied flags. In clubs and cafes cries of 'God Save the King' were received with tremendous cheering ... leaflets and posters were issued by the newspaper offices and distributed ... and although there were no organized demonstrations, numerous parties of soldiers and others were roaming the thoroughfares singing at the top of their voices.[8]

In other cities, such as Agra and Multan, the administrators of towns declared 12 November a public holiday. As a result, law-courts, offices, colleges and schools remained closed.[9] In other towns, educational institutions were encouraged by the administration to organize special meetings. In Aligarh, for example, the "trustees of the *Kayastha Patshala* [school] ... assembled in a meeting and offered congratulations to the British Government on the glorious victory achieved against the enemy".[10] Comparable celebrations were seen in most of the princely states, in many of which the signing of the Armistice was announced by a gun salute. In the state of Ramnagar, government officials assisted in the decoration of shops and the market place, while the troops attached to the State Forces organized a parade.[11]

The festivities continued awhile – well into the fourth week of November – as administrators in the provincial capitals, bigger district headquarters and princely states organized 'victory weeks', wherein the Armistice was commemorated through theatre and musical shows, and special sporting and cultural events for children.[12] In notable cases, special bonuses were awarded to all grades of employees of industrial concerns, after which they were given a day's paid leave to attend the victory ceremonies.[13] However, these celebrations were soon engulfed in a series of acrimonious debates, which began to attract much wider attention than the Armistice itself. These exchanges took on complex forms, often with markedly racist and political connotations. The cessation of hostilities caused an immediate re-definition of what 'loyalism' and 'nationalism' meant, which, in turn, noticeably sharpened the divisions between the European component in India and some sections of the indigenous society.

The relief arising from the end of the war was palpable amongst the Europeans in India. An article in the *Capital*, a European-owned publication, declared, for instance, that:

> It is not easy, this week, to write of anything but the end of the war; it is even harder to say something which has not already been said in thanksgiving that the debauch of destruction is over at last .... The predominant feeling among Europeans was that their kith and kin in the homeland, their relatives and friends in the armies at the front were at last secure of their lives. Those who have had to remain in India during the whole period of

the war, have, it is true, escaped its worst horrors. They have not been terrified by air-raids, there has been no hunger and comparatively little privation . . .[14]

Another European-owned weekly declared that:

After the stress and strain of more than four years of war forced upon the world by the greed and ambition of a single predatory State the prospect of an enduring peace will be welcomed with enthusiasm in every Allied country

xxi "The Lighter Side of Peace - A barrack scene on Armistice Day" – a humorous view of events in India, reproduced from the *Times of India*, in November 1918. (By kind permission of the British Library)

... A great task confronts the Allies, and especially the British Empire. The wastage of war must be repaired. The industries of peace must be repaired.[15]

However, as letters to certain newspapers amply proved, worries about the post-war political and economic scene began to surface almost as soon as the firing stopped. For the European owners of industries which had benefited from the wartime boom, the economic and political future looked less than rosy. Almost everyone questioned the wisdom of the Government of India's decision to impose an Excess Profits Tax after the war had ended.[16] Other worries were also articulated. Some complainants – many of them officials of the Raj – wondered when their salaries would be raised in a period of continued inflation; whereas others concentrated on castigating the more radical elements of the Indian nationalists.[17]

Indeed, the debates regarding the 'value' of the war, what its conclusion held out for India and the choice of indigenous representatives attending the Peace Conference, and became increasingly fractious. On the one hand, the European press regularly highlighted the loyalism of Indian notables who had organized celebrations to mark the Armistice. Their opponents, on the other, questioned the apparent contradictions in Allied – especially British – statesmanship in organizing a meeting to discuss 'freedom' in a post-war world, while balking at offering India greater self-government. A good example of the former was the tone of the reports released by the *Empire* of Calcutta: a programme organized by the Kalighat *Sangit Samaj* [Music Association] to commemorate the end of the war was termed 'befitting';[18] and the distribution of *chudders* [blankets] and alms by notables like Babu Prohladh Chandra Pal, the *Zamindar* of the 'Burdwan Raj', to mark the Armistice was highly appreciated.[19]

The nationalist press, in contrast, tended to unite in downplaying – and even attacking – the prolonged celebration of the Armistice. This compared starkly with the wartime period, when certain Congressmen like M.K. Gandhi lobbied for recruitment into the army, while others, like the Home Rule League headed by Annie Besant, continually criticized British wartime policy. Differences in the nationalist press were now primarily premised on the degree of hostility towards official constitutional policy. The journal edited by Besant, and her Indian political allies, for instance, reported the Armistice in markedly neutral terms,[20] while attacking the lack of constitutional advance thus:

India cannot remain a subject Nation, when all Europe is set free, and when, in Asia, her neighbours also are self-governing. Japan rules herself. China is a Republic. Afghanistan and Persia are self-ruling. Russia in Asia is carving out her own destiny. India, India alone, is left a helot among free peoples, subject to a foreign Nation, to the yoke which Mr. Asquith has declared to be intolerable. Is it possible that this state of things can continue in the most civilised and most proud of Asian nations?[21]

In a more direct attack against official pronouncements after the war, another article declared that:

> India has by her deeds and sacrifices justified her claim to an equality within the British Empire and has, if we understand the Royal Message aright, earned the title to that position of equality by what his message describes as "the bond of brotherhood proved by partnership in trials and triumphs". His Majesty's message has only served to inspire hope in Indian hearts in regard to the future status of India in the Empire. It only behoves, therefore, His Majesty's Ministers to carry out the spirit of the message with reference to India.[22]

Such requests were repeated in other papers as well. For example, the *Leader*, which was published from Lahore, declared that while the announcement by the British and French that an independent government would be established in Syria and Mesopotamia would "thrill the heart of every Indian", it would be a great pity if India, whose soldiers took a great part in conquering these Turkish possessions, were kept out of this "priceless blessing".[23]

In other cases the criticism of the lack of non-official Indian 'leaders' at the Peace Conference was articulated in purely communal terms. For instance, some Muslim-owned papers, including sometimes those considered loyalist by the colonial authorities, complained against the non-selection of any co-religionists in the official deputation.[24] Such fears were also expressed in other arenas. In a special meeting of the Bengal Legislative Council, held on 14 November 1918, at the Government House in Calcutta, designed to discuss the Montagu-Chelmsford Report on Indian constitutional advance, two members, Fazlul Huq and Hasan Suhrawardy (who were to become important all-India political figures in the 1930s and 1940s) reiterated that Muslim interests were not being adequately protected.[25] Although their suggestion that the report be amended was voted out (by 19 votes to 13), their stand revealed the increasing tendency amongst Muslim elites to mobilize support for their policies on religious lines. This constituency's clamour that their community's rights be 'safeguarded' would not go unheard. Indeed, it contributed significantly to the Government of India's eventual decision to introduce separate electorates.

In many cases these debates degenerated into incessantly bitter exchanges, which heightened racial tensions. The frequent complaints made by some Indian newspapers about the "injustice" of not taking a "non-official Indian leader" to Versailles was attacked in the European press. A good example of this was the exchange between the *Bengalee* and the *Empire*. The former had declared that:

> An Anglo Indian journal [the Empire] asks, what has the non-official Indian done to deserve this recognition [of being selected to go to the Peace Conference]? ... It may be said among other things, that but for the

> influence exerted by the non-official leaders, recruiting and war loans would not have been so successful operations [sic].[26]

The *Empire* criticized this standpoint thus: "That the War Loans – whose success the 'Bengalee' attributes to Indian 'leaders' – were successes, was due mainly to the support given the emmissions [sic] by British and Indian merchants, and Indian Princes, none of whom are influenced by Indian politicians".[27]

Resonances of such views could be seen in other public arenas as well. For instance, on 28 November 1918, a meeting of the Bihar Legislative Council seemed to reach an unfavourable conclusion when in response to a speech by Rai Bahadur Dwarka Nath about India's efforts in the war, a Mr. Jameson, representing the planters in the region, said that "All honour" should be due:

> ... to those who really had helped the Empire; the Princes, rajas, zemindars [sic], and those others who had honestly done their best to help but he did not think they could pretend that the mass of Indian people understood or thought much about the war or that the educated and politically active classes had taken any great part in it.[28]

Such animosities often culminated in tasteless caricatures – like the cartoon in the *Empire* (dated 16 November 1918) facetiously recommending, among other things, the gassing of Home Leaguers – which provided further impetus to the acrimonious debates between the protagonists. In other instances they caused the publication of cartoons describing what might have happened to India had the Germans won the war. These actions, often a response to the hostility of Indian opinion, highlight the growing nervousness amongst the Europeans about the current political situation. A notable effect was the renewal of efforts to organize politically, which would ultimately leave an indelible imprint on the form of the Government of India Act of 1919.[29] These acerbic exchanges might also explain the stiffening of the nationalist stance, which caused the isolation of former 'extremists' at the slightest hint of their agreeing to negotiate on the Government of India's terms. A good example of this was the experience of Annie Besant, who was shouted down during a meeting held at Delhi for defending the Montford reforms.[30]

Indian opinions, like European attitudes, were, of course, not conditioned by political factors alone. Economic factors played an important part in shaping the reactions of various sections of society towards the end of the war. Indian industrialists, like their British counterparts, did not welcome the cancellation of war orders and, indeed, opposed the imposition of the Excess Profit Tax.[31] Nonetheless, a great majority of them paraded their loyalty to the British in the face of unprecedented labour activism, which increased in the face of reduced industrial production after the war. The effects of the industrial slowdown were cushioned somewhat by the shortage of labour, but a rapid fall in real incomes – due to the continued inflationary trends and the reductions in the working week – caused workers to become increasingly restive.[32] A series of effective strikes made the owners of the industrial concerns dependent on official mediation and, perhaps more significantly, the state's coercive apparatus. They, therefore, remained in the forefront in the organization – and/or the financing – of many of the programmes designed to celebrate the Armistice.[33]

The reactions of other classes of Indians remained equally mixed. A great majority of the soldiers returning from the war were faced with demobilization, which unsurprisingly caused continuing anxieties about future prospects. While the relief amongst their families about the end of hostilities must have been absolute, especially in areas where recruitment had been achieved by the use of force,[34] the prospect of returning to landed occupations at a time when agriculture was suffering was not welcomed. If anything, the army had provided a regular and stable source of income, which was suddenly being cut off for many following the disbanding of the wartime army. The resulting discontent, which the authorities sought to tackle by the re-employment of soldiers,[35] might explain the not infrequent instances of ex-soldiers participating in, and organizing, nationalist demonstrations in 1919.[36] Economic factors might also explain the sudden upsurge of middle-class interest in nationalist politics. This increasingly vocal and largely urban group had been immediately hit by the rise in prices of foodstuffs, especially as the rate of increase in their salaries lagged far behind the rapid rise in the cost of living.[37] Moreover, the official tendency to stifle their complaints regularly by the use of special censorship regulations, without taking sufficiently effective measures to improve their lot, caused a widespread refusal to endorse the Government's decision to retain wartime restrictions in peace-time and the marked participation of the Indian middle class in the anti-Rowlatt [Sedition] Act agitation organized by Gandhi from 1919 onwards.[37]

In similar fashion, the financial difficulties suffered by all classes of the rural population resulted in a decidedly lukewarm response to the end of the war. More notably, it created a situation where the Congress was able gradually to develop the germs of an organizational network amongst increasingly politically conscious rural constituencies, like the richer elements of the peasantry, from which it had so far enjoyed negligible support. Indeed, in the United Provinces the Congress-controlled *Kisan Sabha* [Peasant Association] expanded rapidly between November 1918 and June 1919: in this period at least 450 branches were formed in 173 *tahsils* [localities]. This was a significant development considering that its first meeting had only been held on 11 November in the city of Allahabad.[39] But the widely varied reactions of Indians to the Armistice is perhaps best highlighted by the reactions of the mass of the rural poor who had suffered terribly from the wartime economic dislocation, and were as a result becoming increasingly aggressive in the post-war period.[40] A great majority remained unaware that the war had ended till special official publicity organizations – created at the height of the war to popularize the Allied war effort amongst urban and rural notables – visited villages with the news. Even more striking was the gist of their message. Grandiose assurances of lasting peace and constitutional progress were avoided and the speakers concentrated instead on promising their audiences, which were usually attracted to attend the meetings by the distribution of free food and cloth, that the financial difficulties that had plagued them would soon cease.[41] Such pledges would then invariably be followed by requests that the views of Congress 'rumour-mongers' be disregarded. The Government's battle-lines against Gandhi were unmistakably being drawn, and the colonial state was now in the awkward position of preparing for a new and difficult struggle while 'celebrating' the successful end of a war.

Endnotes

1 S. Sarkar, *Modern India, 1885–1947* (Delhi, 1983), pp. 168–169.

2 Quoted in A.D.D. Gordon, *Businessmen and Politics: Rising Nationalism and a Modernising Economy in Bombay, 1918–1933* (Delhi, 1978), pp. 33–34.

3 Indeed, an official statistical abstract on prices supplied the following all-India index numbers (1873=100):

1913	1914	1915	1916	1917	1918	1919	1920	1921	1922	1923
143	147	152	152	196	225	276	281	236	232	215

From J. Brown, *Gandhi's Rise to Power: Indian Politics, 1915–1922* (Cambridge, 1972), p. 125.

4 Sarkar, *Modern India*, p. 175.

5 A. Bagchi, *Private Investment in India, 1900–1939* (Cambridge, 1972) and B. Chatterji, *Trade, Tariffs and Empire: Lancashire and British Policy in India 1919–1939* (Delhi, 1992). Also see, P.J. Mead, "Industrial Expansion in Bombay Presidency", *Industrial Handbook, 1919* (Calcutta, 1919), p. 33.

6 *Tribune*, 13 November 1918, Report of 14 November 1918, *Punjab Native Newspaper Reports: 1918*, L/R/5/200, Oriental and India Office Collections, British Museum [hereafter O.I.O.C.].

7 See the *Hamdam* of 13, 14 and 15 November 1918; the *Shakti*, 19 November 1917; the *Cawnpore Samachar*, 17 November 1918, and the *Pratap*, 18 November 1918.

8 "India's Rejoicings", *Pioneer and Indian Weekly News*, 15 November 1918.

9 *Ibid.*

10 *Pioneer and Indian Weekly News*, 22 November 1918.

11 "India's Rejoicings", *Pioneer and Indian Weekly News*, 15 November 1918.

12 *Empire*, 3 December 1918.

13 See, for instance, the report on the India Jute Mills, Serampore (Calcutta), *Empire*, 28 November 1918.

14 "A Ditcher's Diary", *Capital*, 15 November 1918.

15 See Editorial article entitled "Peace at Last", *Pioneer and Indian Weekly News*, 15 November 1918.

16 See, for instance, the complaints of the Madras Chambers of Commerce in *Pioneer Mail and Indian Weekly News*, 13 December 1918.

17 See, for instance, letters to the editor between 15 November 1918 and 27 December 1918 in the *Pioneer Mail and Indian Weekly News*.

18 *Empire*, 2 December 1918.

19 *Empire*, 2 and 3 December 1918.

20 *Commonweal.: A Journal of National Reform*, 15 November 1918.

21 See editorial article entitled "Week of Falling Thrones", *Commonweal.: A Journal of National Reform*, 22 November 1918.

22 See article entitled "Two Recent Pronouncements", *Commonweal.: A Journal of National Reform*, 22 November 1918.

23 *Leader*, 15 November 1918, L/R/5/200, O.I.O.C.
24 See, for instance, the *Mashriq*, 21 November 1918, Report for week ending 16 November 1918, *United Provinces Native Newspaper Reports: 1918*, L/R/5/94, O.I.O.C.
25 *Pioneer and Indian Weekly News*, 22 November 1918.
26 *Pioneer and Indian Weekly News*, 18 November 1918.
27 *Ibid.*
28 *Pioneer and Indian Weekly News*, 6 December 1918.
29 Sarkar, *Modern India*, p.167.
30 Sarkar, *Modern India*, p. 188. For a description of the effect of the Montford reforms on the 'moderates', especially in Bombay, see J. Masselos, "Some Aspects of Bombay City Politics in 1919", in R. Kumar (ed.), *Essays on Gandhian Politics: The Rowlatt Satyagraha of 1919* (Oxford, 1971).
31 See the arguments put forth by the Marwari Chamber of Commerce in *Pioneer Mail and Indian Weekly News*, 13 December 1918.
32 Report on a meeting of the Indian Jute Mill Association, *Empire*, 9 December 1918. Also see, letter to the editor from the mill-labour of Sholapur, dated 8 February 1920, in *The Mahratta*, 15 February 1920.
33 Sarkar, Modern India, pp. 174–176. Also see, A.D.D. Gordon, "Businessmen and Politics in a Developing Colonial Economy: Bombay City, 1918–1933", in C.J. Dewey and A.G. Hopkins (eds), *The Imperial Impact: Studies in the Economic History of Africa and India* (London, 1978); R. Newman, *Worker's and Unions in Bombay, 1918–1929* (Canberra, 1981) and S. Patel, *The Making of Industrial Relations: The Ahmedabad Textile Industry, 1918–39* (Delhi, 1987).
34 Sarkar, *Modern India*, p. 169.
35 *Pioneer Mail and Indian Weekly News*, 27 December 1918. For a description of the fears arising from the impending demobilization, see letter to the editor from "A Professional Man", *ibid.*
36 Sarkar, *Modern India*, pp. 169–224.
37 Their complaints were continually expressed in the Indian press. See, for instance, *Oudh Akhbar*, 20 November 1918, Report for week ending 16 November 1918, *United Provinces Native Newspaper Reports: 1918*, L/R/5/94, O.I.O.C. Also see, *Khalsa Advocate*, 3 December 1918, Report of 14 November 1918, *Punjab Native Newspaper Reports: 1918*, L/R/5/200, O.I.O.C.
38 Sarkar, *Modern India*, pp. 187–204. Also see, R. Kumar (ed.), *The Rowlatt Satyagraha of 1919* (Oxford, 1971).
39 M.H. Siddiqi, *Agrarian Unrest in North India: United Provinces, 1918–1922* (New Delhi, 1978), pp. 122–125. Other good descriptions of the intricacies of the growth of the Congress organizational network are provided by K. Gopal, "The Development of the Indian National Congress as a Mass Organisation, 1918–23", *Journal of Asian Studies*, May 1966 and P.J. Musgrave, "Landlords and Lords of the Land: Estate Management and Social Control in Uttar Pradesh, 1860–1920", *Modern Asian Studies*, July 1972.
40 The dominance of landed interests in the Congress-controlled Kisan Sabha caused some local branches to break away and develop a more marked peasant leadership since, as Majid Siddiqi tells us, it became increasingly difficult for rural operatives to accept the "patient tactics of the United Provinces kisan Sabha". Indeed, in a highly polarized rural context many local *sabha* operatives found it impossible to preach against the landlords, without doing anything to combat their oppression. Siddiqi, *Agrarian Unrest*, p. 125.
41 See, for instance, "Publicity Board Scheme", *Empire*, 26 November 1918.

Chapter Twelve

New Zealand: "The Heroes Lie in France"

Christopher Pugsley

"Colonel Evans of Whangarei, was more to the point as far as we were concerned ... I well recall his final words before we left the ship [to set foot again on New Zealand soil]. 'Remember', he said. 'When you go ashore you are not heroes. The heroes lie in France'".[1]

For men of the New Zealand Division like Bill Taylor who wrote these words, the war and a chapter in their lives came to an end on 11 November 1918. Taylor had been on the Somme in 1916, was wounded at Messines in June 1917, wounded again before Solesmes on 23 October 1918, and he heard the news of the Armistice in the New Zealand No. 2 General Hospital at Walton-on-Thames on 11 November 1918. He "was filled with the same feelings as the poet when he heard everyone burst out singing".[2] It was a view shared by the New Zealand medical staff, one of whom was Gladys Luxford a VAD whose father was one of the New Zealand chaplains to the Hospital. "I will never forget the Matron announcing at dinner time [that] the last shot has been fired. There was absolute silence; & the thought no more soldiers killed, & the return to NZ soon".[3]

In the New Zealand training camps in the United Kingdom, the news came round at about 11.15 a.m. that an armistice had been signed. In Sling Camp, Corporal C.W. Fraser was instructing his squad of reinforcements on the Lewis Gun when the news came through. "Then the fun started , my table with the gun got knocked over. And that was the last we seen of them. They just went mad with joy and off. So we got our guns together, put them away and joined in the fun. And fun it sure was". Canteens were broken into and hogs-heads of beer were rolled into the streets, broached, and when finished the canteens of the nearby British depots were raided, and the drinking continued for three days before the officers and non-commissioned officers got things back under any semblance of control.[4]

For the men with the New Zealand Division in France, it was harder to believe. "In this hour for the first time since facing the enemy my mind allows itself to really believe that I shall see you all again".[5] So wrote Captain George Tuck, Adjutant of the 2nd Auckland Battalion, to his parents on the day after the Armistice of 11 November 1918. A Boer War veteran at 18 and a carpenter by trade, Tuck had immediately enlisted on the declaration of war and sailed with the Main Body of the New Zealand Expeditionary Force in October 1914. He first saw action in the Gallipoli landings on 25 April 1915, as a corporal in No. 7 Platoon of the 6th Hauraki Company, Auckland Battalion. Tuck was wounded on the Somme in September 1916, saw action at Messines in June 1917 and before Passchendaele in October 1917. At the beginning of 1918 he was one of six original members still serving with his battalion. Today what these men went through in those years of war can scarcely be imagined; the green fields and war cemeteries of France and Belgium are too ordered to tell the story. Only the sheer mass of names of the missing and the numbers of graves in a landscape populated by hidden cemeteries help one towards a degree of comprehension.

For men like George Tuck and Bill Taylor, those years were filled with days of surviving amidst a constantly changing parade of faces whose passing through death, mutilation, or nervous collapse, simply became part of life on the Western Front. Friendships were treasured and close comrades mourned with an aching intensity that was lifelong. The mud, stench, fear, the frequent state of exhaustion from broken sleep, night working parties, dawn and dusk stand-to's, forced each man in on himself sensing and fearing most of all, that eventually he too would break and show fear. As Tuck himself had written after the Somme in 1916: "tis a knowledge of these things and of seeing good men flinch from duty when their nerve is gone – that hangs like a waiting beast on its opportunity, that darkens the soul of a man".[6] Now, in November 1918, after months of hard fighting, Tuck's 2nd Auckland Battalion marched through the streets of Solesmes, and, "a message was shown to me which stated that hostilities would cease at the eleventh hour of the eleventh day of the eleventh month. So the end had come".[7]

"There was not even a cheer raised. There had been so many rumours floating about lately that, I think, everyone thought this information but another false yarn...".[8] For 23-year old Gunner Bert Stokes of 13th Battery, New Zealand Field Artillery, moving back with the guns through the Forêt de Mormal, 11 November 1918, was a:

> dull miserable day with misty rain and being in the Forest did not make it any more cheerful. On the way we were told that an Armistice was to be signed at 11.00 a.m. and the war was over. I wrote in a letter home – 'It seems to [sic] wonderful to believe. There is no cheering or excitement, just a feeling of relief. Everything is going on as before, we still have the guns and horses to look after, but of course we miss the screeching shells screaming over from the enemy lines. We all have taken it in a very calm and subdued manner. No one seemed to want to cheer when we first heard the news. We realized that soon we shall see the home shores on the horizon and that is what the armistice means to us. For most of us tired in body and mind and with memories of the tragic field of battle this momentous announcement was too vast to be appreciated at that moment.[9]

For the men of the 'Silent Division' as the New Zealand Division was known, the Armistice was almost an anti-climax to what had been a hard but successful year.[10] No one was more thankful that at last it was over than its commander, Major-General Sir Andrew Russell, who wrote in his diary that night: "News came thro late last night that armistice had been signed, and hostilities ceased at 11 a.m. Thank God!"[11]

It was the end of two-and-a-half years' active service by the New Zealand Division in France and Flanders. This had started at Armentières in May 1916 when the division first went into the line; a raw amateur formation, raised barely three months before, and not yet fit for combat. There were few like Taylor left from those early days in France, even fewer like Tuck who had seen Gallipoli service. The professionalism which was now the hallmark of the Division had been hard won, and the cost high. Twelve thousand, four hundred and eighty three dead and 35,419 wounded; 47,902 out of the total of 59,483 New Zealand casualties suffered in the First World War.[12]

After Passchendaele the New Zealand public believed that the country was being bled white of the best of its manhood. In 1918, a war-weary New Zealand was determined to resist any War Office requests for additional units for overseas service over and above those already raised. Married men with two children had already been balloted to go into training under the Military Services Act, and there was a widespread feeling throughout the country that New Zealand had done enough. Sustaining the forces which were already overseas became New Zealand's priority.[13] In addition to the division in France, there was the New Zealand Mounted Rifles Brigade serving as part of the Anzac Mounted Division in Egypt and Palestine. There was also a range of Corps and Army units in France and administrative and training units in the United Kingdom. In France this included the New Zealand Stationary Hospital at Wisques, an artillery brigade, a tunnelling company, a cyclist battalion and a squadron of Otago Mounted Rifles.[14] In the United Kingdom, New Zealand units included; pay, postal, war records and administrative sections attached to the New Zealand Administrative Headquarters in London. This headquarters controlled three New Zealand General Hospitals at Brockenhurst, Walton-on-Thames, and Codford; the Convalescent Hospital at Hornchurch, as well as various other convalescent homes; training depots at Sling for the Infantry, Brocton for the Rifle Brigade with depots for artillery, engineers, signallers and machine-gunners, together with a Discharge Depot at Torquay.[15] Commanded by Brigadier-General George Spafford Richardson, the New Zealand Expeditionary Force strength in the United Kingdom numbered 26,609 in October 1918, compared to 21,376 in France and Belgium, 17,434 of whom were with the Division. At that time too there were 10,000 men under training in New Zealand.[16]

The New Zealand Division had wintered in the Ypres Salient over Christmas 1917 and by March 1918, after a period in reserve, Russell's New Zealanders were at full strength and trained in open warfare tactics. On 23 March, the Division was rushed forward to fill a dangerous gap in the line of the River Ancre between IV and V British Corps. The *ad hoc* New Zealand formations held the German attacks on their front in the critical days of late

March and early April. Then as part of IV British Corps, Russell's Division held the line from April to August, rotating his battalions out of the line for training in mobile warfare. This was supported by artillery batteries which practised 'leap-frogging' forward to maintain fire support as the infantry practised the advance and attack. All this was in preparation for the 'counter-offensive' which Russell was sure would come.[17]

Although the division was reduced from four to three brigades in January 1918, it still retained the four battalion organization within the Brigade. Russell's division was in the enviable position of being able to maintain its strength with trained reinforcements.[18] The disbanded 4th Infantry Brigade became an Entrenching Group which provided the initial reinforcements to the division in 1918. These reinforcements "comprised a large percentage of men who had previous service in the field. They were of the utmost value and among them were large numbers of NCOs who readily filled the places of those who became casualties".[19] From the March 1918 offensive on, New Zealand brigades each had a bayonet strength equal to most of the now depleted British divisions. This was a major factor in the success of the division as it was equal in infantry strength to some British Corps of three divisions.[20] When the August offensive began, Lieutenant-General G.M. Harper commanding IV Corps had the luxury of being able to pass the New Zealanders through his under-strength British divisions once their set-piece attacks had petered out at the limits of the supporting artillery barrage. Harper gave Russell latitude to plan and fight his division's advance. In turn, Russell gave his brigadiers free rein, 'leap-frogging' brigades forward, with Russell and his reserve brigade commander "keeping in touch with the situation and reconnoitring" ready to pass the next brigade through to keep the momentum going.[21]

Between 21 August and 6 November 1918, the New Zealand Division was the leading division for 49 of the 56 miles advanced on the IV Corps front. In this time it captured 8,756 prisoners, 145 guns, three tanks and 1,263 machine-guns. In an on-going series of operations the New Zealanders showed their superior training and tactical skill. Russell pushed his artillery well forward to support his attacking infantry, instructing his brigades to by-pass centres of population. Where possible, German resistance was also out-flanked or by-passed with firm strictures from Russell to his subordinate commanders to avoid needless casualties at all costs.

By mid-September the British Armies had closed up on the Hindenburg Line. The New Zealand Division attacked on 12 September as part of Third Army in the Battle of Havrincourt. Brigader-General Hart, in command of the 3rd New Zealand Rifle Brigade, recorded in his diary:

> We attacked on a three thousand yard frontage with three battalions in line, each only two-thirds normal strength. The attack commenced very well and we took our first objectives easily ... The enemy stoutly opposed our advance to the second or support trench. Some places we got in and some places we did not. Heavy fighting continued all day and until long after dark. At intervals we turned on artillery and trench mortars to clear up

enemy points of resistance, bombing parties and Lewis gunners were constantly engaged in close combat – he counter-attacked and we re-attacked, and so the battle line swayed to and fro all day. There was more close fighting of this kind than our Division has experienced since Gallipoli... Prisoners came forward steadily until the total reached 502 ... The trenches were crowded with enemy dead, a careful estimate putting the numbers at 250 to 300. Our casualties were only 269 of which at least one half will return to the Field later, the results being that at least five enemy were put permanently out of action to every one of ours, quite apart from the casualties they must have suffered from shell fire ... [22]

In these battles the calibre of German resistance was initially high. "The enemy has been retiring but retiring deliberately in good order with his rear-guards offering fight on selected positions, carefully chosen to give the greatest scope to well placed Machine Guns supported by Field Guns. He has fought cleverly and has always another independently organized screen ready when the first has been broken through".[23] However the growing tactical efficiency of British divisions in 1918 was matched in New Zealand's case by trained reinforcements. It was this that the Germans lacked, and by October 1918 with companies reduced to 60 or less, even the best of German units could not hold their over-stretched defensive fabric together.

Russell knew this and fought his division with consummate skill. The battles of 1918 show his mastery of the advance and encounter battle at divisional level. As a New Zealand platoon commander, Second Lieutenant R.J. Richards wrote: "One way and another we had fighting enough and it was mostly successful – always advancing and always mopping up lots of prisoners and guns ... The attack of the Division was something like a series of waves breaking on the shore, one battalion after another pushing on".[24] This reached a climax with the by-passing and surrender of the fortress town of Le Quesnoy and the Division's rapid advance through the Forêt de Mormal in early November 1918. This marked the end of the fighting on the Western Front for Russell's New Zealanders. They were pulled out of the line to regroup, and it was here that word came that it was over.

Major A.E. Alexander, a signals officer with the New Zealand Division, had served at Gallipoli and on the Western Front. Severely wounded in July 1918, losing the use of an eye, he was engaged in N.Z. Army administration in England in November. His contemporary account presents the reflective comments of a more philosophical mind than would be common, but it is no less interesting in its individuality. On 10 November, he wrote of the Germans: "it is too much to hope that a race of people in whom the national sentiment is so strongly planted, so thoroughly organized and excellently administered should agree to such terms". He hoped that the Armistice would not be signed so that the German people would have to fight in their home-land. He did not write simply in a spirit of vengeance but, by his design, constructively. When the awfulness of war was experienced by Germans: "they will think of the benefits of peace". More interesting still, because here he writes of inner feelings which challenge much received wisdom about the experience of war, Alexander continued:

> It will never be known and it would be unwise to enquire just how many individuals had experienced a sense of freedom, of growth and the fuller meaning of life as a result of the war. Many men prior to the outbreak of war travelled along recognized paths content to live in the rut because they had never known what it was to live anywhere else but suddenly they found their paths widen out and [leading] towards a higher plane – they were drawn out of their humdrum existence and dreary surroundings and placed in an atmosphere of life, animation, thought and inspiration.
>
> Their lives as a result of their wartime experience took on a nobler form, they were influenced by greater and deeper emotions than heretofore, is it to be wondered at that they dread the return to their dull and monotonous existence. They dread the return to their homes not because they fear the possibility of 'love gone out' so much as they shudder at the environment and the dwarfing influences which will inevitably go to kill ambition initiative individuality and mentality.[25]

Whatever may be the wider or deeper application of thoughts which surely express Alexander's own thinking, there seems little doubt however that most New Zealanders in France and in England showed in fact an impatient keenness to get home.

In Palestine, for the New Zealanders of the New Zealand Mounted Rifles Brigade, 1918 had been an exhausting eight months' campaigning in the Jordan Valley. This had seen two unsuccessful raids mounted across the Jordan into the mountains of Moab towards Amman. In the closing month of the campaign, the New Zealand Mounted Rifles Brigade, as part of Chaytor Force, had successfully drawn Turkish reinforcements on them as part of Allenby's deception plan for his break-out battle of Meggido. It succeeded, and now the Anzac Mounted Division advanced down the Amman road for the last time. This road, as Corporal Ted McKay recalled:

> was broad and well-metalled, but littered and disfigured with the cruel wastage that men call war. Dead men and dead animals were sprawled in every attitude: shattered vehicles, wrecked guns, discarded rifles, machine guns and equipment: all spoke eloquently of the demoralising horror of a retreat ... To the best of my recollection we finished this push against our beaten foe at a spot called Ziza, capturing the railway and some trucks laden with food and grain ... We gave what tucker and smokes we could spare to the nearest of the thousands of Turkish prisoners, and with a feeling of satisfaction watched others doing the same. So ended my small share in the war.[26]

The New Zealanders were pulled back to Richon, but the heat and malaria of the Jordan Valley had achieved what the Turks had not been able to do. "In the first 12 days of October the ambulance admitted over 700 cases of malaria, most of it malignant. The New Zealand Brigade lost at least a third of its strength".[27] The diaries of troopers who had soldiered through the Sinai and into the mountains of Palestine end abruptly in blank pages. "Getting plenty of attention. But not feeling to well"[28] is one of the last entries of Trooper Alex McLean before dying of malignant malaria in the tented hospital at Kantara. In such circumstances, "Armistice night – was a quiet affair. Some enthusiasts let off a few fireworks and Verey lights...". [29]

The news that an Armistice was to be signed reached New Zealand at 9 o'clock on Tuesday 12 November 1918. The country was ready to celebrate and had been waiting in anticipation after wild celebrations on the previous Friday which had proved to be a false dawn. As the news spread the main streets of every city and town in the country jammed with people. "Everybody in the streets seemed to have a flag, and everybody in this case meant thousands". Trams stopped running on the crowded streets, businesses and shops emptied of employees and customers, Court sessions were suspended, "picture show managers abandoned any idea of entertaining the public, and liquor was not procurable in the hotels until 4.30 p.m.".[30] Though New Zealand, having celebrated already, was initially extra-cautious in responding to the news of the Armistice, it was a day of wild celebration, tempered by the grim realities of the outbreak of Spanish influenza. Laura Hardy, a housewife of Onehunga, then an outer suburb of Auckland, recalled that: "funerals were passing our house continually all day. Coffins were turned out by the hundred and were just made of rough boards ... To this sad and sorrowing community came the news of the armistice. There were few families which felt like rejoicing".[31] The influenza epidemic was war's terrible epilogue for a sorrowing nation. In the epidemic of 1918–1919 a total of 8,573 New Zealanders died. This included 2,160 Maori out of an estimated Maori population of 51,000.

It took time to adjust to peace both for the citizens at home and especially for the soldiers overseas. Ted McKay, with the Mounted Rifles in Palestine summed it up for most soldiers. " ... we faced the days to come with mingled relief and misgivings. We were fidgety, bored and a trifle fractious ... We gambled a lot of course. There were crown and anchor schools everywhere...". [32] The irksome petty restrictions of soldier life suddenly became unbearable for men anxious to get home to New Zealand. There was discontent and rumblings in the New Zealand Division on receiving word that it was to become part of the British Army of Occupation of the Rhine, but the tight-knit unit cohesiveness formed over four years of war kept any incidents in balance. Russell recognized the temper of the men and recommended his division be returned to New Zealand as soon as possible.

Discontent and friction at continuing theft by local Arabs boiled over among the New Zealand Mounted Rifle Brigade near Richon in Palestine. In the early morning of 10 December 1918, a New Zealander was shot and killed when he surprised thieves in the Brigade tent lines. The men were convinced that the culprits came from the nearby Arab village of Surafend. That evening, after it appeared that the Military Police had been unable to find anything incriminating in the village, the New Zealanders took matters into their own hands. In a carefully planned and coordinated raid; they picketed the village, removed the women and children, then bludgeoned to death all the males and youths they could find. Bodies were thrown into the wells and the village set on fire. A nearby Arab encampment received the same treatment.[33] Allenby publicly berated the New Zealand brigade as cold-blooded murderers, and

xxii The New Zealand Government advertises for new settlers in the Chronicles of the NZEF, November 1918. It was a cruel irony that, by its very nature, the war had robbed New Zealand of many of just the sort of men that she would need to be successful in the post-war world. (Chris Pugsley Collection)

Major-General Sir Edward Chaytor, the New Zealand commander of the Anzac Mounted Division, blamed the brigade's officers for not intervening. A Court of Inquiry could not discover those responsible and New Zealand paid reparation.[34]

Surafend was one of the worst atrocities carried out by British soldiers in this war. The New Zealanders, fiercely protective of their own, acted out of a tribal loyalty when it seemed the authorities were unwilling or unable to act. They took matters into their own hands again soon after when it seemed that their horses, which could not return to New Zealand because of quarantine regulations, were to be sold on the local market in Egypt. After two-and-a-half years of campaigning, these horses had become inseparable from their riders. "I am quite sure they would like to get back to their native land poor creatures where they could have a good feed of green grass and a scamper round the paddock".[35] It was not to be, and rather than see them in Egyptian hands where maltreatment was feared, the New Zealanders "led their faithful friends out on to the sands at Richon and shot them".[36]

There were also riots and incidents in the training camps in England, but, finally in 1919, the men, accompanied in many cases by their wives and children from marriages in England, came home. It seems that the withdrawal of the Division from garrison duty in Cologne was not before time as the staff officer watching the departure of the last trainload of New Zealanders reported that the station platform was crowded with weeping German women bidding farewell.

New Zealand as a nation had paid an enormous price for her involvement in the Great War. From an estimated population in 1914 of 1,158,436, with 243,376 estimated to be men of military age, 124,211 volunteered or were balloted for oversea's military service, and 100,444 sailed from New Zealand's shores. Casualties numbered 18,166 deaths and 41,317 wounded. The nation furthest removed from the fighting had sent almost 10 percent of its total population, 40 percent of its eligible male population, and from these men suffered casualties amounting to 25 percent of New Zealand's eligible male population. After conscription was introduced under the Military Services Act of 1916, 135,282 males were balloted for service from November 1916 onwards; of these, 77,900 were rejected as medically unfit for training, and 57,382 recruits were accepted for training in New Zealand.[37] Conscription guaranteed equality of sacrifice, and few homes were untouched by the impact of war.

Douglas Robb has written that:

> Almost a generation of the best men were wiped out, and throughout my life I have been conscious of this deprivation. In all walks of life many of those who would have been the leaders were missing. The ineptitudes of the decades between the two wars, both in Europe and in New Zealand, may in large measure be due to this. Not only these men, but those who would have been their children are missing, and we have had to do our best without them.[38]

Anzac Day commemorating the landing of the ANZAC Corps on the Gallipoli Peninsula on 25 April became New Zealand's day of mourning. Each year, from 1915 on, there were parades to the cenotaphs remembering 'our boys' in every town and district. It did not have the national overtones that it had in Australia with its parades of living heroes and heroines. In New Zealand it was a sombre day, as bleak and grey as New Zealand life in the years of struggle and depression in the 1920's and 1930's.

FROM THE MODERATE LEAGUE OF NEW ZEALAND.

TO THE

New Zealand Expeditionary Force.

LICENSING REFERENDUM

10th APRIL, 1919.

WHAT HAVE YOU BEEN FIGHTING FOR?

The Soldier's answer is

FREEDOM

Therefore, why forfeit and surrender what you have gained.

The Prohibitionists in New Zealand asked you to leave your families and homes to fight for their

FREEDOM

You have for 4½ years suffered privations to accomplish this, whilst they in return have been at work in your absence in stampeding the Government into granting a

SPECIAL REFERENDUM

on the Liquor Question which will be held on

THURSDAY, 10th APRIL, 1919.

The Prohibitionists hope to secure a catch vote during your absence, and it is their boast when you return it will be to a dry New Zealand.

It is important that you should know that if Prohibition is carried at the Poll on 10th April the people of New Zealand will never have an opportunity of voting again on the subject, as it has been enacted that a Vote of Prohibition **IS FINAL** and the

Question is not again to be submitted to a Referendum.

YOUR VOTE WILL SAVE NEW ZEALAND'S FREEDOM

VOTE FOR CONTINUANCE.

VOTE THUS:

VOTING PAPER.

I Vote for National Continuance.

~~I Vote for National Prohibition with Compensation.~~

DIRECTIONS.

The voter must strike out the proposal for which he does not wish to vote.

If the voter strikes out both or fails to strike out one of the proposals the voting-paper will be void, and his vote will not be recorded.

The voting-paper so marked is to be placed by the voter in the ballot-box prepared for it.

The voter is not allowed to take this voting-paper out of the polling-booth.

Printed and Published by Gillett Bros., Ltd., Walthamstow, England.

xxiii Dissension and division in post-war New Zealand. This poster shows the men of the NZEF becoming caught up in the controversy over plans for prohibition after the war. (Chris Pugsley Collection)

The war had taken the best the nation had, and many of those who returned outwardly without scars would still prove to be its casualties in mental or emotional disablement. Despite Government fears there was plenty of work for skilled men. Rehabilitation loans were offered for housing and resettlement on soldier farming land schemes. But this was an exhausted generation with aspirations which were no longer matched by physical and mental capabilities. Many never settled, and became the generation of rootless men who inhabited the public works camps of the 1930's. Those who settled down, battled with premature physical and nervous breakdown. New Zealand had to cope with a dysfunctional generation, and the burden was placed on the women and children who coped with 'Dad's' spells in the sanitorium and hospital. The cost of war multiplied and by 1938, on the eve of a second Great War, war pensions paid out since the First World War totalled £26,310,564, with an annual liability of over one-and-a-half million pounds to 23,711 pensioners and their children.[39]

The story of the war itself was published in a spate of official and regimental histories in the 1920's, followed by a similar burst of personal reminiscences and autobiographical novels in the 1930's. John A. Lee stories of wartime soldiering and Robin Hyde's *Passport to Hell* stand out.[40] There would have been more, but a lack of local publishers left New Zealand's accounts dependent on British and Australian publishing houses. The best only appeared in the 1960's at the time of the fiftieth anniversaries; and these included Cecil Malthus's *Gallipoli A Retrospect* and Alexander Aitken's understated classic, *Gallipoli to the Somme*.[41]

Yet when the boys came home in 1919, all this was still to come. Bill Taylor went back to the sheep station on the East Coast which he had left to go to war so many years before. "Back on Puketi Station the boss said to me, 'There you were, Bill, all selling your horses and dogs and saddles, going off to the war, and here you are all back again ... '. And I just said, 'Not all of us, Boss'".[42]

Endnotes

1 William Taylor, *The Twilight Hour*, Sutherland, Morrinsville, New Zealand, 1978, p. 107.

2 William Taylor, *The Twilight Hour*, Sutherland, Morrinsville, New Zealand, 1978, p. 105.

3 Gladys Violet Luxford, "How I came to be interested in war & why I went to World War One", Auckland Museum, MS 94/6.

4 Corporal C.W. Fraser, "Through the Mill", Diary and Memoirs, 11 November 1918, QEII Army Museum, RV5299.

5 G.A. Tuck Diaries and Letters, 1914–1919, letter dated 12 November 1918, Copy in the author of this chapter's possession. Also QEII Army Museum and Alexander Turnbull Library, MS140, 712–140, 714.

6 G.A. Tuck Diaries and Letters, 1914–1919, "Battle of the Somme written in England on 12th October 1916", Copy in the author of this chapter's possession. Also QEII Army Museum and Alexander Turnbull Library, MS140, 712–140, 714.

7 G.A. Tuck Diaries and Letters, 1914–1919, Diary 11 November 1918, Copy in

the author of this chapter's possession. Also QEII Army Museum and Alexander Turnbull Library, MS140, 712–140, 714.

8 N.M. Ingram, *Anzac Diary, A Nonentity in Khaki*, Treharne Publishers, Christchurch, ND, p. 137.

9 Bert Stokes, "1914–1918 The Years of World War One", Unpublished memoirs, copy in the author of this chapter's possession, p. 60.

10 This was the title of the only general unofficial history yet written on the New Zealand Division in the First World War, see O.E. Burton, *The Silent Division*, Angus & Robertson, Sydney, 1935.

11 Russell Diary, 11 November 1918, "The Russell Saga", Volume III, compiled by R.F. Gambrill, The Russell Family and Alexander Turnbull.

12 By contrast the nine months of the Gallipoli campaign resulted in 7473 New Zealand casualties including 2721 dead, and in three years of warfare in Sinai and Palestine the New Zealand Mounted Rifle Brigade suffered 1786 casualties including 640 dead. Lt. Colonel John Studholme, *NZEF, Record of Personal Services During the War*, Govt. Printer, Wellington, 1928, p. 383.

13 The one exception was the decision to form a 400-strong New Zealand Tank Battalion. This was interrupted by the German March offensive, and although the unit was sent to England for training, the Armistice took place before it was issued with its tanks.

14 Lt. Colonel John Studholme, *NZEF, Record of Personal Services During the War*, Govt. Printer, Wellington, 1928, p. 15.

15 Lt. Colonel John Studholme, *NZEF, Record of Personal Services During the War*, Govt. Printer, Wellington, 1928, p. 15.

16 Lt. Colonel John Studholme, *NZEF, Record of Personal Services During the War*, Govt. Printer, Wellington, 1928, p. 18.

17 Russell Diary 1 June 1918, "The Russell Saga", Volume III, compiled by R.F. Gambrill, The Russell Family and Alexander Turnbull.

18 In addition there were 7,000 trained reinforcements in depots in the United Kingdom. Reinforcements rates were increased in March to meet the expected increase in casualties from the German March offensive, and by the end of October there were 21,376 personnel in the units in France, the bulk of which 17,431 were with the division. There were 26,609 in the United Kingdom, 9,087 in the training depots, and 16,417 in hospital or convalescing. There were 3,707 in Egypt and Palestine. Lt. Colonel John Studholme, *NZEF, Record of Personal Services During the War*, Govt. Printer, Wellington, 1928, p. 18.

19 HQ N.Z. Division, Report on Operations, July 1 to August 31 1918, WA 20/3/8, National Archives.

20 This may have been a factor in Major-General Russell's diffident response which amounted to a refusal of Haig's offer of command of a British Corps in June 1918, the only Dominion general to be so honoured. "Said I was applying for leave to get repaired, [Broken a bone in foot] and in my case must be allowed to choose my own BGGS so I do not know how it will be taken by D.H. [Douglas Haig]". Russell Diary 1918, "The Russell Saga", Volume III, compiled by R.F. Gambrill, The Russell Family and Alexander Turnbull.

21 Brigadier-General H. Hart Diary, 24 August 1918, copy in the author of this chapter's possession, also QEII Army Museum and Alexander Turnbull Library.

22 Brigadier-General H. Hart Diary, 12 September 1918, copy in the author of this chapter's possession, also QEII Army Museum and Alexander Turnbull Library.

23 1st N.Z. Infantry Brigade 8/155/353 – "Memo on Recent Operations", dated 20 September 1918, National Archives WA1 10/3/7/11.

24 Second Lieutenant R.J. Richards, NZ Rifle Brigade, Diary, "My Own Last Phase", Christ's College, Christchurch, and also QEII Army Museum, RV909.
25 Major A.E. Alexander, Contemporary Account, Liddle Collection, University of Leeds.
26 E.C. McKay, N.Z. Mounted Rifles, Reminiscences, QE II Army Museum, p. 160.
27 A.D. Carbery, *The New Zealand Medical Services in the Great War 1914–1918*, Whitcombe & Tombs, Wellington, 1924, p. 481.
28 Tpr A. McLean, Diary, 25 October 1918, QE II Army Museum, RV 86/02732.
29 E.C. McKay, N.Z. Mounted Rifles, Reminiscences, QE II Army Museum, p. 162.
30 "Germany Signs the Armistice", *Otago Daily Times*, Wednesday 13 November, 1918.
31 "The reminiscences of Laura Mary Hardy as told to her daughter", MS136, Auckland Museum.
32 E.C. McKay, N.Z. Mounted Rifles, Reminiscences, QE II Army Museum, p. 165.
33 Christopher Pugsley, *On the Fringe of Hell*: New Zealanders and Military Discipline in the First World War, Hodder & Stoughton, Auckland, 1991, pp. 285–288.
34 E.C. McKay, N.Z. Mounted Rifles, Reminiscences, QE II Army Museum, p. 167.
35 Lieutenant J.W.V. Masterman, Diary, QE II Army Museum.
36 E.C. McKay, N.Z. Mounted Rifles, Reminiscences, QE II Army Museum, p. 171.
37 "Recruits Examined by Military Medical Boards", H19A *Appendices to the Journals of the House of Representatives*, Govt. Printer, Wellington, 1919, p. 2.
38 Douglas Robb, *Medical Odyssey*, quoted in Keith Sinclair *A History of the University of Auckland 1883–1983*, Auckland University Press, Auckland, 1983, p. 74.
39 New Zealand Government, *New Zealand Year-Book 1938*; Govt. Printer, Wellington, 1937, p. 596.
40 John A. Lee, *Civilian into Soldier*, T. Werner Laurie, London, 1937; Robin Hyde, *Passport to Hell*, Hurst & Blackett, London, 1936. Also *Nor the Years Condemn*, Hurst & Blackett, 1938. See also O.E. Burton, *The Silent Division*, Angus & Robertson, Sydney, 1935.
41 Cecil Malthus, *Gallipoli A Retrospect*, Whitcombe & Tombs, Christchurch, 1965; Alexander Aitken, *Gallipoli to the Somme*, OUP, 1963. John A Lee, *Soldier*, A H & A W Reed, Wellington, 1976.
42 William Taylor, *The Twilight Hour*, Sutherland, Morrinsville, New Zealand, 1978, p. 111.

Chapter Thirteen

Armistice 1915 and 1918: The South African Experience

Bill Nasson

Over three years before 11 November 1918, at a time when preparations were being made for a renewed Allied push at the Dardanelles, and as the Central Powers were breaking Russian and Serbian lines, a German staff officer named Captain Ernst Virmond delivered a sealed envelope to Lieutenant Geoffrey Marsh from the headquarters of General Louis Botha, Premier of the Union of South Africa, and its military Commander-in-Chief. It was 9 July 1915, and Virmond and Marsh were meeting several miles to the north of Otavifontein, an obscure watering-hole deep in the northern interior of German South West Africa. The envelope carried German acceptance of South African surrender terms. For Governor Theodor Seitz and Colonel Victor Franke, commander of the Imperial Army in German South West Africa, the sands had run out: encircled by Botha's invading Expedition Force, Franke's *Schutztruppe* were short of rations, mounted on bony horses and mules, and simply outnumbered and outgunned. Mindful of the strength of Germany's position in Europe, some of Franke's more die-hard subordinates had urged dispersal of German forces and the adoption of guerrilla tactics until the Allies were overcome in the West. Defeat looked especially ignominious if German armies were still advancing in Europe, a consideration which bothered Seitz, who was reluctant to negotiate any cessation of hostilities from a position of German South West African vulnerability.[1]

However, Franke had recognized that the inevitable outcome of continued hostilities would be the destruction of his forces for no achievable purpose. Equally, Botha had no desire for either side to sacrifice more lives. And so, after some desultory dithering over the terms of capitulation, a final armistice was signed by Seitz, Franke and Botha at 10 a.m. on 9 July. Gerald L'Ange, author of the best modern chronicle of the 1914–15 German South West Africa campaign, records that after the signing ceremony (in a tent, amidst thorn trees), the German party was hauled away by a locomotive which trundled off in reverse.[2] It was a rather melancholy footnote to the story of the railway and colonialism in Africa.

German South West Africa, one of the dustier side-shows of the Great War, thus provided South Africans with a kind of premature armistice in miniature. Here, local Allied superiority had obliged the Germans to sue for a binding armistice, ending a bush war which had indeed been short and decisive. In the immediate practical implementation of 1915 armistice conditions, communication and transport exigencies contrived to bring together South African and German adversaries. German Command provided South African officers with rail carriage through their lines, and also permitted Botha the use of Imperial Army telegraph and telephone links to issue cease-fire instructions to Union commanders in the field. Wary of German ability to monitor exchanges in English or Dutch, officers from white Natal units resorted to Zulu; perhaps this was easier than code. With only paroled officers able to retain their horses, some stranded mounted *Schutztruppen* traded bayonets and other small souvenir items for the use of reserve horses held by South African cavalry scouts.[3]

A persistent theme running through many South African letters, diaries and journals is not merely that of an obvious sense of relief and satisfaction at Union victory, but of sympathy for their opponents. Overseeing the disarmament of German soldiers at Otavifontein, a Kimberley Regiment NCO declared, "it was impossible not to feel sorry for them. Poor things! Dealing with Huns who looked so downcast was not much of a tonic. To think I expected this to be the proudest day of my life".[4] Joe Samuels, an under-age Rand Rifles volunteer, recalled "a pitiful sight" of "demoralized" German prisoners who, when offered "*vetkoek* and coffee" before boarding railway trucks, "became sheepish and turned away their eyes as they took food".[5] Such moments of armistice sensitivity and courteous conduct contrasted sharply with Louis Botha's earlier qualms about maintaining restraint and order in South West Africa once Germans had been cornered, given the "too bitter" depth of "feeling between English and Germans".[6]

Botha's own armistice instincts were for humane moderation, and the leniency of Union terms for German forces moved Jan Smuts, his close ally and Minister of Defence, to hope that "our local fire-eaters" would not see this "as rank treachery"; it was his personal view that "Botha's peace terms are very liberal to the conquered enemy".[7] Moderate they most certainly were. German officers would be freed with small arms and allowed open movement and residence anywhere in South West African territory; *Schutztruppen* would be interned and allowed to retain rifles although no ammunition; and the largest army complement, *Landswehr* infantry reservists (mostly farmers and traders), along with paramilitary police were permitted to set out for home to resume their jobs. Moreover, they were authorized to keep their firearms and ammunition stocks for defensive capacity against the possible depredation of Herero and other black inhabitants, whose recent experience in Berlin's "place in the sun" had left them with little love for German colonists. All this, according to Brigadier-General J.J. Collyer of the Union Defence Force, was because "the helplessness of an adversary was a sure passport to General Botha's sympathy".[8]

The Union government certainly believed that swift reconciliation with the

European inhabitants of what had been German territory could and should be eased along. It is equally clear that this approach was not shaped simply by the personal morality of leadership, or by some concept of national magnanimity. In the first place, a non-retributive armistice was possible politically because it did not follow trench warfare and fearsome attrition. German dead numbered just over one hundred, and the 50,000-strong Union Expeditionary Force lost fewer than one hundred killed in action; in fact, the Union Defence Force sustained more deaths in suppressing the 1914–15 domestic republican Afrikaner rebellion.[9] This left a legacy little tainted by bitterness or vengefulness, as Deneys Reitz, Smuts and Botha's liberal and literary Anglo-Boer War comrade, emphasized. "German West" had been a comparatively light campaign in which even the colony's press had reminded settlers that invading Union Afrikaner troops were "neither Russian barbarians nor undisciplined French, but they are men of the same Teutonic extraction as ourselves". For the sacrifice of "fewer casualties than the cost of an average trench raid in France ... for the first time in the Great War, a German commander in the field had laid down his arms".[10]

Second, for the ambitious sub-imperial designs honed by Botha and Smuts, armistice terms inevitably foreshadowed permanent controlling acquisition or annexation of German West territory. This prospect loomed large in Union reaction to the 9 July news, with newspaper editorials and correspondence columns applauding Botha's reconciliatory strategy, "to be wholly commended and congratulated", aimed at pacifying the fears of a surrendered enemy. Not only would "their destitute German families" now be entitled to "the same relief as is afforded to any destitute British subjects of the Union or its destitute German citizens", but, once rapidly re-absorbed into productive civilian roles facilitating the restitution of war damage and restoring 'normal' economic conditions in South West Africa, ex-reservists would reap the benefits of a peace without "the Kaiser and a Germanized autocracy beyond belief". Committed to the healing of war wounds, an incoming Union administration would be more efficient, less rapacious, and better able to control and channel cheap black labour in the interests of renewed colonial enterprise.[11]

A third factor governing the effective 'peace treaty' armistice of 1915 was Pretoria's need to dampen the popular anger of Afrikaner Nationalists and radical republicans over the South West Africa invasion. Politicians, propagandists and rebels within their ranks had expressed anti-British solidarity with the German cause, most belligerently in the case of some northern Cape Afrikaners and Anglo-Boer War *bittereinders* (die-hards) who had decamped for German South West African exile to avoid British dominion after 1902; as a collaborating *Vrijkorps*, they had fought with German forces. In one of the more wry yet poignant armistice moments, the transformed Boer general, Louis Botha, confiscated the old nineteenth century Transvaal republican flag under which German-uniformed *Vrijkorps* combatants had mustered.[12] There was no further humiliation. "Now that we are in strength and completely secure in this country", declared the *Rand Daily Mail*, "vindictiveness is not at all necessary".[13]

Oddly enough, in the ranks of the South African Expeditionary Force there were some who thought that the end of their little war had also heralded the end of the Great War. In Swakopmund, Private Jack Gudgeon weighed up whether to return to Cape Town by troopship, or to secure an immediate discharge as it would be cheaper to sail to Europe from Walfisch Bay. "Now that the Hun has been thrown out", he fancied a walking tour "to see what damage has been done to the richness and grandeur of France and Belgium".[14] With Germany "demolished" and Allied countries "out of all their troubles", another soldier itched for a further round of duty, this time in Europe, "where our fighting forces may now be needed to keep the peace".[15] As news of continued fighting in Flanders and Gallipoli filtered through, several soldiers were uncertain of its authenticity; for one artilleryman, this was assuredly "the machine of Hun propaganda making strenuous mischief".[16] Clearly, in some more wide-eyed part of the soldiering imagination, the outcome on the

The End of the African Lion Hunt.

xxiv South African Prime Minister, Louis Botha, portrayed as a contented lion, having just consumed German forces in South West Africa; a cartoon in the *Diamond Fields Advertiser*, 14 July 1915. (via Bill Nasson) battlefields of German West should have signified a corresponding outcome in Europe. However deluded an estimation of what the Great War would actually entail, on the African imperial periphery it signified beliefs in an imagined war effort which would be short, successful, and require little sacrifice.

For a deeply divided settler state in which the Afrikaner majority of the white population was hostile to participation in the war, and in which most black workers and peasants were conspicuously slow to rally to the flag, July 1915 produced a moment when national experience was in a sense integrated into a rolling war sentiment of victory with peace. Foreshadowing the heightened atmosphere of 1918, it was a rare and unusual occasion of common and concrete home front responses to the achievement of Union war effort. In the imperially-inclined port cities of Cape Town and Durban, ships' sirens blew the news of armistice, along with church and town hall bells. Johannesburg municipality declared an immediate public holiday, while there and in Pretoria, amiable pro-war crowds ran up bunting and spilled around street bands.[17]

Identified as the embodiment of a strong and expanding South Africa, Louis Botha immediately began to be retailed in photographs and flattering cartoons; his residence also drew enthusiastic crowds who had to make do with the allure of Mrs Annie Botha, as the Premier had not yet returned from South West Africa command. Special "German surrender" issues of *The Star* and the *Rand Daily Mail* quickly sold out, while on the Witwatersrand gold mines and Kimberley diamond fields, long blasts on mine company hooters signalled news of the end of hostilities. Given the absence of sources, one can only guess at the likely reactions of African and Afrikaner mine workers, whose bruising experiences in an English-dominated mining system inclined many to fancy the notion that Germany might free them from the grip of 'English' capitalist oppression.[18] On the other hand, Coloured transport riders in the Union invasion force were reported to be "wild" and "delirious"[19] at victory; given what one historian has termed "the undoubted brutality"[20] with which German forces had treated 1914–15 black captives, here there was no mood to bind up the scars of war.

Elsewhere, the South West Africa outcome lifted the spirits of Allied troops entrenched in Flanders, with the African surrender serving as a new taunt in the repertoire of front-line derision. For British and Dominion political leaders and generals, South Africa had passed the test, finally laying the Boer republican ghosts of the past. Asquith declared Botha a "most honoured and cherished" adopted son of Empire, while for his Colonial Secretary, Bonar Law, "instead of South Africa falling away from the British Empire, the forces of South Africa have won a notable victory in the cause of that Empire". Canada's Borden exulted in the surrender of "territory larger than the German Empire itself".[21] Towards the end of July 1915, a symbol of that empire, a captured heavy field gun, disarmed and buffed up, was shipped south for mounting as a war memorial.[22] It was perhaps a touch early for ceremonies and speeches in town squares or municipal parks about the meaning of a post-war era.

In terms of its effect on the overall balance of forces in the war, the German-South African armistice was a blip; unlike the September 1918 Bulgarian surrender, it did not help to shape the central course and outcome of the conflict. That would be decided in Europe, and probably no South African knew this better than General Smuts, whose loyalty to the grandeur of his haunt, Savoy Hotel, was surpassed only by his loyal 1917–18 membership of the British War Cabinet. Serving in the Cabinet up to Armistice, he both developed and aired his thinking on the basis upon which the war should be concluded and, for Smuts, there was never much serious doubt that that basis would be an Allied victory. Convinced that the war was not "drifting on aimlessly", and dismissing beliefs that the "slaughter and exhaustion of mankind" would make victory "no longer possible for us, nor ... possible for anybody", he predicted that the conflict would end not "in a stalemate" but in "decisive results". What really mattered, he argued in a speech in Glasgow in May 1918, was the definition of victory. Presenting himself to his Scottish audience as one "living in a distant part of the British Empire", Smuts reminded them of "people who mean by an Allied victory that we must completely smash the German Army, that we must smash Germany, that we must march to Berlin, occupy the capital of the enemy, and dictate terms of peace there". He was emphatically "not of that opinion". For Smuts, that was "the German view of victory" rather than "our view".

Above all, Smuts saw the coming "measure of victory" in semi-metaphysical terms, not as "a smash-up". For him, this was "much more than a military war. It goes much deeper, and touches deeper forces". Reaching into his homespun reserve of nineteenth century Transvaal stories, he recalled how Paul Kruger had once told him to curb his bullying aggression as a youthful Attorney-General. "That is not the way to deal with your opponent. The way to deal with him is to smack him hard on the one cheek, and to rub him gently on the other".[23] While these views were reported fully by the Glasgow and South African press, metropolitan papers such as *The Times* judiciously omitted Smuts's passages on the undesirability of crushing Germany and dictating peace terms.

Six months later, Armistice confirmed that Smuts's frame of mind was generally shared by others in the Union's governing elite. There was relatively little appetite for harshness towards, or punishment of, Germany; both English and Afrikaner press urgings were for "fair", "good", "honourable", or "higher" armistice terms and peace provisions, for a defeated enemy to be put out of his misery, not for it to be prolonged.[24] In this, there was a striking continuity between 1915 and 1918. Thus, at Armistice, Deneys Reitz recalled meeting a Louis Botha "perturbed by the trend of things". Reminding Reitz how the "sting" and "bitterness" of Boer Republican defeat in 1902, "had been softened by magnanimous peace terms", Botha stressed how much "he and General Smuts were opposed" to "a mistaken policy" of inflicting "humiliating conditions on a beaten enemy" and imposing "a treaty that would leave the Germans a broken people".[25] In an even more forceful reaction, Botha called "the armistice terms ... humiliating. I felt sorry, when I read them, that any nation should stoop so low as to accept such terms. Even

VREDE OP AARDE!
Eindelik vind sij die mensdom gereed om haar te verwelkom

xxv "Peace on Earth! At long last she finds mankind ready to welcome her". An illustration from the Afrikaner nationalist newspaper *De Burger*, on 13 November 1918. (via Bill Nasson) barbarians will not surrender their cattle without a struggle". Likewise, it was apparently more than Smuts's conscience could stand.[26]

One way of seeing this is through A.J.P. Taylor's memorably tart judgement of Smuts as "the great operator of fraudulent idealism".[27] South Africa had been eyeing German South West Africa, and with 'Mandated' annexation about to get the nod, had secured what it wanted of Germany's colonial possessions. Another view would be to recognize that the treatment of peace with Germany was a potentially contentious issue in domestic white electoral politics. While the "Nationalist barometer" had been pushed down by eventual Allied victory, it was even more necessary in 1918 than in 1915 for the Botha-Smuts regime not to fan "the flames of party strife"; this meant reassuring pro-German Afrikaner nationalists that the Union would not support any "excesses" in Armistice arrangements.[28] Nationalist press reaction was in fact mostly taken up with the bleak fate of Germany, having been "dumbfounded by the terms of the armistice". Still, it seemed that there were some strange straws to be grasped. "However disheartening", declared *Het Volk*, "after all it is nevertheless a victory for republicanism, as in any case America was really responsible for the victory".[29]

How the fruits of victory were to be best handled was also of some importance to the politically conscious black population, although here questions of idealism and principle were of a different order. In mining towns like Kimberley which had lost white infantrymen on the Somme, Coloured soldiers in Palestine, and African labour auxiliaries in the English Channel (the latter drowned in the 1917 Mendi sinking), the simple sound of Armistice, blasted on De Beers Company horns, provided a rare binding moment. Perversely, mass warfare provided a reminder of an otherwise lost common humanity between races. While 'native opinion' found such examples encouraging, the great lesson of Armistice was that much more remained to be done. For the South African Native National Congress and the pro-Allied African press, like *iLanga lase Natal* and *Abantu Batho*, the end of the war signalled "the appropriate time to claim the political rights to which the 'loyalty' of their people, and their contribution to the imperial war effort, entitled them". Educated, modernizing African leadership drew encouragement from Woodrow Wilson and Lloyd George's high-flown words over a just settlement and the rights of "subject" nations, anticipating that this might extend to "recognition of the justice of African claims in South Africa". Just as the subjects of the Habsburg Empire could now embrace "national freedom" so Botha's African subjects clamoured for their political dividend. At the same time, for the Coloured social elite, the end of the war was upheld as a vindication of their "selfless" national patriotism despite domestic racial discrimination. Measured against the subversion and treachery of anti-war Afrikaners, their proven "claim to be civilized" now merited recognition in the new world to be made by the peacemakers.[30]

For many South African troops, it was the contrasting *continental* character of combat experience which proved significant in shaping attitudes towards peace relations. For the 1st South African Infantry Brigade on the Franco-Belgian border, years of heavy fighting and a mounting toll of casu-

71. Marshal Józef Pilsudski; in 1918, as Poland emerged independent from the ruins of the German, Austrian and Russian empires, Pilsudski unified into a national army the Polish units which had been fighting for the Austrians, or in the Russian Army or indeed in the Polish Legion under French command. Outside Warsaw in August 1920 this Polish national force repelled the Bolshevik attempt to retake Poland. From a watercolour.
(Mrs A. Kurcz) (Chapter 15 - Central and Eastern Europe)

72. Celebrations following the departure of the Germans from Windau on the Baltic, in August 1919, and the arrival of Lettish troops; an event doubtless of infinitely more importance here than the Armistice in the west, the previous November.
(R.B. Pargiter, Liddle Collection) (Chapter 15 - Central and Eastern Europe)

73. Captain R.B. Pargiter (centre), of the British Military Mission to Lithuania, with Lettish authorities in Windau, August 1919, shortly after independence.

(R.B. Pargiter, Liddle Collection) (Chapter 15 - Central and Eastern Europe)

74. King Ferdinand of Bulgaria, seen here on the left, an inveterate schemer who had led his country to war for territorial and monetary gain.

(Hugh Cecil) (Chapter 16 - Bulgaria)

75. General Lukoff, commanding the Bulgarian 2nd Army, and M.Liaptcheff, Minister of Finance, arrive at Janeš in Macedonia to discuss peace terms, 28 September 1918.

(Liddle collection) (Chapter 16 - Bulgaria)

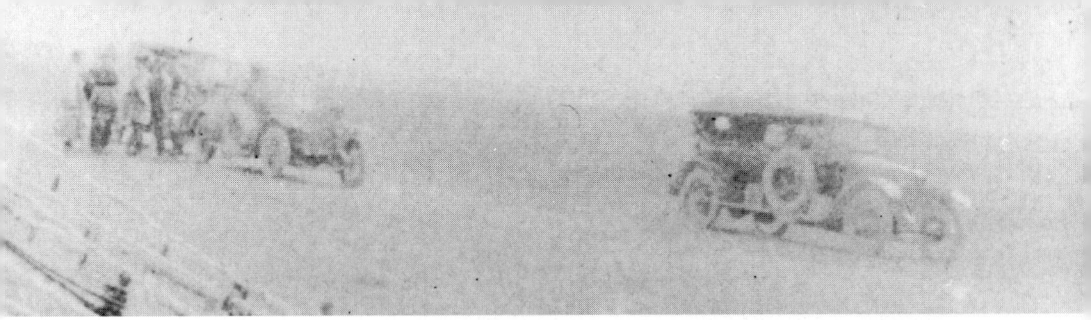

76. Staff cars wait to take away the Bulgarian emissaries, Janes 28 September 1918.
(Liddle Collection) (Chapter 16 - Bulgaria)

77. A Bulgarian officer announces to his men the news of his country's departure from the war.
(via Hugh Cecil) (Chapter 16 - Bulgaria)

78. Victor in the Balkans: General Franchet d'Espérey. (via Hugh Cecil) (Chapter 16 - Bulgaria)

79. A subject city: French and British troops mingle with Turkish citizens in a crowded Constantinople street.
(L. V. White, Liddle Collection)
(Chapter 17 - The Ottoman Empire)

80. Palestinian Arabs, photographed in 1918. What rewards would the Armistice bring for their part in the revolt which assisted in the overthrow of Ottoman rule?
(A.B. Fuller, Liddle Collection)
(Chapter 18 - The Arab World)

81. British troops watching a victory parade, Alexandria, Egypt, November 1918. Captain Eric Smith MC rides the horse with the white blaze.
(E.J. Smith, Liddle Collection)
(Chapter 18 - The Arab World)

alties to the very end did little to produce instinctive goodwill. It was more a case of courtesy deferred than open hands. Nudged to "do our best before eleven o'clock", a private noted with relish that "we did it, wanting to split them". Another Corporal resented the fact that emerging opponents were "so fine looking ... actually offering us cigarettes and wanting to talk. That was a fine nerve". His platoon had "rum and sugar for drinking to our health, not theirs". A Lieutenant Murray Grant wrote of his surprise at being told "not to associate with the Germans, when obviously none of us felt at all inclined to".[31]

By striking contrast, mutual experience of inconclusive and increasingly futile fighting in low intensity African theatres seems to have made armistice relations a good deal less brusque or alienating in the field. In one significant way, at least for European adversaries, 1918 became the mirror image of the German West peace of 1915. Indeed, as South African forces had forced the first localized peace, it was probably appropriate that a Union commander should roll up the last loose ends of 1918. In south-eastern Africa, wire confirmation of a general armistice missed Major-General Paul von Lettow-Vorbeck, whose Africanized German army continued to duck and weave "undefeated" through Mozambique and northern Rhodesia, where he "won the last engagement of the Great War on British territory the day after the armistice".[32] While news of Germany's collapse struck von Lettow-Vorbeck as "improbable", he grudgingly consented to Brigadier-General Jan van Deventer's armistice instructions of "unconditional surrender". One of van Deventer's subordinates observed his commander's "mixed feelings" at having to handle as prisoners of war "Germans who were not really taken but who accepted as their duty to give themselves into our hands". That formal surrender on 25 November saw the German force with fixed bayonets and flag aloft, saw van Deventer apologizing to von Lettow-Vorbeck for having to observe British War Office instructions to treat his troops as prisoners of war, and saw the laying down of arms followed by the laying down of lunch, at which the provision of "jam, chocolate, and other good things for Europeans" tended to dilute "no fraternization" orders.[33]

Adversarial "bad feeling" and "friction" maintained a more resentful line between black German and British *Askaris*: for both, armistice did nothing to resolve running grievances about neglect and lack of proper recompense for their efforts. Mutually deceived and downcast, *Askaris* found that victory and defeat became merely sides of the same grubby coin. For their respective commanders, peace seemed to decree a reassertion of underlying habits of colonial bonding, as the pull of 'Europeanness' in Africa reminded white South African, British and German combatants of their shared social status as overlords.

No less revealing, finally, was the way in which the end of the war in Europe left some South Africans unexpectedly subdued and short of fine words to comprehend the end of the war in the old. Smuts, of course, was waiting as ever for reality to catch up, "all over ... but as to peace in this hour of falling worlds, who could say?"[34] Another whose reach exceeded his grasp was Reitz, for whom the spell of Armistice, "a new era for the world and for my country … splendid visions … which I felt an urge to communicate", fell away. Facing assembled troops, "inspired thoughts of a moment before had vanished completely and I could only stumble through a few halting phrases … at any rate the guns were silent, the war was at an end".[35] While men in the German West of July 1915 had hungered for post-war European vistas, Sergeant Harold Lewin's thoughts now fixed on returning to a country which had not been shattered by war. "It will", he wrote, "be good to get back to civilisation again, and to see my world as it was before, more or less".[36] Here was the consoling logic of Armistice for many servicemen like him. There is little doubt that the state to which they would return presented an appearance of deceptive calm 'Overseas'. It was an appropriate home to the notion of an Armistice Silence, improvised in 1916 in Capetown as an empire ritual of remembrance by the politically influential South African magnate, Sir Percy Fitzpatrick. It is odd that so seminal a ritual should have come from a country which had fought the war mostly at arm's length.

Endnotes

1 R. Hennig, *Deutsch-Südwest im Weltkrieg* (Berlin, Ullstein, 1920), p.129. I am grateful to Veronique Meutey for providing this reference.

2 G. L'Ange, *Urgent Imperial Service: South African Forces in German South West Africa 1914–1915*, (Johannesburg, Ashanti, 1991), p. 329.

3 *Cape Times*, 10 August 1915; *Diamond Fields Advertiser*, 18 August 1915; *The Selbornian*, 4, 1915, p. 23.

4 Rondebosch Boys High School Magazine, 8 (39) 1915, p. 37.

5 Interview with Joseph Samuels (b. 4 November 1897), German South West Africa campaign veteran, University of Cape Town, May, 1995; see also, Nasson, "Joe Samuels: A Springbok on the Somme", *Oral History*, 25 (2) 1997, p. 33. *Vetkoek*: raw bread dough deep-fried in lard – one of the more dubious of Afrikaner camp fire delicacies.

6 Botha to J.C. Smuts, 25 May 1915, in W.K. Hancock and J. van der Poel (eds.), Selections from the *Smuts Papers*, Vol.3 (Cambridge, Cambridge University Press, 1966), p. 283.

7 Smuts to J.X. Merriman, 10 July 1915, in *Smuts Papers*, p. 304.

8 W.S. Rayner and W.W. O'Shaughnessy, *How Botha and Smuts Conquered German South West Africa* (Cape Town, privately published, 1915), p. 238; also, J.J. Collyer, *The Campaign in German South West Africa, 1914–1915* (Pretoria, Government Printer, 1937), p. 166.

9 *Nongquai*, [The Official Journal of the Union Defence Force] October 1915, p. 31; Collyer, *German South West Africa*, p.152; Earl Buxton, *General Botha* (London, John Murray, 1924), p. 122.

10 D. Reitz, *Trekking On* (London, Faber, 1933), pp. 101, 103–4.

11 See, for example, *Cape Times*, 16 July 1915; *Rand Daily Mail*, 15 July 1915; *Natal Witness*, 18 July 1915; Merriman to Smuts, 6 September 1915, in *Smuts Papers*, pp. 311–12.

12 *The Star*, 12 July 1915.

13 *Rand Daily Mail*, 17 July 1915.

14 *The Selbornian*, 8, 1915, p. 31.

15 *Nongquai*, November 1915, p. 43.

16 *Diocesan College Magazine*, 13 (20) 1915, p. 37.

17 *Pretoria News*, 10 July 1915; *The Star*, 11 July 1915; *Rand Daily Mail*, 11 July 1915.

18 For anti-English or pro-German sympathies amongst urban working class Africans, see A. Grundlingh, *Fighting Their Own War: South African Blacks and the First World War* (Johannesburg, Ravan, 1987), pp. 15–17; for poorer Afrikaner disaffection, Nasson, "War Opinion in South Africa, 1914", *Journal of Imperial and Commonwealth History*, 23 (2) 1995, p. 264.

19 *Diamond Fields Advertiser*, 27 July 1915; *The Friend*, 28 July 1915.

20 Grundlingh, *Own War*, p. 87.

21 See L'Ange, *Imperial Service*, p. 196.

22 *Natal Witness*, 29 July 1915.

23 See, 829 Speech (1918) in *Smuts Papers*, pp. 648–52.

24 For example, *Cape Times*, 1 November 1918; *The Star*, 3 November 1918; *De Burger*, 3 November 1918.

25 Reitz, *Trekking On*, p. 341; *No Outspan* (London, Faber, 1943), pp. 13–14.

26 Quoted in S. Weintraub, *A Stillness Heard Around the World: The End of the Great War* (New York, Oxford University Press, 1985), pp. 160–61; Smuts to Lloyd George, 8 June 1918, *Smuts Papers*, p. 661; E.M. Meyntjes, "Suid-Afrika en die Vrede van Versailles", M.A. dissertation, Potchefstroom University, 1973, p. 93.

27 A.J.P. Taylor, *The First World War* (Harmondsworth, Penguin, 1966), p. 263.

28 A.G. Robertson to Smuts, 11 August 1918, *Smuts Papers*, p.670; *Cape Argus*, 31 October 1918; *Natal Mercury*, 7 November 1918.

29 *The Star*, 14 November 1918; *Het Volk*, 15 November 1918.

30 See B. Willan, *Sol Plaatje: A Biography* (Johannesburg, Ravan, 1984), pp. 227–28; M. Adhikari, *Let us Live for Our Children: The Teachers League of South Africa, 1913–1940* (Cape Town, UCT Press, 1993), pp. 47–48.

31 *Diocesan College Magazine*, 13 (26) 1919, p. 3; *Natal Mercury*, 6 December 1918.

32 G. Hodges, "Military Labour in East Africa and its Impact on Kenya", in M.E. Page (ed.), *Africa and the First World War* (London, Macmillan, 1987), p. 139.

33 *The Selbornian*, 12, 1919, p. 44; P. von Lettow-Vorbeck, *My Reminiscences of East Africa* (Nashville, Battery, n.d.), pp. 321–23.

34 Smuts to Gillett, 10 November 1918, *Smuts Papers*, p. 687.

35 Reitz, *Trekking On*, p. 320.

36 *University of Cape Town Quarterly*, March, 1919, p. 246.

The financial support of the Centre for Science Development towards this research is acknowledged with thanks. Argument and opinion are naturally those of the author, and do not necessarily reflect the views of the CSD.

Chapter Fourteen

Detached and Indifferent: The Japanese Response

Naoko Shimazu

Of the belligerent states covered in this study, the Japanese response to the Armistice, as discussed below, may come across as curiously detached and even indifferent. This is intriguing, considering that the Japanese had been involved on the Allied side from the onset of the war in 1914, unlike the United States which was a late entrant. In all justice, Japan's response was conditioned largely by its conception of its war aims on entering the war in August 1914. In Japan, generally speaking, there existed the perception – shared equally by both the government and the public at large – that the First World War was essentially a European war, and only involved them marginally in the Far East. This perception, grounded on its geographical position, far removed from the centre of conflict in Europe, had a profound influence on how the Japanese nation experienced the Armistice. Japan's experience of the Great War was qualitatively different from that of the Allies in Europe, and did not involve the same level of commitment of civilian, military, and finance that the western powers had made to the war. Not surprisingly, then, the Japanese response to the Armistice was not marked by the degree of jubilation evident in Europe. Moreover, the Japanese experience cannot be understood in its entirety without taking into account the popular enthusiasm in Japan for the Paris Peace Conference. What follows, therefore, is an analysis of the Japanese response to the Armistice: first, looking at the limited war aims which influenced attitudes towards it; second, examining the immediate popular response to the coming of peace; and third, analysing the significance of the peace conference for the Japanese public.

Since the Meiji Restoration of 1868, Japan had been building up its national strength in order to maintain its national independence from western imperialism. By 1914, Japan had arguably consolidated its status as the only non-white great power by winning two wars in East Asia, one against China — the traditional hegemonic power in East Asia — in the Sino-Japanese War of 1895, and the other against Russia in 1905, in addition to concluding a military alliance with Britain in 1902. Japan was also fast establishing itself as an imperial power, having acquired two colonies, Taiwan (1895) and Korea (1910), and was waiting for a 'golden' opportunity for further expansion into China and Manchuria especially in the wake of the 1911 Chinese republican revolution which plunged China into political and social chaos. Thus, the outbreak of hostilities in Europe in 1914 was enthusiastically received by many contemporary Japanese political and military leaders, as 'the grace of heaven',[1] a perfect opportunity for Japan to engage in expansionist activities in China. It is within this historical context that we need to understand how Japan responded to the 'call' of the war and to the subsequent armistice in 1918.

Japan's war aims and its participation were tightly circumscribed. They were limited mostly to confronting Germany in East Asia and the Pacific islands. Japan declared war on Germany on 23 August 1914, on the basis of its alliance obligations with Britain.[2] It soon captured the German concessions on the Shantung Peninsula, followed by the German colonies in the Pacific islands (the Micronesian islands). Having attained its war aims swiftly and effortlessly, Japan then effectively sat back and for the next four years waited for the war to end. It was as though Japan had remained in a time warp. Its policy towards the peace remained largely unchanged from 1914 until October 1918, premised as it was on the Japan-Germany Peace Preparatory Committee (Nichidoku kôwa jumbi iinkai) which had been created by the Japanese Foreign Ministry in 1915.[3] The peace terms formulated at that time focused on the permanent retention of the former German concessions and

xxvi Japan's success in November 1914 at Tsing Tao on the Chinese coast, in subduing the German possession there, was to be the high watermark of her military involvement in the war. Japanese troops are shown here in a magazine illustration, resting and having a meal, during the campaign. (*The Great War*, Vol. 3 Chapter 50, H.W. Wilson (ed.), Amalgamated Press, London, 1915) possessions in East Asia which had been in Japan's hands since late–1914. They were made on the assumption that the European Allies would give Japan a free hand in the East Asian settlement if Japan kept out of European matters.[4] To do her justice, Japan did make further contributions to the war effort by dispatching naval assistance in 1916 to the Indian Ocean and the northern Pacific Ocean, and to the Mediterranean in 1917, as well as several new detachments of cruisers to protect shipping in the Indian and South Pacific Oceans.[5] However, these contributions were overshadowed by the difficulties the British had in extracting other assistance from the Japanese government, which would only agree to them on a *quid pro quo* basis.[6] For the Japanese, notwithstanding the concrete gains to be made from the war, it was important from the collective psychological perspective that they were participating as one of the Allied powers in a world war, which reaffirmed their sense of being one of the great powers of the world.

However, Japan's experience of the war was by no means an easy one, in spite of the criticisms made by some, such as British Foreign Secretary Arthur Balfour, to the effect that Japan had only benefited from the war.[7] When Japan came out of the war in November 1918, it felt more isolated internationally than it did in 1914 for a number of reasons. The fear of international isolation weighed heavily upon Japan which was still insecure in her status as a great power. There was a deep-seated distrust of the Japanese by the Anglo-Saxons. Significantly, ever since the Japanese victory over Russia in 1905, the western imperial powers had begun to perceive Japan as a potential threat in East Asia. The British attempted to deal with it through the revision of the Anglo-Japanese Alliance, originally signed in 1902. However, the Americans had no such comfort, not being party to the alliance. Japan's expansionist policy towards China during the First World War had only confirmed the Americans' long-held suspicion of Japan. Most damaging of all was the notorious Twenty-One Demands of 1915, which attempted to reduce China to a semi-colonial status.[8] This act, which was no doubt based on sheer opportunism, branded Japan in the eyes of international public opinion as an aggressive expansionist.[9] Another incident which heightened the Americans' sense of distrust of the Japanese was the Siberian issue in 1918. The Americans had pointedly refused repeated requests made by the Allied powers for Japanese troop deployment in Siberia. Their rejection was based on their fear that the Japanese would use this as a pretext for a long-term military presence there.[10] However, the British suspected that American opposition had also much to do with underlying American racism against at the idea of "using Yellow race to destroy a White one".[11] Needless to say, the Japanese Government became sharply divided between those who supported a limited deployment and those in the minority who wanted a more general deployment.[12] In sum, Japan emerged from the war with a dented international reputation due to its wartime actions which were perceived by the United States in particular as being blatantly opportunistic. Ironically, therefore, Japan's participation as an Allied power did not lead to her increased integration into the western camp, but rather the reverse effect, that of isolating Japan even more than before.

During the war years, whatever the international implications of Japanese wartime actions, the Japanese, on the whole, tended to be more preoccupied with domestic developments than with foreign affairs. This was a reflection of Japan's limited involvement in the war. Economically, Japan had benefited from the conflict. Standards of living were improving, especially in urban areas as people became more interested in enjoying the benefits of modern living. However, in rural areas, conditions remained the same, if not worse, due to the widening gap between the fast-growing industrial sector and the farming sector which was unable to keep up with the pace of the former.[13] Politically, Japan was undergoing an important period of the 'Taishô democracy' led by liberal intellectuals such as Yoshino Sakuzô. The movement was characterized by an increased political awareness at the popular level, as seen in the demands for increased participation in the political system through universal suffrage.[14] In this politically and socially buoyant atmosphere, the Terauchi cabinet came under strong popular criticism especially over its handling of the rice riots in August 1918, and subsequently fell from power. In late-September 1918, the new government under Prime Minister Hara Kei was enthusiastically received by the public, as Hara was the first commoner and the first leader of a political party (Seiyûkai) to head the government. Hara's emergence into power was a significant landmark in the political history of modern Japan. His premiership represented the beginning

xxvii Celebrations in Tokyo, around December 1914, following upon the fall of Tsing Tao. The rejoicing in 1914 can be contrasted with the muted response to the Armistice four years later. (*The Great War*, Vol, 3 Chapter 50, H.W.Wilson (ed.), Amalgamated Press, London, 1915) of the party system, as opposed to the oligarchic clan politics which had dominated the political system since the Meiji Restoration. All in all, it is not too difficult to see that both the Japanese government and the Japanese public were highly preoccupied with domestic events when the Armistice came.

In the light of the above, how did the Japanese public respond immediately to the Armistice? First and foremost, news of the Armistice on 11 November did not reach the Japanese public until 13 November. One of the largest daily newspapers, *Tokyo asahi shimbun*, reported the ceasefire on 13 November based on information from the Associated Press, and gave a fairly detailed report of President Wilson's conditions for peace, and his speech given on 11 November.[15] Also, it reported on the response to the Armistice from capitals around the world, including Paris, New York, Sydney, and interestingly, Mukden (Manchuria) and Tientsin. On the same day, the abdication of Kaiser Wilhelm II was reported from Paris.[16] Interestingly, one newspaper reported that the Tokyo stock exchange which had been depressed, had suddenly shot up, boding well for the postwar period.[17] What is clear overall about the Japanese response on 13 November, the first day the Armistice was reported, was a curious detachment from the war. This is demonstrated by the fact that whilst there were many reports on European jubilation, there was nothing much on the Japanese reaction. Evidently, the time-lag in responding was due to the geographical distance between Japan and Europe. More importantly, this distance underlined the symbolic distance between Japan and the western powers. Japan had always remained on the periphery of what was happening at the centre, Europe, during the whole course of the war.

It was not till 14 and 15 November that the Japanese newspapers started reporting more on the Japanese reactions to the Armistice. Even then, reports were confined to the official celebrations planned by the state and the City of Tokyo on 21 November at Hibiya Park in Tokyo. On that day, there was to be a big celebration in Tokyo which promised to turn the capital into the "city of flags" during the day and "city of lights" at night.[18] There would be flags and illuminations everywhere, including decorations on public transport. The official ceremony was to take place at 1p.m. in the Music Hall where ambassadors from the Allied powers, together with some 2000 dignitaries, would celebrate with *banzai* thrice to the Taishô Emperor, and thrice to the Allied forces.[19] After the official ceremony, Hibiya Park would be opened up to the public, where special events would be organized, including amusements such as moving pictures, balloons, and western crafts. Each street and each district were encouraged to organize individual festive events.

One of the most noteworthy aspects of Japanese newspaper reporting on the armistice was the bemused attitude of the Japanese towards the celebrations of the westerners in Tokyo. One of these took place at the Imperial Hotel in Tokyo:

> The long awaited two words — peace [*hei-wa*] — have turned the foreigners staying at the Imperial Hotel into a frenzy of joy, as on the evening of the 13th, British, Americans, French, Italians and other guests from the Allied powers all came out of their rooms, poured into the lounge, and ordered

more Allied flags to be decorated throughout the hotel. As soon as the dusk came, those who started drinking all rushed to the bar, lined themselves up with red faces on stools and chairs.[20]

It seems that these events were worth reporting precisely because the Japanese were bemused by the westerners' jubilation and happiness about the Armistice, the significance of which the Japanese had obviously failed to share and appreciate. On 17 November, *Osaka asahi shimbun* reported on the victory parade and celebrations in London, which were apparently "so loud that it was impossible to listen to the telephone".[21]

Tokyo hosted the official celebrations on 21 November.[22] According to newspaper reports, both the emperor and the empress were very moved by popular expressions of joy, and had permitted the huge crowd to celebrate with *banzai* within the palace grounds. Outside, there were long torch-lit processions which looked like a "giant fire-dragon" proceeding through the city. The main procession was greeted by the ambassadors and diplomats as it went past the French, British, American, Italian, Belgian, and Russian embassies, ending back in Hibiya Park. The Belgian ambassador and his wife were so jubilant that "they seemed to have gone mad". Citizens of Tokyo celebrated late into the night, and even at midnight, there were streams of people on the streets. There were cars full of foreigners who came to see the celebrations. The press claimed that the impact of these celebrations on the diplomatic corps was extraordinary, as they continued to celebrate, inebriated, far into the night. One American counsellor was reported as giving a toast to every Japanese he bumped into, uttering in a drunken stupor, "My five years of abstinence was broken in a day, and this is how it is!"

In the light of the above, how can we assess the Japanese response to the Armistice? Generally, the dominant impression given in the press reporting was that the 'European' war had ended. For the majority of Japanese, the endless reporting of military advances or retreats on the Western Front in the past four years did not have any impact on their lives; hence, the jubilation over victory which was so prominent in Europe, was conspicuously absent from the Japanese public. Without a doubt, the psychological remoteness of Japan from the European theatres of war played a large part in creating a related response in November 1918. Although Australia and New Zealand were geographically even more remote from Europe, their high-level participation and indeed military presence in France had given them a total sense of identity with the European victors, unlike the Japanese. In fact, the predominant observation which can be gauged from the newspapers in Japan was that the war which appeared to have gone on interminably was finally coming to an end.[23] It was this detachment which made the Japanese seem like observers of, rather than participants in, the war and this characterized Japanese attitudes towards the Armistice. Except on the occasion of the official celebration, there was no general outburst of popular emotion or any passion. From the press reports, moreover, it is possible to detect an underlying sense of anxiety that Japan should be seen as playing its part as an Allied power by organizing the huge state celebration in Hibiya Park to which all foreign dignitaries were invited, and interestingly, to convey the feeling to the Japanese readership that the westerners in Tokyo were enjoying and appreciating the Japanese effort at celebrating the end of the war.

Clearly, Japan's own experiences of the war, being marginal and sporadic in the total scale of the Great War, had important implications on how it viewed the Armistice. Significantly, when the newspaper, *Kokumin shimbun*, reported with an article, "Casualties in the Great War", there was no mention of Japanese casualties or costs of the war.[24] What was missing from the Japanese scene was the popular or the personal experience of the war itself. There was no popular exhilaration as evidenced at the end of the Sino-Japanese War of 1895, or frustration as materialized in the famous Hibiya riots in the aftermath of the Russo-Japanese War of 1905. Consequently, this de-personalization of the war had made it seem more akin to another diplomatic or political event on which Japan had a distant claim.

Because the war did not mean very much to the ordinary Japanese, its end was greeted in a business-like manner. In contrast, it may seem surprising that Japanese public opinion became highly charged and emotional about the ensuing peace conference. Instead of relishing the long-cherished moment of peace, the press on the whole became more concerned about the pragmatic side of what would happen next. Again, this seems to underline the difference between European and Japanese experiences of the Armistice. The prevailing public sentiment was that Japan wanted to get on with the peace which it had been waiting for ever since it captured the German possessions in Shantung and the Pacific islands in 1914. Indeed, it is clear that there was a discrepancy between public opinion which had suddenly decided to take an avid interest in the peace conference issues, and the Hara government which continued to be absorbed in domestic affairs even after the change of direction in public opinion. As this national preoccupation with the peace conference came to typify the Japanese response to the end of the war, it is worth examining in some detail.

Let us first turn to public opinion which led the national debate on the peace conference. Significantly, the first item to appear in the newspapers about the end of the war and the peace conference was the League of Nations and Japan's role within it. In the atmosphere of an impending armistice, the newspaper, *Tokyo asahi shimbun*, published two articles entitled, "The League of Nations" on 2 and 4 November 1918. These articles explored briefly the main ideas behind the League in terms of what the new organization might entail. The fact that the press expressed such an early interest in the League of Nations is highly significant especially as the newly inaugurated Hara government had not yet had the time to reformulate a new peace policy, and was unable to do so until mid-November. Moreover, another newspaper expanded the League question to include racial discrimination when it published an article on 3 November entitled, "The League and racial discrimination — one impediment to permanent peace":

> For Japan the most important question in connection with President Wilson's League of Nations is the mode of dealing with the racial discrim-

ination idea. The object of the League's formation will not be fully realized, it would seem, so long as Japanese and other coloured races are differentially treated in white communities.

The main objects of Mr. Wilson's League are the perpetuation and the freedom and equalization of the races of the world.[25]

The launch of the above article spelt the beginning of a long press and popular campaign to demand the abolition of racial discrimination at the Paris Peace Conference. This campaign continued into December. A stream of articles was published by various intellectuals who expounded their views on the racial equality issue. For example, a controversial intellectual, Fukuda Tokuzô stated that it was important that Japan should stand up to the white race as the representative of the coloured race because President Wilson could not be trusted as his 'beautiful' words on international justice tended to betray reality.[26]

The public debate on the racial equality proposal and the League of Nations continued unabated into 1919, when it hardened in the face of the apparent incompetence of Japanese diplomacy conducted at the peace conference. Many pressure groups were created in February and March 1919 as a means of putting pressure on the government to ensure the successful adoption of the racial equality proposal at Paris. For example, the League to Abolish Racial Discrimination [Jinshu sabetsu teppai kisei taikai] met on a number of occasions during the peace conference in order to make declarations on the racial equality issue.[27] Interestingly, many of these groups attracted members on a cross-party basis, as well as from other professions such as the armed forces and journalism. Not surprisingly, many of the groups expressed the 'pan-Asian' tendency which held that Japan's place rested with Asia and that it was Japan's mission to be the leader of Asia (*tôa no meishu*). Naturally, the government became quite alarmed by the public display of determination to support the racial equality proposal, especially as the negotiations at the peace conference continued to flounder in the face of seemingly insurmountable difficulties.[28]

The broadsheets continued to put pressure on the government through their coverage of the peace conference. Again, it appeared that the public received news from Paris far more quickly than the Government which had to wait for the detailed telegrams to arrive from their delegates. Consequently, the broadsheets were able to report back the happenings in Paris much before the cabinet had any inkling of what was happening. This placed the government in an excruciatingly embarrassing position of not being able to counter press accusations of incompetence with any concrete evidence. The public's unusually high fervour and enthusiasm for the forthcoming peace conference as seen through the broadsheets contrasted sharply with the apparent lack of enthusiasm of the new government.

Another important consideration is that Prime Minister Hara differed considerably in his attitude towards foreign policy from the previous government, which was militarist, led by General Terauchi. Hara was a pro-western internationalist, who believed in the utmost necessity of cooperation with the western powers. His conviction was based on the wartime experience of Japan which had alienated herself from the Anglo-Saxon powers, due to her unpopular, aggressive policies in China. The problem, however, was that he was expected to reverse the previous foreign policy within a very short span of time and as a result, was unable to do so effectively. The only indication in the change of direction in foreign policy was made in Foreign Minister Uchida's policy statement to the National Diet in early October that the new government had considered the Anglo-Japanese Alliance as the cornerstone of Japanese foreign policy, and that it would do its best to cooperate with the western powers over the League of Nations.[29] Surprisingly, the Foreign Ministry until then was unable to detect the change in Allied thinking on peace and, hence, remained oblivious to the fact that by accepting the Armistice, Japan had in principle agreed to base the peace on the Wilsonian Fourteen Points.[30] All this reflected the Japanese government's continued unpreparedness for the new conditions which governed the forthcoming peace conference, and it was jolted into a rude awakening as late as mid-October 1918. Initially, this meant that public opinion led the national debate on the peace conference, as the government stood immobile and silent, desperately trying to formulate its new peace policy. This undermined the Hara government which was often portrayed in the press as being unprepared and incompetent on peace issues, with its basic policy of 'wait and see'.[31] Eventually when the Hara government delivered Japan's peace terms, they consisted of three demands. The first and second demands were territorial in nature, demanding the acquisition of the former German rights and concessions in the Shantung Peninsula as well as the Pacific islands north of the equator. These two demands were considered by the Japanese government as a *fait accompli* mainly due to the fact that Japan had been in *de facto* occupation of these two territories since 1914. Moreover, the existence of a series of secret agreements which Japan had signed with Britain, France, Italy and Russia in 1917, meant that Japan's claims to the Pacific islands were as secure as they possibly could be.[32] The third demand was what became known as the racial equality proposal which insisted that a racial equality principle be inserted into the Covenant of the League of Nations.[33] Effectively, what had happened in the sphere of public opinion was that this third issue became the most important priority for Japan at the Paris Peace Conference. Needless to say, the third demand was also the only new item which encapsulated Prime Minister Hara's desire for increased international cooperation.

In conclusion, it is clear that Japan's experience of the Armistice reflected the reality of her position internationally at the time. In spite of Japan's participation in the First World War as one of the Allied powers, it was still on the periphery of great power politics. By its own limited conception of its war aims, Japan was confining itself to being a 'regional' great power with no real claims on a larger role than it had sought in East Asia. Whilst Japan was content to play a limited role in the war, it had nonetheless developed an underlying desire to gain increased recognition of its status as a great power. This tension became manifestly evident when Japan sought greater equality with the western great powers through what became known as the racial equality proposal at the Paris Peace Conference.

Endnotes

1 Tatsuo Kobayashi, 'Rinji gaikô chôsa iinkai no setchi' [Establishment of the Diplomatic Advisory Council], *Kokusai seiji*, vol. 28, 1964, p. 55.

2 The Anglo-Japanese Alliance of 1902 had been the 'cornerstone' of Japanese foreign policy until its abrogation as a result of the Washington Conference of 1921–22. For an authoritative account of the alliance, consult Ian Hill Nish, *The Anglo-Japanese Alliance: The Diplomacy of Two Island Empires 1894–1907*, London, Athlone Press, 1966 and his *Alliance in Decline: A Study in Anglo-Japanese Relations 1908–1923*, London, Athlone Press, 1972. For controversy surrounding Japan's entry into war, see S. Tamura, 'Dai-ichiji sekai taisen to nihon no sansen' [The First World War and Japan's Entry to War], *Kokusai seiji*, vol. 23, 1963, pp. 1–14.

3 Nagaoka Harukazu, *Nihon gaikô monjo: Nihon gaikô tsuikairoku 1900–1935* [Documents on Japanese Foreign Policy: Diplomatic Memoirs of Nagaoka Harukazu], Diplomatic Records Office, Tokyo, p. 318.

4 Unno Yoshirô, 'Pari kôwa kaigi to gaimushô,' [Paris Conference and the Foreign Ministry] *Rekishi kyôiku*, vol. 15, no. 1, 1967, p. 47.

5 Admiralty Memorandum, 16 February 1917, PRO FO 371/2950, f 36794; FO 371/2950, f 107662.

6 See for instance, Greene to Balfour, 7 January 1918, PRO FO 371/3233, f 33087.

7 Balfour to Milner, 19 January 1918, MS Milner 46, f. 3, *Milner Papers*.

8 Richard Storry, *Japan and the Decline of the West in Asia 1894–1943*, New York, St. Martin's Press, 1979, pp. 108–110.

9 In Britain, *The Manchester Guardian* had leaked the document though *The Times* in London withheld from publishing it. Consult Nish, *Alliance in Decline*, pp. 9–10.

10 Balfour to Milner, 19 January 1918, MS Milner 46, ff. 3–4, *Milner Papers*; House to Balfour, 4 March 1918, F60/2/45, *Lloyd George Papers*; Wiseman to Drummond, 14 June 1918, Additional Manuscripts 49741 f. 81, *Balfour Papers*.

11 Ian Malcolm, 21 June 1918, including Sir William Wiseman's correspondence of 4 March 1918, Box 71, *Davidson Papers*.

12 For the Japanese perspective, see *Gaimusho no hyakunen* [One hundred years of Foreign Ministry], vol.1, pp. 675–85.

13 Hayashi Yûichi and Yasuda Hiroshi, 'Minshû bunka to nashionalizumu' [Popular culture and nationalism], *Kôza nihon rekishi*, vol.9, Tokyo, Tokyo daigaku shuppankai, 1985, pp. 253–4.

14 For the Taishô democracy, consult Mitani Taichirô, *Taishô demokurashiron*, Tokyo, Chûô kôronsha, 1974; Matsuo Takayoshi, 'The Development of Democracy in Japan', *The Developing Economies*, vol. 4, no. 4, 1966, pp. 612–637; Peter Duus, 'Liberal Intellectuals and Social Conflict in Taisho Japan', T. Najita and V. Koschmann, *Conflict in Modern Japanese History*, Princeton, Princeton University Press, 1982; Peter Duus, 'Yoshino Sakuzô', *Journal of Asian Studies*, vol. 4, no. 2, 1978, pp. 301–326.

15 13 November 1918, *Tokyo asahi shimbun*, in *Shimbun shûroku taishôshi*, vol. 6, Tokyo, Taishô shuppan, 1978, pp. 405–6.

16 *ibid.*, pp. 406–8.

17 *ibid.*, 13 November 1918, *Miyako shimbun*, p. 408.

18 *ibid.*, 15 November 1918, p.410.

19 *Banzai* literally means 'ten thousand years'. The closest equivalent in English is 'hip hip hooray'.
20 14 November 1918, *Hochi shimbun* in *Shimbun shûroku taishôshi*, vol. 6, p. 410.
21 *ibid.*, 17 November 1918, *Osaka asahi shimbun*, p. 411.
22 Details from this paragraph are taken from *ibid.*, 23 November 1918, *Tokyo asahi shimbun*, pp. 416–418.
23 The Japanese newspapers (mainly, *Tokyo asahi shimbun*, *Tokyo nichinichi shimbun*, *Yomiuri shimbun*) consulted would give frequent progress reports of the war.
24 18 November 1918, *Kokumin shimbun* in *Shimbun shûroku taishôshi*, vol. 6, p. 414.
25 3 November 1918, *Kokumin shimbun.*
26 15 November 1918, *Tokyo asahi shimbun.*
27 Uchida to Matsui, 31 January, doc. 356, 6 February, doc. 360, 8 February, doc. 361, 15 March, doc. 380, 24 March, doc. 391, 1 April, doc. 398, 25 April, doc. 408, *Nihon gaikô monjo* [Documents on Japanese Foreign Policy], part 1, vol. 3, 1919.
28 Nakano Seigô, *Kôwa kaigi o mokugekishite* [In witnessing the Peace Conference], Tokyo, Tôyô jironsha, 1919, p. 123.
29 8 October 1918, *Yomiuri shimbun.*
30 Shidehara Kijûrô heiwa zaidan ed., *Shidehara Kijûrô*, Tokyo, Shidehara Kijûrô heiwa zaidan, 1955, pp. 135–136; Minutes of Diplomatic Advisory Council, 13 November 1918, Kobayashi Tatsuo, ed., *Suiusô nikki: Itôke monjo*, Tokyo, Hara shobô, 1966.
31 'Gaikô butai tômen no sanhanagata' [The Three Principal Actors on the Diplomatic Stage], *Chûô kôron*, no. 364, 1918, p. 57.
32 Balfour to Greene, 14 February 1917, PRO FO 410/66, Confidential Print 11301, no. 14; J. Grew to Polk, 26 February 1919, SDR 893.77/21A, reel 563, National Archives Microfilm Publication M820.
33 See Naoko Shimazu, *Japan, Race and Equality: The Racial Equality Proposal of 1919*, London, Routledge, 1998.

Part III

The Bulgarian, Turkish and Austrian Armistices, the Balkans and Italy

Central and Eastern Europe in the aftermath of the Great War

Chapter Fifteen

Armistice in Eastern Europe and the Fatal Sequels: Successor States and Wars 1918–23

Imanuel Geiss

For the English-speaking world, 11 November 1918, is firmly linked to Armistice with Germany, the Armistice of World War One. Coming as the climax of the defeat of the Central Powers, following the collapse of the other three, Bulgaria, Turkey and Austria-Hungary, it brought Great Power military hostilities to an end. However, it opened the way to a welter of small successor wars in and between successor states. This chapter offers a survey of these new developments outside Western Europe – that is, in the Balkans, and in the former Russian, Ottoman and Austrian imperial lands; though because Germany, even stricken, was by far the most important of the Central Powers, and was also losing territory to the east, her close involvement in many of these events must not be forgotten.

To the great dismay of the war-weary masses in the Great Power nations, the Armistice did not end the First World War. Regional wars spilled over until the Peace of Lausanne with Turkey in 1923. Today, they seem no longer so incomprehensible, since they followed universal historical patterns, though with bewildering national and regional varieties. The key to making sense of them is through the concept of 'successor states'. Though the term first became current only after 1918 for states emerging from the ruins of the Danube Monarchy, its historical reality can be found in the decline and fall of any power structure, whether large – as in empires[1] – or small – as in African kingdoms.[2] Classical precedents were the 'diadoch empires', called after Alexander's generals and 'diadochs', the latter word meaning 'successors'.

In order not to get lost in a maze of successor states and their wars after the Armistice, it is best to proceed from north to south, starting with those which emerged first, from the revolutions and armistice in Russia 1917, followed by those from Austria-Hungary and the Ottoman Empire

(Armenia), leaving out conflicts to the west (Ireland) and beyond Europe to the east (Arabs, the Middle Eastern Conflict and India).

Regional Conflicts within Global World War

True to its character as the really first global war, the First World War revealed, at its official termination, another deadly feature: it had absorbed older regional conflicts, brought them to explosion point or exacerbated them. Besides the general war between the Great Powers, highlighted by historians and the collective memory of mankind, the Great War also contained many 'little' wars between traditional arch-enemies – the 'Third Balkans War', the ninth Russo-Turkish War, the fourth Bulgaro-Serbian War, the fifth Greco-Turkish War, the fourth Italo-Austrian War since 1820, another Polish-Russian War, and another Japanese war against weak China. A small Irish rebellion against the United Kingdom in Easter, 1916, escalated into the Irish 'troubles' and rebellion from 1918 to 1921/2, the intra-Republican Irish Civil War, and the civil war which has simmered, on and off, in Ulster since that time. In 1915–16 the Great War provided the stage for the third and bloodiest Armenian massacre by the Turks, on a genocidal scale. 'Little' wars or civil wars, as in revolutionary Russia, Germany and Hungary, raged after official armistices, which served to expose the existence of long-standing conflicts.

Post-Imperial Successor States and Successor Wars

Post-imperial successor states after the Great War and the successor wars were a function of the decline and fall of their 'mother' empires, as in many 'zero-sum-games'. Loss of empire meant the appearance of new nationalisms. All provided fascinating 'national' facets of the same universal historical mechanisms – the break-up of empires after severe defeat into successor states, often linked to each other as though by communicating pipes: independence in one place encouraging it elsewhere.

Since Tsarist Russia had collapsed, more than a year before the Central Powers, the Russian Revolutions had had effects in 1917 comparable with those which the armistices were to have on Austria-Hungary, Germany and Turkey in late 1918 but with a marked difference. The February Revolution in Russia triggered national revolutions among non-Russian nationalities, the October Revolution social revolution and civil war against Bolshevism, further escalating national conflicts, while in 1918, social and national revolutions were all telescoped into one. The closest historical parallels are with the European Revolution of 1848–49, when Austria was at breaking-point and national movements were fighting bitterly against each other, once they had been set free; and with the conflicts after the fall of the Soviet Empire 1989–91, amongst peoples and new nations on the fringes of the ex-Soviet Union and in ex-Yugoslavia. In fact the post-communist successor states reverted to the same position as their predecessors of 1917–19.

Post-imperial successor states were either enlarged existing political entities (Rumania and Yugoslavia) or new ones (Czechoslovakia, Hungary, Austria, Poland, Finland, Estonia, Latvia and Lithuania). All remained quiet on the

Western Front after the Armistice, yet all became disquiet on the Eastern Front, for structural reasons: in the West, the victorious Allies felt no need to change their systems of government and could quell any unrest, national or social, with one exception – Ireland. Later, as a result of the post-war peace settlements, one of the victor powers, Italy, felt robbed of her 'victory'. Her 'sacro-egoismo' was not sufficiently served, and in 1922 she plunged into Fascism, to recover her imperial *grandezza*, as if to spite her former allies and with eventual disaster for herself – but this political development lay in the future.

The breakdown of the three dynastic empires to the East – Russia in 1917, Austro-Hungary in 1918, the Ottoman Empire in 1918–20 – and of the 'national' German Empire in 1918 made for chaos among the losers who clashed with those successor states (Poland, Czechoslovakia, Yugoslavia and Rumania) which, by becoming Western allies, profited from imperial decay. As the famous 'Little Entente' or 'Cordon Sanitaire' these Allied successor states were expected to separate the greatest losers, Germany and Russia, to make up for France's loss of her alliance with Russia against Germany, and to prevent the spread of Communism to the West by isolating Soviet Russia.

In the East, from Finland to Armenia, according to historical and political conditions, successor wars for independence and for 'sacred' national frontiers followed instantly after the official end of the Great War – or even preceded it, as in the case of Finland. All claimed the right of national self-determination, usually at the cost of hated neighbours and national minorities of their own. 'Balkanisation' of Eastern Europe was the undesirable but logical by-product of national self-determination, and of the disintegration of empires. Post-imperial successor states had to face great problems – where to draw frontiers, often against hostile fellow-successor states which also had fluid frontiers, and how to deal with the many and heterogeneous national minorities inside the new 'national' states. Because new nation-states were centralist and assimilationist, they repeated, *en miniature*, the deadly mechanisms of their former multi-national 'mother' empires, and this was the case not just with the Habsburg successor states.

1. POST-TSARIST SUCCESSOR STATES

The first Russian Revolution of 1917 started the usual break-up of empire in the outlying provinces with mostly non-Russian populations, further escalated by the October Revolution and armistices with the Central Powers. By 1920, most of these new states were re-absorbed into Bolshevik Russia after the Bolsheviks' victory in the Russian Civil War – the Ukraine, Georgia, Armenia, Central Asia – but they reappeared after the second breakdown of a modern Russian Empire in 1991. Post-Russian Revolution successor states which survived the Bolshevik Reconquista around 1920 were Finland, Estonia, Latvia and Lithuania. Poland, which had formerly been partitioned between three empires, had a predominantly Russian share (about 60%), in contrast to Rumania, whose share of Russian territorial gains was much smaller than that which it took from Austro-Hungary. All these new states were sucked into the maelstrom of revolution and Russian civil war in different ways. When German troops left after the Armistice, the Soviet Red Army or regional Red Guards tried to take over. Thus, fighting took on varying complexions of civil war, 'Reds' against 'Whites' and wars for national independence – in the case of Lithuania complicated by Poland's sub-imperial aspirations. In order to block Communist expansion, the Allies tolerated a continued German military presence in the Baltic countries, until consolidation had been achieved under Allied supervision. The civil war in Russia which followed the October Revolution also merged with regional conflicts in Russia, in Transcaucasia and in Central Asia which, however, are beyond the scope of this chapter.

There is a structural reason behind the attraction of Bolshevism during the years 1918 and 1919 – for countries west of Russia as well: in the agrarian East, the overriding social question was still, as it had been in the West until circa 1848, the pressure of peasants and the landless agrarian proletariat for land of their own. Wherever aristocratic owners of huge estates came from a different nation – in a wide arc from the Baltic provinces via western White Russia and the Ukraine – the Bolshevik programme of expropriating the Polish and German absentee landlords who were extracting the wealth of the soil solely for themselves, had a tremendous appeal, fusing social and national revolt, or inoculating peasants against the national aspirations of their hated foreign landlords, as in the Ukraine and White Russia.

Finland

Because Finland had enjoyed autonomy within the Tsarist Empire since 1809, apart from a short interval 1899–1905, she was first to emerge as a post-Tsarist successor state after the February Revolution 1917 and was already through her share of turmoil by Armistice Day 1918. Yet historical mechanisms were the same as after 11 November 1918. It is worthwhile, therefore, turning aside to look at Finland if only to make comparisons with neighbouring Estonia and Latvia.

In 1916, for the first time in history, Socialists in Finland had won an absolute majority in Parliament in free elections. The Russian Provisional Government extended full autonomy and repealed the oppressive legislation of the past decade. However, when, as early as 18 July 1917, the Finnish *Diet* further extended autonomy by proclaiming itself as the supreme power, except for foreign and military affairs, it was dissolved by the Kerensky Government. In revenge, Finnish socialists helped their Russian comrades and Lenin, after their first coup in neighbouring Petrograd had failed in July 1917, to hide in safety. After the October Revolution, the *Diet*, now with a bourgeois majority, but in an atmosphere of social unrest and Red Guard terror, proclaimed Finnish independence on 6 December, 1917. On 31 December, the Lenin Government was obliged to recognize it, owing to its own weakness, but refused to withdraw Russian troops from Finland. After a coup of the Red Guards against the 'Whites' on 28 January 1918, civil war, along Russian lines, broke out in Finland, in which a German army contingent – in April 1918 – and the Bolshevik Red Army, intervened. Defeat of the 'Reds' by 15 May ended the Finnish Civil War well before Armistice Day, and the

German military presence in Finland continued for some time. Finland remained under pressure from both Germany and Soviet Russia.

The Baltic States

More turbulent than in Finland was the transition from the Great War to small regional wars in the 'Baltic fringe', because the people of that region had no tradition of a state of their own upon which to fall back. Instead, they had lived mostly under the shadow, first of the Germans, then the Russians, and, in the case of Lithuania, of Poland as well. Only the temporary weakness of both imperial nations, the Russians and the Germans, gave them room for short-lived independence during the interwar period, crushed in between the two giants, as well as by the lesser Poland. All three Baltic countries demanded autonomy within the Russian Empire.

The Estonians spoke a language close to the Finns further north, while the Latvians spoke an Indo-european language. Yet the two peoples were alike in that they had never had a state of their own. Since the 13th century, they had been under the rule of German knights and barons – who regarded them as no more than human cattle – and of German burghers in the few cities; yet culturally, through the church and schools, they were influenced by the

Die Wacht im Osten

Nr. 998

Anschrift: Armeezeitung (Wacht im Osten) Deutsche Feldpost 166. □ Verantwortlicher Schriftleiter: Leutnant der Res. Urbach. □ Der Monatsbezug der wöchentlich sechsmal erscheinenden „Wacht im Osten" mit sämtlichen Beilagen kostet im Felde bei

Dienstag, 3. September (Scheiding)

Vorausbezahlung für Unteroffiziere und Mannschaften 0,60 M. Offiziere und Beamte der Armee 1,20 M. □ Bestellungen durch die Truppenteile. □ Postscheckkonto Königsberg 3260. □ Unbefugter Nachdruck verboten. □ Einzelnummer 10 Pfennig — 5 Kopeken.

1918

Abendbericht

Englische Angriffe zwischen Scarpe und Somme. Südöstlich von Arras und nördlich von Peronne gewannen sie Boden. Reserven fingen den Stoß auf. Beiderseits von Bapaume wurde der Feind abgewiesen.

Zwischen Oise und Aisne haben sich am Nachmittag nach schwerstem Feuerkampf französische Angriffe entwickelt.

Deutscher Heeresbericht vom 2. September

Westlicher Kriegsschauplatz

Heeresgruppe Kronprinz Rupprecht und Böhn: Vorfeldkämpfe beiderseits der Lys. Zwischen Scarpe und Somme setzte der Engländer auf der 45 Kilometer breiten Front seine Angriffe fort. Artilleriewirkung gegen die Bereitstellungsräume des Gegners südöstlich von Arras und beiderseits von Bapaume trug wesentlich zu ihrer Abwehr bei. Brennpunkte des Infanteriekampfes waren Hendecourt und Noreuil, die Trichterfelder östlich von Bapaume und zwischen Rancourt und Bouchavesnes. Der Feind, der nördlich von Hendecourt auf Cagnicourt Boden gewann, wurde durch Gegenangriff wieder aus Hendecourt zurückgeworfen. Um Noreuil wurde lange gekämpft; es blieb in unserem Besitz. Beiderseits von Vaulx-Vraucourt vorbrechende Panzerwagen ...

Im Westen

Nur Trümmer und Trichter geschenkt

Berlin, 2. 9. Die Loslösung unserer Truppen vom Feinde in Gegend Bailleul geschah auf die Minute planmäßig und völlig unbemerkt. Den schwachen Patrouillen gelang es, dem Feinde eine starke Besetzung unserer früheren Gräben vorzutäuschen. Erst nach Tagen griffen am 31. 8. vormittags 9 Uhr dichte englische Schützenlinien unsere Nachhuten in dem Berggelände östlich Bailleul an. Der äußerst geschickten Verteidigung gelang es, das Vorgehen des Feindes dermaßen zu verlangsamen, daß der Gegner erst in den Abendstunden die Linie Dranoeter—Ravetzberg erreichte. Die Freude an dem fast kampflos wiedergewonnenen Gelände wird den Engländern wesentlich getrübt werden, wenn sie erkennen, wie planmäßig die Rückzugsbewegung der deutschen Truppen vorbereitet ist. Die Stadt Bailleul, die uns die Engländer im April fast unberührt und voll von Vorräten an Lebensmitteln und Bekleidung überlassen mußten, ist jetzt dank der feindlichen Beschießung ein wüster Trümmerhaufen. Ebenso ist das übrige Gelände, das wir den Gegnern freigegeben haben, wüst und leer. Kaum ein Unterstand blieb ungesprengt. Die Straßen sind an den wichtigsten Punkten durch Sprengungen zerstört. Nicht eine einzige Brücke ist brauchbar geblieben. Die großen englischen Pionierparks mit Holz, Stacheldraht, Eisenbahnschwellen, Zement, die uns bei unserer Offensive wohlgefällig in die Hände fielen, und die wir bis jetzt noch nicht hatten aufbrauchen können, sind zurückgeschafft worden. Zahllose Meter Telephondraht haben unsere Nachrichtentruppen gesammelt und dabei gleichzeitig die Telephonstangen zerstört. Wir haben den Engl... nur Trümmer und Trichter geschenkt.

Die Franzosen drohen

Genf, 1. 9. Das Pariser Auswärtige Amt kündigt an, daß die vom Moskauer Volksrat gegen französische Staatsbürger in Rußland getroffenen Verfügungen, falls sie aufrechterhalten bleiben, dementsprechend Beantwortung finden würden. Eine ministerielle Note enthält Drohungen gegen Lenin und seine Beiräte.

Truppendampfer versenkt

Moskau, 1. 9. An amtlicher Stelle sind hier Nachrichten eingetroffen, daß mehrere feindliche Truppendampfer, die sich auf der Fahrt von Nikolajewsk nach Chabarow befanden, durch bolschewistische Abteilungen von beiden Seiten des Amurflusses aus unter Feuer genommen wurden. Drei Dampfer wurden durch Artilleriefeuer versenkt.

Letzte Nachrichten

Katastrophe in Odessa

Kiew, 1. 9. Bei einer Explosionskatastrophe in Odessa sind dem Vernehmen nach eine Anzahl österreich-ungarische Offiziere und Mannschaften umgekommen. Der Sachschaden ist bedeutend. Ein Teil einer Vorstadt ist vernichtet.

Ein englischer Luftangriff

Wien, 1. 9. Die Marinesektion des Kriegsministeriums teilt amtlich mit: Am Vormittag des 31. 8. versuchten vier englische Landflugzeuge Anlage und Schiffe des Golfs von Vattaro anzugreifen. Ihre Bomben waren wirkungslos und fielen meistenteils in See. Von den vier Flugzeugen entkam nur eins, die anderen drei stürzten ab und zerschellten an den Felsen. Ein verwundeter Flieger konnte geborgen werden, die übrigen sind tot.

xxviii *Die Wacht im Osten,* a newspaper for ethnic Germans living in what were to become the Baltic states, 1918. (Liddle Collection)

Germans. A succession of political overlords – first the Danes, then the Swedes and since 1703–95 the Russians – had followed, but without altering very much the complex arrangement of indirect rule.

Germany had occupied Lithuania and much of Latvia in 1915 – though not Latvia's northern region until November 1917 – and Estonia in February 1918. This difference explains important modifications in the development of both countries after the Russian October Revolution. The German occupying forces had ruled Lithuania and Latvia with an iron fist, through *Oberost*, under Ludendorff, trying to squeeze out more *Lebensraum* for German settlement after victory, while Estonia, after the Russian Revolution, was striving for autonomy and sovereignty. Since that time, Germany had encouraged the 'independence' of the Baltic states outside revolutionary Russia, but inside her own orbit as client states. With the defeat of Germany by the Allies in 1918, the Baltic states were set free to fight for full independence against the Bolshevik government of Russia and the Germans, both trying to manipulate them for their own power-political motives. In the wake of the German retreat, demanded by the Armistice, the Bolsheviks set up ephemeral Soviet Republics in all three Baltic countries during 1918–19. Allied intervention preserved or restored their fragile independence after the Armistice, but was too feeble and confused to save them in 1939–40, once Russia and Germany had re-emerged as first-rate Great Powers.

A) ESTONIA

In April 1917, the Russian Provisional Government had conceded to the Estonians both local autonomy and the right to form their own army. In spite of a massive Russian presence, the Estonians, split between bourgeois and socialist elements, formed a National Council, which first met on 14 July, 1917. After the October Revolution, it declared independence, but was dissolved by the Bolsheviks on 28 November 1917. The Bolshevik grip was broken by a German occupation in February 1918 designed to put pressure on Soviet Russia to accept the German *diktat* of Brest-Litovsk. In April, Germany disbanded the Estonian army. After the Armistice, the German troops withdrew. The power vacuum was filled by Estonian 'Reds', supported by the Soviet Red Army, which occupied most of Estonia and proclaimed a Soviet Republic of Estonia in December 1918. On 14 December, with the help of the re-formed Estonian army, of volunteers from nearby Finland and of a British naval squadron, Tallin, the capital of a 'White' government, was saved. With the assistance of the Russian White North Army, Estonians expelled the 'Reds' from Estonia by February 1919.

B) LATVIA

The Latvian peasants' hatred of the German barons explains why, in the First Russian Revolution of 1905, they had risen against them, why they had rallied politically to the side of Russia, whether Tsarist or Bolshevik, and why Latvian regiments in the Great War had fought bravely against the Germans. After the October Revolution they had a key role as a kind of military police for Lenin. Secretly paid with German gold marks, they recklessly quelled early resistance to the Bolsheviks. In Latvia, native Bolsheviks emerged as the strongest party. When the German Army also occupied Northern Latvia in November 1917, the country was split between a Latvian national bourgeoisie looking towards the Western allies, Bolshevism among the peasants and a minority of leading Germans (barons and burghers), hoping for 'Anschluß' to the greater German Reich. These three elements fought out the future of Latvia, once German troops had to withdraw officially after the Armistice. During this power vacuum, the 'Reds' conquered most of Latvia, including the capital, Riga, by 10 January 1919. Against the Latvian Soviet Republic which they set up, the bourgeois nationalists appealed to the Allies and *Germany* for military help. Germany, being closer at hand, reacted promptly: German officers trained a White Latvian Army, while the German '*Freikorps*' introduced a new military element, organized, paid and armed by Berlin. The *Freikorps* was made up of a mixture of freelance mercenaries seeking to escape massive demobilization at home, and those lured by vague promises of land and Latvian citizenship to settle in Latvia. As a kind of border farmer element (*Grenzbauern* – or *Wehrbauern*), these people would have rescued from the débris of defeat at least part of the German expansionist war aim for more *Lebensraum*. However, the Latvians, for the first time free from German social and economic hegemony, were loath for any of their lands to be part of a Germanic dream which would have subjected them again to control by the country they detested. In a complex three-cornered fight, in which the Russian White Army intervened on the side of the Freikorps, the Bolsheviks were driven out of Latvia by May 1919. However, when the Freikorps, in alliance with Russian Whites under General Yudenich, attacked the Latvian 'White' government in October 1918, Riga held out, relieved by an Anglo-French Baltic naval force. Frustrated *Freikorps* soldiers had to leave and became, after their return to Germany, the first large-scale source of recruits for an élite which would form Hitler's private political army, the S.A.

c) Lithuania

Lithuania had been gradually absorbed by Poland since the late Middle Ages and was annexed by Russia in 1795, with strong elements in and around Vilna of Poles and Jews as its cultural and economic élites. Because the Poles despised the Lithuanians as uncultured peasants, Lithuanian nationalism was as much directed against Poland as against Russian imperial rule. After the Revolution of 1905, Lithuania received limited autonomy. She was occupied by Germany in 1915 and suffered under Ludendorff's oppressive *Oberost* régime. While Lithuanian émigrés had formed a national council in Switzerland in 1916, Ludendorff tried to play them off against the socially dominant Poles by allowing 'independence', under German suzerainty. After the February 1917 Russian Revolution, Germany gave wider scope to Lithuanian nationalists who were actually far from being pro-German collaborateurs.

On 11 December 1917, after the October Revolution, the *Taryba*, the new Lithuanian *Diet*, proclaimed its country's independence and demanded recognition by Germany. In contrast with Latvia, the Bolshevik following in

Lithuania was small, while Poland, which filled the power vacuum after the German retreat in late 1918, remained the stronger power in the region. Thus the proclamation of a Lithuanian Soviet Republic in January 1919, after the conquest of the Vilnius district by the Reds, was only an isolated incident. Poland seized Vilnius for the first time in April 1919. The city remained a bone of contention; it was seized 'unofficially' again by Poles and was annexed by them in 1921.

POLAND

As for Poland, that nation had been divided up in a series of partitions between 1772 and 1815 between Russia, Prussia[3] and Austria. It was the biggest of the successor states and, because of its size, highlighted most of their problems. After the failure of the Polish Uprising of November 1830, the Poles in Russia and Prussia had lost their autonomy, but not in Austrian Galicia. This is why the Polish nationalist and socialist, Józef Pilsudski, could raise Polish Legions in Galicia during the Russian Revolution of 1905–6 and the Great War, which were to be the kernel of a future Polish Army for the liberation of Poland. The World War fulfilled the Polish prayer: "Oh Lord, give us the Great War!", – that is, war between the three partitioning powers at the same time. Their simultaneous downfall in 1917–18 brought about Poland's rebirth. Pilsudski had made a limited military contribution with his Galicia-based 'Polish Legions' against Russia, but fought only on the territory of 'Congress Poland'.[4] In an effort to win over the Poles to the Central Powers, Berlin and Vienna devised a 'Kingdom of Poland' in December 1916 under the joint suzerainty of Germany and Austria-Hungary. However shadowy this was, it did give Poland some constitutional framework for real independence. When Pilsudski refused to collaborate with the Central Powers on a broader military front against Russia, he was banished to the fortress at Magdeburg in 1917 and thus became the Polish national hero.

Polish independence came with the Armistice. On 7 October, a few days after Germany and Austria-Hungary had sued officially for a cease-fire, the Regency Council of the 'Kingdom of Poland' proclaimed the independence of a United Poland. On 6 November, the Galician Poles followed with a Polish Republic in Cracow. Meanwhile, a third Polish insurrection in the Poznan province (the two earlier ones being in 1806 and 1848), challenged German rule from inside the Reich. Thus, in all three parts of partitioned Poland, the flag of national rebirth had been raised. Pilsudski was released and returned to Warsaw on 10 November, one day after the revolution in Berlin and one day before the Armistice which bound Germany to remove her troops from the eastern countries, including emergent Poland. The Regency Council hastened to hand over political power to the new national hero, and Pilsudski became the provisional Head of State of the Second Polish Republic.

Poland was instantly overtaken by the dialectics of national self-determination: by her claim to the frontiers of the multi-national *Rzeczpospolita* of 1772 for the new national state, about 50% of her population would have consisted of minorities. The usual mixture of centralism and assimilation was an invitation to conflict with most of her neighbours apart from Rumania, in

U.S.
4
Miliony
Amerykanów
będzie na frontach Koalicyi
na
przyszłą wiosnę
a
półtora miliona
jest już obecnie na froncie francuskim!
361.

xxx An Allied propaganda leaflet designed to demoralize Polish troops in the Austrian Army, October 1918. It reads "4 million Americans will be on the Allied fronts by next Spring". Without a nation of their own since 1795, Poles fought in nearly all the combatant armies between 1914 and 1918. The Austrians and the Russians had Polish national units, while the French and Italians recruited Polish Legions from the prisoners of war in their camps. Each side promised the restoration of Poland after the war. (via Mark Cornwall) wars to establish the borders of the new Poland – with the Germans over Poznan, West Prussia, Upper Silesia and Gdansk; with the now Communist Russians over western White Russia and the western Ukraine; with the Ukrainians, since 1 November, over Lvov (Lemberg); with the Czechs over Teschen; with the Lithuanians, because Poland refused to recognize their national independence or to let them have Vilna as their capital city.

In the wake of the German retreat came the Red Army, eager to carry world revolution westward, via the Baltic countries and Poland, to Germany, with the help of the newly-founded Polish Communist Party. The overall result was a welter of political, military, social and ethnic conflicts which defy brevity to describe, escalating towards the Soviet-Polish War of 1920, concluded by the compromise Peace of Riga in 1921. This settlement drew the Soviet-Polish border about half-way between the frontiers of 1772, demanded by Poland, and the 'Curzon-line', demanded by the Soviets. The arrangement satisfied neither side, as was the case with all the other new frontiers, and it became a constant reminder to both German and Soviet revisionism to collaborate in making the despised and hated 'seasonal state', Poland, disappear as soon as possible – which was to lead to a second World War.

2. *THE POST-AUSTRO-HUNGARIAN SUCCESSOR STATES*

The successor states which emerged from the former Austro-Hungarian Empire added to the complexities of the European scene. After Tsarist Russia had gone down in military defeat and social revolution in 1917, the Habsburg monarchy followed next in autumn 1918, under the pressure of complex interactions between Allied policy decisions and national movements. On 13 September 1918, the Allied powers, followed by the U.S.A. on 3 October, recognized the Czechoslovak Legion, formed by Czech prisoners-of-war in Russia, as part of the Allied forces; and on 12 October, the Polish National Army under General Haller in the West, made up of Polish deserters and prisoners-of-war in France, was similarly recognized. Meanwhile, Czechoslovakia was accorded 'Ally' status on 3 October.

With the official armistice note of 4 October, time was ripe for action from inside the Austro-Hungarian Empire. First to strike were the traditionally unruly nationalities, the South Slavs and Czechs. On 6 October, the Serb-Croat Coalition in Croatia and the Slovenes formed a National Council, and on 14 October, the Czechs set up a provisional national government. On 21 October, the German Austrian members of the Reichsrat, the National Assembly, constituted themselves as the 'provisional National Assembly of the independent German Austrian state'. After these German Austrian representatives, from the nationality traditionally identified with the Habsburg imperial monarchy, had announced their intention of leaving the Empire, declarations of independence by non-German nationalities only ratified the dissolution of Austria-Hungary in late October – the Rumanians of the Bukovina on 27 October, the Czechs on 28 October, the Croats on 29 October, the Slovaks on 30 October and the Ukrainians in Eastern Galicia on the final day of the month. On that day, too, revolution overturned the *Ancien Régime* in Hungary. Food riots in Vienna and Budapest on 2 November added to the threat of national revolt that of social revolution, now under the banner of Russian Bolshevism.

German Austria

In the death throes of the Monarchy, German Austrian soldiers were the last to continue fighting – against Italy. As in Germany and Hungary, Social Democrats took power provisionally. Because Emperor Karl refused to abdicate, there was a longer period of uncertainty between Austria's armistice on 4 November and the proclamation of the independent Austrian Republic on the twelfth. Some Austrian territory was occupied by Allied troops, and Slovenes occupied southern Styria. In the turbulence following the proclamation of the Republic and in the spring of 1919, two new Soviet Republics, Hungary and Bavaria, pressed on Austria from both east and west, but a Communist victory was prevented. On 4 March 1919, the new National Assembly declared its intention of joining the Weimar Republic. As a small rump state, most Austrians saw their future only in Anschluß, union with the German Empire. Austria became independent by default, but the Greater German logic of Anschluß loomed ominously on the horizon.

Hungary

Since the Compromise of 1867, the Hungarians had been the other imperial nation of the Dual Monarchy. They had been riding high over many nationalities and fell correspondingly low in the autumn of 1918, as a natural consequence of Magyar assimilationist chauvinism which had blocked all attempts of Archduke Francis Ferdinand and, as late as October 1918 by Emperor Karl, to transform the rigid dualist structure of the Monarchy. Even in its death-agony, Magyar sub-imperial chauvinism had prevented the Emperor from extending his promise of autonomy to national minorities in Hungary in his '*Völkermanifest*' of 16 October. With the secession of the crown land of Croatia, certainty of military defeat came home to Hungary, as it did to the Germans of the Reich and in Austria-Hungary. The setting up of Czechoslovakia also meant the loss of Slovakia (often termed 'Upper Hungary').

Reaction, following the normal pattern after defeat, came with a vengeance. After the national revolution of the despised Southern Slavs, there now ensued social revolution from the lower strata of the Hungarians themselves, for the ruling gentry was unwilling and unable to rise to the occasion. Already in late June, Hungary was shaken by a nine-day general strike. On 28 October, police provoked revolution by firing at mass demonstrations in Budapest calling for the installation of a new government under the liberal, Count Károlyi. Workers armed themselves and formed Workers' and Soldiers' Councils. After more mass demonstrations on 30 October, revolution triumphed on the following day in Hungary, but in a complicated situation.

Excluded from the Padua armistice with Italy and the Allies, historic Hungary had to pay very dearly for her leaders' refusal to discard their dreams of Hungarian imperial grandeur. The new coalition government of liberals and social democrats hoped for a lenient Wilsonian peace, but was

439. Liebesgabe zur Armee-Zeitung

Nr. 665 — Wilna, Dienstag, am 3. Scheiding (September) 1918 — 3. Jahrgang

Wer will, dem wird kein Muß zu hart erscheinen,
zum Höchsten hält er stets den Blick gewandt
und such mit Erdgesetzen zu vereinen,
was ihm aus höhern Sphären zuerkannt.
Fritz Buchwald

Von Liedern, die heimlich wanderten . . .

Zur Erinnerung an die Befreiung von Riga am 3. September 1917

Von Robert Albert, Mitau

Heute vor einem Jahre! Als die letzten Kanonenschläge verhallt waren, konnten die Rigenser, wie zwei Jahre vorher auch die Mitauer, einen Weitsprung von 13 Tagen Länge in die Geschichte tun, konnten sie ihren Abreißkalender um volle 13 Tage kürzen und auch ihre Uhren einen Schritt nach vorwärts tun lassen. Der neue Stil ersetzte den alten, westlich wurde gerichtet, was östlich bisher gerichtet war. Aus tiefem Schlaf wurde das Dornröschen von feldgrauen Prinzen erlöst und alles jubelte frohbeglückt: Deutsche Worte hört' ich wieder! . . .

Man muß es an Ort und Stelle erlebt haben,

Alt-Riga

Zur Wiederkehr der Einnahme Alt-Rigas

Ueber die Brücke von Thorensberg
sinnend ich schreite.
Ueber die Düna bis Thorensberg
füll'n alte Glocken die Weite.

Wie vor Jahrhunderten schon kreist der Hahn
St. Petris. Unter den Hauben
der schlanken Giebel schauen ihn an
Fenster voll lichtfrohem Glauben!

Ich schlendere und verträume tief
hinein in das Raunen der Gassen.
Ich lese manch rissige Wand wie 'nen Brief
aus vergangenen Zeiten voll Hassen.

Manch spruch-ummaltes Tor singt leis
von jahrtausendverklungenen Festen.
Das vierschrötig kantige Schloß aber weiß
von ergenen Rittergästen. —

Kriegsfreiw. Alfred Hein

engel umging und die Hoffenden mit Geduld und Mut erfüllte, was bisher nur die wissen, die es mit erlebt, will ich erzählen.

Als die Russen Niederlage auf Niederlage erlitten, rächten sie sich in Riga, wie überall durch eine Deutschenhetze, die man schamhaft „Germano-

te sie die Kinder. Rigenser und baltische Dichter dichteten diese Verse und Zehntausende schrieben sie, da sie ja nicht gedruckt werden durften, heimlich ab und gaben sie an gute Freunde weiter, die sie wiederum abschrieben und weiter verbreiteten — den Häschern zum Trotz, die wildgierig danach fahndeten. Kinder und Jugendliche, Männer, Frauen und Greise — die Verse flogen wie ein Gerücht vom Moskauer zum Petersburger Stadtteil, von der Esplanade bis zur Mitauer Vorstadt. Und ein Gedanke beseelte alle: Die geheime Hoffnung, über die es in einem Gedichte hieß:

Und kommen wird das frische Werde!
das auch bei uns die Nacht besiegt.
Der Tag, da diese deutsche Erde
im Ring des großen Reiches liegt!

Wie falsch beraten doch die Tyrannen waren! Wie immer in der Geschichte haben auch hier die Bedrücker zwar gute Henker, aber schlechte Kundschafter gehabt! Mochten sie immer alles Deutsche unterdrücken — aus den Augen all der Hunderttausend Deutschen in Riga sprach auch unausgesprochen der Wandervers:

Es wird kommen der Tag und mit dem Tag
zu seinem Land der Deutsche kommen,
und wieder sich nehmen mit zürnender Hand,
was raubende Hände ihm heute genommen!

xxix A German newspaper, produced in Vilnius, claimed as a Lithuanian city but culturally Polish and now, in the post-armistice world, finding itself in Poland. (Liddle Collection) bitterly disappointed. Even after becoming democratic, Hungary was still treated as an enemy state and only on 13 November could obtain an armistice, two days after the Armistice with Germany. Furthermore, the Allied blockade remained in force also against republican Hungary. The Allies allowed Rumanians and Czechs to occupy Transylvania and the plains of southern Slovakia, both of which areas contained massive majorities of Hungarians adjacent to the new borders: Hungary lost half of her historic territories, most of them non-Magyar in population and this was ratified by the Peace Treaty of Trianon 1920, although Hungary had the possibility of winning the eastern half of Burgenland from Austria through a plebiscite.

The Hungarian revolution quickly reached a radical extreme in the short-lived Soviet Republic under Béla Kun, from 21 March to 1 August 1919, which even succeeded, for a short time, in establishing a Hungarian Slovak Soviet Republic. However, after withdrawing from Slovakia under Allied pressure, the Hungarian Soviet Republic was put down by Rumanian and Czech troops as well as by Hungarian anti-communist forces under Admiral Hórthy. Henceforth, Hungary belonged to the revisionist states, bent on tearing up the Versailles settlement and ending up as a satellite state of the Third Reich in the Second World War.

The Southern Slavs

The Southern Slavs, whose populations had extended before 1914 over the Ottoman successor state Serbia, over Montenegro and over the Habsburg Empire, never had a common state, but had developed since the 19th century a sense of a common linguistic, cultural, even political, 'Yugoslav' – that is, Southern Slav – identity. In December 1914, Serbia had made her official war aims programme the 'liberation and unification of all our Serb, Croat and Slovene brothers'. Greater Serbian Yugoslavism was upheld by the Serbian Army and state in exile after the German-Austro-Hungarian-Bulgarian conquest of Serbia in 1915, complemented by Croat and Slovene leaders who had fled to the West and set up a 'Yugoslav Committee'. From the start, there was a rift, within the two strands of Yugoslavism, that was destined to destroy both the first Yugoslavia – arising from the First World War – and the second, which re-emerged from the Second World War: the Serbs were for a Greater Serbia, based on Serbian assimilationist centralism, while the Croats and Slovenes stood for federalism amongst the heterogeneous Southern Slav lands, with many other minorities – Muslims, Hungarians, Germans, Albanians and Italians.

On 29 October, the *Narodno Vijecé* in Zagreb proclaimed independence for a state of Serbs, Croats and Slovenes in ex-Habsburg lands. This state, however, became inexorably drawn into the greater Yugoslav union under the hegemony of Serbia, now victor on the side of the Allies, and lost internal autonomy, in the teeth of opposition of the Croats and their Peasants' Party. The Great Serbian Southern Slav union was proclaimed in Belgrade on 1 December and imposed by the Serbian army *manu militaria* in ex-Habsburg lands. Croatian demands for autonomy were ruthlessly quelled by new Serbian authorities trying to recoup their frightful losses from war by rigorously taxing the richer new territories to the north, Croatia and Slovenia, untouched by the war. The Serbian pacification of Croatia also included putting down a nasty hangover from war and defeat, the 'Green cadres' of about 100,000 deserters from the Austro-Hungarian army, who ravaged the countryside, under cover of social revolutionary slogans directed against land owners. In the long run, the Serbs, by their policies of strict centralization and assimilation on the French model only created conflicts which were to rend Yugoslavia in the future, twice – in 1941 under the additional outside pressure of the German invasion and in 1991 after the end of the Cold War.

CZECHOSLOVAKIA

The Czechs, content with their demand for autonomy in Cisleithania (Austria), complicated by the massive presence of Germans in their cities and on the mountainous fringes of Bohemia, had been slow in seceding from the Monarchy. The Slovaks in Transleithania (Greater Hungary) who were politically passive, as rural communities might be expected to be, were kept under the heels of assimilationist Magyar chauvinism. The initiative in the final phase of the Great War came mainly from better educated Czechs abroad under Tomás G. Masaryk in western exile with their Czechoslovak National Council in Lausanne, and from former Czech deserters and prisoners-of-war in Russia. After the October Revolution, the latter had formed the Czechoslovak Legion, soon recognized by the Allies, and from May 1918 had controlled the Trans-Siberian Railway against the Bolsheviks. The Legion became the hard core of the independence movement abroad and of the future Czechoslovak Army.

Between them, political émigrés in the West and military forces of the Legion in the East, seized the opportunities offered by the breakdown of the Monarchy. They shaped the way in which Czechoslovak independence emerged in the wake of armistices by directing the turbulence of national revolution into the calmer waters of political agreements and declarations. Czech politicians in the Austrian parliament, the Reichsrat, who had pressed for internal autonomy, now switched over to the Masaryk line of full independence. From 28 to 31 October 1918, Edouard Benes, later Masaryk's successor as President of the Czechoslovak Republic, negotiated, in neutral Geneva, the assent of politicians on the home front to the Czechoslovak National Council abroad. The Prague National Committee proclaimed its country's independence on 28 October, and this was promptly recognized by the Allies. Three days later, the sole Slovak representative in the Budapest Parliament, Turcansky Sväty Martin, proclaimed his people's secession from Hungary and union with the Czechs. The Slovaks, en masse, endorsed their self-appointed leader.

National revolution for Czechoslovakia was mostly peaceful in Prague and the Czech lands, but, as usual at this time, she had to fight to define her frontiers with neighbouring successor states. When even revolutionary Hungary refused to let the Slovaks go, the Czechs expelled Hungarians who wanted their lost province 'Upper Hungary', to be re-annexed under the international socialist, Béla Kun, and his Soviet Republic. On 21 October, the German fringe, unwilling to live in a Czech republic and claiming the right of national self-determination for themselves, had declared the independence of *'Deutschböhmen'* (German Bohemia) later known as 'the Sudetenland' and demanded *'Anschluß'* to Austria. At the same time the fledgling Czechoslovakia insisted on a maximum extent of national territory, sanctioned by historical precedent, the lands of the crown of St. Wenceslaus, in its entirety. Troops moved into the German districts and put down the threatened secession. Similarly, when Polish troops occupied the district of Teschen on the eastern border of Moravia, the Czechs threw them back, but both countries accepted Allied arbitration, dividing Teschen.

Rumania

There was no peace for Rumania either after Armistice. Just like Poland, she was a three-empire successor state: Moldavia (with Bessarabia) and Wallachia had enjoyed precarious autonomy as an Ottoman vassal state; Transylvania had come under the Habsburgs in 1699, while Bessarabia had been annexed by Russia in 1792 and 1878. Sovereign since 1878, as a post-Ottoman successor state, Rumania won the largest share of her territorial gains in 1918–19 from Austria-Hungary (Transylvania, Bukovina, parts of the Banat), the southern Dobrudja from Bulgaria, and Bessarabia from Russia. Thus, she can be counted here as a mainly post-Austro-Hungarian successor state.

Linked to the Triple Alliance in 1883, but, for fear of hostile national sentiments, only by secret treaty, Rumania had remained neutral in 1914 and joined the Allies in August 1916 in order to win Transylvania, the supreme prize. However, Rumania was swiftly defeated by the Central Powers in late 1916, and to prevent outright conquest, after the Bolsheviks had conceded Russian territory to the Germans, had to conclude the Peace Treaty of Bucharest of 7 May 1918. After Bulgaria's collapse in September 1918, however, the Rumanian Army occupied Transylvania and the Rumanian Government denounced, under Allied pressure, the Bucharest Peace and actually declared war on prostrate Hungary on 10 November, one day before the Armistice with Germany. Thus, for Rumania, the end of the Great War by armistice almost coincided with her local war against Hungary. At the same time, by January 1919, the Rumanian Army had occupied most of the territories promised to her by the Allies in return for entering the war on their side. Greater Rumania was rounded off by the re-annexation of Bessarabia, which, however, Soviet Russia and the Soviet Union never recognized and 'undid' at the earliest opportunity, in 1940, and again in 1944–46. Still, Greater Rumania, as achieved in 1918–19, remained the lodestar for Rumanian patriotism after the fall of communism in 1989–91 too.

3. POST-OTTOMAN SUCCESSOR STATES

The Ottoman Empire in its decay was another hotbed of national movements and nationalisms. The famous Eastern Question, so prominent in the nineteenth century, had raised, among others, the problem of what would happen to the non-Turkish minorities in the Ottoman Empire. After the gruesome massacres of Armenians in 1915 and 1916, and, since 1916, the Arab Revolt, final defeat in September 1918 made the Ottoman Empire ripe for dismemberment. Partition had been secretly envisaged by all the Great Powers, except Germany, which wanted to preserve the Ottoman Empire the better to rule it indirectly. After the Mudros Armistice of 30 October 1918, Allied occupation, which included Italian and Greek forces, foreshadowed the partitioning of Anatolia.

However, the end of Empire did not come so suddenly as in Russia, Austria-Hungary and Germany, but as a complicated and protracted process. In fact, the Sultan was still able to conclude the Peace of Sèvres in 1920, but it became the ultimate challenge to Turkish nationalists to overthrow the Ottoman dynasty and replace it with the new Turkish Republic under Kemal Atatürk. Even before this, however, resistance against Allied plans to carve up Anatolia had crystallized into a Turkish national liberation movement which in 1920 established Turkey, with its Grand National Assembly in Ankara, as the greatest of all Ottoman successor states. It still had large national minorities, above all the Armenians and the Kurds.

At the end of the 'War of Habsburg-Ottoman Succession', many conflicts erupted which are still with us, however transformed. One of the most persistent and spectacular sores opened by the ending of the first World War, is the Middle Eastern conflict, since 1919, between Zionism and Arab nationalism over the Holy Land. It seems likely that, today, we are approaching another phase of great tension between Israel and the autonomous Palestinian State. Elsewhere, after the Great War, the Greeks had started their 'Grand Design' to gain at least the Greek-populated parts of Anatolia, first by occupying Smyrna and its hinterland in 1919. They provoked another Greco-Turkish War 1921–22, when they tried to fill part of the huge power vacuum by pursuing their *fata morgana* of the '*megali* (Great Greece) idea', of restoring Greek imperial power in the footsteps of Alexander the Great and of Byzantium. After the 1920 Peace of Sèvres, their offensives deep into Anatolia were stopped twice by the Turkish nationalists during 1921–22, with the help of Soviet Russia. In a new peace treaty of Lausanne (1923), Greece had to accept defeat, sealed by a transfer of Turkish and Greek populations from both countries, which ended 3,000 years of Greek settlements in Asia Minor. The Yugoslav war, with its added complications of the Bosnian war, Kosovo and Macedonia, both time bombs today and for the near future, are all explosive heritages of the Ottoman Empire, made more deadly by modern nationalism. Here, only one such problem is to be looked at in relative detail – Armenia. Just in passing, the Kurds, divided after war between the Ottoman successor states – Turkey, Iraq and Syria – should also be mentioned, because their parallel tragedy continues on the contemporary scene.

Armenia

After the War of Greek Independence from 1821 to 1829, the Ottoman rulers still regarded the Armenians as the most solidly loyal *millet** of all. Soon,

---

* a religious community of proto-national character with autonomy.

82. Popular celebrations in the Czech capital, Prague, on Independence Day, 28 October 1918. (from *Rosicky, Rakousky Orel Padá*) (Chapter 19 - Austria Hungary)

83. One of the Czech national leaders, Isidor Zahradnìk joins the crowds under the statue of St. Wenceslas, Prague 28 October 1918.
(Rosicky, Rakousky Orel Padá) (Chapter 19 - Austria Hungary)

84. Crowds in Zagreb sing Croatian patriotic songs, having learned that Croatia has severed links with Austria Hungary. 29 October 1918.
(Horvat, *Politicka Povijest Hrvatske)* (Chapter 19 - Austria Hungary)

85. Austrian emissaries arrive at Osteria del Termine in Italy to sign the armistice document, 3 November 1918.
(Reproduced from *With the 48th Division in Italy,* by Lt. Col G.H. Barnett, 1923) (Chapter 20 - Italy)

86. The Austrian party reach the Italian lines, Osteria del Termine, 3 November 1918.
(Reproduced from *With the 48th Division in Italy,* by Lt. Col. G.H. Barnett, 1923) (Chapter 20 - Italy)

87. Italian troops enter Trento around 5 November 1918, shortly after the Armistice on the Italian Front. *(M. Pluviano & I. Guerrini)* (Chapter 20 - Italy)

88. Roger Vercel, author of *Capitaine Conan* published in 1934. Vercel at the time of the Armistice was in Sofia, as a French Army legal officer. He travelled extensively between Budapest, Belgrade, Odessa and Istanbul, and based his literary work on his experiences.
(Hugh Cecil) (Chapter 22 - Armistice in Literature)

89. R.H. Mottram (right), serving with the British Claims Commission (assessing the civilian claims for damage caused by the army) in Belgium, c. 1917.
(Norfolk Record Office, Mottram Collection) (Chapter 22 - Armistice in Literature)

90. Crowds gather on Armistice Day 1920 in Richmond, North Yorkshire.
(Green Howards Regimental Museum, Richmond) (Chapter 23 - A Changing Meaning)

91. A girl bends to lay flowers at the foot of the Cenotaph, while next to her a widow wears her husband's medal ribbons. 11 November 1920.
(Illustrated London News) (Chapter 23 - A Changing Meaning)

92. A service of dedication at the Royal Naval Division memorial, Beaucourt sur Ancre, on Sunday 12 November 1922. Veterans of the division, and Royal Marine bandsmen are present, while behind them the devastation of the battlefield is still apparent.
(E. Wettern, Liddle Collection) (Chapter 23 - A Changing Meaning)

93. A veteran pays his respects at Northampton war memorial, November 1962.
(Liddle Collection) (Chapter 23 - A Changing Meaning)

however, they demanded territorial autonomy as well. When this was denied, the Armenians, from 1860 onwards, rebelled repeatedly. After Turkey's defeat in the eighth Russo-Turkish War, concluded by the Congress of Berlin in 1878 averting the danger of a 'World War' between all the Great Powers, the Turks answered increasingly with a Turkish nationalism *à la française*, combining the preservation of their Empire with Turkish assimilationist nationalism; this only provoked more Armenian uprisings, to which the Turks responded with increasingly larger-scale massacres of Armenians in 1896 and 1909. During the Great War, Armenians in the Ottoman border provinces south of the Caucasus, naturally looked to fellow-Christian Russians for their liberation, which the Turks, in their turn, took as a pretext to 'punish' 'disloyal' Armenians by the most severe repression in the years 1915 and 1916 – mass deportation and murder on a grand scale, partly carried out by some Kurdish tribes – 'ethnic cleansing' on genocidal lines.

It is against that background that the fate of surviving Armenians has to be seen. Even before the war ended, they had been gravely affected by the October Revolution and the Peace of Brest-Litovsk between Russia and the Central Powers. With the victory of the Bolsheviks in Russia, the Russian Army in Transcaucasia had disintegrated, apart from about 20,000 Armenians who defended, as far as was possible, their country against the advancing Turks. After defeating a Turkish Army near Erevan, they proclaimed Armenian independence on 28 May 1918, but were crushed by the return of the Turks in overwhelming superiority, reducing Armenian 'statehood' to a weak Turkish vassal state. The Mudros Armistice and the decay of the Ottoman Empire made possible, with Western financial aid, the return to Armenia of about 200,000 survivors of the Armenian Massacres who had been stranded in far-flung regions of the Ottoman Empire. Moreover, the tiny Armenian Republic could now expand to include Armenian territories to the south within the dying Ottoman Empire. However it was overcrowded with refugees, ravaged by war, landlocked and isolated so that it was difficult for even humanitarian aid to reach a country suffering severe famine. The greatest triumph for the shortlived Armenian Republic was the signing of the Treaty of Sèvres on 10 August, 1920, by which Armenian autonomy within the still formally existing Ottoman Empire was recognized, in the same way as that of the neighbouring Kurds.

In fact this formal diplomatic success proved deceptive: in a joint operation, Kemal Atatürk's nationalist army and the Soviet Red Army attacked the Armenian Republic from two sides in November 1920 and crushed the Armenian – and Kurdish – republics. When, however, the Turkish army again stood before Erevan, the Soviets intervened and offered the northern Armenians a deal: they would be spared Turkish conquest on condition that they assented to the establishment of a Soviet Armenian Republic. This is how the Armenians survived as a small nation, even under Stalinism, while in Turkey, which never admitted the existence of other nationalities than Turkish, Armenians were wiped out by military force or enforced assimilation. Present-day Armenia is the contemporary continuation of former Soviet Armenia, amid a sea of hostile neighbours.

EPILOGUE

This glance aside at Armenia, now on the fringes of post-communist Europe, only confirms the general historical mechanisms at work in Europe at the time of the Armistice ending the First World War: the almost hopeless confusion, of Empire and Nation; of War and Revolution – both national and social – brought about through the agencies of defeat and collapse; of post-imperial successor states and successor wars. A closer look at the Armistice of 1918 with the many sequels to which it gave rise, can also help us to a better understanding of comparable situations – for all their specific differences – such as decolonization and the end of colonial empires; post-colonial successor states and successor wars; the collapse of the Soviet Empire after the Soviet-Afghan War; and the concomitant disintegration of the Titoist sub-empire after the end of the Cold War – in both cases followed by post-communist successor states and successor wars. Many more comparable situations are already with us, as in the Kosovo and Afghanistan, or in the making, as in Ethiopia.

Endnotes

1 For a more detailed, but still brief analysis of the longue durée, see Imanuel Geiss, "Great Powers and Empires: Historical Mechanisms of their Making and Breaking", in Geire Ludestad (ed.), *The Fall of Great Powers. Peace, Stability and Legitimacy*, O.U.P. and Scandinavian University Press, 1994, pp. 23–43.

2 Jan Vansina, *Kingdoms of the savanna*, Madison Wisc., University of Wisconsin Press, 1966; and id., *The Children of Woot: history of the Kuba peoples*, Madison Wisc., University of Wisconsin Press, 1978.

3 Since 1871, therefore, coming under the German Empire.

4 'Congress Poland' consists of those territories constituted as a kingdom of Poland under Romanov rule at the Congress of Vienna.

Apart from the bibliographical section at the end of this volume, the reader is directed to the following sources:

M.S. Anderson, *The Eastern Question, 1774–1923*, London: Macmillan, 1978.

Ludwig Dehio, *Hegemonie oder Gleichgewicht. Betrachtungen über ein Grundproblem der neueren Staatengeschichte*, Krefeld, 1948; new edition, Klaus Hildebrand (ed.), Stuttgart: Deutsche Verlaganstalt, 1997.

Hans Fenske, "Ungeduldige Zuschauer. Die Deutschen und die europäische Expansion 1815–1880", in Wolfgang Reinhard (ed.), *Imperialistische Kontinuität und nationale Ungeduld im 19. Jahrhundert. Geschichte*, Frankfurt am Main: Fischer, 1991.

Imanuel Geiss / Gabriele Intemann, *Der Jugoslawienkrieg*, 2nd edition, Brennpunkt Geschichte, Frankfurt: Diesterweg, 1995.

Marian Kent (ed.), *The Great Powers and the End of the Ottoman Empire*, London: Allen & Unwin, 1984.

Solomon Wank, "The Disintegration of the Habsburg and Ottoman Empires. A comparative Analysis", in Karen Dawisha, Bruce Parrott (eds.), *The End of Empire? The Transformation of the USSR in Comparative Perspective*, N.Y.: Amonk, E. Sharpe, 1997.

Chapter Sixteen

Deprivation, Desperation and Degradation: Bulgaria in Defeat

Richard Crampton

Bulgaria was the last state to join the central powers and the first to leave them when an armistice was signed with the Allies at Salonika on 29 September 1918. But despite the armistice Bulgaria's withdrawal from the war was not a clear, clean-cut affair. There was no immediate transition from war to peace, from turmoil to stability; and there was certainly no jollification or rejoicing. Instead, the signing of the armistice and the ending of the war were the culmination, though by no means the end, of a process of deprivation, desperation and degradation.

The war had never been popular. When Bulgaria entered the conflict in September 1915 the country had already had enough of fighting. In 1912 it had experienced the elation of the first Balkan war with the conquest of what were regarded as historically and ethnically Bulgarian lands in Macedonia and Thrace. In 1913 most of these gains had been lost in the second Balkan war. Just before the country entered the First World War, the leader of the largest popular party, Aleksandûr Stamboliiski of the Bulgarian Agrarian National Union (BANU), had told King Ferdinand that if he joined the conflict it would cost him his throne. For his impertinence Stamboliiski spent the war in prison. Impertinent Stamboliiski may have been, but he was right.

Nevertheless, the war began well for Bulgaria. Alliance with the Ottoman empire meant the gain of some territory in Thrace, the defeat of Serbia meant the occupation of most of Vardar Macedonia, and the elimination of Romania in 1916–17 placed some of the Dobrudja under Bulgarian control. The fact that Bulgaria was in occupation of former enemy territory meant that Sofia, like Berlin, saw little reason to contemplate peace. It also meant that, like its counterparts in Berlin and Vienna, the government in Sofia refused to take sufficient account of the growing social problems affecting the country.

The critical issue was supplies. In this Bulgaria was not unique but the problem in this Balkan state was particularly acute for particular Balkan reasons. The main deployment of Bulgarian forces was in Macedonia and Thrace along a six-hundred kilometre front. The front was relatively easy to defend but its length demanded huge investments of man-power. This, together with the commitment to fighting on the northern front against Romania, meant that Bulgaria mobilized 850,000 men, which represented 19.52% of the entire population and no less than 38.83% of the adult male population, which, Bulgarians have claimed, was the highest figure for any of the countries involved in the First World War.[1] Nor was it only men that were mobilized. The Macedonian front ran mainly along the foothills of the Pirin and Rhodope mountains, an area with almost no modern infrastructure. The huge armies could be supplied for the most part only by carts or even pack animals. By 1917 a quarter of a million draft animals had been taken by the military; the number of such animals left for civilian use was then 22% below the pre-mobilization level, and almost a quarter (24%) of carts had been requisitioned; whereas in 1910 one pair of Bulgarian draft animals worked an average of 58.1 dekars of land, in 1917 the figure was 74.5 dekars. The loss of men and of animals meant that work in the fields had to be carried out mainly by women, children and old men and frequently the work had to be done without the customary draft animals. A contemporary observer reported even in the early stages of the war: "one could see with one's own eyes that the fields contained only women who, surrounded by their numerous children, were ploughing, sowing, reaping, carrying the hay, threshing and so forth...".[2]

The problem was compounded by the activities of the Germans and Austrians. They had been given extensive rights to purchase food, an activity much facilitated by the fact that German currency was legal tender in Bulgaria after December 1915. The Germans were able to pay what were by Bulgarian standards huge prices for food. As scarcity developed at home in Germany the incentive to buy or confiscate in Bulgaria increased; and the opportunity to do so also increased as German units criss-crossed the country installing a new telephone system which the Germans controlled. German acquisitions included not just food but also clothing. By 1918 the Germans had set up a special railway station at Nadezhda, south of Sofia, which was off limits to Bulgarians; here the Germans loaded food and clothes they had acquired in Bulgaria.[3] There was even a special Bulgarian workshop to manufacture the cartons the Germans used to transport these items.[4]

The Bulgarian government attempted to overcome the declining supply situation by establishing a series of authorities, concentrating power at the centre. Military control was also experimented with, but by 1917 this had patently failed and the Directorate of Economic and Social Affairs had been entrusted with the gathering and distribution of food and non-military essentials.[5]

The first food shortages were felt in Sofia in late 1916. Early in 1917 army units had to be called in to persuade peasants to part with food. In April of that year General Protogerov reported that the situation in the army was "critical" with a daily supply of 1,000 tons of grain as opposed to the 1,250 tons that were needed;[6] soldiers on leave were not going home but to areas in northern Bulgaria where food was said to be plentiful so that they might purchase food for their families.[7] Deaths from starvation were reported in western and southern Bulgaria but the situation was far worse in occupied Macedonia and Thrace where in the winter of 1916–17 there had been "thousands of cases of death by starvation".[8]

In 1918 conditions had graduated from "critical" to "hopeless".[9] Figures for the production of grain in quintals per hundred of population tell their own stark story: 1911 – 653.1; 1912 – 589.2; 1913 – 539.6; 1914 – 407.6; 1915 – 482.0; 1916 – 368.1; 1917 – 348.4; 1918 – 241.0.[10] There was little the authorities could do to increase supplies either from internal or external sources. Troops were again used to collect food but this time those employed were taken from the front line in an effort to convince the peasants that what they relinquished would go to the fighting men and not to speculators or for export to Germany. It made little difference. By January 1918 military commanders had scoured the richer agricultural areas; wheat had become all but unobtainable and there was enough maize only until May.[11] There was no alternative but to import food. The end of the war with Russia had raised hopes that supplies might be secured from the Ukraine, but such hopes were soon dashed, the Germans and the Austrians securing a virtual monopoly over produce from that area. As shortages increased, prices rocketed which in turn greatly strengthened the impulse to hoard; in fact few peasants had enough reserves left to hoard but the psychosis of price rises was difficult to dislodge; at one point the Germans even suggested sending trains made up of empty vans from the Ukraine to Bulgaria to make the peasants think that food was being imported.[12] Hopes that the Dobrudja, conquered from Romania in 1916, might provide much needed food were also dashed. The treaty of Bucharest in May 1918 gave Bulgaria sole control over only the relatively infertile northern Dobrudja; the rich southern half was to be under joint German, Austrian and Bulgarian administration, which meant in effect that the Germans and the Austrians took the lion's share of the region's available food reserves.

The quality as well as the quantity of food declined. Bread had to be made from maize or even barley at times. It was coarse and frequently had harmful effects upon those who had to eat it; on 9 July 1918, the head of the censorship section of the General Staff recorded that the bread in Sofia was so bad that it caused "indescribable ... vomiting".[13] Deaths from hunger in Bulgaria in 1918 were, according to one estimate, 182,000 more than the total number of fatalities at the front during the entire war.[14]

Clothing as well as food became ever more difficult to come by. The mobilization of men working in the many small clothing workshops had disrupted supplies, just as general mobilization of men and animals dislocated distribution. And once again the German purchasing agencies were at work. In February 1917 an enquiry in Sofia found that no more than 58% of schoolchildren had their own clothes, 21% came to school in other children's clothes, and a further 21% frequently had to stay away from school because they had no clothes at all.[15] As a sheep-rearing nation Bulgaria produced before the war around 12 million kilograms of wool; but, because of the disruptions of the war and the activities of the German purchasing agencies, in 1917 government procurement officers could secure for domestic use no more than 1.5 million kilograms. The amount doubled in 1918 but by then serious shortages had affected soldier and civilian alike.[16]

As the situation deteriorated, discontent rose. It was expressed by both the civilian population and by the soldiery; the conjunction of the two discontents in the late summer of 1918 precipitated the final collapse of the Bulgarian army. Rising discontent was fuelled by political events as well as by social deprivation. In June the Radoslavov government, which had taken the country to war in 1915, resigned, partly in protest against the treaty of Bucharest. It was widely expected that the new government, headed by the Democratic Party leader, Aleksandûr Malinov, would conclude peace with the Allies. It did not, declaring instead its readiness to pursue the war "to victory". It even sent ministers and MPs to the front line to exhort the troops to greater efforts.[17]

Just as it was women who had been left to bear the burden of work in the fields, so it was with them that the first serious protests began. On 25 February, a crowd of about two hundred women attacked the offices of the Directorate for Economic and Social Affairs in the town of Stanimaka: they demanded an increase in rations and the return of their menfolk. The disorders increased and spread; what was later termed the "women's revolt" had begun. By May it had reached the larger urban centres: on 14 May there were demonstrations in Sofia, on 15 May in Sliven where troops had to be used to restore order, and on 20 May three women were killed when the mayor of Plovdiv fired at women demonstrating in the city. The demands of the demonstrators usually included 'Bread and Peace'; they always included the demand for the return of the men from the front.[18] By August protests by semi-starved women had become a daily occurrence.[19] Other instances of popular anger included the stoning in May near Plovdiv of the train carrying the Emperor Karl and the Empress Zita.[20]

At the front, unrest was growing in equal measure. The military had long been feeling the impact of the intensifying supply crisis. In May 1917 the 11th Army in the mountains of north-western Bulgaria and eastern Serbia was receiving only three quarters of its daily need for flour which therefore had to be adulterated. The shortfall in maize was nearer 60%, in butter 77% and in meat 98%. The only commodity of which there was no shortage was tobacco; but there was almost no decent cigarette paper.[21] As on the home front, conditions deteriorated seriously in 1918. By the summer of 1918 the daily bread ration for the main fighting units on the southern front had been cut to 400 grams per day. Most of this bread was made from flour produced from maize or barley; it looked like the manure briquettes the peasants used to heat their stoves in the winter.[22] It was not merely food that was in short supply. From May 1917 to May 1918 the army received only 10 percent of its needs for fodder, only 9 percent of the greatcoats, 2 percent of the tunics and 2.5 percent of the boots it had ordered.[23]

An aggravating factor for many soldiers was the contrast between their own condition and that of the Germans in nearby trenches. German soldiers were better fed, both in terms of quality and quantity, better clad, better shod, and better supplied with shells and ammunition; they even had ample supplies of good Bulgarian-made cigarette paper. More importantly, the Bulgarian soldier knew that much of the food, especially the wheat flour, available to the Germans also came from Bulgarian sources. Another difference between the Bulgarian soldiers and their German allies was that in the trenches German officers had the same food as their men; in the Bulgarian army most officers were able to procure more and better food from within the country and their pay was docked in advance to allow for this.[24] Even the enemy appeared better off. One Bulgarian officer recalled after capturing and then releasing a few Serbian soldiers: "I took a good look at those prisoners. They were well-dressed ... had new uniforms and fine shoes, and were well-fed".[25] It was not unusual at that time for Bulgarian soldiers to go into action barefoot or with clothing and boots borrowed from other units.[26]

The soldiers were not slow to show their rising anger. Disobedience in parts of the 27th Chepinski Regiment in June reached the level of virtual mutiny.[27] After the MPs and ministers' visit to the front, the government stated publicly that it did not consider conditions to be as bad as the press had made out. This caused a serious decline in discipline both at the front and amongst troops at the rear. A senior official of the Chief Home Administration, when returning from Lovech to Sofia in July, met a crowd of about 300 soldiers from the 9th Pleven Infantry Division who were on leave; they insisted that if peace were not declared by 15 September, the third anniversary of Bulgaria's entry into the war, they would desert and when the official tried to remonstrate with them he was nearly lynched. In the same month General Salabashev heard soldiers from one regiment complaining to those from another that their commander was a rigid disciplinarian given to handing out frequent punishments; the men from the second regiment replied that they had had a similar problem with their commanding officer but they had "bumped him off" and since then had been left alone.[28]

The desertion rate had been growing steadily in 1918 and was particularly high in June and July, the harvest months. In August the 2nd Thracian Infantry Division alone registered 433 NCOs absent without leave: 242 had failed to return from leave, 177 had fled into the interior of Bulgaria, and 14 had gone over to the enemy; and this despite measures against deserters so draconian that they included the internment of the families of the missing men.[29] At the end of August the commander in chief, General Zhekov, described the situation at the front as "very serious".[30]

The most serious danger of all for Bulgaria was the conjunction of domestic and military discontents. In the records of the army censorship authorities from the spring of 1918, there are increasing calls from wives and mothers to their men to abandon the war. After describing the situation at home, one peasant woman urged her husband, "Toma, leave the front and come and see what we are having to put up with"; on a postcard from the village of Tserovo in the Pazardjik region came the desperate cry: "What are you waiting for? Throw away your guns ... your children are dying of starvation".[31] Knowledge of the declining conditions at home was increased when soldiers went on leave in the early summer to help with the harvest. On 22 June during a tour of the front Zhekov and the crown prince, soon to become King Boris

III, were almost attacked by soldiers one of whom reported later, "We are naked, bare-footed and hungry ... It's tough here but we can stand it; what we cannot bear is what is happening in our villages".[32]

Shortly before he was killed on the Macedonian front, a Colonel Drangov had written, "an empty knapsack does not guard a frontier"* and the effect of massive deprivation and the suffering of families at home sapped the morale of the army. Yet that army did not collapse until subjected to an assault so overwhelming that it is doubtful if even an army in the best of fettle could have withstood it. At 7 a.m. on 14 September at Dobro Pole the Allies began a huge artillery barrage which lasted almost twenty-four hours. On 15 September a large scale infantry assault was launched. The Bulgarians could not withstand such numbers and by the end of that day a gap twenty kilometres wide and fifteen kilometres deep had been opened up in the Bulgarian front. The Bulgarians fell back towards the pre-war border but they were broken and no longer able to defend even the core of their homeland.

Morale now collapsed completely. The officer mentioned earlier who had ruefully inspected and then released his Serbian prisoners saw widespread, indiscriminate looting, ever a sign of the total disintegration of discipline; "One of my men", he recalled sadly, "took nine pairs of shoes. He was a Bulgarian from Macedonia. Not one of these soldiers gave a thought to the fact that they were ruining and robbing their fellow Bulgarians ...".[33]

By 24 September the army itself was disintegrating and rebel units appeared at General Staff Headquarters in Kiustendil. Events now moved rapidly on the political front. On 23 September Stamboliiski had been asked to form a government and had agreed to do so on condition that all political detainees be released and that he be given a free hand to conclude a peace. These conditions were refused but Stamboliiski himself was released from prison on 25 September. On that same morning the cabinet met and decided to ask for an armistice and later in the day a delegation, headed by Andrei Liapchev and accompanied by the US minister in Sofia, set out for Salonika.

Whilst this was happening more and more armed units were going over to the mutineers who were congregating in the town of Radomir to the south-west of Sofia. On 26 September Stamboliiski himself set out for Radomir where he tried, in vain, to persuade the soldiers to return to the front, his objectives being perhaps to stabilize the military situation, secure an armistice and then turn upon and depose the King and the government. But the rebellious soldiers refused to listen and instead set out from Radomir to Vladaya, and so confident were they of mass support, military and civilian, that they did not bother to take with them any heavy weapons. It was a mistake. The government had rallied military cadets and some loyal troops under Protogerov, and, with German help, had brought men from the German 217th Infantry Division in Ukraine to Varna and then to Sofia. On 28 September the rebels issued an ultimatum to the government: resign or the rebels would march on Sofia. On 29 September Ferdinand declared a state of

---

* In Bulgarian this is a neat and pithy word-play: 'Prazna ranitsa ne pazi granitsa'.

Д. Н. Фурнаджиевъ.

Прѣдседатель Уилсонъ

Лични спомени

Да се прѣцѣни колко великъ е днесъ г. Удроу Уилсонъ, прѣдседатель на сѣверо-американскитѣ Щати, е невъзможно. Нѣма съмнѣние, обаче, че историята ще впише неговото име между най-великитѣ. За единъ американецъ името Уашингтонъ е най-великото име въ тѣхната история. Той е билъ „първъ въ война, първъ въ миръ и първъ въ сърдцата на

даде или да поиска освѣтление. На студентитѣ той бѣше личенъ приятель, и всички цѣнѣхме високо скжпото му приятелство.

Професоръ д-ръ Уилсонъ е твърдѣ благочестивъ човѣкъ. До избора му за прѣдседатель на Щатитѣ той бѣше дяконъ въ Презвитерианската църква. Въ убѣжденията си той е много силенъ и положителенъ, но и мно-

ла; студентитѣ вземаха участие чрѣзъ свои прѣдставители въ прилагане дисциплината; тѣ участвуваха въ сжденe студенти, които сж нарушили законитѣ на университета, и пр.

Когато доказа способноститѣ си като професоръ, и като администраторъ, като човѣкъ съ прѣвъзходни принципи, самъ честенъ до съвършенство, искренъ, откровенъ безстрашенъ борецъ за правдата и противъ корупцията; по това врѣме щатътъ Ню Джерсей търсѣше губернаторъ, който да прочисти политическия му животъ и поведе готовитѣ му сили въ полезни насоки, Нѣмаше по-добръ отъ Удроу Уилсонъ. Реформитѣ, които неочакваният губернаторъ въведе въ цѣлия щатъ, напълно оправдаха очакванията на приятелитѣ му. До тамъ праведно поведе работитѣ на тази малката държавица, щото отстрани отъ собствената си партия всички провинени водители и други съ съмнителни мотиви.

Тия сж стжпалата, по които г. Уилсонъ се издигна до Прѣдседатель и бѣ избранъ втори пжть за такъвъ. Партизани отъ противнитѣ партии сж гласували за Уилсона, защото вѣрватъ въ достойнството и способността му; Той е демократъ, но хора отъ републиканската партия сж молитствували и работили за избора на Уилсона като прѣдседатель на щатитѣ.

Споредъ насъ г. Уилсонъ е игралъ досега една съвсѣмъ оправдателна роль въ тоя всесвѣтски конфликтъ. Въпрѣки изказани мнѣния въ сената и конгреса, г. Уилсонъ не обяви война на България. Кой е причината на това? Възможно е, че г. Мърфи въ София и господинъ Панаретовъ въ Вашингтонъ заслужаватъ голѣмата признателность на българския народъ, за когото сж работили вѣрно и неуморно прѣдъ г. Уилсона, но щомъ той е устоялъ противъ агитациитѣ и силни наблѣги и отъ страна на неговитѣ съюзници, това е доказъ, че г. Уилсонъ не се води отъ тѣсногърди схващания и егоистични цѣли въ тая война, а е напълно рѣшенъ да използува влиянието и положението си за правда и условия за траенъ миръ на свѣта.

Великъ е народътъ, когото г. Уилсонъ прѣдставлява, и велики сж идеалитѣ съ които самъ той се вдъхновява. Думитѣ му сж за правда и миръ, и той ще изпъл-

xxxi A picture of Woodrow Wilson, published in the Sofia newspaper *Mir* on 24 October 1918, accompanying an admiring article by a Bulgarian who once studied under him at Princeton: "In the person of President Wilson" the author writes hopefully, "America will speak up for justice in the Balkans. Have we stated our case clearly and precisely to him? Let us not delay". (via Richard Crampton) siege in the capital as between six and seven thousand rebels fought their way to Vladaya on its outskirts. Their leader then decided to leave until the morrow his assault upon the city. It was another mistake because on 29 September an armistice was signed in Salonika. Government planes then dropped leaflets to the rebel troops asking them why they wanted to continue fighting when an armistice had been concluded and why they wanted to stay in uniform when they were free to go home. Many did indeed go home forthwith and those who remained were decisively defeated by government forces on 30 September. On 2 October the delegates returned from Salonika and summoned the cabinet. It was decided that Ferdinand must abdicate – which he did the following day.

Neither the departure of Ferdinand, nor the advent of relative political stability, meant an end to the Bulgarians' discomforts. Further tribulations, especially in urban centres, were imposed by steps taken in late October to limit the ravages of Spanish influenza, measures which were all the more necessary because demobilized soldiers were streaming through the towns on their way home. On 24 October, the mayor of Sofia imposed a ban on the sale of certain foodstuffs, including roast sheeps' heads and sausages, whilst on the same day the Directorate of Public Health announced the temporary closure, throughout the country, of every place where the public might congregate in appreciable numbers; these included all schools, theatres, cinemas, cafés, bars, and pubs.[34]

The coming of peace had therefore been a violent process. It had been a peace born of defeat not victory; it was a peace which presaged occupation rather than deliverance; and it was a peace which offered no prospect of security or material improvement. Given these conditions and the political chaos which surrounded them, it was hardly surprising that the conclusion of the war brought no celebrations. The officer whom we followed from the release of his Serbian prisoners to his depressing retreat through Macedonia was in Kiustendil when news of the armistice came through. Though no details were yet known, he wrote, "Everyone understood that there would be no more fighting, but there was no feeling of joy or excitement amongst the men".[35] At one point his unit marched through the town with a military band but once again there was apathy and "Apart from the children no one took any notice of us ... "[36] Nor did peace bring an immediate end to disorder. In Nevrokop the leader of the local Directorate reported that rebels had threatened to kill all local officials associated with the committee; in the town of Sopot disorderly soldiers threw grenades, and on the road to Orhanie there were about a thousand disorganized but armed soldiers in groups of thirty to forty. Not till 15 October was the whole country safe from the violence committed by such groups, and not till 4 November was the state of siege in Sofia lifted.[37]

The appalling shortages and the price inflation which inevitably accompanied them lasted much longer. The harvest of 1918 had proved one of the worst on record and had it not been for the emergency import of American wheat in 1919 Bulgaria would have faced wholesale famine. As it was, the price of a kilogram of wheat-bread rose during 1919 from 1.08 leva to 3.55

leva; the price of pork increased from 7.57 to 31.90 leva, that of beef from 3.45 to 12.92 leva, of sugar from 3.61 to 37.60 leva and that of milk from 2.09 to 5.37 leva per litre. For most families such increases enforced a near-subsistence standard of living.

On the political front the war had discredited the old established parties. Waiting in the wings were the radical forces of the agrarians and the communists. They conducted their battle partly in the polling booth but also on the streets with the major confrontation coming with a communist-backed general strike at the end of 1919. Tough policies by the agrarians ensured that it was they rather than the communists who would dominate the immediate post-war years.[38]

Immediately after the armistice and the restoration of order, Allied troops had begun to occupy Bulgaria. These troops were provided in the main by Italy and France, together with a small contribution from Great Britain. The Italians were concentrated around Sofia, the British on the coast near Varna and the French, one of whose two divisions was composed of colonial troops, took responsibility for the remainder. Some Allied forces were to remain in the country until 1927. Representatives of the Allied reparations commission were also present until the second half of the 1920s. As in all occupations there were examples of misconduct and instances of fraternization. The latter were frowned upon as a number of Italian officers in the port of Dedeagach discovered after they had allowed a Bulgarian military band to enliven their evening, an evening which ended with cries from all concerned of "Vive l'Italie, vive la Bulgarie!"[39]

Much more palpable as a new presence in Bulgaria after the peace were the refugees. In the past Bulgaria had received and treated well many groups of refugees, including Jews from Romania and Russia, Armenians from the Ottoman empire, and political refugees such as sailors from the Potemkin, but most numerous had been fellow-Bulgarians from areas excluded from the Bulgarian state. Never before, however, had refugees appeared in such numbers and by the early 1920s they totalled some 450,000. There were 220,000 from Thrace, 20,000 from the Dobrudja, 11,000 from the western territories handed to Yugoslavia by the peace treaty, and 200,000 from Macedonia. Bulgaria also received a significant number of White Russians who at one time constituted the largest armed force in the land.

The refugees placed an enormous burden on the slender financial resources of the country and in 1926 Bulgaria was granted a League of Nations loan in order to help it settle and succour them. Amongst the incomers were many Macedonians with an implacable determination to overthrow the new Yugoslav or Greek authorities in their homeland. Some factions of them formed an integral part of the conspiracy which in June 1923 overthrew Stamboliiski's radical agrarian government. The incoming Macedonians also gave a boost to the activities of the Bulgarian masonic lodges as, to some extent, did Allied personnel and officers of the occupying armies, particularly the Italians. On occasion this may have been to the advantage of the Bulgarians; British masons on the reparations committee, for example, attended meetings of the Grand Lodge of Bulgaria in 1921 and were thought to have passed information on reparations negotiations to their Bulgarian fellow masons.[40]

The refugees from the Dobrudja, Thrace, the western territories and above all Macedonia were a constant reminder in post war years of Bulgaria's defeat. But the defeat was not merely a military one. The occupation of Macedonia and Thrace by Serbia and Greece seemed to spell the end of Bulgarian aspirations to those areas. The new occupiers would have little truck with any vestiges of Bulgarian culture. In western Thrace the Metropolitan of Giumiurdjina issued an order on 29 March 1920 requiring the Bulgarians to remove from Greek graveyards the bones of all relatives who had died in the preceding three years; if they were not removed they would be dug up. The French made the Metropolitan rescind the order on grounds of health,[41] but it was an indication of the cultural pressures Bulgarians in the lost territories were to endure.

At the close of the war, writes an American historian, "Bitterness settled over Sofia like the city's winter fog."[42] That bitterness was kept sharp by continued economic privation but when even that had passed the refugees helped to sustain the longing for the lost territories. When the next opportunity to regain those territories presented itself in 1941 it proved too tempting to resist. The results were equally fateful; as Churchill was to remark, "Three times in my life has this wretched Bulgaria subjected a peasant population to all the pangs of war and chastisements of defeat."[43]

Endnotes

1 Hristo Hristov, *Revoliutsionnata Kriza v Bûlgariya, 1918–1919*, BAN, Institut za bûlgarskata Istoriya, Sofia 1957, p. 15. Despite its inevitable ideological colouring Hristov's book remains the best source for the events of 1918–1919. Much of its treatment of discontent, civil and military, is based on the archives of the military censorship department.

2 Stiliyan Kovachev, *Zapiski na General na Pehotata, 1876–1918*, Voenno-istoricheski Kompleks "Sv Georgii Pobedonosets," Sofia 1992, pp. 166–7.

3 *ibid*, pp. 179–80.

4 Hristov *op. cit.*, p. 23.

5 For the economic and social impact of the First World War in Bulgaria, and for the government's attempts to regulate the economy and society see Richard J. Crampton, *Bulgaria 1878–1918: A History*, East European Monographs no.138, Boulder, Colorado and New York 1983, pp. 473–510.

6 Hristov *op. cit.*, pp. 26–7.

7 *ibid*, pp. 26–7.

8 *ibid*, p. 37.

9 A word used by a responsible civilian official attached to the general staff. *Ibid*, p. 187.

10 *ibid*, p. 18.

11 Kovachev *op. cit.*, pp. 170–1.

12 *ibid*, pp. 175–6.

13 Hristov, *op. cit.*, p. 188.

14 I. Draev, *Bûlgarskata Osemnadeseta Godina*, Sofia 1970, p. 13.

15 Hristov, *op. cit.*, p. 33.

16 Kovachev, *op. cit.*, pp. 182–3.

17 Yono Mitev, 'Voinishkoto Vûstanie v Bûlgariya prez septemvri 1918 i Uchastieto na germanskite voiski v negovoto Potushavane', in Hristo Hristov et al (eds), *Bûlgarsko-Germanskite Otnosheniya i Vrûzki; Izsledvaniya i Materiali*, vol.i, BAN, Sofia 1972, pp. 279–93, see p. 282.
18 Hristov, *op. cit.*, pp. 198–206.
19 Liubomir Ognyanov, *Voinishkoto Vûstanie 1918*, Nauka i Izkustvo, Sofia 1988, p. 85.
20 Kovachev, *op. cit.*, p. 153.
21 *ibid*, pp. 168–70.
22 *ibid*, pp. 177–8.
23 *ibid*, pp. 183–4.
24 Podpolkovnik o.z. Stoyan Iliev, *Iz Spomenite Mi*, Voennoizdatelski Kompleks, "Sv Georgi Pobedonosets", Sofia 1993, p. 72.
25 *ibid*, p. 65.
26 Hristov, *op. cit.*, p. 196.
27 *ibid*, *op. cit.*, pp. 207–8.
28 Kovachev, *op. cit.*, pp. 156–7.
29 Ognyanov, *op. cit.*, pp. 89–90.
30 Hristov, *op. cit.*, p. 253.
31 *ibid*, *op. cit.*, p. 192.
32 *ibid*, pp. 247–8.
33 Iliev, *op. cit.*, p. 62.
34 *Mir*, 24 October 1918.
35 Iliev op cit., p. 69.
36 *ibid*, p. 70.
37 Ognyanov, *op. cit.*, pp. 148–52.
38 An excellent source for the rule of the agrarian government is, John D. Bell, *Peasants in Power. Alexander Stamboliski and the Bulgarian Agrarian National Union, 1899–1923*, Princeton University Press 1977, especially chapters v-vii.
39 E.L. Woodward and Rohan Butler (eds), *Documents on British Foreign Policy 1919–1939*, 1st series, vol. 1, 131n. 1.
40 Velichko Georgiev, *Masonstvoto v Bûlgariya. Pronikvane, organizatsiya, razvitie in rolya do sredata na tridesette godini na xx vek*, Nauka in Izkustvo, Sofia 1986, 29,140.
41 Staiko Todorov, *Antantata v Trakiya 1919–1920*, Universitetsko Izdatelstvo "Kliment Ohridski", Sofia 1989, p. 227.
42 John R. Lampe, *The Bulgarian Economy in the Twentieth Century*, Croom Helm, London and Sydney 1986, p. 49.
43 In the House of Commons, 2 August 1944.

Chapter Seventeen

The Ottoman Empire and the Armistice of Mudros

Erik Zürcher

Each year Turkey has a day of national mourning on the tenth of November. This, however, has nothing to do with the celebrations and commemorations going on all over Europe one day later. The tenth is the anniversary of Mustafa Kemal Pasha Atatürk (1881–1938), Turkey's first president and the eleventh of November carries no special meaning in the Turkish collective memory.

For the Ottoman Empire the end of the First World War came on 31 October 1918. It was triggered by the almost simultaneous collapse of the Macedonian and the Palestinian fronts. The Allied attack on the Macedonian front, which started on 15 September, resulted in a breakthrough when whole regiments in the Bulgarian army simply left the trenches and revolted. Two weeks later, on 29 September, Bulgaria was forced to sign an unconditional armistice, that is to say: with the terms to be established unilaterally by the Allies. The collapse of the Bulgarian front left European Turkey, including the Dardanelles and the capital Constantinople, open to attack and the Ottomans had no means of defence left as this section of the front was held by less than five weak divisions.[1]

On the Palestinian front, Allenby's forces had broken through on 19 September. The Ottoman forces had to beat a hasty retreat to the north of Aleppo, losing two thirds of their strength.[2] While it was these two collapses which, in the end, made the Ottoman military position untenable, it can be said that the real cause of the collapse was total exhaustion. The Ottoman Empire was essentially an agricultural state which had thrown itself wholesale into something which turned out to be an industrialized war. The result was that, while the empire proved able to put a large and fairly modern conscripted army into the field, it was not really capable of supporting it adequately. Means of transport were completely insufficient. Troops had to be moved on foot and supplies by ox-cart or truck over primitive roads, often took weeks for their journey. As a result, food, clothing (especially shoes) and medical care were totally inadequate, especially on the more distant fronts.

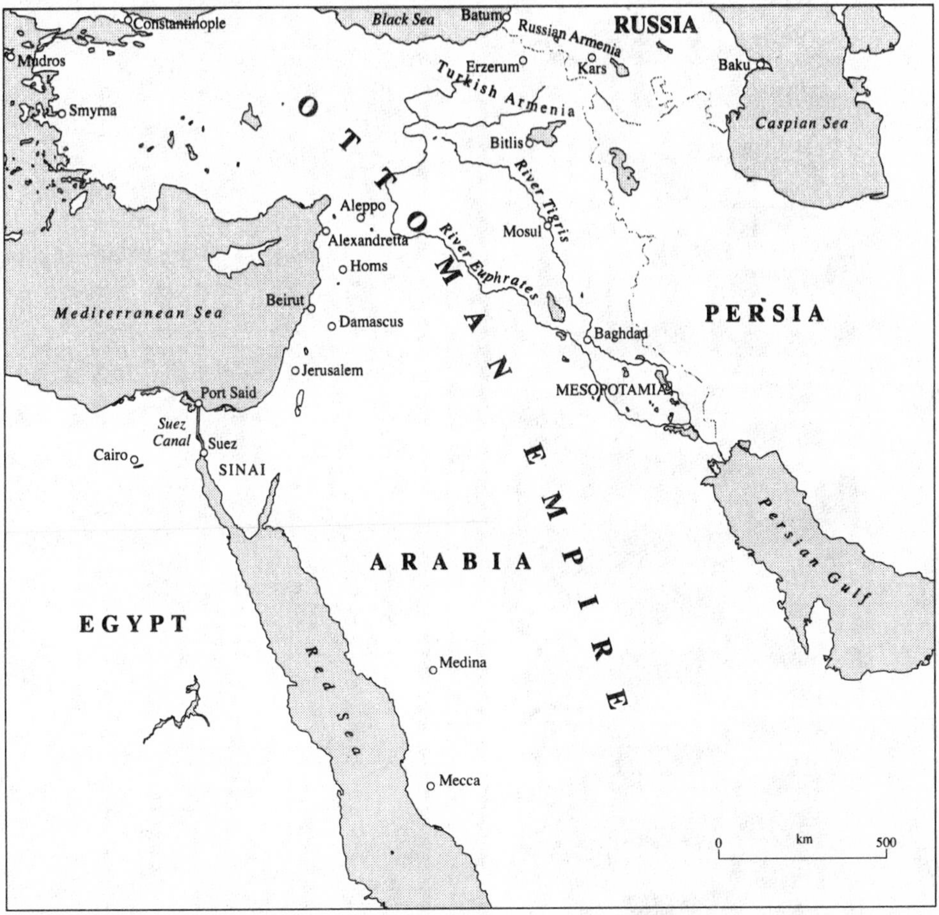

The Ottoman Empire in the Middle East, and bordering territories of the former Russian Empire, November 1918–1920

Armee-Zeitung JILDIRIM

یلدیرم اردو غزته سی

Nr. 36 — **Damaskus, Donnerstag, den 19. September 1918** — **1. Jahrgang**

Die Westfront.

Es wird uns geschrieben:

Im Höhepunkt des Kampfes kann von Frieden nicht gesprochen werden. Dass aber jedes Volk, wie auch immer die Worte seiner Regierung klingen mögen, im Innersten des Herzens den Frieden erwünscht und Friedensmöglichkeiten abwägt, darüber kann kein Zweifel bestehen. Denn nicht nur bei uns herrschen Lebensmittel- und Rohstoffmangel, die das Leben zu Hause schwer machen. Wer Briefe aus England

Man darf nicht vergessen, dass wir diese Taktik bei unserem Siegfriedrückmarsch im März 1917 bereits erprobt haben; jeder, der damals dabei war, weiss, wie leicht er sich für uns gestaltete, wie schwierig dagegen für den Feind, obgleich ihm unsere Bewegung nicht unerwartet kam und er zwischen Roye und Noyon zum Angriff bereit stand. Man vergisst zu leicht, dass wir unser jetziges Ausweichen in genau dem gleichen Abschnitt vornehmen wie damals, dass alle damaligen Massnahmen jetzt also nur zu wiederholen waren. Welche Entlastung und Sicherheit vom Armee- bis zum Kompagnieführer allein durch das Ge-

Feind mit blinder Gewalt und mit schweren eigenen Verlusten angreift. Zweck unserer Kriegführung war und ist immer geblieben, den Feind sich mehr abnutzen zu lassen als uns, und seiner Menschenkraft Schaden zuzufügen durch eine Kampfart, die es ihm nicht gestattet, sein überlegenes Material zur vollen Geltung zu bringen. Der Feind wird seiner angeblich errungenen Siege, die lediglich auf den unvermeidlichen Anfangserfolgen beruhen, nicht froh. Wir erachten den Geländebesitz als ein Nichts, solange wir dadurch unsere Truppen uns erhalten und die feindlichen sich zermürben. Dies sei vor allen Dingen

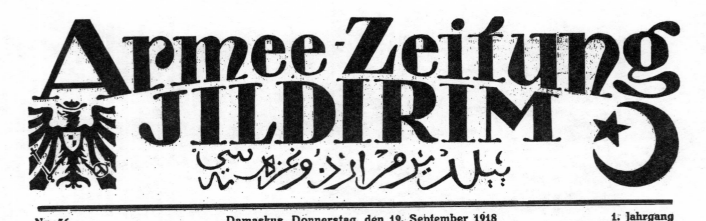

xxxii A daily newspaper produced in Damascus for the officers of the Turko-German army in Palestine. It was the collapse of this army, in the face of Allenby's advance in September 1918, which in part precipitated the Ottoman request for an Armistice. (Liddle Collection)

Diseases like typhus and cholera spread like wildfire, while malaria and scurvy were omnipresent. The conditions in the army affected morale to the extent that, by the end of the war, deserters from the army numbered over 400,000, most of whom had deserted on the way to the front. In October 1918, the army numbered about 100,000 men, or only 15 per cent of its peak strength reached in early 1916.[3]

Conditions in the army were very bad, but, as the needs of the army overrode everything else, the living conditions of the civilian population were if anything worse. Official consumer price inflation during the war was 400 per cent, but many articles were available on the black market only, where prices were, of course, much higher.[4] Shortages of food and fuel made life particularly hard in the cities. Apart from the 'normal' dislocation brought about by the war and mobilization, the persecution of the Armenian and Greek communities also had a detrimental effect on the economy, as the commercial and professional middle classes of the empire hailed to a great extent from these communities.

To sum up the situation: by mid–1918 the empire was exhausted militarily, economically, financially and morally. Public discontent, especially with the visible corruption and profiteering on the part of the protégés of the ruling Committee of Union and Progress (C.U.P.), was rising fast. The Committee recognized this and reacted by lifting political censorship and relaxing its hold over parliament, to allow criticism of profiteers and corrupt officials to be vented.[5]

The breakthrough in Macedonia convinced the Young Turk leadership, and especially Grand Vizier Talât Pasha (who had witnessed the chaos in Bulgaria on his return from Berlin) that the war was lost. The cabinet decided to ask for an armistice and, pinning its hopes on President Wilson's "Fourteen Points", it approached the Americans through Spain's mediation on 5 October. When no reply was received and the British and French troops in Thrace kept moving steadily forward, approaching the Maritza river, the Young Turk cabinet resigned on 8 October. It was succeeded by a cabinet headed by one of the Ottoman Empire's top military officers, Marshal Ahmet İzzet Pasha [Furgaç],[6] who was trusted by the Young Turks as a nationalist, but had never been a member of the C.U.P. himself. His cabinet, which took office on 14 October, was politically neutral and included a small number of important C.U.P. politicians, but none of the people who were closely identified with the war-time policies of the committee.

The new cabinet immediately made another attempt to open negotiations with the Allies, this time by sending General Townshend, who had been held as a prisoner of war on the island of Prinkipo near Constantinople since the fall of Kut in 1916, to meet with Admiral Calthorpe, in command of the Royal Navy in the Eastern Mediterranean. Calthorpe's squadron lay at anchor in Mudros harbour on the island of Lemnos. Five days after the start of Townshend's mission, on 23 October, Calthorpe informed the Ottoman government that he was empowered to negotiate on behalf of the Allies. That he was given this power in spite of the fact that the supreme naval command in the Mediterranean had been in French hands throughout the war, amounted to recognition of Britain's dominant role in the Ottoman war theatre.

The next day, the Ottoman delegation, consisting of Lieutenant-Colonel Sadullah Bey, Chief of Staff of the 8th Army, Reshad Hikmet Bey, from the Foreign Office, and Hüseyin Rauf Bey, Minister of Marine and head of the delegation, left for Mudros, where they arrived on 26 October. The Ottoman delegates were armed with cabinet instructions, which, considering the hopeless situation of the Ottoman army, seemed to display a certain lack of realism. They agreed to the opening of the Straits, but demanded that foreign warships should not remain in the Sea of Marmara for more than a day; they claimed full responsibility for the maintenance of law and order and rejected any foreign interference and the landing of troops; they demanded the preservation of the Sultanate and Caliphate and accepted only administrative, but not political, Allied control in the occupied (that is: Arab) provinces, and they even demanded financial assistance for the Empire.[7]

The actual negotiations took place aboard Calthorpe's flagship, *H.M.S. Agamemnon*, in Mudros harbour. Although the admiral made it known right

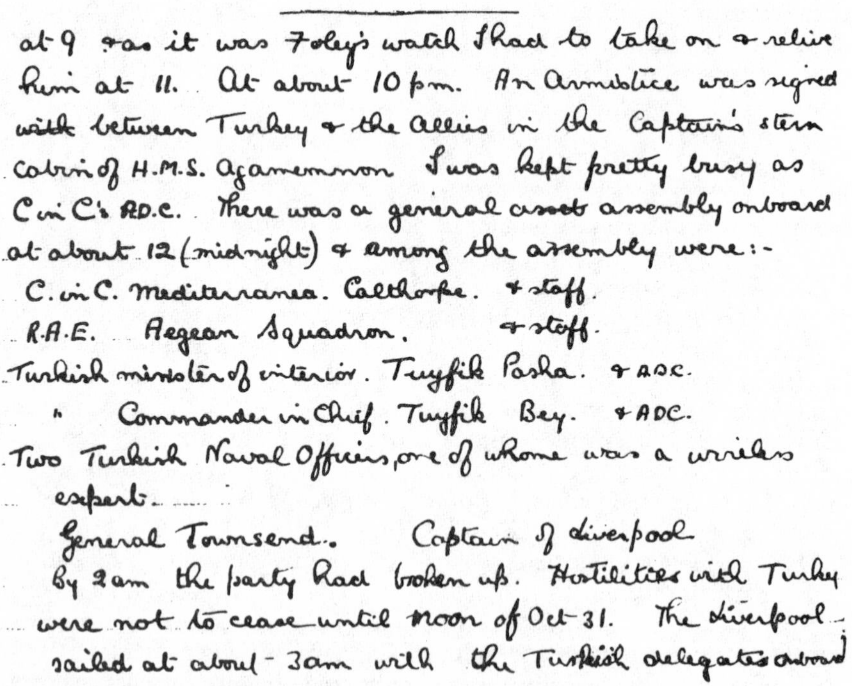
at 9 & as it was Foley's watch I had to take on & relieve him at 11. At about 10 pm. An Armistice was signed with between Turkey & the Allies in the Captain's stern cabin of H.M.S. Agamemnon I was kept pretty busy as C in C's A.D.C. There was a general assot assembly onboard at about 12 (midnight) & among the assembly were:-

C. in C. Mediterranea. Calthorpe. & staff.
R.A.E. Aegean Squadron. & staff.
Turkish minister of interior. Tuyfik Pasha. & ADC.
" Commander in Chief. Tuyfik Bey. & ADC.
Two Turkish Naval Officers, one of whome was a wireless expert.
General Townsend. Captain of Liverpool

By 2am the party had broken up. Hostilities with Turkey were not to cease until noon of Oct 31. The Liverpool sailed at about 3am with the Turkish delegates onboard
So to bed feeling quite important.

xxxiii "So to bed feeling quite important". Midshipman R.H.S. Rodger records in his journal the signing of the Armistice with Turkey, aboard *HMS Agamemnon*. (R.H.S. Rodger, Liddle Collection) at the start that he had a fully worked-out set of conditions agreed by the Allied governments and that no substantial alterations would be acceptable, the talks lasted for four days because the Ottoman side did what it could to mitigate some of the toughest conditions. In doing so it tried to remain in touch with the cabinet in Constantinople, but this proved very difficult. Attempts by a British cable ship to lay a connection to Çesme on the Anatolian mainland failed because of bad weather, so the delegation had to communicate by wireless transmission to the Ottoman wireless station in Okmeydani (Constantinople). The delegation only managed to get instructions regarding the Allied conditions on 29 and again on 30 October. The Ottoman worries, as reflected in these instructions, centred on three points:

1. While they were forced to accept that the fortifications on the Dardanelles and the Bosphorus would be occupied, they tried to get assurances that this occupation would be executed with British and French troops, without the participation of the Italians and particularly of the Greeks.
2. The Ottomans wanted guarantees that the capital, Constantinople itself, would not be occupied.
3. They were extremely worried about possible abuse of articles seven and twenty-four of the armistice agreement. Article seven stated that, when faced with a situation in which their security may be endangered, the Allies would have the right to occupy any strategic point, while article twenty-four stated that, in case of disturbances in the six "Armenian" provinces, the Allies reserved the right to occupy any part of these provinces. In Ottoman eyes, these articles opened the door wide for attempts by Greek or Armenian nationalists to provoke Allied interference. They therefore requested that article twenty-four in particular should be kept secret. This, however, was rejected by Admiral Calthorpe, who pointed out that the principles laid down by President Wilson made secret diplomacy of this kind a thing of the past.[8]

In the end, the Ottoman delegation decided to accept the 25-point armistice text without major alterations, even though it did not have full authorization so to do. It did, however, persuade Admiral Calthorpe to write a personal letter, intended only for the eyes of Rauf Bey, the Grand Vizier and the Sultan, in which he promised, on behalf of the British government, that only British and French troops would be used in the occupation of the Straits fortifications. In addition he wrote that he had strongly recommended to his government that a small number of Ottoman troops would be allowed to stay on in the occupied areas as a symbol of sovereignty. Finally he said that he had conveyed to his government the urgent requests of the Ottoman delegation that no Greek troops be allowed to land either in Constantinople or Izmir and that Constantinople should not be occupied as long as the Ottoman government could protect Allied lives and possessions there.[9]

The delegation left H.M.S. Agamemnon on the evening of 30 October and reached Izmir by noon the next day. After telegraphic communication with

Constantinople they now received the cabinet's approval for the signature of the Armistice.

When we now try to gauge the immediate popular reaction to the conclusion of the Armistice, we have to make a clear distinction between the Muslims of the empire and the Christian communities. The latter were elated. This should cause no surprise. The loyalty of the Greek and Armenian communities to the Ottoman state was in grave doubt even before the war and the ethnic policies of the wartime government, which resulted in the deaths of up to eight hundred thousand Armenians and the flight and expulsion of hundreds of thousand of Greeks, had caused both communities to look upon the Allies as liberators. This had been clear even in 1915, when foreign observers in Constantinople noted the great hopes entertained by the Christians of an Allied breakthrough in Gallipoli and their disappointment when that failed to materialize.[10] It was also apparent in the way the Allied commanders were greeted when they entered Constantinople after the war. When General Franchet d'Esperey, the French commander of the Armée de l'Orient, entered Constantinople, he rode on a white stallion donated by the Greek community and the whole Christian part of the city (Pera, or modern Beyoğlu) was decorated with Greek, Italian, French and British flags.

The Ottoman government was well aware of these sentiments. When the delegation returned to Constantinople on 1 November, Rauf Bey was met by a group of newspaper editors. He agreed to speak to them, but only off the record. He emphasized the delicacy of the situation and implored the editors to avoid publishing anything that could raise tensions between the communities or give the Ottoman Christians (malûm unsurlar or "certain elements") an excuse to start disturbances and call in the help of the Allies under article seven. The newspapers complied and in any case, from the next day, there was another issue which diverted public attention from the Armistice: the flight, during the night and aboard a German submarine, of the wartime leaders Enver, Talât and Cemal. When word of their flight got out on 2 November, the cabinet, which still contained a small number of former members of the Young Turk Committee of Union and Progress, was accused of conniving at their escape. It was the sign for a general assault by the press on the Committee and its wartime policies, in which all the anger and disappointment of the public were vented.[11]

Reactions among the Muslim population varied. Those who bore responsibility for the conduct of the war, such as the leading echelons of the Committee and the members of parliament, were of course disenchanted with the formal recognition that the war was effectively lost, but public opinion seems to have been relieved, rather than anything else, by the Armistice.[12] One can point to several reasons for this.

The main reason obviously was the fact that the war had finally ended. The war had never been popular. A defensive war against the Russians could count on a great deal of popular support, but war against the British and the French, who had enormous prestige and cultural influence among the urban Ottoman elite, even when the empire was linked politically to Germany, was seen by many as unnatural and even suicidal. The hardships endured during the final years of the war had drained away whatever enthusiasm there had been.

Another reason for relief lay in the comparison between the Armistice of Mudros and the Armistice so recently imposed on Bulgaria, which had amounted to an unconditional surrender by that country. Seen in that light, the conditions of the Ottoman Armistice were favourable in that they left the defeated empire with a qualified independence and some dignity.

The fact that the empire survived as an empire with the revered institutions of the Sultanate and Caliphate intact was a consolation. In retrospect, the Ottoman Empire was only one of the great continental empires to disappear in the wake of the First World War, but we should not forget that in 1918 the Ottoman dynasty, unlike that of the Romanovs, the Habsburgs or the Hohenzollerns, did manage to hang on to its throne.

Finally, there was a widespread belief, on the one hand, in British fair play and, on the other hand, in the promises of a new world order based on the principles enunciated by President Wilson. Quite a few members of the Constantinople bourgeoisie enthusiastically joined the "Society of the Friends of England" or the "Wilsonian League" after the war and there was much talk of the benefits of an American mandate.[13]

Perhaps the most striking point, when one reads the contemporary declarations and speeches where the Armistice is discussed, is this: the Armistice was not in itself seen as unjust or unacceptable even by those nationalist Young Turk officers who would go on to lead the national resistance movement in Anatolia and eventually to found the Turkish Republic. There were clear worries about the elasticity of articles seven and twenty-four and, as early as November 1918, the populations in those areas which might be disputed by the Greeks in the west and by the Armenians in the east and south were being mobilized to resist those claims and military commanders on the Syrian and Mesopotamian fronts complained about British transgressions.[14] However, the Armistice as such was not a bone of contention among the Ottoman elite. There was no feeling, as there was to be in Germany, of betrayal or injustice. The reason for this is striking and lies in the way we have been conditioned by Turkish historiography to look at this era contrasting the defeat of 1918 with the triumph of 1922, resulting in the Armistice of Mudanya and then, in 1923, the Peace of Lausanne. Armistice, occupation and the Treaty of Sèvres with its complete dismemberment of the Ottoman state and huge concessions to Greeks, Armenians, Kurds, Italians and French, now all seem part of one dark page in Turkish history. That Hüseyin Rauf Bey, the chief of the Ottoman delegation in Mudros, emerged as the leader of the political opposition against Atatürk in the young Turkish Republic after 1923 and that he was purged in a political trial in 1926, gave added impetus to the tendency to see the Armistice as a piece of treason, to which no true Turk could or should have put his signature.[15]

In reality, the immediate reaction to the Armistice on the part of the Ottoman Muslims was generally one of resignation and, to a certain extent, relief. It was not the Armistice as such, but the Allied policies after its conclusion, culminating in the decision to allow Greek troops to land in Izmir in

May 1919 and the occupation of Constantinople in March 1920, which turned public opinion against the Allies and eventually persuaded the majority to throw in their lot with the nationalist resistance. When we read the speeches and declarations from this period of Mustafa Kemal Pasha Atatürk and other resistance leaders, we see that they were full of complaints and indignation not about the conditions laid down in Mudros, but about the way the Allies, especially the British, abused and exceeded the terms of the Armistice.[16] That the Greek occupation of Izmir galvanized public opinion is well known. It gave rise to mass protest rallies in Constantinople and armed resistance in Anatolia. The occupation of Constantinople, however, was also a very traumatic experience. Both memoirs[17] and novels[18] show the anger and dismay experienced by Ottoman Muslims at the almost 'colonial' way they were treated in their own capital by the officers of the Entente and their Greek and Armenian protégés.

Endnotes

1 Fahri Belen, *Birinci Cihan Harbinde Türk Harbi. 1918 Yılı Hareketleri. Beşinci Cilt*, Ankara: Genelkurmay, 1967, p. 205. [The Turkish War in the First World War. Operations of the Year 1918. Vol. 5].

2 Belen, p. 204.

3 Erik Jan Zürcher, "Little Mehmet in the Desert: the war experience of the Ottoman soldier", in: Hugh Cecil and Peter Liddle (eds.), *Facing Armageddon. The First World War Experienced*, London: Leo Cooper/Pen and Sword, 1996, pp. 230–241. Erik Jan Zürcher, "Between Death and Desertion. The Ottoman Army in World War I", *Turcica* 28 (1996), pp. 235–258.

4 Zafer Toprak, *Türkiye'de "Millî İktisat" (1908–1918)*, Ankara: Yurt, 1982, pp. 313–344.

5 Ahmed Emin [Yalman], *Turkey in the World War*, New Haven: Yale University Press, 1930, p. 265.

6 Names in brackets like this one refer to family names introduced in Turkey in 1934.

7 Belen, p. 209.

8 *The* Turkish source on the negotiations is the serialized version of Hüseyin Rauf [Orbjay]'s memoirs, published in *Yakın Tarihimiz*, Ankara: Türkpetrol, n.d., Vol. 1, pp. 112, 144, 177, 208, 239, 272, 304, 336, 400; Vol. 2, pp. 16–18; 48–50; 80–82. [Our Recent History].

9 Text in *Yakın Tarihimiz*, Vol. 2, p. 49.

10 Cf. Lewis Einstein. *Inside Constantinople. A Diplomatist's Diary during the Dardanelles Expedition*, London: John Murray, 1917, passim. Einstein notes that the majority of the Greeks in the city were Venizelists and thus supported the Entente.

11 *Yakın Tarihimiz*, Vol. 2, pp. 82, 144–146.

12 Belen, p. 215.

13 Tarik Zafer Tunaya, *Türkiye'de Siyasal Partiler. Cilt 2: Mütareke Dönemi*, Istanbul: Hürriyet Vakfı 1986, pp. 245–263; 472–492. [Political Parties in Turkey. Vol. 2 The Armistice Period].

14 The most important one being the occupation by the British of Mosul, the capital of Southern Kurdistan, **after the Armistice had gone into effect**. This later led

Turkey to claim possession of this province, a claim which was officially renounced in 1926.

15 Erik Jan Zürcher, *Opposition in the Early Turkish Republic. The Progressive Republican Party (1924–25)*, Leiden: Brill, 1991, pp. 37–51.

16 See for instance Mustafa Kemal Pasha's speech on his arrival in Ankara on 28 December 1919, in Nimet Unan (ed.), *Atatürk'ün Söylev ve Demeçleri 2 (1906–1938)*, Ankara: Türk Tarih Kurumu, 1959, pp. 4–15.

17 For instance: Halide Edib [Adıvar], *The Turkish Ordeal*, London: The Century, 1928; Falih Rıkı Atay, *Çankaya*, Istanbul: Bateş, 1980.

18 Cf: Yakup Kadri Karaosmanoğlu, *Sodom ve Gomore*, Istanbul: Bilgi, 1966 (original edition: 1928). [Sodom and Gomorrha].

Chapter Eighteen

The Arabs from War to Peace

Avihai Shivtiel

In spite of the active Arab participation in the struggle against the Ottomans, published Arabic scholarship devoted to the theme of the First World War is relatively scanty. This is perhaps not as the result of a shortage of documentation in Arabic but, since the documents and oral testimonies clearly demonstrate the weakness of Arab leadership at the time in negotiation with the Great Powers, many Arab historians have hesitated to give their attention to the subject. Nevertheless, the accusatory finger has been pointed at the West, in particular at Britain and at France, but by politicians more than by historians.

This chapter will attempt to draw a picture of the Arab reaction to the War and the Armistice, based on the writings of some Arab authors and some non-Arab writers whose sources of information are, in the main, based on general works and documentation about the war as well as personal experiences.[1] It is worth mentioning in this context that between 1914 – 1918 the Arab press was generally suppressed by strict censorship imposed by the Ottomans (who in fact executed several leading Arab journalists) and by the tendentious attitude of the Great Powers, who often "helped Arab editors and correspondents express themselves". Thus we find that some of the leading newspapers which were not ready to toe the line dictated by the authorities on both sides stopped being published until the end of all hostilities.[2]

It was Napoleon who 'rediscovered' the Near East in 1798. However, his plans to reap the fruit of his invasion were shortlived, because his greatest rival, Britain, protecting her interests in India, forcibly stifled the French solo performance in the Middle East. However, the serious troubles with the Ottoman Empire, 'the Sick Man of the Bosphorus', indicated that it would only be a matter of time before the Great Powers launched a race for power in the region. In due course, Britain controlled Egypt, the Sudan and Aden; France governed the Maghreb; Italy ruled over Libya, whereas Syria, Palestine, Iraq and the Arabian peninsula remained under Ottoman suzerainty.[3] On the other hand, the other Great Powers in Europe, less successfully, were also drawn into the dangerous illusion that they too should join the game in the Middle East in an attempt to challenge and change the political balance in this area. Encouraged by the European model of independence, some Arab political thinkers had consequently begun to dream about freeing their territories from the hands of the Ottomans and the Europeans. However, the tight clasp of the Ottomans and the firm control of the British and French over the territories under their control left little hope for the Arabs to realize that vision.

The outbreak of war in 1914 gave both parties, that is the Allies *and* the Arabs, a great opportunity to achieve their targets, so far as the Middle East was concerned. The British and the French could, in return for promises to the Arabs they never meant to fulfil, get Arab help in keeping the Turks, with their German allies, busy defending Turkish territories in the Near East. The Arabs, who were encouraged by an eccentric and controversial British officer, T.E. Lawrence, other British liaison officers and small detached British units, and a few political and financial gestures made by the Allies, naïvely believed that their Holy War against the Ottomans would lead to their freedom and independence. What they failed to see was that while the British and the French were ready to help the Arabs to rid themselves of the Ottomans, they had no intention thereafter of vacating the Arab stage.

The Arab Revolt began on 5 June 1916 with the proclamation of war by Sherif (later, King) Hussein. The objective of the war was to liberate Arab lands from the brutal occupation of the hated Ottomans. Led by Hussein's sons and Lawrence, the Arab tribes achieved their aims after a series of engagements which had included defeats as well as successes.[4] So, after capturing the main Turkish garrisons along the route leading to Damascus, this Turkish stronghold fell into the hands of the British and the Arabs on 1 October, 1918. However, though the dazzling victory left no doubt about the Arabs' ability to win battles, their defeat at the negotiating table was soon to be discerned.

The dismembering of the Ottoman Empire began before the end of the war, while the 'patient' was still alive. Numbers of agreements, many of them confidential, most of them based upon verbal exchange and assurances given, were reached, often of a contradictory nature.[5] All these agreements represent a remarkable demonstration of negotiation skills and the art of deception. Describing, for example, the Sykes-Picot Agreement of 16 May, 1916, which "McMahon's pledge to Hussein preceded by six months",[6] two contemporary Arab historians write:

> The Sykes-Picot Agreement is regarded as one of the examples which expose the Great Powers to shame during the First World War, as it indicates their voracity and greed as well as their political hypocrisy ... Although the area was an Arab territory which should have been an independent entity, we see that the Allies were striving for its division in an arbitrary and unnatural way, thus, showing their great insensitivity ... [7]

The scandal involving the Sykes-Picot Agreement was not only because King Hussein was left in the dark for nearly eight months about it, and therefore was made the laughing stock of many of his supporters, but because the earlier agreement reached between him and McMahon had been rendered null and void.

It is ironic that it was the Turks who obtained a copy of the Sykes-Picot Agreement from the Bolsheviks who, after the October Revolution, opened many of the confidential files of the Tsar's foreign office, among which was a copy of the Agreement, and passed it on to Hussein in December 1917. The Turks offered Hussein a new deal: a peace agreement between – as they called it – "Muslim brethren", so that the Turks and the Arabs could protect the entirety of the area against the treacherous intentions of the Allies to "divide and rule" the territories which originally belonged to Islam. The offer also mentioned German support of this plan.

However, Hussein dismissed the indictments levelled against the British and the French and refused to negotiate with the enemy. He instructed his son Faisal to send his negative reply to the Turks, writing at the same time to the British High Commissioner in Cairo, requesting clarifications regarding the Agreement. A few weeks later he received a communication from Arthur Balfour, the British Foreign Secretary, which did not deny the existence of the Agreement, but reminded Hussein that his arch enemies were the Turks, that Britain was his ally and she would continue to support the Arabs' future struggle for independence. Further to appease the Arabs and set their mind at ease, the British troops brought with them an overflow of British products for the starved population. A vivid description of the people's reaction to this is given in Mrs Anbara Salam al-Khalidi's memoirs of Lebanon during the war: "Women, men, youths and children were competing in the soldiers' camps to buy different conserves of meat and sweets and various brands of luxury cigarettes. They bought all those for peanuts, and devoured them to satiate their hunger and their desire for delicious food [and unobtainable delights]".[8]

Another blow landed on the Arabs on 2 November 1917 when the British announced their commitment to the Jews in the form of the Balfour Declaration promising the Jews a National Home in Palestine. Arab reaction was, as expected, frantic. Demonstrations against the Declaration were held in many parts of the Arab world, where slogans and threats against the British were carried by hand and by mouth. The demonstrators called on their leaders to act swiftly, since the British had, yet again, betrayed them. Some Arab historians who blame the British for taking such a crucial decision concerning the future of Palestine, without asking any side involved in the Sykes – Picot Agreement, [including King Hussein and of course the Palestinians], dismiss the three 'traditional' arguments raised by the British to justify the Balfour Declaration, that is to say,

a. luring the Jews to put pressure on America to enter the war;
b. securing Jewish money to help covering the enormous debts of the Allies;

xxxiv His Majesty King Hussein-ibn-Ali, King of the Hejaz. (from the book *Iraq in Wartime*, published by Government Press, Basra)

c. rewarding the Zionist leader, Chaim Weizmann, who had personally contributed to the war effort by inventing a new type of explosive.[9]

Instead, the explanation offered by some Arab historians is that Britain was concerned about the Zionist activities inside Germany which might have led to an agreement between the Jews and Turkey regarding Jewish claim to Palestine. Also, Britain was acutely anxious about the overall war situation and in particular at the likelihood of the Bolsheviks taking Russia out of the war. However, the most important reason was the strategic importance and therefore the vital role of Palestine for the British, who were controlling Egypt, and needing Palestine as a barrier between the French and the Suez Canal.[10]

In the event, Arab apprehensions of the Balfour Declaration were once again defused by the British, who reiterated that a National Home for the Jews did not mean an independent state, but a place where Jews could live peacefully. To avoid further deterioration of the situation and the risk of clashes inside the Allied camp, this explanation was accepted, and the scheme was approved by King Hussein. Hussein's son, Faisal, even met Weizmann and discussed with him the future of the region.

When the dramatic end came in the following year, the Arabs joined the

xxxv Prince Faisal, son of King Hussein, prepares to receive General Allenby after his entry into Damascus. *Le Miroir*'s caption for this illustration, translated, states that "Palestine and Syria have been freed from the Ottoman yoke. Arabia was declared independent in June 1916 ... and Arab formations participated brilliantly in the final victory". (French magazine *Le Miroir*, December 1918)

Allies in their victory festivities, though the celebrations were conducted in the traditional way: feasts extending well into the night and daily *Fantaziyyas*, that is to say, riding camels or horses at great speed, while shooting in the air. Quite apart from the actual end of the war, at the heart of celebrations was the freedom of the Arabs from Turkish servitude and the bright prospect of independence, as promised by their comrades-in-arms, the British and the French. The citizens of Beirut, for example, appointed a team to run the country's affairs, sent a delegation to see the Turkish Governor to ask him to leave at once together with his clerks and hoisted the Arab flag on the Government buildings. However, the celebrations were abruptly interrupted by the British and later the French, who ordered the removal of the Arab 'National' flag, from all masts in Syria and Lebanon, a demand which was accompanied with a warning not to repeat this action. This, of course, infuriated the Arabs, who were simply and categorically informed that the time for independence had not yet arrived.

Instead, the time of settlements and, in particular, 'settling bills' had come and in this it was not just Germany, Austria-Hungary and the Bulgars who would pay but the Arabs too. Faisal tried his best to make the Allies, and in particular, the British keep their promises by fullfilling their obligations to the Arabs. Faisal's case was made still stronger in the light of Wilson's Fourteen Points. However, both Britain and France were busy in exhaustive negotiations concerning the division of the Middle East, and they did not need the presence of Hussein and his son during their power-struggle machinations. The experienced negotiators of the Big Powers knew that independence for any party in the Middle East was out of the question. The area was too important to be left in the hands of its natives. Faisal was only 'allowed in' when Arab rage reached boiling point. Otherwise he was out, exposed to external and internal pressures and 'fait accompli' decisions. Only once, on 6 February, he was allowed to address the Peace Conference in Paris. He presented the Arab demands and defended them; he reminded the participants of the role played by the Arabs in the war, their sacrifices, co-operation and commitment; he referred to the promises given to the Arabs, and stressed the Arabs' legitimate rights in the region; he rejected the Sykes-Picot Agreement and ended his speech with words of thanks to Britain and France for their kind help. The speech was good and clear, but insufficiently convincing for his audience.

Furious, the Arabs held a counter-conference in Damascus on 2 July. The discussions were combative and emotional. The resolutions adopted were: a rejection of the Sykes-Picot agreement, of Balfour and a Jewish National Home, of any division or partition of Iraq, Syria and Palestine, but an acceptance of American or British, but not French financial support for the Arabs.

However, the unequivocal tone of these resolutions had to be softened since Faisal realized that the French were determined to take control of Syria by force as soon as the British evacuated the territories which were occupied by them and which were to be transferred to French hands, in accordance with the Peace Treaty. He therefore went to Paris, and, against his father's wish, agreed with Clemenceau that the French should control the Syrian coastal line up to the Turkish border. This agreement was immediately rejected by other Arab leaders, who accused Faisal of betraying the Arab cause. The accusations were unjustified. Faisal had no choice, other than to let the situation get out of control and in consequence having to confront the French army. If this were to happen – he told his people – no one would come to the rescue of the Arabs.

The San Remo conference in April 1920 was yet another blow for Faisal and the Arabs. Syria was divided, and the Balfour Declaration was to be fullfilled. The Arabs were shocked as "there appears to be a betrayal by the West of an accord the Arabs had written with their blood".[11] Riots in Damascus were unavoidable, and the French retaliated. In consequence, Syria was seized by force by the French and Faisal was exiled to Italy. Clashes with the French spread and reached Iraq, though it was under British rule and was never divided. However, the division within the Arab ranks was the major problem, since many Arabs, mainly the Christians, favoured French rather than British rule in Syria. Anbara al-Khalidi writes: "The overwhelming majority of the Christian community have grown up with the belief that it will never attain security and care from anyone except from France, whom they named 'the loving mother'".[12]

The famous Orientalist, Father Henri Lamans, held the same view. In an article devoted to the history of Franco – Syrian relations, he stressed the emotional link between the two nations and concluded: "The Arabs have erected barriers between the Christians of Syria and France out of fear of foreign influence in their country. Hence, the love of the Syrians for France has remained concealed in the depth of their hearts, like fire under the ashes, flaring up whenever circumstances befit".[13] In an editorial article which appeared in the first issue of *Al-Machriq* after five years of suspension, the editor, Lewis Shikho, wrote a panegyric in which he praised France for the material help and spiritual support given to the Arabs during the war.

> We bow our heads before the triumphant French banner, with its three colours that symbolizes its international merits: the white which symbolizes the purity of its intentions and sincerity of its heart... the red colour which signifies her blood that was willingly shed for the sake of any noble cause and the blue which proclaims its readiness to defend the security and rights of the oppressed, invigorating any enterprise aiming at the welfare of mankind.[14]

The conference in Cairo which was opened on 12 March 1921 at the initiative of Churchill brought some progress and hope. Iraq was awarded independence and Faisal became its King. Abdulla became the first Jordanian monarch, but Egypt and Palestine remained under British rule, the latter as a League of Nations mandate – Egypt because of the importance of the Suez Canal, and the latter because of the British decision to give it to the Jews, "thus making room for a new power that will keep the balance with the Arabs ... and act as a barrier between France and the Suez Canal".[15] The naïvety of the Arabs had again been wholly exploited.

The war had concluded in the Middle East in a confusion of conflicting objectives. The Allies were suspicious of one another, their policies and strategies constantly changing. 'Decisions' were 'ephemeral' while promises were 'inflated' and then disregarded. Consequently, though the Armistice did put an end to a terrible war, the treaties and agreements left many unhappy, feeling that they were deceived and betrayed. Paradoxically, one may conclude that the Great War fathered militarism and the eruption which took place twenty years later is but a sad proof of what unsolved problems may lead to. Moreover, the Arab disappointment with Britain and France, who so easily gave promises and so lightly broke them, had persuaded many Arabs to support Germany during the Second World War. On the other hand, the help and support given to the British by the Jews during the two wars, repaid, again by unfulfilled promises, turned the Jews against the British. Consequently, mistrust, accusations, protest and later military confrontation in Palestine, were unavoidable. This led the British to withdraw from Palestine in 1948 and end their occupation of Egypt in 1954. Other Arab states were freed from foreign influence within a decade or so from the end of the Second World War and it is only the Arabs of Palestine who have remained until now without a state of their own. Even as long as eighty years after the 1918 cease-fire in the Middle East, there is still little confidence that the conflicting aspirations of Arabs and Jews in Palestine, each in turn encouraged by the Allies in the First World War, have been satisfactorily resolved.

Endnotes

1. I am most grateful to Professor T. Khalidi from the University of Cambridge for providing me with some valuable sources on which this chapter is based, including the memoirs of his mother (see the Bibliography).
2. See A. Ayalon, *The Press in the Middle East*, Oxford University Press, London, 1995, pp. 69–72.
3. See G. Lenczowski, *The Middle East in World Affairs*, Cornell University Press, Ithaca, New York, 1952, p. 57.
4. For a detailed account of the various stages of the campaigns in the Middle East during the First World War as seen by a senior ranking Arab officer, see, for example, S.M. Nadim, *The Palestine War*, Dar al-Nibras wa-al-Nashr wa-al-Tawzi`, Baghdad, 1964 (in Arabic).
5. See G. Lenczowski, *op. cit.*, p. 68, and Nadim, *op. cit.*, p. 241.
6. See G. Lenczowski, *op. cit.*, p. 76.
7. See G. Yahya-G. Taha, *Al-`Arab fi al-Ta`rikh al-Hadith*, Minya University, Egypt, 1974, pp. 371–372.
8. See A. Khalidi, *Jawlah fi al-Dhikrayat bayna Lubnan wa-Falastin*, Dar al-Nahar li-al-Nashr, Beirut, 1997, p. 122.
9. See G. Yahya – G. Taha, *op. cit.*, pp. 377–378. For more details on the Arab reaction to the Declaration and the promises made by the British in order to defuse the situation, see, for example, L. Shikho, Al-Sahyuniyyah, *Al-Machriq*, Year 18, No. 10, October 1920, pp. 775–776; and K.M. Khillah, *Palestine under British Mandate 1922–1939*, Palestine Liberation Organization, Beirut, 1974, (In Arabic), Chapters 3 and 4.
10. See G. Antonius, *The Arab Awakening*, Hamish Hamilton, London, 1938, pp. 261–262.

11 See Yahya-Taha, *op. cit.*, p. 397.
12 See A. Khalidi, *op. cit.*, p. 124.
13 See H. Lamans, Faransa wa-Surya, *Al-Machriq*, Year 19, No. 1, January 1921, p. 55.
14 See L. Shikho, Tahiyyat al-Machriq li-qurra`ihi, *Al-Machriq*, Year 18, No. 1, January 1920, pp. 2–3.
15 See G. Yahya – G. Taha, *op. cit.*, p. 403.

Chapter Nineteen

Austria-Hungary

Mark Cornwall

Nowhere was there such a chaotic end to the First World War as in the Austro-Hungarian Empire. On the morning of 4 November 1918, a solemn mass was being celebrated in St Stephen's Cathedral in Vienna in honour of Emperor Karl's name-day, with the whole of what was to be the last Austrian cabinet in attendance. A sombre mood infected those present: Josef Redlich noted in his diary, "the victorious revolution in all of Austria was in striking contrast to the *Te Deum laudamus* and to the words of the national anthem, 'lead us with a wise hand'".[1] In the previous week the Empire had splintered in different directions, and during the mass itself, the Italian army was advancing fast on the south-western front, capturing hundreds of Austro-Hungarian soldiers before the Armistice officially came into force at 3pm. An end to hostilities had been expected by almost everybody for at least six weeks. If some were still unsure in August, even as the Germans were steadily retreating on the western front, or in mid-September when the Foreign Minister, Count István Burián, had despatched a separate peace note to the Entente, few were in doubt by October. On 29 September, Bulgaria had capitulated, exposing the Empire's south-east flank; on 4 October, Austria-Hungary had joined Germany and Turkey in public peace notes to President Wilson, requesting an immediate armistice and peace talks on the basis of the American President's 'Fourteen Points'.

On hearing of this, one loyal Austrian commander on the Italian front wrote to his family: "For us it won't be a fair or satisfactory peace, and for me that takes away most of the joy which otherwise I would feel at this news".[2] Indeed, it might be emphasized that although nobody in the Empire regretted the end of the war – even the High Command had been pressing for it since August – there were sharp distinctions in Austria-Hungary in the way that different sections of the population reacted to the prospect of peace. Some, in the lower strata of society or living in a rural environment, saw the end of the war with simple relief. It meant principally an alleviation of the food crisis and a return to some social normality which would include reunion with loved-ones from the war zones; and for perhaps many of these people, the nationalist turmoil impinged on their concerns only marginally or when it directly invaded their locality. A second swathe of the population, however, viewed peace with excitement, a little anxiety, but generally as the start of a bright new epoch. For these people, who were leading or simply following enthusiastically the formation of new nationalist states from the ruins of the Monarchy, the 'Austro-Hungarian war' had indeed been lost – but it was no longer 'their war'. Their cause was the same as the victors, the Entente, and to differing degrees they envisaged their own liberation as both a nationalist and a social triumph against former oppressors.

In contrast, there was a third group of the population for whom the end of the war was a disaster. For them any relief from wartime stresses was obscured by the complete break-up of the Empire. This group undoubtedly had sympathizers in all corners of Austria-Hungary, but particularly among German-Austrians, many of whom were only reluctantly forced to think of a *Deutschösterreich* entity (or republic) as a result of territorial amputations to the north and south. The group's apparent strength, but actual weakness, was that it was the embodiment of the *kaisertreu* Habsburg elite, those who in the last months were vainly seeking to hold the Empire together before peace was concluded. All the methods attempted in the autumn reveal the degree to which these individuals were largely reacting to events, unable to think in common or with a set of radical or immediate objectives: they lacked, in Helmut Rumpler's words, a "political '*élan vital*'".[3] Not least this was the case with the Emperor's manifesto (16 October) which at the last minute sought to federalize exclusively the Austrian half of the Empire, but this simply served to give imperial sanction to the centrifugal nationalist movements. For the imperial elite too, the end of hostilities was to become one fact in the general whirlwind of domestic events; not surprisingly, one old Austrian diplomat prophesied to Josef Redlich on 19 October that the end of the world was in sight.[4]

As an introduction to assessing how these three major viewpoints overlapped or clashed, one can first study a few incidents in Vienna in the hectic final days of the Monarchy. In a number of different ways, individuals asserted their own allegiance. On 28 October, the imperial couple appeared briefly outside the Hofburg and received ovations from a crowd of hundreds. Franz Brandl, a police official, justifiably questioned this strength of feeling compared to what he perceived as the general indifference of many or the ill-will of a few activists who could quickly whip up such indifference into animosity. By 30 October, outside the Austrian Reichsrat (Parliament) the imperial Austrian flag was being publicly burnt, while red or black-red-golden flags, the latter for *Anschluss* with Germany, were hoisted by the crowds of thousands who gathered on the Ringstrasse. Some heard the German national anthem being sung, others remembered *Wacht am Rhein* coming from one street while the *Marseillaise* was audible from another. Thus the nationalist and socialist messages were competing visibly and audibly.[5]

Emblems also had fast become a touchstone for individuals' allegiance. At the same time as these events were occurring around the Ring, Count Gyula Andrássy was chairing the final Common Ministerial Council of the Empire in a dimly lit Foreign Ministry. The meeting had to be abruptly terminated because of the stormy demonstrations outside, and those present dispersed in their carriages. One carriage, containing the War Minister, General Stöger-Steiner, was intercepted by an enormous 'mob' on the Schwedenplatz; the carriage windows were smashed, Stöger-Steiner slightly injured. But most significantly, the crowd was determined to rip the imperial badges from the uniforms of the minister and his associates before letting them proceed on to the War Ministry where thousands would soon gather in front of the building shouting for 'peace'.[6] This same drama was being enacted in many corners of the city. In the northern railway station, for instance, about fifty youths invaded, removed the emblem from the cap of one soldier, and then turned on two Czech officers and ripped the red-white Czech national emblems from their caps.[7] For many of the victims this might be taken as an assault. Yet for others – in a different environment – to be assailed in this way could actually be uplifting since it reinforced a new and welcome sense of identity. One Czech officer later recalled how in Prague on 28 October, when the Czechoslovak Republic was proclaimed, he encountered a huge crowd singing *Hej Slované*. On seeing him, the crowd stopped singing and a worker stepped forward and asked "kindly" for his cap; he submitted, whereupon the worker tore off the imperial insignia, threw them on the ground, and "with a lovely smile" handed the cap back. The crowd roared their approval, congratulated the soldier, and moved on to further strains of the Czech national anthem.[8]

By this time few civilians could remain untouched by the turmoil caused by the Monarchy's disintegration. On the Italian front, meanwhile, news of domestic chaos had done as much as the new offensive from the enemy, launched on 24 October, to cause mutinies and a subsequent rout of the Austrian forces. Yet for many, until October at least, the horizons had been much more limited, with nationalist sentiments often taking second place to personal crises and a simple longing for peace. Some sense of how these popular viewpoints developed and overlapped can be gleaned from the Monarchy's censor reports on both civilian and military correspondence. In August 1918, reports from all major censorship centres agreed that the food crisis and peace were the predominant concerns. 95% of letters passing through the Vienna censor dealt with the miserable economic situation in Austria; there was no sign of patriotism and no hope of victory.[9] The censor position at Udine, which co-ordinated censorship in the eastern rear of the Italian front, concurred. Apart from an obsession with 'daily bread' and bitterness at requisitioning by the authorities, the correspondence was saturated with thoughts of peace at any price: "There is absolutely no interest in military events, everything has been worn down because the war has lasted so long". Where civilian interest occasionally rose above the mundane in this southern region was in response to Yugoslav agitation filtering into the localities. But many were undoubtedly joining the Yugoslav 'band-wagon' because its message of a brighter future always seemed to be offering some relief from local wartime corruption and hunger. Thus the Monarchy's disintegration was slowly beginning to impinge on the consciousness of all.[10]

„E questi pellirosse, avidi di sangue umano, osano parlare dell' ipocrisia e del gesuitismo austro-ungarico"?

Leggete la Nota pacifista austriaca!

xxxvi Austrian propaganda leaflet intended to demoralize Italian soldiers. It shows America rejecting Austria-Hungary's Peace note'. [Burián's peace offer of 14 September 1918] (Mark Cornwall)

In September 1918, the key themes of the Monarchy's censorship reports continued to be food and peace, with many beginning to shudder at the thought of a fifth winter of war. Certainly, Burián's peace offer of 14 September had also become a point of reference, but the responses to it indicated the growing divergent viewpoints which were so manifest in late October. While some were oblivious to it, others, in Austria proper, greeted it warmly, all the more so as it seemed to represent some independence from the German Reich which was preventing an end to hostilities and pulling the Monarchy down with it. In contrast, Burián's move was dismissed calmly by those who were already in 'nationalist camps'. Many Polish correspondents felt certain and pleased that the peace note would be unsuccessful since they wanted the Polish question to be solved before any peace talks.[11] In the same way, one educated Magyar expressed the feeling of many in Hungary, that the approaching peace needed to be one negotiated not by the old Hungarian elite (Tisza and Wekerle for example), but by new men like Michael Károlyi who would pursue Hungary's real interests. Dr Csepregnis of Nagyvárad wrote:

> Burián's peace move was naïve in the present circumstances. The Entente have to reject this childish stylistic exercise. The Hungarian intelligentsia are increasingly convinced that the Wekerle-Tisza-Burián governing system cannot win the trust of the Entente for peace. Károlyi must come, that is our conviction, for he could get a very fair peace from our enemies.[12]

By October, the level of interest in current affairs was mounting: in the military setbacks, in nationalist agitation, as well as in moves by the elite to stave off disaster (notably the Central Powers' offer of an armistice and the Emperor's manifesto). In Prague, for example, the crowds began to gather again outside press offices in order to keep up to date with the Germans' latest defeats on the Western front. In Zagreb, discussions about the approaching end were perhaps even more intensive in view of the collapse of Bulgaria and the advance of Entente armies in the Balkans; one witness noted the buzz of excitment in the cafés on Jelačič square, similar to the expectant atmosphere in Prague in late 1914 when the Russians had advanced in Galicia.[13] This mood of confidence tempered by anticipation was also picked up by the postal censors. One Croat correspondent observed, "we are approaching the peace and are convinced that our southern Slav question will be solved satisfactorily. We Croats, Slovenes and Serbs maintain that we ourselves are creating our Yugoslav state". All letters seemed to welcome the Central Powers' appeal to Wilson, but there was a more realistic divergence of views when the Emperor's manifesto was discussed. Some Austrian patriots credulously shared the perception of those who had formulated the manifesto, namely that it would, at this eleventh hour, strengthen the Monarchy internally while also helping to preserve it by presenting a more democratic image to the Entente Powers as peace drew nearer. In contrast, Czech and South Slav correspondents could find nothing good in the manifesto.[14] However, a third approach can, as usual, also be glimpsed from other sources. The chief of police in Vienna recorded that the manifesto had not aroused the expected interest, for most of the lower classes were concerned only with food. And even in broader sections of the community, the manifesto was only being discussed in strictly material terms: of whether it would produce a quick peace, and how it would affect food supplies to the starving capital.[15]

If this were the outlook of many in Vienna, their narrow horizon was one which was shared in October by perhaps a majority of soldiers on the Italian front.[16] True, there were commanders like Prince Aloys Schönburg-Hartenstein who were bewildered that the Emperor himself, through his manifesto, had been the one to dissolve the 'Austrian idea'. As peace approached, the Prince grew more alarmed about the fate of 'German-Austria' and who would belong in the new fatherland. A fellow commander wrote similarly on 19 October: "Our lovely old Austria has disappeared".[17] But for many of the rank and file, the concept of peace was largely unconditional. It was stimulated in their minds by news from the interior and from Italian propaganda leaflets which were being scattered over the war zone. But its strongest root, especially since the disastrous offensive of June 1918, was a worsening war-weariness among men who were often expected to serve in rags and famished. One censor position summed up thousands of soldiers' letters:

> The soldier at the front seems to have been awoken from his hopeless apathy by this news [the peace note to Wilson] and to be consciously waiting on events... Even consummately patriotic soldiers of educated classes are, notwithstanding ample regret for the pointless sacrifices and abandonment of the German people, greeting the approaching peace with enthusiasm.

It did not take much to provoke impatience in some of these individuals who thought of 'making peace themselves' should events begin to drag. Amongst others, since so many were civilians in uniform, the same divisions of loyalty as in the hinterland were fast appearing. Joy at the end of the war could indeed be tempered with misgivings about surrendering to the enemy the mountains for which comrades had fought and died. As Feldmarschall Krobatin, the 10th army commander, observed, the more educated men in his sector were alarmed that, in view of uncertainty about the Empire's future, the whole war might have been for nothing.[18] Yet Krobatin was in this way implying that the bulk of the army was *kaisertreu* and of like mind. In fact, for many – Czechs, Poles, Magyars and others – their joy at the approaching peace was not tinged with so much regret except for the waste of life after four years of fighting. Peace was to mean not only their return home to loved-ones, but their chance to participate in a nationalist and social revolution with which a good number of them were certainly sympathetic.

Their viewpoint, and the way in which their depression turned to hope from the late summer, was similar to that of those nationally-conscious civilians living in the rural hinterland. There, as we have noticed in some Yugoslav areas, the thought of peace always had an economic dimension, and that in turn was increasingly bound up with rumours, creeping into their region, of an imminent national-social transformation. The evolution towards this frame of mind can be illustrated from the diary of one Czech councillor, living in the small town of Jaroměř in north-eastern Bohemia. Václav Pácalt kept a diary for the whole of 1918.[19] In much of it he detailed the town's material crisis – the rationing of tobacco, the closure of bakeries, the registering of pigs – but occasionally Czech nationalist agitation invaded the region and widened individuals' horizons. Earlier in the year, Pácalt had noted how on the conclusion of peace against Russia and Romania some civilians had hung out imperial and Czech flags from their houses. However, not until 28 July did he return to the theme of peace, observing that while Germans in neighbouring villages would normally have celebrated the anniversary of the war's outbreak on the twenty-eighth, all were now mute and simply longing for an honourable peace. Two months later, a confident Czech movement was increasingly in evidence, prompted steadily by visits from leading politicians from Prague and Brno. At a service in late September to pray for the fulfilment of national ideals, a great crowd packed the local church to hear a sermon about "the momentous upheavals which are imminent... Today is perhaps the last day that we will celebrate in bondage and without independence".

Many of these Czechs, moreover, clearly shared their national leaders' anxiety about the kind of peace which was approaching. Thus, when on 5 October a false rumour went round that the Armistice had already been signed, Pácalt noted in his diary that "strangely, although everybody longs for an end to the war, nobody was pleasantly surprised except for a few [German] officers, and also nobody believed it". The officers, having bragged that after such a peace the Central Powers in six years would be able to resume the war, were to be dejected a few days later on learning of the reality of the peace note to Wilson. For Czechs too it was an uncertain time. Some were temporarily depressed at the Emperor's manifesto, but, almost immediately their hopes were raised when news arrived that the Czech National Council (*Národní Výbor*) in Prague had rejected the manifesto, and Wilson had effectively embraced Czechoslovak independence (18 October). On 20 October, when the fifth wartime fair was held in Jaroměř, Pácalt could observe that everything was a little merrier than usual with even a traditional goose on display. He concluded that one reason for this was that "everyone believes that the war will end and that it will turn out well": it would be a peace of the victors and the Czechs too were now on the winning side.

In the final weeks, as is clear from Pácalt's diary and from the letter of the Hungarian Dr Csepregnis quoted earlier, educated nationalists in all parts of the Monarchy shared similar feelings to their national leaders about the forthcoming peace. Those national leaders who did not envisage their nationality's post-war future within the framework of Austria-Hungary had one major anxiety from September: namely, that the Monarchy's elite might be able to conclude a peace at the eleventh hour which would preserve the Empire intact. It was vital that they moved to pre-empt this by organizing their own national representative bodies, undermining the authority of Austro-Hungarian institutions, while simultaneously sending a clear message of independence to the Western Powers. In the same way, as we shall see, the imperial elite responded to the approaching peace by seeking to restructure the Monarchy and curry favour in the West. This, however, was a futile and half-hearted refrain, since much of their audience at home and abroad was unsympathetic. Thus the Polish Social Democrat, Ignacy Daszyński, in a turbulent Reichsrat session on 2 October, scorned Burián's peace note as a "false peace which the people won't be able to trust"; he contrasted Bulgaria's actual capitulation a few days earlier with Burián's "scrap of paper", noting that Austria would soon renounce such efforts if the Central Powers' military position improved.[20]

This was undoubtedly true, but an opportunistic stance in the autumn was not solely the preserve of the imperial elite. Most of the national leaders were also weighing their moves carefully, judging the deteriorating military situation, as well as the potential for national concentration when set against a persistently obstinate stance by Habsburg loyalists. In some regions, admittedly, 'national councils' were not simply created in the shadow of the Monarchy's collapse. The Czechs had already organized themselves on 15 July; the Slovenes had proved that they were the vanguard for 'Yugoslavism' by setting up their council in Ljubljana a month later. In Hungary, Michael Károlyi for a long time had been a Cassandra, and in a notorious open letter to his constituents in early September he warned that Hungary should look to its own interests and make a separate peace on the basis of Wilson's 'Fourteen Points'.[21] Yet for other nationalities the collapse of Bulgaria was the catalyst which forced them to take a bolder stance. Not until 10 October would Polish parties organize in Krákow to take over Galicia for a united Polish state. Leaders of Hungary's national minorities moved even slower, partly due to decades of Magyarization. Members of the Slovak intelligentsia did not convene until 30 October and not until 31 October, after a month of demonstrations for peace in Transylvanian towns, did Romanian national and socialist leaders finally unite in a national council of their own.

Developments in the Yugoslav regions illustrate the kind of leadership which these national leaders provided, responding to outside events but also, interacting with and spurred on by the popular mood. Increasingly from 1917, in the face of Austro-Hungarian obstinacy to their claims for more autonomy, Serb, Croat and Slovene politicians had drawn closer together and begun to think of solidarity in the future. By mid-August 1918, the Slovene leaders in Ljubljana had organized a national council as one base for a wider Yugoslav administration which would eventually include Croatia and Bosnia as well.[22] Yet a broader concentration did not materialize until early October. Chiefly this was because the leading political grouping in Croatia, the Serb-Croat Coalition, continued to wait on events. In the meantime, the Slovenes, like the Poles and the Czechs, felt bound to take some stance towards Burián's peace note. On 2 October, their leader, Anton Korošec, duly condemned it in the Reichsrat as a "cry in the wilderness" which ignored the people's right to self-determination and deceived nobody. Austria-Hungary and Germany, he observed, were continuing like two swimmers: "the stronger struggles through the waves and deluge and fights on, but the weaker swimmer sinks in the flood and becomes the prey of fish".[23] It was to ensure that the Yugoslav fish got away safely that the Slovene leadership, excited by Bulgaria's collapse, felt that the time had come to widen their national council with a direct approach to Croatia. With news arriving hourly of Entente (including Serbian) advances in the Balkans, the Serb-Croat Coalition finally ended its 'waiting game' and agreed to enter a 'National Council of Slovenes, Croats and Serbs' in Zagreb (6 October) with representatives from all the Empire's southern Slav regions.

This new body had one common aim, of preparing the ground for a united Yugoslav state which would send its own delegates to the future peace conference. The overriding concern therefore was national concentration as the war ended. This included most Croat and Slovene Social Democrats, who by joining non-socialist parties on the Council had resolved to place their social demands temporarily on the backburner. Their behaviour disgusted the more radical socialist leaders from Bosnia-Hercegovina, who refused to take part and accused their former comrades of collaboration with bourgeois-imperialists; the Bosnian socialists already foresaw that peace meant the start of a new struggle, against a socialist-nationalist clique.[24] Yet among the politicians, such a stand on principle was rare in these weeks. Serb and Croat leaders, who would later be at loggerheads, had set aside their differences about the future structure of their common state. Most were caught up in the common mood, an environment where, for instance, on 21 October in Zagreb, the nationalist tricolour was hoisted spontaneously when news arrived that Wilson had sent a negative response to Austria-Hungary. The Croatian historian Josip Horvat later captured the electric atmosphere:

> Everybody, even the poorest individual, senses that the old world is disintegrating, the loud clash of its collapse whips up our nerves into a new expectation which appears like a great light, like some new golden era which will bring happiness to all. And that future is all the more fascinating when it is compared with reality, with the immediate wartime past of grief, poverty, the whole nightmare of war.[25]

The Council leaders echoed this mood, but at the same time they were anxious to preserve order and prevent any descent into 'Bolshevik anarchy'. This was clear on 29 October, the day when the Croatian Sabor (assembly) met for the last time and to announce formally that Croatia was severing links with the Monarchy and surrendering its sovereignty to the National Council. A huge procession gathered in the old town outside the Sabor building, carrying national and red flags, wholly reminiscent of the pattern of events elsewhere in the Empire. In speeches from the Sabor balcony, the crowd were reminded as much about order – "anarchy is not freedom" – as about the day's significance. Thereupon, the politicians disappeared inside, while the crowd cheered wildly and burst into strains of the Serbian national anthem, Croatian patriotic songs and the *Marseillaise*.[26] The war was already becoming forgotten in the ecstasy of the moment, but the politicians meant to steer the new vibrancy along orderly channels.

Just as the prospect of an end to hostilities had served as a touchstone for nationalist leaders' behaviour in October, so it was for the imperial elite and those who supported them. Their crucial task in the autumn was to secure a favourable peace for Austria-Hungary before the Empire disintegrated or was invaded by Entente forces. Already in late August, Emperor Karl had observed that it was "five minutes to twelve".[27] Yet he himself found it impossible in the following weeks to see the wood for the trees; and when his indecisiveness was compounded by the Monarchy's bureaucratic inertia, by a myriad ministerial claims or objections, it was not surprising that the elite's behaviour became wholly defensive, reacting to events. Well might one minister write later that "we went about in a fog; like consumptive patients we did not believe in our malady, or else we were oppressed by the dull recognition that all hope was vain".[28] Like some of their nationalist opponents, the *kaisertreu* circles were only really shaken to act by Bulgaria's collapse. Andrássy, who at the time was deer-stalking on his Transylvanian estate, was "visibly shrunken" on realizing that a change in fortune was now impossible.[29] In Vienna on 28 September, Josef Redlich confided to his diary the twin themes – peace and reform – which were to beset the elite for the following month:

> I am convinced that the end of the war and our defeat are near: people want peace, even a separate peace. Everything depends on whether we can work fast and set up a government which will bring imperial reform and elicit the trust of the Entente. The Emperor however seems still to be far away from such decisions.[30]

In fact it was precisely these subjects which vexed the Common Ministerial Councils which met on 27 September and 2 October.[31] First, on the issue of peace, the ministers could in general terms agree. Since the United States had already indicated President Wilson's 'Fourteen Points' as a basis for negotiation (in response to Burián's peace note in mid-September), Burián was able on 2 October to gain a consensus from those present that the Monarchy and its allies should immediately turn to Wilson with a peace offer. Yet the attitude of the Hungarians at the meeting was ominous. Not only did the Hungarian Prime Minister, Sándor Wekerle, express his distaste for Wilson's 'Points' in principle; but Burián himself was quite prepared to set a leisurely pace, suggesting placidly "that there could, from our move, gradually develop a conversation about peace possibilities". Once the peace offer was agreed, the eyes of all were to be fixed upon Washington. Redlich noted a "gloomy fear" in press and parliamentary circles about how the Americans would respond.[32]

Indeed, it is clear that the elite, by waiting and setting inordinate store by Wilson's answer, gave less concerted attention in October to the second pressing issue: reform or restructuring of the Empire's government. By the time the Americans replied, almost three weeks had elapsed, and the internal chaos had easily passed the point of no return. There had been fatal delays in implementing domestic reform. Yet even the reforming measures which the elite felt able to take at this time were not really sincere or realistic in the face of the Monarchy's centrifugal disintegration. They were never radical enough to keep abreast of events. To a large degree this was because they were half-hearted or reflex actions, taken simply in order to elicit from Wilson a more sympathetic response to their peace offer. For example, all realized that new, more representative governments were now necessary in Vienna and Budapest, both to present a better image abroad and to rein in the powers of the regional national councils. However, these new alternative 'governments of national concentration' for Austria and Hungary remained a fantasy. In Austria, the Slav nationalities rejected any participation (12 October); in Hungary, the Magyar elite could not bring itself to defer to Károlyi's leadership, let alone to hand over any power to extra-parliamentary radical or socialist forces. As a result, by the middle of October, both the governments of Wekerle and the Austrian Prime Minister, Max Hussarek, though still in office, were viewed on all sides as transitional and had become dead instruments in the leadership of the Empire.

As for constitutional reform before the war ended, the prospect of any meaningful change was even less likely. The elite was moved almost wholly by the impression which such restructuring would make abroad, so that the peace which the Entente would dictate would not mean the dissolution of the Monarchy; to paraphrase Hussarek, "the world will at least think that we are trying to reform".[33] The limits of this, however, particularly those imposed by the elite's own obsession with maintaining the dualist structure of the Empire, were only too apparent in the meetings of the Common Ministerial Council. At the two sessions after Bulgaria's collapse, it was the 'Yugoslav danger' in particular which pressed for some solution before Entente forces marched into that region. Here, as usual, dualism had a fatal impact. The division of the Empire into Austrian and Hungarian halves meant that the Yugoslavs were divided by the Monarchy's rigid structure, and only through its restructuring could they be united. At the Council meetings, however, those present immediately excluded the Slovenes of Austria from any Yugoslav unit – they were, in Burián's words, an "artificial" problem. Thus, from the start, the dualist structure was non-negotiable, and a distinction had been made about any reform for Austria as opposed to Hungary, a split which foreshadowed the limits of Karl's later manifesto.[34] Even when all were agreed that Bosnia and Dalmatia might now be united with Croatia and placed in the Hungarian half of the Empire, Wekerle predictably objected to any common pronouncement, insisting that change should be left to Vienna and Budapest respectively. Nobody agreed with this – Stöger-Steiner, for instance, argued forcefully that "the existence of the Monarchy is at stake" – but Wekerle's procrastinating tactic on 2 October was triumphant. The last chance of a constitutional solution for the whole Empire had been lost.[35]

If Wekerle were either hopelessly optimistic or simply upholding Hungary's interests as he saw them, Hussarek was similarly blinkered in thinking that any reform for Austria could only be along conservative lines. Rather than being the author of a federal Austria, as some historians have imagined,

Hussarek was not prepared to move beyond limited autonomy for the Czechs or Slovenes. Thus it was that the Emperor himself personally took the initiative: with his manifesto of 16 October he pronounced that Austria (excepting Polish areas which would fall to independent Poland) should henceforth become a federal state (*Bundesstaat*). However, this was not as radical a step as it appeared. It is clear, as Helmut Rumpler has convincingly argued,[36] that for the Emperor the manifesto was principally formulated in order to win over Wilson at the eleventh hour; Karl had erratically turned his attention to it on 11 October, when a week had passed and Wilson had sent no reply. What should also be stressed is that any domestic repercussions of the reform seem to have been secondary and therefore ill thought-out. In particular, Karl himself was holding fast to dualism: he never envisaged that the manifesto would include Hungary (the chief criticism of commentators at the time and later), but may well have hoped that the Magyars would manage the Yugoslav problem separately as Wekerle had hinted on 2 October. Thus the manifesto was indeed a "desperate act",[37] and one in no way divorced from the elite's principal aim of finishing the war with the Monarchy intact. It showed again the elite's blindness or despair, particularly that of Karl himself, in the face of domestic realities. For the danger was that the manifesto would accelerate the centrifugal movements. In Budapest, Wekerle had to draw the logical conclusions from such a pronouncement. He announced in the Hungarian Parliament a 'personal union' with Austria, thereby undermining the Magyar elite's own position to the benefit of those democrats around Károlyi who wanted an independent Hungary; they in turn were not slow to proclaim openly in the chamber that they were "friends of the Entente".[38] In Vienna, as Redlich warned, the manifesto, coming before any Austrian 'national government' had been created, simply gave full sanction to the authority of the national councils and shattered any imperial control.[39]

For the elite, however, it was Wilson's reply – not the manifesto – which gave the real *coup de grace* to their hopes.[40] The reply decisively rejected national autonomy within a federalized Empire as a basis for negotiation, acknowledging in effect the claims to independence from Czechoslovaks and Yugoslavs. "The sphinx Wilson has finally spoken", said Burián at the start of a Common Ministerial Council on 22 October. He admitted that the American had "posed a new riddle" for the Monarchy, but even at this twelfth hour he was not wholly pessimistic, suggesting in fact that "a further spinning of the peace threads was possible". To suggest this was to ignore the logic of Wilson's statement, especially since, at the same time, Burián refused to concede any Croat or Slovak secession which would damage the integrity of Hungary. Wekerle fully agreed. Only at the end of the session would he concede that full Yugoslav unity might occur within the Empire, but this was a vague statement of no concrete substance. The meeting's main resolution revealed the elite's true impotence: the two governments were separately to do all they could to prevent the spread of centrifugal Yugoslav forces. Just as these words were being agreed, 30,000 people were marching through Zagreb, acclaiming the American President who had announced a peace on their terms.[41]

SUPPLEMENT TO DAILY NEWS SHEET.

INTELLIGENCE, G.H.Q., BRITISH FORCE IN ITALY.

No. 276(A). **6th NOVEMBER, 1918.**

TERMS OF THE ARMISTICE WITH AUSTRIA.

1. Immediate cessation of hostilities by land, sea and air.

2. Total demobilization of Austro-Hungarian Army and immediate withdrawal of all Austro Hungarian forces operating on the front from the North Sea to Switzerland. Within Austro Hungarian territory, limited as in Clause 3 below, there shall only be maintained as an organised military force a maximum of 20 divisions reduced to pre-war peace effectives. Half of the divisional, corps, and army artillery and equipment shall be collected at points to be indicated by the Allies and the United States of America, for delivery to them, beginning with all such material as exists in the territories to be evacuated by the Austro-Hungarian forces.

3. Evacuation of all territories invaded by Austro-Hungary since the beginning of the war. Withdrawal to take place within such periods as shall be determined by the Commanders-in-Chief of the Allied forces on each front of the Austro-Hungarian Armies behind a line fixed as follows:—From Umbrail to the North of Stelvio it will follow the crest of the Rhetian Alps up to the sources of the Adige and Eisach, passing thence by Mounts Raschen and Brenner and the heights of Oetz and Ziller. Line thence turns South, crossing Mount Toblach and meeting the present frontier of the Carnic Alps. It follows this frontier up to Mount Tarvis, and after Mount Tarvis the watershed of the Julian Alps by the Col of Predil, Mount Mangart, the Tricorno and the watershed of Cols di Podberdo, Podlaniscam and Idviaberg, excluding the whole basin of Save and its tributaries. From the Schwartzenberg it goes down towards the coast in such a way as to include Castro Mattuglia and Volosca in the evacuated territories. It will follow administrative limits of the present Province of Dalmatia, including to the North, Livarica and Frivania, and to the South a territory limited by a line from the shore of Cape Planka to the summits of the watershed eastwards so as to include in the evacuated area all valleys and watercourses flowing towards Sebenico, such as Cicola, Terka, Butisnica and their tributaries. It will also include all the islands in the North and West of Dalmatia from Premuda, Selve, Ulbo, Scherda, Majn, Pago and Patadura in the North up to Meluda in the South, embracing Saint Andrea, Vusi, Lissa, Lesina, Terkola, Curoola, Cazza and Lagosta, as well as neighbouring rocks and islets and spelagosa, only excepting the islands of Great and Small Zirona, Bua, Solta and Drazza. All territories thus evacuated will be occupied by the troops of the Allies and of the United States of America. All military and railway equipment of all kinds, including coal, belonging to or within these territories to be left intact and surrendered to the Allies according to special orders given by the Commander-in-Chief of the forces of the Associated Powers on different fronts. No new destruction, pillage or requisition to be done by enemy troops in the territories to be evacuated by them and occupied by forces of the Associated Powers.

4. The Allies shall have the right of free movement over all road and rail and waterways in Austro-Hungarian territory and the use of the necessary Austrian and Hungarian means of transportation. The armies of the Associated Powers shall occupy such strategic points in Austro-Hungary at such times as they may deem necessary to enable them to conduct military operations or to maintain order. They shall have the right of requisition on payment for the troops of the Associated Powers wherever they may be.

5. Complete evacuation of all German troops within fifteen days, not only from Italian and Balkan fronts, but from all Austro-Hungarian territory. Internment of all German troops that have not left Austria-Hungary within that date.

6. The administration of the evacuated territories of Austro-Hungary will be entrusted to the local authorities under the control of the Allied and Associated Armies of occupation.

7. The immediate repatriation without reciprocity of all Allied prisoners of war and interned subjects and of the civilian populations evacuated from their homes on conditions to be laid down by the Commanders-in-Chief of the Forces of the Associated Powers on the various fronts.

8. Sick and wounded who cannot be removed from evacuated territory will be cared for by the Austro-Hungarian personnel, who will be left on the spot with the medical material required.

xxxvii The terms of the Armistice with Austria. (Liddle Collection)

In contrast, for the Habsburg elite, the end of the war loomed disastrously. Their last hope was that a new Foreign Minister, Andrássy, could secure a separate peace on Wilson's terms yet still salvage something out of the chaos. At the same time, some in Vienna still clutched at the idea of drawing together the regions of Austria on the lines of Karl's manifesto. Both aims, however, were being overtaken by the whirl of events. When on 26 October British troops broke through on the Italian front, the Austro-Hungarian divisions were already disintegrating as news reached them of the nationalist ferment in the rear; Magyar units were some of the first to respond to calls from the hinterland that they should return home.[42] On 28 October, the same day that Andrássy dispatched his note to Wilson, the Emperor at Schönbrunn palace agreed with the High Command to take a shorter road to peace by beginning armistice talks with Italy. In tears, those present signed the documents, since "all the sacrifices had been in vain".[43] Ten days later, Josef Redlich (as Austrian Finance Minister), made a last journey to Schönbrunn for an imperial audience. He thought of the Austro-Hungarian army which had been "shattered into a million atoms", of the Habsburgs who had lost all power, and he mused in the majestic surroundings whether those who came after would understand and continue the old culture. His own government, instead of serving as a 'peace government' had become a 'liquidation body' for the Habsburg Empire. Like so many of his contemporaries, whether joyful or distressed at the collapse of the Monarchy, Redlich now feared that the end of the war would mean social disintegration as well.[44]

Endnotes

1 Josef Redlich, *Schicksalsjahre Österreichs 1908–1919. Das politische Tagebuch Josef Redlichs*, 2 vols, Graz-Cologne, 1954, II, p. 313.

2 Prince Felix Schwarzenberg: quoted in Rudolf Neck (ed.), *Österreich im Jahre 1918. Berichte und Dokumente*, Vienna, 1968, p. 62.

3 Helmut Rumpler, *Max Hussarek. Nationalitäten und Nationalitätenpolitik in Österreich im Sommer des Jahres 1918*, Graz-Cologne, 1965, p. 9.

4 Redlich, *Schicksalsjahre Österreichs*, p. 305.

5 Neck (ed.), *Österreich im Jahre 1918*, pp. 88, 92–3; Ludwig Windischgrätz, *My Memoirs*, London, 1921, p. 302.

6 Carl Freiherr von Bardolff, *Soldat im alten Österreich*, Jena, 1938, pp. 342–3.

7 Neck (ed.), *Österreich im Jahre 1918*, p. 95.

8 V.J. Matina, 'Kadetni škola pražska za světové války', in Alois Žipek (ed.), *Domov za Války. Svědectví Účastníku*, 5 vols, Prague, 1931, V, p. 114.

9 KA [Kriegsarchiv, Vienna], EvB [Evidenzbüro 1918], Faszikel 5759/27805, Zensurstelle Wien to EvB, Na Nr 4500, Beilage 17 and 18, 4 September 1918.

10 *Ibid.*, Nr 28731, Zensurstelle Udine to HGK Feldmarschall von Boroević, Res.Nr 263, 5 September 1918. For a fuller discussion of this unrest see Mark Cornwall, 'The Experience of Yugoslav Agitation in Austria-Hungary, 1917–1918' in H.P. Cecil & P.H. Liddle (eds.), *Facing Armageddon: The First World War Experienced*, London, 1996, pp. 656 ff.

11 KA, EvB 1918, Fasz.5761, Nr 31580, Zensurstelle Wien, report for September 1918, Beilage 21; Nr 32031, Zensurstelle Feldkirch, Beilage 13 ('Polish Question'). For an alternative Polish aristocratic view from Warsaw, see the recently published diary of Princess Maria Lubomirska: Janusz Pajewski (ed.),

Pamiętnik Księżnej Marii Zdzisławowej Lubomirkiej 1914–1918, Poznań, 1997, pp. 670 ff.

12 Letter quoted in *ibid.*, Nr 31730, Zensurstelle Budapest, Na Nr 2582/863, Beilage 14 ('Peace Question'), 26 September 1918. For more mundane views from Hungary, see ibid., Nr 32014, reports of the GZNB Zensurabteilung (which handled correspondence destined for prisoners of war abroad): 'peace at any price' was a common slogan.

13 Jan Hajšman, *Mafie v Rozmachu. Vzpomínky na odboj doma*, Prague, 1933, pp. 384, 387.

14 KA, Zensurstelle Feldkirch, Fasz.5952, October report, Res.Nr 6045, 23 October 1918.

15 Neck (ed.), *Österreich im Jahre 1918*, pp.67–8.

16 For morale at the front, see Mark Cornwall, 'Morale and patriotism in the Austro-Hungarian army, 1914–1918, in *State, Society and Mobilization in Europe during the First World War*, (ed. John Horne), Cambridge, 1997, pp. 188–191; and the reports in Hugo Kerchnawe, *Der Zusammenbruch der österr.-ungar. Wehrmacht im Herbst 1918*, Munich, 1921, pp. 21–33.

17 Neck (ed.), *Österreich im Jahre 1918*, pp. 60–62.

18 KA, Zensurstelle Feldkirch, Fasz.5952, October report, Res.Nr 6045, 23 October 1918; KA, AOK [Armeeoberkommando] 1918 Op.Akten, Fasz.379, Op.Nr 113639, FM Krobatin to HGK GO Erzherzog Joseph, Op.Nr 8012/1, 6 October 1918.

19 Václav Pácalt, 'Jaroměř za světové války 1918', in Žipek (ed.), *Domov za Války*, V, pp. 138–149, 477–484.

20 *Stenographische Protokolle über die Sitzungen des Hauses der Abgeordneten der Österreichischen Reichsrates*, XXII Session, vol. IV, Vienna, 1918: 85. Sitzung, 2 October, p. 4353.

21 Michael Károlyi, *Fighting the World: The Struggle for Peace*, New York, 1925, p. 315. On the difficulty of organizing an alternative 'democratic concentration' in Hungary, see Oszkár Jászi, *Revolution and Counter-Revolution in Hungary*, London, 1924, pp. 19 ff.

22 See Cornwall, 'The Experience of Yugoslav Agitation', pp. 666 ff.

23 *Stenographische Protokolle*, 85. Sitzung, 2 October, p. 4324.

24 Vlado Strugar, *Jugoslavenske Socialdemokratske Stranke 1914–1918*, Zagreb, 1963, pp. 161 ff, 217 ff, 295 ff.

25 Josip Horvat, *Politička Povijest Hrvatske*, 2 vols, Zagreb, 1990 [first published 1936], II, p. 77.

26 *Ibid.*, pp. 83 ff.

27 Redlich, *Schicksalsjahre Österreichs*, p. 290.

28 Windischgrätz, *My Memoirs*, pp .218–9.

29 Károlyi, *Fighting the World*, p. 327.

30 Redlich, *Schicksalsjahre Österreichs*, p. 294.

31 Miklós Komjáthy (ed.), *Protokolle des Gemeinsamen Ministerrates der Österreich-ungarischen Monarchie (1914–1918)*, Budapest, 1966, pp. 680 ff.

32 Redlich, *Schicksalsjahre Österreichs*, p. 298; see also the report of Saxony's minister in Vienna: *Der Zerfall der europäischen Mitte. Staatenrevolution im Donauraum* (eds. A. Opitz & F. Adlgasser), Graz, 1990, p. 178.

33 For this and the following discussion see, Komjáthy (ed.), *Protokolle*, pp. 683–7, 692–5. (Hussarek: p. 686).

34 Helmut Rumpler, *Das Völkermanifest Kaiser Karls vom 16 Oktober 1918. Letzter Versuch zur Rettung des Habsburgerreiches, Vienna, 1966, p.20.*

35 *Ibid.*, p. 26.
36 *Ibid.*, pp. 41 ff.
37 *Ibid.*, p. 63.
38 Károlyi, *Fighting the World*, pp. 368–9.
39 Redlich, *Schicksalsjahre Österreichs*, p.302.
40 See for example the distinction made by Burián, who had sanctioned the manifesto on 15 October: István Burián, *Austria in Dissolution*, London, 1925, pp.408–10; and Ottokar Landwehr, *Die Erschöpfungsjahre der Mittelmächte 1917/18*, Zurich-Leipzig-Vienna, 1931, p. 283.
41 Komjáthy (ed.), *Protokolle*, pp.696–703; Horvat, *Politička Povijest*, p .79.
42 Zoltán Szende, *Die Ungarn im Zusammenbruch. Feldheer/Hinterland*, Oldenburg, 1931, pp. 50–6.
43 Windischgrätz, *My Memoirs*, p. 297. For the subsequent armistice talks, see Manfried Rauchensteiner, *Der Tod des Doppeladlers. Österreich-Ungarn und der Erste Weltkrieg*, Graz-Vienna-Cologne, 1993, pp. 616–22.
44 Redlich, *Schicksalsjahre Österreichs*, pp. 315, 318: at their last session the whole of the Austrian cabinet were in tears.

Chapter Twenty

Italy: A Difficult Peace

Irene Guerrini and Marco Pluviano

Italy reached the Armistice unprepared for the 'outbreak of peace'. Almost no one could imagine that the war would come to an end within the current year but after the failure of the Austrian offensive in June on the Piave and the arresting of the German attacks in France and Flanders, the Italian Supreme Command knew that the Allies were on the road to securing final victory. Although the Italian military leadership wanted to deal the final blow to the Austrian Empire during the spring of 1919, there was no wish to risk the Italian army by a premature offensive against a well-trained and well-positioned enemy. However, there were signs that Austrian strength was weakening. In this context Italy found itself having to face the developing erosion of the enemy fronts in Macedonia, the Middle East and in France without an immediate plan of action for their own front. During the first days of October, after some bitter discussions, the Italian Supreme Command came to a decision for an earlier attack than previously they had envisaged. At 3 a.m. on 24 October, fifty-seven-and-a-half divisions of the Entente (among which there were three British, two French and one Czechoslovakian division), advanced against fifty-eight-and-a-half Austro-Hungarian divisions on the front from Montegrappa to the Piave. After four days of hard fighting, the enemy started to surrender. The following day, 29 October, the Austrians began a disorganized withdrawal. In the afternoon of 3 November, Italian troops entered Trento and disembarked in Trieste. At 6 p.m. the Armistice was signed, establishing a ceasefire at 3 p.m. on 4 November. Even though the Italian units in France continued to fight until 11 November, for the Italians the war was over. After forty-two months of war, Italian casualties were high: more than 600,000 dead and about 650,000 wounded.

Rumour of the signing of the Armistice was spreading to the Italian troops during the first days of November 1918 and the reaction was joyous and triumphal. This reaction is exemplified in four retrospective accounts. Pietro Bera recalled: "... the day came when we were able to scream, crazy with joy; 'it's over, God, it's over in the best of ways'"; Duilio Faustinelli remembered: "In that very moment, you heard about armistice and you didn't exactly know what it was, but my tenant said it was like peace... Around 3 p.m. there came the notice of the end of the war and for us, poor, afflicted yet still miraculously alive, it was like being resurrected"; and Berto Sacco reminisced: "That day the colonel, with a tin hanging from his neck, on which he was banging as if on a drum, was coming down the road and was screaming 'Up with Italy!'" The same witness also remembered the soldiers' reactions: "I saw a lot of bonfires made of Nicolay sacks (full of straw and tar, useful against gas). They were scattered throughout the mountains nearby while trumpets were heard and rockets were fired in the air for enthusiasm". This image of bonfires and rockets occurs over and over again and many people remembered the soldiers organizing dancing parties in the public squares of the villages. Giuseppe Bruno remembered the evening of 4 November: "Trucks full of wine flasks came and even with the bayonet it would have been impossible to hold back the soldiers, a big celebration, like the one for our Patron Saint".

In the survivors' memories, the first nights after the peace were like the rural celebrations for harvesting and hay-making. The participants gave vent to the purest joy of living, to the wonder of still being alive, and celebrated something fantastic: the end of killing and dying. For many, shooting off rockets or setting fire to the sacks in the trenches was not only a manifestation of joy, it was also a way of using the material of war to celebrate the peace.

There were some, like Sergeant Ottone Costantini, who experienced the peace like a purification which resuscitated everything. He wrote to his fiancée on 10 November: "Today everything is born anew, everything rejoices and is transformed. All that yesterday was fading and dying away is today blossoming towards a new joy of colours. All that seemed hazy and uncertain is sparkling with bright light today". But the last days of war had also been days of fighting. Peace came in on a track full of corpses, paved with pain and destruction. Giovanni Brodini, remembering the final offensive, said: "... we figured out the beginning of the operations because in a few hours, the River Piave had turned red with blood... the river was floating away corpses, carcasses of horses and mules, trenches, revetments and empty river barges", and a few days later, referring to 3 November: "The morning following All Souls' Day, we moved on with our tools and, at a certain moment, a French patrol stopped us 'No, you can't go by!' they said, because there were too many dead bodies, all crushed, rotten... there was the danger of an epidemic. Actually the smell fairly took our breath away".

Once the fighting was over, the conditions of the civilians living in the zones occupied by the Germans and Austrians in the autumn of 1917 and in the Hapsburg territories of Trentino shocked everyone with regard to the starvation, the privations, the harshness of the occupying régime, the ruination suffered by villages and towns. The Italian soldiers spent their first days in the lands taken from the Austrians helping the local people. In the letters, diaries, and later interviews with those who were there, the witnesses described in full detail the dreadful conditions under which the Italians had been existing while neglecting the sufferings of the Germans and the Slavs who lived in that same territory. Carlo Verano recalled in his memoirs: "At 4 o' clock on 4 November

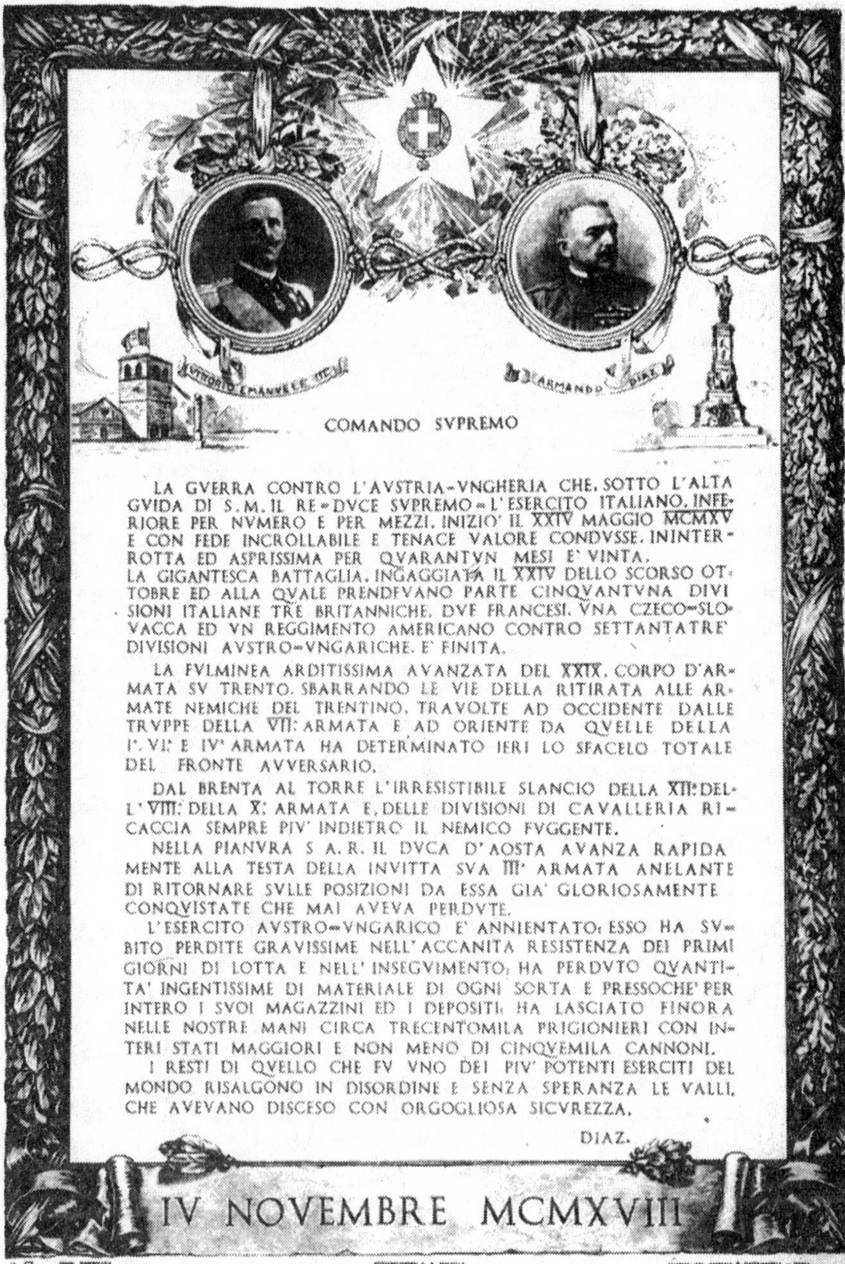

COMANDO SVPREMO

LA GVERRA CONTRO L'AVSTRIA-VNGHERIA CHE, SOTTO L'ALTA GVIDA DI S.M. IL RE-DVCE SVPREMO-L'ESERCITO ITALIANO, INFERIORE PER NVMERO E PER MEZZI, INIZIO' IL XXIV MAGGIO MCMXV E CON FEDE INCROLLABILE E TENACE VALORE CONDVSSE, ININTERROTTA ED ASPRISSIMA PER QVARANTVN MESI E' VINTA.
LA GIGANTESCA BATTAGLIA, INGAGGIATA IL XXIV DELLO SCORSO OTTOBRE ED ALLA QVALE PRENDEVANO PARTE CINQVANTVNA DIVISIONI ITALIANE TRE BRITANNICHE, DVE FRANCESI, VNA CZECO-SLOVACCA ED VN REGGIMENTO AMERICANO CONTRO SETTANTATRE' DIVISIONI AVSTRO-VNGARICHE, E' FINITA.

LA FVLMINEA ARDITISSIMA AVANZATA DEL XXIX. CORPO D'ARMATA SV TRENTO, SBARRANDO LE VIE DELLA RITIRATA ALLE ARMATE NEMICHE DEL TRENTINO, TRAVOLTE AD OCCIDENTE DALLE TRVPPE DELLA VII: ARMATA E AD ORIENTE DA QVELLE DELLA I', VI: E IV' ARMATA HA DETERMINATO IERI LO SFACELO TOTALE DEL FRONTE AVVERSARIO.

DAL BRENTA AL TORRE L'IRRESISTIBILE SLANCIO DELLA XII: DELL' VIII: DELLA X: ARMATA E, DELLE DIVISIONI DI CAVALLERIA RICACCIA SEMPRE PIV' INDIETRO IL NEMICO FVGGENTE.

NELLA PIANVRA S A. R. IL DVCA D'AOSTA AVANZA RAPIDAMENTE ALLA TESTA DELLA INVITTA SVA III' ARMATA ANELANTE DI RITORNARE SVLLE POSIZIONI DA ESSA GIA' GLORIOSAMENTE CONQVISTATE CHE MAI AVEVA PERDVTE.

L'ESERCITO AVSTRO-VNGARICO E' ANNIENTATO: ESSO HA SVBITO PERDITE GRAVISSIME NELL'ACCANITA RESISTENZA DEI PRIMI GIORNI DI LOTTA E NELL'INSEGVIMENTO; HA PERDVTO QVANTITA' INGENTISSIME DI MATERIALE DI OGNI SORTA E PRESSOCHE' PER INTERO I SVOI MAGAZZINI ED I DEPOSITI; HA LASCIATO FINORA NELLE NOSTRE MANI CIRCA TRECENTOMILA PRIGIONIERI CON INTERI STATI MAGGIORI E NON MENO DI CINQVEMILA CANNONI.

I RESTI DI QVELLO CHE FV VNO DEI PIV' POTENTI ESERCITI DEL MONDO RISALGONO IN DISORDINE E SENZA SPERANZA LE VALLI, CHE AVEVANO DISCESO CON ORGOGLIOSA SICVREZZA.

DIAZ.

IV NOVEMBRE MCMXVIII

xxxviii The final despatch of General Diaz, dated 4 November 1918, recounting Italy's part in the defeat of Austria-Hungary. (via Marco Pluviano) we were at the entrance of Trento and we saw all those women and children driven mad by starvation..., we saw all those old abandoned people recalling their sad adventures under Austrian control". Another soldier, Angelo Bonvini, wrote on 6 November to his brother: "These poor people from the Friuli region, who have lived for one year under their dominion, have suffered a lot: they have been left with no underwear, because they took it away, and with no copper to cook with since it was the first thing to be taken to Austria... In these lands there are no more church bells". Also the topic of the old village 'derelict' welcoming the Italian troops is a recurring one. Massimo Imanone, for example, wrote in his memoirs: "In the evening of 29 October we arrived at a village and we met a poor old man who welcomed us and, with reverence, took his hat off, as a sign of greeting and respect for Italian brothers".

The situation in the non-Italian-speaking areas was different. The majority of witnesses described a hostile population. As the months went by, the losers' resentment and the winners' isolation increased the incommunicability between the Italians and the Tyrolese. The Italians were looked upon, and they often acted like, occupation troops.

The Italian soldiers had played their part in the fighting which had led to the collapse of an Austro- Hungarian army which had always been tough to deal with. One witness of the Austrian defeat, Piero Cadenelli, wrote: "The evening of 4 November we arrived at Malles... the Austrians were a never-ending stream of men... great big heavily-built men, but down at heel, some of them wounded or disabled... from time to time they killed a horse and fed themselves a bit... maybe they were happy that the war had come to an end, but from their appearance one couldn't tell".

With the rumour that the Armistice had been signed, the first wish of the soldiers was to return home. Many had written to their families announcing their imminent return, but in fact, this dream came true only for a minority. The others would see their hope postponed for months. Those who went back immediately often had to face difficult situations such as financial problems. Many of those who had lived in the provinces where there had been fighting, faced the additional problem of returning to find their houses destroyed.

In Italy the terrible *Spanish flu* epidemic claimed almost 500,000 victims and was a cruel visitation upon many soldiers who survived the perils of war and returned home to find decimated families. Giovanni Bruno, on coming back to the province of Cuneo at the end of November, found the following situation: "My father who was 62 and my 22 year old sister were dead. My mother was ill in bed and so was my brother". On the other hand Ferruccio Addolori, from Friuli, entered his native village with the liberating troops and found: "The villagers, moved to tears when they saw me, a testimony of their sad past with so cruel and barbarous an enemy... in my house there are no floors and no windows left, nothing else but a few walls". [Letter dated 6 December 1918 addressed to his 'war godmother' correspondent].

As for the Italian prisoners, in total as many as 500,000, a special point must be made. Of these men, almost 100,000 are estimated to have died in prison camps due to the extremely harsh living conditions. Now, the weakened state of the survivors was worsened by the Italian Government's refusal to contribute to their support. Under the circumstances at the end of the war, prisoners were not all able immediately to regain their freedom. Often, former P.O.W.'s who were strong enough, tried to make for Italy, without waiting for someone to organize their repatriation. During the first days of peace, columns of dirty, starved and poorly-dressed men crossed Central Europe in order to reach the territories controlled by the Entente. As Severo Zammarchi recalled in an interview: "We decided to leave and there were one hundred of us. At midnight of 1 November, we started on our way, on foot, on the provincial road from Vienna to Trieste". Giovanni Allino remembered: "One evening, the French came to set us free. All the Germans in the camp had escaped... We started to go through Romania and we ate cauliflowers, apples and goatmeat".

For another witness, the Armistice days coincided with revolution. Bartolomeo Ristorto was in Vienna on 4 November and met "an Austrian soldier who came by, holding a major by the neck, the major's face bleeding... That soldier gave me a gun and told me 'Kill all the officers' [*Herren alles kaputt*]. They made us fight in the war. We were friends and yet they sent us into murderous battle. It was the officers, well now we'll see to them'". In another interview, the ex-prisoner, Pietro Bagnis, remembered the reversal of the roles following upon the news of the peace: "On 4 November 1918, as soon as we knew about the Armistice, we said 'Now we are in command'". Also Battista Rocco recalled that, soon after the Armistice: "The last month we had a great life, we were the leaders of Budapest".

Rocco, in fact, was a witness to an historical event, the murder of the Hungarian Government leader, Count Tisza: "I saw when they killed a minister, I think his name was Tisza. He was in his garden, together with his two daughters, and the rebels took him: he just had time to say goodbye to his family before being shot to death".

In the world of the Italian prisoners of war awaiting the ceasefire, local, regional and international events followed swiftly from the end of October and the first Hungarian revolutionary activity to 11 November and the German surrender. The Italian prisoners' response varied as we have seen. The majority chose to head to Trieste and Trento as fast as possible, going across an Empire that was prey to disturbances and violence between political and national groups. From their letters and interviews, we can see these men travelling anxiously, leaving behind them war destruction of landscape, buildings and men. The words pronounced by Severo Zammarchi, referring to the train bringing them back to Italy, speak for everybody: "Move on train, let's leave in a hurry, get out of this situation." Others chose to wait for the situation to cool down, perhaps attracted by the sight of the collapse of their enemies, now also being faced by revolutionary developments.

The civilians' reaction to the Armistice was even more varied. The majority exulted, invaded the streets and celebrated for days, while, for some people this date marked the beginning of great problems. First we should be mindful of those whose relatives were sick with *Spanish flu* or those who had lost a loved one during the war. All these people were victims of the war. Some had received blows from which they would never completely recover. For these people the days of Armistice celebration had no positive value, but were only another station within their personal calvary.

Among the former Hapsburg subjects of the territories of the new Italian occupation, there were some desolate reactions. For many of them, 4 November did not even bring the hope for an imminent return of their loved ones if they were prisoners in Russia or were located in the Habsburg Empire's eastern borders amidst revolutionary turbulence. It took months, even beyond a year for these soldiers to escape from the areas of political turmoil in Eastern Europe. Some only managed to return as late as 1920. For these people and their families the date of the end of the Italian war was not November 1918; they had months of anguish ahead of them and nothing to celebrate. Others, faithful to Austria, had to submit to the inquisitions of the Italian occupiers and, in some cases, face tough repressive methods. Goffredo de Banfield, star of the Austrian seaplane pilots, had a point to make, even if he exaggerated it in his memoirs: "All of a sudden, some carabinieri came to arrest me... They wanted to keep it secret by making me disappear, as had happened to many others at that time... I remained in prison for forty days and then I was told there was no charge against me".

Another peculiar situation was to be found in the lands invaded by the Austrians after Caporetto. We have already taken into account the soldiers' trauma because of the suffering of the people there, but is there evidence of their reaction to the end of the war? Valeria Bais was a woman from Trento, a prisoner of the Austrians in a camp at Braunau. She recalled in her memoirs: "finis Austriae":

> You can well imagine our consolation, after years of hoping... After a telegram, we were told that we Italians had to leave within fifteen days in order to go back to our beautiful, smiling and peaceful country. After having suffered and been tormented, always holding on to hope, we have arrived safe and happy, in our beautiful country, Italy. Our trip was a bit worrying, because we were thinking of our future.

The parish priest, from Friuli, Giuliano Da Ronco, wrote in his diary about the arrival of the Italian troops:

> 3 November. Ever since the first hours of the morning, we have heard the noise of our machine gun and the echo of well-known military marches. Some are already wearing, hidden under cover, the tricolour shirt. 4 November. The sight of those soldiers brings us all back to life and a smile appears once more on our faces. Our hearts rejoice... crowds of kids run down the village roads – previously still and quiet – the church bells are ringing loudly and inviting everybody to the church. In no time the holy place is over-crowded.

The reaction of the people living in small villages, far from the front and therefore 'secure', was the same all over the national territory. Costantino

Rollandi, in his "chronicle", witnessed the reaction of Manarola, a fishing village in eastern Liguria: "5 November Official News. All the church bells ring. Three celebration days also at the Arsenal. 11 November. In the evening... Germany has also signed the peace conditions. The whole world celebrates... After five years we hear some fireworks. It seems as if the world has changed and people are all happy". Another example refers to a small town in southern Italy, Agropoli. Again in this case, the first thought linked to the peace is the end of danger for the soldiers and their future return home. Antonio Stirone, of a poor farming family, was fourteen at the time and his father was at the front. During a recent interview he said:

> I always remember the last day, when the war was over. I was working near to my house when the oxen got out of my hands and overturned the plough and broke it... My uncle coming from town reached me and I said, 'Uncle look, I've broken the plough' and he said, 'Break the other one too, the war is over!' He had two sons at the front, poor soul, you can imagine what he was going through.

Before looking at what was going on in the big urban centres, it would be helpful to have some general idea of Italy's socio-economic situation. The country was in poor shape with inflation, high State debts and dependence on foreign economic aid. The effect of inflation and the erosion of salary purchasing power had been very serious. As one instance, the salaries in the civil service had gone from a value of 100 to 57.9 in real terms. It is not therefore surprising that in the major production and management centres of the country, the first days of peace coincided with large-scale agitation.

It would be wrong to infer from this that the workers were indifferent to the end of the war and to the victory. For example, in Rome about 40,000 workers of some reserve factories obtained a day off on 5 November and formed a procession in order to show their joy in the very heart of the nation. In Genoa, a procession of workers crossed the town with enthusiastic and spontaneous demonstrations and they also played a large part in the more official ceremonies. On 13 November, a big procession, formed mainly by workers, made for the main offices of the Ansaldo factory in order to acclaim the owners as "admirable builders of those weapons that produced victory".

In Milan, the Socialist Municipal Board ordered the display of Italian flags on all the buildings owned by the Municipality and appropriated the amount of 500,000 Italian liras to support the homecoming of the refugees from Veneto and Friuli who had escaped following upon the Austrian invasion after Caporetto. In La Spezia, an important industrial centre and main naval base in the Tyrhennian Sea, the workers celebrated enthusiastically. They were strongly influenced by the Socialists and the Anarchists, but all of them abstained from going to work on 4, 5, 6, 12 and 13 November in order to commemorate the victorious end of the war.

This acclaim mixed with the social tensions which the strict discipline imposed by the "state of war" had not managed to appease. Worker aims were at the seat of these tensions in the major industrial towns, Genoa, Milan,

Turin, La Spezia, throughout the last weeks of the war. Better working conditions and safety measures in the factories, increase of the "Indemnity food advance", reduction of working hours and half day off on Saturdays [the so called *English Saturday*], these causes were felt with an emotion akin to the working class pride in victory – a powerful demonstration of strength, pride and class autonomy. It is not a coincidence that the ruling class which had earned huge amounts of money from supplying the needs of war, showed strong resistance to the request to pay their workers for those days taken off work to celebrate the end of the war. In some cases, disciplinary measures were taken against workers who had taken time off. The socialist worker, Travesi, from La Spezia, described such measures as "reactionary and directed against the Arsenal workers' organization" and his fellow party member, Dané, asserted that it was necessary "to be ready to fight against the capitalists and the abuses of the ruling class and to respond to violence with violence".

While the echoes of their joyous celebration of victory in the war were still reverberating, the same workers organized demonstrations which became more and more extreme, generating a major fighting movement which involved all the large industrial centres. This movement mixed financial demands, the requirement of social amelioration on a largescale, and revolutionary plans inspired by the Russian revolution. The sufferings and restrictions imposed on workers and all those on the Home Front played a part in this surging call for change. The end of the war represented for the workers the removal of the barriers which had seriously limited their freedom in and outside of the factory. Despite the differences between the General Working Confederation, the Socialist Party and other more radical forces, during the last weeks of the year and the first of 1919, there was an explosion of social conflict which led to some achievements in the line of wage increases, job contracts, and working hours. The struggle of heavy industry workers encouraged the claims of those traditionally more quiet categories of labour, the post and telegraph workers, the municipal employees, those in hospitals, the bakers, and many more. They went on strike for general and specific claims.

While the workers were promoting their offensive in order to obtain some meaningful gains, serious employment problems emerged. Converting to a peacetime economy was drastically reducing the number of working establishments, hitting in particular the less qualified workers, that is the young and women. In Genoa, for example, by 13 December 1918, about 10,000 workers had already been fired and further losses were expected. Of course, the fact that female labour was destined to be cut anyway with the homecoming of the demobilized soldiers, has to be taken into account. Demobilization – almost suspended between February and June 1919 – was delayed because of the necessity to obtain some employment vacancies first.

In this respect the paternalist message of General Emilio De Bono to his soldiers was full of meaning: "Before sending you back home, we have to be sure we can give you an occupation ... There will surely be some work but it is necessary to organize it beforehand". The soldiers wanted to go home. They could not stand military life any longer. The recollections of the uncelebrated may be noted here like those of Luigi Giovannetti, who recalled: "To win a war is worse than to lose it, there was always some territory to occupy: Monastir, Albania, Libia". The soldier, Emilio Barbieri, wrote from Trento to his parents on 6 November 1918: "Our freedom belongs to us and soon we'll come home forever... For the moment no more shootings, we're happy but we're still waiting for some leave".

In the meantime, the demobilized soldiers, the disabled and mutilated, were organizing themselves, laying the foundations of the phenomenon which was to grow in importance during the months and years following the Armistice, the 'ex-servicemen's' attitude. During the final weeks of 1918, about 1,400,000 soldiers were demobilized, the older ones taking priority. The serious problems which they were to face led the powerful "National Association of War Invalids and Crippled" into a concern for the ex-soldier in civilian life and to the idea of promoting an old combattants' association. This association would be aimed at keeping the survivors protected from aggressive nationalism and revolutionary socialism, and at the promotion of a network of relief and social activities to help the reintegration of these old soldiers and give them a significant place in society.

In the 'ex-servicemen's' organizations one could recognize the same attitude of the men at the front at the end of the war: satisfaction, desire to get back to civilian life, fear that all the sacrifices they had made would be forgotten or not acknowledged in any way. As evidence of this, we might take a letter dated 27 November, which testifies to the insecurity of the soldiers about their future: "I have to think of my civilian position. I still don't know what I'll do, if I continue to study or find a good job. We'll wait for events and see also the new measures the Government will issue in favour of those who have fought for their country". The letter to his parents, written on 14 November by another volunteer, the writer Giovanni Comisso, is representative too: "I understand, your joy for the victory is good because it is disinterested and I have rejoiced too... but these days I have more serious matters concerning my future".

The war had wrought change for the small urban middle class which had provided so many of the young officers, and to the farmers' world, which had furnished the majority of the food and fodder for men, horses and mules. These classes were now conscious of their hitherto political and social subordination and they demanded justice and some social change, even though in no organized, structured way. The farmers, in particular, claimed the immediate expropriation and assignment of the state lands and of the uncultivated large estates. The failure of the socialists to realize that their interests and those of the dissatisfied middle class and the farmers had much in common, in terms of positive values, was to be fatal for them and, in retrospect, for the future of Italian democracy.

More generally, the traditional political parties, the socialists and those in the liberal camp and the Catholics who, for the first time, were ready to build a party of their own, were unable to face and solve the problems arising from the end of the war. The nationalist Right reacted to the social disarray by

xxxix An illustration from an Italian war veteran's account, published in 1931. In this book - and during the Fascist period in general - the Italian soldier was lionised. The everyday hardships endured by the troops - and the fact that by the time of the Armistice the men were nearly at breaking point – were played down. (Liddle Collection) stressing the unachieved expansionist goals of the Italian war. In tune with the Government led by Orlando and the Foreign Minister, Sonnino, they claimed the full enforcement of the "London Agreement" of April 1915. In this way the Right introduced to the nation its own recipe – acquisition of almost all of Dalmatia, control of the Adriatic Sea and territorial expansion to the Near East.

Italy emerged from the war with credit for the part it had played and yet the evidence shown here reveals a nation in crisis. Almost 400,000 prisoners of war were returning, dispirited and in bad physical condition. Some hundreds of thousands of war disabled, many of whom were unable to work and who faced tremendous difficulties in being reaccepted in society, were to be handled by a welfare system that was demonstrably inadequate. Industry and commerce proved completely incapable of taking on all the demobilized servicemen and so the unemployment situation worsened.

The prospects were far from bright and people seemed quickly to realize it. There was exultation for the victory and even more so for the end of the war but, after a couple of days of excitement, Italian attention seemed to focus on immediate and future anxieties. In those first months not many were concerned about the danger of a 'mutilated' victory.

Accounts contemporary with the period and those obtained later confirm that the majority of the Italian soldiers did what they thought was their duty in the war, without being in conscious agreement over the reasons for going to war. There was great satisfaction and pride in having overcome a very tough test, rather than an indulgence in nationalist euphoria. The soldiers hoped that the victory would bring them an allotment of land, social justice and welfare support, – all the key-words of the official propaganda – and a few were interested in imperialist aims. However, civilians and servicemen seemed convinced that this must be the last war and many thought that society had to change radically, perhaps by revolution. Only the political shortsightedness of the ideologically committed parties and the Government's incapacity to adapt its own territorial demands to the changed international political atmosphere, allowed, within a year, the nationalist Right to spread through the population the myth of the 'mutilated victory', in place of the hope for a 'just peace' which most had seen as the goal. On the future of the country there was some hint of the violence of the extreme Right, soon to rehearse its bid for power with the Fiume exploit.

Endnotes

In our translation of the personal experience testimony quoted here we have eliminated dialect and slang terms and corrected the grammar, but we have tried to keep to the writer's style. In the course of our research, we have examined hundreds of testimonies: the ones we have chosen to quote (the names of the witnesses are in capital letters) are taken from the following published texts and archives, with the names of 'our' witnesses shown in capital letters.

SACCO: S. Pedemonte, *Verso casa. Cronache di soldati isolesi. 1805–1947*, Isola del Cantone, Centro Culturale, 1995.

G. BRUNO, P. BAGNIS, G. ALLINO, B. RISTORTO: N. Revelli, *Il mondo dei vinti*, 2 v., Torino, Einaudi, 1977.
O. COSTANTINI: C. Costantini, *Un contabile alla guerra*, Torino, Paravia, 1996.
C. VERANO, M. IMANONE, C. ROLLANDI, G. MAZZONI, E. BARBIERI: these documents are kept in the Ligurian Archive of Popular Writing, at the Department of Contemporary History, University of Genoa.
L. GIOVANNETTI, D. FAUSTINELLI, S. ZAMMARCHI, B. ROCCO, A. BONVINI, G. BRODINI, P. BERA, P. CADENELLI: S. Fontana and M. Pierretti – eds. – , *La grande guerra.Operai e contadini lombardi nel primo conflitto mondiale*, Milano, Silvana, 1980.
V. BAIS: Q. Antonelli – ed. by – , *Scritture di guerra*, vol. 4, Trento, Museo storico in Trento; Rovereto, Museo storico italiano della guerra, 1996.
Don G. DA RONCO: L. Fabi – ed. – , *La gente e la guerra. Documenti*, Udine, Il Campo, 1990.
A. STIRONE: private archive.
G. COMISSO: L. Urettini, *Il giovane Comisso e le sue lettere a casa*, Abano Terme, Francisci, 1985.
G. DE BANFIELD: *L'aquila di Trieste*, Trieste, LINT, 1984.
Historical Archive of the Museo del Risorgimento di Milano: Generale E. DE BONO, Alcuni consigli ai miei soldati, novembre 1918, typescript, A.S.C. 23/18567; F. ADDOLORI, letter, A.S.C., 28/19670.
Record Office of Genova, file Prefettura, boxes 304 – Prefect's report – and 296 – Social unrests, strikes, riots -.
Italian daily newspapers: *Il Secolo XIX*; *Corriere della Sera*.

Part IV

The Legacy

Chapter Twenty-One

The European and International Consequences of the Armistice

John Bourne

The last shot is fired: The slaughter is over: The enemy people are in revolution: What will come of it?

Diary of Florence Lockwood, 12 November 1918.[1]

The principal consequence of the Armistice for Europe and the world was simple. German acceptance of the Allied terms was a recognition of defeat. The Central Powers had lost the war. The Allies had won. The victors, especially the 'Big Three' – Great Britain, France and the United States of America, would decide the peace. This would be shaped by idealism, pragmatism and fear. The idealism would be largely (though not entirely) American, the pragmatism largely (though not entirely) British, and the fear largely (though not entirely) French.

German surrender made it inevitable that the map of Europe would be redrawn. The Armistice terms themselves left no room for doubt. The German Armistice delegation had hoped for sympathetic treatment, but they were soon disabused of this by the intransigent Allied *generalissimo*, Marshal Ferdinand Foch. The harshness of the Armistice terms was designed to prevent Germany from pausing for breath and beginning the war again. The terms also pre-figured the peace settlement which would be signed at Versailles in June 1919. Germany was required to evacuate all occupied territory, to retreat to points twenty-five miles east of the Rhine and to surrender territory on its left bank, including river crossings and bridgeheads of at least 30 kilometres in radius at Mainz, Coblenz and Cologne. Huge quantities of war materials, including the whole of the German submarine fleet, were to be surrendered. The costs of the Allied occupation were to be born entirely by Germany.

Foch's statue now dominates the forest clearing in which the German surrender took place. The Armistice represented a personal triumph and a moment to savour for his country. France had, perhaps, suffered most among the Allies. The war had been a martyrdom and an epic of national resistance.

French casualties were among the highest proportionately of any belligerent. A tenth of French soil had been under enemy occupation for more than four years. Its industrial capacity and mineral wealth had been systematically exploited and, during the final German retreat, systematically wrecked. At the very least France had the right to expect, and the power to demand, the restoration of Belgian sovereignty, the recovery of Alsace-Lorraine and German financial restitution for the damage inflicted on French soil – 'reparations'.

The French, however, did not have long to enjoy their moment of triumph. Harvesting the fruits of victory would be as difficult as the victory itself. Foch and his prime minister, Georges Clemenceau, were both aware that even in defeat Germany would remain larger, more populous and more productive than France and with an industrial infrastructure largely untouched by the ravages of war. How long before Germany once more became a threat, five years, ten, twenty? Foch was willing to contemplate the dismemberment of

REUNITED

Strasbourg, December 8th, 1918.

xl The spirit of France reunited with her lost city of Strasbourg. (From *Mr Punch's History of the Great War*)

Germany. Clemenceau favoured annexation of the Rhineland, the key to future French security, and at the very least its demilitarization. In the event, however, when the map of Europe was redrawn, Germany would only be marginally affected, though the loss of territory was enough to fuel the spirit of *revanchism* from which fascism would draw both inspiration and support. The full price of defeat would be felt, instead, by Germany's allies, Austria-Hungary and Turkey. French hopes of ensuring long-term security against her powerful neighbour would founder on Anglo-Saxon sensibilities and widespread fear of the Bolshevik menace in the East.

The First World War has had a bad press, especially in the English-speaking world. During the 1920s and 30s a considerable literature of disillusionment derided wartime idealism as naïve, even reprehensible. Patriotism was not enough. These views lodged themselves firmly in popular memory where the war is commonly recalled as avoidable, mismanaged and futile. They were reinforced by the perceived experience of the Second World War as an inevitable and necessary struggle against evil and tyranny, a 'people's war' which achieved a 'people's peace'. Distance may lend perspective but it can also distort. For those who fought it, the First World War was clearly about something. It mattered who won and who lost. This was not simply a matter of patriotism and national survival, so clear-cut in countries like Belgium, France and Serbia, which had been invaded and occupied by enemy forces. It was also a question of ideology. The ideological nature of the war is consistently underestimated. It was the Last Crusade of nineteenth-century liberalism. This was nowhere more true than in Great Britain and, eventually, the United States.

Of course, this aspect of the war subsisted alongside others, more pragmatic. The British statesmen who took their country to war in 1914 were not embarking on a liberal crusade. They were seeking to achieve the survival and long-term security of the British Empire. This, they believed, was fundamental to the future prosperity and stability of Britain and could only be achieved by British belligerency. If Britain stayed out of the war, there were dangers not only from a German victory but also a French and Russian one. France and Russia, after all, were Britain's chief imperial rivals, not Germany. The British statesmen who would negotiate the Versailles settlement had these aims firmly in view. They could not be achieved simply by winning the war. It was also necessary to win the peace. Unfortunately for the British government, it was not a free agent. The interests of its Allies would have to be considered. And so would domestic and international opinion. This was often ambiguous and contradictory, but nevertheless real.

British victory in the Great War required the mass mobilization of the British people and they had ideas of their own about why the war was being fought and what it should eventually achieve. These ideas were often of a traditional nature, 'King and Country' certainly, 'King and Empire' perhaps. There were plenty of people about in the aftermath of the Armistice who wanted to hang the Kaiser and turn Germany into a disarmed pastoral society incapable ever again of disturbing the peace. One of the first domestic consequences of the Armistice was that the coalition government called a snap

'Khaki election'. Its rhetoric appealed to the basest instincts. Germany would be made to pay and, if necessary, squeezed until the pips squeaked.

But these ideas existed alongside others, often equally traditional, to do with fair play and a sense of justice. For some, the concept of the just cause remained almost subliminal; for others, particularly amongst the educated, informed, articulate middle classes who flooded into the army in unprecedented numbers, it was carefully thought out and passionately held. H.S. Lawson, a headmaster in his thirties when the war began, read all the published documentation about the outbreak of war before he volunteered. Convinced of Germany's 'guilt', he devoted the rest of his life, until his death in action in 1918 as a 41 year-old artillery lieutenant, to the destruction of German militarism.[2] Lawson had no wish, however, to inflict a Carthaginian peace on Germany. He fought an ideological war but he wanted an idealistic peace in which such tragedies would never again be allowed to recur.

For Lawson, and for many others who shared his views, the defining moment was German violation of Belgian neutrality. It is difficult to overestimate the importance of this act. Opposition to the war in Britain virtually disappeared overnight. British and, to a great extent, Allied belligerency camped on the moral high ground of world opinion for the rest of the war and was made impregnable by repeated German acts seen as morally outrageous, the shooting of hostages, the wanton destruction of the great medieval library at Louvain,[3] the military use of poison gas, the sinking of unarmed merchant ships, unrestricted submarine warfare, aerial bombing of civilian targets. Germany became, increasingly, an international pariah. By the time of the Armistice, she was at war with no fewer than 28 countries. These included, of course, the United States of America.

The Great War began as a nineteenth-century 'Cabinet war' on the Bismarckian model, but the collapse of the Schlieffen Plan, the 'miracle of the Marne' and the onset of trench warfare punctured this delusion. The cost of the military means had an almost immediate political effect. The effect was inflationary. Mass mobilization and mass sacrifice required something more substantial to sustain them than discredited diplomatic abstractions like 'the balance of power'. Increasingly, the war came to be seen as a struggle between value systems, between parliamentary government and autocracy, between freedom and tyranny, between civilization and barbarism. Subtle and sophisticated Allied propaganda, much of it British, came increasingly to portray the war in this way to both domestic and neutral audiences. Germany found herself isolated and defensive in the face of this moral onslaught, especially in the United States.

The great embarrassment for those liberals and democrats who viewed the war in moral absolutes was, of course, the presence in the Allied camp of the world's greatest autocracy, Russia. The collapse of Tsarism during the February revolution of 1917 seemed to clarify the issues once and for all. American entry into the war, the following April, was undoubtedly facilitated by events in Russia. It also did much to reinforce the idea of the war as a crusade, bringing to the forefront of world events the chief crusader, President Woodrow Wilson.

Wilson was determined that his country would play a decisive role in the outcome of the Great War. This meant, as he came painfully to recognize, that the United States itself would actually have to go to war. Without participating in the struggle America would lack the moral authority and political influence to decide the peace. Deciding the peace was vital for Wilson. The United States did not enter the war simply to play the 'great game' of power diplomacy. This was reflected in the status she accepted, not that of an Ally but of an Associated Power. The United States would be Associated with the Allies only so far as they were prepared to share the Wilsonian view of the war and, more importantly, of the peace. These views were encapsulated in his famous 'Fourteen Points', first enunciated in January 1918. They had an immediate impact on the conduct of the war and on the way it was perceived by the Allies, the Central Powers and neutrals alike.

Until then the British government had avoided any clarification or specification of its war aims. This, it was felt, was as likely to undermine as it was to maintain the moral consensus which underpinned the British war effort. The policy became unsustainable during the final winter of the war. The British government had wind of Wilson's intentions. On 5 January 1918, significantly before an audience of trade unionists, the British prime minister David Lloyd George testified to the disinterested idealism of Britain's cause and her determination to effect a just and lasting peace based on the sanctity of international law, the right of national self-determination and the creation of an international organization to 'limit the burden of armaments and diminish the probability of war'.[4] It was now, officially, a 'war to end all wars'. In aligning the British and American positions Lloyd George did much to restore flagging Allied morale, but this alignment meant that in the aftermath of any Allied victory, which then seemed remote, idealism as well as self-interest would have to be allowed its say.

The promulgation of Wilson's 'Fourteen Points' played its part in undermining German resistance. Their existence made it more likely that Germany would seek an Armistice in the autumn of 1918. In Ludendorff's case, this arose from the deluded belief that Germany would be able to obtain better Armistice terms by dealing with the Americans than with the French and British, a point of view daily undermined by his continuing presence at the head of German affairs and by the actions of Germany's army and U-boat commanders. In the case of those who came to power in Germany in October 1918, it arose out of a sincere desire for peace on Wilsonian terms. At the heart of these terms was the principle of self-determination. The principle was, in Wilson's view, universal. It could not be denied to Germany simply because she had been defeated. Germany would have to pay a price for defeat, but that price was unlikely to include dismemberment. Germany was, after all, inhabited almost entirely by Germans. Under what arrangements should they live other than in a German state? This state would, doubtless, have to divest itself of its autocratic superstructure, indeed had already done so even before the Armistice was signed. Germany would have to give up its conquests in Belgium and France. Bismarck's annexations would have to be restored to France and Denmark. Painful losses would have to be endured in the east to facilitate the restoration of an independent Polish state, the thirteenth of Wilson's 'Fourteen Points'. The British would certainly demand the secession of all Germany's colonies, but these were mostly worthless and a distraction. Massive reductions in military strength would be imposed. But Germany itself would remain largely united and intact, a powerful country at the heart of

RECONSTRUCTION: A NEW YEAR'S TASK

xli The awesome scale of the task facing the world in 1919, as seen in *Mr Punch's History of the Great War*.

Europe, and one whose national aspirations could not forever be set aside. France would continue to live in the shadow of a mighty neighbour.

Neither Wilsonian liberalism nor fears of Bolshevism, however, contained comfort for Germany's allies, the multi-ethnic empires of Austria-Hungary and Turkey. These empires were already in an advanced state of disintegration before the German Armistice was signed. It would have been difficult, perhaps impossible, for the Allied and Associated powers to maintain them even had they wanted to, but the Armistice signed their death warrant. The principle of self-determination ensured their dismemberment and this was particularly significant in the case of the Austro-Hungarian Empire. This empire had appeared, to its detractors, increasingly anachronistic, a medieval relic with no place in a new world order of nation states defined by commonality of race, language and religion. The Armistice made inevitable the fall of the Habsburgs. No one understood this better than the last emperor, Karl, who had been trying to avoid it by seeking a compromise peace ever since he came to the throne at the end of 1916, though – ambiguous to the end – he indulged the fantasy of a return to power until his death in exile on Madeira at the age of 35 in 1922. The Hungarian component of the Dual Monarchy would lose out even more than the Austrian. Two-thirds of its territory and a third of its population would be ceded to Czechoslovakia, Yugoslavia and (especially) Romania at the peace of Trianon in June 1920. The other Central Power, Bulgaria, would lose territory to Yugoslavia and Greece. Four independent states, Finland, Estonia, Latvia and Lithuania, would also be created on the territory of the former Russian Empire. These were all areas ceded to the Germans in the punitive treaty of Brest-Litovsk in March 1918. Russia, too, thus paid the price for defeat. Its new Bolshevik government was considered beyond the pale and would be allowed no part in the post-Armistice peace negotiations.

Satisfying Slav national aspirations at the expense of a defeated enemy was one thing; reconciling them with the territorial ambitions of an ally, however, was another. Italy had been attracted to the Allied side in May 1915 principally by the prospect of territorial aggrandizement in the Adriatic. She would, however, be disappointed by the eventual size of her reward. Italy ended the war socially and politically divided and by 1922 had succumbed to fascist dictatorship. Even the fruits of victory could be bitter.

The Ottoman Empire ceased to exist four days after the signing of the German Armistice. Imperialism, however, rather than self-determination would prove the decisive motive in its redistribution. The British had been willing to sponsor Arab nationalism during the war and a British officer, Colonel T.E. Lawrence, had forged a legend in its support. But Arab national aspirations would find less sympathy among the peacemakers at Versailles than those of Slavs. The British and French had long conspired to carve up the middle-east after the war and they largely did so, the British even choosing to intrude a new element of uncertainty into the area by their eccentric patronage of Zionism. What was true of the middle east was even more true of the 'third world'. Germany's colonies in South-West and East Africa and the Pacific would be absorbed into the British Empire, either under direct

British control or under the control of the British Dominions, principally South Africa and Australia. A war which had been publicly fought on principles of national self-determination and the rights of small nations would result in one of the biggest expansions of colonial control in British history.

The peace settlements which followed the Armistice would, nevertheless, do much to complete the nationalist agenda of nineteenth-century European liberalism. However, the nationalisms which the victors blessed were rarely forged from the progressive, democratic metal of Garibaldi or Mazzini, but were often narrow, mean-spirited affairs, rooted in ancient tribal hatreds and ethnic tensions, with much capacity for future mischief. As for the 'third world', they would have to wait for another war and the destructive impact of Japanese arms to realize their dreams of national self-determination.

Internationalism was also central to the agenda of nineteenth-century European liberalism and Wilsonian idealism, but creating a supra-national body to police the new world order would prove even more difficult than

OVERWEIGHTED

PRESIDENT WILSON: "Here's your olive branch. Now get busy."
DOVE OF PEACE: "Of course, I want to please everybody, but isn't this a bit thick?"

xlii An ominous portent for the future of the League of Nations. (From *Mr Punch's History of the Great War*) nation-building. President Wilson would not even be able to deliver his own country's support. The United States Congress would repudiate the Covenant of the League of Nations and refuse to ratify the Treaty of Versailles. The Soviet Union would be excluded from the League and so, for some years, would Germany. The only effective instrument available to the League would be the French Army. This would prove increasingly frail in the post-war world, and France's victory too, would begin to look less and less significant in the years ahead. The degree of security offered by the pre-war alliance with Russia would find no effective substitute among the turbulent and avaricious successor states of Austria-Hungary's Balkan dominions. Anglo-American support would be grudging and unreliable. France would be left to contemplate her material inferiority to Germany, her lack of powerful friends – and, to remember her sacrifices in the Great War. France's catastrophic collapse in the spring of 1940 was as much moral as physical; its author was as much Erich von Falkenhayn as the 'Panzer generals'.

The eventual outcome of German defeat would represent a much more satisfactory state of affairs for the British than the French. The British representative on the Armistice commission was, significantly, a sailor, Admiral Sir Roslyn Weymss. British naval superiority was fundamental to her power in the world. Naval supremacy had permitted the despatch of great armies to France, to Salonika, to Palestine, to Mesopotamia; it had kept Britain safe from invasion and famine; it had allowed her to impose an increasingly ruthless economic blockade against Germany, a blockade which she would not lift until the ink was dry on a final settlement. The Armistice delivered the German fleet into British hands. Within a few months it would be resting at the bottom of the North Sea, scuttled by its own crews. British enthusiasm for Wilsonian idealism would not extend to any agreement which would limit her ability to use the naval weapon in a future war. Whatever shape the new world order took, it would have to make a place for the Royal Navy and the Empire which it protected.

If the consequences of the Armistice were to prove ambiguous and difficult for the victors, for the vanquished political and military elites of Germany and Austria-Hungary, they would be immediate and catastrophic. Defeat would bring in its train precisely those transformations which the war was designed to prevent. The Armistice signalled the end of an era for central European aristocracy and monarchy, an historic verdict which would prove irreversible. Wilhelm II was bounced into abdication by Prince Max of Baden on 9 November, a decision which would be formally ratified seventeen days after the Armistice, and fled to ignominious exile in Holland where his entourage was met by an obstructive border guard and a minor display of Dutch disapproval. It was a melancholy end for the Supreme War Lord. He left behind him not a stable political entity shorn of an inconvenient monarch, but a country in turmoil, facing the prospect of revolution and disintegration.

Defeat did not fall equally on all Germans. For some, especially on the Left, it represented opportunity. In Bavaria, as early as 7 November, socialists led by Kurt Eisner threatened to begin the dismemberment of Germany from within by declaring a Bavarian People's Republic. Philip Scheidemann, one of the leaders of the Social Democrats, fearing being outflanked by the radical Spartacists led by Karl Liebknecht and Rosa Luxemburg, proclaimed a German republic from the balcony of the Reichstag on 9 November. Scheidemann and his leader, Friedrich Ebert, were not revolutionaries. They believed that a Republic was essential to bring about an Armistice, to maintain order and to deliver Germany from the tightening grip of famine. Their views brought them into increasing conflict with the advocates of radical change. Liebknecht would engineer a Berlin uprising in January 1919 and be crushed within a fortnight. Elections for a National Assembly would be held later in the month and a new constitution proclaimed at Weimar in August. A weak, sickly, pluralistic democracy, dominated by the socialists and trades unionists whom Germany's traditional ruling elite despised, would take its place in the centre of Europe. Born in defeat and civil war, it inherited the burden of the Versailles settlement and its economic depredations. Its prospects did not look encouraging.

The European and international consequences of the Armistice were not only political but also economic. The Great War destroyed the old economic order. Most governments believed the war would be short. This was not because they were complacent, but because they believed that sustaining the economic burden of modern industrial war for any length of time would be impossible without incurring national bankruptcy. They may have been right about the bankruptcy but they were wrong about the timescale. This would take years rather than weeks. It proved not only necessary but also possible for governments to intervene in economic management, to organize shifts of resources from domestic consumption to armaments production, to finance these by increasing taxation, by borrowing and by printing money. Nineteenth-century governments had been notably prudent. During the war governmental thrift went out of season. In Germany military expenditure alone rose to a colossal 53 per cent of GDP by 1917. This kind of big spending was common to all belligerent powers. Adherence to the traditional instrument of financial probity, the Gold Standard, was an early victim of war economics. So, too, was the pattern of international trade. By 1914 Britain, France and Germany were the source of about 60 per cent of the world's exports of manufactured goods. During the war the transfer of industrial production to war-related industries meant that Britain, France and Germany were unable to supply the world's manufacturing needs as well. The world did not wait for the return of peace, but looked instead to the industries of the United States and Japan and to increased domestic production to supply the deficit. The belligerents' need to expand industrial production in war-related industries also had the effect of displacing agriculture from its privileged fiscal position. Import duties, designed to protect the domestic agricultural sector, were abandoned in the search for access to cheap overseas supplies.

If the economic consequences of the war were profound, so too were the consequences of its conclusion. There was little understanding of the need for a new economic order to go with a new political order. On the contrary, there was much nostalgic desire to return to economic 'normalcy' when currencies were tied to the price of gold, taxation was low, government expenditures were small, cotton and coal were 'King' and the London money markets ruled the world. It was not to be. The genie was out of the bottle and would never be put back. The Armistice would render much industrial capacity in the belligerent nations surplus overnight. Readjustment of industrial economies to the patterns of peacetime production and consumption would prove extremely difficult. Economic readjustment would be handicapped by the burden of debt, by the damage inflicted on transport infrastructures and other physical assets and in, Germany's case, also by reparations. The redrawing of the map of Europe in the aftermath of the Central Powers' defeat would be done with little regard to economic considerations. The successor states of the Russian and Austro-Hungarian empires would seek to overcome their inheritance of economic weakness by policies of self-sufficiency. Domestic production would be protected by tariff barriers and exports encouraged. This would simultaneously impose new restrictions on world trade and lead to a glut of cheap exports on the world market. Artificially high food prices would collapse. Agriculture would join industry in the economic doldrums. The spectre of depression, unemployment and economic nationalism would begin to take shape.

Florence Lockwood, whose diary is quoted at the beginning of this chapter, was a Liberal, a feminist, a suffragist and a pacifist. She opposed the war. She consistently advocated a negotiated peace. When the Armistice was announced, she refused to celebrate. Despite a life devoted to achieving women's political rights, she could not even raise the enthusiasm to vote in the general election in December. Hers was not the predominant response. The civilian populations of the victorious powers would erupt into an orgy of celebration. But when they sobered up, their considered views would fall more into line with Mrs Lockwood's. The last shot had been fired. The slaughter had stopped. But the killing was not over. More than a thousand people would die in the Berlin uprising. Allied soldiers would continue to die in fruitless anti-Bolshevik interventions. Within a year the British Army would again find itself at war on a familiar battlefield, Afghanistan. The legacy of the Armistice would not only be peace but also revolution, civil war, economic dislocation, political and social unrest. Few who lived astride the Great War failed to recognize that they had witnessed the end of an era. Some looked back with longing. Some looked forward with hope. Many looked forward with foreboding. What would come of it?

Endnotes

1 Quoted in Tom Foulerton, 'A Critical Edition of the Diary of Florence Elizabeth Lockwood, 1915–16', Unpublished B.A. Dissertation, University of Birmingham, 1998, p. xv. The diary is now in the Liddle Collection, University of Leeds.

2 H.S. Lawson, *Letters of a Headmaster Soldier*, London, H.R. Allenson, n.d., p. 12.

3 The importance of this event was brought home to me at the Christening of the youngest daughter of my friend and colleague, Carl Chinn, in 1996. One of the child's given names was 'Louvain'. When I asked why this was, Carl replied

that it was in memory of his grandmother, universally known as 'Lou', who died early in the year. His grandmother was born in November 1914 in working-class Aston, her name a commemoration of the destruction of Louvain cathedral.

4 D. Lloyd George, *War Memoirs* (2 vols., London: Odhams, [1938]), II, pp. 1492–93.

Chapter Twenty-Two

'I say it *is* a victory': The Armistice in British, French, German and American Literature

Hugh Cecil

In this historical survey of literary reactions to the Armistice, good and bad writers alike are considered here for the evidence they provide and little judgement is passed on their quality. Many of the poems and novels listed here express jubilation or grief – as one would expect – and have contributed to the familiar image of the Armistice in modern memory. Others are more surprising – those which record soldiers' disappointment that the war is ending, for example. There are features common to the writings from all four countries which are being considered here, but obviously those from Britain and France were composed from the standpoint of victors heavily committed to the war and with much cause to rejoice, while the Germans' thoughts were on defeat, domestic instability and food shortages. The German writers mention no celebrations save a few flowers thrown to glum returning regiments and the occasional orgy of alcohol and sex, though it should not be forgotten that many of the troops received a heartfelt welcome home from civilians who were astonished by their high morale.[1]

Some well-known writers from the U.S.A., for all that their country was among the victors, viewed the end of the war ironically: only a modest percentage of the American soldiers who had been mobilized actually saw service; and as members of a nation which had gone to war in the cause of personal freedom, they deeply resented being under military discipline for a moment longer than hostilities lasted. Americans are probably quicker to swing into party mode than most other great nations, but as with the British, there were a number who were repelled by the blatant triumphalism of their compatriots, among whom aggressive patriotism – "spread-eagleism" – had been whipped into a frenzy.

As has been shown elsewhere in this book, the impact of the war's end was complex, even within a single nation; Britain, though hardly touched by direct assaults on her country, bore the scars of her great losses in the field for years to come, albeit less so than France or Germany. It was difficult for any of those who had been in the trenches during a great battle to understand what had been won or lost by it, knowing only the carnage and triumphs in their short section of the line. Victory, assuredly, was far better than defeat, but what of the cost in lives, in bad memories, in dislocation?

As in reality, so in the literature of these four nations, the reaction to the coming of the Armistice was often alloyed or negative. From all countries, of course, writers mourned lost comrades and perceived a sanctity in the sacrifice that their soldiers had made for their country; but there were also those – sometimes the same authors – who questioned the value of the cause for which they had fought. In some cases, the unhappy Armistice scenes in novels and poems written by English or American authors long after the event reflected their subsequent disillusion with the post-war world rather than their vision in November 1918. Frequently, however, the jaundiced view of the war's end they presented was an accurate picture of their immediate feelings at the time. Thomas Hardy, for instance, ever sceptical, ever tragic in his views, had felt no reassurance, as Britain's elder statesman of letters, that God's benign purposes were at work in the war or the victory. Published on Armistice Day 1920, his poem 'And There was a Great Calm', looked sadly back at the signature of the peace terms. The last verse ran:

> Calm fell. From Heaven distilled a clemency;
> There was peace on earth, and silence in the sky;
> Some could, some could not, shake off misery:
> The Sinister Spirit sneered: "It had to be!"
>
> And again the Spirit of Pity whispered, 'Why?'[2]

Some writers recorded only a feeling of numbness and disbelief at the news of the Armistice. One such was the British novelist Henry Williamson, in *A Test to Destruction* (1960), the eighth volume of his great *roman fleuve* on 20th century life, the *Chronicle of Ancient Sunlight*. His protagonist, Phillip Maddison, an infantry subaltern, is past caring about the outcome. Consumed with anxiety about having venereal disease, he hardly absorbs what has happened.[3] It was a typical response of a war-exhausted soldier, such as Williamson had been in November 1918, but looking back over forty years and the failure of his misguided fascist hopes, Williamson doubtless also overstressed the irony.

More movingly, Pamela Hinkson, in *The Ladies' Road* (1932), a semi-autobiographical best-selling account of grief and separation in wartime western Ireland, describes the unresponsive reaction of her heroine, Stella, a young girl whose brother has been killed a few weeks before. On 11 November she goes for a morning ride with a yeomanry captain from a battalion camped near her home:

> In the field the other side they heard shouting from the camp. She had forgotten that they had been waiting for that. Letting the horses crop grass, they listened for a moment, then turned and looked at each other.
>
> "Well, its over", he said.

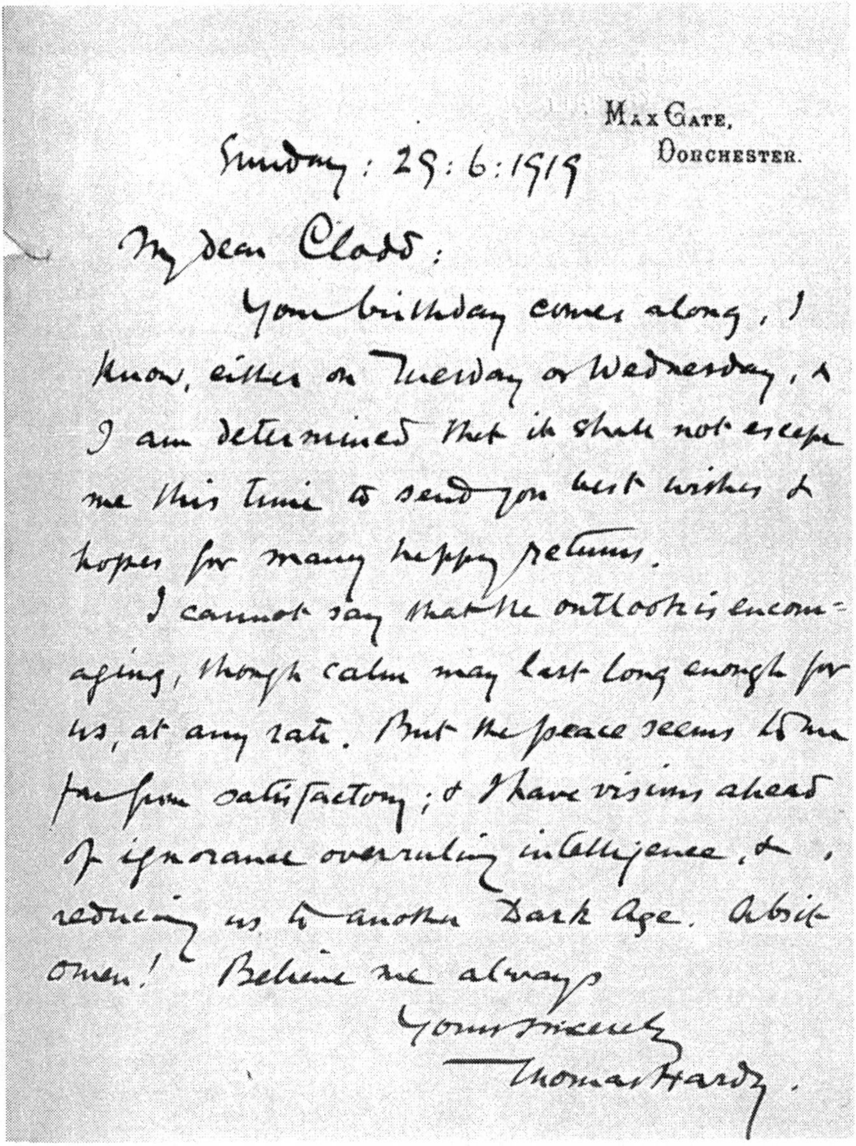

Max Gate,
Dorchester.

Sunday: 29:6:1919

My dear Clodd:

Your birthday comes along, I know, either on Tuesday or Wednesday, & I am determined that it shall not escape me this time to send you best wishes & hopes for many happy returns.

I cannot say that the outlook is encouraging, though calm may last long enough for us, at any rate. But the peace seems to me far from satisfactory; & I have visions ahead of ignorance overruling intelligence, &, reducing us to another Dark Age. Absit omen! Believe me always

Yours sincerely

Thomas Hardy.

xliii Thomas Hardy, writing in 1919, expresses his misgivings about the recently concluded Peace Settlement of Versailles. (Brotherton Collection, Leeds University Library)

He took out a cigarette and stooped, lighting it. If his face showed anything, it was hidden from her. He could always keep his eyes closed anyway, hiding his thoughts....

"I don't feel anything," she said. "Do you?"

She sat holding the reins, watching him as though he might help her...

"Well, I suppose a lot of good fellows' lives will be saved" and he wondered how many had gone over before eleven o'clock that morning. He wished he was in France. That would be the place to feel something. He looked at Stella sympathetically, knowing why she felt nothing, and they rode slowly along the field with the November sky, blue and white over them... [4]

For Stella the peace has come too late, as it has for Lieutenant Skene, R.H. Mottram's leading character in the disenchanted British novel *Sixty -four, Ninety -four!* Hearing news of the impending Armistice on 10 November, "Skene pulled off his boots and got into his blankets. 'Too long' he thought. 'Who cares now?' He had forgotten that this was victory".[5]

It was hard for many service personnel to believe that the war had ended and indeed for most it was only fighting, not soldiering, which was over. Although their publication dates were ten years apart, in two American novels, the celebrated *Three Soldiers* (1921)[6] by John Dos Passos, and *"It's a Great War"* (1930),[7] by Mary Lee, the main preoccupation, even on Armistice Day itself, was the same – that military life, with its petty restrictions and injustices was dragging miserably on. In contrast, Warwick Deeping, in *Seven Men Came Back* (1934), a realistic, if somewhat sentimental and banal, study of postwar adjustment, enlists the reader's sympathies on the side of those anxious to keep discipline. The disagreable Second Lieutenant Bastable tries to take advantage of what he thinks is his new freedom:

"Hallo, B.P., who gave you permission to sit?"

Bastable's upward look was a sulky glare.

"Not you, Steel".

"Not bloody likely. When your seniors are on their feet".

"Bastable's sallow face seemed to swell. The turgid arrogance of the man concealed for so long under that thick skin, showed a sudden, savage ooze.

"Indeed! – Seniors? – All that superstition was washed away at 11 a.m. I'm not taking orders from any bank clerk".[8]

A French writer, Roger Vercel, in a more distinguished novel, *Capitaine Conan*,[9] written the same year, 1934, describes regiments of the French Army in Salonika taking part, after the eleventh of November, in continued campaigning in Bulgaria (where fighting had officially stopped in late September) and in Bessarabia, against the Bolsheviks. For all except hard-bitten ex-*groupes francs* ('storm troop' units), re-formed into machine-gun companies since the Bulgarian Armistice, the prospect is a nightmare. The book is based on Vercel's own experience as a legal officer during that bizarre campaign. Two Germans, Ernst von Saloman in *The Outlaws*,[10] and Kurt Heuser, in *The Inner Journey* (both 1931), wrote of their forces fighting on in Latvia after the war. In Heuser's romantic tale, a veteran of that campaign describes it as "the most dreadful time of my life".[11]

Another immediate reaction to the coming of peace which appears repeatedly in literature, is the devastating sense of loss among so many who served. In *Goodbye to All That*, the poet Robert Graves has related how after learning of the deaths of friends, including Wilfred Owen, he went out walking on Armistice night near his camp in Wales, "cursing and sobbing and thinking of the dead".[12] Similarly, at the start of Erich Maria Remarque's *The Road Back* (1931), his equally heightened sequel to *All Quiet on the Western Front*, a sudden thrill of realization that peace is on the way is overshadowed by the soldiers' sorrow about comrades who have not lived to see this miraculous end.[13]

Remarque's actual knowledge of the fighting has been questioned, but the problems he described in *The Road Back*, of trying to settle down after the war were true to his experience and reflected that of millions of men in all countries – "What does life hold for us? Will we find employment again? Is there a place for us in a peaceful society?" Such apprehensions are recorded by many other authors. Vera Brittain's novel *Account Rendered* (1945) describes, with the hindsight of one who had witnessed the social upheavals between the wars, a group of soldiers hearing the news of the Armistice from their commanding officer: "A long silence followed his departure as the little gathering of officers tried to realize the incredible fact. For nearly all of them peace had its problems hardly less than war; readjustment, domestic dilemmas, financial difficulties, the uncertainty of employment, confronted one or another in the now imminent future".[14]

For years Captain Sherring, the dedicated company commander in Warwick Deeping's *Seven Men Came Back*, finds no place for himself in postwar society. On the day of the Armistice itself, he has intimations of the bleak times ahead, in a scene that reads like a bad film script of the early talkies:

> "It's the end of our world, Kettle".
> "There's still old Blighty sir!'
> "... 'It'll be a different Blighty, Kettle, somehow".
> "Different, Sir?"
> "Not the place we went on leave to, but the place we've got to live in".[15]

Some books remind us that there was a minority for whom killing became a way of life and who did not wish the war to end. One is the fire-eating company-commander in Remarque's *The Road Back*, Heel, who, hours before the Armistice, is forcing his men into a desperate counter-attack; after it, cheated by the cease-fire of an outlet for his aggression, he becomes a *Freikorps* officer, shooting down political demonstrators in his own country.[16]

Another example is the eponymous main character of Roger Vercel's *Capitaine Conan*, the tough Breton war hero, who blithely tells his fellow-officer, Norbert, that, Armistice or no Armistice, the French troops in Bulgaria will be in the war for another year.[17] At the book's end, set in Brittany, ten years after the war, Norbert tracks down Conan to a local café in his home town, and finds him a husk of his former self. The lesson of this *Prix Goncourt*-winning book is that war creates a morality quite different from that of peace. Conan and his band of trained killers, crack troops of the French expeditionary force in Macedonia, are courageous and dependable soldiers, but in many cases ex-criminals, capable of frightful atrocities. Once returned to civilian life, they revert to crime, or, like Conan, for whom peace spells disaster, are simply burnt out. The French director, Bernard Tavernier, has recently tackled the same subject in a much-acclaimed film of the book.

In the popular writer Pierre Benoit's romantic novel, *Axelle* (1928),[18] General von Reichendorff, refuses to accept the Armistice when told of it in his remote East Prussian castle, not because he wants the fighting to continue, for he is elderly and retired, but because he cannot face admitting that his three sons have died in vain at the front. The French prisoner-of-war, Dumaine, who works at the castle and has become close to the family, also has mixed feelings about the coming of peace; he is in love with the general's niece, Axelle, and is reluctant to leave her when offered the chance of returning immediately to France.

Another reaction, which Remarque emphasizes in his characteristically over-sensational fashion, is the isolation felt by the war generation in post-war society. The mental agony which ex-combatants would continue to suffer after the war is stressed in *A Man Could Stand Up* (1926) the third volume of Ford Maddox Ford's novel tetralogy, *Parades End*, now part of Britain's war literary canon. On Armistice Day, Valentine Wannop overhears her lover, Christopher Tietjens, confessing how haunted he is by the horrors and pains of the war. She realizes the degree to which ex-soldiers must forever be separated from non-combatants by their memories: "Hitherto, she had thought of the war as physical suffering only: now she saw it only as mental torture... Men might stand up on hills but the mental torture could not be expelled".[19]

Similarly, in *The Ladies' Road*, Pamela Hinkson highlights the particular problem of isolation affecting returned prisoners-of-war:

> After the Armistice, prisoners newly set free from work behind the lines ... went back without jubilation, without enthusiasm. A certain dullness of expression, common to all prisoners, marked them. They were almost indistinguishable from German prisoners still in camps in England. The War was over, but they had lost touch.... "who are you?" was a question they hardly knew how to answer.[20]

Of all the negative emotions felt at the time of the Armistice, one of the strongest described by some writers is the sense of betrayal: the ex-R.A.F. pilot in Duncan Grinnell-Milne's short story 'Looking Back: Armistice', (1931) feels betrayed by *fate* because just before the cease-fire he is blinded, through an act of carelessness he would never have committed if he had not been feeling so confident about the German defeat.[21]

Among the Germans there were naturally many who felt let down by their leaders over the Armistice agreement that they had negotiated. At the beginning of his autobiographical novel, *The Outlaws* (1931), Ernst von Saloman recalls his horror at "these appalling terms" which he sees posted on a local newspaper building. What upsets him above all is that there will be no resistance to the French taking over his home town.[22] Later, German troops return from the front, past a crowd which, though passionately wishing them well, is unable to summon up more than a few hoarse shouts. Saloman has a blinding conviction that these exhausted but still unbowed soldiers are the nation for which he must henceforth fight. He immediately joins, as a sixteen-year-old soldier, the Hamburg *Freikorps* fighting in the Baltic states.[23]

Unusually for an Englishman, Phillip Maddison, in Henry Williamson's, *A Test to Destruction*, also deplores the terms imposed on the Germans. On Armistice Day, Phillip hears of German U-Boat commanders, as required by the agreement, going through the humiliation of surrendering their vessels at East Coast ports. "Such weariness,such sadness", he reflects.[24] Williamson had a strong fellow-feeling with the Germans ever since he had taken part in the unofficial 'Christmas truce' of 1914 in the trenches, and after the war he preached reconciliation, a path which led him disastrously towards Fascism and an admiration for Adolf Hitler.[25]

In Ford Madox Ford's *The Last Post*, Mark Tietjens, the brother of Christopher Tietjens, and wartime British Minister of Transport, takes the opposite position. He is so enraged by the failure of the Armistice terms to break Germany completely that he is made speechless by a stroke.[26]

Even among those Germans who were not on the far right and who accepted the Armistice because what they desired above all was peace, there was a strong feeling that the German army had been let down. In *The Road Back*, Remarque shows his disgust with the brutal treatment, by revolutionary mobs, of loyal officers who refused to remove their shoulder straps – the symbol of their responsible position;[27] and the whole book is a tale of how honest fighting men have been betrayed by former teachers, employers, wives and girl friends. Ludwig Renn, at the end of his autobiographical novel, *War* (1929), which the London *Mercury* described as "much better than *All Quiet on the Western Front*", expressed his bitterness, too, at the terms of the Armistice. One of his group, the radical Corporal Mehling, is pleased that the war has ended and that the German military machine has been broken, "but" writes Renn, "I felt sad. The damned old Fatherland was still dear to me!"[28]

For the Germans, one of the worst aspects of the Armistice agreement, was that it brought no end to the crippling food blockade. The nation's desperation is recorded by such novelists as Hans Fallada in *Iron Gustav* (1938)[29]and Ludwig Renn in *War*;[30] in Remarque's *The Road Back*, Breyer and his men eagerly hand over their insignia to American soldiers, in exchange for food. The wounded Breyer himself even trades in his squalid crepe-paper bandages, the Doughboys being delighted to have a German *ersatz* dressing covered with genuine German officer's blood.[31]

The German writer, Karl Wilke, has given an account, *Prisoner Halm* (1933), of what happened to German prisoners captured by the French in the last stages of the war. Halm and his fellow-prisoners are beaten by their guards and given starvation rations; their first thought when the Armistice is declared is whether they will get something to eat. They fight each other for bread; a German sergeant and ambulance-man contract cholera from wolfing down some half-rotten sardines from a rubbish bin.[32] For the rest of the year, Halm and his fellows are interned in an horrific 'reprisal camp' at Candor where hundreds die – which, if Wilke's account can be believed, set an evil precedent for the future.

A deep disgust at the crudity and tastelessness of Armistice celebrations was particularly evident in the literature of Britain and the U.S.A. Siegfried Sassoon travelled to London on Armistice Day, to persuade himself that peace had truly come, "and found masses of people in streets and congested Tubes, all waving flags and making fools of themselves – an outburst of mob patriotism. It was a wretched wet night, and very mild. It is a loathsome ending to the loathsome tragedy of the last four years".[33] A friend of his, the poet Wilfrid Gibson, then in the Army Service Corps,[34] whose poetry owed much to Sassoon, wrote a poem, 'Bacchanal', at that time, expressing wonder at the pagan frenzy of Armistice night:

> Lads who so long have looked death in the face,
> Girls who so long have tended death's machines,
> Released from the long terror, shriek and prance;
> And watching them, I see the outrageous dance,
> The frantic torches and the tambourines
> Tumultuous on the midnight hills of Thrace.[35]

Cruder and more farcical was the revelry described in the American John Dos Passos' *Three Soldiers*, a work in which the comic moments are better handled than the author's tragic anti-war message. Corporal John Andrews is recovering from his wound in hospital when the major in charge rushes into the ward:

> "Men", he shouted in the deep roar of one announcing baseball scores, "the war ended this morning... The Armistice is signed. To hell with the Kaiser!" Then he rang the dinner bell madly and danced along the aisle between the rows of cots, holding the head nurse by one hand who held a little yellow-headed lieutenant by the other hand, who, in turn, held another nurse and so on. The Line advanced jerkily into the ward; the front part was singing "The Star Spangled Banner", and the rear "The Yanks are Coming", and through it all the Major rang his brass bell. The men who were well enough sat up in bed and yelled. The others rolled restlessly about, sickened by the din.[36]

After the major has left, the wounded men continue to shout and sing and bang their bed pans together; but, shortly afterwards, the enraged officer returns to tell them "If I hear any more noise from this ward, I'll chuck every one of you men out of the hospital; if you can't walk you'll have to crawl... the war may be over, but you men are in the Army and don't you forget it". He leaves them silenced, while outside whistles are blowing and church bells are ringing madly.

Most squalid of all is the account of Armistice Day by a fellow-American, James Taylor Farrell, in the novel *Studs Lonigan* (1932). 'Studs', a poor Irish-American boy of sixteen living in Chicago, joins in the riotous jubilations. Doomed all his short life to be captivated by the fourth-rate and meretricious, he leaps on an elevated railway car where the drunken crowd is singing *The Star Spangled Banner* and yelling "TO HELL WITH THE KAISER":

> A female body pressed against Studs. From the corner of his eye he lamped the woman; her face was wrinkling she must be forty or over, almost old enough to be his grandmother, but she excited him as much as if she was a young jane, perspiration beaded his broad, planed face... She'd been giving him the works all right, and he didn't care about her age, and he'd liked it ... He wished he was alone with her; he'd bet she knew her onions, and could teach him plenty that he ought to know... [37]

However, in the jostling, crowded carriage, Studs is pushed aside and loses his opportunity to carry on with the 'grandmother'. Caught up in the hysteria, he continues to follow the rampaging mob round the town, but is bitterly aware that his lack of a uniform makes it much harder for him to attract the 'janes'.

In a German work, Remarque's *The Road Back*, there is another orgiastic passage, but here it is not a case of rejoicing being polluted by lust so much as of simple earthiness being spoiled by war-created cynicism. Breyer and his companions stop on the way home at the first German inn they find as they cross the border. There they drink heavily and some eagerly seek to alleviate the bitterness of defeat in amorous antics with local women, but are disillusioned afterwards to find that they are expected to pay for their fun.[38]

Wilfrid Ewart, whose solemn and sentimental tale of upper-class life in wartime, *Way of Revelation* (1921)[39] was a best seller, set its melodramatic climax at the Grand Victory Ball. There were many people at the time who regarded this event, which took place at the Albert Hall on 19 November and was attended by a fashionable crowd of many nationalities, as tastless in the extreme, a kind of *danse macabre* on the graves of the men who had perished on the Western Front. Ewart himself writes in this spirit: looking on, his leading character, Adrian Knoyle, has a momentary vision of an accusing army of the dead joining the dancers.

However, despite this and the other examples given above, much of the literature leaves a more positive impression of feelings at the time of the Armistice. Even Ewart, as he sets the scene for the Victory Ball, is clearly bewitched by the strange beauty of the romantic and carnival-like atmosphere:

It was as though some magic window opened in material earth, ushering from the hard and the real into realms of the unreal, the mystical, the make-believe; as though some glorious glittering cavern exposed its secret life to human gaze; as though a curtain lifted upon some grand, portentous drama of the legendary past... Everywhere displayed were the flags and banners of the Allied Nations – billowing across the roof, covering all spaces round the walls between and beside the boxes, over the entrances and exits... The dancers! all costumes of all periods of all countries... Crusaders in mail, and casque, long sword, shield marked with the Red Cross, dancing with old-fashioned English country girls in big straw hats, tied under chin... here were Court Jesters dancing with Bacchantes, Chinamen waltzing with shepherdesses, the Comic Ass with the Elephant and the Kangaroo... among all these came and went foreign uniforms, from the sky-blue of French officers, the grey of Italy, and the mauve-blue of Rumania to American khaki-yellow and the red-striped dark blue of British officers.[40]

Not all the feasting – or even the sexual licence – has been remembered as something unworthy or base. In *Theophilus North* (1973), the novelist Thornton Wilder, recounts, with charm, how a young U.S. corporal hearing, prematurely, as it turns out, that the peace has been signed, celebrates the triumph of life over death by spending the night with an alluring lady he has just met.[41]

Although some soldiers at the fighting fronts often found it hard – understandably – to react to the news of the peace,[42] there were also others, in life and in literature, who were eager for festivities. Vercel's *Capitaine Conan* begins with infantrymen of a French battalion ravaged by dysentery, somewhere in Bulgaria, being dragged out of their miserable snow-covered tents on a dark November afternoon, to be told of the cease-fire. The colonel has even assembled a band:

Music! It astonished us far more than the news of the Armistice, that the music of the regiment, which none of us had seen or heard, which people talked of as though of a legend, that this music actually existed and was here with us, when the regimental standard bearer himself had been drowned with his mule when we crossed the Vardar. Now there really were twelve musicians, with their eyes anxiously fixed on the band-master, twelve musicians who cautiously put their lips to the strangely battered brass. The cornet player sucked his cold fingers methodically, one by one, the bugler had already raised his instrument to his lips, the cymbalist was ready to clash...

"Fa fa fa si... " murmured the band-master.

And the music burst out!

The gale from Russia smote us, every branch of the forest leaned southwards, and the clouds scurried overhead. We stood there, presenting arms, hemmed in by the baleful wood, while the wind whipped up the waves on the gloomy river! But we were oblivious to all this, listening only to the Marseillaise which the band-master was conducting with his arms and body. Far more stirring than the lofty phrases of the communiqué, the pulsing roar of the band achieved a miracle: drooping heads were held high, emaciated faces filled out, wretched bodies were galvanised into life.[43]

Sadly, however, the bandsmen have lost their musical scores on the march, and the Marseillaise peters out miserably, leaving the soldiers without other means of celebration; no wine, only water, stained pink with disinfectant. It is not for weeks, when the whole French force finally reaches Bucharest, that they are allowed, first, a triumphal march – before the Rumanian royal family, "with shivers running down our backs, our nerves as tight as the drum-skins, and the massed bands of six regiments belting out the *Sambre-et-Meuse* march"[44] – and then forays for food, alcohol and prostitutes. Even so, for this French army, the fighting – now against the Bolsheviks – still continues.

For those nearer home, the efforts to celebrate were usually easier. William Barnett Logan, in his autobiographical novel of naval life in wartime, *Dress of the Day*, finds the riotous rejoicing "noisy, stupid, unexpected"; but it is in its way, right – as is the reaction of his wife, who hits on the appropriate means to signify the end of a long period of gloom:

> At home Betty turns on all the lights and pulls up all the blinds, and cries with a queer excited break in her voice.
>
> 'Now let them come! They'll see London again all right tonight, Bill! Oh, I wish we'd a hundred windows, and I'd leave them all brilliantly lit!'[45]

The lamps were beginning to go on all over Europe. In France, the poet Paul Geraldy described the ecstatic response of crowds in Alsace-Lorraine as the French troops march through the towns: "To give an idea of how it was, one needs to borrow the most torrid and fervid words from the language of love, to dare to use the speech of amorous passion, for we have truly just witnessed a population and an army clasped to one another, surrendering themselves in one great cry to the embrace of a spiritual marriage".[46]

In the same spirit is the riotous Armistice scene with which the Old Etonian and ultra-patriot Gilbert Frankau finishes his best-selling novel *Peter Jackson, Cigar Merchant* (1920). Peter, recovered from shell-shock after a harrowing war career in the R.F.A., drives with his cousin Francis and their wives to join the festivities in the metropolis. Loaded down with "food, fizz and flags", they race each other in their Rolls-Royce and Crossley cars down the Thames Valley, and enter the capital just in time, Peter sounding his horn, his former commanding officer, General 'Weasel' Stark, straddling the radiator of the Crossley, thumping it with his cane, shouting "Forrard away! Forrard away!" and Francis yelling: "Well rowed, E-ton!" at the top of his voice: "Their own car was dancing: her cushions were dancing; they could feel her engine dancing. They themselves were dancing: they could feel their hearts dancing inside them: the blood was dancing in their veins, dancing and dancing... ".[47]

There was something forced about this, as there was about Geraldy's purple passages. Frankau approved of such extravagant demonstrations but they also provided a happy ending to please the 1920 reader, who, just after a war, wanted something consolingly triumphant. The bizarre end of Ford Madox Ford's *A Man Could Stand Up*, parodies the undignified behaviour of the kind Frankau applauds, though it is not without its own message of hope as well as of loss. The elephantine Christopher Tietjens, gasping like a huge carp, dances with his beloved Valentine and a motley assembly of shell-shocked and maimed companions-in-arms, in a crazy ecstasy, round his house, from which he has sold the only remaining furniture left to him by his faithless, rapacious wife.[48]

John Brophy's account in *The World went Mad* (1934) is ironical but cheerful. Brophy, an infantryman, recorded in another novel his regrets at the loss of his youthful idealism, though taking comfort in the self-sacrifice and duty involved. In two chapters of *The World went Mad* he sums up the Armistice – the first through the eyes of British soldiers marching triumphantly through Belgium; and the second through those of a boy who has never served at the front. For one of the soldiers, there is a feeling for the first time of genuine glamour and romance – something he had hoped for in 1914, when he joined up originally, but did not see for four long years. He is momentarily attracted to a girl who is standing aloof from the mob of cheering locals. Ignoring a warning that she has been a collaborator, he longs to reassure her, but she spurns him coolly and disappears – a momentary dimming of his mood of radiant joy. In the other chapter, the boy joins the noisy jubilation around Piccadilly and finds to his delight that his O.T.C. uniform wins him the undeserved admiration of a voluptuous young woman; the scene has a light touch which makes it very different from the comparable passage, quoted above, from J.T. Farrell's remorseless social tract, *Studs Lonigan*.[49]

If there were no Trafalgars to celebrate, it was the British Navy, of all the Allied forces, which came closest to such a triumph, shortly after the Armistice, when it accepted the surrender of the German Grand Fleet. William Barnett Logan recalled the moment, in his autobiographical novel, *Dress of the Day*:

> a Lieutenant-Commander coming up to where I stand says in a queerly choked voice that is none too steady:
>
> "My God, what a signal! '09.40. Battle Fleet meets the German Fleet!' It's worth something to be alive to see that at last!"... for this *is* victory. A vengeance so tremendous, a surrender so abject because of its completeness ... this magnificent fighting machine... this boasted Navy... and hardly a blow struck or a shot fired! Instead this scene in the North Sea, a pageant indeed, and for us a vindication past our wildest dreams![50]

It was in a quieter mood, however, that many writers conveyed their gratitude for the victory. In *Lament for Adonis* (1934), the novelist, poet and wartime padre, Edward Thompson M.C., describes an intimate and informal Armistice Day service of thanksgiving in Beirut. This is attended by British officers and members of a Methodist mission to the American Relief

Force. It is momentarily disturbed when a man bursts out with a passionate expression of pity for the Kaiser: A young woman missionary seethes with indignation, but says nothing; for she hears in her mind the voice of her beloved, the 'Adonis' himself, Captain Warren Remfry, lately killed on the Western Front: "Don't – *don't* – let yourself be fussed, sweetheart! People either understand, or they don't. Its no use talking to those who don't. But you and I understand". The meeting closes with a prayer that God should be close to all those "whose hearts have been left bereaved by the long agony of the War just finished".[51]

Thankfulness is the theme of two versifiers, who could only have been civilians and whose Armistice sentiments must seem to many of today's generation almost incomprehensibly old-fashioned: first, Robert Bridges, the British Poet Laureate of the time, who wrote 'Harvest -Home' to honour the American people on Thanksgiving Day, 28 November, for their part in the victory, when together the U.S.A. and Britain, "Fought hell in the mirth/Of Shakespeare's spirit".

A Toast for West and East
Drink on this Thursday Feast
Last in November,
The year when Albion's lands
Across the sea join hands –
Drink and remember![52]

It was not the best verse of which the celebrated wordsmith was capable, at the age of seventy-four in 1918; nor was his 'Der Tag: Nelson and Beatty, a Broadsheet',[53] which celebrated the surrender of the German fleet; nor was his 'Britannia Victrix' (23 November),[54] in which the handsome old traditionalist praised Britain's great achievement in the war. However they were not mere crude triumphalism, for Kipling-like, he delivered a warning: sloth and complacency have led Britain into war. Greed and failure to live up to Christian ideals of love and truth may lead her into another.

Conveying a similar message, but in even more religiously charged language, are the poems of the now hardly remembered John (later Sir John) Stanhope Arkwright – once the most read, or rather sung, of all the poets of the Great War. The author of the famous 'The Supreme Sacrifice' (1917), more commonly known by its first line, "O Valiant Hearts",[55] Arkwright articulated for the British people the potent myth – destined to endure for forty years and still faintly resonant – of war and horror redeemed through sacrifice, the soldier's ordeal being equated with Jesus's crucifixion. Sung to a haunting tune, the hymn still gives a sombre emotional power to such church services as continue to use it on Remembrance Sunday. Eton College, Arkwright's *Alma Mater*, anxious to purge the school's religion of what one of its provosts styled '*bushido*' (way of the warrior) elements, has for years ceased to include 'The Supreme Sacrifice' in services and has recently removed it from the school hymn book:[56]

These were His servants; in His steps they trod
Following through death the martyr'd Son of God:
Victor He rose; Victorious too shall rise
They who have drunk His cup of Sacrifice.

'Buckingham Palace' (11 November 1918), Arkwright's tribute to George V on that day, is a straightforward thanksgiving for leading Britain "by wise and faithful ways/Through war's long years of Hell"[57] but his poem 'Armistice' is in the spirit of "O Valiant Hearts".

Bow down, Old Land, at the altar-steps of God;
Thank Him for Peace – thank Him for Victory;
But chiefly thank Him that thy feet have trod
The path of honour in the Agony.[58]

Clearly Arkwright's response to war and peace, though many today may find it alien, was something a widely mourning population wanted. For the many men of the German army who felt pride in their achievement, defeat notwithstanding, there was a need for equivalent sentiments expressed in verse, though the 'higher purpose' with which death in battle was identified was the Fatherland rather than the Saviour. One such work was 'To the Last Man', a little poem (unattributed) published just before the end of the war, and quoted by an artillery officer, Herbert Sulzbach, in his diary, when he read it on 11 November:

He who has locked the gates of Death,
And sealed the peace with blood and breath,
He shall be one of the chosen... [59]

Equally, people after the war wanted to look to the future. The optimistic belief that a new and better world was now beginning stirred many writers at the time of the Armistice. One poem inspired by this, and generally thought to be the purest utterance of joy about the war's end, is Siegfried Sassoon's 'Everyone Sang'.

Everyone suddenly burst out singing;
And I was filled with such delight
As prisoned birds must find in freedom,
Winging wildly across the white
Orchards and dark green fields; on – on – and out of sight.

Everyone's voice was suddenly lifted;
And beauty came like the setting sun:
My heart was shaken with tears and horror
Drifted away... O, but Everyone
Was a bird; and the song was wordless; the singing will never be done.[60]

John Masefield called this verse "the only adequate peace celebration he had seen". Since people have always chosen to treat it as such, he was right, though, in fact, this was not Sassoon's conscious intention. As we have seen, his feelings on 11 November were more sombre. He actually composed the poem later, on "a sultry spring night" in mid-April 1919. In his memoir, he was at pains to point out that the poem was not about soldiers singing on the march at the end of the war, but about his hopes of a glorious social revolution – in what form, he admitted, he was far from clearly perceiving.[61]

The most passionate plea for a new world order, free from war, came from the former British war correspondent, Philip Gibbs, soon to be knighted for his work on the Western Front. Gibbs felt profoundly guilty about having presented, because of military censorship, an anodyne picture of the war to readers back at home. His experience at the time of the Armistice set him on the path he was to follow for the next twenty years. He has recalled the "wonderful days"[62] in Belgium when the British troops entered the liberated country. However, there were ugly sides to the liberation: the shaving of the heads of women who had slept with the invaders and the lynching of '*Flamagands*' – Belgians who had collaborated. When the British Army reached Germany, he thought the Rhinelanders sensible and dignified in defeat. He was now repelled by the pitiless hatred which the French felt towards the Germans and was stirred by Sir Douglas Haig's plea for a just peace without vengeance. A year afterwards, Gibbs's conclusions took shape in a highly successful novel *Back to Life* (1920).[63] This powerful and moving work called for reconciliation among the belligerents notwithstanding what he saw as the terrible injustices of the Versailles Treaty signed in July 1919. Prophetic in its analysis of the ill-consequences that would follow, *Back to Life* continued to be reprinted into the 1930's. Gibbs wrote other books on similar themes to stir up public awareness – such as *Blood Relations* (1935) in which he argued that the widespread idealistic hopes at the time of the Armistice – "a comradeship of youth across the frontiers... A chance for a new era of human history"[64] – were undermined by the Treaty of Versailles, leading inevitably to the nightmare of the Third Reich.

Some German authors, too, looked forward. Amid the ruins of the Hohenzollern imperial order, there was an initial euphoria among writers and artists of the Expressionist movement in the last months of 1918. One of these was Franz Werfel, whose war verse, in *Day of Judgement*, published a few months after the coming of peace, expressed both his despair about the futility of the war and his hopes for a better life and the brotherhood of man, which, he believed, would be realized through revolution. Disillusionment set in fairly quickly, though his social conscience re-awoke later in resistance to Nazism. Other idealistic responses to the Armistice appeared in more conservative works. In *Otto Babendiek* (1933), Gustav Frenssen's 'nordic blood and soil' tale of a young man's early life on the coast of Holstein, and his passage through the war, he describes his own feelings. He discounts the fact of Germany's defeat: "We have no need to feel ashamed, for we have suffered a thousand times more, both officers and men, and have been a thousand times braver, than our enemies. So let us march back covered with laurels from the front... back to our homes under old Hindenburg! Friends... perhaps when we get back, a new world will come into being".[65]

Frenssen, as a creative writer well above military age, was in many ways removed from the harshest impact of his country's ordeal. He took a long, epoch-surveying view of world affairs, typical of later nineteenth-century German thinkers, and was optimistic that a new age lay ahead for his tried and tested nation; this would not be along the path of communism but through a reinforced sense of national rootedness in Germanic moral and cultural values.

Such authors saw the coming peace as bringing a new age in human consciousness. In 1932, penetrating more deeply, Herbert Read, the modernist art critic, reflected in a long poem, *The End of a War*, published as a single volume, on the significance of the conflict. His setting for the piece is the aftermath of a tragic incident during the liberation of a French town on 10 November 1918: a British force is ambushed, with great loss of life, through the treachery of a wounded German officer who tells them the town is unoccupied by Germans. Into the mouth of an English officer, joyful and thankful to be alive, Read puts the chief dilemma for himself and for many others: has the war been devoid of meaning and only a sign of man's inability to escape his barbarism – or has it been in some way a test, set by God, part of a plan to raise man to a higher plane? Read, himself, who gained the M.C. and D.S.O. as a junior officer in the Green Howards, certainly valued the war as a test of his spirit, despite strong pacifist leanings. In *The End of a War*, coming down on the side of hope, he put the position to his readers:

> No I see, either the world is mechanic force
> and this the last tragic act, portending
> endless hate and blind reversion
> back to the tents and healthy lusts
> of animal men: or we act
> God's purpose in an obscure way.
> Evil can only to the Reason stand
> in scheme and scope beyond the human man.
> God seeks the perfect man, planned
> to love him as a friend: our savage fate
> a fire to burn our dross
> to temper us to finer stock
> man emerging in some inconceived span
> as something more than remnant of a dream.[66]

Such questions needed to be considered at some distance in time from the event. They disturb us to this day. Peace, however, the blessed cessation of strife, was an undisputed fact for most on Armistice Day, even if it were destined to be short-lived. What authors have communicated, above all, in writing of the cease-fire, is the sheer relief of millions that it had happened, victory or no victory. As the distinguished novelist John Galsworthy wrote in his diary, "*Armistice signed. Peace at last. Thank all the Gods that be*".[67] John

Freeman, the eminent Georgian poet, who earned his living as a director of the London Victoria Friendly Society, expressed the profundity of that feeling of peace, compared with which even the natural life and rhythms of the universe seemed, at that moment, almost hectic.

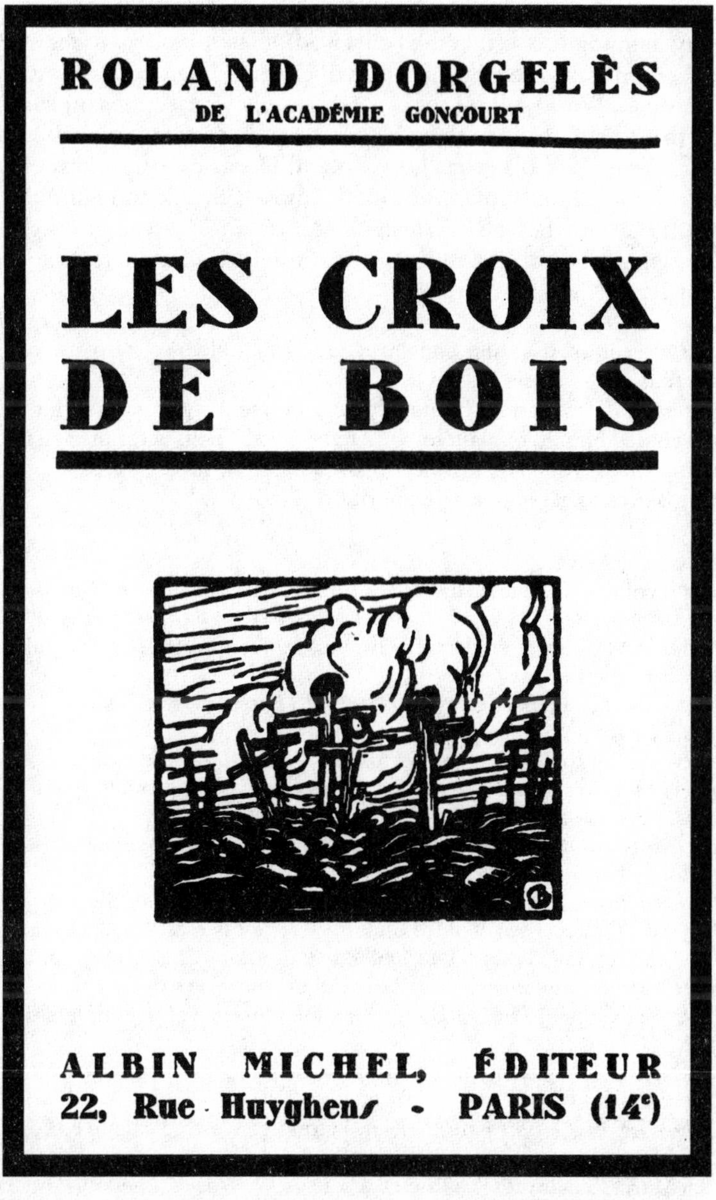

xliv The cover of Roland Dorgelès' *Les Croix de Bois*. (via Hugh Cecil)

Earth's pulse still was beating,
The bright stars circling;
Only our tongues were hushing.
While Time ticked silent on, men drew
A deeper breath than passion knew.[68]

Whether or not they felt otherwise positive about the Armistice, for each individual who had taken part in the fighting and was still alive, there was one overwhelming fact – they had survived. "The tide", as Richard Blaker, Second Lieutenant in the Royal Field Artillery and, later, best-selling novelist, puts it in *Medal Without Bar* (1930), "had simply washed them up with bones and breath and blood still in them".[69] At the end of the famous prize-winning novel, *Les Croix de Bois* (1921), by Roland Dorgelès, his central character, Sulphart, a poor infantryman, has made himself drunk enough in a café to feel cheerful, even when he overhears a man saying: "Peace or no peace, it's come too late... For all the rest of us it's a defeat". Sulphart disagrees – "I say it *is* a victory".

> The drinker looked at him and shrugged his shoulders: "Why do you say that – that it's a victory?"
>
> Sulphart, disconcerted, hesitated for a moment, groping for the words which eluded him, to explain his wild happiness. Then, without even understanding the terrible significance of his statement he answered simply: "I think it's a victory because I've got out of it alive... ".[70]

Endnotes

1 See this volume, Chapter 3 and, for example, Herbert Sulzbach, *With the German Guns: Four Years on the Western Front, 1914–1918*, tr. Richard Thonger, London, Leo Cooper / Frederick Warne, 1973/81, pp. 253–255, (1st pub. as Zwei lebende Mauern, 1935).

2 James Gibson, ed., *The Complete Poems of Thomas Hardy*, London, Macmillan, 1976, p. 590.

3 Henry Williamson, *A Test to Destruction*, London, Macdonald 1960, p. 340.

4 Pamela Hinkson, *The Ladies Road,* Harmondsworth, Penguin, 1946 (1st Pub. 1932), pp. 208–211.

5 R.H. Mottram, *Sixty-four, Ninety-four!*, Vol. 2 of *the Spanish Farm Trilogy*, London, Chatto & Windus, 1927, p. 535.

6 John Dos Passos, *Three Soldiers: a Novel*, London, Hurst & Blackett, 1922.

7 Mary Lee, *"It's a Great War"*, London, George Allen & Unwin, 1930.

8 Warwick Deeping, *Seven Men Came Back,* London, Cassel, 1934, p. 11.

9 Roger Vercel, *Capitaine Conan,* Paris, Albin Michel, 1934.

10 Ernst von Saloman, *The Outlaws*, tr. Ian F.D. Morrow, London, Jonathan Cape, 1931.

11 Kurt Heuser, *The Inner Journey,* tr. Edwin Muir, London, Secker & Warburg, 1932, pp. 104–106.

12 Robert Graves, *Goodbye to All That,* Harmondsworth, Penguin edn., 1960 (1st pub. 1929), p. 228.

13 Erich Maria Remarque, The Road Back, tr. A.W. Wheen, London, Putnam 1931, pp. 22–24.

14 Vera Brittain, *Account Rendered*,London, Macmillan, 1945, pp. 45–46.
15 Deeping, p. 5.
16 Remarque, pp. 16–18, 256–250.
17 Vercel, p. 20.
18 Pierre Benoit, *Axelle*, Paris, Albin Michel, 1928.
19 Ford Madox Ford, *A Man Could Stand Up*, London, The Bodley Head, 1963 (1st pub. 1926), pp. 435–470.
20 Hinkson, p. 212.
21 Duncan Grinnell Milne, *Fortune of War*, London, John lane, The Bodley Head, 1931, p. 251 et seq.
22 Saloman, pp. 20–21.
23 *Ibid.*, pp. 28–30.
24 Williamson, p. 341.
25 See Hugh Cecil, *The Flower of Battle: How Britain Wrote the Great War*, South Royalton, Vermont, The Steerforth Press, 1996, pp. 71, 74–6.
26 Ford Madox Ford, *The Last Post*, New York, The Literary Guild of America, 1928, pp. 33–34.
27 Remarque, pp. 58–59.
28 Ludwig Renn, *War*, tr.Willa & Edwin Muir, London, Martin Secker, 1930, p. 357; the comment by *The London Mercury* is on the dust jacket.
29 Hans Fallada, *Iron Gustav*, tr. Philip Owens, London, Putnam, 1940 (1st pub. 1938), p. 181.
30 Renn, p. 356.
31 Remarque, p. 31.
32 Karl Wilke, *Prisoner Halm,* London, Hutchinson, 1933, pp. 141–56.
33 Siegfried Sassoon, *Diaries, 1913–1918,* ed. Rupert Hart-Davis, London Book Club Assocs., by arrangement with Faber & Faber,1983, p. 282.
34 Siegfried Sassoon, *Siegfried's Journey*, London, Faber & Faber, 1945, pp. 97–108.
35 W. Keane Seymour, ed., *A Miscellany of Poetry,* Cecil Palmer and Hayward, 1919, p. 54.
36 Dos Passos, pp. 186–187.
37 James Taylor Farrell, *Studs Lonigan*, 1st English edn., London, Constable, 1932, p. 178.
38 Remarque, pp. 40–46.
39 Wilfid Ewart, *Way of Revelation*, London, Putnam, 1921.
40 *Ibid.*, pp. 509–511.
41 Thornton Wilder, *Theophilus North*, London, Allen Lane, 1974, pp. 351–353.
42 See, for example, Guy Chapman, *A Passionate Prodigality*, London, Ivor Nicholson &Watson, 1933, pp. 335–336.
43 Vercel, pp. 17–18.
44 *Ibid.*, pp. 34–40.
45 William Barnett Logan, *Dress of the Day: War – and After Reminiscences of the British Navy*, London, Albert Marriott, 1930, p. 220.
46 Paul Geraldy, *La Guerre, Madame*, Paris, G. Crès et Cie, 1922, p. 123.
47 Gilbert Frankau, *Peter Jackson, Cigar Merchant*, London, Hutchinson, 1920, pp. 393–399.
48 Ford Madox Ford, *A Man Could Stand Up*, pp. 468–470.
49 John Brophy, *The Word Went Mad,* London, Jonathan Cape, 1934, pp. 272–286; see also by the same author, *The Bitter End*, London, J.M. Dent, 1928.
50 Logan, pp. 250–251.

51 Edward Thompson, *Lament for Adonis*, London, Ernest Benn, 1932, pp. 282–285.
52 Robert Bridges, *October and Other Poems, with occasional verses on the War*, London, Heinemann, 1920, p. 40.
53 *Ibid.*, pp. 51–55.
54 *Ibid.*, pp. 47–50.
55 John S. Arkwright, *The Supreme Sacrifice, and Other Poems in Time of War*, London, Skeffington & Son, 1919.
56 I am grateful to Penny Hatfield, College Archivist, Eton College Library and the late Lord David Cecil for this information. It was Lord Quickswood, devout Christian and Provost of Eton over the Second World War period, who used the phrase 'Bushido' to describe the military influence on public school religion.
57 Arkwright, p. 43.
58 *Ibid.*, p. 44.
59 Sulzbach, *With the German Guns*, p. 248.
60 Dominic Hibberd and John Onions, *The Poetry of the Great War: an Anthology*, London, Macmillan 1986, pp. 178–9.
61 Sassoon, *Siegfried's Journey*, pp. 140–142.
62 Philip Gibbs, *The Pageant of the Years: an Autobiography*, London, Heinemann, 1946, pp. 232–235.
63 Philip Gibbs, *Back to Life*, London, Hutchinson, 1930, (1st pub. 1920).
64 Philip Gibbs, *Blood Relations*, London, Hutchinson, 1935, pp. 340–341.
65 Gustav Frenssen, *Otto Babendiek*, tr. Huntley Paterson, London, George G. Harrap, 1930, p. 457.
66 Herbert Read, *Collected Poems*, London, Faber & Faber, 1946, p. 73.
67 H.V. Marrot, *The Life and Letters of John Galsworthy*, London, Heinemann, 1935, p. 445.
68 I.M. Parsons, ed., *Men Who March Away: Poems of the First World War*, London, Heinemann, 1965, p. 173.
69 Richard Blaker, *Medal Without Bar*, London, Hodder & Stoughton, 1930, pp. 636–7.
70 Roland Dorgelès, *Les Croix de Bois*, Paris, Albin Michel, 1931 (1st pub. 1919), pp. 370–371.

My thanks are due to Jenny Moores for typing this chapter; to George Sassoon for permission to print 'Everyone Sang' by Siegfried Sassoon; and to Benedict Read for permission to quote from Herbert Read's *The End of a War*.

Chapter Twenty-Three

A Changing Meaning for Armistice Day

Matthew Richardson

In this concluding chapter the reasons behind the continuing resonance of the Armistice down the decades to the present day, and indeed why commemoration is such a particularly British phenomenon, will be examined. Why does Armistice Day mean so much more in these isles and also in the former dominions, than it does for example in France or the United States – those co-belligerents who might reasonably be expected to accord it an equal place in their national life? It is the intention to detail the part that memories of the events of that misty November morning in 1918 have played in the British psyche and consciousness in the intervening 80 years, to look at changing attitudes both official and public, to examine how remembrance withstood the emotion of the 1920's, the controversies of the 1930's, the rigours of the Second World War, and to follow the fluctuating social significance of the event ever since. In short, to chart the rise, fall, and rise again of Armistice Day.

"The news for which the world has been so anxiously waiting has come at last, and the war which started, so far as Great Britain is concerned, on the night of August 4th 1914, came to an end this morning".[1] So the *Nottingham Evening Post* broached the news of the day's momentous events to its readers late on Monday 11 November 1918. The war, and more especially its ending, was to prove a watershed. On that historic morning the doors of an old way of life closed, and those of another opened, and in consequence the day itself would continue to hold a special significance. As Marshal Foch told the Allied armies in his communiqué the following morning, "*La Posterité vous garde sa reconnaissance*"[2] – you will have with you always the gratitude of posterity, or translated in a more liberal way perhaps, "posterity will forever remember you".

In July 1919, a victory parade was staged in London, Britain's military and political leaders heading a triumphalist march along Whitehall to mark the signing of the peace treaty of Versailles. In November, the first anniversary of Armistice Day, the commemorative ceremonies and the national mood were to be in marked contrast to the summer celebration. It had soon become apparent that the mood of the nation favoured a more sombre event, based instead upon the ideas of remembrance of the fallen and sober reflection. *The Times* commented that, "Today is the first anniversary of the day on which the military power of Germany confessed itself humbled, on which right triumphed in a terrible struggle, and it is but right that the sacrifice and cost should be fittingly remembered... this morning there will be more than mere thanksgiving for peace, more even than a tribute to the dead". 'Old Thunderer' continued, "The Empire will never forget, and today's ceremony is but the first of a never ending series of yearly homages".[3] *The Yorkshire Post's* correspondent reported from the capital that wreaths sent to the service in Whitehall by HM King George V and the Prime Minister had been laid on their behalf, and "a great crowd assembled at the Cenotaph and a continuous stream of people made the pilgrimage from long before eleven o'clock onwards, to lay floral tributes at the foot of the memorial. So great was the crush that the majority were unable to reach the Cenotaph itself and their wreaths were handed over the heads of the crowd".[4] Later a great procession marched down Whitehall, headed by the 'Comrades of the Great War', and disabled ex-servicemen. Assembled, formed up in three sides of a square around the monument, they listened to an address by the Chaplain General to the Forces.

This inaugural Armistice parade in fact saw the Cenotaph used for wreath laying for the first time. Initially intended only as a temporary creation, Sir Edwin Lutyens' wood and plaster vision of the empty tomb – placed in the centre of Whitehall – so captured the public imagination that it was to become a permanent feature. The memorial had originally been intended as the centre-piece of the march-past of the victorious armies in July 1919, but such was the public demand that the temporary structure was retained for the proceedings of November that year, and the following November, 1920, the Portland stone obelisk was unveiled. It has remained the focus of British remembrance and commemoration up to the present day. As cultural historian Jay Winter has observed, the design was without romantic or patriotic, or indeed Christian symbolism:

> an abstract architectural form had somehow managed to transform a victory parade, a moment of high politics, into a time when millions contemplate the timeless, the eternal, the inexorable reality of death in war... Lutyens' cenotaph is a work of genius largely because of its simplicity. It says so much because it says so little. It is a form on which anyone could inscribe his or her own thoughts, reveries, sadnesses.[5]

Indeed one might remember that this form was not settled upon by chance or without prior thought – the purpose of the Cenotaph was after all to act as a focus for mourning for those of whatever faith or creed, and perhaps we might identify this as a part of a long British tradition of secularism and tolerance.

Another permanent feature to emerge from that November 1919 ceremony was the two minutes' silence, which was asked of the nation by the King in a royal proclamation published on 7 November . Here something without precedent was being asked. In an age before mass communication, a national silence would be a difficult thing to organize and indeed with the possible exception of the death of Queen Victoria there were few occasions which had led to what we could call "mass mourning" which might be signified in such a manner. The King himself felt that "no elaborate organization appears to be necessary", as the silence could be orchestrated on a local and *ad hoc* basis, and the Home Secretary added that "no general instructions can ensure the success of a ceremony which can only be truly impressive if it is universal and spontaneous".[6] As it was, the terrible weight of that first silence, as the hands of Big Ben ticked around to two minutes past eleven, was overpowering. It has been evocatively described by Jonathan Vance: "In the Imperial capital, the response was astonishing: all traffic paused, power was cut to trolleys, factories ceased operations, all pedestrians in the street stopped and removed their hats".[7] Away from the bustle of urban life, a country housekeeper, Mrs Kinsey, was equally moved and recorded in her diary for 11 November 1919: "At 11 there was an impressive 2 minutes silence over the whole of the [district]. We stood in the garden to hear the silence! Vera went to Lansdowne to see the crowds of men bareheaded. Every moving machine stopped dead even to express trains – in memory of those who died to save our country".[8] Another significant feature of this day was the 'civil' rather than religious feel of the ceremony not only in Whitehall but throughout the land – although there was a service of thanksgiving in St Paul's Cathedral that day, as Adrian Gregory comments, "Royalty and politicians, rather than religious acts were the focus".[9] This tended to be a feature throughout the 1920's and 1930's – the religious aspect tended to come in the church services of the Sunday usually preceding the eleventh. The shift in emphasis towards religion was really to emerge after 1945, as we shall see later.

The following year, on 11 November 1920, came the Armistice commemoration which was without doubt the one most heavily charged with emotion, for it witnessed the interment of the body of the Unknown Warrior in Westminster Abbey. The symbolism in the air that day was so heavy as to be almost unbearable for all but the most emotionally resilient – the body had been selected at random from several brought from battlefields all over France and Belgium. It was conveyed across the Channel in the destroyer *HMS Verdun*, another reference to the sacrifices of the war, and to the Anglo-French alliance. The word "warrior" was a deliberate choice, for included among those originally selected had been soldiers, sailors (presumably of the Royal Naval Division), and airmen.[10] The corpse was identified neither by name nor rank, and all that was known about him was simply that he was British. The coffin, flanked by Victoria Cross winners, and by Field Marshals, generals, statesmen and archbishops, was borne through Westminster Abbey to the graveside. As it was lowered into the grave, the King scattered earth from the battlefields of France onto the coffin. The body lay in the company of the mightiest kings, the greatest writers, and the most celebrated churchmen in the long history of these islands, and so the nation offered the highest honour it could bestow to one who might easily have been born in one of its lowliest slums. The irony, not to mention the heady atmosphere of emotion hanging almost like incense in the air, was not lost on Horatio Bottomley, a journalist not naturally given to self restraint, who was at the Abbey. Bottomley, for all the dubiousness of his reputation in 1918, wrote poignantly of what he had seen that day:

> Of what shall I write?
>
> Shall it be of the weeping woman at my side, whose whole frame quivers with emotion, but who signals away the attention of a kindly nurse who approaches her with smelling salts?
>
> Shall it be of the strong man, sitting near, with set face, struggling hard to suppress the tears which are running down his cheeks?
>
> Or shall it be of that poor, sad soul of a woman over there, in deep mourning, who never takes her eyes away from the open grave, and is, beyond all doubt, saying "That is for my boy"?[11]

In 1921 came another feature of Armistice which has remained and is familiar to us today – artificial poppies in symbolic association with the flower which had so often sprung up on recently shelled ground or the graves of soldiers. From time to time a *cri de coeur* has risen from some about why can we not organize the sale of real poppies in November instead of plastic and paper imitations, but this is to miss the point: poppies had at first been made by hand in the devastated areas of France by women, who sold them for the benefit of children. However, "in the summer of 1921... a French woman named Madame Guerin, called at the offices of the British Legion... She suggested to them that hand made artificial poppies might be sold in support of their work... Rather hesitantly they agreed and a few weeks later... Eight million hastily manufactured poppies were sold".[12] The poppies were used to support the Earl Haig Fund for ex-servicemen – Haig's fund was set up in 1921, and the poppies continue to bear the Field Marshal's name.

The British Legion came in due course to organize the production of all red poppies sold on Armistice Day, and they were manufactured by disabled ex-servicemen working in the Legion's own factories. In order to avoid charges of hypocrisy in honouring the dead, the Legion strongly emphasized the fact that by buying a poppy one was actively doing something to help the living. This is still an argument which the RBL uses today, but in the 1920's and 1930's the anger of numbers of ex-servicemen at the commemoration of the dead as a cheaper substitute for supporting properly their living dependants was widespread – C.E. Leatherland was one such ex-soldier who wrote in the Birmingham *Town Crier* of his disgust at the proposal by that city to spend half a million pounds on a Hall of Memory, "the first cry of the National Union [of ex-servicemen] is 'houses for heroes' and when the whole of the ex-servicemen of Birmingham are properly housed, and when every widow and child of those of our unfortunate comrades who lie in Flanders have been brought out of the workhouse and provided with homes of their own... then and not till then may they be expected to consider the scheme which is before the city today". In his counter-proposal, a garden suburb, "there would be no

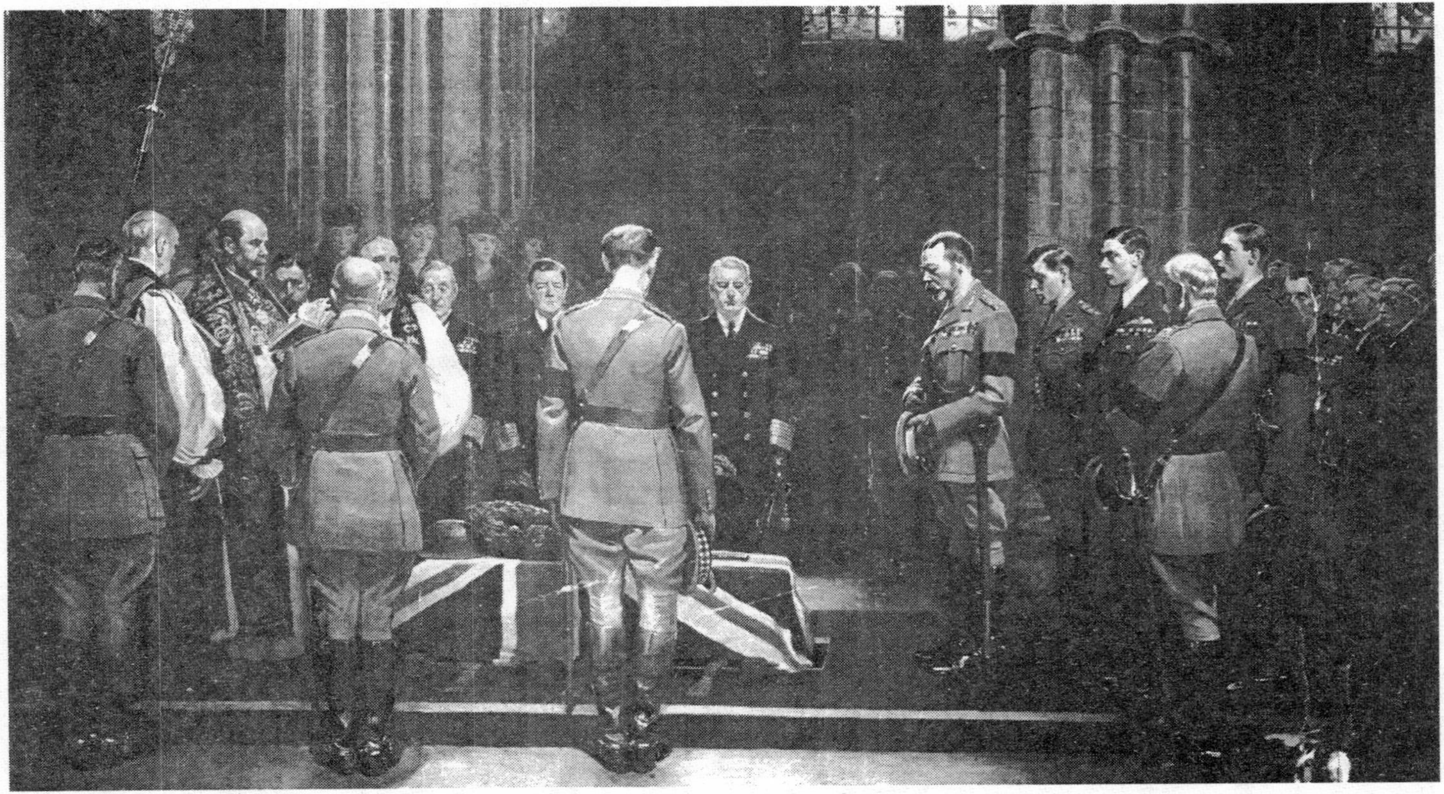

xlv HM King George V, Admiral Beatty, and other figures pictured at the burial of the Unknown Warrior in Westminster Abbey, 11 November 1920. From a contemporary print. (Liddle Collection) danger of the memorial being stigmatised by posterity as having been built by the conscience money of the profiteers".[13]

However, the bitterness of some ex-servicemen at their treatment was to be pulled into sharp focus more than once on Armistice Days that followed. Vance has written that "Postwar discontents emerged from the peace, not the war; the evils of the 1920s and 1930s were born not on the Somme and at Passchendaele, but at Versailles".[14] This is undoubtedly true as most servicemen remained proud of the part that they played in the war. However, as Germany brooded resentfully over her humiliation (and later emerged rearmed), it became apparent that the economic slump would mean that there would be no homes fit for heroes but instead the same slums and unemployment. Frank Richards, author of *Old Soldiers Never Die*, in a chapter entitled "Rewards for War Service", commented, "living not far from me ... is what the papers call one of the Old Contemptibles, and indeed no man has been treated with greater contempt than what he has".[15] Richards related that the man received no pension at all for his disabilities incurred while on active service for his country. Armistice parades in some cities were marred by protests from ex-servicemen that local authorities would rather spend money on war memorials than on providing for destitute ex-servicemen or their widows. Other ex-servicemen railed against the apparent unfairness of their treatment. Richards continued,

> It is Armistice Day today [1932], and the ex-servicemen are on parade wearing their war medals. The men who served at the Bases a hundred miles behind the front line are wearing their medals more proudly than the men who served in the firing line... and there are some on parade today wearing war medals on their breasts as if to say that they have been in action – but the only action they were ever in was with some of the charming damsels in the Red Lamps behind the Front and down at the Bases where they served.[16]

Clearly Armistice Day revealed not only the fissures between those who had served in the forces and those who had stayed at home, but as significantly, the fault line of resentment between those who had seen action and those who had not. Intriguingly, the same phenomenon may be observed among those veterans who returned from the Second World War.

For the 20 years between the end of one war and the beginning of the next, the eleventh of November was to be one of the most potent and meaningful dates of the year. Mrs Kinsey again wrote in her diary, this time on Sunday 11 November 1923, that she had heard the former Bishop of Liverpool, the Right Reverend F.J. Chavasse, give a sermon, "the hurry & bit of excitement & then the emotion one could not help feeling made me very bad in the church & I didn't know what was going to happen to me for a bit, but I carried on".[17] To us today, the power of that moment at 11a.m. cannot easily be imagined. Traffic stopped, offices ceased work, conversation was stilled. As Vance has pointed out, the effect was all the more dramatic because the eleventh of November was not a public holiday – it was an ordinary working day, and so the contrast of these two minutes among the everyday hustle and bustle was all the more visible.[18]

To understand this phenomenon more fully we must look at British society in the 1930's. The parents of the war generation were very much alive, mostly in their sixties and seventies. The number of bereaved mothers was high. Then there were the children, perhaps in their teens or early twenties, whose fathers had been lost in the war. Lastly, there were the men who had served in the war themselves, generally in their forties (and so many British servicemen who returned had lost a brother), and there were the widows of those who had not returned. To this might be added the maimed, disfigured, and those institutionalized by reason of their wounds or mental instability. This then was the scale of grief and disadvantage – the war had had a direct impact on perhaps three quarters of the adult population. Dyer comments:

> while this made the human cost of the war more apparent, the scale of loss, it turned out, could actually be comforting. The pain of mothers, wives and fathers was subsumed in a list of names whose sheer scale was numbing ... realizing that grief could be rendered more manageable if simultaneously divided and shared by a million, the scale of sacrifice was emphasized. Publicising the scale of loss was the best way to make it bearable.[19]

In other words, in a rather perverse way, for a mother or widow to know that there were thousands of others like her and that she was not alone, made grief for some at least more tolerable.

The silence of the eleventh hour of the eleventh day was an expression of the grief which touched almost everyone. It drew together a number of themes in the 1930's – the "lost generation", the "men marched away", the empty chair, the empty place. Nearly every home in the land had a bronze memorial plaque in the best or 'front' room, in memory of one who did not return. In an extraordinary but little known film made in the 1930's called "Forgotten Men", in one household, a setting is regularly laid at the table for one such young man, who returns in the film as a ghostly figure to take up his place.[20]

Throughout the 1920's and 1930's, Armistice was associated with the "returning dead" – a concept which appears in various forms again and again. Bill Grant, an Australian at the Cenotaph in 1919, wrote to his family that he had imagined he saw "a Great Phantom army" passing the monument, "Swiftly, Silently & singing as they went a song of triumph or victory".[21] In 1928 the former war artist, Captain Will Longstaff, painted "The Immortal Shrine" which depicts the spirits of dead soldiers marching past the Cenotaph.[22] Others, like Fabian Ware, of the Imperial War Graves Commission, calculated that it would take the fallen, if they marched four abreast down Whitehall, three-and-a-half days to pass the Cenotaph.[23] It could be argued that in many ways this was also a manifestation of a sense of collective guilt among the British people. For those who actually served, the concept of the "guilt of the survivor" is well documented, but, amid those who did not, we might seek to identify a subconscious guilt at the terrible price paid by others on their behalf. The "returning army" is almost the stuff of nightmares – a ghostly skeletal army returning from the battlefields to their homeland, indeed Longstaff painted other works which depicted such skeletal warriors rising from their graves. In perhaps its strangest and most extreme incarnation, the idea of the "returning dead" became associated with the spiritualist movement of the 1920's. With so many young sons killed, there was an enormous upsurge of interest in mediums, table-tapping and attempting to contact those on the "other side". Sir Arthur Conan Doyle was one famous acolyte, while, according to Robert Graves, Siegfried Sassoon's mother was given to holding seances to try to contact her other son, who had been killed in the Dardanelles.[24] Many of the mediums professed that on Armistice Day they could actually *see* the dead at the Cenotaph ceremony, and one claimed to be able to take "spirit photographs" in which the souls of the dead soldiers are apparently visible above the Armistice crowd.[25]

At war memorials up and down the land, veterans, widows, and bereaved parents gathered. The language of these events often sought to put the nature of the sacrifice into context – to give meaning to a national loss on a scale which was almost incomprehensible. The form of the ceremony during the 1930's usually involved a procession to a district war memorial, led by local worthies and dignitaries, some of whom would have served in the war. The emphasis was usually two-fold. It was not triumphalist – the names of generals were not read out, but instead the names of the dead, the ordinary people who had participated, then came the solemn vow – "at the going down of the sun, and in the morning, we *will* remember them". This was the primary emphasis – *remembrance*. The second was *indebtedness*, an appeal that their selflessness should not be wasted.[26] The speeches talked of war to end war, that the sacrifice must be justified through the lives of those who had been spared. All of society must comport itself and behave in a way which fitted the memory of those who had not lived – a better society, a changed society. "Their sacrifice must not be in vain" came the exhortation. General Sir Arthur Currie, in an Armistice Day address for 1933, wrote: "has the world... in the fifteen years since the Armistice kept its promised faith with the unreturning dead?" Currie concluded sadly that it had not, "Bitterness and hate, selfishness and greed are still entrenched in our social, economic and political life".[27]

However, as the 1930's drew to a close, and especially after Munich in 1938, the notion of "War to end wars" came to have a hollow ring to it. Germany was elbow deep in the civil war in Spain, which had seen, among a range of other atrocities, the indiscriminate bombing of civilians. Italy was busy using poison gas in its attempt to conquer Abyssinia and to carve itself out an African empire. The world had plainly not been made safe for democracy and freedom, and on Armistice Day of that year of 1938, one newspaper asked the question: "Can we say today, 'They did not die in vain?' Can we chant this phrase in unison about the Cenotaph and mock their names with pious recitations of our faith? Can we go on hiding our shame behind sloppy platitudes to their glory? Or would it be better to bare the record and admit our failure?"[28] However, to many families, even at this late stage to suggest

xlvi In this newspaper cartoon, which appeared on 9 November 1930, a soldier of the Great War hangs his head in sorrow at the decadence of the 1920s. (*Sunday Express*) that they had died in vain, was to insult the memory of the fallen. What else did the bereaved have to cling to but this?

The moral high ground of the Armistice commemoration by the late 1930's was wrestled for by the growing pacifist movement on one side, and those who retained "traditional" views of the meaning of the eleventh of November on the other. Traditional observances, "invariably included hymns that strongly emphasized the religious interpretation of the war. Standards like 'God of our Fathers', 'O Valiant Hearts' and 'O God Our Help in Ages Past' reminded worshippers that God had fought on the Allied side, and they affirmed that the war had been a simple struggle between good and evil".[29] They stressed that the war had been worthwhile and 'right'. The rise of the pacifist movement by contrast was based upon a rejection of these ideas and the ensuing conflict was typified by the controversy over the white poppy. The 1920's and especially the 1930's saw arguably the biggest rise in pacifist sentiment and anti-war feeling in British history and indeed the official response to this was to scale down the military presence at Armistice parades. Armistice Day in the 1930's regularly provoked debate over a range of issues centring around the role of the League of Nations, collective security, British rearmament and so on. In fact, it is probably fair to say that in the 1930's most British people would have classified themselves as "anti-war" to some degree. In 1933, the Women's Co-operative Guild produced and sold the first white poppies. The organization had been involved in disseminating pacifist propaganda since the mid 1920's and the white poppy, symbolizing peace, was the idea of Edith Pavitt of the Guild. In 1936, it was taken up by the newly-founded Peace Pledge Union. According to the PPU, the white poppy stood for all who had died in the war – military and civilian, Allied and enemy, while at the same time they claimed that the Legion's red poppies "glorified" only the British dead. Of course their opponents pointed out that a donation for a white poppy went to a political cause, while that for a red poppy went to help dependants and disabled, but the strength of the "peace movement" in the 1930's was undeniable – their rallies at Hyde Park and at other venues on the eleventh of November drew enormous crowds, and what might be called an "alternative armistice day" came into being. Some people attempted to support both causes by wearing red and white poppies, but nevertheless, the "out and out" pacifists faced considerable hostility from some quarters of mainstream society. There is evidence that white poppy wearers were verbally abused, and wreaths of white poppies laid at war memorials in the 1930's were frequently removed and trampled or destroyed. At the heart of the argument lay the fact that the PPU was drawn from the organizations and groups which had opposed the war at the time, and Gregory concludes:

> above all, the symbolism of the white poppy jarred. Veterans' pacifism was based on personal experience and sacrifice. It could not accept the moral equivalence of conscientious objectors with servicemen, let alone any claim to the superiority of the former. The peace movement revered the memory of the war resisters of 1914–18; for the ex-servicemen they would always

be damned as 'conchies'. The red poppy symbolised the experience of veterans' suffering. The white poppy was too close to the white feather for comfort.[30]

As the 1930's drew to a close, the PPU represented only one element of those opposed to the future of Armistice Day – in spite of notions of "collective grief" discussed earlier, there was in fact a quite widespread feeling that it was simply too painful an occasion for many people to bear, and a considerable number felt that it was wrong to subject the bereaved to official torment in this way each year. Mrs Margaret More, whose own husband had survived the war, wrote in her diary for Armistice Day 1936, "We listened to the Armistice Day programme which upset Mrs Edgington because her husband died of war wounds".[31] The Mass Observation surveys of the late 1930's had a distinctly left-wing political agenda which has led some to question their validity but they included questions about public perceptions of Armistice, and here at least they tend to reinforce this argument. These surveys reveal a perhaps surprising level of antipathy towards the ceremony and the two minutes' silence, though not by any means through what one might consider pacifistic views. One woman commented: "my sister's husband was killed. She goes all to pieces that day... they ought to stop it". Another said, "I think them as lost anybody go through hell that day, its all brought back".[32]

When the Second World War began, observance of Armistice Day was put into abeyance. The sheer dislocation experienced by much of the population – round the clock shifts, evacuation, conscription and training, not to mention dehousing caused by bombing – meant that there was no Cenotaph ceremony or two minutes' silence,[33] although poppy selling continued.[34] Some ceremonies were still held in schools. Middlesborough schoolgirl, Margaret Pykett, recalled:

> I can distinctly remember two. Tuesday 11th Nov 1940 and Wednesday 11th November 1941. All the girls moved quietly into the hall... an appropriate prayer or passage was read just before 11 o'clock when we became silent. Miss Murray never failed to ensure that it was absolute silence. After the two minutes silence we sang 'Oh God our help in ages past' and then quietly returned to our classrooms.[35]

In fact, Miss Murray, the headmistress, had lost two of her brothers in the Great War and we can only speculate on her feelings on the eleventh, manifesting themselves perhaps in her strictly enforced observance of the silence. Girl Guides and Boy Scouts also seem to have attended war memorials regularly on the eleventh, but the large scale attendances of the 1930's were no more. In the armed forces it is difficult to find any evidence of an awareness of Armistice or of its observance during the years 1939–45, the servicemen of a new generation were doubtless too preoccupied with trying to avoid death in the freezing night sky over Germany or perhaps wading waist deep in water through the jungles of Burma to spend much time reflecting upon the ironies of history. Yet on the Home Front there did come the realization during the war that things would not be the same again, that the First World War and the Armistice would now be viewed through the tinted lens of the second conflict with Germany. After a Sunday service in church on 10 November 1940, Mrs Ada Reece noted in her diary, "sermon... was preached by the padre of the Worcestershires, an Irishman whose name is Cowley and his theme: Love never forgets – also of how we long to forget – of tomorrow's poppies, of the soldiers of today being deeply religious, of the communions so gladly made in the Belgian campaign, daily always a few, sometimes as many as 60".[36] *Of tomorrow's poppies* – already the symbols of Armistice were being transferred and applied to the new conflict, and today we regard the poppy as symbolizing all British servicemen and women who die in war.

After the war, the question arose as to the future of Armistice commemoration. The Labour Government of 1945 had to deal with this problem. Even before the end of the war in Europe, in early May 1945, the coalition government had been in consultation with archbishops and the British Legion over the future of Armistice Day,[37] and to try to settle on a national day of remembrance which would include both world wars. It was felt in some quarters that to continue with the eleventh of November was in effect to diminish the importance of the Second World War and those who had died in it.

The Home Office began to consider other options – the possibilities included the eighth of May (VE Day), the sixth of June (D-Day), and the fifteenth of June (signing of Magna Carta in 1215 – seemingly a rather incongruous choice), as well as the fifteenth of August (VJ Day), and the third of September (outbreak of war in 1939).[38] Objections were raised to all of these dates in one quarter or another for a variety of reasons, for example the Australians objected to the European War dates, in which they had played a smaller part. For similar reasons, it was felt that dates linked to the Pacific War were not sufficiently emotive for the British people. The eleventh of November re-emerged as the only date on which there was consensus, or at least a minimum of dissent, and a Cenotaph ceremony was held on Sunday 11 November 1945. In January 1946, the Home Office agreed to the Bishop of Westminster's view that the two wars should be commemorated on Remembrance Sunday, i.e. the Sunday before 11 November, or 11 or 12 November if one of these happened to be a Sunday. Attlee announced this to the Commons in June 1946, stating that "the Government felt that this view would commend itself to all quarters in the country. I am glad to be able to say that it has now found general acceptance here and has been approved by The King".[39] That year, there was no "Armistice Day" as such. The Cenotaph ceremony was held on Remembrance Sunday as it is today, as was the two minutes' silence, and so the religious service which had traditionally accompanied the secular and civil ceremony of the eleventh of November came to eclipse it, and this has continued to be the case for over fifty years.

There had been a change in national sentiment – not so much actively against any form of commemoration, but clearly the dissolution of any unifying certainty that it was necessary and important. By the 1950's, the two minutes' silence had effectively gone. With Armistice commemoration moved to the nearest Sunday, it was observed only as part of a church service or a ceremony at the Cenotaph in London or at a local war memorial. The concept of the nation breaking from daily routine to remember the war dead was no more. The difficulties of making Armistice relevant to a generation almost too young to remember the Second World War, let alone the First, were addressed by Ada Reece's Vicar in a sermon on 12 November 1950: "Mr Sharp preached on Fellowship to the old who remembered and the young who were facing so different a world".[40]

In 1960, the Vicar of Kenilworth, the Reverend John Thomson, told his Remembrance Sunday congregation how much he regretted the discontinuation of the two minutes' silence on the eleventh hour, day and month[41] – clearly he felt that it was moving out of local consciousness. Three years later, in the same parish on Remembrance Sunday, another clergyman, the Reverend J.C. Dunham, acknowledged the difficulties of reaching a new generation – "we not only remember; we also rejoice in victory. The welfare state has clouded the minds of many young people today. Do they realize what defeat would have been like?"[42]

In the 1960's, Armistice Day slid into disrepute as the war which had originated it slid into disrepute, as a war in which, it was alleged, the young were cynically misled and slaughtered by the old. The writer and critic, Keith Sagar, described Armistice Day as, "part of the process whereby the nation promises to remember for one day a year in order to forget with a clear conscience for the other three hundred and sixty four; the process whereby the nation accepts with pride the slaughter of a whole generation of its youth. The rhetoric of the cenotaph ceremony is a continuance in solemn guise of the lying jingoism [of the First World War]".[43]

Of course the ex-servicemen of the Great War knew differently, but by the late 1960s their numbers were in serious decline. In 1968, C.E. Crutchley, who had served in the war, produced a pamphlet entitled "Remembering... 50 years after". Crutchley wrote in his introduction:

> Instead of curtailing or abolishing remembrance as some would have it, I would like to see the existing sacred ceremony of Remembrance become international in character, so that realization of what war means is brought home to peoples of all nations. Remembrance Day, if it is to serve the purpose for which it was created, must act as a warning – as well as a reminder of man's past deeds of shame. I am aware that every generation must live with its own problems, but I do not accept the assumption of some people – that the young folk of today are not interested in what we are remembering".[44]

It seems that Crutchley was wide of the mark in this last comment, for the decline in the importance of the eleventh of November in the national calendar continued inexorably throughout the 1970's. The names on village or town war memorials were increasingly becoming just that – names. There were fewer and fewer men or women who could remember them when they were alive, when they were more than just names carved in stone or in grimy bronze relief. In a Warwickshire town, Leamington Spa, by no means alone in this, there was additionally municipal indifference and an attempt by town hall bureaucrats to diminish the ceremony even further in 1970: "Last year's break with tradition... a brief ceremony at the memorial... struck a discordant note which prompted civic and other leaders to reintroduce the more acceptable form of service this year".[45] Finally, at the end of the decade, as if struggling vainly to hold back a tide, a local minister, the Reverend Michael Mansbridge is quoted as protesting that: "the occasion was not an empty show, but a meaningful and important event".[46] Over the whole country, The Royal British Legion and the Second World War veterans continued to mark the occasion, but as far as being a major part of national life was concerned, Armistice remembrance was no more. Intellectual or liberal opinion felt that the First World War had all been futile and a waste, and that all should be ashamed of it. There was nothing there to commemorate, as this would imply a respect for the period that a later enlightened generation could not hold.

What might be described as the "rise again" of Armistice Day came in the 1980's, with the huge upsurge in public interest in the Great War. The first milestone identifiable on this road is probably the foundation of the Western Front Association in 1980 by the author, John Giles. What was unique and indeed extraordinary about the WFA was that it was the first, and undoubtedly the most successful First World War-linked association whose members had predominantly not served in that conflict, but who were drawn to it from scholarly or genealogical interest.[47] The WFA began to promote anniversaries both locally and nationally, and to raise money for memorials to the Great War – the first since the 1920's. Most important of all, it sought to raise awareness again of the need to mark the November Armistice on the day itself.

Some aspects of the November commemoration have remained controversial – in 1981 the then Labour Party leader, Michael Foot, aroused anger when he attended the Cenotaph ceremony in a donkey jacket – the *Daily Telegraph* reported that he laid his wreath with "all the reverent dignity of a tramp bending down to inspect a cigarette end".[48] In the mid 1980's, white poppies were again sold to compete with red ones, which it was still argued by some in the pacifist movement "glorified" war. This upsurge in white poppy popularity was in no small part linked to the emergence of green politics, Greenpeace, the "peace protests" outside Greenham Common US airbase in the mid 1980s, and the fleeting re-emergence of CND as a political force, developments which in themselves were reactions to the strongly right-wing Thatcher governments of those years.

However, in 1995 and again in 1996, an extraordinary event took place. In both these years, two minutes' silence was observed by a substantial proportion of the nation on the morning of the eleventh itself. Not all public or private institutions were willing to take part by any means, but a goodly

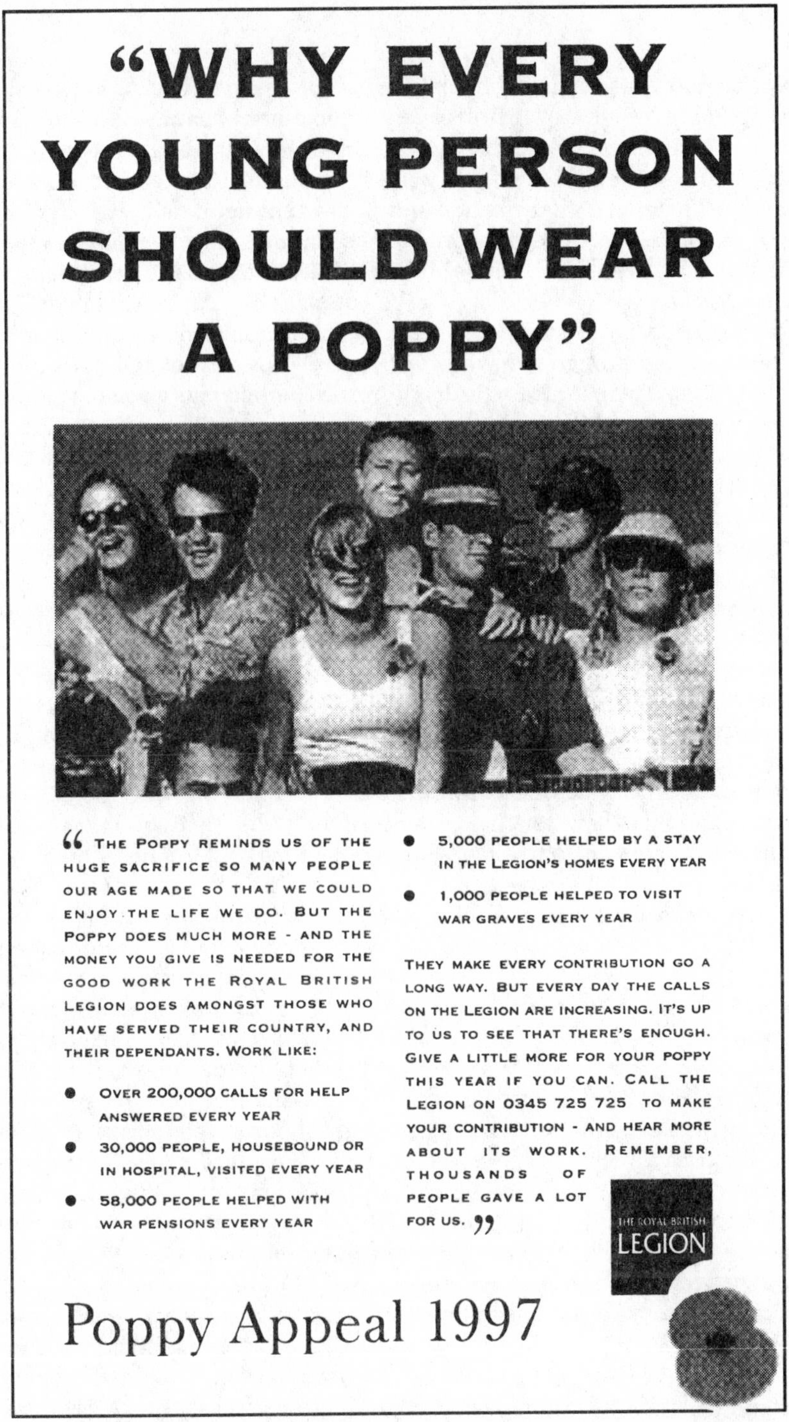
"WHY EVERY YOUNG PERSON SHOULD WEAR A POPPY"
"The Poppy reminds us of the huge sacrifice so many people our age made so that we could enjoy the life we do. But the Poppy does much more - and the money you give is needed for the good work the Royal British Legion does amongst those who have served their country, and their dependants. Work like:
• Over 200,000 calls for help answered every year
• 30,000 people, housebound or in hospital, visited every year
• 58,000 people helped with war pensions every year
• 5,000 people helped by a stay in the Legion's homes every year
• 1,000 people helped to visit war graves every year
They make every contribution go a long way. But every day the calls on the Legion are increasing. It's up to us to see that there's enough. Give a little more for your poppy this year if you can. Call the Legion on 0345 725 725 to make your contribution - and hear more about its work. Remember, thousands of people gave a lot for us."
THE ROYAL BRITISH LEGION
Poppy Appeal 1997

xlvii The British Legion's 1997 appeal focused its attention on younger people and on involving them in marking the Armistice commemoration. (Royal British Legion) portion, including McDonalds and J. Sainsbury, were. The new move, argued for strongly by the Royal British Legion, had once again placed the silence back in the context of everyday work. On an average Sunday morning a fair proportion of the British population is not even out of bed by 11a.m., but to break off from one's daily routine for just two minutes on a weekday in this way prompts sober reflection among those observing it. The move to restore Armistice Day to the eleventh at present lacks official backing, although the RBL is strongly in favour of it, but the popularity of the move is undeniable. There is widespread support in the business community,[49] and this in turn reflects renewed interest in the event and the history of the 20th century among British people generally. In 1997, the Legion's campaign to restore the silence was named 'Public Relations Campaign of the Year' by the industry magazine *PR Week,* after judges felt that the RBL had managed to re-establish the silence in the national consciousness.

There is still criticism of Armistice commemoration today from some quarters – the author Julian Putkowski has commented recently that, "nationalist politicians and militarists milk Armistice Day for all it's politically worth. It's changed to suit whatever politicians reckon will gain them a vote or avoid taking responsibility for their role in the killing... Armistice Day is also used as a means to stifle criticism of the responsibility of the ruling class for the slaughter in the 'Great' (and most other) wars",[50] and "Armistice Day is not a conspiracy by politicians, it's a photo opportunity – differing from most others in that they are not expected to smile at the cameras. It is part of a political agenda which seeks legitimation by identifying with the dead who were supposed to have fought in defence of the nation".[51] Such a verdict seems extreme, even when contrasted with the opinions of those of a similar political hue to Putkowski himself. The columnist and commentator Martin Kettle, in an eloquent article in *The Guardian* on 16 November 1996, described an extraordinary pause for two minutes at 11a.m. on the eleventh, during an editorial meeting. Kettle revealed that at the offices of that newspaper he was not aware of this ever taking place before, and indeed that this was not the kind of newspaper that one would immediately associate with this sort of event: "Doubtless there will be those on the left who will offer a facile explanation. They will see it as just another in a long line of compromises with the culture of the English establishment", comments Kettle, but perceptively he goes on to describe a subtle but profound shift in British society as we near the end of the 20th century. It is part of an underlying and unspoken realization that in spite of all the assaults on the fabric of our culture this century – the First World War itself and its aftermath, the rise and fall of fascism and communism, withdrawal from Empire, loss of world status, economic recession and unemployment, we are still bound together by a sense of community: "The era in which such remembrance events could be depicted as merely right wing, nationalistic, and private to those who had fought has long gone ... The two minutes is only a gesture. But its existence – and in particular its revival – is nothing less than a popular triumph against the odds".[52] November the eleventh 1997 saw the two minutes' silence more widely observed than at any other time since the 1930's. Supermarkets, banks, railway stations and airports all ceased in their activities for a moment of reflection, an act which spanned barriers of both class and generation.

Thus, seemingly against the run of events, Armistice Day has survived seven decades and is almost certain still to be with us at the close of the century. It has endured and survived discredit derived from the disillusion of the war generation and others who came after, and the stigma of the almost unbearable pain it could bring about. It has survived indifference, both official and public. It has survived precisely because its meaning has changed yet again, and it now symbolizes something much broader than its Georgian originators can ever have imagined. Today Armistice Day is in many ways stronger than it has been at any time in the latter half of this century. It is commemorated by a society which is now much more at ease with itself. Less riven by internal conflict, although more culturally diverse than hitherto, British society, in numerous ways is more homogeneous than ever before and this is reflected by the manner in which an event like Armistice commemoration finds such widespread approval.

Endnotes

All references marked L.C. are from the Liddle Collection, Brotherton Library, University of Leeds, U.K.

1 *Nottingham Evening Post*, 11.11.18, L.C.
2 Marshal F. Foch, communiqué to Allied Armies 12.11.18 (quoted in D. Ward, *The 56th Division*, John Murray, London, 1921, p. 314).
3 *The Times*, 11.11.19, L.C.
4 *The Yorkshire Post*, 12.11.19, L.C.
5 Jay Winter, *Sites of Memory, Sites of Mourning*, Cambridge University Press, Cambridge, 1995, p. 104.
6 *The Times*, 7.11.19, L.C.
7 Jonathan Vance, *Death So Noble – Memory, Meaning and the First World War*, U.B.C. Press, Vancouver, 1997, p. 213.
8 Mrs Mary Kinsey, diary 11.11.19, L.C.
9 Gregory, Adrian, The Silence of Memory: Armistice Day 1919–46, Berg Publishers, Oxford/Providence, 1994, p. 15.
10 Martin Middlebrook, *The Somme Battlefields*, Viking, 1991, p. 43 has an interesting version of the selection procedure. See also *Sunday Express*, 9.11.30.
11 *The Daily Mirror*, 12.11.20, L.C.
12 G. Palmer, "Poppy Day & the YMCA" pamphlet, undated, L.C.
13 *Town Crier*, 9.1.20, L.C.
14 Jonathan Vance, *op. cit.*, p. 222.
15 Frank Richards, *Old Soldiers Never Die*, Faber & Faber, London, 1933, p. 322.
16 ibid, p. 323.
17 Mary Kinsey, diary, 11.11.23, L.C.
18 Jonathan Vance, *op. cit.*, p. 213.
19 Geoff Dyer, *The Missing of the Somme*, Penguin, London, 1994, p. 26.
20 "Forgotten Men: The War as it Was", 1934, Associated British Picture Corporation. [Directed by Norman Lee].
21 Adrian Gregory, *op. cit.*, p. 15.
22 Jay Winter, *op. cit.*, p. 60.
23 Quoted in Geoff Dyer, *op. cit.*, p. 22.

24 Robert Graves, *Goodbye to All That*, Penguin, London, pp. 191–2.
25 Jay Winter, *op. cit.*, p. 69.
26 *ibid*, p. 97.
27 Jonathan Vance, *op. cit.*, p. 222.
28 *Globe*, Toronto, 11.11.38.
29 Jonathan Vance, *op. cit.*, p. 217.
30 Adrian Gregory, *op. cit.*, p. 157.
31 M.L. More, diary, 11.11.36, L.C.
32 Mass Observation interviews, Fulham, October 1938. Quoted in Gregory, *op. cit.*, p. 166.
33 M.L. More, diary, 11.11.40, L.C.
34 Lydia Reece, diary, 11.11.44, L.C.
35 Margaret Pykett, Manuscript recollections, L.C.
36 Ada Reece, diary, 10.11.40, L.C.
37 Adrian Gregory, *op. cit.*, p. 216
38 *ibid*, p. 218.
39 Hansard 424 H.C.DEB. 5 S., p. 179.
40 Ada Reece, diary, 12.11.50, L.C.
41 *Leamington Spa Courier*, 18.11.60, L.C.
42 *ibid*, 12.11.63.
43 Quoted in Geoff Dyer, *op. cit.*, p. 29.
44 C.E. Crutchley, "Remembering... 50 years after", pamphlet copy, L.C.
45 *Leamington Spa Courier*, 14.11.71, L.C.
46 *ibid*, 12.11.78, L.C.
47 See the excellent journal of the Western Front Association, "Stand To!".
48 *Daily Telegraph*, 15.11.81.
49 *Daily Mail*, 6.10.97.
50 Julian Putkowski, comments made on WW1-L Internet discussion site, 21.5.97.
51 *ibid.*
52 *The Guardian*, 16.11.96.

BIBLIOGRAPHY

GENERAL

Inevitably there is overlap in a subdivided bibliography and it is recommended that those readers examining the 'National' sections should also look in the General Section.

Armistice et paix: 1918, Catalogue de l'exposition, 9 novembre 1978 - 15 janvier 1979, Hotel national des Invalides (Nanterre) to Universités de Paris, Bibliothèque de documentation international contemporaine, Musée des deux guerres mondiales, Paris, 1978.

Barclay, Brigadier C.N., *Armistice 1918*, London: J.M. Dent, 1968.

Brook-Shepherd, Gordon. *November 1918: The Last Act of the Great War*, London: Collins, 1981.

Debergh, François and Gaillard, André, *Les Chemins de l'armistice*, Paris: Edition France-empire, 1968.

Dufresne, Claude, *Ce jour-là. La victoire: 1918*, Paris: Librairie academique Perrin, 1988.

Lowry, Bullitt, *Armistice 1918*, Kent: Kent State University Press, 1996.

Marhefka, Edmond (ed.), *Der Waffenstillstand 1914–1919. Das Dokumentenmaterial der Waffenstillstandsverhandlungen vom Compiègne, Spa, Trier und Brüssel.* 3 vols., Berlin, 1928.

Mermeix [Gabriel Terrail], *Les négociations secrètes et les quatre armistices*, Paris: Ollendorff, [1922].

Maurice, Frederick Barton, *The Armistices of 1918*, New York and London: Oxford University Press, 1943.

Nicolson, Harold, *Peacemaking 1919*, London: Constable, 1933.

Rudin, Harry R., *Armistice 1918*, New Haven: Yale University Press, 1944.

Stevenson, David, *The First World War and International Politics*, Oxford: Oxford University Press, 1987.

Watt, Richard M., *The King's Depart*, London: Weidenfeld and Nicolson, 1968.

Weintraub, Stanley, *A Stillness Heard Round the World: The End of the Great War: November 1918*, New York: Truman Talley / E.P. Dutton, 1985.

OFFICIAL HISTORIES

FRANCE

Ministère de la guerre. État-major de l'armée. Service historique. *Les armées françaises dans la Grande Guerre.* Tome 7. *Le campagne offensive de 1918 et la marche au Rhin (18 juillet 1918–28 juin 1919).* 2 vols. plus 1 vol. of annexed documents and 2 vols. of maps. Paris: Imprimerie nationale, 1938.

Ministère de la guerre. État-major de l'armée. Service historique. *Les armées françaises dans la Grande Guerre.* Tome 8. *Le campagne d'Orient.* 3 vols. plus 3 vols. of documents and 1 vol. of maps. Paris: Imprimerie nationale, 1934.

Ministère des armées. État-major de l'armée de terre. Service historique. *Les armées françaises en Orient après l'armistice de 1918.* By General Jean Bernachot. 2 vols. Paris: Imprimerie nationale, 1970.

GERMANY

Reichskanzlei. *Vorgeschichte des Waffenstillstand*, Berlin: R. Hobbing, 1919. Translated as: *Preliminary History of the Armistice.* Translated by Carnegie Endowment for International Peace. New York: Oxford University Press, 1924.

Waffenstillstandkommission, 1918–1919. *Der Waffenstillstand: 1918–1919.* 3 vols. Berlin: Deutsche Verlagsgesellschaft für Politik und Geschichte, 1928.

GREAT BRITAIN

Military Operations, France and Belgium, 1918. By J.E. Edmonds and R. Maxwell-Hyslop. 5 vols. London: H.M. Stationery Office, 1947.

Military Operations, Italy, 1915–1919. By J.E. Edmonds and H.R. Davies. 4 vols. in 1. London: H.M. Stationery Office, 1949.

Committee of Imperial Defence. Historical Section. *The Campaign in Mesopotamia 1914–18.* By F.J. Moberley. Vol. 4. London: H.M. Stationery Office, 1927.

Committee of Imperial Defence. Historical Section. *Military Operations, Macedonia.* By Cyril Falls. 2 vols. London: H.M. Stationery Office, 1935.

Military Operations, Egypt and Palestine. By Cyril Falls and A.F. Becke. From June 1917 to the end of the war. Part II. London: H.M. Stationery Office, 1930.

Naval Operations, Vol. 5, *From April 1917 to the End of the War.* By Henry Newbolt. London: Longmans, Green, 1931.

United States
Department of the Army, *The United States Army in the World War*. 17 vols. Washington, Government Printing Office, 1947.

STUDIES BY PARTICIPANTS

Bliss, Tasker, "The Armistices", *American Journal of International Law* 16 (1922), pp. 509–522.
Erzberger, Mathias, *Erlebnisse im Weltkrieg*, Stuttgart and Berlin: Deutsche Verlagsanstalt, 1920.
Foch, Ferdinand, *Mémoires pour servir à l'histoire de la Guerre de 1914–1918*. 2 vols. Paris: Plon, 1931.
[Haig, Douglas], *The Private Papers of Douglas Haig: 1914–1919*. Edited by Robert Blake. London: Eyre and Spottiswoode, 1952.
Hankey, Lord, *The Supreme Command, 1914–1918*. 2 vols. London: George Allen and Unwin, 1961.
Hindenburg, Paul von, *Aus meinen Leben*. Trans. as *Out of My Life*. Trans. by F.A. Holt. 2 vols. New York: Cassell, 1920.
Lloyd George, David, *Memoirs of the Peace Conference*. 2 vols. New Haven: Yale University Press, 1939.
Lloyd George, David, *War Memoirs*. 6 vols. London: Ivor Nicholson and Watson, 1933–1936.
Ludendorff, Erich, *Urkunden der Obersten Heeresleitung über ihre Tätigkeit 1916–1918*. Trans. as *The General Staff and Its Problems*. Trans. by F.A. Holt. 2 vols. London: Hutchinson, 1920.
Ludendorff, Erich, *Meine Kriegserinnerungen*. 2 vols. Berlin: 1919. Trans. as *My War Memories, 1914–1918*. 2 vols. London: Hutchinson, 1919.
Ludendorff, Erich, *Das Verschrieben der Verantwortlichkeit*, Berlin: Mittler, 1919.
Mordacq, Henri, *L'Armistice du 11 novembre 1918: récit d'un témoin*, Paris: Plon, 1930–1937.
Mordacq, Henri, *Le ministère Clemenceau: journal d'un témoin*. 4 vols. Paris: Plon, 1930–1931.
Mordacq, Henri, *Pouvait-on signer l'armistice à Berlin?* Paris: Grasset, [1930].
Mordacq, Henri, *La vérité sur l'armistice*, Paris: Tallandier, 1929.
Weygand, Maxime, *Le onze novembre*. Paris: Flammarion, 1958.
Weygand, Maxime, *Mémoires*. Vol. 1, *Idéal vécu*. Vol. 2, *Mirages et réalité*, Paris: Flammarion, 1953–1957.
Weygand, Maxime, *Foch*, Paris: Flammarion, 1947.

STUDIES OF PARTICIPANTS

Azan, Paul, *Franchet d'Espérey*, Paris: Flammarion, 1949.
Beaverbrook, Lord [W.M. Aitken], *The Decline and Fall of Lloyd George*, New York: Duell, Sloan and Pearce, 1963.
Callwell, Maj-Gen [Sir] C.E, *Field Marshal Sir Henry Wilson, His Life and Diaries*. 2 vols. London: Cassell, 1927.

Chalmers, W.S, *The Life and Letters of David, Earl Beatty*, London: Hodder and Stoughton, 1951.
Duroselle, Jean-Baptiste, *Clemenceau*, Paris: Fayard, 1988.
L'Hôpital, Réné M.M, *Foch, l'armistice et la paix*, Paris: Plon, 1938.
Newhall, David S., *Clemenceau: A Life at War*, Lewiston, New York: Edwin Mellen Press, 1991.
Seymour, Charles (ed.), *The Intimate Papers of Colonel House*. 4 vols. Boston and New York: Houghton Mifflin, 1926–1928.
Smythe, Donald, *Pershing: General of the Armies*, Bloomington: Indiana University Press, 1986.

OTHERS

Gelfand, L.E., *The Inquiry*, American Preparations for Peace, 1917–19, New Haven: Yale University Press, 1963.
Lutz, Ralph Haswell (ed.), *The Fall of the German Empire, 1914–1918*. 2 vols. Stanford: Stanford University Press, 1932.
Petkov, Petko M., *The United States and Bulgaria in World War I*, Boulder, Colorado: East European Monographs, 306/Distributed by Columbia University Press, 1991.
Stevenson, David, *French War Aims against Germany, 1914–1919*, Oxford: Clarendon Press, 1982.

IN THE LONGER TERM (two books with opposing theses):

Keynes, John Maynard, *The Economic Consequences of the Peace*, London: Macmillan, 1920.
Mantoux, Etienne, *The Carthaginian Peace or The Economic Consequences of Mr Keynes*, London: Oxford University Press, 1946. [reprint, London: Serif, projected 1999]

FURTHER PRINTED SOURCES

Albrecht-Carrié, René *Italy at the Paris Peace Conference*, New York: Columbia University Press, 1938; reprint, Hamden: Archon, 1977.
Gen. Jean Bernachot, *Les armées françaises en Orient après l'armistice de 1918*, Ministère des armées, État-major de l'armée de terre, Service historique. 3 vols. Paris: Imprimerie nationale, 1970–72.
[Germany. Reichskanzlei]. *Preliminary History of the Armistice*, Carnegie Endowment for International Peace, New York: Oxford University Press, 1924.
Bogdan Krizman, "The Belgrade Armistice of 13 November 1918", *Slavonic and East European Review* 48 (1970): pp. 67–87.
United States. Department of State. *Papers Relating to the Foreign Relations of the United States, 1918*, Supplement I, *The World War*. 2 vols. Washington: Government Printing Office, 1933.
United States. Department of State. *Foreign Relations of the United States, 1919*, The Paris Peace Conference. 13 vols. Washington: Government Printing Office, 1942–47.

Wheeler-Bennett, Sir John, *Hindenburg: The Wooden Titan*, London: Macmillan, 1936.
Winter, Jay, and Robert, Jean-Louis (eds)., *Capital Cities at War: Paris, London, Berlin 1914–1919*, Cambridge: Cambridge University Press, 1997.

GERMANY

Prinz Max von Baden, *Erinnerungen und Dokumente*, Golo Mann and Andreas Burckhardt, (new ed.) with an introduction by Golo Mann, Stuttgart: 1968. [First published 1928].
Berghahn, Volker R., *Sarajewo, 28. Juni 1914. Der Untergang des alten Europa*, München: 1997.
Bessel, Richard, *Germany after the First World War*, Oxford: O.U.P., 1993.
Groener, Wilhelm, *Lebenserinnerungen. Jugend, Generalstab, Weltkrieg*, Friedrich Freiherr Hiller von Gaertringen (ed.), Göttingen: 1957.
Heinemann, Ulrich, *Die verdröngte Niederlage*, Göttingen: 1983.
Kielmansegg, Peter Graf von, *Deutschland und der Erste Weltkrieg*, Frankfurt am Main: 1980 (2nd Edition).
Kluge, Ulrich, *Die deutsche Revolution 1918/19*, Frankfurt am Main: 1985.
Kruse, Wolfgang (ed.), *Eine Welt von Feinden. Der Grosse Krieg 1914–1918*, Frankfurt am Main: 1997.
Michalka, Wolfgang (Hg.), *Der Erste Weltkrieg. Wirkung, Wahrenehmung, Analyse*, München: 1994.
Mommsen, Wolfgang J., *Bürgerstolz und Weltmachtstreben*, Berlin: 1995.
Stumpf, Richard, *Erinnerungen aus dem deutsch-englischen Seekriege auf S.M.S. Helgoland*. Das Werk des Untersuchungsausschusses der Verfassunggebenden Deutschen Nationalversammlung und des Deutschen Reichstages 1919–1928. IV. Reihe Band 10, 2. Halbband, Berlin: 1928.
Thaer, Albrecht von, *Generalstabschef an der Front und in der OHL. Aus Briefen und Tagebuchaufzeichnungen 1915–1919*, Siegfried A. Kaehler (ed.), Göttingen: 1958.
Ullrich, Volker, *Die nervöse Grossmacht. Aufstieg und Untergang des deutschen Kaiserreichs 1871–1918*, Frankfurt am Main: 1997.
Ulrich, Bernd and Ziemann, Benjamin (eds.), *Frontalltag im Ersten Weltkrieg: Wahn und Wirklichkeit; Quellen und Dokumente*, Frankfurt am Main: Fischer Taschenbuch Verlag, 1994.
Winkler, Heinrich August, "Vom Kaiserreich zur Republik. Der historische Ort der Revolution von 1918/19", in: Heinrich August Winkler, *Streitfragen der deutschen Geschichte*, München: 1997, pp. 52–70.

THE UNITED KINGDOM

Bourne, J.M., *Britain and the Great War 1914–18*, London: Edward Arnold, 1989.
Garrett, Richard, *The Final Betrayal: The Armistice 1918 and Afterwards*, London: Buchan & Enright, 1989.

Marwick, Arthur, *The Deluge: British Society and the First World War*, London: Bodley Head, 1965.
Pitt, Barrie, *1918: The Last Act*, London: Cassell, 1962.
Terraine, John, *To Win A War, 1918: The Year of Victory*, London: Sidgwick & Jackson, 1978.
Wilson, Trevor, *The Myriad Faces of War: Britain and the Great War*, Cambridge: Polity Press, 1986.
Winter, J.M., *The Great War and the British People*, London: Macmillan, 1985.

FRANCE

Baudrillart, Alfred de, *Les carnets du Cardinal de ... , 1er août 1914–31 décembre 1918*, Paris: Du Cerf, 1994.
Delvert, capitaine, *Les carnets d'un fantassin*, Paris: du Mémorial, 1981.
Dorgelès, R., *Les Croix de bois*, Paris: Albin Michel, 1919.
Duroselle, J.B., *La grande guerre des Français, 1914–1918*, Paris: Perrin, 1994.
Ducasse, A., Meyer, J., *Mémoires pour servir à l'histoire de la guerre 1914–1918*, Paris: Hachette, 1962.
Husser, Philippe, *Journal d'un instituteur 1914–1951*, Hachette, collection: Livre de poche, 1989.
Mayer, Jean, *Le 11 novembre*, Hachette, 1964.
Miquel, P., *La Grande Guerre*, Paris: Fayard, 1983.
Mordacq, général, *Les Grandes Heures de la guerre de 14*, 3 vols., Plon, 1938.
Nobécourt, R.G., *L'année du 11 novembre*, Paris: Robert Laffont, 1968.
Pédroncini, Guy, *Journal de marche de Joffre (1916–1919)*, documents présenté, par la Service historique de l'Armée de Terre, Vincennes: 1990.
Poincaré, Raymond, *Au service de la France. Victoire et armistice*, Paris: Plon, 1939.
Pierrefeu, Jean de., *G.Q.G. Secteur 1, L'édition française illustrée*, 2 tomes, Paris: G. Crès, 1920.
Radiguet, R., *Le Diable au corps*, Grasset, 1923.
Renouvin, P., *11 Novembre-L'Armistice de Rethondes*, Collection: Trente journées qui ont fait la France, Paris: Gallimard, 1968.
Tournes, René, *Histoire de la guerre mondiale, Foch et la victoire des Alliés, 1918*, Paris: Payout, 1936.

ARTICLES

Cadras, Louis, "L'Armistice du 11 novembre 1918", in *Les Cahiers de l'Histoire*, no. 80, November 1968, pp. 87–112.
Defrasne, Colonel, "L'offensive de Lorraine et l'Armistice", November 1918, in *Revue historique de l'Armée*, special issue: Fiftieth Anniversary of the 1918 Victory, 24th year, no. 4, pp. 97–112.
du Chesne, Lieutenant-Colonel Mabille, "Paris en 1918", in *Revue historique de l'Armée,* Ministère des Armées, special issue: Fiftieth Anniversary of the 1918 Victory, 24th year, no. 4, pp. 113–118.
Nobécourt, R.G., "La Onzième Heure", in *Revue historique de l'Armée*,

Ministère des Armées, special issue: Fiftieth Anniversary of the 1918 Victory, 24th year, no. 4, pp. 173–179.

BELGIUM

België en de Eerste Wereldoorlog. Bibliografie, (P. Lefèvre and J. Lorette eds.), Brussels: 1987.
Deflo, F., *De literaire oorlog. De Vlaamse prozaliteratuur over de Eerste Wereldoorlog*, Aartrijke: 1991.
Dolderer, W., *Deutscher Imperialismus und belgischer Nationalitätenkonflikt. Die Rezeption der Flamenfrage in der deutschen Öffentlichkeit und deutsch-flämische Kontakte 1890–1920*, Messungen: 1989.
Durnez, G., *Zeg mij waar de bloemen zijn. Beelden uit de Eerste Wereldoorlog in Vlaanderen*, Leuven: 1988.
Haag, H., "La Belgique en novembre 1918", *Revue d'histoire moderne et contemporaine*, Jan-March 1969, pp. 153–160.
Haag, H., "Le choix du roi Albert à Loppem", in *Actes du colloque Roi Albert. Bruxelles Bibliothèque royale Albert Ier 26–29 mai 1975* (C. Wyffels ed.), Brussels: 1976, pp. 170–191.
Haag, H., *Le comte Charles de Broqueville, Ministre d'État et les luttes pour le pouvoir (1910–1940)*, Louvain-la-Neuve Brussels: 1990.
van Hoonacker, E., *Kortrijk 14–18. Een stad tijdens de Eerste Wereldoorlog*, Kortrijk: 1994.
Jacobs, M., *Zij, die vielen als helden: Inventaris van de oorlogsgedenktekens van de twee wereldoorlogen in West-Vlaanderen*. 2 vols. Brugge: 1996.
Kossmann, E.H., *The Low Countries 1780–1940*, Oxford: 1978.
Pirenne, H., *La Belgique et la guerre mondiale*, Paris-New Haven: 1928.
de Schaepdrijver, S., *De Groote Oorlog. Het koninkrijk België tijdens de Eerste Wereldoorlog*, Amsterdam Antwerpen: 1997.
Schepens, L., *14/18 Een oorlog in Vlaanderen*, Tielt: 1984.
Schepens, L., "België in de eerste wereldoorlog", in *Algemene Geschiedenis der Nederlanden*, Haarlem 1979, vol. XIV, pp. 19–39.
Stengers, J., "La Belgique", in *Les Sociétés européennes et la guerre de 1914–1918. Actes du colloque organisé à Nanterre et à Amiens du 8 au 11 décembre 1988*, Nanterre: 1990, pp. 75–91.
Vanacker, D., *Het Aktivistisch avontuur*, Gent 1991.
Van den Grooten Oorlog. Volksboek, (Elfnovembergroep ed.), Kemmel: 1978.
Verschaeve, C., *Oorlogsindrukken* (D. Vanacker & R. Vanlandschoot eds.), Gent: 1996.
de Vos, L., *De Eerste Wereldoorlog*, Leuven: 1996.
Weemaes, M., *De l'Yser à Bruxelles. Offensive libératrice de l'Armée belge le 28 septembre 1918*, Marcinelle: 1969.
Wils, L., *Flamenpolitik en activisme. Vlaanderen tegenover België in de Eerste Wereldoorlog*, Leuven: 1974.
van Ypersele, L., *Le roi Albert. Histoire d'un mythe*, Ottignies - Louvain-la-Neuve: 1995.

THE UNITED STATES

In dealing with the Armistice of November 1918, the Americans have the same problem that they do in understanding their role in the Great War. World War One is sandwiched between two great, defining events in American history: the Civil War (1861–1865), and World War Two (1941–1945). The former left deep scars on the land, while the latter forced the United States reluctantly to abandon isolation for a prominent role in post-war affairs. Most historians have dealt with the Armistice in the context of President Woodrow Wilson's actions at Versailles and the failure of the United States to ratify the Versailles Treaty. Changing the focus to Americans rather than their President and the Armistice presents problems. Of primary importance, however, is David M. Kennedy, *Over Here: The First World War and American Society* (New York: Oxford University Press, 1980). While Kennedy's work spans the entire American war effort, his insights into the Armistice are clear and coherent. Frank Friedel's *Over There: The Story of America's Great Overseas Crusade* (New York: McGraw-Hill, 1990) has some insight into the impact of 11 November on soldiers and civilians alike. For a soldier's view of his comrades, the war, and the Armistice, one still consults Lawrence Stallings, *The Doughboys: The Story of the AEF, 1917–1918* (New York: Doubleday, 1963).

The biographies of General of the Armies, John Pershing, shed some light on the Armistice. Frank Vandiver's *Black Jack: The Life and Times of John J. Pershing*, 2 vols., (College Station: Texas A&M Press, 1977) and the late Donald Smythe, *Pershing: General of the Armies* (Bloomington: Indiana University Press, 1986) both discuss the immediate impact of 11 November on the General and the AEF. David F. Trask's *The AEF and Coalition Warmaking, 1917–1918* (Lawrence: University of Kansas Press, 1993) discusses the effects of the Armistice on those who formulated higher policy in their capitals and at Versailles.

There are glimpses of the reaction to the end of fighting in France. James J. Cooke's *The Rainbow Division in the Great War, 1917–1919* (Westport: Praeger, 1994) and *The U.S. Air Service in the Great War, 1917–1919* (Westport: Praeger, 1996) relate the individual serviceman's reaction to the news of the end of combat. Beyond the short discussion of the Armistice in newer works, much can be gleaned from the number of published diaries and memoirs of soldiers who served in the AEF. Most of these remembrances were published in the 1920's and 1930's, and they vary greatly in content and substantive comment. Contemporary newspaper accounts are wildly inaccurate about the processes of the Armistice, and they report a standard fare of description of the celebrations. The story of the Armistice for the United States, then, still needs to be researched and published.

AUSTRALIA

Bean, C.E.W., *The Australian Imperial Force in France During the Allied Offensive, 1918*, vol. VI, *The Official History of Australia in the War of 1914–1918*, 12 vols, Sydney: Angus & Robertson, 1942.

Bean, C.E.W., *Anzac to Amiens*, Canberra: Australian War Memorial, 1983 [first published 1946].

Beaumont, Joan (ed.), *Australia's War, 1914–18*, St Leonards, NSW: Allen & Unwin, 1995.

Butler, A.G., *The Western Front*, vol. II, *The Australian Army Medical Services in the War of 1914–1918*, 3 vols, Melbourne: Australian War Memorial, 1940.

Butler, A.G., *Special Problems and Services*, vol. III, *The Australian Army Medical Services in the War of 1914–1918*, 3 vols, Melbourne: Australian War Memorial, 1943.

Gammage, Bill, *The Broken Years: Australian Soldiers in the Great War*, Ringwood: Vic & Harmondsworth, Penguin, 1975 [first published 1974].

Lewis, Brian, *Our War: Australia during World War I*, Melbourne: Melbourne University Press, 1980.

Lloyd, Clem and Rees, Jacqui, *The Last Shilling: A History of Repatriation in Australia*, Melbourne: Melbourne University Press, 1994.

McKernan, Michael, *The Australian People and the Great War*, Melbourne: Nelson, 1980.

Scott, Ernest, *Australia During the War*, Vol. XI, *The Official History of Australia in the War of 1914–1918*, 12 vols, Sydney: Angus and Robertson, 1939.

Wilcox, Craig (ed.), assisted by Aldridge, Janice, *The Great War: Gains and Losses - ANZAC and Empire*, Canberra: The Australian War Memorial and The Australian National University, 1995.

CANADA

The essential starting place for any study of Canada in the First World War is G.W.L. Nicholson's official history, *Canadian Expeditionary Force, 1914–1919* (Ottawa: 1962). There are several academic accounts, most of them now rather dated, but John Swettenham, *The Canadian Corps in World War I: To Seize the Victory* (Toronto: 1965) stands out for its breadth of coverage and writing style. Desmond Morton and J.L. Granatstein, *Marching to Armageddon: Canadians and the Great War, 1914–1919* (Toronto: 1989) is a popular, picture-filled tome which is also based on sound research and deft writing. It is the best brief account of the war.

For the meaning of the war experience for Canada and Canadians, Jonathan F. Vance, *Death So Noble: Memory, Meaning, and the First World War* (Vancouver: 1997) is essential, along with John Herd Thompson's classic, *The Harvests of War: The Prairie West, 1914–1918* (Toronto: 1978). Robert Craig Brown and Ramsay Cook, *Canada 1896–1921: A Nation Transformed* (Toronto: 1974) provides the necessary context for both Vance and Thompson. A volume in the prestigious Canadian Centenary Series by McClelland and Stewart, that of Brown and Cook, provides a fine period survey.

Published first hand accounts of the war are numerous but, in general, are of poor quality. Several accounts by Will R. Bird, especially *Ghosts Have Warm Hands* (Toronto: 1968), are considered among the best. A comprehensive listing can be found in O.A. Cooke, *The Canadian Military Experience, 1867–1995: A Bibliography* (3rd edition, Ottawa: 1997). Regimental histories and biographies, also of mixed quality, help make up the difference. David Pierce Beatty, *Memories of the Forgotten War: The World War I Diary of Pte. V.E. Goodwin* (Port Elgin, New Brunswick: 1986) is a fine example of the better sort. Desmond Morton's collective biography, *When Your Number's Up: The Canadian Soldier in the First World War* (Toronto: 1993) is brilliant and indispensable. For primary unpublished accounts, one's goal should be the National Archives of Canada, located on 395 Wellington Street, Ottawa, Ontario, K1A 0N3.

BRITISH INDIA

Bagchi, A., *Private Investment in India, 1900–1939*, Cambridge: Cambridge University Press, 1972.

Barrier, N.G., *Banned: Controversial Literature and Political Control in British India 1907–1947*, Columbia: University of Missouri Press, 1974.

Bayly, C.A., *The Local Roots of Indian Politics: Allahabad, 1880–1920*, Oxford: Oxford University Press, 1975.

Brass, P., *Indian National Congress and Indian Society, 1885–1985: Ideology, Social Structure and Political Dominance*, Delhi: Chanakya Publishers, 1987.

Brown, J., *Gandhi's Rise to Power: Indian Politics, 1915–1922*, Cambridge, Cambridge University Press, 1972.

Brown, J., *Modern India: The Origins of an Asian Democracy*, Delhi: Oxford University Press, 1984.

Chatterji, B., *Trade, Tariffs and Empire: Lancashire and British Policy in India 1919–1939*, Delhi: Oxford University Press, 1992.

Chirol, V., *India*, London: Ernest Benn, 1926.

Crawley, W.F., "Kisan Sabhas and Agrarian Revolt in the United Provinces", *Modern Asian Studies*, Cambridge: Cambridge University Press, Vol. 5, 1971.

Das, A.N., *Agrarian Unrest and Socio-economic change in Bihar, 1900–1980*, New Delhi: Manohar, 1983.

Das, S., *Communal Riots in Bengal, 1905–1947*, New Delhi: Oxford University Press, 1993.

Gordon, A.D.D., *Businessmen and Politics: Rising Nationalism and a Modernising Economy in Bombay, 1918–1933*, Delhi: Manohar, 1978.

Gordon, A.D.D., "Businessmen and Politics in a Developing Colonial Economy: Bombay City, 1918–1933", in C.J. Dewey and A.G. Hopkins (eds.), *The Imperial Impact: Studies in the Economic History of Africa and India*, London: Athlone Press for the Institute of Commonwealth Studies, 1978.

Henningham, S., *Peasant Movements in Colonial India; North Bihar 1917–1942*, Canberra: Australian National University, 1982.

Irschik, E.F., *Politics and Social Conflict in South India: The Non-Brahman Movement and Tamil Separatism, 1916–29*, California: Stanford University Press, 1972.

Israel, M., *Communications and power: Propaganda and the press in the Indian nationalist struggle, 1920–1947*, Cambridge: Cambridge University Press, 1994.
Kumar, R. (ed.), *Essays on Gandhian Politics: The Rowlatt Satyagraha of 1919*, Oxford: Clarendon Press, 1971.
Low, D.A. (ed.), *Congress and the Raj*, London: Heinemann, 1977.
Musgrave, P.J., "Landlords and Lords of the Land: Estate Management and Social Control in Uttar Pradesh, 1860–1920", *Modern Asian Studies*, Cambridge: Cambridge University Press, Vol. 6, July 1972.
Narain, D., *The Impact of price movements on areas under selected crops in India: 1900–39*, Cambridge: Cambridge University Press, 1965.
Newman, R., *Workers and Unions in Bombay, 1918–1929*, Canberra: Australian National University, 1981.
Patel, S., *The Making of Industrial Relations: The Ahmedabad Textile Industry, 1918–39*, Delhi: Oxford University Press, 1987.
Reeves, P., "The Politics of Order", *Journal of Asian Studies*, 1966.
Sarkar, S., *Modern India, 1885–1947*, Delhi: Macmillan, 1983.
Siddiqi, M., *Agrarian Unrest in North India: United Provinces, 1918–1922*, New Delhi: Vikas, 1978.
Stokes, E.T., "The Structure of Landholding in Uttar Pradesh, 1860–1948", *Indian Economic and Social History Review*, New Delhi: Sage, April-June 1975.
Woodruff, P., *The men who ruled India. The Guardians*, London: Cape, 1954.

NEW ZEALAND

Baker, Paul, *King and Country Call*, Auckland: Auckland University Press, 1988.
Burton, O.E., *The Silent Division*, Sydney: Angus & Robertson, 1935.
Pugsley, Christopher, *On the Fringe of Hell*, Auckland: Hodder & Stoughton, 1991.
Pugsley et al, *Scars on the Heart: Two Centuries of New Zealand at War*, Auckland: David Bateman, 1996.
Stewart, Col H., *The Zealand Division, 1916–1919*, Wellington: Whitcombe & Tombs, 1921.

SOUTH AFRICA

Hancock, W.K., *Smuts: The Sanguine Years, 1870–1919*, Cambridge: Cambridge University Press, 1962.
Hancock, W.K. and van der Poel, Jean (eds.), *Selections from the Smuts Papers*, Vol. 4, Cambridge: Cambridge University Press, 1966.
Meintjies, Johannes, *General Louis Botha*, London: Cassell, 1970.

JAPAN

The following bibliography has been restricted to materials available in the English language. For primary sources, there is a good deal of material in the Public Record Office, Kew Gardens, in the Foreign Office files (FO 371), as well as in the private papers of many of the key politicians of the period such as Arthur Balfour (British Library), Lloyd George (House of Lords Records Office), Alfred Milner (The Bodleian Library), Jan Smuts (Cambridge University Library) to name but a few. As far as secondary sources are concerned, there is a dearth of material on Japan and the First World War.

Fifield, Russell H., *Woodrow Wilson and the Far East: The Diplomacy of the Shantung Question*, New York: Thomas Y. Crowell Co., 1952.

Lowe, Peter, *Great Britain and Japan 1911–15: A Study of British Far Eastern Policy*, London: Macmillan, 1969.

Nish, Ian, *The Anglo-Japanese Alliance: The Diplomacy of Two Island Empires 1894–1907*, London: Athlone Press, 1966.

Nish, Ian, *Alliance in Decline: A Study in Anglo-Japanese Relations 1908–1923*, London: Athlone Press, 1972.

Nish, Ian (ed.), *Anglo-Japanese Alienation 1919–1952*, Cambridge: Cambridge University Press, 1982.

Shimazu, Naoko, *Japan, Race and Equality: The Racial Equality Proposal of 1919*, London: Routledge, 1998.

BULGARIA

The historiography of the events of November 1918 in Bulgaria has been dominated by two concerns. The first, which prevailed particularly in the immediate post war years, was to explain Bulgaria's defeat. The second, which was prevalent throughout the period of communist domination (1944–89), was to highlight the military revolt of September 1918 and to place it within the framework of the marxist canon of historical law.

In the early 1920's the workings and actions of the final wartime government were laid before the public in *Doklad ot parlamentarnata izpitelna komisiya za anketirane upravlenieto na bivshiya kabinet Al Malinov-Kosturkov* (Report of the parliamentary commission of enquiry into the administration of the former cabinet of Al[exander] Malinov-Kosturkov) [details]; although clearly prepared with political and judicial purposes in view the Report nevertheless provides much basic documentation. Other propagandist works which attempted to point the finger of blame for the national catastrophe included: L Maleev, *Prinos kûm instinata za katastrofata na Bûlgariya prez semtemvri 1918*, (Contribution[?] to the truth concerning the catastrophe in Bulgaria in September 1918) Sofia 1921; D Petkov, *Vinovnitsite za pogroma na Bûlgariya prez septemvri 1918 god vuz osnova na istoricheski dokumenti i fakti* (The culprits for Bulgaria's collapse in September 1918 on the basis of historic documents and facts) [details]; and St Noikov, *Zashto ne pobedihme? 1915–1918* (Why did we not prevail? 1915–1918), 1st edition 1921, 2nd 1922.

For more disinterested discussions of the social and economic impact of the war see: G T Danaillow, *Les effects de la guerre en Bulgarie*, Paris, 1933; Hans Loewnefeld-Russ, *Die Regelung der Volksnährung im Krieg*, Economic and Social History of the World War, Vienna, 1926; and Richard J Crampton, *Bulgaria 1878–1918; A History*, East European Monographs No.138, Boulder, Colorado and New York, 1983, pp. 473–510.

The standard history of the 1918 military revolt remains Hristo Hristov, *Revoliutsionnite Krize v Bûlgariya, 1918–1919* (The Revolutionary Crisis in Bulgaria, 1918–1919), Sofia, 1957. Although produced during the relatively early stages of communist rule Hristov's book is a mine of information. It is based largely on archival material created by Bulgarian censorship of letters between soldiers and their families, and its material is therefore authentic and immediate. Many subsequent works rely heavily on Hristov's book; such works include: I Draev, *Bûlgarskata osemnadeseta godina* (Bulgaria's '18) Sofia, 1970; Yono Mitev, "Voinishkoto vûstanie v Bûlgariya prez septemvri 1918 i uchastieto na germanskite voiski v negovoto potushavane" ("The military rebellion in Bulgaria in September 1918 and the part played by German forces in suppressing it"), in Hristo Hristov et al (eds), *Bûlgarsko-Germanskite Otnosheniya i Vrûzki; Izsledvaniya i Materiali*, (Bulgarian-German Relations and Connections; Studies and Documentation), vol. i, Sofia, 1972, pp. 279–93; and Liubomir Ognyanov, *Voinishkoto V–stanie 1918* (The military revolt of 1918), Sofia, 1988.

Since the fall of the totalitarian regime in 1989 Bulgarian historians and publishers have naturally been much less inhibited in what they are prepared to produce. This has meant the appearance both of a number of memoirs of people other than those who took part in the military rebellion, and of monographs on themes previously too sensitive to receive a public airing. Amongst the former are Stiliyan Kovachev, *Zapiski na General na Pehotata, 1876–1918*, (Notes of an infantry general, 1876–1918), Sofia, 1992 and Stoyan Iliev, *Iz Spomenite mi* (From my memoirs), Sofia, 1993. One of the studies which would have been unpublishable during the communist period is Staiko Todorov, *Antantata v Trakiya 1919–1920* (The entente in Thrace 1919–1920), Sofia, 1989.

THE OTTOMAN EMPIRE

Atay, Falih Rifki, *Cankaya*, Istanbul: Bates, 1980.

Belen, Fahri, *Birinci Cihan Harbinde Türk Harbi. 1918 Yih Hareketleri. Besinci Cilt*, Ankara: Gelenkurmay, 1967. [The Turkish War in the First World War. Operations of the Year 1918. Vol. 5].

Criss, Nur Bilge, *Isgal Altinda Istanbul*, Istanbul: Iletisim, 1994. [Istanbul under occupation].

Edib, Halide [Adivar], *The Turkish Ordeal*, London: The Century, 1928.

Einstein, Lewis, *Inside Constantinople. A Diplomatist's Diary During the Dardanelles Expedition*, London: John Murray, 1917.

Emin, Ahmed [Yalman], *Turkey in the World War*, New Haven: Yale University Press, 1930.

Karaosmanoglu, Yakup Kadri, *Sodom ve Gomore*, Istanbul: Bilgi, 1966 (original edition 1928) [Sodom and Gomorrha - a novel].

Orbay, Hüseyin, Rauf, *Hatiralari* [His memoirs], in Feridun Kandemir (ed.), Yakin Tarihimiz, Vol. 1 and 2, Ankara: Türkpetrol, n.d. [Our Recent History].

Toprak, Zafer, Türkiye'de Milli Iktisat (1908–1918), Ankara: Yurt, 1982.

Tunaya, Tarik Zafer, *Türkiye'de Siyasal Partiler. Cilt 2. Mütareke Dünemi*,

Istanbul: Hürriyet Vakfi, 1986 [Political parties in Turkey. Vol. 2. The Armistice Period].
Unan, Nimet (ed.), *Atatürk'ün S"ylev ve Demecleri 2 (1906–1938)*, Ankara: Türk Tarih Kurumu, 1959.
Zürcher, Erik Jan, "Little Mehmet in the Desert: the war experience of the Ottoman soldier", in Hugh Cecil and Peter Liddle (eds.), *Facing Armageddon. The First World War Experienced*, London: Leo Cooper / Pen and Sword, 1996, pp. 230–241.
Zürcher, Erik Jan, "Between Death and Desertion. The Ottoman Army in World War I". *Tucica* 28 (1996), pp. 235–258.

THE ARAB PEOPLES

Aldington, R., *Lawrence of Arabia: a Bibliographical Enquiry*, London: Collins, 1955.
Antonius, G., *The Arab Awakening*, London: Hamish Hamilton, 1938.
Atiyah E., *The Arabs*, Edinburgh: Penguin, 1955.
Ayalon, A., *The Press in the Middle East,* Oxford: Oxford University Press, 1995.
Ende, W., "Iraq in World War I: the Turks, the Germans and the Shi`ite Mujtahids` call for Jihad", in Peters, R., (ed.), *Proceedings of the Ninth Congress of the Union Européenne des Arabisants et Islamisants*, Leiden: Brill, 1981.
Hourani, A., *Islam in European Thought*, Cambridge: Cambridge University Press, 1991.
Khalidi, A. S., *Jawlah fi al-dhikrayat bayn lubnan wa-falastin*, Beirut: al-Nahar, 1979.
Khalidi, R., *Palestinian Identity*, New York: Columbia University Press, 1997.
Khillah, K.M., *Palestine under British Mandate*, Beirut: Palestine Liberation Organization, 1974.
Lamans, H., Faransa wa-surya, *al-Machriq*, Year 19, No. 1, January 1921, pp. 49–55.
Lawrence, T.E., *Seven Pillars of Wisdom*, London: Jonathan Cape, 1935.
Lenczowski, G., *The Middle East in World Affairs*, New York: Cornell University Press, 1952.
Nadim, S.M., *Harb falastin,* (The War for Palestine), Baghdad: Sharikat al-Nibras li-al-Nashr wa-al-Tawzi, 1964. [in Arabic]
Nadim, S.M., *Harb al-`Iraq*, (The Iraqi War), Baghdad: Matba `at Dar al-Tadamun, 1967. [in Arabic]
Nutting, A., *Lawrence of Arabia*, London: Mayfair, 1947.
Parry, V.J. and Yapp, M.E., *War, Technology and Society in the Middle East*, Oxford: Oxford University Press, 1975.
Shikho, L., tahiyyat al-Machriq li-qurra`ihi, *al-Machriq*, Year 18, No. 1, January 1920, pp. 1–3.
Shikho, L., A`zam ṭāmmah fi al-harb al-`ammah: baritanya al-`uzmah, *al-Machriq*, Year 18, No. 4, March 1920, pp. 288–296.

Shikho, L., Al-Sahyuniyyah (Zionism), *Al-Machriq*, Year 18, No. 10, October 1920, pp. 768–778.
Tauber, E., *The Arab Movements in World War I*, London: Frank Cass, 1993.
Yapp, M.E., *The Near East since the First World War*, Cambridge: Cambridge University Press, 1985.
Yahya, G. and Taha, G, *Al-`Arab fi al-Ta`rikh al-Hadith*, Egypt: Minya University, 1974.

AUSTRIA-HUNGARY, CENTRAL, EASTERN, SOUTH EASTERN EUROPE AND ASIA MINOR

Amtliche Urkunden zur Vorgeschichte des Waffenstillstandes 1918. Auf Grund der Akten der Reichskanzlei, des Auswörtigen Amtes und des Reichsarchivs, hrsg. vom Auswörtigen Amt und vom Reichsministerium des Innern. - 4. Aufl. - Berlin: Deutscher Verlag für Politik und Geschichte, 1927. [Reprint Frankfurt am Main, 1988].
Berghahn, Volker, *Der Tirpitz-Plan. Genesis und Verfall einer innenpolitischen Krisenstrategie unter Wilhelm II*, Düsseldorf: Droste, 1971.
Cornwall, Mark (ed), *The Last Years of Austria-Hungary*, Exeter: Exeter University Press, 1998
Fischer, Fritz, *Germany's Aims in the First World War*, London: Chatto & Windus, 1967.
Förster, Stig, 'Der deutsche Generalstab und die Illusion des kurzen Krieges, 1871–1914. Metakritik eines Mythos', in Burckhardt, Johannes, et. al., *Lange und kurze Wege in den Ersten Weltkrieg. Vier Augsburger Beiträge zur Kriegsursachenerforschung*, Munich: Ernst Vögel, 1996, pp. 115–158.
Geiss, Imanuel, *Der lange Weg in die Katastrophe. Die vorgeschichte des Ersten Weltkriegs 1815–1914*, Munich: Serie Piper 943, 1990.
Geiss, Imanuel (ed.), *July 1914*, London: Batsford, 1967.
Glaise-Horstenau, Edmund von, *The Collapse of the Austro-Hungarian Empire*, London & Toronto: Dent, 1930.
Glaise-Horstenau, Edmund von & Kiszling, Rudolf (eds.), *Österreich-Ungarns letzter Krieg 1914–1918, Band VII: Das Kriegsjahr 1918*, Vienna: Verlag für Militärwissenschaftlichen Mitteilungen, 1938.
Kerchnawe, Hugo, *Der Zusammenbruch der sterr.-ungar. Wehrmacht im Herbst 1918*, Munich: Lehmann, 1921.
Krizman, Bogdan, *Raspad Austro-Ugarske i Stvaranje Jugoslavenske Drzave*, Zagreb: Školska knjiga, 1977.
Mitev, A.J., 'L'entente et l'armistice de 1918', in *Études balkaniques* 24/3, 1988, S. 80 ff.
Neck, Rudolf (ed.), *Österreich im Jahre 1918. Berichte und Dokumente*, Vienna: Verlag für Geschichte und Politik, 1968.
Nowak, Karl, *Der Sturz der Mittelmächte*, Munich: Callwey, 1921.
Opočenský, Jan, *Konec Monarchie Rakousko-Uherské*, Prague: Orbis-Čin, 1928.
Peroutka, Ferdinand, *Budování Stútu. I: Rok 1918*, Prague: Borový, 1933.

Plaschka, Richard, *Cattaro-Prag. Revolte und Revolution*, Graz-Cologne: Böhlau, 1963.
Plaschka, Richard & Mack, Karlheinz (eds.), *Die Auflösung des Habsburgerreiches. Zusammenbruch und Neuorientierung im Donauraum*, Munich: 1970.
Rauchensteiner, Manfried, *Der Tod des Doppeladlers. Österreich-Ungarn und der Erste Weltkrieg*, Graz: Verlag Styria, 1993.
Redlich, Josef, *Schicksalsjahre Österreichs. Das politische Tagebuch Josef Redlichs* (ed. Fritz Fellner), vol. II, Graz-Cologne: Böhlau, 1954.
Rošický, Jaroslav, *Rakouský Orel Padá*, Prague: Forejt, 1933.
Rumpler, Helmut, *Das Völkermanifest Kaiser Karls vom 16. Oktober 1918. Letzter Versuch zur Rettung des Habsburgerreiches*, Vienna: Verlag für Politik und Geschichte, 1966.
Siklós, András, *Revolution in Hungary and the Dissolution of the Multinational State 1918*, Budapest: Akadémiai Kiadó, 1988.
Taylor, A.J.P. and Roberts, J.M. (eds.), History of the 20th Century, London: Purnell, 1968.
Vilain, Charles, *Les Quatre armistices de 1918*, Paris: Edition France-empire, 1968.
Wagner, Bruno, *Der Waffenstillstand von Villa Giusti, 3. November 1918*, Vienna: 1970 [phil.Diss].

ITALY

Burgwyn, H.J., *The Legend of the Mutilated Victory. Italy, the Great War and the Paris Peace Conference 1915–1918*, Westport, Connecticut and London: 1993.
Candeloro, G. *Storia dell'Italia moderna*, vol. 8, Milano: Feltrinelli, 1978.
Fabi, L., *Gente di trincea*, Milano: Mursia, 1994.
Gibelli, *L'officina della guerra*, Torino: Boringhieri, 1991.
Melograni, *Storia politica della grande guerra*, 2 vols., Bari: Laterza, 1977.
Procacci, G., *Soldati e prigionieri italiani nella grande guerra*, Roma: Editori riuniti, 1993.
Sabbatucci, G., *I combattenti nel primo dopoguerra*, Bari: Laterza, 1974.

BRITISH, FRENCH, GERMAN AND AMERICAN LITERATURE

Biography and memoirs:
Brittain, Vera, *Testament of Youth: an Autobiographical Study of the Years 1900–1925*, London: Victor Gollancz, 1933.
Chapman, Guy, *A Passionate Prodigality*, London: Ivor Nicholson &Watson, 1933.
Dos Passos, John, *The Best Times: an informal memoir*, London: André Deutsch, 1968.
Graves, Robert, *Goodbye to All That*, Harmondsworth, Middlesex: Penguin edn., 1960 (1st pub. 1929).
Lanoux, Armand, *Adieu la vie, adieu l'amour*, Paris: Albin Michel, 1977 (on Roland Dorgelès).
Sassoon, Siegfried, *Siegfried's Journey*, London: Faber and Faber, 1945.

Sulzbach, Herbert, *With the German Guns: Four Years on the Western Front, 1914–1918*, tr. Richard Thonger, London: Leo Cooper / Frederick Warne, 1973/81 (1st pub. as *Zwei lebende Mauern*, 1935).

CULTURAL HISTORY AND ANTHOLOGIES:
Cecil, Hugh, *The Flower of Battle: How Britain Wrote the Great War*, South Royalton, Vermont: The Steerforth Press, 1996.
Chapman, Guy (ed.), *Vain Glory*, London: Cassell, 1968
Hibberd, Dominic, and Onions, John, *The Poetry of the Great War: an Anthology*, London: Macmillan, 1986.
Moore, Harry T., *Twentieth Century German Literature*, London: Heinemann, 1971.
Parsons, I.M. (ed.), *Men Who March Away: Poems of the First World War*, London: Heinemann, 1965.
Stephen, Martin, *Everyman Poems of the First World War: 'Never Such Innocence'*, London: Everyman, 1993.
Stephen, Martin, *The Price of Pity: Poetry, History and Myth in the Great War*, London: Leo Cooper, 1996.
Tuohy, Ferdinand, *Occupied 1918–1930: a Postscript to the Western Front*, London: Thornton Butterworth, 1931.
Weinstein, Joan, *Art and the November Revolution in Germany, 1918–19*, Chicago: University of Chicago Press, 1990.

COMMEMORATION
Dyer, Geoff, *The Missing of the Somme*, London: Penguin, 1995.
Gavaghan, Michael, *The Story of the Unknown Warrior*, Cambridge: Cambridge University Press, 1995.
Gregory, Adrian, *The Silence of Memory: Armistice Day 1919–1946*, Oxford: Berg, 1994.
Vance, Jonathan F., *Death So Noble, Memory, Meaning, and the First World War*, Vancouver: UBC Press, 1997.
Winter, J.M., *Sites of Memory, Sites of Mourning*, Cambridge: Cambridge University Press, 1995.

Notes on Contributors

Colonel Allain Bernède [Paul Valéry University, Montpellier]
Allain Bernède is a Professor of History at the Direction de l'enseignement militaire supérieur de l'Armée de Terre in Paris and Director of a Department of Historical Research at Paul Valéry University in Montpellier. He has published books on the French Army and contributed to research publications and conferences on this subject.

Dr Sanjoy Bhattacharya [Sheffield Hallam University]
Sanjoy Bhattacharya, a Wellcome Trust Fellow, has contributed chapters to several books and articles on the 20th century political / military history of the Indian sub-continent.

Dr John M. Bourne [The University of Birmingham]
John Bourne is the author of *Great Britain and the First World War*. He contributed to *Facing Armageddon: the First World War Experienced*, to *Passchendaele in Perspective* and is one of the team working on a computer-based study of British Army divisions and their commanders in the First World War.

Dr Hugh Cecil [The University of Leeds]
Hugh Cecil is an acknowledged authority on the literature of the First World War. He is the author of numerous articles and books including, *The Flower of Battle: How Britain wrote the First World War* [US edition 1996] and was the co-editor of *Facing Armageddon: the First World War Experienced* [1996].

Dr James J. Cooke [The University of Mississippi, Oxford Campus]
James Cooke's publications include *The Rainbow Division in the Great War 1917–19* [1994]. He contributed to *Facing Armageddon: The First World*

War Experienced, and his most recent book is entitled, *Pershing and his Generals* [1997].

DR MARK CORNWALL [THE UNIVERSITY OF DUNDEE]
Mark Cornwall was the editor of a book of essays on *The Last Years of Austria-Hungary* [1990] and is currently working upon military propaganda in this field. He also contributed to *Facing Armageddon: the First World War Experienced.*

PROFESSOR RICHARD CRAMPTON [ST EDMUND HALL, UNIVERSITY OF OXFORD]
Richard Crampton, a Fellow of St Edmund Hall, is a leading expert on Bulgaria. He has recently written *A Concise History of Bulgaria* [1997] and is also the author of *Eastern Europe in the Twentieth Century - and After* [1997].

MARK DEREZ [THE ARCHIVES OF THE CATHOLIC UNIVERSITY OF LEUVEN]
Mark Derez is a Belgian archivist whose speciality is the history of his University. He contributed to the volumes, *Facing Armageddon: the First World War Experienced* and *Passchendaele in Perspective.*

ASHLEY EKINS [THE AUSTRALIAN WAR MEMORIAL, CANBERRA]
Ashley Ekins, who is completing a study of discipline and punishment within the Australian army during the First World War, is an historian with the Official History Unit at the War Memorial working on Australia's involvement in the Vietnam War. He is co-author of a forthcoming volume in the series.

PROFESSOR IMANUEL GEISS [THE UNIVERSITY OF BREMEN]
Imanuel Geiss first achieved eminence through research into Germany and the origins of the First World War *July 1914* [1967 English translation]. More recently he has published an 'accessible' multi-volume world history, *Geschicte griffbereit* [1993], and contributed to *Facing Armageddon: the First World War Experienced.*

DR IRENE GUERRINI [THE LIBRARY, GENOA UNIVERSITY]
Irene Guerrini works collaboratively on Italian popular writing during the wars of the 20th century and has published articles on 'the organization of consent' during the Fascist period. Her book on the celebrated Italian fighter pilot, Francesco Baracca, will be published in 1998.

DR HEINZ HAGENLÜCKE [HEINRICH HEINE UNIVERSITY, DÜSSELDORF]
Dr Hagenlücke has published on aspects of German party political activity in the 19th and 20th centuries, *Die Deutsche Vaterlandspartei* [1996]. He contributed to *Passchendaele in Perspective* and is currently working to produce a published edition of Wolfgang Kapp's 1914–18 papers.

DR PETER H. LIDDLE [THE LIDDLE COLLECTION, THE UNIVERSITY OF LEEDS]
Peter Liddle is Founder and Keeper of the World War personal experience archive in the University of Leeds. His publications include, *The Battle of the Somme*; *The Worst Ordeal: Britons at Home and Abroad 1914–18*; *Facing Armageddon: the First World War Experienced* [co-edited] and, as editor, *Passchendaele in Perspective* [1997].

DR BULLITT LOWRY [THE UNIVERSITY OF NORTH TEXAS, DENTON, TEXAS]
Bullitt Lowry has written extensively on the First World War. His most recent book is entitled *Compiègne 1918* [1997]. He contributed to *Facing Armageddon: The First World War Experienced* and is currently researching the period between the Armistice and the Peace Treaties.

PROFESSOR BILL NASSON [THE UNIVERSITY OF CAPETOWN]
Bill Nasson has written journal articles and a book on The South African War 1899–1902 and has also published work on aspects of South African service in the First World War. He contributed to *Passchendaele in Perspective.*

DR DEAN F. OLIVER [SENIOR HISTORIAN, CANADIAN WAR MUSEUM, OTTAWA]
Dean Oliver is in a new appointment following upon his research fellowship at the Norman Paterson School of International Affairs, Carleton University, Ottawa, and External Affairs and National Defence contributor for the Canadian Annual Review of Politics and Public Affairs. He contributed to *Passchendaele in Perspective.*

DR MARCO PLUVIANO [ITALIAN FEDERATION OF ARCHIVES OF POPULAR WRITING, GENOA]
Marco Pluviano collaborates with the historical museum of Trento and has published widely in the area of soldier welfare and worker compliance in the First World War and on the Italian people under Fascism.

CHRISTOPHER PUGSLEY [THE UNIVERSITY OF NEW ENGLAND, ARMIDALE, NEW SOUTH WALES]
Christopher Pugsley served as an officer in the New Zealand Army and has lectured on aspects of New Zealand's military history at Waikato and Massey Universities. He has published, *Gallipoli: The New Zealand Story*; *On the Fringe of Hell: New Zealanders and Military Discipline in the First World War* and *Scars on the Heart* [1996], the subject of a permanent exhibition [for which he was the curator at the Auckland War Memorial Museum] on two centuries of New Zealand at War.

MATTHEW RICHARDSON [THE LIDDLE COLLECTION, THE UNIVERSITY OF LEEDS]
Matthew Richardson, is the Assistant Keeper of the Liddle Collection. He has written articles for *Stand To: the Journal of the Western Front Association*

and his interest in recollected testimony has led to the publication with Peter Liddle of an article in the *Journal of Contemporary History* [1996]. He contributed to *Passchendaele in Perspective*.

DR NAOKO SHIMAZU [BIRKBECK COLLEGE, UNIVERSITY OF LONDON]
Naoko Shimazu lectures in Japanese history. She obtained her D.Phil at Oxford University. She is the author of *Japan, Race and Equality* [1998] and is currently working on a cultural history of the Russo-Japanese war of 1904–5.

DR AVIHAI SHIVTIEL [UNIVERSITY OF CAMBRIDGE]
Avi Shivtiel is currently Senior Research Associate in the Library of the University of Cambridge. He was formerly head of the Department of Modern Arabic Studies at the University of Leeds and his research covers aspects of Middle Eastern culture.

PROFESSOR ERIK J. ZÜRCHER [THE UNIVERSITY OF LEIDEN, THE NETHERLANDS]
Erik Zürcher holds the Chair in Turkish Studies at Leiden. He has published articles on the political and social history of the late Ottoman Empire and the Turkish Republic. He contributed to *Facing Armageddon: the First World War Experienced* and is working on the social history of the Turkish Army.

Index